Karl Marx

F. Engels

KARL MARX AND FREDERICK ENGELS

SELECTED WORKS

In One Volume

KARL MARX
and
FREDERICK ENGELS

SELECTED WORKS

In One Volume

PROGRESS PUBLISHERS
MOSCOW

LAWRENCE & WISHART
LONDON

This one-volume edition of *Selected Works* of
Marx and Engels was prepared, edited and published
in 1968 by Progress Publishers, Moscow, U.S.S.R.,
and simultaneously published in London by Lawrence
and Wishart Ltd., and in New York by International
Publishers Inc.

*Printed in the Union of Soviet Socialist Republics
by Progress Publishers*

CONTENTS

PUBLISHERS' NOTE

These selections from the voluminous writings of Karl Marx and Frederick Engels present the essentials of their thinking. It is hoped that *Selected Works* will prove a useful source book for the student of Marxism. The selections have been made with a view to providing in a single volume the basic theories of the founders of Marxism in philosophy and political economy, and of history, social change and communism.

The shorter fundamental works are given in full, including those most often used in the study of Marxism. The larger works, such as *Capital*, are represented by the author's introduction or by a chapter. From the extensive correspondence of Marx and Engels, a number of germinal letters have been chosen.

In lieu of an introduction, it was thought best to open the volume with three essays on the significance of Marxism by V. I. Lenin, its leading exponent in the 20th century.

For the most part, the writings are given in chronological order, with the correspondence in a separate section. The volume is supplied with reference notes as well as name and subject indexes.

Lawrence and Wishart
London

V. I. Lenin

From the Article KARL MARX

A BRIEF BIOGRAPHICAL SKETCH
WITH AN EXPOSITION OF MARXISM

Marx, Karl, was born on May 5, 1818 (New Style) in the city of Trier (Rhenish Prussia). His father was a lawyer, a Jew, who in 1824 adopted Protestantism. The family was well-to-do, cultured, but not revolutionary. After graduating from a *Gymnasium* in Trier, Marx entered the university, first at Bonn and later in Berlin, where he read law, majoring in history and philosophy. He concluded his university course in 1841, submitting a doctoral thesis on the philosophy of Epicurus. At the time Marx was a Hegelian idealist in his views. In Berlin, he belonged to the circle of "Left Hegelians" (Bruno Bauer and others) who sought to draw atheistic and revolutionary conclusions from Hegel's philosophy.

After graduating, Marx moved to Bonn, hoping to become a professor. However, the reactionary policy of the government, which deprived Ludwig Feuerbach of his chair in 1832, refused to allow him to return to the university in 1836, and in 1841 forbade young Professor Bruno Bauer to lecture at Bonn, made Marx abandon the idea of an academic career. Left Hegelian views were making rapid headway in Germany at the time. Ludwig Feuerbach began to criticise theology, particularly after 1836, and turn to materialism, which in 1841 gained the ascendancy in his philosophy (*The Essence of Christianity*). The year 1843 saw the appearance of his *Principles of the Philosophy of the Future*. "One must himself have experienced the liberating effect" of these books, Engels subsequently wrote of these works of Feuerbach. "We" (i.e., the Left Hegelians, including Marx) "all became at once Feuerbachians."* At that time, some radical bourgeois in the Rhineland, who were in touch with the Left Hegelians, founded, in Cologne, an opposition paper called *Rheinische Zeitung* (the first issue appeared on January 1, 1842). Marx and Bruno Bauer were invited to be the chief contributors, and in October 1842 Marx became Editor-in-Chief and moved from Bonn to Cologne. The newspaper's revolutionary-democratic trend became more and more pronounced

---

* F. Engels, *Ludwig Feuerbach and the End of Classical German Philosophy* (see p. 592 of this volume).—*Ed.*

under Marx's editorship, and the government first imposed double and triple censorship on the paper, and then on January 1, 1843, decided to suppress it. Marx had to resign the editorship before that date, but his resignation did not save the paper, which suspended publication in March 1843. Of the major articles Marx contributed to *Rheinische Zeitung*, Engels notes, in addition to those indicated below (see *Bibliography**), an article on the condition of peasant vine-growers in the Moselle Valley.** Marx's journalistic activities convinced him that he was insufficiently acquainted with political economy, and he zealously set out to study it.

In 1843, Marx married, at Kreuznach, Jenny von Westphalen, a childhood friend he had become engaged to while still a student. His wife came of a reactionary family of the Prussian nobility, her elder brother being Prussia's Minister of the Interior during a most reactionary period—1850-58. In the autumn of 1843, Marx went to Paris in order to publish a radical journal abroad, together with Arnold Ruge (1802-1880; Left Hegelian; in prison in 1825-30; a political exile following 1848, and a Bismarckian after 1866-70). Only one issue of this journal, *Deutsch-Französische Jahrbücher*, appeared; publication was discontinued owing to the difficulty of secretly distributing it in Germany, and to disagreement with Ruge. Marx's articles in this journal showed that he was already a revolutionary, who advocated "merciless criticism of everything existing", and in particular the "criticism by weapon", and appealed to the *masses* and to the *proletariat*.

In September 1844 Frederick Engels came to Paris for a few days, and from that time on became Marx's closest friend. They both took a most active part in the then seething life of the revolutionary groups in Paris (of particular importance at the time was Proudhon's doctrine, which Marx pulled to pieces in his *Poverty of Philosophy*, 1847); waging a vigorous struggle against the various doctrines of petty-bourgeois socialism, they worked out the theory and tactics of revolutionary *proletarian socialism*, or communism (Marxism). See Marx's works of this period, 1844-48, in the *Bibliography*. At the insistent request of the Prussian government, Marx was banished from Paris in 1845, as a dangerous revolutionary. He went to Brussels. In the spring of 1847 Marx and Engels joined a secret propaganda society called the Communist League; they took a prominent part in the League's Second Congress (London, November 1847), at whose request they drew up the celebrated *Communist Manifesto*, which appeared in February

---

* Lenin means the bibliography which he compiled for his work *Karl Marx*. —*Ed.*

** Reference is to Marx's article *Rechtfertigung des Korrespondenten von der Mosel* (see Marx/Engels, *Werke*, Bd. 1, Dietz Verlag, Berlin, 1958, S. 172-99).—*Ed.*

1848. With the clarity and brilliance of genius, this work outlines a new world conception, consistent materialism, which also embraces the realm of social life; dialectics, as the most comprehensive and profound doctrine of development; the theory of the class struggle and of the world-historic revolutionary role of the proletariat—the creator of a new, communist society.

On the outbreak of the Revolution of February 1848, Marx was banished from Belgium. He returned to Paris, whence, after the March Revolution, he went to Cologne, Germany, where *Neue Rheinische Zeitung* was published from June 1, 1848 to May 19, 1849, with Marx as Editor-in-Chief. The new theory was splendidly confirmed by the course of the revolutionary events of 1848-49, just as it has been subsequently confirmed by all proletarian and democratic movements in all countries of the world. The victorious counter-revolutionaries first instigated court proceedings against Marx (he was acquitted on February 9, 1849), and then banished him from Germany (May 16, 1849). First Marx went to Paris, was again banished after the demonstration of June 13, 1849, and then went to London, where he lived till his death.

His life as a political exile was a very hard one, as the correspondence between Marx and Engels (published in 1913) clearly reveals. Poverty weighed heavily on Marx and his family; had it not been for Engels's constant and selfless financial aid, Marx would not only have been unable to complete *Capital* but would have inevitably been crushed by want. Moreover, the prevailing doctrines and trends of petty-bourgeois socialism, and of non-proletarian socialism in general, forced Marx to wage a continuous and merciless struggle and sometimes to repel the most savage and monstrous personal attacks (*Herr Vogt*)*. Marx, who stood aloof from circles of political exiles, developed his materialist theory in a number of historical works (see *Bibliography*), devoting himself mainly to a study of political economy. Marx revolutionised this science (see "The Marxist Doctrine", below) in his *Contribution to the Critique of Political Economy* (1859) and *Capital* (Vol. I, 1867).

The revival of the democratic movements in the late fifties and in the sixties recalled Marx to practical activity. In 1864 (September 28) the International Working Men's Association—the celebrated First International—was founded in London. Marx was the heart and soul of this organisation, and author of its first Address** and of a host of resolutions, declarations and manifestos. In uniting the labour movement of various countries, striving to channel into joint activity the various forms of non-proletarian, pre-Marxist

---

* See Marx/Engels, *Werke*, Bd. 14, Dietz Verlag, Berlin, 1961, S. 381-686.—*Ed.*
** K. Marx, *Inaugural Address of the Working Men's International Association* (see Marx and Engels, *Selected Works*, Vol. I, Moscow, 1962, pp. 377-85).—*Ed.*

socialism (Mazzini, Proudhon, Bakunin, liberal trade-unionism in Britain, Lassallean vacillations to the right in Germany, etc.), and in combating the theories of all these sects and schools, Marx hammered out a uniform tactic for the proletarian struggle of the working class in the various countries. Following the downfall of the Paris Commune (1871)—of which Marx gave such a profound, clear-cut, brilliant, *effective* and revolutionary analysis (*The Civil War in France*, 1871)—and the Bakuninist-caused cleavage in the International, the latter organisation could no longer exist in Europe. After the Hague Congress of the International (1872), Marx had the General Council of the International transferred to New York. The First International had played its historical part, and now made way for a period of a far greater development of the labour movement in all countries in the world, a period in which the movement grew in *scope*, and *mass* socialist working-class parties in individual national states were formed.

Marx's health was undermined by his strenuous work in the International and his still more strenuous theoretical occupations. He continued work on the refashioning of political economy and on the completion of *Capital*, for which he collected a mass of new material and studied a number of languages (Russian, for instance). However, ill-health prevented him from completing *Capital*.

His wife died on December 2, 1881, and on March 14, 1883, Marx passed away peacefully in his armchair. He lies buried next to his wife at Highgate Cemetery in London. Of Marx's children some died in childhood in London, when the family were living in destitute circumstances. Three daughters married English and French socialists: Eleanor Aveling, Laura Lafargue and Jenny Longuet. The latter's son is a member of the French Socialist Party.

Written in July-November 1914

Abridged version published in 1915
in the Granat Encyclopaedic
Dictionary, 7th edition, Vol. 28

Collected Works, Vol. 21,
pp. 46-50

V. I. Lenin

FREDERICK ENGELS

> What a torch of reason ceased to burn,
> What a heart has ceased to beat!*

On August 5 (New Style), 1895, Frederick Engels died in London. After his friend Karl Marx (who died in 1883), Engels was the finest scholar and teacher of the modern proletariat in the whole civilised world. From the time that fate brought Karl Marx and Frederick Engels together, the two friends devoted their life's work to a common cause. And so to understand what Frederick Engels has done for the proletariat, one must have a clear idea of the significance of Marx's teaching and work for the development of the contemporary working-class movement. Marx and Engels were the first to show that the working class and its demands are a necessary outcome of the present economic system, which together with the bourgeoisie inevitably creates and organises the proletariat. They showed that it is not the well-meaning efforts of noble-minded individuals, but the class struggle of the organised proletariat that will deliver humanity from the evils which now oppress it. Marx and Engels were the first to explain in their scientific works that socialism is not the invention of dreamers, but the final aim and necessary result of the development of the productive forces in modern society. All recorded history hitherto has been a history of class struggle, of the succession of the rule and victory of certain social classes over others. And this will continue until the foundations of class struggle and of class domination—private property and anarchic social production—disappear. The interests of the proletariat demand the destruction of these foundations, and therefore the conscious class struggle of the organised workers must be directed against them. And every class struggle is a political struggle.

These views of Marx and Engels have now been adopted by all proletarians who are fighting for their emancipation.

But when in the forties the two friends took part in the socialist literature and the social movements of their time, they were absolutely novel. There were then many people, talented and

---

* N. A. Nekrasov, *In Memory of Dobrolyubov.*—*Ed.*

without talent, honest and dishonest, who, absorbed in the struggle
for political freedom, in the struggle against the despotism of kings,
police and priests, failed to observe the antagonism between the
interests of the bourgeoisie and those of the proletariat. These
people would not entertain the idea of the workers acting as an
independent social force. On the other hand, there were many
dreamers, some of them geniuses, who thought that it was only
necessary to convince the rulers and the governing classes of the
injustice of the contemporary social order, and it would then be
easy to establish peace and general well-being on earth. They
dreamt of a socialism without struggle. Lastly, nearly all the
socialists of that time and the friends of the working class generally regarded the proletariat only as an *ulcer*, and observed with
horror how it grew with the growth of industry. They all, therefore, sought for a means to stop the development of industry and
of the proletariat, to stop the "wheel of history". Marx and Engels
did not share the general fear of the development of the proletariat; on the contrary, they placed all their hopes on its continued
growth. The more proletarians there are, the greater is their
strength as a revolutionary class, and the nearer and more possible does socialism become. The services rendered by Marx and
Engels to the working class may be expressed in a few words thus:
they taught the working class to know itself and be conscious of
itself, and they substituted science for dreams.

That is why the name and life of Engels should be known to
every worker. That is why in this collection of articles, the aim
of which, as of all our publications, is to awaken class-conscious-
ness in the Russian workers, we must give a sketch of the life and
work of Frederick Engels, one of the two great teachers of the
modern proletariat.

Engels was born in 1820 in Barmen, in the Rhine Province of
the kingdom of Prussia. His father was a manufacturer. In 1838
Engels, without having completed his high-school studies, was
forced by family circumstances to enter a commercial house in
Bremen as a clerk. Commercial affairs did not prevent Engels from
pursuing his scientific and political education. He had come to hate
autocracy and the tyranny of bureaucrats while still at high school.
The study of philosophy led him further. At that time Hegel's
teaching dominated German philosophy, and Engels became his
follower. Although Hegel himself was an admirer of the autocratic
Prussian state, in whose service he was as a professor at Berlin
University, Hegel's *teachings* were revolutionary. Hegel's faith in
human reason and its rights, and the fundamental thesis of
Hegelian philosophy that the universe is undergoing a constant
process of change and development, led some of the disciples of
the Berlin philosopher—those who refused to accept the existing

situation—to the idea that the struggle against this situation, the struggle against existing wrong and prevalent evil, is also rooted in the universal law of eternal development. If all things develop, if institutions of one kind give place to others, why should the autocracy of the Prussian king or of the Russian tsar, the enrichment of an insignificant minority at the expense of the vast majority, or the domination of the bourgeoisie over the people, continue for ever ? Hegel's philosophy spoke of the development of the mind and of ideas; it was *idealistic*. From the development of the mind it deduced the development of nature, of man, and of human, social relations. While retaining Hegel's idea of the eternal process of development,* Marx and Engels rejected the preconceived idealist view; turning to life, they saw that it is not the development of mind that explains the development of nature but that, on the contrary, the explanation of mind must be derived from nature, from matter.... Unlike Hegel and the other Hegelians, Marx and Engels were materialists. Regarding the world and humanity materialistically, they perceived that just as material causes underlie all natural phenomena, so the development of human society is conditioned by the development of material forces, the productive forces. On the development of the productive forces depend the relations into which men enter with one another in the production of the things required for the satisfaction of human needs. And in these relations lies the explanation of all the phenomena of social life, human aspirations, ideas and laws. The development of the productive forces creates social relations based upon private property, but now we see that this same development of the productive forces deprives the majority of their property and concentrates it in the hands of an insignificant minority. It abolishes property, the basis of the modern social order, it itself strives towards the very aim which the socialists have set themselves. All the socialists have to do is to realise which social force, owing to its position in modern society, is interested in bringing socialism about, and to impart to this force the consciousness of its interests and of its historical task. This force is the proletariat. Engels got to know the proletariat in England, in the centre of English industry, Manchester, where he settled in 1842, entering the service of a commercial firm of which his father was a shareholder. Here Engels not only sat in the factory office but wandered about the slums in which the workers were cooped up, and saw their poverty and misery with his own eyes. But he did not confine

---

* Marx and Engels frequently pointed out that in their intellectual development they were much indebted to the great German philosophers, particularly to Hegel. "Without German philosophy," Engels says, "scientific socialism would never have come into being." [See p. 246 of this volume.—*Ed.*]

himself to personal observations. He read all that had been revealed before him about the condition of the British working class
and carefully studied all the official documents he could lay his
hands on. The fruit of these studies and observations was the
book which appeared in 1845: *The Condition of the Working Class
in England.* We have already mentioned what was the chief service
rendered by Engels in writing *The Condition of the Working Class
in England.* Even before Engels, many people had described the
sufferings of the proletariat and had pointed to the necessity of
helping it. Engels was the *first* to say that the proletariat is *not
only* a suffering class; that it is, in fact, the disgraceful economic
condition of the proletariat that drives it irresistibly forward and
compels it to fight for its ultimate emancipation. And the fighting
proletariat *will help itself.* The political movement of the working
class will inevitably lead the workers to realise that their only
salvation lies in socialism. On the other hand, socialism will
become a force only when it becomes the aim of the *political
struggle of the working class.* Such are the main ideas of Engels's
book on the condition of the working class in England, ideas which
have now been adopted by all thinking and fighting proletarians,
but which at that time were entirely new. These ideas were set out
in a book written in absorbing style and filled with most authentic
and shocking pictures of the misery of the English proletariat. The
book was a terrible indictment of capitalism and the bourgeoisie
and created a profound impression. Engels's book began to be
quoted everywhere as presenting the best picture of the condition
of the modern proletariat. And, in fact, neither before 1845 nor
after has there appeared so striking and truthful a picture of the
misery of the working class.

It was not until he came to England that Engels became a
socialist. In Manchester he established contacts with people active
in the English labour movement at the time and began to write
for English socialist publications. In 1844, while on his way back
to Germany, he became acquainted in Paris with Marx, with whom
he had already started to correspond. In Paris, under the influence
of the French socialists and French life, Marx had also become
a socialist. Here the friends jointly wrote a book entitled *The Holy
Family, or Critique of Critical Critique.* This book, which appeared
a year before *The Condition of the Working Class in England,* and
the greater part of which was written by Marx, contains the foundations of revolutionary materialist socialism, the main ideas of
which we have expounded above. "The holy family" is a facetious
nickname for the Bauer brothers, the philosophers, and their followers. These gentlemen preached a criticism which stood above
all reality, above parties and politics, which rejected all practical
activity, and which only "critically" contemplated the surrounding

world and the events going on within it. These gentlemen, the Bauers, looked down on the proletariat as an uncritical mass. Marx and Engels vigorously opposed this absurd and harmful tendency. In the name of a real, human person—the worker, trampled down by the ruling classes and the state—they demanded, not contemplation, but a struggle for a better order of society. They, of course, regarded the proletariat as the force that is capable of waging this struggle and that is interested in it. Even before the appearance of *The Holy Family*, Engels had published in Marx's and Ruge's *Deutsch-Französische Jahrbücher* his "Critical Essays on Political Economy,"* in which he examined the principal phenomena of the contemporary economic order from a socialist standpoint, regarding them as necessary consequences of the rule of private property. Contact with Engels was undoubtedly a factor in Marx's decision to study political economy, the science in which his works have produced a veritable revolution.

From 1845 to 1847 Engels lived in Brussels and Paris, combining scientific work with practical activities among the German workers in Brussels and Paris. Here Marx and Engels established contact with the secret German Communist League, which commissioned them to expound the main principles of the socialism they had worked out. Thus arose the famous *Manifesto of the Communist Party* of Marx and Engels, published in 1848. This little booklet is worth whole volumes; to this day its spirit inspires and guides the entire organised and fighting proletariat of the civilised world.

The revolution of 1848, which broke out first in France and then spread to other West-European countries, brought Marx and Engels back to their native country. Here, in Rhenish Prussia, they took charge of the democratic *Neue Rheinische Zeitung* published in Cologne. The two friends were the heart and soul of all revolutionary-democratic aspirations in Rhenish Prussia. They fought to the last ditch in defence of freedom and of the interests of the people against the forces of reaction. The latter, as we know, gained the upper hand. The *Neue Rheinische Zeitung* was suppressed. Marx, who during his exile had lost his Prussian citizenship, was deported; Engels took part in the armed popular uprising, fought for liberty in three battles, and after the defeat of the rebels fled, via Switzerland, to London.

Marx also settled in London. Engels soon became a clerk again, and then a shareholder, in the Manchester commercial firm in which he had worked in the forties. Until 1870 he lived in Manchester, while Marx lived in London, but this did not prevent their

---

* Frederick Engels, "Umrisse zu einer Kritik der Nationalökonomie." Marx/Engels, *Werke*, Band 1, Dietz Verlag, Berlin, 1956, S. 499-524.—*Ed.*

maintaining a most lively interchange of ideas: they corresponded almost daily. In this correspondence the two friends exchanged views and discoveries and continued to collaborate in working out scientific socialism. In 1870 Engels moved to London, and their joint intellectual life, of the most strenuous nature, continued until 1883, when Marx died. Its fruit was, on Marx's side, *Capital*, the greatest work on political economy of our age, and on Engels's side, a number of works both large and small. Marx worked on the analysis of the complex phenomena of capitalist economy. Engels, in simply written works, often of a polemical character, dealt with more general scientific problems and with diverse phenomena of the past and present in the spirit of the materialist conception of history and Marx's economic theory. Of Engels's works we shall mention: the polemical work against Dühring (analysing highly important problems in the domain of philosophy, natural science and the social sciences),* *The Origin of the Family, Private Property and the State* (translated into Russian, published in St. Petersburg, 3rd ed., 1895), *Ludwig Feuerbach* (Russian translation and notes by G. Plekhanov, Geneva, 1892), an article on the foreign policy of the Russian Government (translated into Russian in the Geneva *Sotsial-Demokrat* Nos. 1 and 2), splendid articles on the housing question, and finally, two small but very valuable articles on Russia's economic development (*Frederick Engels on Russia*, translated into Russian by Zasulich, Geneva, 1894). Marx died before he could put the final touches to his vast work on capital. The draft, however, was already finished, and after the death of his friend, Engels undertook the onerous task of preparing and publishing the second and the third volumes of *Capital*. He published Volume II in 1885 and Volume III in 1894 (his death prevented the preparation of Volume IV). These two volumes entailed a vast amount of labour. Adler, the Austrian Social-Democrat, has rightly remarked that by publishing volumes II and III of *Capital* Engels erected a majestic monument to the genius who had been his friend, a monument on which, without intending it, he indelibly carved his own name. Indeed these two volumes of *Capital* are the work of two men: Marx and Engels. Old legends contain various moving instances of friendship. The European proletariat may say that its science was created by two scholars and fighters, whose relationship to each other surpasses the most moving stories of the ancients about human friendship. Engels

---

* This is a wonderfully rich and instructive book. Unfortunately, only a small portion of it, containing a historical outline of the development of socialism, has been translated into Russian (*The Development of Scientific Socialism*, 2nd ed., Geneva, 1892). [Reference is to Engels's books *Anti-Dühring* and *Socialism: Utopian and Scientific.—Ed.*]

always—and, on the whole, quite justly—placed himself after Marx. "In Marx's lifetime," he wrote to an old friend, "I played second fiddle."* His love for the living Marx, and his reverence for the memory of the dead Marx were boundless. This stern fighter and austere thinker possessed a deeply loving soul.

After the movement of 1848-49, Marx and Engels in exile did not confine themselves to scientific research. In 1864 Marx founded the International Working Men's Association, and led this society for a whole decade. Engels also took an active part in its affairs. The work of the International Association, which, in accordance with Marx's idea, united proletarians of all countries, was of tremendous significance in the development of the working-class movement. But even with the closing down of the International Association in the seventies, the unifying role of Marx and Engels did not cease. On the contrary, it may be said that their importance as the spiritual leaders of the working-class movement grew continuously, because the movement itself grew uninterruptedly. After the death of Marx, Engels continued alone as the counsellor and leader of the European socialists. His advice and directions were sought for equally by the German socialists, whose strength, despite government persecution, grew rapidly and steadily, and by representatives of backward countries, such as the Spaniards, Rumanians and Russians, who were obliged to ponder and weigh their first steps. They all drew on the rich store of knowledge and experience of Engels in his old age.

Marx and Engels, who both knew Russian and read Russian books, took a lively interest in the country, followed the Russian revolutionary movement with sympathy and maintained contact with Russian revolutionaries. They both became socialists after being *democrats*, and the democratic feeling of *hatred* for political despotism was exceedingly strong in them. This direct political feeling, combined with a profound theoretical understanding of the connection between political despotism and economic oppression, and also their rich experience of life, made Marx and Engels uncommonly responsive *politically*. That is why the heroic struggle of the handful of Russian revolutionaries against the mighty tsarist government evoked a most sympathetic echo in the hearts of these tried revolutionaries. On the other hand, the tendency, for the sake of illusory economic advantages, to turn away from the most immediate and important task of the Russian socialists, namely, the winning of political freedom, naturally appeared suspicious to them and was even regarded by them as a direct betrayal of the great cause of the social revolution. "The emancipation of the workers must be the

---

* Engels's letter to J. F. Becker dated October 15, 1884.—*Ed.*

act of the working class itself"—Marx and Engels constantly taught.* But in order to fight for its economic emancipation, the proletariat must win itself certain *political* rights. Moreover, Marx and Engels clearly saw that a political revolution in Russia would be of tremendous significance to the West-European working-class movement as well. Autocratic Russia had always been a bulwark of European reaction in general. The extraordinarily favourable international position enjoyed by Russia as a result of the war of 1870, which for a long time sowed discord between Germany and France, of course only enhanced the importance of autocratic Russia as a reactionary force. Only a free Russia, a Russia that had no need either to oppress the Poles, Finns, Germans, Armenians or any other small nations, or constantly to set France and Germany at loggerheads, would enable modern Europe, rid of the burden of war, to breathe freely, would weaken all the reactionary elements in Europe and strengthen the European working class. That was why Engels ardently desired the establishment of political freedom in Russia for the sake of the progress of the working-class movement in the West as well. In him the Russian revolutionaries have lost their best friend.

Let us always honour the memory of Frederick Engels, a great fighter and teacher of the proletariat!

Written in autumn 1895

First published in 1896
in the miscellany *Rabotnik*
No. 1-2

Collected Works, Vol. 2,
pp. 19-27

---

* Marx and Engels, *Manifesto of the Communist Party*, and Karl Marx, *General Rules of the International Working Men's Association* (Marx and Engels, *Selected Works*, Vol. I, Moscow, 1962, pp. 32 and 386).—*Ed.*

V. I. Lenin

THE THREE SOURCES AND THREE COMPONENT PARTS OF MARXISM

Throughout the civilised world the teachings of Marx evoke the utmost hostility and hatred of all bourgeois science (both official and liberal), which regards Marxism as a kind of "pernicious sect". And no other attitude is to be expected, for there can be no "impartial" social science in a society based on class struggle. In one way or another, *all* official and liberal science *defends* wage-slavery, whereas Marxism has declared relentless war on that slavery. To expect science to be impartial in a wage-slave society is as foolishly naïve as to expect impartiality from manufacturers on the question of whether workers' wages ought not to be increased by decreasing the profits of capital.

But this is not all. The history of philosophy and the history of social science show with perfect clarity that there is nothing resembling "sectarianism" in Marxism, in the sense of its being a hidebound, petrified doctrine, a doctrine which arose *away from* the high road of the development of world civilisation. On the contrary, the genius of Marx consists precisely in his having furnished answers to questions already raised by the foremost minds of mankind. His doctrine emerged as the direct and immediate *continuation* of the teachings of the greatest representatives of philosophy, political economy and socialism.

The Marxist doctrine is omnipotent because it is true. It is comprehensive and harmonious, and provides men with an integral world outlook irreconcilable with any form of superstition, reaction, or defence of bourgeois oppression. It is the legitimate successor to the best that man produced in the nineteenth century, as represented by German philosophy, English political economy and French socialism.

It is these three sources of Marxism, which are also its component parts, that we shall outline in brief.

I

The philosophy of Marxism is *materialism*. Throughout the modern history of Europe, and especially at the end of the eighteenth century in France, where a resolute struggle was conducted against every kind of medieval rubbish, against serfdom in institutions and ideas, materialism has proved to be the only philosophy that is consistent, true to all the teachings of natural science and hostile to superstition, cant and so forth. The enemies of democracy have, therefore, always exerted all their efforts to "refute", undermine and defame materialism, and have advocated various forms of philosophical idealism, which always, in one way or another, amounts to the defence or support of religion.

Marx and Engels defended philosophical materialism in the most determined manner and repeatedly explained how profoundly erroneous is every deviation from this basis. Their views are most clearly and fully expounded in the works of Engels, *Ludwig Feuerbach* and *Anti-Dühring*, which, like the *Communist Manifesto*, are handbooks for every class-conscious worker.

But Marx did not stop at eighteenth-century materialism: he developed philosophy to a higher level. He enriched it with the achievements of German classical philosophy, especially of Hegel's system, which in its turn had led to the materialism of Feuerbach. The main achievement was *dialectics*, i.e., the doctrine of development in its fullest, deepest and most comprehensive form, the doctrine of the relativity of the human knowledge that provides us with a reflection of eternally developing matter. The latest discoveries of natural science—radium, electrons, the transmutation of elements—have been a remarkable confirmation of Marx's dialectical materialism despite the teachings of the bourgeois philosophers with their "new" reversions to old and decadent idealism.

Marx deepened and developed philosophical materialsm to the full, and extended the cognition of nature to include the cognition of *human society*. His *historical materialism* was a great achievement in scientific thinking. The chaos and arbitrariness that had previously reigned in views on history and politics were replaced by a strikingly integral and harmonious scientific theory, which shows how, in consequence of the growth of productive forces, out of one system of social life another and higher system develops—how capitalism, for instance, grows out of feudalism.

Just as man's knowledge reflects nature (i.e., developing matter), which exists independently of him, so man's *social knowledge* (i.e., his various views and doctrines—philosophical, religious, political and so forth) reflects the *economic system* of society. Political institutions are a superstructure on the economic foundation. We see, for example, that the various political forms of the modern European states serve to strengthen the domination of the bourgeoisie over the proletariat.

Marx's philosophy is a consummate philosophical materialism which has provided mankind, and especially the working class, with powerful instruments of knowledge.

II

Having recognised that the economic system is the foundation on which the political superstructure is erected, Marx devoted his greatest attention to the study of this economic system. Marx's principal work, *Capital*, is devoted to a study of the economic system of modern, i.e., capitalist, society.

Classical political economy, before Marx, evolved in England, the most developed of the capitalist countries. Adam Smith and David Ricardo, by their investigations of the economic system, laid the foundations of the *labour theory of value*. Marx continued their work; he provided a proof of the theory and developed it consistently. He showed that the value of every commodity is determined by the quantity of socially necessary labour time spent on its production.

Where the bourgeois economists saw a relation between things (the exchange of one commodity for another) Marx revealed a *relation between people*. The exchange of commodities expresses the connection between individual producers through the market. Money *signifies* that the connection is becoming closer and closer, inseparably uniting the entire economic life of the individual producers into one whole. *Capital* signifies a further development of this connection: man's labour-power becomes a commodity. The wage-worker sells his labour-power to the owner of land, factories and instruments of labour. The worker spends one part of the day covering the cost of maintaining himself and his family (wages), while the other part of the day he works without remuneration, creating for the capitalist *surplus-value*, the source of profit, the source of the wealth of the capitalist class.

The doctrine of surplus-value is the corner-stone of Marx's economic theory.

Capital, created by the labour of the worker, crushes the worker, ruining small proprietors and creating an army of unemployed. In industry, the victory of large-scale production is immediately apparent, but the same phenomenon is also to be observed in agriculture, where the superiority of large-scale capitalist agriculture is enhanced, the use of machinery increases and the peasant economy, trapped by money-capital, declines and falls into ruin under the burden of its backward technique. The decline of small-scale production assumes different forms in agriculture, but the decline itself is an indisputable fact.

By destroying small-scale production, capital leads to an increase in productivity of labour and to the creation of a monopoly position for the associations of big capitalists. Production itself becomes more and more social—hundreds of thousands and millions of workers become bound together in a regular economic organism—

but the product of this collective labour is appropriated by a handful of capitalists. Anarchy of production, crises, the furious chase after markets and the insecurity of existence of the mass of the population are intensified.

By increasing the dependence of the workers on capital, the capitalist system creates the great power of united labour.

Marx traced the development of capitalism from embryonic commodity economy, from simple exchange, to its highest forms, to large-scale production.

And the experience of all capitalist countries, old and new, year by year demonstrates clearly the truth of this Marxian doctrine to increasing numbers of workers.

Capitalism has triumphed all over the world, but this triumph is only the prelude to the triumph of labour over capital.

III

When feudalism was overthrown, and *"free"* capitalist society appeared in the world, it at once became apparent that this freedom meant a new system of oppression and exploitation of the working people. Various socialist doctrines immediately emerged as a reflection of and protest against this oppression. Early socialism, however, was *utopian* socialism. It criticised capitalist society, it condemned and damned it, it dreamed of its destruction, it had visions of a better order and endeavoured to convince the rich of the immorality of exploitation.

But utopian socialism could not indicate the real solution. It could not explain the real nature of wage-slavery under capitalism, it could not reveal the laws of capitalist development, or show what *social force* is capable of becoming the creator of a new society.

Meanwhile, the stormy revolutions which everywhere in Europe, and especially in France, accompanied the fall of feudalism, of serfdom, more and more clearly revealed the *struggle of classes* as the basis and the driving force of all development.

Not a single victory of political freedom over the feudal class was won except against desperate resistance. Not a single capitalist country evolved on a more or less free and democratic basis except by a life-and-death struggle between the various classes of capitalist society.

The genius of Marx lies in his having been the first to deduce from this the lesson world history teaches and to apply that lesson consistently. The deduction he made is the doctrine of the *class struggle*.

People always have been the foolish victims of deception and self-deception in politics, and they always will be until they have learnt to seek out the *interests* of some class or other behind all moral, religious, political and social phrases, declarations and promises. Champions of reforms and improvements will always be fooled by the defenders of the old order until they realise that every old institution, however barbarous and rotten it may appear to be, is kept going by the forces of certain ruling classes. And there is *only one* way of smashing the resistance of those classes, and that is to find, in the very society which surrounds us, the forces which can—and, owing to their social position, *must*—constitute the power capable of sweeping away the old and creating the new, and to enlighten and organise those forces for the struggle.

Marx's philosophical materialism alone has shown the proletariat the way out of the spiritual slavery in which all oppressed classes have hitherto languished. Marx's economic theory alone has explained the true position of the proletariat in the general system of capitalism.

Independent organisations of the proletariat are multiplying all over the world, from America to Japan and from Sweden to South Africa. The proletariat is becoming enlightened and educated by waging its class struggle; it is ridding itself of the prejudices of bourgeois society; it is rallying its ranks ever more closely and is learning to gauge the measure of its successes; it is steeling its forces and is growing irresistibly.

Prosveshcheniye No. 3,
March 1913

Collected Works, Vol. 19,
pp. 23-28

Karl Marx

THESES ON FEUERBACH[1]

THREE SOURCES AND THREE COMPONENT PARTS OF MARXISM

I

The chief defect of all hitherto existing materialism—that of Feuerbach included—is that the thing [*Gegenstand*], reality, sensuousness, is conceived only in the form of the *object* [*Objekt*] or of *contemplation* [*Anschauung*], but not as *human sensuous activity, practice*, not subjectively. Hence it happened that the *active* side, in contradistinction to materialism, was developed by idealism—but only abstractly, since, of course, idealism does not know real, sensuous activity as such. Feuerbach wants sensuous objects, really differentiated from the thought objects, but he does not conceive human activity itself as *objective* [*gegenständliche*] activity. Hence, in the *Essence of Christianity*, he regards the theoretical attitude as the only genuinely human attitude, while practice is conceived and fixed only in its dirty-judaical form of appearance. Hence he does not grasp the significance of "revolutionary," of "practical-critical," activity.

II

The question whether objective [*gegenständliche*] truth can be attributed to human thinking is not a question of theory but is a *practical* question. In practice man must prove the truth, that is, the reality and power, the this-sidedness [*Diesseitigkeit*] of his thinking. The dispute over the reality or non-reality of thinking which is isolated from practice is a purely *scholastic* question.

III

The materialist doctrine that men are products of circumstances and upbringing, and that, therefore, changed men are products of other circumstances and changed upbringing, forgets that it is men that change circumstances and that the educator himself needs educating. Hence, this doctrine necessarily arrives at dividing society into two parts, of which one is superior to society (in Robert Owen, for example).

The coincidence of the changing of circumstances and of human activity can be conceived and rationally understood only as *revolutionising practice*.

IV

Feuerbach starts out from the fact of religious self-alienation, the duplication of the world into a religious, imaginary world and a real one. His work consists in the dissolution of the religious world into its secular basis. He overlooks the fact that after completing this work, the chief thing still remains to be done. For the fact that the secular foundation detaches itself from itself and establishes itself in the clouds as an independent realm is really only to be explained by the self-cleavage and self-contradictoriness of this secular basis. The latter must itself, therefore, first be understood in its contradiction and then, by the removal of the contradiction, revolutionised in practice. Thus, for instance, once the earthly family is discovered to be the secret of the holy family, the former must then itself be criticised in theory and revolutionised in practice.

V

Feuerbach, not satisfied with *abstract thinking*, appeals to *sensuous contemplation*; but he does not conceive sensuousness as *practical*, human-sensuous activity.

VI

Feuerbach resolves the religious essence into the *human* essence. But the human essence is no abstraction inherent in each single individual. In its reality it is the ensemble of the social relations.

Feuerbach, who does not enter upon a criticism of this real essence, is consequently compelled:

1. To abstract from the historical process and to fix the religious sentiment [*Gemüt*] as something by itself and to presuppose an abstract—*isolated*—human individual.

2. The human essence, therefore, can with him be comprehended only as a "genus", as an internal, dumb generality which merely naturally unites the many individuals.

VII

Feuerbach, consequently, does not see that the "religious sentiment" is itself a *social product*, and that the abstract individual whom he analyses belongs in reality to a particular form of society.

VIII

Social life is essentially *practical*. All mysteries which mislead theory to mysticism find their rational solution in human practice and in the comprehension of this practice.

IX

The highest point attained by *contemplative* materialism, that is, materialism which does not understand sensuousness as practical activity, is the contemplation of single individuals in "civil society."

X

The standpoint of the old materialism is "*civil*" society; the standpoint of the new is *human* society, or socialised humanity.

XI

The philosophers have only *interpreted* the world, in various ways; the point, however, is to *change* it.

Written by Marx in the spring of 1845

Originally published by Engels in 1888 in the Appendix to the separate edition of his *Ludwig Feuerbach and the End of Classical German Philosophy*

Printed according to the text of the separate 1888 edition and checked with the ms. of Karl Marx

Translated from the German

Karl Marx and Frederick Engels

MANIFESTO OF THE COMMUNIST PARTY[2]

PREFACE TO THE GERMAN EDITION OF 1872

The Communist League,[3] an international association of workers, which could of course be only a secret one under the conditions obtaining at the time, commissioned the undersigned, at the Congress held in London in November 1847, to draw up for publication a detailed theoretical and practical programme of the Party. Such was the origin of the following Manifesto, the manuscript of which travelled to London, to be printed, a few weeks before the February Revolution[4]. First published in German, it has been republished in that language in at least twelve different editions in Germany, England and America. It was published in English for the first time in 1850 in the *Red Republican*,[5] London, translated by Miss Helen Macfarlane, and in 1871 in at least three different translations in America. A French version first appeared in Paris shortly before the June insurrection of 1848[6] and recently in *Le Socialiste*[7] of New York. A new translation is in the course of preparation. A Polish version appeared in London shortly after it was first published in German. A Russian translation was published in Geneva in the sixties. Into Danish, too, it was translated shortly after its first appearance.

However much the state of things may have altered during the last twenty-five years, the general principles laid down in this Manifesto are, on the whole, as correct today as ever. Here and there some detail might be improved. The practical application of the principles will depend, as the Manifesto itself states, everywhere and at all times, on the historical conditions for the time being existing, and, for that reason, no special stress is laid on the revolutionary measures proposed at the end of Section II. That passage would, in many respects, be very differently worded today. In view of the gigantic strides of Modern Industry in the last twenty-five years, and of the accompanying improved and extended party organisation of the working class, in view of the practical experience gained, first in the February Revolution, and then, still more, in the Paris Commune,[8] where the proletariat for the first time held political power for two whole months, this programme has in some details become antiquated. One thing especially was proved by the Commune, *viz.*, that "the working class cannot simply lay hold of the ready-made State machinery, and wield it for its own purposes." (See *The Civil War in France; Address of the General Council of the International Working Men's Association*, London, Truelove, 1871, p. 15, where this point is further developed.*) Further, it is self-evident that the criticism of socialist literature is deficient in relation to the present time, because it comes down only to 1847; also, that the remarks on the relation of the Communists to the various opposition parties (Section IV), although in principle still correct, yet in practice are antiquated, because the political situation has been entirely changed, and the progress of history has swept from off the earth the greater portion of the political parties there enumerated.

But, then, the Manifesto has become a historical document which we have no longer any right to alter. A subsequent edition may perhaps appear with an introduction bridging the gap from 1847 to the present day; this reprint was too unexpected to leave us time for that.

Karl Marx   Frederick Engels

London, June 24, 1872

Written by Marx and Engels
for the German edition which
appeared in Leipzig in 1872

Printed according to the 1872
edition
Translated from the German

FROM THE PREFACE TO THE GERMAN EDITION
OF 1890

The Manifesto has had a history of its own. Greeted with enthusiasm, at the time of its appearance, by the then still not at all numerous vanguard of scientific socialism (as is proved by the translations mentioned in the first preface**), it was soon forced into the background by the reaction that began with the defeat of the Paris workers in June 1848, and was finally excommunicated "according to law" by the conviction of the Cologne Communists in November 1852.[9] With the disappearance from the public scene of the workers' movement that had begun with the February Revolution, the Manifesto too passed into the background.

When the working class of Europe had again gathered sufficient strength for a new onslaught upon the power of the ruling classes, the International Working Men's Association came into being. Its

---

* See p. 285 of this volume.—*Ed.*
** See p. 31 of this volume.—*Ed.*

aim was to weld together into *one* huge army the whole militant working class of Europe and America. Therefore it could not *set out* from the principles laid down in the Manifesto. It was bound to havè a programme which would not shut the door on the English trade unions, the French, Belgian, Italian and Spanish Proudhonists and the German Lassalleans.* This programme—the preamble to the Rules of the International**—was drawn up by Marx with a master hand acknowledged even by Bakunin and the Anarchists. For the ultimate triumph of the ideas set forth in the Manifesto Marx relied solely and exclusively upon the intellectual development of the working class, as it necessarily had to ensue from united action and discussion. The events and vicissitudes in the struggle against capital, the defeats even more than the successes, could not but demonstrate to the fighters the inadequacy hitherto of their universal panaceas and make their minds more receptive to a thorough understanding of the true conditions for the emancipation of the workers. And Marx was right. The working class of 1874, at the dissolution of the International, was altogether different from that of 1864, at its foundation. Proudhonism in the Latin countries and the specific Lassalleanism in Germany were dying out, and even the then arch-conservative English trade unions were gradually approaching the point where in 1887 the chairman of their Swansea Congress*** could say in their name: "Continental Socialism has lost its terrors for us." Yet by 1887 Continental Socialism was almost exclusively the theory heralded in the Manifesto. Thus, to a certain extent, the history of the Manifesto reflects the history of the modern working-class movement since 1848. At present it is doubtless the most widely circulated, the most international product of all socialist literature, the common programme of many millions of workers of all countries, from Siberia to California.

Nevertheless, when it appeared we could not have called it a *Socialist* Manifesto. In 1847 two kinds of people were considered Socialists. On the one hand were the adherents of the various Utopian systems, notably the Owenites in England and the Fourierists in France, both of whom at that date had already dwindled to mere sects gradually dying out. On the other, the manifold

---

* Lassalle personally, to us, always acknowledged himself to be a "disciple" of Marx, and, as such, stood, of course, on the ground of the Manifesto. Matters were quite different with regard to those of his followers who did not go beyond his demand for producers' co-operatives supported by state credits and who divided the whole working class into supporters of state assistance and supporters of self-assistance. [*Note by Engels.*]

** K. Marx, *General Rules of the International Working Men's Association* (see Marx and Engels, *Selected Works*, Vol. I, Moscow, 1962, pp. 386-89).—*Ed.*

*** W. Bevan.—*Ed.*

types of social quacks who wanted to eliminate social abuses through their various universal panaceas and all kinds of patchwork, without hurting capital and profit in the least. In both cases, people who stood outside the labour movement and who looked for support rather to the "educated" classes. The section of the working class, however, which demanded a radical reconstruction of society, convinced that mere political revolutions were not enough, then called itself *Communist*. It was still a rough-hewn, only instinctive, and frequently somewhat crude communism. Yet it was powerful enough to bring into being two systems of Utopian Communism—in France the "Icarian" communism of Cabet, and in Germany that of Weitling. Socialism in 1847 signified a bourgeois movement, communism a working-class movement. Socialism was, on the Continent at least, quite respectable, whereas communism was the very opposite. And since we were very decidedly of the opinion as early as then that "the emancipation of the workers must be the act of the working class itself," we could have no hesitations as to which of the two names we should choose. Nor has it ever occurred to us since to repudiate it.

"Working men of all countries, unite!" But few voices responded when we proclaimed these words to the world forty-two years ago, on the eve of the first Paris Revolution in which the proletariat came out with demands of its own.[10] On September 28, 1864, however, the proletarians of most of the Western European countries united to form the International Working Men's Association of glorious memory. True, the International itself lived only nine years. But that the eternal union of the proletarians of all countries created by it is still alive and lives stronger than ever, there is no better witness than this day. Because today,[11] as I write these lines, the European and American proletariat is reviewing its fighting forces, mobilised for the first time, mobilised as *one* army, under *one* flag, for *one* immediate aim: the standard eight-hour working day, to be established by legal enactment, as proclaimed by the Geneva Congress of the International in 1866, and again by the Paris Workers' Congress in 1889. And today's spectacle will open the eyes of the capitalists and landlords of all countries to the fact that today the working men of all countries are united indeed.

If only Marx were still by my side to see this with his own eyes!

F. Engels

London, May 1, 1890

Written by Engels for the German edition which appeared in London in 1890

Printed according to the 1890 edition
Translated from the German

MANIFESTO OF THE COMMUNIST PARTY[2]

A spectre is haunting Europe—the spectre of Communism. All the Powers of old Europe have entered into a holy alliance to exorcise this spectre: Pope and Czar, Metternich and Guizot, French Radicals and German police-spies.

Where is the party in opposition that has not been decried as Communistic by its opponents in power? Where the Opposition that has not hurled back the branding reproach of Communism, against the more advanced opposition parties, as well as against its reactionary adversaries?

Two things result from this fact.

I. Communism is already acknowledged by all European Powers to be itself a Power.

II. It is high time that Communists should openly, in the face of the whole world, publish their views, their aims, their tendencies, and meet this nursery tale of the Spectre of Communism with a Manifesto of the party itself.

To this end, Communists of various nationalities have assembled in London, and sketched the following Manifesto, to be published in the English, French, German, Italian, Flemish and Danish languages.

I

BOURGEOIS AND PROLETARIANS*

The history of all hitherto existing society** is the history of class struggles.

Freeman and slave, patrician and plebeian, lord and serf, guild-

---

* By bourgeoisie is meant the class of modern Capitalists, owners of the means of social production and employers of wage-labour. By proletariat, the class of modern wage-labourers who, having no means of production of their own, are reduced to selling their labour-power in order to live. [*Note by Engels to the English edition of 1888.*]

** That is, all *written* history. In 1847, the pre-history of society, the social organisation existing previous to recorded history, was all but unknown. Since

master* and journeyman, in a word, oppressor and oppressed, stood in constant opposition to one another, carried on an uninterrupted, now hidden, now open fight, a fight that each time ended, either in a revolutionary re-constitution of society at large, or in the common ruin of the contending classes.

In the earlier epochs of history, we find almost everywhere a complicated arrangement of society into various orders, a manifold gradation of social rank. In ancient Rome we have patricians, knights, plebeians, slaves; in the Middle Ages, feudal lords, vassals, guild-masters, journeymen, apprentices, serfs; in almost all of these classes, again, subordinate gradations.

The modern bourgeois society that has sprouted from the ruins of feudal society has not done away with class antagonisms. It has but established new classes, new conditions of oppression, new forms of struggle in place of the old ones.

Our epoch, the epoch of the bourgeoisie, possesses, however, this distinctive feature: it has simplified the class antagonisms. Society as a whole is more and more splitting up into two great hostile camps, into two great classes directly facing each other: Bourgeoisie and Proletariat.

From the serfs of the Middle Ages sprang the chartered burghers of the earliest towns. From these burgesses the first elements of the bourgeoisie were developed.

The discovery of America, the rounding of the Cape, opened up fresh ground for the rising bourgeoisie. The East-Indian and Chinese markets, the colonisation of America, trade with the colonies, the increase in the means of exchange and in commodities generally, gave to commerce, to navigation, to industry, an impulse never before known, and thereby, to the revolutionary element in the tottering feudal society, a rapid development.

The feudal system of industry, under which industrial production was monopolised by closed guilds, now no longer sufficed for the growing wants of the new markets. The manufacturing system

---

then, Haxthausen discovered common ownership of land in Russia, Maurer proved it to be the social foundation from which all Teutonic races started in history, and by and by village communities were found to be, or to have been the primitive form of society everywhere from India to Ireland. The inner organisation of this primitive Communistic society was laid bare, in its typical form, by Morgan's crowning discovery of the true nature of the *gens* and its relation to the *tribe*. With the dissolution of these primaeval communities society begins to be differentiated into separate and finally antagonistic classes. I have attempted to retrace this process of dissolution in: "Der Ursprung der Familie, des Privateigenthums und des Staats" [*The Origin of the Family, Private Property and the State.* See pp. 449-583 of this volume.—*Ed.*], 2nd edition, Stuttgart 1886. [*Note by Engels to the English edition of 1888.*]

* Guild-master, that is, a full member of a guild, a master within, not a head of a guild. [*Note by Engels to the English edition of 1888.*]

took its place. The guild-masters were pushed on one side by the manufacturing middle class; division of labour between the different corporate guilds vanished in the face of division of labour in each single workshop.

Meantime the markets kept ever growing, the demand ever rising. Even manufacture no longer sufficed. Thereupon, steam and machinery revolutionised industrial production. The place of manufacture was taken by the giant, Modern Industry, the place of the industrial middle class, by industrial millionaires, the leaders of whole industrial armies, the modern bourgeois.

Modern industry has established the world-market, for which the discovery of America paved the way. This market has given an immense development to commerce, to navigation, to communication by land. This development has, in its turn, reacted on the extension of industry; and in proportion as industry, commerce, navigation, railways extended, in the same proportion the bourgeoisie developed, increased its capital, and pushed into the background every class handed down from the Middle Ages.

We see, therefore, how the modern bourgeoisie is itself the product of a long course of development, of a series of revolutions in the modes of production and of exchange.

Each step in the development of the bourgeoisie was accompanied by a corresponding political advance of that class. An oppressed class under the sway of the feudal nobility, an armed and self-governing association in the mediaeval commune*; here independent urban republic (as in Italy and Germany), there taxable "third estate" of the monarchy (as in France), afterwards, in the period of manufacture proper, serving either the semi-feudal or the absolute monarchy as a counterpoise against the nobility, and, in fact, corner-stone of the great monarchies in general, the bourgeoisie has at last, since the establishment of Modern Industry and of the world-market, conquered for itself, in the modern representative State, exclusive political sway. The executive of the modern State is but a committee for managing the common affairs of the whole bourgeoisie.

The bourgeoisie, historically, has played a most revolutionary part.

---

* "Commune" was the name taken, in France, by the nascent towns even before they had conquered from their feudal lords and masters local self-government and political rights as the "Third Estate". Generally speaking, for the economical development of the bourgeoisie, England is here taken as the typical country; for its political development, France. [*Note by Engels to the English edition of 1888.*]

This was the name given their urban communities by the townsmen of Italy and France, after they had purchased or wrested their initial rights of self-government from their feudal lords. [*Note by Engels to the German edition of 1890.*]

The bourgeoisie, wherever it has got the upper hand, has put an end to all feudal, patriarchal, idyllic relations. It has pitilessly torn asunder the motley feudal ties that bound man to his "natural superiors," and has left remaining no other nexus between man and man than naked self-interest, than callous "cash payment." It has drowned the most heavenly ecstasies of religious fervour, of chivalrous enthusiasm, of philistine sentimentalism, in the icy water of egotistical calculation. It has resolved personal worth into exchange value, and in place of the numberless indefeasible chartered freedoms, has set up that single, unconscionable freedom— Free Trade. In one word, for exploitation, veiled by religious and political illusions, it has substituted naked, shameless, direct, brutal exploitation.

The bourgeoisie has stripped of its halo every occupation hitherto honoured and looked up to with reverent awe. It has converted the physician, the lawyer, the priest, the poet, the man of science, into its paid wage-labourers.

The bourgeoisie has torn away from the family its sentimental veil, and has reduced the family relation to a mere money relation

The bourgeoisie has disclosed how it came to pass that the brutal display of vigour in the Middle Ages, which Reactionists so much admire, found its fitting complement in the most slothful indolence. It has been the first to show what man's activity can bring about. It has accomplished wonders far surpassing Egyptian pyramids, Roman aqueducts, and Gothic cathedrals; it has conducted expeditions that put in the shade all former Exoduses of nations and crusades.[12]

The bourgeoisie cannot exist without constantly revolutionising the instruments of production, and thereby the relations of production, and with them the whole relations of society. Conservation of the old modes of production in unaltered form, was, on the contrary, the first condition of existence for all earlier industrial classes. Constant revolutionising of production, uninterrupted disturbance of all social conditions, everlasting uncertainty and agitation distinguish the bourgeois epoch from all earlier ones. All fixed, fast-frozen relations, with their train of ancient and venerable prejudices and opinions, are swept away, all new-formed ones become antiquated before they can ossify. All that is solid melts into air, all that is holy is profaned, and man is at last compelled to face with sober senses, his real conditions of life, and his relations with his kind.

The need of a constantly expanding market for its products chases the bourgeoisie over the whole surface of the globe. It must nestle everywhere, settle everywhere, establish connexions everywhere.

The bourgeoisie has through its exploitation of the world-market given a cosmopolitan character to production and consumption in every country. To the great chagrin of Reactionists, it has drawn from under the feet of industry the national ground on which it stood. All old-established national industries have been destroyed or are daily being destroyed. They are dislodged by new industries, whose introduction becomes a life and death question for all civilised nations, by industries that no longer work up indigenous raw material, but raw material drawn from the remotest zones; industries whose products are consumed, not only at home, but in every quarter of the globe. In place of the old wants, satisfied by the productions of the country, we find new wants, requiring for their satisfaction the products of distant lands and climes. In place of the old local and national seclusion and self-sufficiency, we have intercourse in every direction, universal inter-dependence of nations. And as in material, so also in intellectual production. The intellectual creations of individual nations become common property. National one-sidedness and narrow-mindedness become more and more impossible, and from the numerous national and local literatures, there arises a world literature.

The bourgeoisie, by the rapid improvement of all instruments of production, by the immensely facilitated means of communication, draws all, even the most barbarian, nations into civilisation. The cheap prices of its commodities are the heavy artillery with which it batters down all Chinese walls, with which it forces the barbarians' intensely obstinate hatred of foreigners to capitulate. It compels all nations, on pain of extinction, to adopt the bourgeois mode of production; it compels them to introduce what it calls civilisation into their midst, i.e., to become bourgeois themselves. In one word, it creates a world after its own image.

The bourgeoisie has subjected the country to the rule of the towns. It has created enormous cities, has greatly increased the urban population as compared with the rural, and has thus rescued a considerable part of the population from the idiocy of rural life. Just as it has made the country dependent on the towns, so it has made barbarian and semi-barbarian countries dependent on the civilised ones, nations of peasants on nations of bourgeois, the East on the West.

The bourgeoisie keeps more and more doing away with the scattered state of the population, of the means of production, and of property. It has agglomerated population, centralised means of production, and has concentrated property in a few hands. The necessary consequence of this was political centralisation. Independent, or but loosely connected provinces, with separate interests, laws, governments and systems of taxation, became lumped together into one nation, with one government, one code of laws, one national class-interest, one frontier and one customs-tariff.

The bourgeoisie, during its rule of scarce one hundred years, has created more massive and more colossal productive forces than have all preceding generations together. Subjection of Nature's forces to man, machinery, application of chemistry to industry and agriculture, steam-navigation, railways, electric telegraphs, clearing of whole continents for cultivation, canalisation of rivers, whole populations conjured out of the ground—what earlier century had even a presentiment that such productive forces slumbered in the lap of social labour?

We see then: the means of production and of exchange, on whose foundation the bourgeoisie built itself up, were generated in feudal society. At a certain stage in the development of these means of production and of exchange, the conditions under which feudal society produced and exchanged, the feudal organisation of agriculture and manufacturing industry, in one word, the feudal relations of property became no longer compatible with the already developed productive forces; they became so many fetters. They had to be burst asunder; they were burst asunder.

Into their place stepped free competition, accompanied by a social and political constitution adapted to it, and by the economical and political sway of the bourgeois class.

A similar movement is going on before our own eyes. Modern bourgeois society with its relations of production, of exchange and of property, a society that has conjured up such gigantic means of production and of exchange, is like the sorcerer, who is no longer able to control the powers of the nether world whom he has called up by his spells. For many a decade past the history of industry and commerce is but the history of the revolt of modern productive forces against modern conditions of production, against the property relations that are the conditions for the existence of the bourgeoisie and of its rule. It is enough to mention the commercial crises that by their periodical return put on its trial, each time more threateningly, the existence of the entire bourgeois society. In these crises a great part not only of the existing products, but also of the previously created productive forces, are periodically destroyed. In these crises there breaks out an epidemic that, in all earlier epochs, would have seemed an absurdity—the epidemic of over-production. Society suddenly finds itself put back into a state of momentary barbarism; it appears as if a famine, a universal war of devastation had cut off the supply of every means of subsistence; industry and commerce seem to be destroyed; and why? Because there is too much civilisation, too much means of subsistence, too much industry, too much commerce. The productive forces at the disposal of society no longer tend to further the development of the conditions of bourgeois property; on the contrary, they have become too powerful for these conditions, by which they are fettered, and so soon as they overcome these fetters, they bring disorder into the whole of bourgeois society, endanger the existence of bourgeois property. The conditions of bourgeois society are too narrow to comprise the wealth created by them. And how does the bourgeoisie get over these crises? On the one hand by enforced destruction of a mass of productive forces; on the other, by the conquest of new markets, and by the more thorough exploitation of the old ones. That is to say, by paving the way for more extensive and more destructive crises, and by diminishing the means whereby crises are prevented.

The weapons with which the bourgeoisie felled feudalism to the ground are now turned against the bourgeoisie itself.

But not only has the bourgeoisie forged the weapons that bring death to itself; it has also called into existence the men who are to wield those weapons—the modern working class—the proletarians.

In proportion as the bourgeoisie, *i.e.*, capital, is developed, in the same proportion is the proletariat, the modern working class, developed—a class of labourers, who live only so long as they find work, and who find work only so long as their labour increases capital. These labourers, who must sell themselves piecemeal, are a commodity, like every other article of commerce, and are consequently exposed to all the vicissitudes of competition, to all the fluctuations of the market.

Owing to the extensive use of machinery and to division of labour, the work of the proletarians has lost all individual character, and, consequently, all charm for the workman. He becomes an appendage of the machine, and it is only the most simple, most monotonous, and most easily acquired knack, that is required of him. Hence, the cost of production of a workman is restricted, almost entirely, to the means of subsistence that he requires for his maintenance, and for the propagation of his race. But the price of a commodity, and therefore also of labour,[13] is equal to its cost of production. In proportion, therefore, as the repulsiveness of the work increases, the wage decreases. Nay more, in proportion as the use of machinery and division of labour increases, in the same proportion the burden of toil also increases, whether by prolongation of the working hours, by increase of the work exacted in a given time or by increased speed of the machinery, etc.

Modern industry has converted the little workshop of the patriarchal master into the great factory of the industrial capitalist. Masses of labourers, crowded into the factory, are organised like soldiers. As privates of the industrial army they are placed under the command of a perfect hierarchy of officers and sergeants. Not only are they slaves of the bourgeois class, and of the bourgeois State; they are daily and hourly enslaved by the machine, by the overlooker, and, above all, by the individual bourgeois manufacturer himself. The more openly this despotism proclaims gain to be its end and aim, the more petty, the more hateful and the more embittering it is.

The less the skill and exertion of strength implied in manual labour, in other words, the more modern industry becomes developed, the more is the labour of men superseded by that of women. Differences of age and sex have no longer any distinctive social validity for the working class. All are instruments of labour, more or less expensive to use, according to their age and sex.

No sooner is the exploitation of the labourer by the manufacturer, so far, at an end, and he receives his wages in cash, than he is set upon by the other portions of the bourgeoisie, the landlord, the shopkeeper, the pawnbroker, etc.

The lower strata of the middle class—the small tradespeople, shopkeepers, and retired tradesmen generally, the handicraftsmen and peasants—all these sink gradually into the proletariat, partly because their diminutive capital does not suffice for the scale on which Modern Industry is carried on, and is swamped in the competition with the large capitalists, partly because their specialised skill is rendered worthless by new methods of production. Thus the proletariat is recruited from all classes of the population.

The proletariat goes through various stages of development. With its birth begins its struggle with the bourgeoisie. At first the contest is carried on by individual labourers, then by the workpeople of a factory, then by the operatives of one trade, in one locality, against the individual bourgeois who directly exploits them. They direct their attacks not against the bourgeois conditions of production, but against the instruments of production themselves; they destroy imported wares that compete with their labour, they smash to pieces machinery, they set factories ablaze, they seek to restore by force the vanished status of the workman of the Middle Ages.

At this stage the labourers still form an incoherent mass scattered over the whole country, and broken up by their mutual competition. If anywhere they unite to form more compact bodies, this is not yet the consequence of their own active union, but of the union of the bourgeoisie, which class, in order to attain its own political ends, is compelled to set the whole proletariat in motion, and is moreover yet, for a time, able to do so. At this stage, therefore, the proletarians do not fight their enemies, but the enemies of their enemies, the remnants of absolute monarchy, the landowners, the non-industrial bourgeois, the petty bourgeoisie. Thus the whole historical movement is concentrated in the hands of the bourgeoisie; every victory so obtained is a victory for the bourgeoisie.

But with the development of industry the proletariat not only increases in number; it becomes concentrated in greater masses, its strength grows, and it feels that strength more. The various interests and conditions of life within the ranks of the proletariat are more and more equalised, in proportion as machinery obliterates all distinctions of labour, and nearly everywhere reduces wages to the same low level. The growing competition among the bourgeois, and the resulting commercial crises, make the wages of the workers ever more fluctuating. The unceasing improvement of machinery, ever more rapidly developing, makes their livelihood more and more precarious; the collisions between individual workmen and individual bourgeois take more and more the character of collisions between two classes. Thereupon the workers begin to form combinations (Trades' Unions) against the bourgeois; they club together in order to keep up the rate of wages; they found permanent associations in order to make provision beforehand for these occasional revolts. Here and there the contest breaks out into riots.

Now and then the workers are victorious, but only for a time. The real fruit of their battles lies, not in the immediate result, but in the ever-expanding union of the workers. This union is helped on by the improved means of communication that are created by modern industry and that place the workers of different localities in contact with one another. It was just this contact that was needed to centralise the numerous local struggles, all of the same character, into one national struggle between classes. But every class struggle is a political struggle. And that union, to attain which the burghers of the Middle Ages, with their miserable highways, required centuries, the modern proletarians, thanks to railways, achieve in a few years.

This organisation of the proletarians into a class, and consequently into a political party, is continually being upset again by the competition between the workers themselves. But it ever rises up again, stronger, firmer, mightier. It compels legislative recognition of particular interests of the workers, by taking advantage of the divisions among the bourgeoisie itself. Thus the ten-hours' bill in England was carried.

Altogether collisions between the classes of the old society further, in many ways, the course of development of the proletariat. The bourgeoisie finds itself involved in a constant battle. At first with the aristocracy; later on, with those portions of the bourgeoisie itself, whose interests have become antagonistic to the progress of industry; at all times, with the bourgeoisie of foreign countries. In all these battles it sees itself compelled to appeal to the proletariat, to ask for its help, and thus, to drag it into the political arena. The bourgeoisie itself, therefore, supplies the pro-

letariat with its own elements of political and general education,
in other words, it furnishes the proletariat with weapons for fighting the bourgeoisie.

Further, as we have already seen, entire sections of the ruling
classes are, by the advance of industry, precipitated into the proletariat, or are at least threatened in their conditions of existence.
These also supply the proletariat with fresh elements of enlightenment and progress.

Finally, in times when the class struggle nears the decisive hour,
the process of dissolution going on within the ruling class, in fact
within the whole range of old society, assumes such a violent,
glaring character, that a small section of the ruling class cuts itself
adrift, and joins the revolutionary class, the class that holds the
future in its hands. Just as, therefore, at an earlier period, a section
of the nobility went over to the bourgeoisie, so now a portion of
the bourgeoisie goes over to the proletariat, and in particular, a
portion of the bourgeois ideologists, who have raised themselves to
the level of comprehending theoretically the historical movement
as a whole.

Of all the classes that stand face to face with the bourgeoisie
today, the proletariat alone is a really revolutionary class. The
other classes decay and finally disappear in the face of Modern
Industry; the proletariat is its special and essential product.

The lower middle class, the small manufacturer, the shopkeeper,
the artisan, the peasant, all these fight against the bourgeoisie, to
save from extinction their existence as fractions of the middle
class. They are therefore not revolutionary, but conservative. Nay
more, they are reactionary, for they try to roll back the wheel of
history. If by chance they are revolutionary, they are so only in view
of their impending transfer into the proletariat, they thus defend
not their present, but their future interests, they desert their own
standpoint to place themselves at that of the proletariat.

The "dangerous class," the social scum, that passively rotting
mass thrown off by the lowest layers of old society, may, here and
there, be swept into the movement by a proletarian revolution, its
conditions of life, however, prepare it far more for the part of a
bribed tool of reactionary intrigue.

In the conditions of the proletariat, those of old society at large
are already virtually swamped. The proletarian is without property; his relation to his wife and children has no longer anything
in common with the bourgeois family-relations; modern, industrial
labour, modern subjection to capital, the same in England as in
France, in America as in Germany, has stripped him of every trace
of national character. Law, morality, religion, are to him so many
bourgeois prejudices, behind which lurk in ambush just as many
bourgeois interests.

All the preceding classes that got the upper hand, sought to fortify their already acquired status by subjecting society at large to their conditions of appropriation. The proletarians cannot become masters of the productive forces of society, except by abolishing their own previous mode of appropriation, and thereby also every other previous mode of appropriation. They have nothing of their own to secure and to fortify; their mission is to destroy all previous securities for, and insurances of, individual property.

All previous historical movements were movements of minorities, or in the interests of minorities. The proletarian movement is the self-conscious, independent movement of the immense majority, in the interests of the immense majority. The proletariat, the lowest stratum of our present society, cannot stir, cannot raise itself up, without the whole superincumbent strata of official society being sprung into the air.

Though not in substance, yet in form, the struggle of the proletariat with the bourgeoisie is at first a national struggle. The proletariat of each country must, of course, first of all settle matters with its own bourgeoisie.

In depicting the most general phases of the development of the proletariat, we traced the more or less veiled civil war, raging within existing society, up to the point where that war breaks out into open revolution, and where the violent overthrow of the bourgeoisie lays the foundation for the sway of the proletariat.

Hitherto, every form of society has been based, as we have already seen, on the antagonism of oppressing and oppressed classes. But in order to oppress a class, certain conditions must be assured to it under which it can, at least, continue its slavish existence. The serf, in the period of serfdom, raised himself to membership in the commune, just as the petty bourgeois, under the yoke of feudal absolutism, managed to develop into a bourgeois. The modern labourer, on the contrary, instead of rising with the progress of industry, sinks deeper and deeper below the conditions of existence of his own class. He becomes a pauper, and pauperism develops more rapidly than population and wealth. And here it becomes evident, that the bourgeoisie is unfit any longer to be the ruling class in society, and to impose its conditions of existence upon society as an over-riding law. It is unfit to rule because it is incompetent to assure an existence to its slave within his slavery, because it cannot help letting him sink into such a state, that it has to feed him, instead of being fed by him. Society can no longer live under this bourgeoisie, in other words, its existence is no longer compatible with society.

The essential condition for the existence, and for the sway of the bourgeois class, is the formation and augmentation of capital; the condition for capital is wage-labour. Wage-labour rests exclusively on competition between the labourers. The advance of industry, whose involuntary promoter is the bourgeoisie, replaces the isolation of the labourers, due to competition, by their revolutionary combination, due to association. The development of Modern Industry, therefore, cuts from under its feet the very foundation on which the bourgeoisie produces and appropriates products. What the bourgeoisie, therefore, produces, above all, is its own grave-diggers. Its fall and the victory of the proletariat are equally inevitable.

II

PROLETARIANS AND COMMUNISTS

In what relation do the Communists stand to the proletarians as a whole ?

The Communists do not form a separate party opposed to other working-class parties.

They have no interests separate and apart from those of the proletariat as a whole.

They do not set up any sectarian principles of their own, by which to shape and mould the proletarian movement.

The Communists are distinguished from the other working-class parties by this only: 1. In the national struggles of the proletarians of the different countries, they point out and bring to the front the common interests of the entire proletariat, independently of all nationality. 2. In the various stages of development which the struggle of the working class against the bourgeoisie has to pass through, they always and everywhere represent the interests of the movement as a whole.

The Communists, therefore, are on the one hand, practically, the most advanced and resolute section of the working-class parties of every country, that section which pushes forward all others; on the other hand, theoretically, they have over the great mass of the proletariat the advantage of clearly understanding the line of march, the conditions, and the ultimate general results of the proletarian movement.

The immediate aim of the Communists is the same as that of all the other proletarian parties: formation of the proletariat into a class, overthrow of the bourgeois supremacy, conquest of political power by the proletariat.

The theoretical conclusions of the Communists are in no way based on ideas or principles that have been invented, or discovered, by this or that would-be universal reformer.

They merely express, in general terms, actual relations springing from an existing class struggle, from a historical movement going on under our very eyes. The abolition of existing property relations is not at all a distinctive feature of Communism.

All property relations in the past have continually been subject to historical change consequent upon the change in historical conditions.

The French Revolution,[14] for example, abolished feudal property in favour of bourgeois property.

The distinguishing feature of Communism is not the abolition of property generally, but the abolition of bourgeois property. But modern bourgeois private property is the final and most complete expression of the system of producing and appropriating products, that is based on class antagonisms, on the exploitation of the many by the few.

In this sense, the theory of the Communists may be summed up in the single sentence: Abolition of private property.

We Communists have been reproached with the desire of abolishing the right of personally acquiring property as the fruit of a man's own labour, which property is alleged to be the groundwork of all personal freedom, activity and independence.

Hard-won, self-acquired, self-earned property! Do you mean the property of the petty artisan and of the small peasant, a form of property that preceded the bourgeois form? There is no need to abolish that; the development of industry has to a great extent already destroyed it, and is still destroying it daily.

Or do you mean modern bourgeois private property?

But does wage-labour create any property for the labourer? Not a bit. It creates capital, *i.e.*, that kind of property which exploits wage-labour, and which cannot increase except upon condition of begetting a new supply of wage-labour for fresh exploitation. Property, in its present form, is based on the antagonism of capital and wage-labour. Let us examine both sides of this antagonism.

To be a capitalist, is to have not only a purely personal, but a social *status* in production. Capital is a collective product, and only by the united action of many members, nay, in the last resort, only by the united action of all members of society, can it be set in motion.

Capital is, therefore, not a personal, it is a social power.

When, therefore, capital is converted into common property, into the property of all members of society, personal property is not thereby transformed into social property. It is only the social character of the property that is changed. It loses its class-character.

Let us now take wage-labour.

The average price of wage-labour is the minimum wage, *i.e.*, that quantum of the means of subsistence, which is absolutely requisite to keep the labourer in bare existence as a labourer. What, therefore, the wage-labourer appropriates by means of his labour, merely suffices to prolong and reproduce a bare existence. We by no means intend to abolish this personal appropriation of the products of labour, an appropriation that is made for the maintenance and reproduction of human life, and that leaves no surplus wherewith to command the labour of others. All that we want to do away with, is the miserable character of this appropriation, under which the labourer lives merely to increase capital, and is allowed to live only in so far as the interest of the ruling class requires it.

In bourgeois society, living labour is but a means to increase accumulated labour. In Communist society, accumulated labour is but a means to widen, to enrich, to promote the existence of the labourer.

In bourgeois society, therefore, the past dominates the present; in Communist society, the present dominates the past. In bourgeois society capital is independent and has individuality, while the living person is dependent and has no individuality.

And the abolition of this state of things is called by the bourgeois, abolition of individuality and freedom! And rightly so. The abolition of bourgeois individuality, bourgeois independence, and bourgeois freedom is undoubtedly aimed at.

By freedom is meant, under the present bourgeois conditions of production, free trade, free selling and buying.

But if selling and buying disappears, free selling and buying disappears also. This talk about free selling and buying, and all the other "brave words" of our bourgeoisie about freedom in general, have a meaning, if any, only in contrast with restricted selling and buying, with the fettered traders of the Middle Ages, but have no meaning when opposed to the Communistic abolition of buying and selling, of the bourgeois conditions of production, and of the bourgeoisie itself.

You are horrified at our intending to do away with private property. But in your existing society, private property is already done away with for nine-tenths of the population; its existence for the few is solely due to its non-existence in the hands of those nine-tenths. You reproach us, therefore, with intending to do away with a form of property, the necessary condition for whose existence is the non-existence of any property for the immense majority of society.

In one word, you reproach us with intending to do away with your property. Precisely so; that is just what we intend.

From the moment when labour can no longer be converted into capital, money, or rent, into a social power capable of being monopolised, *i.e.*, from the moment when individual property can no longer be transformed into bourgeois property, into capital, from that moment, you say, individuality vanishes.

You must, therefore, confess that by "individual" you mean no other person than the bourgeois, than the middle-class owner of property. This person must, indeed, be swept out of the way, and made impossible.

Communism deprives no man of the power to appropriate the products of society; all that it does is to deprive him of the power to subjugate the labour of others by means of such appropriation.

It has been objected that upon the abolition of private property all work will cease, and universal laziness will overtake us.

According to this, bourgeois society ought long ago to have gone to the dogs through sheer idleness; for those of its members who work, acquire nothing, and those who acquire anything, do not work. The whole of this objection is but another expression of the tautology: that there can no longer be any wage-labour when there is no longer any capital.

All objections urged against the Communistic mode of producing and appropriating material products, have, in the same way, been urged against the Communistic modes of producing and appropriating intellectual products. Just as, to the bourgeois, the disappearance of class property is the disappearance of production itself, so the disappearance of class culture is to him identical with the disappearance of all culture.

That culture, the loss of which he laments, is, for the enormous majority, a mere training to act as a machine.

But don't wrangle with us so long as you apply, to our intended abolition of bourgeois property, the standard of your bourgeois notions of freedom, culture, law, &c. Your very ideas are but the outgrowth of the conditions of your bourgeois production and bourgeois property, just as your jurisprudence is but the will of your class made into a law for all, a will, whose essential character and direction are determined by the economical conditions of existence of your class.

The selfish misconception that induces you to transform into eternal laws of nature and of reason, the social forms springing from your present mode of production and form of property—historical relations that rise and disappear in the progress of production—this misconception you share with every ruling class that has preceded you. What you see clearly in the case of ancient property, what you admit in the case of feudal property, you are of course forbidden to admit in the case of your own bourgeois form of property.

Abolition of the family! Even the most radical flare up at this infamous proposal of the Communists.

On what foundation is the present family, the bourgeois family, based? On capital, on private gain. In its completely developed form this family exists only among the bourgeoisie. But this state of things finds its complement in the practical absence of the family among the proletarians, and in public prostitution.

The bourgeois family will vanish as a matter of course when its complement vanishes, and both will vanish with the vanishing of capital.

Do you charge us with wanting to stop the exploitation of children by their parents? To this crime we plead guilty.

But, you will say, we destroy the most hallowed of relations, when we replace home education by social.

And your education! Is not that also social, and determined by the social conditions under which you educate, by the intervention, direct or indirect, of society, by means of schools, &c.? The Communists have not invented the intervention of society in education: they do but seek to alter the character of that intervention, and to rescue education from the influence of the ruling class.

The bourgeois clap-trap about the family and education, about the hallowed co-relation of parent and child, becomes all the more disgusting, the more, by the action of Modern Industry, all family ties among the proletarians are torn asunder, and their children transformed into simple articles of commerce and instruments of labour.

But you Communists would introduce community of women, screams the whole bourgeoisie in chorus.

The bourgeois sees in his wife a mere instrument of production. He hears that the instruments of production are to be exploited in common, and, naturally, can come to no other conclusion than that the lot of being common to all will likewise fall to the women.

He has not even a suspicion that the real point aimed at is to do away with the status of women as mere instruments of production.

For the rest, nothing is more ridiculous than the virtuous indignation of our bourgeois at the community of women which, they pretend, is to be openly and officially established by the Communists. The Communists have no need to introduce community of women; it has existed almost from time immemorial.

Our bourgeois, not content with having the wives and daughters of their proletarians at their disposal, not to speak of common prostitutes, take the greatest pleasure in seducing each other's wives.

Bourgeois marriage is in reality a system of wives in common and thus, at the most, what the Communists might possibly be reproached with, is that they desire to introduce, in substitution for a hypocritically concealed, an openly legalised community of women. For the rest, it is self-evident that the abolition of the present system of production must bring with it the abolition of the community of women springing from that system, i.e., of prostitution both public and private.

The Communists are further reproached with desiring to abolish countries and nationality.

The working men have no country. We cannot take from them what they have not got. Since the proletariat must first of all acquire political supremacy, must rise to be the leading class of the nation, must constitute itself *the* nation, it is, so far, itself national, though not in the bourgeois sense of the word.

National differences and antagonisms between peoples are daily more and more vanishing, owing to the development of the bourgeoisie, to freedom of commerce, to the world-market, to uniformity in the mode of production and in the conditions of life corresponding thereto.

The supremacy of the proletariat will cause them to vanish still faster. United action, of the leading civilised countries at least, is one of the first conditions for the emancipation of the proletariat.

In proportion as the exploitation of one individual by another is put an end to, the exploitation of one nation by another will also be put an end to. In proportion as the antagonism between classes within the nation vanishes, the hostility of one nation to another will come to an end.

The charges against Communism made from a religious, a philosophical, and, generally, from an ideological standpoint, are not deserving of serious examination.

Does it require deep intuition to comprehend that man's ideas, views and conceptions, in one word, man's consciousness, changes with every change in the conditions of his material existence, ir his social relations and in his social life ?

What else does the history of ideas prove, than that intellectual production changes its character in proportion as material production is changed? The ruling ideas of each age have ever been the ideas of its ruling class.

When people speak of ideas that revolutionise society, they do but express the fact, that within the old society, the elements of a new one have been created, and that the dissolution of the old ideas keeps even pace with the dissolution of the old conditions of existence.

When the ancient world was in its last throes, the ancient religions were overcome by Christianity. When Christian ideas succumbed in the 18th century to rationalist ideas, feudal society fought its death battle with the then revolutionary bourgeoisie. The ideas of religious liberty and freedom of conscience merely gave expression to the sway of free competition within the domain of knowledge.

"Undoubtedly," it will be said, "religious, moral, philosophical and juridical ideas have been modified in the course of historical development. But religion, morality, philosophy, political science, and law, constantly survived this change."

"There are, besides, eternal truths, such as Freedom, Justice, etc., that are common to all states of society. But Communism abolishes eternal truths, it abolishes all religion, and all morality, instead of constituting them on a new basis; it therefore acts in contradiction to all past historical experience."

What does this accusation reduce itself to? The history of all past society has consisted in the development of class antagonisms, antagonisms that assumed different forms at different epochs.

But whatever form they may have taken, one fact is common to all past ages, *viz.*, the exploitation of one part of society by the other. No wonder, then that the social consciousness of past ages, despite all the multiplicity and variety it displays, moves within certain common forms, or general ideas, which cannot completely vanish except with the total disappearance of class antagonisms.

The Communist revolution is the most radical rupture with traditional property relations; no wonder that its development involves the most radical rupture with traditional ideas.

But let us have done with the bourgeois objections to Communism.

We have seen above, that the first step in the revolution by the working class, is to raise the proletariat to the position of ruling class, to win the battle of democracy.

The proletariat will use its political supremacy to wrest, by degrees, all capital from the bourgeoisie, to centralise all instruments of production in the hands of the State, *i.e.*, of the proletariat organised as the ruling class; and to increase the total of productive forces as rapidly as possible.

Of course, in the beginning, this cannot be effected except by means of despotic inroads on the rights of property, and on the conditions of bourgeois production; by means of measures, therefore, which appear economically insufficient and untenable, but which, in the course of the movement, outstrip themselves, necessitate further inroads upon the old social order, and are unavoidable as a means of entirely revolutionising the mode of production.

These measures will of course be different in different countries.

Nevertheless in the most advanced countries, the following will be pretty generally applicable.

1. Abolition of property in land and application of all rents of land to public purposes.

2. A heavy progressive or graduated income tax.

3. Abolition of all right of inheritance.

4. Confiscation of the property of all emigrants and rebels.

5. Centralisation of credit in the hands of the State, by means of a national bank with State capital and an exclusive monopoly.

6. Centralisation of the means of communication and transport in the hands of the State.

7. Extension of factories and instruments of production owned by the State; the bringing into cultivation of waste-lands, and the improvement of the soil generally in accordance with a common plan.

8. Equal liability of all to labour. Establishment of industrial armies, especially for agriculture.

9. Combination of agriculture with manufacturing industries; gradual abolition of the distinction between town and country, by a more equable distribution of the population over the country.

10. Free education for all children in public schools. Abolition of children's factory labour in its present form. Combination of education with industrial production, &c., &c.

When, in the course of development, class distinctions have disappeared, and all production has been concentrated in the hands of a vast association of the whole nation, the public power will lose its political character. Political power, properly so called, is merely the organised power of one class for oppressing another. If the proletariat during its contest with the bourgeoisie is compelled, by the force of circumstances, to organise itself as a class, if, by means of a revolution, it makes itself the ruling class, and, as such, sweeps away by force the old conditions of production, then it will, along with these conditions, have swept away the conditions for the existence of class antagonisms and of classes generally, and will thereby have abolished its own supremacy as a class.

In place of the old bourgeois society, with its classes and class antagonisms, we shall have an association, in which the free development of each is the condition for the free development of all.

III

SOCIALIST AND COMMUNIST LITERATURE

1. REACTIONARY SOCIALISM

A. FEUDAL SOCIALISM

Owing to their historical position, it became the vocation of the aristocracies of France and England to write pamphlets against modern bourgeois society. In the French revolution of July 1830, and in the English reform[15] agitation, these aristocracies again succumbed to the hateful upstart. Thenceforth, a serious political contest was altogether out of question. A literary battle

alone remained possible. But even in the domain of literature the
old cries of the restoration period* had become impossible.

In order to arouse sympathy, the aristocracy were obliged to
lose sight, apparently, of their own interests, and to formulate
their indictment against the bourgeoisie in the interest of the exploited working class alone. Thus the aristocracy took their revenge by singing lampoons on their new master, and whispering
in his ears sinister prophecies of coming catastrophe.

In this way arose Feudal Socialism: half lamentation, half lam-
poon; half echo of the past, half menace of the future; at times, by
its bitter, witty and incisive criticism, striking the bourgeoisie to
the very heart's core; but always ludicrous in its effect, through
total incapacity to comprehend the march of modern history.

The aristocracy, in order to rally the people to them, waved
the proletarian alms-bag in front for a banner. But the people,
so often as it joined them, saw on their hindquarters the old feudal
coats of arms, and deserted with loud and irreverent laughter.

One section of the French Legitimists[17] and "Young England"[18]
exhibited this spectacle.

In pointing out that their mode of exploitation was different to that
of the bourgeoisie, the feudalists forget that they exploited under
circumstances and conditions that were quite different, and that are
now antiquated. In showing that, under their rule, the modern
proletariat never existed, they forget that the modern bourgeoisie
is the necessary offspring of their own form of society.

For the rest, so little do they conceal the reactionary character of their criticism that their chief accusation against the bourgeoisie amounts to this, that under the bourgeois *régime* a class
is being developed, which is destined to cut up root and branch
the old order of society.

What they upbraid the bourgeoisie with is not so much that
it creates a proletariat, as that it creates a *revolutionary* proletariat.

In political practice, therefore, they join in all coercive measures against the working class; and in ordinary life, despite their
high-falutin phrases, they stoop to pick up the golden apples
dropped from the tree of industry, and to barter truth, love, and
honour for traffic in wool, beetroot-sugar, and potato spirits.**

---

* Not the English Restoration 1660 to 1689, but the French Restoration 1814
to 1830.[16] [*Note by Engels to the English edition of 1888.*]

** This applies chiefly to Germany where the landed aristocracy and squirearchy[19] have large portions of their estates cultivated for their own account by
stewards, and are, moreover, extensive beetroot-sugar manufacturers and distil-
lers of potato spirits. The wealthier British aristocracy are, as yet, rather above
that; but they, too, know how to make up for declining rents by lending their
names to floaters of more or less shady joint-stock companies. [*Note by Engels
to the English edition of 1888.*]

As the parson has ever gone hand in hand with the landlord, so has Clerical Socialism with Feudal Socialism.

Nothing is. easier than to give Christian asceticism a Socialist tinge. Has not Christianity declaimed against private property, against marriage, against the State? Has it not preached in the place of these, charity and poverty, celibacy and mortification of the flesh, monastic life and Mother Church? Christian Socialism is but the holy water with which the priest consecrates the heart-burnings of the aristocrat.

B. PETTY-BOURGEOIS SOCIALISM

The feudal aristocracy was not the only class that was ruined by the bourgeoisie, not the only class whose conditions of existence pined and perished in the atmosphere of modern bourgeois society. The mediaeval burgesses and the small peasant proprietors were the precursors of the modern bourgeoisie. In those countries which are but little developed, industrially and commercially, these two classes still vegetate side by side with the rising bourgeoisie.

In countries where modern civilisation has become fully developed, a new class of petty bourgeois has been formed, fluctuating between proletariat and bourgeoisie and ever renewing itself as a supplementary part of bourgeois society. The individual members of this class, however, are being constantly hurled down into the proletariat by the action of competition, and, as modern industry develops, they even see the moment approaching when they will completely disappear as an independent section of modern society, to be replaced, in manufactures, agriculture and commerce, by overlookers, bailiffs and shopmen.

In countries like France, where the peasants constitute far more than half of the population, it was natural that writers who sided with the proletariat against the bourgeoisie, should use, in their criticism of the bourgeois *régime*, the standard of the peasant and petty bourgeois, and from the standpoint of these intermediate classes should take up the cudgels for the working class. Thus arose petty-bourgeois Socialism. Sismondi was the head of this school, not only in France but also in England.

This school of Socialism dissected with great acuteness the contradictions in the conditions of modern production. It laid bare the hypocritical apologies of economists. It proved, incontrovertibly, the disastrous effects of machinery and division of labour; the concentration of capital and land in a few hands; overproduction and crises; it pointed out the inevitable ruin of the petty bourgeois and peasant, the misery of the proletariat, the anarchy in production, the crying inequalities in the distribution of wealth, the

industrial war of extermination between nations, the dissolution
of old moral bonds, of the old family relations, of the old nationalities.

In its positive aims, however, this form of Socialism aspires
either to restoring the old means of production and of exchange,
and with them the old property relations, and the old society, or
to cramping the modern means of production and of exchange,
within the framework of the old property relations that have been,
and were bound to be, exploded by those means. In either case,
it is both reactionary and Utopian.

Its last words are: corporate guilds for manufacture, patriarchal
relations in agriculture.

Ultimately, when stubborn historical facts had dispersed all
intoxicating effects of self-deception, this form of Socialism ended
in a miserable fit of the blues.

C. GERMAN, OR "TRUE," SOCIALISM

The Socialist and Communist literature of France, a literature
that originated under the pressure of a bourgeoisie in power, and
that was the expression of the struggle against this power, was
introduced into Germany at a time when the bourgeoisie, in that
country, had just begun its contest with feudal absolutism.

German philosophers, would-be philosophers, and *beaux esprits*,
eagerly seized on this literature, only forgetting, that when these
writings immigrated from France into Germany, French social
conditions had not immigrated along with them. In contact with
German social conditions, this French literature lost all its immediate practical significance, and assumed a purely literary aspect.
Thus, to the German philosophers of the eighteenth century, the
demands of the first French Revolution were nothing more than
the demands of "Practical Reason" in general, and the utterance
of the will of the revolutionary French bourgeoisie signified in
their eyes the laws of pure Will, of Will as it was bound to be.
of true human Will generally.

The work of the German *literati* consisted solely in bringing
the new French ideas into harmony with their ancient philosophical conscience, or rather, in annexing the French ideas without
deserting their own philosophic point of view.

This annexation took place in the same way in which a foreign
language is appropriated, namely, by translation.

It is well known how the monks wrote silly lives of Catholic
Saints *over* the manuscripts on which the classical works of ancient heathendom had been written. The German *literati* reversed
this process with the profane French literature. They wrote their
philosophical nonsense beneath the French original. For instance,

beneath the French criticism of the economic functions of money, they wrote "Alienation of Humanity," and beneath the French criticism of the bourgeois State they wrote "Dethronement of the Category of the General," and so forth.

The introduction of these philosophical phrases at the back of the French historical criticisms they dubbed "Philosophy of Action," "True Socialism," "German Science of Socialism," "Philosophical Foundation of Socialism," and so on.

The French Socialist and Communist literature was thus completely emasculated. And, since it ceased in the hands of the German to express the struggle of one class with the other, he felt conscious of having overcome "French one-sidedness" and of representing, not true requirements, but the requirements of Truth; not the interests of the proletariat, but the interests of Human Nature, of Man in general, who belongs to no class, has no reality, who exists only in the misty realm of philosophical fantasy.

This German Socialism, which took its schoolboy task so seriously and solemnly, and extolled its poor stock-in-trade in such mountebank fashion, meanwhile gradually lost its pedantic innocence.

The fight of the German, and, especially, of the Prussian bourgeoisie, against feudal aristocracy and absolute monarchy, in other words, the liberal movement, became more earnest.

By this, the long wished-for opportunity was offered to "True" Socialism of confronting the political movement with the Socialist demands, of hurling the traditional anathemas against liberalism, against representative government, against bourgeois competition, bourgeois freedom of the press, bourgeois legislation, bourgeois liberty and equality, and of preaching to the masses that they had nothing to gain, and everything to lose, by this bourgeois movement. German Socialism forgot, in the nick of time, that the French criticism, whose silly echo it was, presupposed the existence of modern bourgeois society, with its corresponding economic conditions of existence, and the political constitution adapted thereto, the very things whose attainment was the object of the pending struggle in Germany.

To the absolute governments, with their following of parsons, professors, country squires and officials, it served as a welcome scarecrow against the threatening bourgeoisie.

It was a sweet finish after the bitter pills of floggings and bullets with which these same governments, just at that time, dosed the German working-class risings.

While this "True" Socialism thus served the governments as a weapon for fighting the German bourgeoisie, it, at the same time, directly represented a reactionary interest, the interest of the German Philistines. In Germany the *petty-bourgeois* class, a relic of the sixteenth century, and since then constantly cropping up again under various forms, is the real social basis of the existing state of things.

To preserve this class is to preserve the existing state of things in Germany. The industrial and political supremacy of the bourgeoisie threatens it with certain destruction; on the one hand, from the concentration of capital; on the other, from the rise of a revolutionary proletariat. "True" Socialism appeared to kill these two birds with one stone. It spread like an epidemic.

The robe of speculative cobwebs, embroidered with flowers of rhetoric, steeped in the dew of sickly sentiment, this transcendental robe in which the German Socialists wrapped their sorry "eternal truths," all skin and bone, served to wonderfully increase the sale of their goods amongst such a public.

And on its part, German Socialism recognised, more and more, its own calling as the bombastic representative of the petty-bourgeois Philistine.

It proclaimed the German nation to be the model nation, and the German petty Philistine to be the typical man. To every villainous meanness of this model man it gave a hidden, higher, Socialistic interpretation, the exact contrary of its real character. It went to the extreme length of directly opposing the "brutally destructive" tendency of Communism, and of proclaiming its supreme and impartial contempt of all class struggles. With very few exceptions, all the so-called Socialist and Communist publications that now (1847) circulate in Germany belong to the domain of this foul and enervating literature.*

2. CONSERVATIVE, OR BOURGEOIS, SOCIALISM

A part of the bourgeoisie is desirous of redressing social grievances, in order to secure the continued existence of bourgeois society.

To this section belong economists, philanthropists, humanitarians, improvers of the condition of the working class, organisers of charity, members of societies for the prevention of cruelty to animals, temperance fanatics, hole-and-corner reformers of every imaginable kind. This form of Socialism has, moreover, been worked out into complete systems.

We may cite Proudhon's *Philosophie de la Misère* as an example of this form.

---

* The revolutionary storm of 1848[20] swept away this whole shabby tendency and cured its protagonists of the desire to dabble further in Socialism. The chief representative and classical type of this tendency is Herr Karl Grün. [*Note by Engels to the German edition of 1890.*]

The Socialistic bourgeois want all the advantages of modern social conditions without the struggles and dangers necessarily resulting therefrom. They desire the existing state of society minus its revolutionary and disintegrating elements. They wish for a bourgeoisie without a proletariat. The bourgeoisie naturally conceives the world in which it is supreme to be the best; and bourgeois Socialism develops this comfortable conception into various more or less complete systems. In requiring the proletariat to carry out such a system, and thereby to march straightway into the social New Jerusalem,[21] it but requires in reality, that the proletariat should remain within the bounds of existing society, but should cast away all its hateful ideas concerning the bourgeoisie.

A second and more practical, but less systematic, form of this Socialism sought to depreciate every revolutionary movement in the eyes of the working class, by showing that no mere political reform, but only a change in the material conditions of existence, in economical relations, could be of any advantage to them. By changes in the material conditions of existence, this form of Socialism, however, by no means understands abolition of the bourgeois relations of production, an abolition that can be effected only by a revolution, but administrative reforms, based on the continued existence of these relations; reforms, therefore, that in no respect affect the relations between capital and labour, but, at the best, lessen the cost, and simplify the administrative work, of bourgeois government.

Bourgeois Socialism attains adequate expression, when, and only when, it becomes a mere figure of speech.

Free trade: for the benefit of the working class. Protective duties: for the benefit of the working class. Prison Reform: for the benefit of the working class. This is the last word and the only seriously meant word of bourgeois Socialism.

It is summed up in the phrase: the bourgeois is a bourgeois— for the benefit of the working class.

3. CRITICAL-UTOPIAN SOCIALISM AND COMMUNISM

We do not here refer to that literature which, in every great modern revolution, has always given voice to the demands of the proletariat, such as the writings of Babeuf and others.

The first direct attempts of the proletariat to attain its own ends, made in times of universal excitement, when feudal society was being overthrown, these attempts necessarily failed, owing to the then undeveloped state of the proletariat, as well as to the absence of the economic conditions for its emancipation, conditions that had yet to be produced, and could be produced by the impending bourgeois epoch alone. The revolutionary literature that accompanied these first movements of the proletariat had necessarily a reactionary character. It inculcated universal asceticism and social levelling in its crudest form.

The Socialist and Communist systems properly so called, those of Saint-Simon, Fourier, Owen and others, spring into existence in the early undeveloped period, described above, of the struggle between proletariat and bourgeoisie (see Section I. Bourgeoisie and Proletariat).

The founders of these systems see, indeed, the class antagonisms, as well as the action of the decomposing elements, in the prevailing form of society. But the proletariat, as yet in its infancy, offers to them the spectacle of a class without any historical initiative or any independent political movement.

Since the development of class antagonism keeps even pace with the development of industry, the economic situation, as they find it, does not as yet offer to them the material conditions for the emancipation of the proletariat. They therefore search after a new social science, after new social laws, that are to create these conditions.

Historical action is to yield to their personal inventive action, historically created conditions of emancipation to fantastic ones, and the gradual, spontaneous class-organisation of the proletariat to an organisation of society specially contrived by these inventors. Future history resolves itself, in their eyes, into the propaganda and the practical carrying out of their social plans.

In the formation of their plans they are conscious of caring chiefly for the interests of the working class, as being the most suffering class. Only from the point of view of being the most suffering class does the proletariat exist for them.

The undeveloped state of the class struggle, as well as their own surroundings, causes Socialists of this kind to consider themselves far superior to all class antagonisms. They want to improve the condition of every member of society, even that of the most favoured. Hence, they habitually appeal to society at large, without distinction of class; nay, by preference, to the ruling class. For how can people, when once they understand their system, fail to see in it the best possible plan of the best possible state of society?

Hence, they reject all political, and especially all revolutionary, action; they wish to attain their ends by peaceful means, and endeavour, by small experiments, necessarily doomed to failure, and by the force of example, to pave the way for the new social Gospel.

Such fantastic pictures of future society, painted at a time when the proletariat is still in a very undeveloped state and has but a fantastic conception of its own position, correspond with the first instinctive yearnings of that class for a general reconstruction of society.

But these Socialist and Communist publications contain also a critical element. They attack every principle of existing society. Hence they are full of the most valuable materials for the enlightenment of the working class. The practical measures proposed in them—such as the abolition of the distinction between town and country, of the family, of the carrying on of industries for the account of private individuals, and of the wage system, the proclamation of social harmony, the conversion of the functions of the State into a mere superintendence of production, all these proposals point solely to the disappearance of class antagonisms which were, at that time, only just cropping up, and which, in these publications, are recognised in their earliest, indistinct and undefined forms only. These proposals, therefore, are of a purely Utopian character.

The significance of Critical-Utopian Socialism and Communism bears an inverse relation to historical development. In proportion as the modern class struggle develops and takes definite shape, this fantastic standing apart from the contest, these fantastic attacks on it, lose all practical value and all theoretical justification. Therefore, although the originators of these systems were, in many respects, revolutionary, their disciples have, in every case, formed mere reactionary sects. They hold fast by the original views of their masters, in opposition to the progressive historical development of the proletariat. They, therefore, endeavour, and that consistently, to deaden the class struggle and to reconcile the class antagonisms. They still dream of experimental realisation of their social Utopias, of founding isolated "*phalanstères*," of establishing "Home Colonies," of setting up a "Little Icaria"*—duodecimo editions of the New Jerusalem—and to realise all these castles in the air, they are compelled to appeal to the feelings and purses of the bourgeois. By degrees they sink into the category of the reactionary conservative Socialists depicted above, differing from these only by more systematic pedantry, and by their fanatical and superstitious belief in the miraculous effects of their social science.

They, therefore, violently oppose all political action on the part of the working class; such action, according to them, can only result from blind unbelief in the new Gospel.

---

* *Phalanstères* were Socialist colonies on the plan of Charles Fourier; *Icaria* was the name given by Cabet to his Utopia and, later on, to his American Communist colony. [*Note by Engels to the English edition of 1888.*]

"Home colonies" were what Owen called his Communist model societies. *Phalanstères* was the name of the public palaces planned by Fourier. *Icaria* was the name given to the Utopian land of fancy, whose Communist institutions Cabet portrayed. [*Note by Engels to the German edition of 1890.*]

The Owenites in England, and the Fourierists in France, respectively, oppose the Chartists[22] and the *Réformistes*.[23]

IV

POSITION OF THE COMMUNISTS IN RELATION TO THE VARIOUS EXISTING OPPOSITION PARTIES

Section II has made clear the relations of the Communists to the existing working-class parties, such as the Chartists in England and the Agrarian Reformers in America.

The Communists fight for the attainment of the immediate aims, for the enforcement of the momentary interests of the working class; but in the movement of the present, they also represent and take care of the future of that movement. In France the Communists ally themselves with the Social-Democrats,* against the conservative and radical bourgeoisie, reserving, however, the right to take up a critical position in regard to phrases and illusions traditionally handed down from the great Revolution.

In Switzerland they support the Radicals, without losing sight of the fact that this party consists of antagonistic elements, partly of Democratic Socialists, in the French sense, partly of radical bourgeois.

In Poland they support the party that insists on an agrarian revolution as the prime condition for national emancipation, that party which fomented the insurrection of Cracow in 1846.[25]

In Germany they fight with the bourgeoisie whenever it acts in a revolutionary way, against the absolute monarchy, the feudal squirearchy, and the petty bourgeoisie.

But they never cease, for a single instant, to instil into the working class the clearest possible recognition of the hostile antagonism between bourgeoisie and proletariat, in order that the German workers may straightway use, as so many weapons against the bourgeoisie, the social and political conditions that the bourgeoisie must necessarily introduce along with its supremacy, and in order that, after the fall of the reactionary classes in Germany, the fight against the bourgeoisie itself may immediately begin.

---

* The party then represented in Parliament by Ledru-Rollin, in literature by Louis Blanc, in the daily press by the *Réforme*.[24] The name of Social-Democracy signified, with these its inventors, a section of the Democratic or Republican party more or less tinged with Socialism. [*Note by Engels to the English edition of 1888.*]

The party in France which at that time called itself Socialist-Democratic was represented in political life by Ledru-Rollin and in literature by Louis Blanc; thus it differed immeasurably from present-day German Social-Democracy. [*Note by Engels to the German edition of 1890.*]

The Communists turn their attention chiefly to Germany, because that country is on the eve of a bourgeois revolution that is bound to be carried out under more advanced conditions of European civilisation, and with a much more developed proletariat, than that of England was in the seventeenth, and of France in the eighteenth century, and because the bourgeois revolution in Germany will be but the prelude to an immediately following proletarian revolution.

In short, the Communists everywhere support every revolutionary movement against the existing social and political order of things.

In all these movements they bring to the front, as the leading question in each, the property question, no matter what its degree of development at the time.

Finally, they labour everywhere for the union and agreement of the democratic parties of all countries.

The Communists disdain to conceal their views and aims. They openly declare that their ends can be attained only by the forcible overthrow of all existing social conditions. Let the ruling classes tremble at a Communistic revolution. The proletarians have nothing to lose but their chains. They have a world to win.

WORKING MEN OF ALL COUNTRIES, UNITE!

Written by Marx and Engels in
December 1847-January 1848

Originally published in German
in London in February 1848

Printed according to the 1888
English edition

Karl Marx

WAGE LABOUR AND CAPITAL[26]

INTRODUCTION BY FREDERICK ENGELS

The following work appeared as a series of leading articles in the *Neue Rheinische Zeitung*[27] from April 4, 1849 onwards. It is based on the lectures delivered by Marx in 1847 at the German Workers' Society in Brussels.[28] The work as printed remained a fragment; the words at the end of No. 269: "To be continued," remained unfulfilled in consequence of the events which just then came crowding one after another: the invasion of Hungary[29] by the Russians, the insurrections in Dresden, Iserlohn, Elberfeld, the Palatinate and Baden[30], which led to the suppression of the newspaper itself (May 19, 1849). The manuscript of the continuation was not found among Marx's papers after his death.[31]

Wage Labour and Capital has appeared in a number of editions as a separate publication in pamphlet form, the last being in 1884, by the Swiss Co-operative Press, Hottingen-Zurich. The editions hitherto published retained the exact wording of the original. The present new edition, however, is to be circulated in not less than 10,000 copies as a propaganda pamphlet, and so the question could not but force itself upon me whether under these circumstances Marx himself would have approved of an unaltered reproduction of the original.

In the forties, Marx had not yet finished his critique of political economy. This took place only towards the end of the fifties. Consequently, his works which appeared before the first part of *A Contribution to the Critique of Political Economy* (1859) differ in some points from those written after 1859, and contain expressions and whole sentences which, from the point of view of the later works, appear unfortunate and even incorrect. Now, it is self-evident that in ordinary editions intended for the general public this earlier point of view also has its place, as a part of the intellectual development of the author, and that both author and public have an indisputable right to the unaltered reproduction of these older works. And I should not have dreamed of altering a word of them.

It is another thing when the new edition is intended practically exclusively for propaganda among workers. In such a case Marx would certainly have brought the old presentation dating from 1849 into harmony with his new point of view. And I feel certain of acting as he would have done in undertaking *for this edition* the few alterations and additions which are required in order to attain this object in all essential points. I therefore tell the reader beforehand: this is not the pamphlet as Marx wrote it in 1849 but approximately as he would have written it in 1891. The actual text, moreover, is circulated in so many copies that this will suffice until I am able to reprint it again, unaltered, in a later complete edition.

My alterations all turn on one point. According to the original, the worker sells his *labour* to the capitalist for wages; according to the present text he sells his labour *power*. And for this alteration I owe an explanation. I owe it to the workers in order that they may see it is not a case here of mere juggling with words, but rather of one of the most important points in the whole of political economy. I owe it to the bourgeois, so that they can convince themselves how vastly superior the uneducated workers, for whom one can easily make comprehensible the most difficult economic analyses, are to our supercilious "educated people" to whom such intricate questions remain insoluble their whole life long.

Classical political economy[32] took over from industrial practice the current conception of the manufacturer, that he buys and pays for the *labour* of his workers. This conception had been quite adequate for the business needs, the book-keeping and price calculations of the manufacturer. But, naively transferred to political economy, it produced there really wondrous errors and confusions.

Economics observes the fact that the prices of all commodities, among them also the price of the commodity that it calls "labour," are continually changing; that they rise and fall as the result of the most varied circumstances, which often bear no relation whatever to the production of the commodities themselves, so that prices seem, as a rule, to be determined by pure chance. As soon, then, as political economy made its appearance as a science,[33] one of its first tasks was to seek the law which was concealed behind this chance apparently governing the prices of commodities, and which, in reality, governed this very chance. Within the prices of commodities, continually fluctuating and oscillating, now upwards and now downwards, political economy sought for the firm central point around which these fluctuations and oscillations turned. In a word, it started from the *prices* of commodities in order to look for the *value* of the commodities as the law controlling prices, the value by which all fluctuations in price are to be explained and to which finally they are all to be ascribed.

Classical economics then found that the value of a commodity is determined by the labour contained in it, requisite for its production. With this explanation it contented itself. And we also can pause here for the time being. I will only remind the reader, in order to avoid misunderstandings, that this explanation has nowadays become totally inadequate. Marx was the first thoroughly to investigate the value-creating quality of labour and he discovered in so doing that not all labour apparently, or even really, necessary for the production of a commodity adds to it under all circumstances a magnitude of value which corresponds to the quantity of. labour expended. If therefore today we say offhandedly with economists like Ricardo that the value of a commodity is determined by the labour necessary for its production, we always in so doing imply the reservations made by Marx. This suffices here; more is to be found in Marx's *A Contribution to the Critique of Political Economy,* 1859, and the first volume of *Capital.*

But as soon as the economists applied this determination of value by labour to the commodity "labour," they fell into one contradiction after another. How is the value of "labour" determined? By the necessary labour contained in it. But how much labour is contained in the labour of a worker for a day, a week, a month, a year? The labour of a day, a week, a month, a year. If labour is the measure of all values, then indeed we can express the "value of labour" only in labour. But we know absolutely nothing about the value of an hour of labour, if we only know that it is equal to an hour of labour. This brings us not a hair's breadth nearer the goal; we keep on moving in a circle.

Classical economics, therefore, tried another tack. It said: The value of a commodity is equal to its cost of production. But what is the cost of production of labour? In order to answer this question, the economists have to tamper a little with logic. Instead of investigating the cost of production of labour itself, which unfortunately cannot be ascertained, they proceed to investigate the cost of production of the *worker.* And this can be ascertained It varies with time and circumstance, but for a given state of society, a given locality and a given branch of production, it too is given, at least within fairly narrow limits. We live today under the domination of capitalist production, in which a large, ever-increasing class of the population can live only if it works for the owners of the means of production—the tools, machines, raw materials and means of subsistence—in return for wages. On the basis of this mode of production, the cost of production of the worker consists of that quantity of the means of subsistence—or their price in money—which, on the average, is necessary to make him capable of working, keep him capable of working, and to replace him, after his departure by reason of old age, sickness or death, with a new worker—that is to say, to propagate the working class in the necessary numbers. Let us assume that the money price of these means of subsistence averages three marks a day.

Our worker, therefore, receives a wage of three marks a day from the capitalist who employs him. For this, the capitalist makes him work, say, twelve hours a day, calculating roughly as follows:

Let us assume that our worker—a machinist—has to make a part of a machine which he can complete in one day. The raw material—iron and brass in the necessary previously prepared form—costs twenty marks. The consumption of coal by the steam engine, and the wear and tear of this same engine, of the lathe and the other tools which our worker uses represent for one day, and reckoned by his share of their use, a value of one mark. The wage for one day, according to our assumption, is three marks. This makes twenty-four marks in all for our machine part. But the capitalist calculates that he will obtain, on an average, twenty-seven marks from his customers in return, or three marks more than his outlay.

Whence came the three marks pocketed by the capitalist? According to the assertion of classical economics, commodities are, on the average, sold at their values, that is, at prices corresponding to the amount of necessary labour contained in them. The average price of our machine part—twenty-seven marks—would thus be equal to its value, that is, equal to the labour embodied in it. But of these twenty-seven marks, twenty-one marks were values already present before our machinist began work. Twenty marks were contained in the raw materials, one mark in the coal consumed during the work, or in the machines and tools which were used in the process and which were diminished in their efficiency by the value of this sum. There remain six marks which have been added to the value of the raw material. But according to the assumption of our economists themselves, these six marks can only arise from the labour added to the raw material by our worker. His twelve hours' labour has thus created a new value of six marks. The value of his twelve hours' labour would, therefore, be equal to six marks. And thus we would at last have discovered what the "value of labour" is.

"Hold on there!" cries our machinist. "Six marks? But I have received only three marks! My capitalist swears by all that is holy that the value of my twelve hours' labour is only three marks, and if I demand six he laughs at me. How do you make that out?"

If previously we got into a vicious circle with our value of labour, we are now properly caught in an insoluble contradiction. We looked for the value of labour and we have found more than we can use. For the worker, the value of the twelve hours' labour is three marks, for the capitalist it is six marks, of which he pays three to the worker as wages and pockets three for himself. Thus labour would have not one but two values and very different values into the bargain!

The contradiction becomes still more absurd as soon as we reduce to labour time the values expressed in money. During the twelve hours' labour a new value of six marks is created. Hence, in six hours three marks—the sum which the worker receives for twelve hours' labour. For twelve hours' labour the worker receives as an equivalent value the product of six hours' labour. Either, therefore, labour has two values, of which one is double the size of the other, or twelve equals six! In both cases we get pure nonsense.

Turn and twist as we will, we cannot get out of this contradiction, as long as we speak of the purchase and sale of labour and of the value of labour. And this also happened to the economists. The last offshoot of classical economics, the Ricardian school, was wrecked mainly by the insolubility of this contradiction. Classical economics had got into a blind alley. The man who found the way out of this blind alley was Karl Marx.

What the economists had regarded as the cost of production of "labour" was the cost of production not of labour but of the living worker himself. And what this worker sold to the capitalist was not his labour. "As soon as his labour actually begins," says Marx, "it has already ceased to belong to him; it can therefore no longer be sold by him."* At the most, he might sell his *future* labour, that is, undertake to perform a certain amount of work in a definite time. In so doing, however, he does not sell labour (which would first have to be performed) but puts his labour power at the disposal of the capitalist for a definite time (in the case of time-work) or for the purpose of a definite output (in the case of piece-work) in return for a definite payment: he hires out, or sells, his *labour power*. But this labour power is intergrown with his person and inseparable from it. Its cost of production, therefore, coincides with his cost of production; what the economists called the cost of production of labour is really the cost of production of the worker and therewith of his labour power. And so we can go back from the cost of production of labour power to the *value* of labour power and determine the amount of socially necessary labour requisite for the production of labour power of a particular quality, as Marx has done in the chapter on the buying and selling of labour power (*Kapital*, Band IV, 3).

Now what happens after the worker has sold his labour power to· the capitalist, that is, placed it at the disposal of the latter in return for a wage—day wage or piece wage—agreed upon beforehand? The capitalist takes the worker into his workshop or factory, where all the things necessary for work—raw materials, auxiliary materials (coal, dyes, etc.), tools, machines—are already to be found. Here the worker begins to drudge. His daily wage may be, as above, three marks—and in this connection it does not make any difference whether he earns it as day wage or piece wage. Here also we again assume that in twelve hours the worker by his labour adds a new value of six marks to the raw materials used up, which new value the capitalist realises on the sale of the finished piece of work. Out of this he pays the worker his three

---

* K. Marx, *Capital*, Moscow, 1965, Vol. I, p. 537.—*Ed.*

marks; the other three marks he keeps for himself. If, now, the worker creates a value of six marks in twelve hours, then in six hours he creates a value of three marks. He has, therefore, already repaid the capitalist the counter-value of the three marks contained in his wages when he has worked six hours for him. After six hours' labour they are both quits, neither owes the other a pfennig.

"Hold on there!" the capitalist now cries. "I have hired the worker for a whole day, for twelve hours. Six hours, however, are only half a day. So go right on working until the other six hours are up—only then shall we be quits!" And, in fact, the worker has to comply with his contract "voluntarily" entered into, according to which he has pledged himself to work twelve whole hours for a labour product which costs six hours of labour.

It is just the same with piece wages. Let us assume that our worker makes twelve items of a commodity in twelve hours. Each of these costs two marks in raw materials and depreciation and is sold at two and a half marks. Then the capitalist, on the same assumptions as before, will give the worker twenty-five pfennigs per item; that makes three marks for twelve items, to earn which the worker needs twelve hours. The capitalist receives thirty marks for the twelve items; deduct twenty-four marks for raw materials and depreciation and there remain six marks, of which he pays three marks to the worker in wages and pockets three marks. It is just as above. Here, too, the worker works six hours for himself, that is, for replacement of his wages (half an hour in each of the twelve hours) and six hours for the capitalist.

The difficulty over which the best economists came to grief, so long as they started out from the value of "labour," vanishes as soon as we start out from the value of "labour *power*" instead. In our present-day capitalist society, labour power is a commodity, a commodity like any other, and yet quite a peculiar commodity. It has, namely, the peculiar property of being a value-creating power, a source of value, and, indeed, with suitable treatment, a source of more value than it itself possesses. With the present state of production, human labour power not only produces in one day a greater value than it itself possesses and costs; with every new scientific discovery, with every new technical invention, this surplus of its daily product over its daily cost increases, and therefore that portion of the labour day in which the worker works to produce the replacement of his day's wage decreases; consequently, on the other hand, that portion of the labour day in which he has to *make a present* of his labour to the capitalist without being paid for it increases.

And this is the economic constitution of the whole of our present-day society: it is the working class alone which produces all values. For value is cnly another expression for labour, that expression whereby in our present-day capitalist society is designated the amount of socially necessary labour contained in a particular commodity. These values produced by the workers do not, however, belong to the workers. They belong to the owners of the raw materials, machines, tools and the reserve funds which allow these owners to buy the labour power of the working class. From the whole mass of products produced by it, the working class, therefore, receives back only a part for itself. And as we have just seen, the other part, which the capitalist class keeps for itself and at most has to divide with the class of landowners, becomes larger with every new discovery and invention, while the part falling to the share of the working class (reckoned per head) either increases only very slowly and inconsiderably or not at all, and under certain circumstances may even fall.

But these discoveries and inventions which supersede each other at an ever-increasing rate, this productivity of human labour which rises day by day to an extent previously unheard of, finally give rise to a conflict in which the present-day capitalist economy must perish. On the one hand are immeasurable riches and a superfluity of products which the purchasers cannot cope with; on the other hand, the great mass of society proletarianised, turned into wage-workers, and precisely for that reason made incapable of appropriating for themselves this superfluity of products. The division of society into a small, excessively rich class and a large, propertyless class of wage-workers results in a society suffocating from its own superfluity, while the great majority of its members is scarcely, or even not at all, protected from extreme want. This state of affairs becomes daily more absurd and—more unnecessary. It *must* be abolished, it *can* be abolished. A new social order is possible in which the present class differences will have disappeared and in which—perhaps after a short transitional period involving some privation, but at any rate of great value morally—through the planned utilisation and extension of the already existing enormous productive forces of all members of society, and with uniform obligation to work, the means for existence, for enjoying life, for the development and employment of all bodily and mental faculties will be available in an equal measure and in ever-increasing fulness. And that the workers are becoming more and more determined to win this new social order will be demonstrated on both sides of the ocean by May the First, tomorrow, and by Sunday, May 3.[34]

Frederick Engels

London, April 30, 1891

Published as supplement to
Vorwärts No. 109, May 13, 1891,
and in the pamphlet: Karl Marx.
Lohnarbeit und Kapital,
Berlin, 1891

Printed according to the text
of the 1891 pamphlet

Translated from the German

WAGE LABOUR AND CAPITAL[26]

From various quarters we have been reproached with not having presented the *economic relations* which constitute the material foundation of the present class struggles and national struggles. We have designedly touched upon these relations only where they directly forced themselves to the front in political conflicts.

The point was, above all, to trace the class struggle in current history, and to prove empirically by means of the historical material already at hand and which is being newly created daily, that, with the subjugation of the working class that February[4] and March[35] had wrought, its opponents were simultaneously defeated —the bourgeois republicans in France and the bourgeois and peasant classes which were fighting feudal absolutism throughout the continent of Europe; that the victory of the "honest republic" in France was at the same time the downfall of the nations that had responded to the February Revolution by heroic wars of independence; finally, that Europe, with the defeat of the revolutionary workers, had relapsed into its old double slavery, the *Anglo-Russian* slavery. The June struggle in Paris,[6] the fall of Vienna, the tragicomedy of Berlin's November 1848,[36] the desperate exertions of Poland, Italy and Hungary,[37] the starving of Ireland into submission—these were the chief factors which characterised the European class struggle between bourgeoisie and working class and by means of which we proved that every revolutionary upheaval, however remote from the class struggle its goal may appear to be, must fail until the revolutionary working class is victorious, that every social reform remains a utopia until the proletarian revolution and the feudalistic counter-revolution measure swords in a *world war*. In our presentation, as in reality, *Belgium* and *Switzerland* were tragicomic genre-pictures akin to caricature in the great historical tableau, the one being the model state of the bourgeois monarchy, the other the model state of the bourgeois republic, both of them states which imagine themselves to be as independent of the class struggle as of the European revolution.

Now, after our readers have seen the class struggle develop in colossal political forms in 1848, the time has come to deal more closely with the economic relations themselves on which the existence of the bourgeoisie and its class rule, as well as the slavery of the workers, are founded.

We shall present in three large sections: 1) the relation of *wage labour to capital*, the slavery of the worker, the domination of the capitalist; 2) *the inevitable destruction of the middle bourgeois classes and of the so-called peasant estate under the present system*; 3) *the commercial subjugation and exploitation of the bourgeois classes of the various European nations* by the despot of the world market—*England*.

We shall try to make our presentation as simple and popular as possible and shall not presuppose even the most elementary notions of political economy. We wish to be understood by the workers. Moreover, the most remarkable ignorance and confusion of ideas prevails in Germany in regard to the simplest economic relations, from the accredited defenders of the existing state of things down to the *socialist miracle workers* and the *unrecognised political geniuses* in which fragmented Germany is even richer than in sovereign princes.

Now, therefore, for the first question:

What are wages?
How are they determined?

If workers were asked: "How much are your wages?" one would reply: "I get a mark a day from my employer"; another, "I get two marks," and so on. According to the different trades to which they belong, they would mention different sums of money which they receive from their respective employers for the performance of a particular piece of work, for example, weaving a yard of linen or type-setting a printed sheet. In spite of the variety of their statements, they would all agree on one point: wages are the sum of money paid by the capitalist for a particular labour time or for a particular output of labour.

The capitalist, it seems, therefore, *buys* their labour with money. They *sell* him their labour for money. But this is merely the appearance. In reality what they sell to the capitalist for money is their labour *power*. The capitalist buys this labour power for a day, a week, a month, etc. And after he has bought it, he uses it by having the workers work for the stipulated time. For the same sum with which the capitalist has bought their labour power, for example, two marks, he could have bought two pounds of sugar or a definite amount of any other commodity. The two marks, with which he bought two pounds of sugar, are the *price* of the two pounds of sugar. The two marks, with which he bought twelve hours' use of labour power, are the price of twelve hours' labour. Labour power, therefore, is a commodity, neither more nor less than sugar. The former is measured by the clock, the latter by the scales.

The workers exchange their commodity, labour power, for the

commodity of the capitalist, for money, and this exchange takes place in a definite ratio. So much money for so long a use of labour power. For twelve hours' weaving, two marks. And do not the two marks represent all the other commodities which I can buy for two marks? In fact, therefore, the worker has exchanged his commodity, labour power, for other commodities of all kinds and that in a definite ratio. By giving him two marks, the capitalist has given him so much meat, so much clothing, so much fuel, light, etc., in exchange for his day's labour. Accordingly, the two marks express the ratio in which labour power is exchanged for other commodities, the *exchange value* of his labour power. The exchange value of a commodity, reckoned in *money*, is what is called its *price*. *Wages* are only a special name for the price of labour power, commonly called the *price of labour*, for the price of this peculiar commodity which has no other repository than human flesh and blood.

Let us take any worker, say, a weaver. The capitalist supplies him with the loom and yarn. The weaver sets to work and the yarn is converted into linen. The capitalist takes possession of the linen and sells it, say, for twenty marks. Now are the wages of the weaver a *share* in the linen, in the twenty marks, in the product of his labour? By no means. Long before the linen is sold, perhaps long before its weaving is finished, the weaver has received his wages. The capitalist, therefore, does not pay these wages with the money which he will obtain from the linen, but with money already in reserve. Just as the loom and the yarn are not the product of the weaver to whom they are supplied by his employer, so likewise with the commodities which the weaver receives in exchange for his commodity, labour power. It was possible that his employer found no purchaser at all for his linen. It was possible that he did not get even the amount of the wages by its sale. It is possible that he sells it very profitably in comparison with the weaver's wages. All that has nothing to do with the weaver. The capitalist buys the labour power of the weaver with a part of his available wealth, of his capital, just as he has bought the raw material—the yarn—and the instrument of labour—the loom—with another part of his wealth. After he has made these purchases, and these purchases include the labour power necessary for the production of linen, he produces only with the *raw materials and instruments of labour belonging to him*. For the latter include now, true enough, our good weaver as well, who has as little share in the product or the price of the product as the loom has.

Wages are, therefore, not the worker's share in the commodity produced by him. Wages are the part of already existing commodities with which the capitalist buys for himself a definite amount of productive labour power.

Labour power is, therefore, a commodity which its possessor, the wage-worker, sells to capital. Why does he sell it? In order to live.

But the exercise of labour power, labour, is the worker's own life-activity, the manifestation of his own life. And this *life-activity* he sells to another person in order to secure the necessary *means of subsistence*. Thus his life-activity is for him only a means to enable him to exist. He works in order to live. He does not even reckon labour as part of his life, it is rather a sacrifice of his life. It is a commodity which he has made over to another. Hence, also, the product of his activity is not the object of his activity. What he produces for himself is not the silk that he weaves, not the gold that he draws from the mine, not the palace that he builds. What he produces for himself is *wages*, and silk, gold, palace resolve themselves for him into a definite quantity of the means of subsistence, perhaps into a cotton jacket, some copper coins and a lodging in a cellar. And the worker, who for twelve hours weaves, spins, drills, turns, builds, shovels, breaks stones, carries loads, etc. —does he consider this twelve hours' weaving, spinning, drilling, turning, building, shovelling, stone breaking as a manifestation of his life, as life? On the contrary, life begins for him where this activity ceases, at table, in the public house, in bed. The twelve hours' labour, on the other hand, has no meaning for him as weaving, spinning, drilling, etc., but as *earnings*, which bring him to the table, to the public house, into bed. If the silk worm were to spin in order to continue its existence as a caterpillar, it would be a complete wage-worker. Labour power was not always a *commodity*. Labour was not always wage labour, that is, *free labour*. The *slave* did not sell his labour power to the slave owner, any more than the ox sells its services to the peasant. The slave, together with his labour power, is sold once and for all to his owner. He is a commodity which can pass from the hand of one owner to that of another. He is *himself* a commodity, but the labour power is not *his* commodity. The *serf* sells only a part of his labour power. He does not receive a wage from the owner of the land; rather the owner of the land receives a tribute from him.

The serf belongs to the land and turns over to the owner of the land the fruits thereof. The *free labourer*, on the other hand, sells himself and, indeed, sells himself piecemeal. He sells at auction eight, ten, twelve, fifteen hours of his life, day after day, to the highest bidder, to the owner of the raw materials, instruments of labour and means of subsistence, that is, to the capitalist. The worker belongs neither to an owner nor to the land, but eight, ten, twelve, fifteen hours of his daily life belong to him who buys them. The worker leaves the capitalist to whom he hires himself whenever he likes, and the capitalist discharges him whenever he thinks fit, as soon as he no longer gets any profit out of him, or not the anticipated profit. But the worker, whose sole source of livelihood is the sale of his labour power, cannot leave the *whole class of purchasers, that is, the capitalist class*, without renouncing his existence. He belongs not to this or that capitalist but to the *capitalist class*, and, moreover, it is his business to dispose of himself, that is, to find a purchaser within this capitalist class.

Now, before going more closely into the relation between capital and wage labour, we shall present briefly the most general relations which come into consideration in the determination of wages.

Wages, as we have seen, are the *price* of a definite commodity, of labour power. Wages are, therefore, determined by the same laws that determine the price of every other commodity. The question, therefore, is, *how is the price of a commodity determined?*

By What Is the Price of a Commodity Determined?

By competition between buyers and sellers, by the relation of inquiry to delivery, of demand to supply. Competition, by which the price of a commodity is determined, is *three-sided*.

The same commodity is offered by various sellers. With goods of the same quality, the one who sells most cheaply is certain of driving the others out of the field and securing the greatest sale for himself. Thus, the sellers mutually contend among themselves for sales, for the market. Each of them desires to sell, to sell as much as possible and, if possible, to sell alone, to the exclusion of the other sellers. Hence, one sells cheaper than another. Consequently, *competition* takes place *among the sellers*, which *depresses* the price of the *commodities* offered by them.

But *competition* also takes place *among the buyers*, which in its turn *causes* the commodities offered to *rise* in price.

Finally *competition* occurs *between buyers and sellers*; the former desire to buy as cheaply as possible, the latter to sell as dearly as possible. The result of this competition between buyers and sellers will depend upon how the two above-mentioned sides of the competition are related, that is, whether the competition is stronger in the army of buyers or in the army of sellers. Industry leads two armies into the field against each other, each of which again carries on a battle within its own ranks, among its own troops. The army whose troops beat each other up the least gains the victory over the opposing host.

Let us suppose there are 100 bales of cotton on the market and at the same time buyers for 1,000 bales of cotton. In this case, therefore, the demand is ten times as great as the supply. Competition will be very strong among the buyers, each of whom desires to get one, and if possible all, of the hundred bales for himself. This example is no arbitrary assumption. We have experienced periods of cotton crop failure in the history of the trade when a few capitalists in alliance have tried to buy, not one hundred bales, but all the cotton stocks of the world. Hence, in the example mentioned, one buyer will seek to drive the other from the field by offering a relatively higher price per bale of cotton. The cotton sellers, who see that the troops of the enemy army are engaged in the most violent struggle among themselves and that the sale of all their hundred bales is absolutely certain, will take good care not to fall out among themselves and depress the price of cotton at the moment when their adversaries are competing with one another to force it up. Thus, peace suddenly descends on the army of the sellers. They stand facing the buyers as one man, fold their arms philosophically, and there would be no bounds to their demands were it not that the offers of even the most persistent and eager buyers have very definite limits.

If, therefore, the supply of a commodity is lower than the demand for it, then only slight competition, or none at all, takes place among the sellers. In the same proportion as this competition decreases, competition increases among the buyers. The result is a more or less considerable rise in commodity prices.

It is well known that the reverse case with a reverse result occurs more frequently. Considerable surplus of supply over demand; desperate competition among the sellers; lack of buyers; disposal of goods at ridiculously low prices.

But what is the meaning of a rise, a fall in prices; what is the meaning of high price, low price? A grain of sand is high when examined through a microscope, and a tower is low when compared with a mountain. And if price is determined by the relation between supply and demand, what determines the relation between supply and demand?

Let us turn to the first bourgeois we meet. He will not reflect for an instant but, like another Alexander the Great, will cut this metaphysical knot[38] with the multiplication table. If the production of the goods which I sell has cost me 100 marks, he will tell us, and if I get 110 marks from the sale of these goods, within the year of course—then that is sound, honest, legitimate profit. But if I get in exchange 120 or 130 marks, that is a high profit; and if I get as much as 200 marks, that would be an extraordinary, an enormous profit. What, therefore, serves the bourgeois as his *measure* of profit? The *cost of production* of his commodity. If he receives in exchange for this commodity an amount of other commodities which it has cost less to produce, he has lost. If he receives in exchange for his commodity an amount of other commodities the production of which has cost more, he has gained. And he calculates the rise or fall of the profit according to the degree in which the exchange value of his commodity stands above or below zero—the *cost of production*.

We have thus seen how the changing relation of supply and demand causes now a rise and now a fall of prices, now high, now low prices. If the price of a commodity rises considerably because of inadequate supply or disproportionate increase of the demand, the price of some other commodity must necessarily have fallen proportionately, for the price of a commodity only expresses in money the ratio in which other commodities are given in exchange for it. If, for example, the price of a yard of silk material rises from five marks to six marks, the price of silver in relation to silk material has fallen and likewise the prices of all other commodities that have remained at their old prices have fallen in relation to the silk. One has to give a larger amount of them in exchange to get the same amount of silks. What will be the consequence of the rising price of a commodity? A mass of capital will be thrown into that flourishing branch of industry and this influx of capital into the domain of the favoured industry will continue until it yields the ordinary profits or, rather, until the price of its products, through overproduction, sinks below the cost of production.

Conversely, if the price of a commodity falls below its cost of production, capital will be withdrawn from the production of this commodity. Except in the case of a branch of industry which has become obsolete and must, therefore, perish, the production of such a commodity, that is, its supply, will go on decreasing owing to this flight of capital until it corresponds to the demand, and consequently its price is again on a level with its cost of production or, rather, until the supply has sunk below the demand, that is, until its price rises again above its cost of production, *for the current price of a commodity is always either above or below its cost of production.*

We see how capital continually migrates in and out, out of the domain of one industry into that of another. High prices bring too great an immigration and low prices too great an emigration.

We could show from another point of view how not only supply but also demand is determined by the cost of production. But this would take us too far away from our subject.

We have just seen how the fluctuations of supply and demand continually bring the price of a commodity back to the cost of production. *The real price of a commodity, it is true, is always above or below its cost of production; but rise and fall reciprocally balance each other*, so that within a certain period of time, taking the ebb and flow of the industry together, commodities are exchanged for one another in accordance with their cost of production, their price, therefore, being determined by their cost of production.

This determination of price by cost of production is not to be understood in the sense of the economists. The economists say that the *average price* of commodities is equal to the cost of production; that this is a *law*. The anarchical movement, in which rise is compensated by fall and fall by rise, is regarded by them as chance. With just as much right one could regard the fluctuations as the law and the determination by the cost of production as chance, as has actually been done by other economists. But it is solely these fluctuations, which, looked at more closely, bring with them the most fearful devastations and, like earthquakes, cause bourgeois society to tremble to its foundations—it is solely in the course of these fluctuations that prices are determined by the cost of production. The total movement of this disorder is its order. In the course of this industrial anarchy, in this movement in a circle, competition compensates, so to speak, for one excess by means of another.

We see, therefore, that the price of a commodity is determined by its cost of production in such manner that the periods in which the price of this commodity rises above its cost of production are compensated by the periods in which it sinks below the cost of production, and vice versa. This does not hold good, of course, for separate, particular industrial products but only for the whole branch of industry. Consequently, it also does not hold good for the individual industrialist but only for the whole class of industrialists.

The determination of price by the cost of production is equivalent to the determination of price by the labour time necessary for the manufacture of a commodity, for the cost of production consists of 1) raw materials and depreciation of instruments, that is, of industrial products the production of which has cost a certain amount of labour days and which, therefore, represent a certain amount of labour time, and 2) of direct labour, the measure of which is, precisely, time.

Now, the same general laws that regulate the price of commodities in general of course also regulate *wages*, the *price of labour*.

Wages will rise and fall according to the relation of supply and demand, according to the turn taken by the competition between the buyers of labour power, the capitalists, and the sellers of labour power, the workers. The fluctuations in wages correspond in general to the fluctuations in prices of commodities. *Within these fluctuations, however, the price of labour will ·be determined by the cost of production, by the labour time necessary to produce this commodity—labour power.*

What, then, is the cost of production of labour power?

It is the cost required for maintaining the worker as a worker and of developing him into a worker.

The less the period of training, therefore, that any work requires the smaller is the cost of production of the worker and the lower is the price of his labour, his wages. In those branches of industry in which hardly any period of apprenticeship is required and where the mere bodily existence of the worker suffices, the cost necessary for his production is almost confined to the commodities necessary for keeping him alive and capable of working. The *price of his labour* will, therefore, be determined by the *price of the necessary means of subsistence*.

Another consideration, however, also comes in. The manufacturer in calculating his cost of production and, accordingly, the price of the products takes into account the wear and tear of the instruments of labour. If, for example, a machine costs him 1,000 marks and wears out in ten years, he adds 100 marks annually to the price of the commodities so as to be able to replace the worn-out machine by a new one at the end of ten years. In the same way, in calculating the cost of production of simple labour power, there must be included the cost of reproduction, whereby the race of workers is enabled to multiply and to replace worn-out workers by new ones. Thus the depreciation of the worker is taken into account in the same way as the depreciation of the machine.

The cost of production of simple labour power, therefore, amounts to the *cost of existence and reproduction of the worker*. The price of this cost of existence and reproduction constitutes wages. Wages so determined are called the *wage minimum*. This wage minimum, like the determination of the price of commodities by the cost of production in general, does not hold good for the *single individual* but for the *species*. Individual workers, millions of workers, do not get enough to be able to exist and reproduce themselves; *but the wages of the whole working class* level down, within their fluctuations, to this minimum.

Now that we have arrived at an understanding of the most general laws which regulate wages like the price of any other commodity, we can go into our subject more specifically.

Capital consists of raw materials, instruments of labour and means of subsistence of all kinds, which are utilised in order to produce new raw materials, new instruments of labour and new means of subsistence. All these component parts of capital are creations of labour, products of labour, *accumulated labour*. Accumulated labour which serves as a means of new production is capital.

So say the economists.

What is a Negro slave? A man of the black race. The one explanation is as good as the other.

A Negro is a Negro. He only becomes a slave in certain relations. A cotton-spinning jenny is a machine for spinning cotton. It becomes *capital* only in certain relations. Torn from these relationships it is no more capital than gold in itself is *money* or sugar the price of sugar.

In production, men not only act on nature but also on one another. They produce only by co-operating in a certain way and mutually exchanging their activities. In order to produce, they enter into definite connections and relations with one another and only within these social connections and relations does their action on nature, does production, take place.

These social relations into which the producers enter with one another, the conditions under which they exchange their activities and participate in the whole act of production, will naturally vary according to the character of the means of production. With the invention of a new instrument of warfare, firearms, the whole internal organisation of the army necessarily changed; the relationships within which individuals can constitute an army and act as an army were transformed and the relations of different armies to one another also changed.

Thus the social relations within which individuals produce, *the social relations of production, change, are transformed, with the change and development of the material means of production, the productive forces. The relations of production in their totality constitute what are called the social relations, society, and, specifically, a society at a definite stage of historical development,* a society with a peculiar, distinctive character. *Ancient* society, *feudal* society, *bourgeois* society are such totalities of production relations, each of which at the same time denotes a special stage of development in the history of mankind.

Capital, also, is a social relation of production. *It is a bourgeois production relation*, a production relation of bourgeois society. Are not the means of subsistence, the instruments of labour, the raw materials of which capital consists, produced and accumulated under given social conditions, in definite social relations? Are they not utilised for new production under given social conditions, in definite social relations? And is it not just this definite social character which turns the products serving for new production into *capital*?

Capital consists not only of means of subsistence, instruments of labour and raw materials, not only of material products; it consists just as much of *exchange values*. All the products of which it consists are *commodities*. Capital is, therefore, not only a sum of material products; it is a sum of commodities, of exchange values, *of social magnitudes*.

Capital remains the same, whether we put cotton in place of wool, rice in place of wheat or steamships in place of railways, provided only that the cotton, the rice, the steamships—the body of capital—have the same exchange value, the same price as the wool, the wheat, the railways in which it was previously incorporated. The body of capital can change continually without the capital suffering the slightest alteration.

But while all capital is a sum of commodities, that is, of exchange values, not every sum of commodities, of exchange values, is capital.

Every sum of exchange values is an exchange value. Every separate exchange value is a sum of exchange values. For instance, a house that is worth 1,000 marks is an exchange value of 1,000 marks. A piece of paper worth a pfennig is a sum of exchange values of one-hundred hundredths of a pfennig. Products which are exchangeable for others are *commodities*. The particular ratio in which they are exchangeable constitutes their *exchange value* or, expressed in money, their *price*. The quantity of these products can change nothing in their quality of being *commodities* or representing an *exchange value* or having a definite price. Whether a tree is large or small it is a tree. Whether we exchange iron for other products in ounces or in hundredweights, does this make any difference in its character as commodity, as exchange value? It is a commodity of greater or lesser value, of higher or lower price, depending upon the quantity.

How, then, does any amount of commodities, of exchange values, become capital?

By maintaining and multiplying itself as an independent social *power*, that is, as the power *of a portion of society*, by means of its *exchange for direct, living labour power*. The existence of a class which possesses nothing but its capacity to labour is a necessary prerequisite of capital.

It is only the domination of accumulated, past, materialised labour over direct, living labour that turns accumulated labour into capital.

Capital does not consist in accumulated labour serving living labour as a means for new production. It consists in living labour serving accumulated labour as a means for maintaining and multiplying the exchange value of the latter.

What takes place in the exchange between capitalist and wage-worker?

The worker receives means of subsistence in exchange for his labour power, but the capitalist receives in exchange for his means of subsistence labour, the productive activity of the worker, the creative power whereby the worker not only replaces what he consumes but *gives to the accumulated labour a greater value than it previously possessed*. The worker receives a part of the available means of subsistence from the capitalist. For what purpose do these means of subsistence serve him? For immediate consumption. As soon, however, as I consume the means of subsistence, they are irretrievably lost to me unless I use the time during which I am kept alive by them in order to produce new means of subsistence, in order during consumption to create by my labour new values in place of the values which perish in being consumed. But it is just this noble reproductive power that the worker surrenders to the capitalist in exchange for means of subsistence received. He has, therefore, lost it for himself.

Let us take an example: a tenant farmer gives his day labourer five silver groschen a day. For these five silver groschen the labourer works all day on the farmer's field and thus secures him a return of ten silver groschen. The farmer not only gets the value replaced that he has to give the day labourer; he doubles it. He has therefore employed, consumed, the five silver groschen that he gave to the labourer in a fruitful, productive manner. He has bought with the five silver groschen just that labour and power of the labourer which produces agricultural products of double value and makes ten silver groschen out of five. The day labourer, on the other hand, receives in place of his productive power, the effect of which he has bargained away to the farmer, five silver groschen, which he exchanges for means of subsistence, and these he consumes with greater or less rapidity. The five silver groschen have, therefore, been consumed in a double way, *reproductively* for capital, for they have been exchanged for labour power* which produced ten silver groschen, *unproductively* for the worker, for they have been exchanged for means of subsistence which have disappeared forever and the value of which he can only recover by repeating the same exchange with the farmer. *Thus capital presupposes wage labour; wage labour presupposes capital. They reciprocally condition the existence of each other; they reciprocally bring forth each other.*

Does a worker in a cotton factory produce merely cotton textiles? No, he produces capital. He produces values which serve afresh to command his labour and by means of it to create new values.

Capital can only increase by exchanging itself for labour power, by calling wage labour to life. The labour power of the wage-worker can only be exchanged for capital by increasing capital, by strengthening the power whose slave it is. *Hence, increase of capital is increase of the proletariat, that is, of the working class.*

The interests of the capitalist and those of the worker are, therefore, *one and the same*, assert the bourgeois and their economists. Indeed! The worker perishes if capital does not employ him. Capital perishes if it does not exploit labour power, and in order to exploit it, it must buy it. The faster capital intended for production, productive capital, increases, the more, therefore, industry prospers, the more the bourgeoisie enriches itself and the better business is, the more workers does the capitalist need, the more dearly does the worker sell himself.

---

* The term "labour power" was not added here by Engels but had already been in the text Marx published in the *Neue Rheinische Zeitung.*—Ed.

The indispensable condition for a tolerable situation of the worker *is, therefore, the fastest possible growth of productive capital.*

But what is the growth of productive capital? Growth of the power of accumulated labour over living labour. Growth of the domination of the bourgeoisie over the working class. If wage labour produces the wealth of others that rules over it, the power that is hostile to it, capital, then the means of employment, that is, the means of subsistence, flow back to it from this hostile power, on condition that it makes itself afresh into a part of capital, into the lever which hurls capital anew into an accelerated movement of growth.

To say that the interests of capital and those of the workers are one and the same is only to say that capital and wage labour are two sides of one and the same relation. The one conditions the other, just as usurer and squanderer condition each other.

As long as the wage-worker is a wage-worker his lot depends upon capital. That is the much-vaunted community of interests between worker and capitalist.

If capital grows, the mass of wage labour grows, the number of wage-workers grows; in a word, the domination of capital extends over a greater number of individuals. Let us assume the most favourable case: when productive capital grows, the demand for labour grows; consequently, the price of labour, wages, goes up.

A house may be large or small; as long as the surrounding houses are equally small it satisfies all social demands for a dwelling. But let a palace arise beside the little house, and it shrinks from a little house to a hut. The little house shows now that its owner has only very slight or no demands to make; and however high it may shoot up in the course of civilisation, if the neighbouring palace grows to an equal or even greater extent, the occupant of the relatively small house will feel more and more uncomfortable, dissatisfied and cramped within its four walls.

A noticeable increase in wages presupposes a rapid growth of productive capital. The rapid growth of productive capital brings about an equally rapid growth of wealth, luxury, social wants, social enjoyments. Thus, although the enjoyments of the worker have risen, the social satisfaction that they give has fallen in comparison with the increased enjoyments of the capitalist, which are inaccessible to the worker, in comparison with the state of development of society in general. Our desires and pleasures spring from society; we measure them, therefore, by society and not by the objects which serve for their satisfaction. Because they are of a social nature, they are of a relative nature.

In general, wages are determined not only by the amount of commodities for which I can exchange them. They embody various relations.

What the workers receive for their labour power is, in the first place, a definite sum of money. Are wages determined only by this money price?

In the sixteenth century, the gold and silver circulating in Europe increased as a result of the discovery of richer and more easily worked mines in America. Hence, the value of gold and silver fell in relation to other commodities. The workers received the same amount of coined silver for their labour power as before. The money price of their labour remained the same, and yet their wages had fallen, for in exchange for the same quantity of silver they received a smaller amount of other commodities. This was one of the circumstances which furthered the growth of capital and the rise of the bourgeoisie in the sixteenth century.

Let us take another case. In the winter of 1847, as a result of a crop failure, the most indispensable means of subsistence, cereals, meat, butter, cheese, etc., rose considerably in price. Assume that the workers received the same sum of money for their labour power as before. Had not their wages fallen? Of course. For the same money they received less bread, meat, etc., in exchange. Their wages had fallen, not because the value of silver had diminished, but because the value of the means of subsistence had increased.

Assume, finally, that the money price of labour remains the same while all agricultural and manufactured goods have fallen in price owing to the employment of new machinery, a favourable season, etc. For the same money the workers can now buy more commodities of all kinds. Their wages, therefore, have risen, just because the money value of their wages has not changed.

Thus, the money price of labour, nominal wages, do not coincide with real wages, that is, with the sum of commodities which is actually given in exchange for the wages. If, therefore, we speak of a rise or fall of wages, we must keep in mind not only the money price of labour, the nominal wages.

But neither nominal wages, that is, the sum of money for which the worker sells himself to the capitalist, nor real wages, that is, the sum of commodities which he can buy for this money, exhaust the relations contained in wages.

Wages are, above all, also determined by their relation to the gain, to the profit of the capitalist—comparative, relative wages.

Real wages express the price of labour in relation to the price of other commodities; relative wages, on the other hand, express the share of direct labour in the new value it has created in relation to the share which falls to accumulated labour, to capital.

We said above, page 14*: "Wages are not the worker's share in the commodity produced by him. Wages are the part of already

_____
* See p. 73 of this volume.—*Ed.*

existing commodities with which the capitalist buys for himself
a definite amount of productive labour power." But the capitalist
must replace these wages out of the price at which he sells the
product produced by the worker; he must replace it in such a way
that there remains to him, as a rule, a surplus over the cost of
production expended by him, a profit. For the capitalist, the selling
price of the commodities produced by the worker is divided int'
three parts: *first*, the replacement of the price of the raw materiais
advanced by him together with replacement of the depreciation of
the tools, machinery and other means of labour also advanced by
him; *secondly*, the replacement of the wages advanced by him,
and *thirdly*, the surplus left over, the capitalist's profit. While the
first part only replaces *previously existing values*, it is clear that
both the replacement of the wages and also the surplus profit of
the capitalist are, on the whole, taken from the *new value created
by the worker's labour* and added to the raw materials. And *in this
sense*, in order to compare them with one another, we can regard
both wages and profit as shares in the product of the worker.

Real wages may remain the same, they may even rise, and yet
relative wages may fall. Let us suppose, for example, that all means
of subsistence have gone down in price by two-thirds while wages
per day have only fallen by one-third, that is to say, for example,
from three marks to two marks. Although the worker can command a greater amount of commodities with these two marks
than he previously could with three marks, yet his wages have
gone down in relation to the profit of the capitalist. The profit of
the capitalist (for example, the manufacturer) has increased by
one mark; that is, for a smaller sum of exchange values which
he pays to the worker, the latter must produce a greater amount
of exchange values than before. The share of capital relative to
the share of labour has risen. The division of social wealth between
capital and labour has become still more unequal. With the same
capital, the capitalist commands a greater quantity of labour. The
power of the capitalist class over the working class has grown, the
social position of the worker has deteriorated, has been depressed
one step further below that of the capitalist.

*What, then, is the general law which determines the rise and fall
of wages and profit in their reciprocal relation?*

*They stand in inverse ratio to each other. Capital's share, profit,
rises in the same proportion as labour's share, wages, falls, and vice
versa. Profit rises to the extent that wages fall; it falls to the extent
that wages rise.*

The objection will, perhaps, be made that the capitalist can profit
by a favourable exchange of his products with other capitalists, by
increase of the demand for his commodities, whether as a result of
the opening of new markets, or as a result of a momentarily increased

demand in the old markets, etc.; that the capitalist's profit can, therefore, increase by overreaching other capitalists, independently of the rise and fall of wages, of the exchange value of labour power; or that the capitalist's profit may also rise owing to the improvement of the instruments of labour, a new application of natural forces, etc.

First of all, it will have to be admitted that the result remains the same, although it is brought about in reverse fashion. True, the profit has not risen because wages have fallen, but wages have fallen because the profit has risen. With the same amount of other people's labour, the capitalist has acquired a greater amount of exchange values, without having paid more for the labour on that account; that is, therefore, labour is paid less in proportion to the net profit which it yields the capitalist.

In addition, we recall that, in spite of the fluctuations in prices of commodities, the average price of every commodity, the ratio in which it is exchanged for other commodities, is determined by its *cost of production*. Hence the overreachings within the capitalist class necessarily balance one another. The improvement of machinery, new application of natural forces in the service of production, enable a larger amount of products to be created in a given period of time with the same amount of labour and capital, but not by any means a larger amount of exchange values. If, by the use of the spinning jenny, I can turn out twice as much yarn in an hour as before its invention, say, one hundred pounds instead of fifty, then in the long run I will receive for these hundred pounds no more commodities in exchange than formerly for the fifty pounds, because the cost of production has fallen by one-half, or because I can deliver double the product at the same cost.

Finally, in whatever proportion the capitalist class, the bourgeoisie, whether of one country or of the whole world market, shares the net profit of production within itself, the total amount of this net profit always consists only of the amount by which, on the whole, accumulated labour has been increased by direct labour. This total amount grows, therefore, in the proportion in which labour augments capital, that is, in the proportion in which profit rises in comparison with wages.

We see, therefore, that even if we remain *within the relation of capital and wage labour, the interests of capital and the interests of wage labour are diametrically opposed.*

A rapid increase of capital is equivalent to a rapid increase of profit. Profit can only increase rapidly if the price of labour, if relative wages, decrease just as rapidly. Relative wages can fall although real wages rise simultaneously with nominal wages, with the money value of labour, if they do not rise, however, in the same proportion as profit. If, for instance, in times when business is good, wages rise by five per cent, profit on the other hand by thirty per cent, then the comparative, the relative wages, have not *increased* but *decreased*.

Thus if the income of the worker increases with the rapid growth of capital, the social gulf that separates the worker from the capitalist increases at the same time, and the power of capital over labour, the dependence of labour on capital, likewise increases at the same time.

To say that the worker has an interest in the rapid growth of capital is only to say that the more rapidly the worker increases the wealth of others, the richer will be the crumbs that fall to him, the greater is the number of workers that can be employed and called into existence, the more can the mass of slaves dependent on capital be increased.

We have thus seen that:

Even the *most favourable situation* for the working class, the *most rapid possible growth of capital*, however much it may improve the material existence of the worker, does not remove the antagonism between his interests and the interests of the bourgeoisie, the interests of the capitalists. *Profit and wages* remain as before in *inverse proportion.*

If capital is growing rapidly, wages may rise; the profit of capital rises incomparably more rapidly. The material position of the worker has improved, but at the cost of his social position. The social gulf that divides him from the capitalist has widened.

Finally:

To say that the most favourable condition for wage labour is the most rapid possible growth of productive capital is only to say that the more rapidly the working class increases and enlarges the power that is hostile to it, the wealth that does not belong to it and that rules over it, the more favourable will be the conditions under which it is allowed to labour anew at increasing bourgeois wealth, at enlarging the power of capital, content with forging for itself the golden chains by which the bourgeoisie drags it in its train.

Are *growth of productive capital and rise of wages* really so inseparably connected as the bourgeois economists maintain? We must not take their word for it. We must not even believe them when they say that the fatter capital is, the better will its slave be fed. The bourgeoisie is too enlightened, it calculates too well, to share the prejudices of the feudal lord who makes a display by the brilliance of his retinue. The conditions of existence of the bourgeoisie compel it to calculate.

We must, therefore, examine more closely:

How does the growth of productive capital affect wages?

If, on the whole, the productive capital of bourgeois society grows, a *more manifold* accumulation of labour takes place. The capitals increase in number and extent. The *numerical increase* of the capitals increases the *competition between the capitalists.* The *increasing extent* of the capitals provides the means for *bringing more powerful labour armies with more gigantic instruments of war into the industrial battlefield.*

One capitalist can drive another from the field and capture his capital only by selling more cheaply. In order to be able to sell more cheaply without ruining himself, he must produce more cheaply, that is, raise the productive power of labour as much as possible. But the productive power of labour is raised, above all, by *a greater division of labour,* by a more universal introduction and continual improvement of *machinery.* The greater the labour army among whom labour is divided, the more gigantic the scale on which machinery is introduced, the more does the cost of production proportionately decrease, the more fruitful is labour. Hence, a general rivalry arises among the capitalists to increase the division of labour and machinery and to exploit them on the greatest possible scale.

If, now, by a greater division of labour, by the utilisation of new machines and their improvement, by more profitable and extensive exploitation of natural forces, one capitalist has found the means of producing with the same amount of labour or of accumulated labour a greater amount of products, of commodities, than his competitors, if he can, for example, produce a whole yard of linen in the same labour time in which his competitors weave half a yard, how will this capitalist operate?

He could continue to sell half a yard of linen at the old market price; this would, however, be no means of driving his opponents from the field and of enlarging his own sales. But in the same measure in which his production has expanded, his need to sell has also increased. The more powerful and costly means of production that he has called into life *enable* him, indeed, to sell his commodities more cheaply, they *compel* him, however, at the same time *to sell more commodities,* to conquer a much *larger* market for his commodities; consequently, our capitalist will sell his half yard of linen more cheaply than his competitors.

The capitalist will not, however, sell a whole yard as cheaply as his competitors sell half a yard, although the production of the whole yard does not cost him more than the half yard costs the others. Otherwise he would not gain anything extra but only get back the cost of production by the exchange. His possibly greater income would be derived from the fact of having set a larger capital into motion, but not from having made more of his capital than the others. Moreover, he attains the object he wishes to attain, if he puts the price of his goods only a small percentage lower than that of his competitors. He drives them from the field, he wrests from them at least a part of their sales, by *underselling* them. And, finally, it will be remembered that the current price always stands *above or below the cost of production*, according to whether the sale of the commodity occurs in a favourable or unfavourable industrial season. The percentage at which the capitalist who has employed new and more fruitful means of production sells above his real cost of production will vary, depending upon whether the market price of a yard of linen stands below or above its hitherto customary cost of production.

However, the *privileged position* of our capitalist is not of long duration; other competing capitalists introduce the same machines, the same division of labour, introduce them on the same or on a larger scale, and this introduction will become so general that the price of linen *is reduced* not only *below its old*, but *below its new cost of production*.

The capitalists find themselves, therefore, in the same position relative to one another as *before* the introduction of the new means of production, and if they are able to supply by these means double the production at the same price, they are *now* forced to supply the double product *below* the old price. On the basis of this new cost of production, the same game begins again. More division of labour, more machinery, enlarged scale of exploitation of machinery and division of labour. And again competition brings the same counteraction against this result.

We see how in this way the mode of production and the means of production are continually transformed, revolutionised, *how the division of labour is necessarily followed by greater division of labour, the application of machinery by still greater application of machinery, work on a large scale by work on a still larger scale.*

That is the law which again and again throws bourgeois production out of its old course and which compels capital to intensify the productive forces of labour, *because* it has intensified them, it, the law which gives capital no rest and continually whispers in its ear: "Go on! Go on!"

This law is none other than that which, within the fluctuations of trade periods, necessarily *levels out* the price of a commodity to its *cost of production*.

However powerful the means of production which a capitalist brings into the field, competition will make these means of production universal and from the moment when it has made them universal, the only result of the greater fruitfulness of his capital is that he must now supply *for the same price* ten, twenty, a hundred times as much as before. But, as he must sell perhaps a thousand times as much as before in order to outweigh the lower selling price by the greater amount of the product sold, because a more extensive sale is now necessary, not only in order to make more profit but in order to replace the cost of production—the instrument of production itself, as we have seen, becomes more and more expensive—and because this mass sale becomes a question of life and death not only for him but also for his rivals, the old struggle begins again *all the more violently the more fruitful the already discovered means of production are. The division of labour and the application of machinery, therefore, will go on anew on an incomparably greater scale.*

Whatever the power of the means of production employed may be, competition seeks to rob capital of the golden fruits of this power by bringing the price of the commodities back to the cost of production, by thus making cheaper production—the supply of ever greater amounts of products for the same total price—an imperative law to the same extent as production can be cheapened, that is, as more can be produced with the same amount of labour. Thus the capitalist would have won nothing by his own exertions but the obligation to supply more in the same labour time, in a word, *more difficult conditions for the augmentation of the value of his capital.* While, therefore, competition continually pursues him with its law of the cost of production and every weapon that he forges against his rivals recoils against himself, the capitalist continually tries to get the better of competition by incessantly introducing new machines, more expensive, it is true, but producing more cheaply, and new division of labour in place of the old, and by not waiting until competition has rendered the new ones obsolete.

If now we picture to ourselves this feverish simultaneous agitation on the *whole world market*, it will be comprehensible how the growth, accumulation and concentration of capital results in an uninterrupted division of labour, and in the application of new and the perfecting of old machinery precipitately and on an ever more gigantic scale.

But how do these circumstances, which are inseparable from the growth of productive capital, affect the determination of wages?

The greater *division of labour* enables *one* worker to do the work of five, ten or twenty; it therefore multiplies. competition among the workers fivefold, tenfold and twentyfold. The workers do not only compete by one selling himself cheaper than another; they compete by *one* doing the work of five, ten, twenty; and the *division of labour*, introduced by capital and continually increased, compels the workers to compete among themselves in this way.

Further, as the *division of labour* increases, labour *is simplified.* The special skill of the worker becomes worthless. He becomes transformed into a simple, monotonous productive force that does not have to use intense bodily or intellectual faculties. His labour becomes a labour that anyone can perform. Hence, competitors crowd upon him on all sides, and besides we remind the reader that the more simple and easily learned the labour is, the lower

he cost of production needed to master it, the lower do wages sink,
or, like the price of every other commodity, they are determined
by the cost of production.

*Therefore, as labour becomes more unsatisfying, more repul-
sive, competition increases and wages decrease.* The worker tries
to keep up the amount of his wages by working more, whether
by working longer hours or by producing more in one hour. Driv-
en by want, therefore, he still further increases the evil effects of
the division of labour. The result is that *the more he works the
less wages he receives*, and for the simple reason that he competes
to that extent with his fellow workers, hence makes them into so
many competitors who offer themselves on just the same bad terms
as he does himself, and that, therefore, in the last resort he *competes
with himself, with himself as a member of the working class.*

Machinery brings about the same results on a much greater scale,
by replacing skilled workers by unskilled, men by women, adults by
children. It brings about the same results, where it is newly introduced, by throwing the hand workers on to the streets in masses,
and, where it is developed, improved and replaced by more productive machinery, by discharging workers in smaller batches. We
have portrayed above, in a hasty sketch, the industrial war of the
capitalists among themselves; *this war has the peculiarity that its
battles are won less by recruiting than by discharging the army of
labour. The generals, the capitalists, compete with one another as
to who can discharge most soldiers of industry.*

The economists tell us, it is true, that the workers rendered
superfluous by machinery find *new* branches of employment.

They dare not assert directly that the same workers who are
discharged find places in the new branches of labour. The facts
cry out too loudly against this lie. They really only assert that
new means of employment will open up for *other component sections of the working class*, for instance, for the portion of the
young generation of workers that was ready to enter the branch
of industry which has gone under. That is, of course, a great
consolation for the disinherited workers. The worshipful capitalists
will never want for fresh exploitable flesh and blood, and will let
the dead bury their dead. This is a consolation which the bourgeois
give themselves rather than one which they give the workers. If
the whole class of wage-workers were to be abolished owing to
machinery, how dreadful that would be for capital which, without
wage labour, ceases to be capital!

Let us suppose, however, that those directly driven out of their
jobs by machinery, and the entire section of the new generation
that was already on the watch for this employment, *find a new
occupation.* Does any one imagine that it will be as highly paid as
that which has been lost? *That would contradict all the laws of*

economics. We have seen how modern industry always brings with
it the substitution of a more simple, subordinate occupation for the
more complex and higher one.

How, then, could a mass of workers who have been thrown out
of one branch of industry owing to machinery find refuge in another,
unless the latter *is lower, worse paid?*

The workers who work in the manufacture of machinery itself
have been cited as an exception. As soon as more machinery is
demanded and used in industry, it is said, there must necessarily
be an increase of machines, consequently of the manufacture of
machines, and consequently of the employment of workers in the
manufacture of machines; and the workers engaged in this branch
of industry are claimed to be skilled, even educated workers.

Since the year 1840 this assertion, which even before was only
half true, has lost all semblance of truth because ever more versatile
machines have been employed in the manufacture of machinery,
no more and no less than in the manufacture of cotton yarn, and
the workers employed in the machine factories, confronted by highly
elaborate machines, can only play the part of highly unelaborate
machines.

But in place of the man who has been discharged owing to the
machine, the factory employs maybe *three* children and *one* woman. And did not the man's wages have to suffice for the three
children and a woman? Did not the minimum of wages have to
suffice to maintain and to propagate the race? What, then, does
this favourite bourgeois phrase prove? Nothing more than that now
four times as many workers' lives are used up in order to gain a
livelihood for *one* worker's family.

Let us sum up: *The more productive capital grows, the more
the division of labour and the application of machinery expands.
The more the division of labour and the application of machinery
expands, the more competition among the workers expands and the
more their wages contract.*

In addition, the working class gains recruits from the *higher
strata of society* also; a mass of petty industrialists and small
rentiers are hurled down into its ranks and have nothing better
to do than urgently stretch out their arms alongside those of the
workers. Thus the forest of uplifted arms demanding work becomes
ever thicker, while the arms themselves become ever thinner.

That the small industrialist cannot survive in a contest one of
the first conditions of which is to produce on an ever greater scale,
that is, precisely to be a large and not a small industrialist, is self-
evident.

That the interest on capital decreases in the same measure as
the mass and number of capitals increase, as capital grows; that,
therefore, the small rentier can no longer live on his interest but

must throw himself into industry, and, consequently, help to swell the ranks of the small industrialists and thereby of candidates for the proletariat—all this surely requires no further explanation.

Finally, as the capitalists are compelled, by the movement described above, to exploit the already existing gigantic means of production on a larger scale and to set in motion all the mainsprings of credit to this end, there is a corresponding increase in industrial earthquakes, in which the trading world can only maintain itself by sacrificing a part of wealth, of products and even of productive forces to the gods of the nether world—in a word, *crises* increase. They become more frequent and more violent, if only because, as the mass of production, and consequently the need for extended markets, grows, the world market becomes more and more contracted, fewer and fewer new markets remain available for exploitation, since every preceding crisis has subjected to world trade a market hitherto unconquered or only superficially exploited. But capital does not *live* only on labour. A lord, at once aristocratic and barbarous, it drags with it into the grave the corpses of its slaves, whole hecatombs of workers who perish in the crises. Thus we see: *if capital grows rapidly, competition among the workers grows incomparably more rapidly, that is, the means of employment, the means of subsistence, of the working class decrease proportionately so much the more, and, nevertheless, the rapid growth of capital is the most favourable condition for wage labour.*

Written by Marx on the basis of lectures delivered by him in the latter half of December 1847

Published in the *Neue Rheinische Zeitung* Nos. 264-67 and 269, of April 5-8 and 11, 1849

Appeared as a separate pamphlet, prefaced and edited by Engels, in Berlin in 1891

Printed according to the text of the pamphlet
Translated from the German

Karl Marx

THE EIGHTEENTH BRUMAIRE OF LOUIS BONAPARTE[39]

F. ENGELS'S PREFACE
TO THE THIRD GERMAN EDITION

The fact that a new edition of *The Eighteenth Brumaire* has become necessary, thirty-three years after its first appearance, proves that even today this little book has lost none of its value.

It was in truth a work of genius. Immediately after the event that struck the whole political world like a thunderbolt from the blue, that was condemned by some with loud cries of moral indignation and accepted by others as salvation from the revolution and as punishment for its errors, but was only wondered at by all and understood by none—immediately after this event Marx came out with a concise, epigrammatic exposition that laid bare the whole course of French history since the February days in its inner interconnection, reduced the miracle of December 2[40] to a natural, necessary result of this interconnection and in so doing did not even need to treat the hero of the *coup d'état* otherwise than with the contempt he so well deserved. And the picture was drawn with such a master hand that every fresh disclosure since made has only provided fresh proofs of how faithfully it reflected reality. This eminent understanding of the living history of the day, this clear-sighted appreciation of events at the moment of happening, is indeed without parallel.

But for this, Marx's thorough knowledge of French history was needed. France is the land where, more than anywhere else, the historical class struggles were each time fought out to a decision, and where, consequently, the changing political forms within which they move and in which their results are summarised have been stamped in the sharpest outlines. The centre of feudalism in the Middle Ages, the model country of unified monarchy, resting on estates, since the Renaissance,[41] France demolished feudalism in the Great Revolution and established the unalloyed rule of the bourgeoisie in a classical purity unequalled by any other European land. And the struggle of the upward-striving proletariat against the ruling bourgeoisie appeared here in an acute form unknown elsewhere. This was the reason why Marx not only studied the past history of France with particular predilection, but also followed her current history in every detail, stored up the material for future use and, consequently, events never took him by surprise.

In addition, however, there was still another circumstance. It was precisely Marx who had first discovered the great law of motion of history, the law according to which all historical struggles, whether they proceed in the political, religious, philosophical or some other ideological domain, are in fact only the more or less clear expression of struggles of social classes, and that the existence of and thereby the collisions, too, between these classes are in turn conditioned by the degree of development of their economic position, by the mode of their production and of their exchange determined by it. This law, which has the same significance for history as the law of the transformation of energy has for natural science —this law gave him here, too, the key to an understanding of the history of the Second French Republic.[42] He put his law to the test on these historical events, and even after thirty-three years we must still say that it has stood the test brilliantly.

Frederick Engels

Written in 1885

Published in the book:
Karl Marx. *Der Achtzehnte Brumaire des Louis Bonaparte*, Hamburg, 1885

Printed according to the text of the book
Translated from the German

THE EIGHTEENTH BRUMAIRE
OF LOUIS BONAPARTE[39]

I

Hegel remarks somewhere that all facts and personages of great importance in world history occur, as it were, twice. He forgot to add: the first time as tragedy, the second as farce. Caussidière for Danton, Louis Blanc for Robespierre, the *Montagne* of 1848 to 1851 for the *Montagne* of 1793 to 1795,[43] the Nephew for the Uncle. And the same caricature occurs in the circumstances attending the second edition of the eighteenth Brumaire![44]

Men make their own history, but they do not make it just as they please; they do not make it under circumstances chosen by themselves, but under circumstances directly encountered, given and transmitted from the past. The tradition of all the dead generations weighs like a nightmare on the brain of the living. And just when they seem engaged in revolutionising themselves and things, in creating something that has never yet existed, precisely in such periods of revolutionary crisis they anxiously conjure up the spirits of the past to their service and borrow from them names, battle cries and costumes in order to present the new scene of world history in this time-honoured disguise and this borrowed language. Thus Luther donned the mask of the Apostle Paul, the Revolution of 1789 to 1814 draped itself alternately as the Roman republic and the Roman empire, and the Revolution of 1848 knew nothing better to do than to parody, now 1789, now the revolutionary tradition of 1793 to 1795. In like manner a beginner who has learnt a new language always translates it back into his mother tongue, but he has assimilated the spirit of the new language and can freely express himself in it only when he finds his way in it without recalling the old and forgets his native tongue in the use of the new.

Consideration of this conjuring up of the dead of world history reveals at once a salient difference. Camille Desmoulins, Danton, Robespierre, Saint-Just, Napoleon, the heroes as well as the parties and the masses of the old French Revolution, performed the task of their time in Roman costume and with Roman phrases, the task of unchaining and setting up modern *bourgeois* society. The first ones knocked the feudal basis to pieces and mowed off the feudal heads which had grown on it. The other created inside France the conditions under which alone free competition could be developed, parcelled landed property exploited and the unchained industrial productive power of the nation employed; and beyond the French borders he everywhere swept the feudal institutions away, so far as was necessary to furnish bourgeois society in France with a suitable up-to-date environment on the European Continent. The new social formation once established, the antediluvian Colossi disappeared and with them resurrected Romanity— the Brutuses, Gracchi, Publicolas, the tribunes, the senators, and Caesar himself. Bourgeois society in its sober reality had begotten its true interpreters and mouthpieces in the Says, Cousins, Royer-Collards, Benjamin Constants and Guizots; its real military leaders sat behind the office desks, and the hogheaded Louis XVIII was its political chief. Wholly absorbed in the production of wealth and in peaceful competitive struggle, it no longer comprehended that ghosts from the days of Rome had watched over its cradle. But unheroic as bourgeois society is, it nevertheless took heroism, sacrifice, terror, civil war and battles of peoples to bring it into being. And in the classically austere traditions of the Roman republic its gladiators found the ideals and the art forms, the self-deceptions that they needed in order to conceal from themselves the bourgeois limitations of the content of their struggles and to keep their enthusiasm on the high plane of the great historical tragedy. Similarly, at another stage of development, a century earlier, Cromwell and the English people had borrowed speech, passions and illusions from the Old Testament[45] for their bourgeois revolution.[46] When the real aim had been achieved, when the bourgeois transformation of English society had been accomplished, Locke supplanted Habakkuk.

Thus the awakening of the dead in those revolutions served the purpose of glorifying the new struggles, not of parodying the old; of magnifying the given task in imagination, not of fleeing from its solution in reality; of finding once more the spirit of revolution, not of making its ghost walk about again.

From 1848 to 1851 only the ghost of the old revolution walked about, from Marrast, the *républicain en gants jaunes,** who disguised himself as the old Bailly, down to the adventurer, who hides his commonplace repulsive features under the iron death mask of Napoleon. An entire people, which had imagined that by means of a revolution it had imparted to itself an accelerated power of motion, suddenly finds itself set back into a defunct epoch and, in order that no doubt as to the relapse may be possible, the old dates arise again, the old chronology, the old names, the old edicts, which had long become a subject of antiquarian erudition, and the old minions of the law, who had seemed long

---

* Republican in yellow gloves.—*Ed.*

decayed. The nation feels like that mad Englishman in Bedlam[47]
who fancies that he lives in the times of the ancient Pharaohs
and daily bemoans the hard labour that he must perform in the
Ethiopian mines as a gold digger, immured in this subterranean
prison, a dimly burning lamp fastened to his head, the overseer
of the slaves behind him with a long whip, and at the exits a
confused welter of barbarian mercenaries, who understand neither
the forced labourers in the mines nor one another, since they
speak no common language. "And all this is expected of me,"
sighs the mad Englishman, "of me, a freeborn Briton, in order to
make gold for the old Pharaohs." "In order to pay the debts of
the Bonaparte family," sighs the French nation. The Englishman,
so long as he was in his right mind, could not get rid of the fixed
idea of making gold. The French, so long as they were engaged
in revolution, could not get rid of the memory of Napoleon, as the
election of December 10[48] proved. They hankered to return from
the perils of revolution to the flesh-pots[49] of Egypt, and December 2, 1851[40] was the answer. They have not only a caricature of
the old Napoleon, they have the old Napoleon himself, caricatured
as he must appear in the middle of the nineteenth century.

The social revolution of the nineteenth century cannot draw its
poetry from the past, but only from the future. It cannot begin
with itself before it has stripped off all superstition in regard to
the past. Earlier revolutions required recollections of past world
history in order to drug themselves concerning their own content.
In order to arrive at its own content, the revolution of the nineteenth century must let the dead bury their dead. There the phrase
went beyond the content; here the content goes beyond the phrase.

The February Revolution was a surprise attack, a *taking* of the
old society *unawares*, and the people proclaimed this unexpected
stroke as a deed of world importance, ushering in a new epoch. On
December 2 the February Revolution is conjured away by a card-
sharper's trick, and what seems overthrown is no longer the monarchy
but the liberal concessions that were wrung from it by centuries of
struggle. Instead of *society* having conquered a new content for
itself, it seems that the *state* only returned to its oldest form, to the
shamelessly simple domination of the sabre and the cowl. This is
the answer to the *coup de main** of February 1848, given by the
*coup de tête*** of December 1851. Easy come, easy go. Meanwhile
the interval of time has not passed by unused. During the years
1848 to 1851 French society has made up, and that by an abbreviated
because revolutionary method, for the studies and experiences which,
in a regular, so to speak, textbook course of development, would

* *Coup de main*: Unexpected stroke.—*Ed.*
** *Coup de tête:* Rash act.—*Ed.*

have had to precede the February Revolution, if it was to be more than a ruffling of the surface. Society now seems to have fallen back behind its point of departure; it has in truth first to create for itself the revolutionary point of departure, the situation, the relations, the conditions under which alone modern revolution becomes serious.

Bourgeois revolutions, like those of the eighteenth century, storm swiftly from success to success; their dramatic effects outdo each other; men and things seem set in sparkling brilliants; ecstasy is the everyday spirit; but they are short-lived; soon they have attained their zenith, and a long crapulent depression lays hold of society before it learns soberly to assimilate the results of its storm-and-stress period. On the other hand, proletarian revolutions, like those of the nineteenth century, criticise themselves constantly, interrupt themselves continually in their own course, come back to the apparently accomplished in order to begin it afresh, deride with unmerciful thoroughness the inadequacies, weaknesses and paltrinesses of their first attempts, seem to throw down their adversary only in order that he may draw new strength from the earth and rise again, more gigantic, before them, recoil ever and anon from the indefinite prodigiousness of their own aims, until a situation has been created which makes all turning back impossible, and the conditions themselves cry out:

Hic Rhodus, hic salta!
Here is the rose, here dance![50]

For the rest, every fairly competent observer, even if he had not followed the course of French development step by step, must have had a presentiment that an unheard-of fiasco was in store for the revolution. It was enough to hear the self-complacent howl of victory with which Messieurs the Democrats congratulated each other on the expected gracious consequences of the second Sunday in May 1852.[51] In their minds the second Sunday in May 1852 had become a fixed idea, a dogma, like the day on which Christ should reappear and the millennium begin, in the minds of the Chiliasts.[52] As ever, weakness had taken refuge in a belief in miracles, fancied the enemy overcome when he was only conjured away in imagination, and it lost all understanding of the present in a passive glorification of the future that was in store for it and of the deeds it had *in petto* but which it merely did not want to carry out as yet. Those heroes who seek to disprove their demonstrated incapacity by mutually offering each other their sympathy and getting together in a crowd had tied up their bundles, collected their laurel wreaths in advance and were just then engaged in discounting on the exchange market the republics *in partibus*[53] for which they had already providently organised the government personnel with all the calm of their unassuming disposition. December 2 struck

them like a thunderbolt from a clear sky, and the peoples that in periods of pusillanimous depression gladly let their inward apprehension be drowned out by the loudest bawlers will perchance have convinced themselves that the times are past when the cackle of geese could save the Capitol.[54]
The Constitution, the National Assembly, the dynastic parties, the blue and the red republicans, the heroes of Africa,[55] the thunder from the platform, the sheet lightning of the daily press, the entire literature, the political names and the intellectual reputations, the civil law and the penal code, the *liberté, égalité, fraternité* and the second Sunday in May 1852—all has vanished like a phantasmagoria before the spell of a man whom even his enemies do not make out to be a magician. Universal suffrage seems to have survived only for a moment, in order that with its own hand it may make its last will and testament before the eyes of all the world and declare in the name of the people itself: All that exists deserves to perish.*
It is not enough to say, as the French do, that their nation was taken unawares. A nation and a woman are not forgiven the unguarded hour in which the first adventurer that came along could violate them. The riddle is not solved by such turns of speech, but merely formulated differently. It remains to be explained how a nation of thirty-six millions can be surprised and delivered unresisting into captivity by three swindlers.
Let us recapitulate in general outline the phases that the French Revolution went through from February 24, 1848, to December 1851.
Three main periods are unmistakable: *the February period*; May 4, 1848, to May 28, 1849: *the period of the constitution of the republic,* or *of the Constituent National Assembly*; May 28, 1849, to December 2, 1851: *the period of the constitutional republic* or *of the Legislative National Assembly.*
The *first period,* from February 24, or the overthrow of Louis Philippe. to May 4, 1848, the meeting of the Constituent Assembly, the *February period* proper, may be described as the *prologue* to the revolution. Its character was officially expressed in the fact that the government improvised by it itself declared that it was *provisional* and, like the government, everything that was mooted, attempted or enunciated during this period proclaimed itself to be only *provisional.* Nothing and nobody ventured to lay claim to the right of existence and of real action. All the elements that had prepared or determined the revolution, the dynastic opposition,[56] the republican bourgeoisie, the democratic-republican petty bourgeoisie and the social-democratic workers, provisionally found their place in the February *government.*

* Mephistopheles in Goethe's *Faust.—Ed.*

It could not be otherwise. The February days originally intended an electoral reform, by which the circle of the politically privileged among the possessing class itself was to be widened and the exclusive domination of the aristocracy of finance overthrown. When it came to the actual conflict, however, when the people mounted the barricades, the National Guard maintained a passive attitude, the army offered no serious resistance and the monarchy ran away, the republic appeared to be a matter of course. Every party construed it in its own way. Having secured it arms in hand, the proletariat impressed its stamp upon it and proclaimed it to be a *social republic*. There was thus indicated the general content of the modern revolution, a content which was in most singular contradiction to everything that, with the material available, with the degree of education attained by the masses, under the given circumstances and relations, could be immediately realised in practice. On the other hand, the claims of all the remaining elements that had collaborated in the February Revolution were recognised by the lion's share that they obtained in the government. In no period do we, therefore, find a more confused mixture of high-flown phrases and actual uncertainty and clumsiness, of more enthusiastic striving for innovation and more deeply-rooted domination of the old routine, of more apparent harmony of the whole of society and more profound estrangement of its elements. While the Paris proletariat still revelled in the vision of the wide prospects that had opened before it and indulged in seriously-meant discussions on social problems, the old powers of society had grouped themselves, assembled, reflected and found unexpected support in the mass of the nation, the peasants and petty bourgeois, who all at once stormed on to the political stage, after the barriers of the July monarchy had fallen.[57]

The *second period*, from May 4, 1848, to the end of May 1849, is the period of the *constitution*, the *foundation, of the bourgeois republic*. Directly after the February days not only had the dynastic opposition been surprised by the republicans and the republicans by the Socialists, but all France by Paris. The National Assembly, which met on May 4, 1848, had emerged from the national elections and represented the nation. It was a living protest against the pretensions of the February days and was to reduce the results of the revolution to the bourgeois scale. In vain the Paris proletariat, which immediately grasped the character of this National Assembly, attempted on May 15,[58] a few days after it met, forcibly to negate its existence, to dissolve it, to disintegrate again into its constituent parts the organic form in which the proletariat was threatened by the reacting spirit of the nation. As is known, May 15 had no other result save that of removing Blanqui and his comrades, that is, the real leaders of the proletarian party, from the public stage for the entire duration of the cycle we are considering.

The *bourgeois monarchy* of Louis Philippe can be followed only by a *bourgeois republic*, that is to say, whereas a limited section of the bourgeoisie ruled in the name of the king, the whole of the bourgeoisie will now rule on behalf of the people. The demands of the Paris proletariat are utopian nonsense, to which an end must be put. To this declaration of the Constituent National Assembly the Paris proletariat replied with the *June Insurrection,*[6] the most colossal event in the history of European civil wars. The bourgeois republic triumphed. On its side stood the aristocracy of finance, the industrial bourgeoisie, the middle class, the petty bourgeois, the army, the *lumpenproletariat** organised as the Mobile Guard, the intellectual lights, the clergy and the rural population. On the side of the Paris proletariat stood none but itself. More than three thousand insurgents were butchered after the victory, and fifteen thousand were transported without trial. With this defeat the proletariat passes into the *background* of the revolutionary stage. It attempts to press forward again on every occasion, as soon as the movement appears to make a fresh start, but with ever decreased expenditure of strength and always slighter results. As soon as one of the social strata situated above it gets into revolutionary ferment, the proletariat enters into an alliance with it and so shares all the defeats that the different parties suffer, one after another. But these subsequent blows become the weaker, the greater the surface of society over which they are distributed. The more important leaders of the proletariat in the Assembly and in the press successively fall victims to the courts, and ever more equivocal figures come to head it. In part it throws itself into *doctrinaire experiments, exchange banks and workers' associations, hence into a movement in which it renounces the revolutionising of the old world by means of the latter's own great, combined resources, and seeks, rather, to achieve its salvation behind society's back, in private fashion, within its limited conditions of existence, and hence necessarily suffers shipwreck.* It seems to be unable either to rediscover revolutionary greatness in itself or to win new energy from the connections newly entered into, until *all classes* with which it contended in June themselves lie prostrate beside it. But at least it succumbs with the honours of the great, world-historic struggle; not only France, but all Europe trembles at the June earthquake, while the ensuing defeats of the upper classes are so cheaply bought that they require barefaced exaggeration by the victorious party to be able to pass for events at all, and become the more ignominious the further the defeated party is removed from the proletarian party.

---

* See K. Marx, *The Class Struggles in France, 1848 to 1850* (Marx and Engels, *Selected Works*, Vol. I, Moscow, 1962, p. 155).—*Ed.*

THE EIGHTEENTH BRUMAIRE OF LOUIS BONAPARTE 103

The defeat of the June insurgents, to be sure, had now prepared, had levelled the ground on which the bourgeois republic could be founded and built up, but it had shown at the same time that in Europe the questions at issue are other than that of "republic or monarchy." It had revealed that here *bourgeois republic* signifies the unlimited despotism of one class over other classes. It had proved that in countries with an old civilisation, with a developed formation of classes, with modern conditions of production and with an intellectual consciousness in which all traditional ideas have been dissolved by the work of centuries, *the republic* signifies *in general only the political form of revolution of bourgeois society* and not its *conservative form of life*, as, for example, in the United States of North America, where, though classes already exist, they have not yet become fixed, but continually change and interchange their elements in constant flux, where the modern means of production, instead of coinciding with a stagnant surplus population, rather compensate for the relative deficiency of heads and hands, and where, finally, the feverish, youthful movement of material production, which has to make a new world its own, has left neither time nor opportunity for abolishing the old spirit world.

During the June days all classes and parties had united in the *party of Order* against the proletarian class as the *party of Anarchy*, of socialism, of communism. They had "saved" society from "*the enemies of society*." They had given out the watchwords of the old society, "*property, family, religion, order*," to their army as passwords and had proclaimed to the counter-revolutionary crusaders: "By this sign thou shalt conquer!"[59] From that moment, as soon as one of the numerous parties which had gathered under this sign against the June insurgents seeks to hold the revolutionary battlefield in its own class interest, it goes down before the cry: "Property, family, religion, order." Society is saved just as often as the circle of its rulers contracts, as a more exclusive interest is maintained against a wider one. Every demand of the simplest bourgeois financial reform, of the most ordinary liberalism, of the most formal republicanism, of the most shallow democracy, is simultaneously castigated as an "attempt on society" and stigmatised as "socialism." And, finally, the high priests of "the religion of order" themselves are driven with kicks from their Pythian tripods,[60] hauled out of their beds in the darkness of night, put in prison-vans, thrown into dungeons or sent into exile; their temple is razed to the ground, their mouths are sealed, their pens broken, their law torn to pieces in the name of religion, of property, of the family, of order. Bourgeois fanatics for order are shot down on their balconies by mobs of drunken soldiers, their domestic sanctuaries profaned, their houses bombarded for amusement—in the name of property, of the family, of religion and of order. Finally, the scum of bourgeois society

forms the *holy phalanx of order* and the hero Crapulinski* installs
himself in the Tuileries as the *"saviour of society."*

II

Let us pick up the threads of the development once more.

The history of the *Constituent National Assembly* since the June
days is the *history of the domination and the disintegration of the
republican faction of the bourgeoisie*, of that faction which is
known by the names of tricolour republicans, pure republicans,
political republicans, formalist republicans, etc.

Under the bourgeois monarchy of Louis Philippe it had formed
the *official* republican *opposition* and consequently a recognised
component part of the political world of the day. It had its representatives in the Chambers and a considerable sphere of influence
in the press. Its Paris organ, the *National*,[61] was considered just as
respectable in its way as the *Journal des Débats*.[62] Its character
corresponded to this position under the constitutional monarchy.
It was not a faction of the bourgeoisie held together by great common interests and marked off by specific conditions of production.
It was a clique of republican-minded bourgeois, writers, lawyers,
officers and officials that owed its influence to the personal antipathies of the country against Louis Philippe, to memories of the
old republic, to the republican faith of a number of enthusiasts,
above all, however, to *French nationalism*, whose hatred of the
Vienna treaties[63] and of the alliance with England it stirred up perpetually. A large part of the following that the *National* had under
Louis Philippe was due to this concealed imperialism, which could
consequently confront it later, under the republic, as a deadly rival
in the person of Louis Bonaparte. It fought the aristocracy of
finance, as did all the rest of the bourgeois opposition. Polemics
against the budget, which were closely connected in France with
fighting the aristocracy of finance, procured popularity too cheaply
and material for puritanical leading articles too plentifully, not to
be exploited. The industrial bourgeoisie was grateful to it for its
slavish defence of the French protectionist system, which it accepted,
however, more on national grounds than on grounds of national
economy; the bourgeoisie as a whole, for its vicious denunciation of
communism and socialism. For the rest, the party of the *National*
was *purely republican*, that is, it demanded a republican instead of
a monarchist form of bourgeois rule and, above all, the lion's share
of this rule. Concerning the conditions of this transformation it was

---

* Louis Bonaparte.—*Ed.*

by no means clear in its own mind. On the other hand, what was clear as daylight to it and was publicly acknowledged at the reform banquets in the last days of Louis Philippe, was its unpopularity with the democratic petty bourgeois and, in particular, with the revolutionary proletariat. These pure republicans, as is, indeed, the way with pure republicans, were already on the point of contenting themselves in the first instance with a regency of the Duchess of Orleans, when the February Revolution[4] broke out and assigned their best-known representatives a place in the Provisional Government. From the start, they naturally had the confidence of the bourgeoisie and a majority in the Constituent National Assembly. The *socialist* elements of the Provisional Government were excluded forthwith from the Executive Commission which the National Assembly formed when it met, and the party of the *National* took advantage of the outbreak of the June insurrection to discharge the *Executive Commission* also, and therewith to get rid of its closest rivals, the *petty-bourgeois,* or *democratic, republicans* (Ledru-Rollin, etc.). Cavaignac, the general of the bourgeois republican party who commanded the June massacre, took the place of the Executive Commission with sort of dictatorial powers. Marrast, former editor-in-chief of the *National,* became the perpetual president of the Constituent National Assembly, and the ministries, as well as all other important posts, fell to the portion of the pure republicans.

The republican bourgeois faction, which had long regarded itself as the legitimate heir of the July monarchy, thus found its fondest hopes exceeded; it attained power, however, not as it had dreamed under Louis Philippe, through a liberal revolt of the bourgeoisie against the throne, but through a rising of the proletariat against capital, a rising laid low with grape-shot. What it had pictured to itself as the *most revolutionary* event turned out in reality to be the *most counter-revolutionary.* The fruit fell into its lap, but it fell from the tree of knowledge, not from the tree of life.

The exclusive *rule of the bourgeois republicans* lasted only from June 24 to December 10, 1848. It is summed up in the *drafting of a republican constitution* and in the *state of siege of Paris.*

The new *Constitution* was at bottom only the republicanised edition of the constitutional Charter[64] of 1830. The narrow electoral qualification of the July monarchy, which excluded even a large part of the bourgeoisie from political rule, was incompatible with the existence of the bourgeois republic. In lieu of this qualification, the February Revolution had at once proclaimed direct universal suffrage. The bourgeois republicans could not undo this event. They had to content themselves with adding the limiting proviso of a six months' residence in the constituency. The old organisation of the administration, of the municipal system, of the judicial system, of the army, etc., continued to exist inviolate, or, where the Constitution changed them, the change concerned the table of contents, not the contents; the name, not the subject matter.

The inevitable general staff of the liberties of 1848, personal liberty, liberty of the press, of speech, of association, of assembly, of education and religion, etc., received a constitutional uniform, which made them invulnerable. For each of these liberties is proclaimed as the *absolute* right of the French *citoyen*, but always with the marginal note that it is unlimited so far as it is not limited by the "*equal rights of others* and the *public safety*" or by "laws" which are intended to mediate just this harmony of the individual liberties with one another and with the public safety. For example: "The citizens have the right of association, of peaceful and unarmed assembly, of petition and of expressing their opinions, whether in the press or in any other way. *The enjoyment of these rights has no limit save the equal rights of others and the public safety,*" (Chapter II of the French Constitution, §8.)—"Education is free. Freedom of education shall be *enjoyed* under the conditions fixed by law and under the supreme control of the state." (*Ibidem*, §9.)— "The home of every citizen is inviolable *except* in the forms prescribed by law." (Chapter II, §3.) Etc., etc.—The Constitution, therefore, constantly refers to future *organic* laws which are to put into effect those marginal notes and regulate the enjoyment of these unrestricted liberties in such manner that they will collide neither with one another nor with the public safety. And later, these organic laws were brought into being by the friends of order and all those liberties regulated in such manner that the bourgeoisie in its enjoyment of them finds itself unhindered by the equal rights of the other classes. Where it forbids these liberties entirely to "the others" or permits enjoyment of them under conditions that are just so many police traps, this always happens solely in the interest of "*public safety,*" that is, the safety of the bourgeoisie, as the Constitution prescribes. In the sequel, both sides accordingly appeal with complete justice to the Constitution: the friends of order, who abrogated all these liberties, as well as the democrats, who demanded all of them. For each paragraph of the Constitution contains its own antithesis, its own Upper and Lower House, namely, liberty in the general phrase, abrogation of liberty in the marginal note. Thus, so long as the *name* of freedom was respected and only its actual realisation prevented, of course in a legal way, the constitutional existence of liberty remained intact, inviolate, however mortal the blows dealt to its existence *in actual life*.

This Constitution, made inviolable in so ingenious a manner, was nevertheless, like Achilles, vulnerable in one point, not in the heel, but in the head, or rather in the two heads in which it wound up— the *Legislative Assembly*, on the one hand, the *President*, on the other. Glance through the Constitution and you will find that only the paragraphs in which the relationship of the President to the Legislative Assembly is defined are absolute, positive, non-contradictory, incapable of distortion. For here it was a question of the bourgeois republicans safeguarding themselves. §§ 45-70 of the Constitution are so worded that the National Assembly can remove the President constitutionally, whereas the President can remove the National Assembly only unconstitutionally, only by setting aside the Constitution itself. Here, therefore, it challenges its forcible destruction. It not only sanctifies the division of powers, like the Charter of 1830, it widens it into an intolerable contradiction. The *play of the constitutional powers*, as Guizot termed the parliamentary squabble between the legislative and executive power, is in the Constitution of 1848 continually played *va-banque*.* On one side are seven hundred and fifty representatives of the people, elected by universal suffrage and eligible for re-election; they form an uncontrollable, indissoluble, indivisible National Assembly, a National Assembly that enjoys legislative omnipotence, decides in the last instance on war, peace and commercial treaties, alone possesses the right of amnesty and, by its permanence, perpetually holds the front of the stage. On the other side is the President, with all the attributes of royal power, with authority to appoint and dismiss his ministers independently of the National Assembly, with all the resources of the executive power in his hands, bestowing all posts and disposing thereby in France of the livelihoods of at least a million and a half people, for so many depend on the five hundred thousand officials and officers of every rank. He has the whole of the armed forces behind him. He enjoys the privilege of pardoning individual criminals, of suspending National Guards, of discharging, with the concurrence of the Council of State, general, cantonal and municipal councils elected by the citizens themselves. Initiative and direction are reserved to him in all treaties with foreign countries. While the Assembly constantly performs on the boards and is exposed to daily public criticism, he leads a secluded life in the Elysian Fields,[65] and that with Article 45 of the Constitution before his eyes and in his heart, crying to him daily *"Frère, il faut mourir!"*** Your power ceases on the second Sunday of the lovely month of May in the fourth year after your election! Then your glory is at an end, the piece is not played twice and if you have debts, look to it betimes that you pay them off with the six hundred thousand francs granted you by the Constitution, unless, perchance, you should prefer to go to Clichy[66] on the second Monday of the lovely month of May!— Thus, whereas the Constitution assigns actual power to the President, it seeks to secure moral power for the National Assembly. Apart

---

 * *Va-banque*: Staking one's all.—*Ed.*
 ** "Brother, you must die!"—*Ed.*

from the fact that it is impossible to create a moral power by paragraphs of law, the Constitution here abrogates itself once more by
having the President elected by all Frenchmen through direct suffrage. While the votes of France are split up among the seven
hundred and fifty members of the National Assembly, they are here,
on the contrary, concentrated on a single individual. While each
separate representative of the people represents only this or that
party, this or that town, this or that bridgehead, or even only the
mere necessity of electing some one of the seven hundred and fifty,
in which neither the cause nor the man is closely examined, *he* is
the elect of the nation and the act of his election is the trump
that the sovereign people plays once every four years. The elected
National Assembly stands in a metaphysical relation, but the elected
President in a personal relation, to the nation. The National Assembly, indeed, exhibits in its individual representatives the manifold aspects of the national spirit, but in the President this national
spirit finds its incarnation. As against the Assembly, he possesses
a sort of divine right; he is President by the grace of the people.

Thetis, the sea goddess, had prophesied to Achilles that he would
die in the bloom of youth. The Constitution, which, like Achilles,
had its weak spot, had also, like Achilles, its presentiment that it
must go to an early death. It was sufficient for the constitution-
making pure republicans to cast a glance from the lofty heaven of
their ideal republic at the profane world to perceive how the arrogance of the royalists, the Bonapartists, the Democrats, the Communists as well as their own discredit grew daily in the same measure as they approached the completion of their great legislative work
of art, without Thetis on this account having to leave the sea and
communicate the secret to them. They sought to cheat destiny by a
catch in the Constitution, through §III of it, according to which
every motion for a *revision of the Constitution* must be supported
by at least three-quarters of the votes, cast in three successive
debates between which an entire month must always lie, with the
added proviso that not less than five hundred members of the National Assembly must vote. Thereby they merely made the impotent attempt still to exercise, when only a parliamentary minority,
as which they already saw themselves prophetically in their mind's
eye, a power which at the present moment, when they commanded
a parliamentary majority and all the resources of governmental
authority, was slipping daily more and more from their feeble hands.

Finally the Constitution, in a melodramatic paragraph, entrusts
itself "to the vigilance and the patriotism of the whole French
people and every single Frenchman," after it had previously entrusted in another paragraph the "vigilant" and "patriotic" to the
tender, most painstaking care of the High Court of Justice, the
"haute cour," invented by it for the purpose.

Such was the Constitution of 1848, which on December 2, 1851, was not overthrown by a head, but fell down at the touch of a mere hat; this hat, to be sure, was a three-cornered Napoleonic hat.

While the bourgeois republicans in the Assembly were busy devising, discussing and voting this Constitution, Cavaignac outside the Assembly maintained the *state of siege of Paris*. The state of siege of Paris was the midwife of the Constituent Assembly in its travail of republican creation. If the Constitution is subsequently put out of existence by bayonets, it must not be forgotten that it was likewise by bayonets, and these turned against the people, that it had to be protected in its mother's womb and by bayonets that it had to be brought into existence. The forefathers of the "respectable republicans" had sent their symbol, the tricolour,[67] on a tour round Europe. They themselves in turn produced an invention that of itself made its way over the whole Continent, but returned to France with ever renewed love until it has now become naturalised in half her Departments—the *state of siege*. A splendid invention, periodically employed in every ensuing crisis in the course of the French Revolution. But barrack and bivouac, which were thus periodically laid on French society's head to compress its brain and render it quiet; sabre and musket, which were periodically allowed to act as judges and administrators, as guardians and censors, to play policemen and do night watchman's duty; moustache and uniform, which were periodically trumpeted forth as the highest wisdom of society and as its rector—were not barrack and bivouac, sabre and musket, moustache and uniform finally bound to hit upon the idea of rather saving society once and for all by proclaiming their own regime as the highest and freeing civil society completely from the trouble of governing itself? Barrack and bivouac, sabre and musket, moustache and uniform were bound to hit upon this idea all the more as they might then also expect better cash payment for their higher services, whereas from the merely periodical state of siege and the transient rescues of society at the bidding of this or that bourgeois faction little of substance was gleaned save some killed and wounded and some friendly bourgeois grimaces. Should not the military at last one day play state of siege in their own interest and for their own benefit, and at the same time besiege the citizens' purses? Moreover, be it noted in passing, one must not forget that *Colonel Bernard*, the same military commission president who under Cavaignac had 15,000 insurgents deported without trial, is at this moment again at the head of the military commissions active in Paris.

Whereas, with the state of siege in Paris, the respectable, the pure republicans planted the nursery in which the praetorians of December 2, 1851[68] were to grow up, they on the other hand deserve praise for the reason that, instead of exaggerating the national sentiment as under Louis Philippe, they now, when they had command of the national power, crawled before foreign countries, and, instead of setting Italy free, let her be reconquered by Austrians and Neapolitans.[69] Louis Bonaparte's election as President on December 10, 1848, put an end to the dictatorship of Cavaignac and to the Constituent Assembly.

In §44 of the Constitution it is stated: "The President of the French Republic must never have lost his status of a French citizen." The first President of the French republic, L. N. Bonaparte, had not merely lost his status of a French citizen, had not only been an English special constable, he was even a naturalised Swiss.[70]

I have worked out elsewhere the significance of the election of December 10.* I will not revert to it here. It is sufficient to remark here that it was a *reaction of the peasants*, who had had to pay the costs of the February Revolution, against the remaining classes of the nation, a *reaction of the country against the town*. It met with great approval in the army, for which the republicans of the *National* had provided neither glory nor additional pay, among the big bourgeoisie, which hailed Bonaparte as a bridge to monarchy, among the proletarians and petty bourgeois, who hailed him as a scourge for Cavaignac. I shall have an opportunity later of going more closely into the relationship of the peasants to the French Revolution.

The period from December 20, 1848, until the dissolution of the Constituent Assembly, in May 1849, comprises the history of the downfall of the bourgeois republicans. After having founded a republic for the bourgeoisie, driven the revolutionary proletariat out of the field and reduced the democratic petty bourgeoisie to silence for the time being, they are themselves thrust aside by the mass of the bourgeoisie, which justly impounds this republic as *its property*. This bourgeois mass was, however, *royalist*. One section of it, the large landowners, had ruled during the *Restoration*[16] and was accordingly *Legitimist*.[17] The other, the aristocrats of finance and big industrialists, had ruled during the July Monarchy and was consequently *Orleanist*.[71] The high dignitaries of the army, the university, the church, the bar, the academy and of the press were to be found on either side, though in various proportions. Here, in the bourgeois republic, which bore neither the name *Bourbon* nor the name *Orleans*, but the name *Capital*, they had found the form of state in which they could rule *conjointly*. The June Insurrection had already united them in the "party of Order."[72] Now it was necessary, in the first place, to remove the coterie of bourgeois republicans who still occupied the seats of the National Assembly.

---

* See K. Marx, *The Class Struggles in France, 1848 to 1850* (Marx and Engels, *Selected Works,* Vol. I, Moscow, 1962, pp. 174-76).—*Ed.*

Just as brutal as these pure republicans had been in their misuse of physical force against the people, just as cowardly, mealy-mouthed, broken-spirited and incapable of fighting were they now in their retreat, when it was a question of maintaining their republicanism and their legislative rights against the executive power and the royalists. I need not relate here the ignominious history of their dissolution. They did not succumb; they passed out of existence. Their history has come to an end forever, and, both inside and outside the Assembly, they figure in the following period only as memories, memories that seem to regain life whenever the mere name of Republic is once more the issue and as often as the revolutionary conflict threatens to sink down to the lowest level. I may remark in passing that the journal which gave its name to this party, the *National*, was converted to socialism in the following period.

Before we finish with this period we must still cast a retrospective glance at the two powers, one of which annihilated the other on December 2, 1851, whereas from December 20, 1848, until the exit of the Constituent Assembly, they had lived in conjugal relations. We mean Louis Bonaparte, on the one hand, and the party of the coalesced royalists, the party of Order, of the big bourgeoisie, on the other. On acceding to the presidency, Bonaparte at once formed a ministry of the party of Order, at the head of which he placed Odilon Barrot, the old leader, *nota bene*, of the most liberal faction of the parliamentary bourgeoisie. M. Barrot had at last secured the ministerial portfolio, the spectre of which had haunted him since 1830, and what is more, the premiership in the ministry; but not, as he had imagined under Louis Philippe, as the most advanced leader of the parliamentary opposition,[56] but with the task of putting a parliament to death, and as the confederate of all his arch-enemies, Jesuits and Legitimists. He brought the bride home at last, but only after she had been prostituted. Bonaparte seemed to efface himself completely. This party acted for him.

The very first meeting of the council of ministers resolved on the expedition to Rome, which, it was agreed, should be undertaken behind the back of the National Assembly and the means for which were to be wrested from it by false pretences. Thus they began by swindling the National Assembly and secretly conspiring with the absolutist powers abroad against the revolutionary Roman republic. In the same manner and with the same manoeuvres Bonaparte prepared his *coup* of December 2 against the royalist Legislative Assembly and its constitutional republic. Let us not forget that the same party which formed Bonaparte's ministry on December 20, 1848, formed the majority of the Legislative National Assembly on December 2, 1851.

In August the Constituent Assembly had decided to dissolve only after it had worked out and promulgated a whole series of organic laws that were to supplement the Constitution. On January 6, 1849, the party of Order had a deputy named Rateau move that the Assembly should let the organic laws go and rather decide on its *own dissolution.* Not only the ministry, with Odilon Barrot at its head, but all the royalist members of the National Assembly told it in bullying accents then that its dissolution was necessary for the restoration of credit, for the consolidation of order, for putting an end to the indefinite provisional arrangements and for establishing a definitive state of affairs; that it hampered the productivity of the new government and sought to prolong its existence merely out of malice; that the country was tired of it. Bonaparte took note of all this invective against the legislative power, learnt it by heart and proved to the parliamentary royalists, on December 2, 1851, that he had learnt from them. He reiterated their own catchwords against them.

The Barrot ministry and the party of Order went further. They caused *petitions to the National Assembly* to be made throughout France, in which this body was politely requested to decamp. They thus led the unorganised popular masses into the fire of battle against the National Assembly, the constitutionally organised expression of the people. They taught Bonaparte to appeal against the parliamentary assemblies to the people. At length, on January 29, 1849, the day had come on which the Constituent Assembly was to decide concerning its own dissolution. The National Assembly found the building where its sessions were held occupied by the military; Changarnier, the general of the party of Order, in whose hands the supreme command of the National Guard and troops of the line had been united, held a great military review in Paris, as if a battle were impending, and the royalists in coalition threateningly declared to the Constituent Assembly that force would be employed if it should prove unwilling. It was willing, and got only the very short extra term of life it bargained for. What was January 29 but the *coup d'état* of December 2, 1851, only carried out by the royalists with Bonaparte against the republican National Assembly? The gentlemen did not observe, or did not wish to observe, that Bonaparte availed himself of January 29, 1849, to have a portion of the troops march past him in front of the Tuileries, and seized with avidity on just this first public summoning of the military power against the parliamentary power to foreshadow Caligula.[73] They, to be sure, saw only their Changarnier.

A motive that particularly actuated the party of Order in forcibly cutting short the duration of the Constituent Assembly's life was the *organic* laws supplementing the Constitution, such as the education law, the law on religious worship, etc. To the royalists in coalition it was most important that they themselves should make these laws and not let them be made by the republicans, who had grown mistrustful. Among these organic laws, however, was also a law on the responsibility of the President of the republic. In 1851 the Legislative Assembly was occupied with the drafting of just such a law, when Bonaparte anticipated this *coup* with the *coup* of December 2. What would the royalists in coalition not have given in their parliamentary winter campaign of 1851 to have found the Responsibility Law ready to hand, and drawn up, at that, by a mistrustful, hostile, republican Assembly!

After the Constituent Assembly had itself shattered its last weapon on January 29, 1849, the Barrot ministry and the friends of order hounded it to death, left nothing undone that could humiliate it and wrested from the impotent, self-despairing Assembly laws that cost it the last remnant of respect in the eyes of the public. Bonaparte, occupied with his fixed Napoleonic idea, was brazen enough to exploit publicly this degradation of the parliamentary power. For when on May 8, 1849, the National Assembly passed a vote of censure of the ministry because of the occupation of Civitavecchia by Oudinot, and ordered it to bring back the Roman expedition to its alleged purpose, Bonaparte published the same evening in the *Moniteur*[74] a letter to Oudinot, in which he congratulated him on his heroic exploits and, in contrast to the ink-slinging parliamentarians, already posed as the generous protector of the army. The royalists smiled at this. They regarded him simply as their dupe. Finally, when Marrast, the President of the Constituent Assembly, believed for a moment that the safety of the National Assembly was endangered and, relying on the Constitution, requisitioned a colonel and his regiment, the colonel declined, cited discipline in his support and referred Marrast to Changarnier, who scornfully refused him with the remark that he did not like *baïonnettes intelligentes*.* In November 1851, when the royalists in coalition wanted to begin the decisive struggle with Bonaparte, they sought to put through in their notorious *Questors' Bill*[75] the principle of the direct requisition of troops by the President of the National Assembly. One of their generals, Le Flô, had signed the bill. In vain . did Changarnier vote for it and Thiers pay homage to the far-sighted wisdom of the former Constituent Assembly. The *War Minister, Saint-Arnaud*, answered him as Changarnier had answered Marrast —and to the acclamation of the *Montagne*!

Thus the *party of Order*, when it was not yet the National Assembly, when it was still only the ministry, had itself stigmatised the *parliamentary regime*. And it makes an outcry when December 2, 1851 banished this regime from France!

We wish it a happy journey.

---

* Intellectual bayonets.—*Ed.*

III

On May 28, 1849, the Legislative National Assembly met. On December 2, 1851, it was dispersed. This period covers the span of life of the *constitutional, or parliamentary, republic.*

In the first French Revolution the rule of the *Constitutionalists* is followed by the rule of the *Girondins* and the rule of the *Girondins* by the rule of the *Jacobins.*[76] Each of these parties relies on the more progressive party for support. As soon as it has brought the revolution far enough to be unable to follow it further, still less to go ahead of it, it is thrust aside by the bolder ally that stands behind it and sent to the guillotine. The revolution thus moves along an ascending line.

It is the reverse with the Revolution of 1848. The proletarian party appears as an appendage of the petty-bourgeois-democratic party. It is betrayed and dropped by the latter on April 16,[77] May 15,[58] and in the June days. The democratic party, in its turn, leans on the shoulders of the bourgeois-republican party. The bourgeois-republicans no sooner believe themselves well established than they shake off the troublesome comrade and support themselves on the shoulders of the party of Order. The party of Order hunches its shoulders, lets the bourgeois-republicans tumble and throws itself on the shoulders of armed force. It fancies it is still sitting on its shoulders when, one fine morning, it perceives that the shoulders have transformed themselves into bayonets. Each party kicks back at the one behind, which presses upon it, and leans against the one in front, which pushes backwards. No wonder that in this ridiculous posture it loses its balance and, having made the inevitable grimaces, collapses with curious capers. The revolution thus moves in a descending line. It finds itself in this state of retrogressive motion before the last February barricade has been cleared away and the first revolutionary authority constituted.

The period that we have before us comprises the most motley mixture of crying contradictions: constitutionalists who conspire openly against the Constitution; revolutionists who are confessedly constitutional; a National Assembly that wants to be omnipotent and always remains parliamentary; a *Montagne* that finds its vocation in patience and counters its present defeats by prophesying future victories; royalists who form the *patres conscripti**
of the republic and are forced by the situation to keep the hostile royal houses, to which they adhere, abroad, and the republic, which they hate, in France; an executive power that finds its strength in its very weakness and its respectability in the contempt that it calls forth; a republic that is nothing but the combined

---

* *Patres conscripti*: Senators.—*Ed.*

infamy of two monarchies, the Restoration and the July Monarchy,[57] with an imperial label—alliances whose first proviso is separation; struggles whose first law is indecision; wild, inane agitation in the name of tranquillity, most solemn preaching of tranquillity in the name of revolution; passions without truth, truths without passion; heroes without heroic deeds, history without events; development, whose sole driving force seems to be the calendar, wearying with constant repetition of the same tensions and relaxations; antagonisms that periodically seem to work themselves up to a climax only to lose their sharpness and fall away without being able to resolve themselves; pretentiously paraded exertions and philistine terror at the danger of the world coming to an end, and at the same time the pettiest intrigues and court comedies played by the world redeemers, who in their *laisser aller*[*] remind us less of the Day of Judgement than of the times of the Fronde[78]—the official collective genius of France brought to naught by the artful stupidity of a single individual; the collective will of the nation, as often as it speaks through universal suffrage, seeking its appropriate expression through the inveterate enemies of the interests of the masses, until at length it finds it in the self-will of a filibuster. If any section of history has been painted grey on grey, it is this. Men and events appear as inverted Schlemihls, as shadows that have lost their bodies. The revolution itself paralyses its own bearers and endows only its adversaries with passionate forcefulness. When the "red spectre," continually conjured up and exorcised by the counter-revolutionaries, finally appears, it appears not with the Phrygian cap[79] of anarchy on its head, but in the uniform of order, in *red breeches*.

We have seen that the ministry which Bonaparte installed on December 20, 1848, on his Ascension Day, was a ministry of the party of Order, of the Legitimist and Orleanist coalition. This Barrot-Falloux ministry had outlived the republican Constituent Assembly, whose term of life it had more or less violently cut short, and found itself still at the helm. Changarnier, the general of the allied royalists, continued to unite in his person the general command of the First Army Division and of the National Guard of Paris. Finally, the general elections had secured the party of Order a large majority in the National Assembly. Here the deputies and peers of Louis Philippe encountered a hallowed host of Legitimists, for whom many of the nation's ballots had become transformed into admission cards to the political stage. The Bonapartist representatives of the people were too sparse to be able to form an independent parliamentary party. They appeared merely as the *mauvaise queue*[**] of

---

[*] *Laisser aller*: Letting things take their course.—*Ed.*
[**] *Mauvaise queue*: Evil appendage.—*Ed.*

the party of Order. Thus the party of Order was in possession of the governmental power, the army and the legislative body, in short, of the whole of the state power; it had been morally strengthened by the general elections, which made its rule appear as the will of the people, and by the simultaneous triumph of the counter-revolution on the whole continent of Europe.

Never did a party open its campaign with greater resources or under more favourable auspices.

The shipwrecked *pure republicans* found that they had melted down to a clique of about fifty men in the Legislative National Assembly, the African generals Cavaignac, Lamoricière and Bedeau at their head.[55] The great opposition party, however, was formed by the *Montagne*. The *social-democratic* party had given itself this parliamentary baptismal name. It commanded more than two hundred of the seven hundred and fifty votes of the National Assembly and was consequently at least as powerful as any one of the three factions of the party of Order taken by itself. Its numerical inferiority compared with the entire royalist coalition seemed compensated by special circumstances. Not only did the elections in the Departments show that it had gained a considerable following among the rural population. It counted in its ranks almost all the deputies from Paris; the army had made a confession of democratic faith by the election of three non-commissioned officers, and the leader of the *Montagne*, Ledru-Rollin, in contradistinction to all the representatives of the party of Order, had been raised to the parliamentary peerage by five Departments, which had pooled their votes for him. In view of the inevitable clashes of the royalists among themselves and of the whole party of Order with Bonaparte, the *Montagne* thus seemed to have all the elements of success before it on May 28, 1849. A fortnight later it had lost everything, honour included.

Before we pursue parliamentary history further, some remarks are necessary to avoid common misconceptions regarding the whole character of the epoch that lies before us. Looked at with the eyes of democrats, the period of the Legislative National Assembly is concerned with what the period of the Constituent Assembly was concerned with: the simple struggle between republicans and royalists. The movement itself, however, they sum up in the one shibboleth: *"reaction"*—night, in which all cats are grey and which permits them to reel off their night watchman's commonplaces. And, to be sure, at first sight the party of Order reveals a maze of different royalist factions, which not only intrigue against each other —each seeking to elevate its own pretender to the throne and exclude the pretender of the opposing faction—but also all unite in common hatred of, and common onslaughts on, the "republic." In opposition to this royalist conspiracy the *Montagne*, for its part, appears as the representative of the "republic." The party of Order appears to be perpetually engaged in a "reaction," directed against press, association and the like, neither more nor less than in Prussia, and which, as in Prussia, is carried out in the form of brutal police intervention by the bureaucracy, the *gendarmerie* and the law courts. The "*Montagne*," for its part, is just as continually occupied in warding off these attacks and thus defending the "eternal rights of man" as every so called people's party has done, more or less, for a century and a half. If one looks at the situation and the parties more closely, however, this superficial appearance, which veils the *class struggle* and the peculiar physiognomy of this period, disappears.

Legitimists and Orleanists, as we have said, formed the two great factions of the party of Order. Was that which held these factions fast to their pretenders and kept them apart from one another nothing but lily[80] and tricolour, House of Bourbon and House of Orleans, different shades of royalism, was it at all the confession of faith of royalism? Under the Bourbons, *big landed property* had governed, with its priests and lackeys; under the Orleans, high finance, large-scale industry, large-scale trade, that is, *capital*, with its retinue of lawyers, professors and smooth-tongued orators. The Legitimate Monarchy was merely the political expression of the hereditary rule of the lords of the soil, as the July Monarchy was only the political expression of the usurped rule of the bourgeois *parvenus*. What kept the two factions apart, therefore, was not any so-called principles, it was their material conditions of existence, two different kinds of property, it was the old contrast between town and country, the rivalry between capital and landed property. That at the same time old memories, personal enmities, fears and hopes, prejudices and illusions, sympathies and antipathies, convictions, articles of faith and principles bound them to one or the other royal house, who is there that denies this? Upon the different forms of property, upon the social conditions of existence, rises an entire superstructure of distinct and peculiarly formed sentiments, illusions, modes of thought and views of life. The entire class creates and forms them out of its material foundations and out of the corresponding social relations. The single individual, who derives them through tradition and upbringing, may imagine that they form the real motives and the starting-point of his activity. While Orleanists and Legitimists, while each faction sought to make itself and the other believe that it was loyalty to their two royal houses which separated them, facts later proved that it was rather their divided interests which forbade the uniting of the two royal houses. And as in private life one differentiates between what a man thinks and says of himself and what he really is and does, so in historical struggles one must distinguish still more the phrases and fancies of parties from their real organism and their real interests, their conception of themselves, from their reality. Orleanists and Legitimists found themselves side by side in the republic, with equal claims. If each side wished to effect the *restoration* of its *own* royal house against the other, that merely signified that each of the *two great interests* into which the *bourgeoisie* is split—landed property and capital—sought to restore its own supremacy and the subordination of the other. We speak of two interests of the bourgeoisie, for large landed property, despite its feudal coquetry and pride of race, has been rendered thoroughly bourgeois by the development of modern society. Thus the Tories[81] in England long imagined that they were enthusiastic about monarchy, the church and the beauties of the old English Constitution, until the day of danger wrung from them the confession that they are enthusiastic only about *ground rent.*

The royalists in coalition carried on their intrigues against one another in the press, in Ems, in Claremont,[82] outside parliament. Behind the scenes they donned their old Orleanist and Legitimist liveries again and once more engaged in their old tourneys. But on the public stage, in their grand performances of state, as a great parliamentary party, they put off their respective royal houses with mere obeisances and adjourn the restoration of the monarchy *ad infinitum.** They do their real business as the *party of Order,* that is, under a *social,* not under a *political* title; as representatives of the bourgeois world-order, not as knights of errant princesses; as the bourgeois class against other classes, not as royalists against the republicans. And as the party of Order they exercised more unrestricted and sterner domination over the other classes of society than ever previously under the Restoration or under the July Monarchy, a domination which, in general, was only possible under the form of the parliamentary republic, for only under this form could the two great divisions of the French bourgeoisie unite, and thus put the rule of their class instead of the regime of a privileged faction of it on the order of the day. If, nevertheless, they, as the party of Order, also insulted the republic and expressed their repugnance to it, this happened not merely from royalist memories. Instinct taught them that the republic, true enough, makes their political rule complete, but at the same time undermines its social foundation, since they must now confront the subjugated classes and contend against them without mediation, without the concealment afforded by the crown, without being able to divert the national interest by their subordinate struggles among themselves and with the monarchy. It was a feeling of weakness that caused them to recoil from the pure conditions of their own class rule and to yearn for the former more incomplete, more undeveloped and precisely on

---

* To infinity.—*Ed.*

that account less dangerous forms of this rule. On the other hand, every time the royalists in coalition come in conflict with the pretender that confronts them, with Bonaparte, every time they believe their parliamentary omnipotence endangered by the executive power, every time, therefore, that they must produce their political title to their rule, they come forward as *republicans* and not as *royalists*, from the Orleanist Thiers, who warns the National Assembly that the republic divides them least, to the Legitimist Berryer, who, on December 2, 1851,[40] as a tribune swathed in a tricoloured sash, harangues the people assembled before the town hall of the tenth *arrondissement* in the name of the republic. To be sure, a mocking echo calls back to him: Henry V! Henry V!

As against the coalesced bourgeoisie, a coalition between petty bourgeois and workers had been formed, the so-called *social-democratic* party. The petty bourgeois saw that they were badly rewarded after the June days of 1848, that their material interests were imperilled and that the democratic guarantees which were to ensure the effectuation of these interests were called in question by the counter-revolution. Accordingly, they came closer to the workers. On the other hand, their parliamentary representation, the *Montagne*, thrust aside during the dictatorship of the bourgeois republicans, had in the last half of the life of the Constituent Assembly reconquered its lost popularity through the struggle with Bonaparte and the royalist ministers. It had concluded an alliance with the socialist leaders. In February 1849, banquets celebrated the reconciliation. A joint programme was drafted, joint election committees were set up and joint candidates put forward. From the social demands of the proletariat the revolutionary point was broken off and a democratic turn given to them; from the democratic claims of the petty bourgeoisie the purely political form was stripped off and their socialist point thrust forward. Thus arose the Social-Democracy. The new *Montagne*, the result of this combination, contained, apart from some supernumeraries from the working class and some socialist sectarians, the same elements as the old *Montagne*, only numerically stronger. However, in the course of development, it had changed with the class that it represented. The peculiar character of the Social-Democracy is epitomised in the fact that democratic-republican institutions are demanded as a means, not of doing away with two extremes, capital and wage labour, but of weakening their antagonism and transforming it into harmony. However different the means proposed for the attainment of this end may be, however much it may be trimmed with more or less revolutionary notions, the content remains the same. This content is the transformation of society in a democratic way, but a transformation within the bounds of the petty bourgeoisie. Only one must not form the narrow-minded notion that the petty bourgeoisie, on principle, wishes to enforce an egoistic class interest. Rather, it believes that the *special* conditions of its emancipation are the *general* conditions within the frame of which alone modern society can be saved and the class struggle avoided. Just as little must one imagine that the democratic representatives are indeed all shopkeepers or enthusiastic champions of shopkeepers. According to their education and their individual position they may be as far apart as heaven from earth. What makes them representatives of the petty bourgeoisie is the fact that in their minds they do not get beyond the limits which the latter do not get beyond in life, that they are consequently driven, theoretically, to the same problems and solutions to which material interest and social position drive the latter practically. This is, in general, the relationship between the *political* and *literary representatives* of a class and the class they represent.

After the analysis given, it is obvious that if the *Montagne* continually contends with the party of Order for the republic and the so-called rights of man, neither the republic nor the rights of man are its final end, any more than an army which one wants to deprive of its weapons and which resists has taken the field in order to remain in possession of its own weapons.

Immediately, as soon as the National Assembly met, the party of Order provoked the *Montagne*. The bourgeoisie now felt the necessity of making an end of the democratic petty bourgeois, just as a year before it had realised the necessity of settling with the revolutionary proletariat. Only the situation of the adversary was different. The strength of the proletarian party lay in the streets, that of the petty bourgeois in the National Assembly itself. It was therefore a question of decoying them out of the National Assembly into the streets and causing them to smash their parliamentary power themselves, before time and circumstances could consolidate it. The *Montagne* rushed headlong into the trap.

The bombardment of Rome by the French troops* was the bait that was thrown to it. It violated Article V of the Constitution which forbids the French republic to employ its military forces against the freedom of another people. In addition to this, Article 54 prohibited any declaration of war on the part of the executive power without the assent of the National Assembly, and by its resolution of May 8, the Constituent Assembly had disapproved of the Roman expedition. On these grounds Ledru-Rollin brought in a bill of impeachment against Bonaparte and his ministers on June 11, 1849. Exasperated by the wasp stings of Thiers, he actually let himself be carried away to the point of threatening that he would

---

* See K. Marx, *The Class Struggles in France, 1848 to 1850* (Marx and Engels, *Selected Works*, Vol. I, Moscow, 1962, pp. 186-88).—*Ed.*

defend the Constitution by every means, even with arms in hand.
The *Montagne* rose to a man and repeated this call to arms. On June
12, the National Assembly rejected the bill of impeachment, and the
Montagne left the parliament. The events of June 13 are known:
the proclamation issued by a section of the *Montagne*, declaring Bonaparte and his ministers "outside the Constitution"; the street procession of the democratic National Guards, who, unarmed as they
were, dispersed on encountering the troops of Changarnier, etc., etc.
A part of the *Montagne* fled abroad; another part was arraigned
before the High Court at Bourges, and a parliamentary regulation
subjected the remainder to the schoolmasterly surveillance of the
President of the National Assembly. Paris was again declared in a
state of siege and the democratic part of its National Guard dissolved. Thus the influence of the *Montagne* in parliament and the
power of the petty bourgeois in Paris were broken.

Lyons, where June 13 had given the signal for a bloody insurrection of the workers, was, along with the five surrounding Departments, likewise declared in a state of siege, a condition that has
continued up to the present moment.

The bulk of the *Montagne* had left its vanguard in the lurch,
having refused to subscribe to its proclamation. The press had
deserted, only two journals having dared to publish the *pronun-
ciamento*. The petty bourgeois betrayed their representatives, in
that the National Guards either stayed away or, where they appeared, hindered the erection of barricades. The representatives had
duped the petty bourgeois, in that the alleged allies from the army
were nowhere to be seen. Finally, instead of gaining an accession
of strength from it, the democratic party had infected the proletariat
with its own weakness and, as is usual with the great deeds of
democrats, the leaders had the satisfaction of being able to charge
their "people" with desertion, and the people the satisfaction of
being able to charge its leaders with humbugging it.

Seldom had an action been announced with more noise than the
impending campaign of the *Montagne*, seldom had an event been
trumpeted with greater certainty or longer in advance than the
inevitable victory of the democracy. Most assuredly, the democrats
believe in the trumpets before whose blasts the walls of Jericho[83]
fell down. And as often as they stand before the ramparts of despotism, they seek to imitate the miracle. If the *Montagne* wished to
triumph in parliament, it should not have called to arms. If it called
to arms in parliament, it should not have acted in parliamentary
fashion in the streets. If the peaceful demonstration was meant
seriously, then it was folly not to foresee that it would be given a
war-like reception. If a real struggle was intended, then it was a
queer idea to lay down the weapons with which it would have to
be waged. But the revolutionary threats of the petty bourgeois and

their democratic representatives are mere attempts to intimidate the antagonist. And when they have run into a blind alley, when they have sufficiently compromised themselves to make it necessary to give effect to their threats, then this is done in an ambiguous fashion that avoids nothing so much as the means to the end and tries to find excuses for succumbing. The blaring overture that announced the contest dies away in a pusillanimous snarl as soon as the struggle has to begin, the actors cease to take themselves *au sérieux*, and the action collapses completely, like a pricked bubble.

No party exaggerates its means more than the democratic, none deludes itself more light-mindedly over the situation. Since a section of the army had voted for it, the *Montagne* was now convinced that the army would revolt for it. And on what occasion? On an occasion which, from the standpoint of the troops, had no other meaning than that the revolutionists took the side of the Roman soldiers against the French soldiers. On the other hand, the recollections of June 1848 were still too fresh to allow of anything but a profound aversion on the part of the proletariat towards the National Guard and a thoroughgoing mistrust of the democratic chiefs on the part of the chiefs of the secret societies. To iron out these differences, it was necessary for great, common interests to be at stake. The violation of an abstract paragraph of the Constitution could not provide these interests. Had not the Constitution been repeatedly violated, according to the assurance of the democrats themselves? Had not the most popular journals branded it as counter-revolutionary botch-work? But the democrat, because he represents the petty bourgeoisie, that is, a *transition class*, in which the interests of two classes are simultaneously mutually blunted, imagines himself elevated above class antagonism generally. The democrats concede that a privileged class confronts them, but they, along with all the rest of the nation, form the *people*. What they represent is the *people's rights;* what interests them is the *people's interest*. Accordingly, when a struggle is impending, they do not need to examine the interests and positions of the different classes. They do not need to weigh their own resources too critically. They have merely to give the signal and the *people,* with all its inexhaustible resources, will fall upon the *oppressors*. Now, if in the performance their interests prove to be uninteresting and their potency impotence, then either the fault lies with pernicious sophists, who split the *indivisible people* into different hostile camps, or the army was too brutalised and blinded to comprehend that the pure aims of democracy are the best thing for it itself, or the whole thing has been wrecked by a detail in its execution, or else an unforeseen accident has this time spoilt the game. In any case, the democrat comes out of the most disgraceful defeat just as immaculate as he was innocent when he went into it, with the newly-won conviction that he is bound to win, not that he himself and his party have to give up the old standpoint, but, on the contrary, that conditions have to ripen to suit him.

Accordingly, one must not imagine the *Montagne*, decimated and broken though it was, and humiliated by the new parliamentary regulation, as being particularly miserable. If June 13 had removed its chiefs, it made room, on the other hand, for men of lesser calibre, whom this new position flattered. If their impotence in parliament could no longer be doubted, they were entitled now to confine their actions to outbursts of moral indignation and blustering declamation. If the party of Order affected to see embodied in them, as the last official representatives of the revolution, all the terrors of anarchy, they could in reality be all the more insipid and modest. They consoled themselves, however, for June 13 with the profound utterance: But if they dare to attack universal suffrage, well then —then we'll show them what we are made of! *Nous verrons!**

So far as the *Montagnards* who fled abroad are concerned, it is sufficient to remark here that Ledru-Rollin, because in barely a fortnight he had succeeded in ruining irretrievably the powerful party at whose head he stood, now found himself called upon to form a French government *in partibus*[53]; that to the extent that the level of the revolution sank and the official bigwigs of official France became more dwarf-like, his figure in the distance, removed from the scene of action, seemed to grow in stature; that he could figure as the republican pretender for 1852, and that he issued periodical circulars to the Wallachians and other peoples, in which the despots of the Continent are threatened with the deeds of himself and his confederates. Was Proudhon altogether wrong when he cried to these gentlemen: *"Vous n'êtes que des blagueurs"*?**

On June 13, the party of Order had not only broken the *Montagne*, it had effected the *subordination of the Constitution to the majority decisions of the National Assembly*. And it understood the republic thus: that the bourgeoisie rules here in parliamentary forms, without, as in a monarchy, encountering any barrier such as the veto power of the executive or the right to dissolve parliament. This was a *parliamentary republic*, as Thiers termed it. But whereas on June 13 the bourgeoisie secured its omnipotence within the house of parliament, did it not afflict parliament itself, as against the executive authority and the people, with incurable weakness by expelling its most popular part? By surrendering numerous deputies without further ado on the demand of the courts, it abolished its own parliamentary immunity. The humiliating regulations to which it subjected the *Montagne* exalted the President of the republic in

---

* We shall see. –*Ed.*
** "You are nothing but windbags."—*Ed.*

the same measure as they degraded the individual representatives of the people. By branding an insurrection for the protection of the constitutional charter an anarchic act aiming at the subversion of society, it precluded the possibility of its appealing to insurrection should the executive authority violate the Constitution in relation to it. And by the irony of history, the general who on Bonaparte's instructions bombarded Rome and thus provided the immediate occasion for the constitutional revolt of June 13, that very *Oudinot* had to be the man offered by the party of Order imploringly and unavailingly to the people as general on behalf of the Constitution against Bonaparte on December 2, 1851. Another hero of June 13, *Vieyra*, who was lauded from the tribune of the National Assembly for the brutalities that he had committed in the democratic newspaper offices at the head of a gang of National Guards belonging to high finance circles—this same Vieyra had been initiated into Bonaparte's conspiracy and he essentially contributed to depriving the National Assembly in the hour of its death of any protection by the National Guard.

June 13 had still another meaning. The *Montagne* had wanted to force the impeachment of Bonaparte. Its defeat was therefore a direct victory for Bonaparte, his personal triumph over his democratic enemies. The party of Order gained the victory; Bonaparte had only to cash in on it. He did so. On June 14 a proclamation could be read on the walls of Paris in which the President, reluctantly, against his will, as it were, compelled by the sheer force of events, comes forth from his cloistered seclusion and, posing as misunderstood virtue, complains of the calumnies of his opponents and, while he seems to identify his person with the cause of order, rather identifies the cause of order with his person. Moreover, the National Assembly had, it is true, subsequently approved the expedition against Rome, but Bonaparte had taken the initiative in the matter. After having re-installed the High Priest Samuel in the Vatican, he could hope to enter the Tuileries[84] as King David. He had won the priests over to his side.

The revolt of June 13 was confined, as we have seen, to a peaceful street procession. No war laurels were, therefore, to be won against it. Nevertheless, at a time as poor as this in heroes and events, the party of Order transformed this bloodless battle into a second Austerlitz.[85] Platform and press praised the army as the power of order, in contrast to the popular masses, representing the impotence of anarchy, and extolled Changarnier as the "bulwark of society," a deception in which he himself finally came to believe. Surreptitiously, however, the corps that seemed doubtful were transferred from Paris, the regiments which had shown at the elections the most democratical sentiments were banished from France to Algiers, the turbulent spirits among the troops were relegated to penal detachments, and finally the isolation of the press from the barracks and of the barracks from bourgeois society was systematically carried out.

Here we have reached the decisive turning-point in the history of the French National Guard. In 1830 it was decisive in the overthrow of the Restoration.[86] Under Louis Philippe every rebellion miscarried in which the National Guard stood on the side of the troops. When in the February days of 1848 it evinced a passive attitude towards the insurrection and an equivocal one towards Louis Philippe, he gave himself up for lost and actually was lost. Thus the conviction took root that the revolution could not be victorious *without* the National Guard, nor the army *against* it. This was the superstition of the army in regard to civilian omnipotence. The June days of 1848, when the entire National Guard, with the troops of the line, put down the insurrection, had strengthened the superstition. After Bonaparte's assumption of office, the position of the National Guard was to some extent weakened by the unconstitutional union, in the person of Changarnier, of the command of its forces with the command of the First Army Division.

Just as the command of the National Guard appeared here as an attribute of the military commander-in-chief, so the National Guard itself appeared as only an appendage of the troops of the line. Finally, on June 13 its power was broken, and not only by its partial disbandment, which from this time on was periodically repeated all over France, until mere fragments of it were left behind. The demonstration of June 13 was, above all, a demonstration of the democratic National Guards. They had not, to be sure, borne their arms, but worn their uniforms against the army; precisely in this uniform, however, lay the talisman. The army convinced itself that this uniform was a piece of woollen cloth like any other. The spell was broken. In the June days of 1848, bourgeoisie and petty bourgeoisie had united as the National Guard with the army against the proletariat; on June 13, 1849, the bourgeoisie let the petty-bourgeois National Guard be dispersed by the army; on December 2, 1851, the National Guard of the bourgeoisie itself had vanished, and Bonaparte merely registered this fact when he subsequently signed the decree for its disbandment. Thus the bourgeoisie had itself smashed its last weapon against the army, but it had to smash it the moment the petty bourgeoisie no longer stood behind it as a vassal, but before it as a rebel, as in general it was bound to destroy all its means of defence against absolutism with its own hand as soon as it had itself become absolute.

Meanwhile, the party of Order celebrated the reconquest of a power that seemed lost in 1848 only to be found again, freed from its restraints, in 1849, celebrated by means of invectives against the republic and the Constitution, of curses on all future, present and past revolutions, including that which its own leaders had made, and in laws by which the press was muzzled, association destroyed and the state of siege regulated as an organic institution. The National Assembly then adjourned from the middle of August to the middle of October, after having appointed a permanent commission for the period of its absence. During this recess the Legitimists intrigued with Ems, the Orleanists—with Claremont, Bonaparte—by means of princely tours, and the Departmental Council—in deliberations on a revision of the Constitution: incidents which regularly recur in the periodic recesses of the National Assembly and which I propose to discuss only when they become events. Here it may merely be remarked, in addition, that it was impolitic for the National Assembly to disappear for considerable intervals from the stage and leave only a single, albeit a sorry, figure to be seen at the head of the republic, that of Louis Bonaparte, while to the scandal of the public the party of Order fell asunder into its royalist component parts and followed its conflicting desires for Restoration. As often as the confused noise of *parliament* grew silent during these recesses and its body dissolved in the nation, it became unmistakably clear that only one thing was still wanting to complete the true form of this republic: to make the *former's* recess permanent and replace the *latter's* inscription: Liberté, Égalité, Fraternité by the unambiguous words: Infantry, Cavalry, Artillery!

IV

In the middle of October 1849, the National Assembly met once more. On November 1, Bonaparte surprised it with a message in which he announced the dismissal of the Barrot-Falloux ministry and the formation of a new ministry. No one has ever sacked lackeys with less ceremony than Bonaparte his ministers. The kicks that were intended for the National Assembly were given in the meantime to Barrot and Co.

The Barrot ministry, as we have seen, had been composed of Legitimists and Orleanists, a ministry of the party of Order. Bonaparte had needed it to dissolve the republican Constituent Assembly, to bring about the expedition against Rome and to break the democratic party. Behind this ministry he had seemingly effaced himself, surrendered governmental power into the hands of the party of Order and donned the modest character mask that the responsible editor of a newspaper wore under Louis Philippe, the mask of the *homme de paille.** He now threw off a mask which was no longer the light veil behind which he could hide his physiognomy, but an iron mask which prevented him from displaying

---

* *Homme de paille*: man of straw.—*Ed.*

a physiognomy of his own. He had appointed the Barrot ministry in order to blast the republican National Assembly in the name of the party of Order; he dismissed it in order to declare his own name independent of the National Assembly of the party of Order.

Plausible pretexts for this dismissal were not lacking. The Barrot ministry neglected even the decencies that would have let the President of the republic appear as a power side by side with the National Assembly. During the recess of the National Assembly Bonaparte published a letter to Edgar Ney in which he seemed to disapprove of the illiberal attitude of the Pope,* just as in opposition to the Constituent Assembly he had published a letter in which he commended Oudinot for the attack on the Roman republic.** When the National Assembly now voted the budget for the Roman expedition, Victor Hugo, out of alleged liberalism, brought up this letter for discussion. The party of Order with scornfully incredulous outcries stifled the idea that Bonaparte's ideas could have any political importance. Not one of the ministers took up the gauntlet for him. On another occasion Barrot, with his well-known hollow rhetoric, let fall from the platform words of indignation concerning the "abominable intrigues" that, according to his assertion, went on in the immediate entourage of the President. Finally, while the ministry obtained from the National Assembly a widow's pension for the Duchess of Orleans it rejected any proposal to increase the Civil List of the President. And in Bonaparte the imperial pretender was so intimately bound up with the adventurer down on his luck that the one great idea, that he was called to restore the empire, was always supplemented by the other, that it was the mission of the French people to pay his debts.

The Barrot-Falloux ministry was the first and last *parliamentary ministry* that Bonaparte brought into being. Its dismissal forms, accordingly, a decisive turning-point. With it the party of Order lost, never to reconquer it, an indispensable post for the maintenance of the parliamentary regime, the lever of executive power. It is immediately obvious that in a country like France, where the executive power commands an army of officials numbering more than half a million individuals and therefore constantly maintains an immense mass of interests and livelihoods in the most absolute dependence; where the state enmeshes, controls, regulates, superintends and tutors civil society from its most comprehensive manifestations of life down to its most insignificant stirrings, from its most general modes of being to the private existence of individuals; where through the most extraordinary centralisation this parasitic

---

* Pius IX.—*Ed.*
** See K. Marx, *The Class Struggles in France, 1848 to 1850* (Marx and Engels, *Selected Works*, Vol. I, Moscow, 1962, p. 188).—*Ed.*

body acquires a ubiquity, an omniscience, a capacity for accelerated mobility and an elasticity which finds a counterpart only in the helpless dependence, in the loose shapelessness of the actual body politic—it is obvious that in such a country the National Assembly forfeits all real influence when it loses command of the ministerial posts, if it does not at the same time simplify the administration of the state, reduce the army of officials as far as possible and, finally, let civil society and public opinion create organs of their own, independent of the governmental power. But it is precisely with the maintenance of that extensive state machine in its numerous ramifications that the *material interests* of the French bourgeoisie are interwoven in the closest fashion. Here it finds posts for its surplus population and makes up in the form of state salaries for what it cannot pocket in the form of profit, interest, rents and honorariums. On the other hand, its *political interests* compelled it to increase daily the repressive measures and therefore the resources and the personnel of the state power, while at the same time it had to wage an uninterrupted war against public opinion and mistrustfully mutilate, cripple, the independent organs of the social movement, where it did not succeed in amputating them entirely. Thus the French bourgeoisie was compelled by its class position to annihilate, on the one hand, the vital conditions of all parliamentary power, and therefore, likewise, of its own, and to render irresistible, on the other hand, the executive power hostile to it.

The new ministry was called the d'Hautpoul ministry. Not in the sense that General d'Hautpoul had received the rank of Prime Minister. Rather, simultaneously with Barrot's dismissal, Bonaparte abolished this dignity, which, true enough, condemned the President of the republic to the status of the legal nonentity of a constitutional monarch, but of a constitutional monarch without throne or crown, without sceptre or sword, without irresponsibility, without imprescriptible possession of the highest state dignity, and, worst of all, without a Civil List. The d'Hautpoul ministry contained only one man of parliamentary standing, the moneylender *Fould*, one of the most notorious of the high financiers. To his lot fell the ministry of finance. Look up the quotations on the Paris *bourse* and you will find that from November 1, 1849 onwards, the French *fonds** rise and fall with the rise and fall of Bonapartist stocks. While Bonaparte had thus found his ally in the *bourse*, he at the same time took possession of the police by appointing Carlier Police Prefect of Paris.

Only in the course of development, however, could the consequences of the change of ministers come to light. To begin with, Bonaparte had taken a step forward only to be driven backward all the more conspicuously. His brusque message was followed by

* *Fonds*: Government securities.—*Ed.*

the most servile declaration of allegiance to the National Assembly. As often as the ministers dared to make a diffident attempt to introduce his personal fads as legislative proposals, they themselves seemed to carry out, against their will only and compelled by their position, comical commissions of whose fruitlessness they were persuaded in advance. As often as Bonaparte blurted out his intentions behind the ministers' backs and played with his "*idées napoléoniennes*,"[87] his own ministers disavowed him from the tribune of the National Assembly. His usurpatory longings seemed to make themselves heard only in order that the malicious laughter of his opponents might not be muted. He behaved like unrecognised genius, whom all the world takes for a simpleton. Never did he enjoy the contempt of all classes in fuller measure than during this period. Never did the bourgeoisie rule more absolutely, never did it display more ostentatiously the insignia of domination.

I have not here to write the history of its legislative activity, which is summarised during this period in two laws: in the law re-establishing the *wine tax* and the *education law* abolishing unbelief. If wine drinking was made harder for the French, they were presented all the more plentifully with the water of true life. If in the law on the wine tax the bourgeoisie declared the old, hateful French tax system to be inviolable, it sought through the education law to ensure among the masses the old state of mind that put up with the tax system. One is astonished to see the Orleanists, the liberal bourgeois, these old apostles of Voltairianism and eclectic philosophy, entrust to their hereditary enemies, the Jesuits, the superintendence of the French mind. However, in regard to the pretenders to the throne, Orleanists and Legitimists could part company, they understood that to secure their united rule necessitated the uniting of the means of repression of two epochs, that the means of subjugation of the July Monarchy had to be supplemented and strengthened by the means of subjugation of the Restoration.

The peasants, disappointed in all their hopes, crushed more than ever by the low level of grain prices on the one hand, and by the growing burden of taxes and mortgage debts on the other, began to bestir themselves in the Departments. They were answered by a drive against the schoolmasters, who were made subject to the clergy, by a drive against the *maires*,* who were made subject to the prefects, and by a system of espionage, to which all were made subject. In Paris and the large towns reaction itself has the physiognomy of its epoch and challenges more than it strikes down. In the countryside it becomes dull, coarse, petty, tiresome and vexatious; in a word, the *gendarme*. One comprehends how three

---

* *Maires*: Mayors.—*Ed.*

years of the regime of the *gendarme*, consecrated by the regime of the priest, were bound to demoralise immature masses.

Whatever amount of passion and declamation might be employed by the party of Order against the minority from the tribune of the National Assembly, its speech remained as monosyllabic as that of the Christians, whose words were to be: Yea, yea; nay, nay! As monosyllabic on the platform as in the press. Flat as a riddle whose answer is known in advance. Whether it was a question of the right of petition or the tax on wine, freedom of the press or free trade, the clubs or the municipal charter, protection of personal liberty or regulation of the state budget, the watchword constantly recurs, the theme remains always the same, the verdict is ever ready and invariably reads: "*Socialism!*" Even bourgeois liberalism is declared *socialistic*, bourgeois enlightenment socialistic, bourgeois financial reform socialistic. It was socialistic to build a railway, where a canal already existed, and it was socialistic to defend oneself with a cane when one was attacked with a rapier.

This was not merely a figure of speech, fashion or party tactics. The bourgeoisie had a true insight into the fact that all the weapons which it had forged against feudalism turned their points against itself, that all the means of education which it had produced rebelled against its own civilisation, that all the gods which it had created had fallen away from it. It understood that all the so-called bourgeois liberties and organs of progress attacked and menaced its *class rule* at its social foundation and its political summit simultaneously, and had therefore become "*socialistic*". In this menace and this attack it rightly discerned the secret of socialism, whose import and tendency it judges more correctly than so-called socialism knows how to judge itself; the latter can, accordingly, not comprehend why the bourgeoisie callously hardens its heart against it, whether it sentimentally bewails the sufferings of mankind, or in Christian spirit prophesies the millennium and universal brotherly love, or in humanistic style twaddles about mind, education and freedom, or in doctrinaire fashion excogitates a system for the conciliation and welfare of all classes. What the bourgeoisie did not grasp, however, was the logical conclusion that its *own parliamentary regime*, that its *political rule* in general, was now also bound to meet with the general verdict of condemnation as being *socialistic*. As long as the rule of the bourgeois class had not been organised completely, as long as it had not acquired its pure political expression, the antagonism of the other classes, likewise, could not appear in its pure form, and where it did appear could not take the dangerous turn that transforms every struggle against the state power into a struggle against capital. If in every stirring of life in society it saw "tranquillity" imperilled, how could it want to maintain at the head of society a *regime of unrest*, its own regime, the *parliamentary regime*, this regime that, according to the expression of one of its spokesmen, lives in struggle and by struggle? The parliamentary regime lives by discussion; how shall it forbid discussion? Every interest, every social institution, is here transformed into general ideas, debated as ideas; how shall any interest, any institution, sustain itself above thought and impose itself as an article of faith? The struggle of the orators on the platform evokes the struggle of the scribblers of the press; the debating club in parliament is necessarily supplemented by debating clubs in the salons and the pothouses; the representatives, who constantly appeal to public opinion, give public opinion the right to speak its real mind in petitions. The parliamentary regime leaves everything to the decision of majorities; how shall the great majorities outside parliament not want to decide? When you play the fiddle at the top of the state, what else is to be expected but that those down below dance?

Thus, by now stigmatising as *"socialistic"* what it had previously extolled as *"liberal,"* the bourgeoisie confesses that its own interests dictate that it should be delivered from the danger of its *own rule*; that, in order to restore tranquillity in the country, its bourgeois parliament must, first of all, be given its quietus; that in order to preserve its social power intact, its political power must be broken; that the individual bourgeois can continue to exploit the other classes and to enjoy undisturbed property, family, religion and order only on condition that their class be condemned along with the other classes to like political nullity; that in order to save its purse, it must forfeit the crown, and the sword that is to safeguard it must at the same time be hung over its own head as a sword of Damocles.

In the domain of the interests of the general citizenry, the National Assembly showed itself so unproductive that, for example, the discussions on the Paris-Avignon railway, which began in the winter of 1850, were still not ripe for conclusion on December 2, 1851. Where it did not repress or pursue a reactionary course it was stricken with incurable barrenness.

While Bonaparte's ministry partly took the initiative in framing laws in the spirit of the party of Order, and partly even outdid that party's harshness in their execution and administration, he, on the other hand, by childishly silly proposals sought to win popularity, to bring out his opposition to the National Assembly, and to hint at a secret reserve that was only temporarily prevented by conditions from making its hidden treasures available to the French people. Such was the proposal to decree an increase in pay of four sous a day to the non-commissioned officers. Such was the proposal of an honour system loan bank for the workers. Money as a gift and money as a loan, it was with prospects such as these that he hoped to allure the masses. Donations and loans—the financial science of the *lumpenproletariat*, whether of high degree or low, is restricted to this. Such were the only springs which Bonaparte knew how to set in action. Never has a pretender speculated more stupidly on the stupidity of the masses.

The National Assembly flared up repeatedly over these unmistakable attempts to gain popularity at its expense, over the growing danger that this adventurer, whom his debts spurred on and no established reputation held back, would venture a desperate *coup*. The discord between the party of Order and the President had taken on a threatening character when an unexpected event threw him back repentant into its arms. We mean the *by-elections of March 10, 1850*. These elections were held for the purpose of filling the representatives' seats that after June 13 had been rendered vacant by imprisonment or exile. Paris elected only social-democratic candidates. It even concentrated most of the votes on an insurgent of June 1848, on Deflotte. Thus did the Parisian petty bourgeoisie, in alliance with the proletariat, revenge itself for its defeat on June 13, 1849. It seemed to have disappeared from the battlefield at the moment of danger only to reappear there on a more propitious occasion with more numerous fighting forces and with a bolder battle cry. One circumstance seemed to heighten the peril of this election victory. The army voted in Paris for the June insurgent against La Hitte, a minister of Bonaparte's, and in the Departments largely for the *Montagnards*, who here, too, though indeed not so decisively as in Paris, maintained the ascendancy over their adversaries.

Bonaparte saw himself suddenly confronted with revolution once more. As on January 29, 1849, as on June 13, 1849, so on March 10, 1850, he disappeared behind the party of Order. He made obeisance, he pusillanimously begged pardon, he offered to appoint any ministry it pleased at the behest of the parliamentary majority, he even implored the Orleanist and Legitimist party leaders, the Thiers, the Berryers, the Broglies, the Molés, in brief, the so-called burgraves,[88] to take the helm of state themselves. The party of Order proved unable to take advantage of this opportunity that would never return. Instead of boldly possessing itself of the power offered, it did not even compel Bonaparte to reinstate the ministry dismissed on November 1; it contented itself with humiliating him by its forgiveness and adjoining *M. Baroche* to the d'Hautpoul ministry. As public prosecutor this Baroche had stormed and raged before the High Court at Bourges, the first time against the revolutionists of May 15, the second time against the democrats of June 13, both times because of an attempt on the life of the National Assembly. None of Bonaparte's ministers subsequently contributed more to the degradation of the National Assembly, and after

December 2, 1851, we meet him once more as the comfortably installed and highly paid Vice-President of the Senate. He had spat in the revolutionists' soup in order that Bonaparte might eat it up. The social-democratic party, for its part, seemed only to try to find pretexts for putting its own victory once again in doubt and for blunting its point. Vidal, one of the newly elected representatives of Paris, had been elected simultaneously in Strasbourg. He was induced to decline the election for Paris and accept it for Strasbourg. And so, instead of making its victory at the polls conclusive and thereby compelling the party of Order at once to contest it in parliament, instead of thus forcing the adversary to fight at the moment of popular enthusiasm and favourable mood in the army, the democratic party wearied Paris during the months of March and April with a new election campaign, let the aroused popular passions wear themselves out in this repeated provisional election game, let the revolutionary energy satiate itself with constitutional successes, dissipate itself in petty intrigues, hollow declamations and sham movements, let the bourgeoisie rally and make its preparations, and, lastly, weakened the significance of the March elections by a sentimental commentary in the April by-election, that of Eugène Sue. In a word, it made an April Fool of March 10.

The parliamentary majority understood the weakness of its antagonists. Its seventeen burgraves—for Bonaparte had left to it the direction of and responsibility for the attack—drew up a new electoral law, the introduction of which was entrusted to M. Faucher, who solicited this honour for himself. On May 8 he introduced the law by which universal suffrage was to be abolished, a residence of three years in the locality of the election to be imposed as a condition on the electors and, finally, the proof of this residence made dependent in the case of workers on a certificate from their employers.

Just as the democrats had, in revolutionary fashion, agitated the minds and raged during the constitutional election contest, so now, when it was requisite to prove the serious nature of that victory arms in hand, did they in constitutional fashion preach order, majestic calm (*calme majestueux*), lawful action, that is to say, blind subjection to the will of the counter-revolution, which imposed itself as the law. During the debate the Mountain put the party of Order to shame by asserting, against the latter's revolutionary passionateness, the dispassionate attitude of the philistine who keeps within the law, and by felling that party to earth with the fearful reproach that it proceeded in a revolutionary manner. Even the newly elected deputies were at pains to prove by their decorous and discreet action what a misconception it was to decry them as anarchists and construe their election as a victory for revolution. On May 31, the new electoral law went through. The *Montagne* contented itself with smuggling a protest into the pocket of the President. The electoral law was followed by a new press law, by which the revolutionary newspaper press[89] was entirely suppressed. It had deserved its fate. The *National*[61] and *La Presse*,[90] two bourgeois organs, were left behind after this deluge as the most advanced outposts of the revolution.

We have seen how during March and April the democratic leaders had done everything to embroil the people of Paris in a sham fight, how after May 8 they did everything to restrain them from a real fight. In addition to this, we must not forget that the year 1850 was one of the most splendid years of industrial and commercial prosperity, and the Paris proletariat was therefore fully employed. But the election law of May 31, 1850, excluded it from any participation in political power. It cut it off from the very arena of the struggle. It threw the workers back into the position of pariahs which they had occupied before the February Revolution. By letting themselves be led by the democrats in face of such an event and forgetting the revolutionary interests of their class for momentary ease and comfort, they renounced the honour of being a conquering power, surrendered to their fate, proved that the defeat of June 1848 had put them out of the fight for years and that the historical process would for the present again have to go on *over* their heads. So far as the petty-bourgeois democracy is concerned, which on June 13 had cried: "But if once universal suffrage is attacked, then we'll show them," it now consoled itself with the contention that the counter-revolutionary blow which had struck it was no blow and the law of May 31 no law. On the second Sunday in May 1852, every Frenchman would appear at the polling place with ballot in one hand and sword in the other. With this prophecy it rested content. Lastly, the army was disciplined by its superior officers for the elections of March and April 1850, just as it had been disciplined for those of May 28, 1849. This time, however, it said decidedly: "The revolution shall not dupe us a third time."

The law of May 31, 1850, was the *coup d'état* of the bourgeoisie. All its conquests over the revolution hitherto had only a provisional character. They were endangered as soon as the existing National Assembly retired from the stage. They depended on the hazards of a new general election, and the history of elections since 1848 irrefutably proved that the bourgeoisie's moral sway over the mass of the people was lost in the same measure as its actual domination developed. On March 10, universal suffrage declared itself directly against the domination of the bourgeoisie; the bourgeoisie answered by outlawing universal suffrage. The law of May 31 was, therefore, one of the necessities of the class struggle. On the other hand, the Constitution required a minimum of two million votes to make an election of the President of the republic valid. If none of the candidates for the presidency received this minimum, the National Assembly was to choose the President from among the three candidates to whom the largest number of votes would fall. At the time when the Constituent Assembly made this law, ten million electors were registered on the rolls of voters. In its view, therefore, a fifth of the people entitled to vote was sufficient to make the presidential election valid. The law of May 31 struck at least three million votes off the electoral rolls, reduced the number of people entitled to vote to seven million and, nevertheless, retained the legal minimum of two million for the presidential election. It therefore raised the legal minimum from a fifth to nearly a third of the effective votes, that is, it did everything to smuggle the election of the President out of the hands of the people and into the hands of the National Assembly. Thus through the electoral law of May 31 the party of Order seemed to have made its rule doubly secure, by surrendering the election of the National Assembly and that of the President of the republic to the stationary section of society.

V

As soon as the revolutionary crisis had been weathered and universal suffrage abolished, the struggle between the National Assembly and Bonaparte broke out again.

The Constitution had fixed Bonaparte's salary at 600,000 francs. Barely six months after his installation he succeeded in increasing this sum to twice as much, for Odilon Barrot wrung from the Constituent National Assembly an extra allowance of 600,000 francs a year for so-called representation moneys. After June 13, Bonaparte had caused similar requests to be voiced, this time without eliciting response from Barrot. Now, after May 31, he at once availed himself of the favourable moment and caused his ministers to propose a Civil List of three millions in the National Assembly. A long life of adventurous vagabondage had endowed him with the most developed antennae for feeling out the weak moments when he might squeeze money from his bourgeois. He practised regular *chantage*.*
The National Assembly had violated the sovereignty of the people with his assistance and his cognizance. He threatened to denounce its crime to the Tribunal of the people unless it loosened its purse-strings and purchased his silence with three million a year. It had robbed three million Frenchmen of their franchise. He demanded, for every Frenchman out of circulation, a franc in circulation, precisely three million francs. He, the elect of six millions, claimed damages for the votes out of which he said he had retrospectively been cheated. The Commission of the National Assembly refused the

---

* *Chantage*: Blackmail.—*Ed.*

importunate one. The Bonapartist press threatened. Could the
National Assembly break with the President of the republic at a
moment when in principle it had definitely broken with the mass of
the nation ? It rejected the annual Civil List, it is true, but it granted,
for this once, an extra allowance of two million one hundred and
sixty thousand francs. It thus rendered itself guilty of the double
weakness of granting the money and of showing at the same time
by its vexation that it granted it unwillingly. We shall see later
for what purpose Bonaparte needed the money. After this vexatious
aftermath, which followed on the heels of the abolition of universal
suffrage and in which Bonaparte exchanged his humble attitude
during the crisis of March and April for challenging impudence to
the usurpatory parliament, the National Assembly adjourned for
three months, from August 11 to November 11. In its place it left
behind a Permanent Commission of twenty-eight members, which
contained no Bonapartists, but did contain some moderate republicans. The Permanent Commission of 1849 had included only Order
men and Bonapartists. But at that time the party of Order declared
itself in permanence against the revolution. This time the parliamentary republic declared itself in permanence against the President. After the law of May 31, this was the only rival that still
confronted the party of Order.

When the National Assembly met once more in November 1850,
it seemed that, instead of the petty skirmishes it had hitherto had
with the President, a great and ruthless struggle, a life-and-death
struggle between the two powers, had become inevitable.

As in 1849 so during this year's parliamentary recess, the party
of Order had broken up into its separate factions, each occupied
with its own Restoration intrigues, which had obtained fresh nutriment through the death of Louis Philippe. The Legitimist king,
Henry V, had even nominated a formal ministry which resided
in Paris and in which members of the Permanent Commission held
seats. Bonaparte, in his turn, was therefore entitled to make tours
of the French Departments, and according to the disposition of
the town that he favoured with his presence, now more or less
covertly, now more or less overtly, to divulge his own restoration
plans and canvass votes for himself. On these processions, which
the great official *Moniteur* and the little private *Moniteurs* of Bonaparte naturally had to celebrate as triumphal processions, he was
constantly accompanied by persons affiliated with the *Society of
December 10*. This society dates from the year 1849. On the pretext
of founding a benevolent society, the *lumpenproletariat* of Paris
had been organised into secret sections, each section being led by
Bonapartist agents, with a Bonapartist general at the head of the
whole. Alongside decayed *roués* with dubious means of subsistence
and of dubious origin, alongside ruined and adventurous offshoots

of the bourgeoisie, were vagabonds, discharged soldiers, discharged jailbirds, escaped galley slaves, swindlers, mountebanks, *lazzaroni*,[91] pickpockets, tricksters, gamblers, *maquereaus*,* brothel keepers, porters, *literati*, organ-grinders, rag-pickers, knife grinders, tinkers, beggars—in short, the whole indefinite, disintegrated mass, thrown hither and thither, which the French term *la bohème* ; from this kindred element Bonaparte formed the core of the Society of December 10. A "benevolent society"—in so far as, like Bonaparte, all its members felt the need of benefiting themselves at the expense of the labouring nation. This Bonaparte, who constitutes himself *chief of the lumpenproletariat*, who here alone rediscovers in mass form the interests which he personally pursues, who recognises in this scum, offal, refuse of all classes the only class upon which he can base himself unconditionally, is the real Bonaparte, the Bonaparte *sans phrase*. An old crafty *roué*, he conceives the historical life of the nations and their performances of state as comedy in the most vulgar sense, as a masquerade where the grand costumes, words and postures merely serve to mask the pettiest knavery. Thus on his expedition to Strasbourg, where a trained Swiss vulture had played the part of the Napoleonic eagle. For his irruption into Boulogne he puts some London lackeys into French uniforms. They represent the army.[92] In this Society of December 10, he assembles ten thousand rascally fellows, who are to play the part of the people, as Nick Bottom that of the lion.** At a moment when the bourgeoisie itself played the most complete comedy, but in the most serious manner in the world, without infringing any of the pedantic conditions of French dramatic etiquette, and was itself half deceived, half convinced of the solemnity of its own performance of state, the adventurer, who took the comedy as plain comedy, was bound to win. Only when he has eliminated his solemn opponent, when he himself now takes his imperial role seriously and under the Napoleonic mask imagines he is the real Napoleon, does he become the victim of his own conception of the world, the serious buffoon who no longer takes world history for a comedy but his comedy for world history. What the national *ateliers*·*** were for the socialist workers, what the *Gardes mobiles*·*) were for the bourgeois republicans, the Society of December 10, the party fighting force characteristic of Bonaparte, was for him. On his journeys the detachments of this society packing the railways had to improvise a public for him, stage public enthusiasm, roar *vive l'Empereur*,

---

* *Maquereaus*: Procurers.—*Ed.*
** The reference is to Shakespeare's comedy: *A Midsummer Night's Dream.*—*Ed.*
*** See K. Marx, *The Class Struggles in France, 1848 to 1850* (Marx and Engels, *Selected Works*, Vol. I, Moscow, 1962, p. 156).—*Ed.*
*) Ibid., p. 155.—*Ed.*

insult and thrash republicans, of course under the protection of the police. On his return journeys to Paris they had to form the advance guard, forestall counter-demonstrations or disperse them. The Society of December 10 belonged to him, it was *his* work, his very own idea. Whatever else he appropriates is put into his hands by the force of circumstances : whatever else he does, the circumstances do for him or he is content to copy from the deeds of others. But Bonaparte with official phrases about order, religion, family and property in public, before the citizens, and with the secret society of the Schufterles and Spiegelbergs, the society of disorder, prostitution and theft, behind him—that is Bonaparte himself as original author, and the history of the Society of December 10 is his own history.

Now it had happened by way of exception that people's representatives belonging to the party of Order came under the cudgels of the Decembrists. Still more. Yon, the Police Commissioner assigned to the National Assembly and charged with watching over its safety, acting on the deposition of a certain Alais, advised the Permanent Commission that a section of the Decembrists had decided to assassinate General Changarnier and Dupin, the President of the National Assembly, and had already designated the individuals who were to perpetrate the deed. One comprehends the terror of M. Dupin. A parliamentary enquiry into the Society of December 10, that is, the profanation of the Bonapartist secret world, seemed inevitable. Just before the meeting of the National Assembly Bonaparte providently disbanded his society, naturally only on paper, for in a detailed memoir at the end of 1851 Police Prefect Carlier still sought in vain to move him to really break up the Decembrists.

The Society of December 10 was to remain the private army of Bonaparte until he succeeded in transforming the public army into a Society of December 10. Bonaparte made the first attempt at this shortly after the adjournment of the National Assembly, and precisely with the money just wrested from it. As a fatalist, he lives in the conviction that there are certain higher powers which man, and the soldier in particular, cannot withstand. Among these powers he counts, first and foremost, cigars and champagne, cold poultry and garlic sausage. Accordingly, to begin with, he treats officers and non-commissioned officers in his Elysée apartments to cigars and champagne, to cold poultry and garlic sausage. On October 3 he repeats this manoeuvre with the mass of the troops at the St. Maur review, and on October 10 the same manoeuvre on a still larger scale at the Satory army parade. The Uncle remembered the campaigns of Alexander in Asia, the Nephew the triumphal marches of Bacchus in the same land. Alexander was a demigod, to be sure, but Bacchus was a god and moreover the tutelary deity of the Society of December 10.

After the review of October 3, the Permanent Commission summoned War Minister d'Hautpoul. He promised that these breaches of discipline should not recur. We know 'how on October 10 Bonaparte kept d'Hautpoul's word. As Commander-in-Chief of the Paris army, Changarnier had commanded at both reviews. He, at once a member of the Permanent Commission, chief of the National Guard, the "saviour" of January 29 and June 13, the "bulwark of society," the candidate of the party of Order for presidential honours, the suspected Monk of two monarchies, had hitherto never acknowledged himself as the subordinate of the War Minister, had always openly derided the republican Constitution and had pursued Bonaparte with an ambiguous lordly protection. Now he was consumed with zeal for discipline against the War Minister and for the Constitution against Bonaparte. While on October 10 a section of the cavalry raised the shout: *"Vive Napoléon! Vivent les saucissons!"** Changarnier arranged that at least the infantry marching past under the command of his friend Neumayer should preserve an icy silence. As a punishment. the War Minister relieved General Neumayer of his post in Paris at Bonaparte's instigation, on the pretext of appointing him commanding general of the fourteenth and fifteenth military divisions. Neumayer refused this exchange of posts and so had to resign. Changarnier, for his part, published an order of the day on November 2, in which he forbade the troops to indulge in political outcries or demonstrations of any kind while under arms. The Elysée newspapers[93] attacked Changarnier; the papers of the party of Order attacked Bonaparte; the Permanent Commission held repeated secret sessions in which it was repeatedly proposed to declare the country in danger; the army seemed divided into two hostile camps, with two hostile general staffs, one in the Elysée, where Bonaparte resided, the other in the Tuileries, the quarters of Changarnier. It seemed that only the meeting of the National Assembly was needed to give the signal for battle. The French public judged this friction between Bonaparte and Changarnier like that English journalist who characterised it in the following words:

"The political housemaids of France are sweeping away the glowing lava of the revolution with old brooms and wrangle with one another while they do their work."

Meanwhile, Bonaparte hastened to remove the War Minister, d'Hautpoul, to pack him off in all haste to Algiers and to appoint General Schramm War Minister in his place. On November 12, he sent to the National Assembly a message of American prolixity, overloaded with detail, redolent of order, desirous of reconcilia-

---

* "Hurrah for Napoleon! Hurrah for the sausages!"—*Ed.*

tion, constitutionally acquiescent, treating of all and sundry, but
not of the *questions brûlantes** of the moment. As if in passing, he
made the remark that according to the express provisions of the
Constitution the President alone could dispose of the army. The
message closed with the following words of great solemnity:

"*Above all things, France demands tranquillity.... But bound by an oath, I
shall keep within the narrow limits that it has set for me....* As far as I am
concerned, elected by the people and owing my power to it alone, I shall always
bow to its lawfully expressed will. Should you resolve at this session on a revision of the Constitution, a Constituent Assembly will regulate the position of the
executive power. If not, then the people will solemnly pronounce its decision in
1852. But whatever the solutions of the future may be, let us come to an understanding, so that passion, surprise or violence may never decide the destiny of a
great nation.... What occupies my attention, above all, is not who will rule
France in 1852, but how to employ the time which remains at my disposal so
that the intervening period may pass by without agitation or disturbance. I have
opened my heart to you with sincerity; you will answer my frankness with your
trust, my good endeavours with your co-operation, and God will do the rest."

The respectable, hypocritically moderate, virtuously commonplace
language of the bourgeoisie reveals its deepest meaning in the mouth
of the autocrat of the Society of December 10 and the picnic hero of
St. Maur and Satory.

The burgraves of the party of Order did not delude themselves
for a moment concerning the trust that this opening of the heart
deserved. About oaths they had long been *blasé*; they numbered
in their midst veterans and virtuosos of political perjury. Nor had
they failed to hear the passage about the army. They observed with
annoyance that in its discursive enumeration of lately enacted laws
the message passed over the most important law, the electoral law,
in studied silence, and moreover, in the event of there being no
revision of the Constitution, left the election of the President in
1852 to the people. The electoral law was the leaden ball chained
to the feet of the party of Order, which prevented it from walking
and so much the more from storming forward! Moreover, by the
official disbandment of the Society of December 10 and the dismissal of the War Minister d'Hautpoul, Bonaparte had with his
own hand sacrificed the scapegoats on the altar of the country. He
had blunted the edge of the expected collision. Finally, the party
of Order itself anxiously sought to avoid, to mitigate, to gloss over
any decisive conflict with the executive power. For fear of losing
their conquests over the revolution, they allowed their rival to carry
off the fruits thereof. "Above all things, France demands tranquillity." This was what the party of Order had cried to the revolution
since February,** this was what Bonaparte's message cried to the

---

* *Questions brûlantes*: Burning questions.—*Ed.*
** 1848.—*Ed.*

party of Order. "Above all things, France demands tranquillity." Bonaparte committed acts that aimed at usurpation, but the party of Order committed "unrest" if it raised a row about these acts and construed them hypochondriacally. The sausages of Satory were quiet as mice when no one spoke of them. "Above all things, France demands tranquillity." Bonaparte demanded, therefore, that he be left in peace to do as he liked and the parliamentary party was paralysed by a double fear, by the fear of again evoking revolutionary unrest and by the fear of itself appearing as the instigator of unrest in the eyes of its own class, in the eyes of the bourgeoisie. Consequently, since France demanded tranquillity above all things, the party of Order dared not answer "war" after Bonaparte had talked "peace" in his message. The public, which had anticipated scenes of great scandal at the opening of the National Assembly, was cheated of its expectations. The opposition deputies, who demanded the submission of the Permanent Commission's minutes on the October events, were outvoted by the majority. On principle, all debates that might cause excitement were eschewed. The proceedings of the National Assembly during November and December 1850 were without interest.

At last, towards the end of December, guerrilla warfare began over a number of prerogatives of parliament. The movement got bogged in petty squabbles regarding the prerogatives of the two powers, since the bourgeoisie had done away with the class struggle for the moment by abolishing universal suffrage.

A judgement for debt had been obtained from the court against Mauguin, one of the People's Representatives. In answer to the enquiry of the President of the Court, the Minister of Justice, Rouher, declared that a *capias* should be issued against the debtor without further ado. Mauguin was thus thrown into the debtors' jail. The National Assembly flared up when it learned of the assault. Not only did it order his immediate release, but it even had him fetched forcibly from Clichy[66] the same evening, by its *greffier*.* In order, however, to confirm its faith in the sanctity of private property and with the idea at the back of its mind of opening, in case of need, an asylum for *Montagnards* who had become troublesome, it declared imprisonment of People's Representatives for debt permissible after previously obtaining its consent. It forgot to decree that the President might also be locked up for debt. It destroyed the last semblance of the immunity that enveloped the members of its own body.

It will be remembered that, acting on the information given by a certain Alais, Police Commissioner Yon had denounced a section of the Decembrists for planning the murder of Dupin and Changar-

* *Greffier*: Clerk.—*Ed.*

nier. In reference to this, at the very first sitting the questors made the proposal that parliament should form a police force of its own, paid out of the private budget of the National Assembly and absolutely independent of the police prefect. The Minister of the Interior, Baroche, protested against this invasion of his domain. A miserable compromise on this matter was concluded, according to which, true, the police commissioner of the Assembly was to be paid out of its private budget and to be appointed and dismissed by its questors, but only after previous agreement with the Minister of the Interior. Meanwhile criminal proceedings had been taken by the government against Alais, and here it was easy to represent his information as a hoax and through the mouth of the public prosecutor to cast ridicule upon Dupin, Changarnier, Yon and the whole National Assembly. Thereupon, on December 29, Minister Baroche writes a letter to Dupin in which he demands Yon's dismissal. The Bureau of the National Assembly decides to retain Yon in his position, but the National Assembly, alarmed by its violence in the Mauguin affair and accustomed when it has ventured a blow at the executive power to receive two blows from it in return, does not sanction this decision. It dismisses Yon as a reward for his official zeal and robs itself of a parliamentary prerogative indispensable against a man who does not decide by night in order to execute by day, but who decides by day and executes by night.

We have seen how on great and striking occasions during the months of November and December the National Assembly avoided or quashed the struggle with the executive power. Now we see it compelled to take it up on the pettiest occasions. In the Mauguin affair it confirms the principle of imprisoning People's Representatives for debt, but reserves the right to have it applied only to representatives obnoxious to itself and wrangles over this infamous privilege with the Minister of Justice. Instead of availing itself of the alleged murder plot to decree an enquiry into the Society of December 10 and irredeemably unmasking Bonaparte before France and Europe in his true character of chief of the Paris *lumpenproletariat,* it lets the conflict be degraded to a point where the only issue between it and the Minister of the Interior is which of them has the authority to appoint and dismiss a police commissioner. Thus, during the whole of this period, we see the party of Order compelled by its equivocal position to dissipate and disintegrate its struggle with the executive power in petty jurisdictional squabbles, pettifoggery, legalistic hairsplitting, and delimitational disputes, and to make the most ridiculous matters of form the substance of its activity. It does not dare to take up the conflict at the moment when this has significance from the standpoint of principle, when the executive power has really exposed itself and the cause of the National Assembly would be the cause of the nation. By so doing it would give the nation its marching orders, and it fears nothing more than that the nation should move. On such occasions it accordingly rejects the motions of the *Montagne* and proceeds to the order of the day. The question at issue in its larger aspects having thus been dropped, the executive power calmly bides the time when it can again take up the same question on petty and insignificant occasions, when this is, so to speak, of only local parliamentary interests. Then the repressed rage of the party of Order breaks out, then it tears away the curtain from the coulisses, then it denounces the President, then it declares the republic in danger, but then, also, its fervour appears absurd and the occasion for the struggle seems a hypocritical pretext or altogether not worth fighting about. The parliamentary storm becomes a storm in a teacup, the fight becomes an intrigue, the conflict a scandal. While the revolutionary classes gloat with malicious joy over the humiliation of the National Assembly, for they are just as enthusiastic about the parliamentary prerogatives of this Assembly as the latter is about the public liberties, the bourgeoisie outside parliament does not understand how the bourgeoisie inside parliament can waste time over such petty squabbles and imperil tranquillity by such pitiful rivalries with the President. It becomes confused by a strategy that makes peace at the moment when all the world is expecting battles, and attacks at the moment when all the world believes peace has been made.

On December 20, Pascal Duprat interpellated the Minister of the Interior concerning the Gold Bars Lottery. This lottery was a "daughter of Elysium."[94] Bonaparte with his faithful followers had brought her into the world and Police Prefect Carlier had placed her under his official protection, although French law forbids all lotteries with the exception of raffles for charitable purposes. Seven million lottery tickets at a franc apiece, the profits ostensibly to be devoted to shipping Parisian vagabonds to California. On the one hand, golden dreams were to supplant the socialist dreams of the Paris proletariat; the seductive prospect of the first prize, the doctrinaire right to work. Naturally, the Paris workers did not recognise in the glitter of the California gold bars the inconspicuous francs that were enticed out of their pockets. In the main, however, the matter was nothing short of a downright swindle. The vagabonds who wanted to open California gold mines without troubling to leave Paris were Bonaparte himself and his debt-ridden Round Table. The three millions voted by the National Assembly had been squandered in riotous living; in one way or another the coffers had to be replenished. In vain had Bonaparte opened a national subscription for the building of so-called *cités ouvrières,** and figured at the head of the list himself with a considerable sum.

---

* *Cités ouvrières*: Workers' settlements.—*Ed.*

The hard-hearted bourgeois waited mistrustfully for him to pay
up his share and since this, naturally, did not ensue, the speculation in socialist castles in the air fell straightway to the ground.
The gold bars proved a better draw. Bonaparte & Co. were not
content to pocket part of the excess of the seven millions over the
bars to be allotted in prizes; they manufactured false lottery tickets;
they issued ten, fifteen and even twenty tickets with the same
number—a financial operation in the spirit of the Society of December 10! Here the National Assembly was confronted not with
the fictitious President of the republic, but with Bonaparte in the
flesh. Here it could catch him in the act, in conflict not with the
Constitution but with the *Code pénal*. If on Duprat's interpella-
tion it proceeded to the order of the day, this did not happen merely
because Girardin's motion that it should declare itself *"satisfait"*
reminded the party of Order of its own systematic corruption. The
bourgeois and, above all, the bourgeois inflated into a statesman,
supplements his practical meanness by theoretical extravagance.
As a statesman he becomes, like the state power that confronts him, a
higher being that can only be fought in a higher, consecrated fashion.

Bonaparte, who precisely because he was a Bohemian, a princely
lumpenproletarian, had the advantage over a rascally bourgeois in
that he could conduct the struggle meanly, now saw, after the Assembly had itself guided him with its own hand across the slippery
ground of the military banquets, the reviews, the Society of December 10, and, finally, the *Code pénal*, that the moment had come
when he could pass from an apparent defensive to the offensive.
The minor defeats meanwhile sustained by the Minister of Justice,
the Minister of War, the Minister of the Navy and the Minister of
Finance, through which the National Assembly signified its snarling
displeasure, troubled him little. He not only prevented the ministers
from resigning and thus recognising the sovereignty of parliament
over the executive power, but could now consummate what he had
begun during the recess of the National Assembly: the severance
of the military power from parliament, the *removal of Changarnier*.

An Elysée paper published an order of the day alleged to have
been addressed during the month of May to the First Military
Division, and therefore proceeding from Changarnier, in which the
officers were recommended, in the event of an insurrection, to give
no quarter to the traitors in their own ranks, but to shoot them
immediately and refuse the National Assembly the troops, should
it requisition them. On January 3, 1851, the Cabinet was interpellated
concerning this order of the day. For the investigation of this matter
it requests a breathing space, first of three months, then of a week,
finally of only twenty-four hours. The Assembly insists on an immediate explanation. Changarnier rises and declares that there never
was such an order of the day. He adds that he will always hasten

to comply with the demands of the National Assembly and that in case of a clash it can count on him. It receives his declaration with indescribable applause and passes a vote of confidence in him. It abdicates, it decrees its own impotence and the omnipotence of the army by placing itself under the private protection of a general; but the general deceives himself when he puts at its command against Bonaparte a power that he only holds as a fief from the same Bonaparte and when, in his turn, he expects to be protected by this parliament, by his own protégé in need of protection. Changarnier, however, believes in the mysterious power with which the bourgeoisie has endowed him since January 29, 1849. He considers himself the third power, existing side by side with both the other state powers. He shares the fate of the rest of this epoch's heroes, or rather saints, whose greatness consists precisely in the biassed great opinion of them that their party creates in its own interests and who shrink to everyday figures as soon as circumstances call on them to perform miracles. Unbelief is, in general, the mortal enemy of these reputed heroes and real saints. Hence their majestically moral indignation at the dearth of enthusiasm displayed by wits and scoffers.

The same evening, the ministers were summoned to the Elysée; Bonaparte insists on the dismissal of Changarnier; five ministers refuse to sign it; the *Moniteur*[74] announces a ministerial crisis, and the press of the party of Order threatens to form a parliamentary army under Changarnier's command. The party of Order had constitutional authority to take this step. It merely had to appoint Changarnier President of the National Assembly and requisition any number of troops it pleased for its protection. It could do so all the more safely as Changarnier still actually stood at the head of the army and the Paris National Guard and was only waiting to be requisitioned together with the army. The Bonapartist press did not as yet even dare to question the right of the National Assembly directly to requisition troops, a legal scruple that in the given circumstances did not promise any success. That the army would have obeyed the orders of the National Assembly is probable when one bears in mind that Bonaparte had to search all Paris for eight days in order, finally, to find two generals—Baraguey d'Hilliers and Saint-Jean d'Angely—who declared themselves ready to countersign Changarnier's dismissal. That the party of Order, however, would have found in its own ranks and in parliament the necessary number of votes for such a resolution is more than doubtful, when one considers that eight days later two hundred and eighty-six votes detached themselves from the party and that in December 1851, at the last hour for decision, the *Montagne* still rejected a similar proposal. Nevertheless, the burgraves might, perhaps, still have suc-

ceeded in spurring the mass of their party to a heroism that consisted in feeling themselves secure behind a forest of bayonets and
accepting the services of an army that had deserted to their camp
Instead of this, on the evening of January 6 Messrs. the Burgraves
betook themselves to the Elysée in order to make Bonaparte desist
from dismissing Changarnier by using statesmanlike phrases and
urging considerations of state. Whomever one seeks to persuade,
one acknowledges as master of the situation. On January 12, Bonaparte, assured by this step, appoints a new ministry in which the
leaders of the old ministry, Fould and Baroche, remain. Saint-Jean
d'Angely becomes War Minister, the *Moniteur* publishes the decree
dismissing Changarnier, and his command is divided between Baraguey d'Hilliers, who receives the First Army Division, and Perrot,
who receives the National Guard. The bulwark of society has been
discharged, and while this does not cause any tiles to fall from the
roofs, quotations on the *bourse* are, on the other hand, going up.

By repulsing the army, which places itself in the person of Changarnier at its disposal, and so surrendering the army irrevocably
to the President, the party of Order declares that the bourgeoisie
has forfeited its vocation to rule. A parliamentary ministry no longer
existed. Having now indeed lost its grip on the army and National
Guard, what forcible means remained to it with which simultaneously to maintain the usurped authority of parliament over the
people and its constitutional authority against the President? None.
Only the appeal to forceless principles remained to it now, to principles that it had itself always interpreted merely as general rules.
which one prescribes for others in order to be able to move all the
more freely oneself. The dismissal of Changarnier and the falling
of the military power into Bonaparte's hands closes the first part of
the period we are considering, the period of struggle between the
party of Order and the executive power. War between the two
powers has now been openly declared, is openly waged, but only
after the party of Order has lost both arms and soldiers. Without
the ministry, without the army, without the people, without public
opinion, after its Electoral Law of May 31 no longer the
representative of the sovereign nation, *sans* eyes, *sans* ears, *sans*
teeth, *sans* everything, the National Assembly had undergone a
gradual transformation into an *ancient French Parliament*[95] that has
to leave action to the government and content itself with growling
remonstrances *post festum.**

The party of Order receives the new ministry with a storm of
indignation. General Bedeau recalls to mind the mildness of the
Permanent Commission during the recess, and the excessive consideration it had shown by waiving the publication of its minutes.

---

* *Post festum*: After the feast, that is, belatedly.—*Ed.*

The Minister of the Interior now himself insists on the publication of these minutes, which by this time have naturally become as dull as ditchwater, disclose no fresh facts and have not the slightest effect on the *blasé* public. Upon Rémusat's proposal the National Assembly retires into its bureaux and appoints a "Committee for Extraordinary Measures." Paris departs the less from the rut of its everyday routine, since at this moment trade is prosperous, manufactories are busy, corn prices low, foodstuffs overflowing and the savings banks receive fresh deposits daily. The "extraordinary measures" that parliament has announced with so much noise fizzle out on January 1℃ in a no-confidence vote against the ministry without General Changarnier even being mentioned. The party of Order had been forced to frame its motion in this way in order to secure the votes of the republicans, as of all the measures of the ministry, Changarnier's dismissal is precisely the only one which the republicans approve of, while the party of Order is in fact not in a position to censure the other ministerial acts, which it had itself dictated.

The no-confidence vote of January 18 was passed by four hundred and fifteen votes to two hundred and eighty-six. Thus, it was carried only by a *coalition* of the extreme Legitimists and Orleanists with the pure republicans and the *Montagne*. Thus it proved that the party of Order had lost in conflicts with Bonaparte not only the ministry, not only the army, but also its independent parliamentary majority, that a squad of representatives had deserted from its camp, out of fanaticism for conciliation, out of fear of the struggle, out of lassitude, out of family regard for the state salaries so near and dear to them, out of speculation on ministerial posts becoming vacant (Odilon Barrot), out of sheer egoism, which makes the ordinary bourgeois always inclined to sacrifice the general interest of his class for this or that private motive. From the first, the Bonapartist representatives adhered to the party of Order only in the struggle against revolution. The leader of the Catholic party, Montalembert, had already at that time thrown his influence into the Bonapartist scale, since he despaired of the parliamentary party's prospects of life. Lastly, the leaders of this party, Thiers and Berryer, the Orleanist and the Legitimist, were compelled openly to proclaim themselves republicans, to confess that their hearts were royalist but their heads republican, that the parliamentary republic was the sole possible form for the rule of the bourgeoisie as a whole. Thus they were compelled, before the eyes of the bourgeois class itself, to stigmatise the Restoration plans, which they continued indefatigably to pursue behind parliament's back as an intrigue as dangerous as it was brainless.

The no-confidence vote of January 18 hit the ministers and not the President. But it was not the ministry, it was the President

who had dismissed Changarnier. Should the party of Order impeach
Bonaparte himself? On account of his restoration desires? The
latter merely supplemented their own. On account of his conspiracy
in connection with the military reviews and the Society of December 10? They had buried these themes long since under simple
orders of the day. On account of the dismissal of the hero of
January 29 and June 13, the man who in May 1850 threatened to
set fire to all four corners of Paris in the event of a rising? Their
allies of the *Montagne* and Cavaignac did not even allow them to
raise the fallen bulwark of society by means of an official attesta-
tion of sympathy. They themselves could not deny the President
the constitutional authority to dismiss a general. They only raged
because he made an unparliamentary use of his constitutional right.
Had they not continually made an unconstitutional use of their parliamentary prerogative, particularly in regard to the abolition of
universal suffrage? They were therefore reduced to moving within
strictly parliamentary limits. And it took that peculiar malady which
since 1848 has raged all over the Continent, *parliamentary cretinism*,
which holds those infected by it fast in an imaginary world and
robs them of all sense, all memory, all understanding of the rude
external world—it took this parliamentary cretinism for those who
had destroyed all the conditions of parliamentary power with their
own hands, and were bound to destroy them in their struggle with
the other classes, still to regard their parliamentary victories as
victories and to believe they hit the President by striking at his
ministers. They merely gave him the opportunity to humiliate the
National Assembly afresh in the eyes of the nation. On January 20
the *Moniteur* announced that the resignation of the entire ministry
had been accepted. On the pretext that no parliamentary party any
longer had a majority, as the vote of January 18, this fruit of the
coalition between *Montagne* and royalists, proved, and pending the
formation of a new majority, Bonaparte appointed a so-called
transition ministry, not one member of which was a member of parliament, all being absolutely unknown and insignificant individuals,
a ministry of mere clerks and copyists. The party of Order could
now work to exhaustion playing with these marionettes; the executive power no longer thought it worth while to be seriously
represented in the National Assembly. The more his ministers were
pure dummies, the more manifestly Bonaparte concentrated the
whole executive power in his own person and the more scope he
had to exploit it for his own ends.

In coalition with the *Montagne*, the party of Order revenged
itself by rejecting the grant to the President of one million eight
hundred thousand francs, which the chief of the Society of December 10 had compelled his ministerial clerks to propose. This
time a majority of only a hundred and two votes decided the

matter; thus twenty-seven fresh votes had fallen away since January 18; the dissolution of the party of Order was making progress. At the same time, in order that there might not for a moment be any mistake about the meaning of its coalition with the *Montagne*, it scorned even to consider a proposal signed by a hundred and eighty-nine members of the *Montagne* calling for a general amnesty of political offenders. It sufficed for the Minister of the Interior, a certain Vaïsse, to declare that the tranquillity was only apparent, that in secret great agitation prevailed, that in secret ubiquitous societies were being organised, the democratic papers were preparing to come out again, the reports from the Departments were unfavourable, the Geneva refugees were directing a conspiracy spreading by way of Lyons over all the south of France, France was on the verge of an industrial and commercial crisis, the manufacturers of Roubaix had reduced working hours, that the prisoners of Belle Isle[96] were in revolt—it sufficed for even a mere Vaïsse to conjure up the red spectre and the party of Order rejected without discussion a motion that would certainly have won the National Assembly immense popularity and thrown Bonaparte back into its arms. Instead of letting itself be intimidated by the executive power with the prospect of fresh disturbances, it ought rather to have allowed the class struggle a little elbowroom, so as to keep the executive power dependent on itself. But it did not feel equal to the task of playing with fire.

Meanwhile, the so-called transition ministry continued to vegetate until the middle of April. Bonaparte wearied and befooled the National Assembly with continual new ministerial combinations. Now he seemed to want to form a republican ministry with Lamartine and Billault, now a parliamentary one with the inevitable Odilon Barrot, whose name may never be missing when a dupe is necessary, then a Legitimist ministry with Vatimesnil and Benoist d'Azy, and then again an Orleanist one with Maleville. While he thus kept the different factions of the party of Order in tension against one another and alarmed them as a whole by the prospect of a republican ministry and the consequent inevitable restoration of universal suffrage, he at the same time engendered in the bourgeoisie the conviction that his honest efforts to form a parliamentary ministry were being frustrated by the irreconcilability of the royalist factions. The bourgeoisie, however, cried out all the louder for a "strong government"; it found it all the more unpardonable to leave France "without administration," the more a general commercial crisis seemed now to be approaching and won recruits for socialism in the towns, just as the ruinously low price of corn did in the countryside. Trade became daily slacker, the unemployed hands increased perceptibly, ten thousand workers, at least, were breadless in Paris, innumerable factories stood idle in Rouen, Mul-

house, Lyons, Roubaix, Tourcoing, St. Etienne, Elbeuf, etc. Unde
these circumstances Bonaparte could venture, on April 11, to restor
the ministry of January 18: Messrs. Rouher, Fould, Baroche, etc
reinforced by M. Léon Faucher, whom the Constituent Assembl
during its last days had, with the exception of five votes cast b
ministers, unanimously stigmatised by a vote of no-confidence fo
sending out false telegrams. The National Assembly had therefor
gained a victory over the ministry on January 18, had struggled wit
Bonaparte for three months, only to have Fould and Baroche o
April 11 admit the puritan Faucher as a third party into thei
ministerial alliance.

In November 1849, Bonaparte had contented himself with a
unparliamentary ministry, in January 1851 with an *extra-parliamentary* one, and on April 11 he felt strong enough to form ar
anti-parliamentary ministry, which harmoniously combined in itsel
the no-confidence votes of both Assemblies, the Constituent anc
the Legislative, the republican and the royalist. This gradation o
ministries was the thermometer with which parliament could
measure the decrease of its own vital heat. By the end of Apri
the latter had fallen so low that Persigny, in a personal interview,
could urge Changarnier to go over to the camp of the President.
Bonaparte, he assured him, regarded the influence of the National
Assembly as completely destroyed, and the proclamation was already prepared that was to be published after the *coup d'état*, which
was kept steadily in view but was by chance again postponed.
Changarnier informed the leaders of the party of Order of the obit-
uary notice, but who believes that bedbug bites are fatal? And
parliament, stricken, disintegrated and death-tainted as it was, could
not prevail upon itself to see in its duel with the grotesque chief of
the Society of December 10 anything but a duel with a bedbug.
But Bonaparte answered the party of Order as Agesilaus did King
Agis:

"*I seem to thee an ant, but one day I shall be a lion.*"[97]

VI

The coalition with the *Montagne* and the pure republicans, to
which the party of Order saw itself condemned in its unavailing
efforts to maintain possession of the military power and to
reconquer supreme control of the executive power, proved incontrovertibly that it had forfeited its independent *parliamentary
majority*. On May 28, the mere power of the calendar, of the hour
hand of the clock, gave the signal for its complete disintegration.
With May 28, the last year of the life of the National Assembly
began. It had now to decide for continuing the Constitution
unaltered or for revising it. But revision of the Constitution, that

mplied not only rule of the bourgeoisie or of the petty-bourgeois
democracy, democracy or proletarian anarchy, parliamentary republic or Bonaparte, it implied at the same time Orleans or Bourbon! Thus fell in the midst of parliament the apple of discord that
was bound to inflame openly the conflict of interests which split
the party of Order into hostile factions. The party of Order was a
combination of heterogeneous social substances. The question of
revision generated a political temperature at which the product again
decomposed into its original constituents.

The interest of the Bonapartists in a revision was simple. For
them it was above all a question of abolishing Article 45, which
forbade Bonaparte's re-election and the prorogation of his authority. No less simple appeared the position of the republicans. They
unconditionally rejected any revision; they saw in it a universal
conspiracy against the republic. Since they commanded *more than
a quarter of the votes* in the National Assembly and, according to
the Constitution, three-quarters of the votes were required for a
resolution for revision to be legally valid and for the convocation
of a revising Assembly, they only needed to count their votes to
be sure of victory. And they were sure of victory.

As against these clear positions, the party of Order found itself
caught in inextricable contradictions. If it should reject revision, it
would imperil the *status quo*, since it would leave Bonaparte only
one way out, that of force, and since on the second Sunday in May
1852, at the decisive moment, it would be surrendering France to
revolutionary anarchy, with a President who had lost his authority,
with a parliament which for a long time had not possessed it and
with a people that meant to reconquer it. If it voted for constitutional revision, it knew that it voted in vain and would be bound
to fail constitutionally because of the veto of the republicans. If it
unconstitutionally declared a simple majority vote to be binding,
then it could hope to dominate the revolution only if it subordinated
itself unconditionally to the sovereignty of the executive power, then
it would make Bonaparte master of the Constitution, of its revision
and of itself. Only a partial revision which would prolong the
authority of the President would pave the way for imperial usurpation. A general revision which would shorten the existence of the
republic would bring the dynastic claims into unavoidable conflict,
for the conditions of a Bourbon and the conditions of an Orleanist
Restoration were not only different, they were mutually exclusive.

The parliamentary republic was more than the neutral territory
on which the two factions of the French bourgeoisie, Legitimists
and Orleanists, large landed property and industry, could dwell
side by side with equality of rights. It was the unavoidable condition of their *common* rule, the sole form of state in which their
general class interest subjected to itself at the same time both the

claims of their particular factions and all the remaining classes of
society. As royalists they fell back into their old antagonism, into
the struggle for the supremacy of landed property or of money, and
the highest expression of this antagonism, its personification, was
their kings themselves, their dynasties. Hence the resistance of the
party of Order to the *recall of the Bourbons*.

The Orleanist and people's representative Creton had in 1849,
1850 and 1851 periodically introduced a motion for the revocation
of the decree exiling the royal families. Just as regularly parliament presented the spectacle of an Assembly of royalists that ob-
durately barred the gates through which their exiled kings might
return home. Richard III had murdered Henry VI, remarking that
he was too good for this world and belonged in heaven. They declared France too bad to possess her kings again. Constrained by
force of circumstances, they had become republicans and repeatedly
sanctioned the popular decision that banished their kings from
France.

A revision of the Constitution—and circumstances compelled
taking it into consideration—called in question, along with the
republic, the common rule of the two bourgeois factions, and revived, with the possibility of a monarchy, the rivalry of the interests
which it had predominantly represented by turns, the struggle
for the supremacy of one faction over the other. The diplomats of
the party of Order believed they could settle the struggle by an
amalgamation of the two dynasties, by a so-called *fusion* of the
royalist parties and their royal houses. The real fusion of the
Restoration and the July Monarchy was the parliamentary republic,
in which Orleanist and Legitimist colours were obliterated and the
various species of bourgeois disappeared in the bourgeois as such,
in the bourgeois genus. Now, however, Orleanist was to become
Legitimist and Legitimist Orleanist. Royalty, in which their antagonism was personified, was to embody their unity; the expression
of their exclusive factional interests was to become the expression
of their common class interest; the monarchy was to do that which
only the abolition of two monarchies, the republic, could do and had
done. This was the philosopher's stone, to produce which the doctors
of the party of Order racked their brains. As if the Legitimist
monarchy could ever become the monarchy of the industrial
bourgeois or the bourgeois monarchy ever become the monarchy
of the hereditary landed aristocracy. As if landed property and
industry could fraternise under *one* crown, when the crown could
only descend to one head, the head of the elder brother or of the
younger. As if industry could come to terms with landed property
at all, so long as landed property does not decide itself to become
industrial. If Henry V should die tomorrow, the Count of Paris
would not on that account become the king of the Legitimists unless

he ceased to be the king of the Orleanists. The philosophers of
fusion, however, who became more vociferous in proportion as the
question of revision came to the fore, who had provided themselves
with an official daily organ in the *Assemblée Nationale*[98] and who
are again at work even at this very moment (February 1852), considered the whole difficulty to be due to the opposition and rivalry
of the two dynasties. The attempts to reconcile the Orleans family
with Henry V, begun since the death of Louis Philippe, but, like
the dynastic intrigues generally, played at only while the National
Assembly was in recess, during the *entr'actes*, behind the scenes,
sentimental coquetry with the old superstition rather than seriously-
meant business, now became grand performances of state, enacted
by the party of Order on the public stage, instead of in amateur
theatricals, as hitherto. The couriers sped from Paris to Venice,[99]
from Venice to Claremont, from Claremont to Paris. The Count of
Chambord issues a manifesto in which "with the help of all the
members of his family" he announces not his, but the "national"
Restoration. The Orleanist Salvandy throws himself at the feet of
Henry V. The Legitimist chiefs, Berryer, Benoist d'Azy, Saint-Priest,
travel to Claremont in order to persuade the Orleans set, but in
vain. The fusionists perceive too late that the interests of the two
bourgeois factions neither lose exclusiveness nor gain pliancy when
they become accentuated in the form of family interests, the interests of two royal houses. If Henry V were to recognise the Count
of Paris as his successor—the sole success that the fusion could
achieve at best—the House of Orleans would not win any claim
that the childlessness of Henry V had not already secured to it, but
it would lose all claims that it had gained through the July Revolution. It would waive its original claims, all the titles that it had
wrested from the older branch of the Bourbons in almost a hundred
years of struggle; it would barter away its historical prerogative,
the prerogative of the modern kingdom, for the prerogative of its
genealogical tree. The fusion, therefore, would be nothing but a
voluntary abdication of the House of Orleans, its resignation to
Legitimacy, repentant withdrawal from the Protestant state church
into the Catholic. A withdrawal, moreover, that would not even
bring it to the throne which it had lost, but to the throne's steps,
on which it had been born. The old Orleanist ministers, Guizot, Duchâtel, etc., who likewise hastened to Claremont to advocate the
fusion, in fact represented merely the *Katzenjammer** over the July
Revolution, the despair felt in regard to the bourgeois kingdom and
the kingliness of the bourgeois, the superstitious belief in Legitimacy as the last charm against anarchy. Imagining themselves
mediators between Orleans and Bourbon, they were in reality merely

---

* *Katzenjammer*: The "morning-after" feeling.—*Ed.*

Orleanist renegades, and the prince of Joinville received them a
such. On the other hand, the viable, bellicose section of the Orleanists, Thiers, Baze, etc., convinced Louis Philippe's family al
the more easily that if any directly monarchist restoration presupposed the fusion of the two dynasties and if any such fusion, however, presupposed abdication of the House of Orleans, it was, on
the contrary, wholly in accord with the tradition of their forefathers
to recognise the republic for the moment and wait until events
permitted the conversion of the presidential chair into a throne.
Rumours of Joinville's candidature were circulated, public curiosity
was kept in suspense and, a few months later, in September, after
the rejection of revision, his candidature was publicly proclaimed.

The attempt at a royalist fusion of Orleanists with Legitimists
had thus not only failed; it had destroyed their *parliamentary
fusion*, their common republican form, and had broken up the party
of Order into its original component parts; but the more the
estrangement between Claremont and Venice grew, the more their
settlement broke down and the Joinville agitation gained ground, so
much the more eager and earnest became the negotiations between
Bonaparte's minister Faucher and the Legitimists.

The disintegration of the party of Order did not stop at its original
elements. Each of the two great factions, in its turn, underwent
decomposition anew. It was as if all the old nuances that had
formerly fought and jostled one another within each of the two
circles, whether Legitimist or Orleanist, had thawed out again like
dry infusoria on contact with water, as if they had acquired anew
sufficient vital energy to form groups of their own and independent
antagonisms. The Legitimists dreamed that they were back among
the controversies between the Tuileries and the Pavillon Marsan,
between Villèle and Polignac.[100] The Orleanists relived the golden
days of the tourneys between Guizot, Molé, Broglie, Thiers and
Odilon Barrot.

That part of the party of Order which was eager for revision,
but was divided again on the limits to revision, a section composed
of the Legitimists led by Berryer and Falloux, on the one hand,
and by La Rochejaquelein, on the other, and of the conflict-weary
Orleanists led by Molé, Broglie, Montalembert and Odilon Barrot,
agreed with the Bonapartist representatives on the following indefinite and broadly framed motion:

"With the object of restoring to the nation the full exercise of its sovereignty,
the undersigned Representatives move that the Constitution be revised."

At the same time, however, they unanimously declared through
their reporter Tocqueville that the National Assembly had not the
right to move the *abolition of the republic*, that this right was vested

olely in the Revising Chamber. For the rest, the Constitution might
be revised only in a *"legal"* *manner*, hence only if the constitution-
lly prescribed three-quarters of the number of votes were cast in
avour of revision. On July 19, after six days of stormy debate,
evision was rejected, as was to be anticipated. Four hundred and
orty-six votes were cast for it, but two hundred and seventy-eight
gainst. The extreme Orleanists, Thiers, Changarnier, etc., voted
with the republicans and the *Montagne*.

Thus the majority of parliament declared against the Constitu-
:ion, but this Constitution itself declared for the minority and that
its vote was binding. But had not the party of Order subordinated
the Constitution to the parliamentary majority on May 31, 1850,
and on June 13, 1849? Up to now, was not its whole policy based
on the subordination of the paragraphs of the Constitution to the
decisions of the parliamentary majority? Had it not left to the
democrats the antediluvian superstitious belief in the letter of the
law, and castigated the democrats for it? At the present moment,
however, revision of the Constitution meant nothing but continuation of the presidential authority, just as continuation of the Constitution meant nothing but Bonaparte's deposition. Parliament had
declared for him, but the Constitution declared against parliament.
He therefore acted in the sense of parliament when he tore up the
Constitution, and he acted in the sense of the Constitution when he
dispersed parliament.

Parliament had declared the Constitution and, with the latter,
its own rule to be "beyond the majority"; by its vote it had abolished the Constitution and prorogued the presidential power, while
declaring at the same time that neither can the one die nor the
other live so long as it itself continues to exist. Those who were
to bury it were standing at the door. While it debated on revision,
Bonaparte removed General Baraguey d'Hilliers, who had proved
irresolute, from the command of the First Army Division and
appointed in his place General Magnan, the victor of Lyons, the
hero of the December days, one of his creatures, who under Louis
Philippe had already compromised himself more or less in Bonaparte's favour on the occasion of the Boulogne expedition.

The party of Order proved by its decision on revision that it
knew neither how to rule nor how to serve; neither how to live
nor how to die; neither how to suffer the republic nor how to overthrow it; neither how to uphold the Constitution nor how to throw
it overboard; neither how to co-operate with the President nor how
to break with him. To whom, then, did it look for the solution of
all the contradictions? To the calendar, to the course of events.
It ceased to presume to sway the events. It therefore challenged
the events to assume sway over it, and thereby challenged the power
to which in the struggle against the people it had surrendered one

attribute after another until it itself stood impotent before thi power. In order that the head of the executive power might be able the more undisturbedly to draw up his plan of campaign against it, strengthen his means of attack, select his tools and fortify his positions, it resolved precisely at this critical moment to retire from the stage and adjourn for three months, from August 10 to November 4.

The parliamentary party was not only dissolved into its two great factions, each of these factions was not only split up within itself, but the party of Order in parliament had fallen out with the party of Order *outside* parliament. The spokesmen and scribes of the bourgeoisie, its platform and its press, in short, the ideologists of the bourgeoisie and the bourgeoisie itself, the representatives and the represented, faced one another in estrangement and no longer understood one another.

The Legitimists in the provinces, with their limited horizon and their unlimited enthusiasm, accused their parliamentary leaders, Berryer and Falloux, of deserting to the Bonapartist camp and of defection from Henry V. Their fleur-de-lis minds believed in the fall of man, but not in diplomacy.

Far more fateful and decisive was the breach of the commercial bourgeoisie with its politicians. It reproached them, not as the Legitimists reproached theirs, with having abandoned their principles, but, on the contrary, with clinging to principles that had become useless.

I have already indicated above that since Fould's entry into the ministry the section of the commercial bourgeoisie which had held the lion's share of power under Louis Philippe, namely, the *aristocracy of finance*, had become Bonapartist. Fould represented not only Bonaparte's interests in the *bourse*, he represented at the same time the interests of the *bourse* before Bonaparte. The position of the aristocracy of finance is most strikingly depicted in a passage from its European organ, the London *Economist*.[101] In its number of February 1, 1851, its Paris correspondent writes:

"Now we have it stated from numerous quarters that above all things France demands tranquillity. The President declares it in his message to the Legislative Assembly; it is echoed from the tribune; it is asserted in the journals; it is announced from the pulpit; *it is demonstrated by the sensitiveness of the public funds at the least prospect of disturbance, and their firmness the instant it is made manifest that the executive is victorious.*"

In its issue of November 29, 1851, *The Economist* declares in its own name:

"*The President is the guardian of order, and is now recognised as such on every Stock Exchange of Europe.*"

The aristocracy of finance, therefore, condemned the parliamentary struggle of the party of Order with the executive power as a *disturbance of order*, and celebrated every victory of the President over its ostensible representatives as a *victory of order*. By the aristocracy of finance must here be understood not merely the great loan promoters and speculators in public funds, in regard to whom it is immediately obvious that their interests coincide with the interests of the state power. All modern finance, the whole of the banking business, is interwoven in the closest fashion with public credit. A part of their business capital is necessarily invested and put out at interest in quickly convertible public funds. Their deposits, the capital placed at their disposal and distributed by them among merchants and industrialists, are partly derived from the dividends of holders of government securities. If in every epoch the stability of the state power signified Moses and the prophets to the entire money market and to the priests of this money market, why not all the more so today, when every deluge threatens to sweep away the old states, and the old state debts with them?

The *industrial bourgeoisie*, too, in its fanaticism for order, was angered by the squabbles of the parliamentary party of Order with the executive power. After their vote of January 18 on the occasion of Changarnier's dismissal, Thiers, Anglès, Sainte-Beuve, etc., received from their constituents in precisely the industrial districts public reproofs in which particularly their coalition with the *Montagne* was scourged as high treason to order. If, as we have seen, the boastful taunts, the petty intrigues which marked the struggle of the party of Order with the President merited no better reception, then, on the other hand, this bourgeois party, which required its representatives to allow the military power to pass from its own parliament to an adventurous pretender without offering resistance, was not even worth the intrigues that were squandered in its interests. It proved that the struggle to maintain its *public* interests, its own *class interests*, its *political power*, only troubled and upset it, as it was a disturbance of private business.

With barely an exception, the bourgeois dignitaries of the Departmental towns, the municipal authorities, the judges of the Commercial Courts, etc., everywhere received Bonaparte on his tours in the most servile manner, even when, as in Dijon, he made an unrestrained attack on the National Assembly, and especially on the party of Order.

When trade was good, as it still was at the beginning of 1851, the commercial bourgeoisie raged against any parliamentary struggle, lest trade be put out of humour. When trade was bad, as it continually was from the end of February 1851, the commercial bourgeoisie accused the parliamentary struggles of being the cause of stagnation and cried out for them to stop in order that trade might start again. The revision debates came on just in this bad period. Since the question here was whether the existing form of state was to be or not to be, the bourgeoisie felt itself all the more justified in demanding from its Representatives the ending of this torturous provisional arrangement and at the same time the maintenance of the *status quo*. There was no contradiction in this. By the end of the provisional arrangement it understood precisely its continuation, the postponement to a distant future of the moment when a decision had to be reached. The *status quo* could be maintained in only two ways: prolongation of Bonaparte's authority or his constitutional retirement and the election of Cavaignac. A section of the bourgeoisie desired the latter solution and knew no better advice to give its Representatives than to keep silent and leave the burning question untouched. They were of the opinion that if their Representatives did not speak, Bonaparte would not act. They wanted an ostrich parliament that would hide its head in order to remain unseen. Another section of the bourgeoisie desired, because Bonaparte was already in the presidential chair, to leave him sitting in it, so that everything might remain in the same old rut. They were indignant because their parliament did not openly infringe the Constitution and abdicate without ceremony.

The General Councils of the Departments, those provincial representative bodies of the big bourgeoisie, which met from August 25 on during the recess of the National Assembly, declared almost unanimously for revision, and thus against parliament and in favour of Bonaparte.

Still more unequivocally than in its falling out with its *parliamentary representatives* the bourgeoisie displayed its wrath against its literary representatives, its own press. The sentences to ruinous fines and shameless terms of imprisonment, on the verdicts of bourgeois juries, for every attack of bourgeois journalists on Bonaparte's usurpationist desires, for every attempt of the press to defend the political rights of the bourgeoisie against the executive power, astonished not merely France, but all Europe.

While the *parliamentary party of Order*, by its clamour for tranquillity, as I have shown, committed itself to quiescence, while it declared the political rule of the bourgeoisie to be incompatible with the safety and existence of the bourgeoisie, by destroying with its own hands in the struggle against the other classes of society all the conditions for its own regime, the parliamentary regime, the *extra-parliamentary mass of the bourgeoisie*, on the other hand, by its servility towards the President, by its vilification of parliament, by its brutal maltreatment of its own press, invited Bonaparte to suppress and annihilate its speaking and writing section, its politicians and its *literati*, its platform and its press, in order that it might then be able to pursue its private affairs with full confidence in the protection of a strong and unrestricted government. It declared unequivocally that it longed to get rid of its own political rule in order to get rid of the troubles and dangers of ruling.

And this extra-parliamentary bourgeoisie, which had already rebelled against the purely parliamentary and literary struggle for the rule of its own class and betrayed the leaders of this struggle, now dares after the event to indict the proletariat for not having risen in a bloody struggle, a life-and-death struggle on its behalf! This bourgeoisie, which every moment sacrificed its general class interests, that is, its political interests, to the narrowest and most sordid private interests, and demanded a similar sacrifice from its Representatives, now moans that the proletariat has sacrificed its [the bourgeoisie's] ideal political interests to its [the proletariat's] material interests. It poses as a lovely being that has been misunderstood and deserted in the decisive hour by the proletariat misled by Socialists. And it finds a general echo in the bourgeois world. Naturally, I do not speak here of German shyster politicians and riffraff of the same persuasion. I refer, for example, to the already quoted *Economist*, which as late as November 29, 1851, that is, four days prior to the *coup d'état*, had declared Bonaparte to be the "guardian of order," but the Thiers and Berryers to be "anarchists," and on December 27, 1851, after Bonaparte had quieted these anarchists, is already vociferous concerning the treason to "the skill, knowledge, discipline, mental influence, intellectual resources and moral weight of the middle and upper ranks" committed by the masses of "ignorant, untrained, and stupid *proletaires*." The stupid, ignorant and vulgar mass was none other than the bourgeois mass itself.

In the year 1851, France, to be sure, had passed through a kind of minor trade crisis. The end of February showed a decline in exports compared with 1850; in March trade suffered and factories closed down; in April the position of the industrial Departments appeared as desperate as after the February days; in May business had still not revived; as late as June 28 the holdings of the Bank of France showed, by the enormous growth of deposits and the equally great decrease in advances on bills of exchange, that production was at a standstill, and it was not until the middle of October that a progressive improvement of business again set in. The French bourgeoisie attributed this trade stagnation to purely political causes, to the struggle between parliament and the executive power, to the precariousness of a merely provisional form of state, to the terrifying prospect of the second Sunday in May 1852. I will not deny that all these circumstances had a depressing effect on some branches of industry in Paris and the Departments. But in any case this influence of the political conditions was only local and inconsiderable. Does this require further proof than the fact that the improvement of trade set in towards the middle of October, at the very moment when the political situation grew worse, the political horizon darkened and a thunderbolt from Elysium was expected at any moment? For the rest, the French bourgeois, whose "skill, knowledge, spiritual insight and intellectual resources" reach no further than his nose, could throughout the period of the Industrial Exhibition[102] in London have found the cause of his commercial misery right under his nose. While in France factories were closed down, in England commercial bankruptcies broke out. While in April and May the industrial panic reached a climax in France, in April and May the commercial panic reached a climax in England. Like the French woollen industry, so the English woollen industry suffered, and as French silk manufacture, so did English silk manufacture. True, the English cotton mills continued working, but no longer at the same profits as in 1849 and 1850. The only difference was that the crisis in France was industrial, in England commercial; that while in France the factories stood idle, in England they extended operations, but under less favourable conditions than in preceding years; that in France it was exports, in England imports which were hardest hit. The common cause, which is naturally not to be sought within the bounds of the French political horizon, was obvious. The years 1849 and 1850 were years of the greatest material prosperity and of an over-production that appeared as such only in 1851. At the beginning of this year it was given a further special impetus by the prospect of the Industrial Exhibition. In addition there were the following special circumstances: first, the partial failure of the cotton crop in 1850 and 1851, then the certainty of a bigger cotton crop than had been expected; first the rise, then the sudden fall, in short, the fluctuations in the price of cotton. The crop of raw silk, in France at least, had turned out to be even below the average yield. Woollen manufacture, finally, had expanded so much since 1848 that the production of wool would not keep pace with it and the price of raw wool rose out of all proportion to the price of woollen manufactures. Here, then, in the raw material of three industries for the world market, we have already threefold material for a stagnation in trade. Apart from the special circumstances, the apparent crisis of 1851 was nothing else but the halt which over-production and over-speculation invariably make in describing the industrial cycle, before they summon all their strength in order to rush feverishly through the final phase of this cycle and arrive once more at their starting-point, the *general trade crisis*. During such intervals in the history of trade commercial bankruptcies break out in England, while in France industry itself is reduced to idleness, being partly forced into retreat by the competition, just then becoming intolerable, of the English in all markets, and being partly singled out for attack as a luxury industry by every business stagnation. Thus, besides the general crisis, France goes through national trade crises of her own, which are nevertheless determined and conditioned far more by the general state of the world market than by French local influences. It will not be without interest to contrast the judgement of the English bourgeois with the prejudice of the French bourgeois. In its annual trade report for 1851, one of the largest Liverpool houses writes:

"Few years have more thoroughly belied the anticipations formed at their commencement than the one just closed; instead of the great prosperity which was almost unanimously looked for it has proved one of the most discouraging that has been seen for the last quarter of a century—this, of course, refers to the mercantile, not to the manufacturing classes. And yet there certainly were grounds for anticipating the reverse at the beginning of the year—stocks of produce were moderate, money was abundant, and food was cheap, a plentiful harvest well secured, unbroken peace on the Continent and no political or fiscal disturbances at home; indeed, the wings of commerce were never more unfettered.... To what source, then, is this disastrous result to be attributed? We believe in *over-trading* both in imports and exports. Unless our merchants will put more stringent limits to their freedom of action, nothing but a *triennial* panic can keep us in check."*

Now picture to yourself the French bourgeois, how in the throes of this business panic his trade-crazy brain is tortured, set in a whirl and stunned by rumours of *coups d'état* and the restoration of universal suffrage, by the struggle between parliament and the executive power, by the Fronde war between Orleanists and Legitimists, by the communist conspiracies in the south of France, by alleged *Jacqueries* in the Departments of Nièvre and Cher, by the advertisements of the different candidates for the presidency, by the cheapjack slogans of the journals, by the threats of the republicans to uphold the Constitution and universal suffrage by force of arms, by the gospel-preaching émigré heroes *in partibus*,[53] who announced that the world would come to an end on the second Sunday in May 1852—think of all this and you will comprehend why in this unspeakable, deafening chaos of fusion, revision, prorogation, constitution, conspiration, coalition, emigration, usurpation and revolution, the bourgeois madly snorts at his parliamentary republic: "*Rather an end with terror than terror without end!*"

Bonaparte understood this cry. His power of comprehension was sharpened by the growing turbulence of creditors who, with each sunset which brought settling day, the second Sunday in May 1852,[51] nearer, saw a movement of the stars protesting their earthly bills of exchange. They had become veritable astrologers. The National Assembly had blighted Bonaparte's hopes of a constitutional prorogation of his authority; the candidature of the Prince of Joinville forbade further vacillation.

* *The Economist*, January 10, 1852, pp. 29-30.—*Ed.*

If ever an event has, well in advance of its coming, cast its shadow before, it was Bonaparte's *coup d'état*. As early as January 29, 1849, barely a month after his election, he had made a proposal about it to Changarnier. In the summer of 1849 his own Prime Minister, Odilon Barrot, had covertly denounced the policy of *coups d'état*; in the winter of 1850 Thiers had openly done so. In May 1851, Persigny had sought once more to win Changarnier for the *coup*; the *Messager de l'Assemblée*[103] had published an account of these negotiations. During every parliamentary storm, the Bonapartist journals threatened a *coup d'état*, and the nearer the crisis drew, the louder grew their tone. In the orgies that Bonaparte kept up every night with men and women of the "swell mob," as soon as the hour of midnight approached and copious potations had loosened tongues and fired imaginations, the *coup d'état* was fixed for the following morning. Swords were drawn, glasses clinked, the Representatives were thrown out of the window, the imperial mantle fell upon Bonaparte's shoulders, until the following morning banished the spook once more and astonished Paris learned, from vestals of little reticence and from indiscreet paladins, of the danger it had once again escaped. During the months of September and October rumours of a *coup d'état* followed fast one after the other. Simultaneously, the shadow took on colour, like a variegated daguerreotype. Look up the September and October copies of the organs of the European daily press and you will find, word for word, intimations like the following: "Paris is full of rumours of a *coup d'état*. The capital is to be filled with troops during the night, and the next morning is to bring decrees which will dissolve the National Assembly, declare the Department of the Seine in a state of siege, restore universal suffrage and appeal to the people. Bonaparte is said to be seeking ministers for the execution of these illegal decrees." The letters that bring these tidings always end with the fateful word "*postponed*." The *coup d'état* was ever the fixed idea of Bonaparte. With this idea he had again set foot on French soil. He was so obsessed by it that he continually betrayed it and blurted it out. He was so weak that, just as continually, he gave it up again. The shadow of the *coup d'état* had become so familiar to the Parisians as a spectre that they were not willing to believe in it when it finally appeared in the flesh. What allowed the *coup d'état* to succeed was, therefore, neither the reticent reserve of the chief of the Society of December 10 nor the fact that the National Assembly was caught unawares. If it succeeded, it succeeded despite *his* indiscretion and with *its* foreknowledge, a necessary, inevitable result of antecedent development.

On October 10 Bonaparte announced to his ministers his decision to restore universal suffrage; on the sixteenth they handed in their resignations, on the twenty-sixth Paris learned of the formation of the Thorigny ministry. Police Prefect Carlier was simultaneously replaced by Maupas; the head of the First Military Division, Magnan, concentrated the most reliable regiments in the capital. On November 4, the National Assembly resumed its sittings. It had nothing better to do than to recapitulate in a short, succinct form the course it had gone through and to prove that it was buried only after it had died.

The first post that it forfeited in the struggle with the executive power was the ministry. It had solemnly to admit this loss by accepting at full value the Thorigny ministry, a mere shadow cabinet. The Permanent Commission had received M. Giraud with laughter when he presented himself in the name of the new ministers. Such a weak ministry for such strong measures as the restoration of universal suffrage! Yet the precise object was to get nothing through *in* parliament, but everything *against* parliament.

On the very first day of its re-opening, the National Assembly received the message from Bonaparte in which he demanded the restoration of universal suffrage and the abolition of the law of May 31, 1850. The same day his ministers introduced a decree to this effect. The National Assembly at once rejected the ministry's motion of urgency and rejected the law itself on November 13 by three hundred and fifty-five votes to three hundred and forty-eight. Thus, it tore up its mandate once more; it once more confirmed the fact that it had transformed itself from the freely elected representatives of the people into the usurpatory parliament of a class; it acknowledged once more that it had itself cut in two the muscles which connected the parliamentary head with the body of the nation.

If by its motion to restore universal suffrage the executive power appealed from the National Assembly to the people, the legislative power appealed by its Questors' Bill from the people to the army. This Questors' Bill was to establish its right of directly requisitioning troops, of forming a parliamentary army. While it thus designated the army as the arbitrator between itself and the people, between itself and Bonaparte, while it recognised the army as the decisive state power, it had to confirm, on the other hand, the fact that it had long given up its claim to dominate this power. By debating its right to requisition troops, instead of requisitioning them at once, it betrayed its doubts about its own powers. By rejecting the Questors' Bill, it made public confession of its impotence. This bill was defeated, its proponents lacking 108 votes of a majority. The *Montagne* thus decided the issue. It found itself in the position of Buridan's ass, not, indeed, between two bundles of hay with the problem of deciding which was the more attractive, but between two showers of blows with the problem of deciding which was the harder. On the one hand, there was the fear of Changarnier; on the

other, the fear of Bonaparte. It must be confessed that the position
was no heroic one.

On November 18, an amendment was moved to the law on municipal elections introduced by the party of Order, to the effect that
instead of three years', one year's domicile should suffice for municipal electors. The amendment was lost by a single vote, but this
one vote immediately proved to be a mistake. By splitting up into
its hostile factions, the party of Order had long ago forfeited its
independent parliamentary majority. It showed now that there was
no longer any majority at all in parliament. The National Assembly
had become *incapable of transacting business*. Its atomic constituents were no longer held together by any force of cohesion; it had
drawn its last breath; it was dead.

Finally, a few days before the catastrophe, the extra-parliamentary mass of the bourgeoisie was solemnly to confirm once more its
breach with the bourgeoisie in parliament. Thiers, as a parliamentary hero infected more than the rest with the incurable disease of
parliamentary cretinism, had, after the death of parliament, hatched
out, together with the Council of State, a new parliamentary intrigue, a Responsibility Law by which the President was to be firmly
held within the limits of the Constitution. Just as, on laying the
foundation stone of the new market halls in Paris on September 15,
Bonaparte, like a second Masaniello, had enchanted the *dames des
halles*, the fishwives—to be sure, one fishwife outweighed seventeen
burgraves in real power; just as after the introduction of the Questors' Bill he enraptured the lieutenants he regaled in the Elysée, so
now, on November 25, he swept off their feet the industrial bourgeoisie, which had gathered at the circus to receive at his hands
prize medals for the London Industrial Exhibition. I shall give
the significant portion of his speech as reported in the *Journal des
Débats*[62]:

"With such unhoped-for successes, I am justified in reiterating how great the
French republic would be if it were permitted to pursue its real interests and
reform its institutions, instead of being constantly disturbed by demagogues, on
the one hand, and by monarchist hallucinations, on the other. (Loud, stormy and
repeated applause from every part of the amphitheatre.) The monarchist hallucinations hinder all progress and all important branches of industry. In place of
progress nothing but struggle. One sees men who were formerly the most zealous
supporters of the royal authority and prerogative become partisans of a Convention merely in order to weaken the authority that has sprung from universal
suffrage. (Loud and repeated applause.) We see men who have suffered most
from the Revolution, and have deplored it most, provoke a new one, and merely
in order to fetter the nation's will.... I promise you tranquillity for the future,
etc., etc. (Bravo, bravo, a storm of bravos.)"

Thus the industrial bourgeoisie applauds with servile bravos the
coup d'état of December 2, the annihilation of parliament, the

downfall of its own rule, the dictatorship of Bonaparte The thunder of applause on November 25 had its answer in the thunder of cannon on December 4, and it was on the house of Monsieur Sallandrouze, who had clapped most, that they clapped most of the bombs.

Cromwell, when he dissolved the Long Parliament,[104] went alone into its midst, drew out his watch in order that it should not continue to exist a minute after the time limit fixed by him, and drove out each one of the members of parliament with hilariously humorous taunts. Napoleon, smaller than his prototype, at least betook himself on the eighteenth Brumaire to the legislative body and read out to it, though in a faltering voice, its sentence of death. The second Bonaparte, who, moreover, found himself in possession of an executive power very different from that of Cromwell or Napoleon, sought his model not in the annals of world history, but in the annals of the Society of December 10, in the annals of the criminal courts. He robs the Bank of France of twenty-five million francs, buys General Magnan with a million, the soldiers with fifteen francs apiece and liquor, comes together with his accomplices secretly like a thief in the night, has the houses of the most dangerous parliamentary leaders broken into and Cavaignac, Lamoricière, Le Flô, Changarnier, Charras, Thiers, Baze, etc., dragged from their beds, the chief squares of Paris and the parliamentary building occupied by troops, and cheapjack placards posted early in the morning on all the walls, proclaiming the dissolution of the National Assembly and the Council of State, the restoration of universal suffrage and the placing of the Seine Department in a state of siege. In like manner, he inserted a little later in the *Moniteur* a false document which asserted that influential parliamentarians had grouped themselves round him and formed a state *consulta*.

The rump parliament, assembled in the *mairie* building of the tenth *arrondissement* and consisting mainly of Legitimists and Orleanists, votes the deposition of Bonaparte amid repeated cries of "Long live the Republic," unavailingly harangues the gaping crowds before the building and is finally led off in the custody of African sharpshooters, first to the d'Orsay barracks, and later packed into prison vans and transported to the prisons of Mazas, Ham and Vincennes. Thus ended the party of Order, the Legislative Assembly and the February Revolution. Before hastening to close, let us briefly summarise the latter's history:

I. *First period.* From February 24 to May 4, 1848. February period. Prologue. Universal brotherhood swindle.

II. *Second period.* Period of constituting the republic and of the Constituent National Assembly.

1. May 4 to June 25, 1848. Struggle of all classes against the proletariat. Defeat of the proletariat in the June days.

2. June 25 to December 10, 1848. Dictatorship of the pure bourgeois-republicans. Drafting of the Constitution. Proclamation of a state of siege in Paris. The bourgeois dictatorship set aside on December 10 by the election of Bonaparte as President.

3. December 20, 1848 to May 28, 1849. Struggle of the Constituent Assembly with Bonaparte and with the party of Order in alliance with him. Passing of the Constituent Assembly. Fall of the republican bourgeoisie.

III. *Third period.* Period of the *constitutional republic* and of the *Legislative National Assembly.*

1. May 28, 1849 to June 13, 1849. Struggle of the petty bourgeoisie with the bourgeoisie and with Bonaparte. Defeat of the petty-bourgeois democracy.

2. June 13, 1849 to May 31, 1850. Parliamentary dictatorship of the party of Order. It completes its rule by abolishing universal suffrage, but loses the parliamentary ministry.

3. May 31, 1850 to December 2, 1851. Struggle between the parliamentary bourgeoisie and Bonaparte.

(a) May 31, 1850 to January 12, 1851. Parliament loses the supreme command of the army.

(b) January 12 to April 11, 1851. It is worsted in its attempts to regain the administrative power. The party of Order loses its independent parliamentary majority. Its coalition with the republicans and the *Montagne.*

(c) April 11, 1851 to October 9, 1851. Attempts at revision, fusion, prorogation. The party of Order decomposes into its separate constituents. The breach between the bourgeois parliament and press and the mass of the bourgeoisie becomes definite.

(d) October 9 to December 2, 1851. Open breach between parliament and the executive power. Parliament performs its dying act and succumbs, left in the lurch by its own class, by the army and by all the remaining classes. Passing of the parliamentary regime and of bourgeois rule. Victory of Bonaparte. Parody of restoration of empire.

VII

On the threshold of the February Revolution, the *social republic* appeared as a phrase, as a prophecy. In the June days of 1848, it was drowned in the blood of the *Paris proletariat*, but it haunts the subsequent acts of the drama like a ghost. The *democratic republic* announces its arrival. On June 13, 1849, it is dissipated together with its *petty bourgeois*, who have taken to their heels, but in its flight it blows its own trumpet with redoubled boastfulness. The *parliamentary republic*, together with the bourgeoisie, takes possession of the entire stage; it enjoys its existence to the full, but December 2, 1851 buries it to the accompaniment of the anguished cry of the royalists in coalition: "Long live the Republic!"

The French bourgeoisie balked at the domination of the working proletariat; it has brought the *lumpenproletariat* to domination, with the chief of the Society of December 10 at the head. The bourgeoisie kept France in breathless fear of the future terrors of red anarchy; Bonaparte discounted this future for it when, on December 4, he had the eminent bourgeois of the Boulevard Montmartre and the Boulevard des Italiens shot down at their windows by the liquor-inspired army of order. It apotheosised the sword; the sword rules it. It destroyed the revolutionary press; its own press has been destroyed. It placed popular meetings under police supervision; its salons are under the supervision of the police. It disbanded the democratic National Guards; its own National Guard is disbanded. It imposed a state of siege; a state of siege is imposed upon it. It supplanted the juries by military commissions; its juries are supplanted by military commissions. It subjected public education to the sway of the priests; the priests subject it to their own education. It transported people without trial; it is being transported without trial. It repressed every stirring in society by means of the state power; every stirring in its society is suppressed by means of the state power. Out of enthusiasm for its purse, it rebelled against its own politicians and men of letters; its politicians and men of letters are swept aside, but its purse is being plundered now that its mouth has been gagged and its pen broken. The bourgeoisie never wearied of crying out to the revolution what Saint Arsenius cried out to the Christians: "*Fuge, tace, quiesce!* Flee, be silent, keep still!" Bonaparte cries to the bourgeoisie: "*Fuge, tace, quiesce!* Flee, be silent, keep still!"

The French bourgeoisie had long ago found the solution to Napoleon's dilemma: "*Dans cinquante ans l'Europe sera républicaine ou cosaque.*"* It had found the solution to it in the "*république cosaque.*" No Circe, by means of black magic, has distorted that work of art, the bourgeois republic, into a monstrous shape. That republic has lost nothing but the semblance of respectability. Present-day** France was contained in a finished state within the parliamentary republic. It only required a bayonet thrust for the bubble to burst and the monster to spring forth before our eyes.

Why did the Paris proletariat not rise in revolt after December 2?

The overthrow of the bourgeoisie had as yet been only decreed; the decree had not been carried out. Any serious insurrection of the proletariat would at once have put fresh life into the bourgeoisie,

---

* "In fifty years Europe will be republican or Cossack."—*Ed.*
** i.e., after the *coup d'état* of 1851.—*Ed.*

would have reconciled it with the army and ensured a second June defeat for the workers.

On December 4 the proletariat was incited by bourgeois and *épicier* to fight. On the evening of that day several legions of the National Guard promised to appear, armed and uniformed, on the scene of battle. For the bourgeois and the *épicier* had got wind of the fact that in one of his decrees of December 2 Bonaparte abolished the secret ballot and enjoined them to record their "yes" or "no" in the official registers after their names. The resistance of December 4 intimidated Bonaparte. During the night he caused placards to be posted on all the street corners of Paris, announcing the restoration of the secret ballot. The bourgeois and the *épicier* believed that they had gained their end. Those who failed to appear next morning were the bourgeois and the *épicier*.

By a *coup de main* during the night of December 1 to 2, Bonaparte had robbed the Paris proletariat of its leaders, the barricade commanders. An army without officers, averse to fighting under the banner of the *Montagnards* because of the memories of June 1848 and 1849 and May 1850, it left to its vanguard, the secret societies, the task of saving the insurrectionary honour of Paris, which the bourgeoisie had so unresistingly surrendered to the soldiery that, later on, Bonaparte could sneeringly give as his motive for disarming the National Guard—his fear that its arms would be turned against it itself by the anarchists!

"*C'est le triomphe complet et définitif du Socialisme!*"* Thus Guizot characterised December 2. But if the overthrow of the parliamentary republic contains within itself the germ of the triumph of the proletarian revolution, its immediate and palpable result was *the victory of Bonaparte over parliament, of the executive power over the legislative power, of force without phrases over the force of phrases.* In parliament the nation made its general will the law, that is, it made the law of the ruling class its general will. Before the executive power it renounces all will of its own and submits to the superior command of an alien will, to authority. The executive power, in contrast to the legislative power, expresses the heteronomy of a nation, in contrast to its autonomy. France, therefore, seems to have escaped the despotism of a class only to fall back beneath the despotism of an individual, and, what is more, beneath the authority of an individual without authority. The struggle seems to be settled in such a way that all classes, equally impotent and equally mute, fall on their knees before the rifle butt.

But the revolution is thoroughgoing. It is still journeying through purgatory. It does its work methodically. By December 2, 1851, it had completed one half of its preparatory work; it is now completing

---

* "This is the complete and final triumph of socialism!"—*Ed.*

the other half. First it perfected the parliamentary power, in order to be able to overthrow it. Now that it has attained this, it perfects the *executive power*, reduces it to its purest expression, isolates it, sets it up against itself as the sole target, in order to concentrate all its forces of destruction against it. And when it has done this second half of its preliminary work, Europe will leap from its seat and exultantly exclaim: Well grubbed, old mole!*

This executive power with its enormous bureaucratic and military organisation, with its ingenious state machinery, embracing wide strata, with a host of officials numbering half a million, besides an army of another half million, this appalling parasitic body, which enmeshes the body of French society like a net and chokes all its pores, sprang up in the days of the absolute monarchy, with the decay of the feudal system, which it helped to hasten. The seignorial privileges of the landowners and towns became transformed into so many attributes of the state power, the feudal dignitaries into paid officials and the motley pattern of conflicting mediaeval plenary powers into the regulated plan of a state authority whose work is divided and centralised as in a factory. The first French Revolution, with its task of breaking all separate local, territorial, urban and provincial powers in order to create the civil unity of the nation, was bound to develop what the absolute monarchy had begun: centralisation, but at the same time the extent, the attributes and the agents of governmental power. Napoleon perfected this state machinery. The Legitimist monarchy and the July monarchy added nothing but a greater division of labour, growing in the same measure as the division of labour within bourgeois society created new groups of interests, and, therefore, new material for state administration. Every *common* interest was straightway severed from society, counterposed to it as a higher, *general* interest, snatched from the activity of society's members themselves and made an object of government activity, from a bridge, a schoolhouse and the communal property of a village community to the railways, the national wealth and the national university of France. Finally, in its struggle against the revolution, the parliamentary republic found itself compelled to strengthen, along with the repressive measures, the resources and centralisation of governmental power. All revolutions perfected this machine instead of smashing it. The parties that contended in turn for domination regarded the possession of this huge state edifice as the principal spoils of the victor.

But under the absolute monarchy, during the first Revolution, under Napoleon, bureaucracy was only the means of preparing the class rule of the bourgeoisie. Under the Restoration, under Louis Philippe, under the parliamentary republic, it was the

* Shakespeare, *Hamlet*, Act I, Scene V.—*Ed.*

instrument of the ruling class, however much it strove for power of its own.

Only under the second Bonaparte does the state seem to have made itself completely independent. As against civil society, the state machine has consolidated its position so thoroughly that the chief of the Society of December 10 suffices for its head, an adventurer blown in from abroad, raised on the shield by a drunken soldiery, which he has bought with liquor and sausages, and which he must continually ply with sausage anew. Hence the downcast despair, the feeling of most dreadful humiliation and degradation that oppresses the breast of France and makes her catch her breath. She feels dishonoured.

And yet the state power is not suspended in mid air. Bonaparte represents a class, and the most numerous class of French society at that, the *small-holding* [*Parzellen*] *peasants*.

Just as the Bourbons were the dynasty of big landed property and just as the Orleans were the dynasty of money, so the Bonapartes are the dynasty of the peasants, that is, the mass of the French people. Not the Bonaparte who submitted to the bourgeois parliament, but the Bonaparte who dispersed the bourgeois parliament is the chosen of the peasantry. For three years the towns had succeeded in falsifying the meaning of the election of December 10 and in cheating the peasants out of the restoration of the empire. The election of December 10, 1848, has been consummated only by the *coup d'état* of December 2, 1851.

The small-holding peasants form a vast mass, the members of which live in similar conditions but without entering into manifold relations with one another. Their mode of production isolates them from one another instead of bringing them into mutual intercourse. The isolation is increased by France's bad means of communication and by the poverty of the peasants. Their field of production, the small holding, admits of no division of labour in its cultivation, no application of science and, therefore, no diversity of development, no variety of talent, no wealth of social relationships. Each individual peasant family is almost self-sufficient; it itself directly produces the major part of its consumption and thus acquires its means of life more through exchange with nature than in intercourse with society. A small holding, a peasant and his family; alongside them another small holding, another peasant and another family. A few score of these make up a village, and a few score of villages make up a Department. In this way, the great mass of the French nation is formed by simple addition of homologous magnitudes, much as potatoes in a sack form a sack of potatoes. In so far as millions of families live under economic conditions of existence that separate their mode of life, their interests and their culture from those of the other classes, and put them in hostile opposition to the latter, they form a class. In so far as there is merely a local inter-connection among these small-holding peasants, and the identity of their interests begets no community, no national bond and no polit-ical organisation among them, they do not form a class. They are consequently incapable of enforcing their class interests in their own name, whether through a parliament or through a convention. They cannot represent themselves, they must be represented. Their rep-resentative must at the same time appear as their master, as an authority over them, as an unlimited governmental power that pro-tects them against the other classes and sends them rain and sun-shine from above. The political influence of the small-holding peas-ants, therefore, finds its final expression in the executive power subordinating society to itself.

Historical tradition gave rise to the belief of the French peasants in the miracle that a man named Napoleon would bring all the glory back to them. And an individual turned up who gives himself out as the man because he bears the name of Napoleon, in consequence of the *Code Napoléon*, which lays down that *la recherche de la pa-ternité est interdite.** After a vagabondage of twenty years and after a series of grotesque adventures, the legend finds fulfilment and the man becomes Emperor of the French. The fixed idea of the Nephew was realised, because it coincided with the fixed idea of the most numerous class of the French people.

But, it may be objected, what about the peasant risings in half of France, the raids on the peasants by the army, the mass incar-ceration and transportation of peasants?

Since Louis XIV, France has experienced no similar persecution of the peasants "on account of demagogic practices."

But let there be no misunderstanding. The Bonaparte dynasty rep-resents not the revolutionary, but the conservative peasant; not the peasant that strikes out beyond the condition of his social existence, the small holding, but rather the peasant who wants to consolidate this holding, not the country folk who, linked up with the towns, want to overthrow the old order through their own energies, but on the contrary those who, in stupefied seclusion within this old order, want to see themselves and their small holdings saved and favoured by the ghost of the empire. It represents not the enlightenment, but the superstition of the peasant; not his judgement, but his preju-dice; not his future, but his past; not his modern Cévennes,[105] but his modern Vendée.

The three years' rigorous rule of the parliamentary republic had freed a part of the French peasants from the Napoleonic illusion and had revolutionised them, even if only superficially; but the

---

* Inquiry into paternity is forbidden.—*Ed.*

bourgeoisie violently repressed them, as often as they set themselves
in motion. Under the parliamentary republic the modern and the
traditional consciousness of the French peasant contended for mastery. This progress took the form of an incessant struggle between
the schoolmasters and the priests. The bourgeoisie struck down the
schoolmasters. For the first time the peasants made efforts to behave
independently in the face of the activity of the government. This was
shown in the continual conflict between the *maires* and the prefects.
The bourgeoisie deposed the *maires*. Finally, during the period of
the parliamentary republic, the peasants of different localities rose
against their own offspring, the army. The bourgeoisie punished
them with states of siege and punitive expeditions. And this same
bourgeoisie now cries out about the stupidity of the masses, the vile
multitude, that has betrayed it to Bonaparte. It has itself forcibly
strengthened the empire sentiments [*Imperialismus*] of the peasant
class, it conserved the conditions that form the birthplace of this
peasant religion. The bourgeoisie, to be sure, is bound to fear the
stupidity of the masses as long as they remain conservative, and
the insight of the masses as soon as they become revolutionary.

In the risings after the *coup d'état*, a part of the French peasants
protested, arms in hand, against their own vote of December 10,
1848. The school they had gone through since 1848 had sharpened
their wits. But they had made themselves over to the underworld
of history; history held them to their word, and the majority was
still so prejudiced that in precisely the reddest Departments the
peasant population voted openly for Bonaparte. In its view, the
National Assembly had hindered his progress. He had now merely
broken the fetters that the towns had imposed on the will of the
countryside. In some parts the peasants even entertained the
grotesque notion of a convention side by side with Napoleon.[106]

After the first revolution had transformed the peasants from semi-
villeins into freeholders, Napoleon confirmed and regulated the conditions on which they could exploit undisturbed the soil of France
which had only just fallen to their lot and slake their youthful passion for property. But what is now causing the ruin of the French
peasant is his small holding itself, the division of the land, the form
of property which Napoleon consolidated in France. It is precisely
the material conditions which made the feudal peasant a small-
holding peasant and Napoleon an emperor. Two generations have
sufficed to produce the inevitable result: progressive deterioration
of agriculture, progressive indebtedness of the agriculturist. The
"Napoleonic" form of property, which at the beginning of the nineteenth century was the condition for the liberation and enrichment
of the French country folk, has developed in the course of this century into the law of their enslavement and pauperisation. And precisely this law is the first of the "*idées napoléoniennes*" which the

second Bonaparte has to uphold. If he still shares with the peasants the illusion that the cause of their ruin is to be sought, not in this small-holding property itself, but outside it, in the influence of secondary circumstances, his experiments will burst like soap bubbles when they come in contact with the relations of production.

The economic development of small-holding property has radically changed the relation of the peasants to the other classes of society. Under Napoleon, the fragmentation of the land in the countryside supplemented free competition and the beginning of big industry in the towns. The peasant class was the ubiquitous protest against the landed aristocracy which had just been overthrown. The roots that small-holding property struck in French soil deprived feudalism of all nutriment. Its landmarks formed the natural fortifications of the bourgeoisie against any surprise attack on the part of its old overlords. But in the course of the nineteenth century the feudal lords were replaced by urban usurers; the feudal obligation that went with the land was replaced by the mortgage; aristocratic landed property was replaced by bourgeois capital. The small holding of the peasant is now only the pretext that allows the capitalist to draw profits, interest and rent from the soil, while leaving it to the tiller of the soil himself to see how he can extract his wages. The mortgage debt burdening the soil of France imposes on the French peasantry payment of an amount of interest equal to the annual interest on the entire British national debt. Small-holding property, in this enslavement by capital to which its development inevitably pushes forward, has transformed the mass of the French nation into troglodytes. Sixteen million peasants (including women and children) dwell in hovels, a large number of which have but one opening, others only two and the most favoured only three. And windows are to a house what the five senses are to the head. The bourgeois order, which at the beginning of the century set the state to stand guard over the newly arisen small holding and manured it with laurels, has become a vampire that sucks out its blood and brains and throws them into the alchemistic cauldron of capital. The *Code Napoléon* is now nothing but a *codex* of distraints, forced sales and compulsory auctions. To the four million (including children, etc.) officially recognised paupers, vagabonds, criminals and prostitutes in France must be added five million who hover on the margin of existence and either have their haunts in the countryside itself or, with their rags and their children, continually desert the countryside for the towns and the towns for the countryside. The interests of the peasants, therefore, are no longer, as under Napoleon, in accord with, but in opposition to the interests of the bourgeoisie, to capital. Hence the peasants find their natural ally and leader in the *urban proletariat*, whose task is the overthrow of the bourgeois order. But *strong and unlimited government*—and this is

the second "*idée napoléonienne*", which the second Napoleon has to
carry out—is called upon to defend this "material" order by force.
This "*ordre matériel*" also serves as the catchword in all of Bonaparte's proclamations against the rebellious peasants.

Besides the mortgage which capital imposes on it, the small holding is burdened by taxes. Taxes are the source of life for the bureaucracy, the army, the priests and the court, in short, for the whole
apparatus of the executive power. Strong government and heavy
taxes are identical. By its very nature, small-holding property forms
a suitable basis for an all-powerful and innumerable bureaucracy.
It creates a uniform level of relationships and persons over the whole
surface of the land. Hence it also permits of uniform action from
a supreme centre on all points of this uniform mass. It annihilates
the aristocratic intermediate grades between the mass of the people
and the state power. On all sides, therefore, it calls forth the direct
interference of this state power and the interposition of its immediate organs. Finally, it produces an unemployed surplus population for which there is no place either on the land or in the towns,
and which accordingly reaches out for state offices as a sort of respectable alms, and provokes the creation of state posts. By the new
markets which he opened at the point of the bayonet, by the plundering of the Continent, Napoleon repaid the compulsory taxes with
interest. These taxes were a spur to the industry of the peasant,
whereas now they rob his industry of its last resources and complete his inability to resist pauperism. And an enormous bureaucracy, well-gallooned and well-fed, is the "*idée napoléonienne*"
which is most congenial of all to the second Bonaparte. How could
it be otherwise, seeing that alongside the actual classes of society he
is forced to create an artificial caste, for which the maintenance of
his regime becomes a bread-and-butter question? Accordingly, one
of his first financial operations was the raising of officials' salaries
to their old level and the creation of new sinecures.

Another "*idée napoléonienne*" is the domination of the *priests* as
an instrument of government. But while in its accord with society,
in its dependence on natural forces and its submission to the authority which protected it from above, the small holding that had
newly come into being was naturally religious, the small holding that
is ruined by debts, at odds with society and authority, and driven
beyond its own limitations naturally becomes irreligious. Heaven
was quite a pleasing accession to the narrow strip of land just won,
more particularly as it makes the weather; it becomes an insult as
soon as it is thrust forward as substitute for the small holding. The
priest then appears as only the anointed bloodhound of the earthly
police—another "*idée napoléonienne*." On the next occasion, the expedition against Rome will take place in France itself, but in a sense
opposite to that of M. de Montalembert.

Lastly, the culminating point of the *"idées napoléoniennes"* is the preponderance of the *army*. The army was the *point d'honneur** of the small-holding peasants, it was they themselves transformed into heroes, defending their new possessions against the outer world, glorifying their recently won nationhood, plundering and revolutionising the world. The uniform was their own state dress: war was their poetry; the small holding, extended and rounded off in imagination, was their fatherland, and patriotism the ideal form of the sense of property. But the enemies against whom the French peasant has now to defend his property are not the Cossacks; they are the *huissiers*** and the tax collectors. The small holding lies no longer in the so-called fatherland, but in the register of mortgages. The army itself is no longer the flower of the peasant youth; it is the swamp-flower of the peasant *lumpenproletariat*. It consists in large measure of *remplaçants*, of substitutes, just as the second Bonaparte is himself only a *remplaçant*, the substitute for Napoleon. It now performs its deeds of valour by hounding the peasants in masses like chamois, by doing *gendarme* duty, and if the internal contradictions of his system chase the chief of the Society of December 10 over the French border, his army, after some acts of brigandage, will reap, not laurels, but thrashings.

One sees: *all* "idées napoléoniennes" *are ideas of the undeveloped small holding in the freshness of its youth*; for the small holding that has outlived its day they are an absurdity. They are only the hallucinations of its death struggle, words that are transformed into phrases, spirits transformed into ghosts. But the parody of the empire *[des Imperialismus]* was necessary to free the mass of the French nation from the weight of tradition and to work out in pure form the opposition between the state power and society. With the progressive undermining of small-holding property, the state structure erected upon it collapses. The centralisation of the state that modern society requires arises only on the ruins of the military-bureaucratic government machinery which was forged in opposition to feudalism.***

The condition of the French peasants provides us with the answer to the riddle of the *general elections of December 20 and 21,*

---

* Matter of honour, a point of special touch.—*Ed.*
** *Huissiers*: Bailiffs.—*Ed.*
*** In the 1852 edition this paragraph ended with the following lines, which Marx omitted in the 1869 edition: "The demolition of the state machine will not endanger centralisation. Bureaucracy is only the low and brutal form of a centralisation that is still afflicted with its opposite, with feudalism. When he is disappointed in the Napoleonic Restoration, the French peasant will part with his belief in his small holding, the entire state edifice erected on this small holding will fall to the ground and *the proletarian revolution will obtain that chorus without which its solo song becomes a swan song in all peasant countries.*" —*Ed.*

which bore the second Bonaparte up Mount Sinai,[107] not to receive laws, but to give them.

Manifestly, the bourgeoisie had now no choice but to elect Bonaparte. When the puritans at the Council of Constance[108] complained of the dissolute lives of the popes and wailed about the necessity of moral reform, Cardinal Pierre d'Ailly thundered at them: "Only the devil in person can still save the Catholic Church, and you ask for angels." In like manner, after the *coup d'état*, the French bourgeoisie cried: Only the chief of the Society of December 10 can still save bourgeois society! Only theft can still save property; only perjury, religion; bastardy, the family; disorder, order!

As the executive authority which has made itself an independent power, Bonaparte feels it to be his mission to safeguard "bourgeois order." But the strength of this bourgeois order lies in the middle class. He looks on himself, therefore, as the representative of the middle class and issues decrees in this sense. Nevertheless, he is somebody solely due to the fact that he has broken the political power of this middle class and daily breaks it anew. Consequently, he looks on himself as the adversary of the political and literary power of the middle class. But by protecting its material power, he generates its political power anew. The cause must accordingly be kept alive; but the effect, where it manifests itself, must be done away with. But this cannot pass off without slight confusions of cause and effect, since in their interaction both lose their distinguishing features. New decrees that obliterate the border line. As against the bourgeoisie, Bonaparte looks on himself, at the same time, as the representative of the peasants and of the people in general, who wants to make the lower classes of the people happy within the frame of bourgeois society. New decrees that cheat the "True Socialists"[109] of their statecraft in advance. But, above all, Bonaparte looks on himself as the chief of the Society of December 10, as the representative of the *lumpenproletariat* to which he himself, his entourage, his government and his army belong, and whose prime consideration is to benefit itself and draw California lottery prizes from the state treasury. And he vindicates his position as chief of the Society of December 10 with decrees, without decrees and despite decrees.

This contradictory task of the man explains the contradictions of his government, the confused groping about which seeks now to win, now to humiliate first one class and then another and arrays all of them uniformly against him, whose practical uncertainty forms a highly comical contrast to the imperious, categorical style of the government decrees, a style which is faithfully copied from the Uncle.

Industry and trade, hence the business affairs of the middle class, are to prosper in hothouse fashion under the strong government. The grant of innumerable railway concessions. But the Bonapartist *lumpenproletariat* is to enrich itself. The initiated play *tripotage** on the *bourse* with the railway concessions. But no capital is forthcoming for the railways. Obligation of the Bank to make advances on railway shares. But, at the same time, the Bank is to be exploited for personal ends and therefore must be cajoled. Release of the Bank from the obligation to publish its report weekly. Leonine agreement of the Bank with the government. The people are to be given employment. Initiation of public works. But the public works increase the obligations of the people in respect of taxes. Hence reduction of the taxes by an onslaught on the *rentiers*, by conversion of the five per cent bonds to four-and-a-half per cent. But, once more, the middle class must receive a *douceur.*** Therefore doubling of the wine tax for the people, who buy it *en détail*, and halving of the wine tax for the middle class, who drink it *en gros*. Dissolution of the actual workers' associations, but promises of miracles of association in the future. The peasants are to be helped. Mortgage banks that expedite their getting into debt and accelerate the concentration of property. But these banks are to be used to make money out of the confiscated estates of the House of Orleans. No capitalist wants to agree to this condition, which is not in the decree, and the mortgage bank remains a mere decree, etc., etc.

Bonaparte would like to appear as the patriarchal benefactor of all classes. But he cannot give to one class without taking from another. Just as at the time of the Fronde it was said of the Duke of Guise that he was the most *obligeant* man in France because he had turned all his estates into his partisans' obligations to him, so Bonaparte would fain be the most *obligeant* man in France and turn all the property, all the labour of France into a personal obligation to himself. He would like to steal the whole of France in order to be able to make a present of her to France or, rather, in order to be able to buy France anew with French money, for as the chief of the Society of December 10 he must needs buy what ought to belong to him. And all the state institutions, the Senate, the Council of State, the legislative body, the Legion of Honour, the soldiers' medals, the washhouses, the public works, the railways, the *état-major**** of the National Guard to the exclusion of privates, and the confiscated estates of the House of Orleans—all become parts of the institution of purchase. Every place in the army and in the government machine becomes a means of purchase. But the most important feature

---

* *Tripotage*: Hanky-panky.—*Ed.*
** *Douceur*: Sop.—*Ed.*
*** *État-major*: General Staff.—*Ed.*

of this process, whereby France is taken in order to give to
her, is the percentages that find their way into the pockets of the
head and the members of the Society of December 10 during the
turnover. The witticism with which Countess L., the mistress of M.
de Morny, characterised the confiscation of the Orleans estates:
"*C'est le premier vol* de l'aigle*"** is applicable to every flight of
this *eagle,* which is more like a *raven.* He himself and his adherents call out to one another daily like that Italian Carthusian
admonishing the miser who, with boastful display, counted up the
goods on which he could yet live for years to come. "*Tu fai conto
sopra i beni, bisogna prima far il conto sopra gli anni.*"*** Lest they
make a mistake in the years, they count the minutes. A bunch of
blokes push their way forward to the court, into the ministries, to
the head of the administration and the army, a crowd of the best
of whom it must be said that no one knows whence he comes, a
noisy, disreputable, rapacious bohème that crawls into gallooned
coats with the same grotesque dignity as the high dignitaries of
Soulouque. One can visualise clearly this upper stratum of the
Society of December 10, if one reflects that *Uéron-Crevel**) is its
preacher of morals and *Granier de Cassagnac* its thinker. When
Guizot, at the time of his ministry, utilised this Granier on a hole-
and-corner newspaper against the dynastic opposition, he used to
boast of him with the quip: "*C'est le roi des drôles,*" "he is the king
of buffoons." One would do wrong to recall the Regency[110] or Louis
XV in connection with Louis Bonaparte's court and clique. For
"often already, France has experienced a government of mistresses;
but never before a government of *hommes entretenus.*"**)
Driven by the contradictory demands of his situation and being
at the same time, like a conjurer, under the necessity of keeping
the public gaze fixed on himself, as Napoleon's substitute, by springing constant surprises, that is to say, under the necessity of executing a *coup d'état en miniature* every day, Bonaparte throws the
entire bourgeois economy into confusion, violates everything that
seemed inviolable to the Revolution of 1848, makes some tolerant of
revolution, others desirous of revolution, and produces actual anarchy in the name of order, while at the same time stripping its halo
from the entire state machine, profanes it and makes it at once loath-

---

* *Vol* means flight and theft. [*Note by Marx.*]
** "It is the first flight (theft) of the eagle."—*Ed.*
*** "Thou countest thy goods, thou shouldst first count thy years." [*Note by
Marx.*]
*) In his work, *Cousine Bette,* Balzac delineates the thoroughly dissolute
Parisian philistine in Crevel, a character which he draws after the model of
Dr. Véron, the proprietor of the *Constitutionnel.* [*Note by Marx.*]
**) The words quoted are those of Madame Girardin. [*Note by Marx.*] *Hommes
entretenus*: Kept men.—*Ed.*

some and ridiculous. The cult of the Holy Tunic of Treves[111] he duplicates at Paris in the cult of the Napoleonic imperial mantle. But when the imperial mantle finally falls on the shoulders of Louis Bonaparte, the bronze statue of Napoleon will crash from the top of the Vendôme Column.[112]

Written by Marx in December 1851-
March 1852

Published in the first issue
of the journal *Die Revolution*,
New York, 1852

Signed: *Karl Marx*

Printed according to the 1869
edition checked with the 1852
and 1885 editions

Translated from the German

Karl Marx

PREFACE TO *A CONTRIBUTION TO THE CRITIQUE OF POLITICAL ECONOMY*[113]

I examine the system of bourgeois economics in the following order: *capital, landed property, wage labour; state, foreign trade, world market.* Under the first three headings, I investigate the economic conditions of life of the three great classes into which modern bourgeois society is divided; the interconnection of the three other headings is obvious at a glance. The first section of the first book, which deals with capital, consists of the following chapters: 1. Commodities; 2. Money, or simple circulation; 3. Capital in general. The first two chapters form the contents of the present part. The total material lies before me in the form of monographs, which were written at widely separated periods, for self-clarification, not for publication, and whose coherent elaboration according to the plan indicated will be dependent on external circumstances.

I am omitting a general introduction[114] which I had jotted down because on closer reflection any anticipation of results still to be proved appears to me to be disturbing, and the reader who on the whole desires to follow me must be resolved to ascend from the particular to the general. A few indications concerning the course of my own politico-economic studies may, on the other hand, appear in place here.

I was taking up law, which discipline, however, I only pursued as a subordinate subject along with philosophy and history. In the year 1842-43, as editor of the *Rheinische Zeitung,*[115] I experienced for the first time the embarrassment of having to take part in discussions on so-called material interests. The proceedings of the Rhenish Landtag on thefts of wood and parcelling of landed property, the official polemic which Herr von Schaper, then *Oberpräsident* of the Rhine Province, opened against the *Rheinische Zeitung* on the conditions of the Moselle peasantry, and finally debates on free trade and protective tariffs provided the first occasions for occupying myself with economic questions. On the other hand, at that time when the good will "to go further" greatly outweighed knowledge of the subject, a philosophically weakly tinged

echo of French socialism and communism made itself audible in the
Rheinische Zeitung. I declared myself against this amateurism, but
frankly confessed at the same time in a controversy with the *Allgemeine Augsburger Zeitung*[116] that my previous studies did not permit
me even to venture any judgement on the content of the French
tendencies. Instead, I eagerly seized on the illusion of the managers
of the *Rheinische Zeitung*, who thought that by a weaker attitude on
the part of the paper they could secure a remission of the death
sentence passed upon it, to withdraw from the public stage into the
study.

The first work which I undertook for a solution of the doubts
which assailed me ˛was a critical review of the Hegelian philosophy of right,* a work the introduction** to which appeared in 1844
in the *Deutsch-Französische Jahrbücher*,[117] published in Paris. My
investigation led to the result that legal relations as well as forms
of state are to be grasped neither from themselves nor from the
so-called general development of the human mind, but rather have
their roots in the material conditions of life, the sum total of
which Hegel, following the example of the Englishmen and
Frenchmen of the eighteenth century, combines under the name
of "civil society," that, however, the anatomy of civil society is to
be sought in political economy. The investigation of the latter,
which I began in Paris, I continued in Brussels, whither I had
emigrated in consequence of an expulsion order of M. Guizot. The
general result at which I arrived and which, once won, served
as a guiding thread for my studies, can be briefly formulated as
follows: In the social production of their life, men enter into definite relations that are indispensable and independent of their
will, relations of production which correspond to a definite stage
of development of their material productive forces. The sum total
of these relations of production constitutes the economic structure
of society, the real foundation, on which rises a legal and political
superstructure and to which correspond definite forms of social
consciousness. The mode of production of material life conditions
the social, political and intellectual life process in general. It is
not the consciousness of men that determines their being, but, on
the contrary, their social being that determines their consciousness. At a certain stage of their development, the material productive forces of society come in conflict with the existing relations of production, or—what is but a legal expression for the
same thing—with the property relations within which they have
been at work hitherto. From forms of development of the produc-

---

* K. Marx, *Contribution to the Critique of Hegel's Philosophy of Right.—Ed.*
** K. Marx, *Contribution to the Critique of Hegel's Philosophy of Right.
Introduction* (see Marx and Engels, *On Religion*, Moscow, 1962, pp. 41-58).—*Ed.*

tive forces these relations turn into their fetters. Then begins an epoch of social revolution. With the change of the economic foundation the entire immense superstructure is more or less rapidly transformed. In considering such transformations a distinction should always be made between the material transformation of the economic conditions of production, which can be determined with the precision of natural science, and the legal, political, religious, aesthetic or philosophic—in short, ideological forms in which men become conscious of this conflict and fight it out. Just as our opinion of an individual is not based on what he thinks of himself, so can we not judge of such a period of transformation by its own consciousness; on the contrary, this consciousness must be explained rather from the contradictions of material life, from the existing conflict between the social productive forces and the relations of production. No social order ever perishes before all the productive forces for which there is room in it have developed; and new, higher relations of production never appear before the material conditions of their existence have matured in the womb of the old society itself. Therefore mankind always sets itself only such tasks as it can solve; since, looking at the matter more closely, it will always be found that the task itself arises only when the material conditions for its solution already exist or are at least in the process of formation. In broad outlines Asiatic, ancient, feudal, and modern bourgeois modes of production can be designated as progressive epochs in the economic formation of society. The bourgeois relations of production are the last antagonistic form of the social process of production—antagonistic not in the sense of individual antagonism, but of one arising from the social conditions of life of the individuals; at the same time the productive forces developing in the womb of bourgeois society create the material conditions for the solution of that antagonism. This social formation brings, therefore, the prehistory of human society to a close.

Frederick Engels, with whom, since the appearance of his brilliant sketch on the criticism of the economic categories* (in the *Deutsch-Französische Jahrbücher*), I maintained a constant exchange of ideas by correspondence, had by another road (compare his *The Condition of the Working Class in England in 1844*) arrived at the same result as I, and when in the spring of 1845 he also settled in Brussels, we resolved to work out in common the opposition of our view to the ideological view of German philosophy, in fact, to settle accounts with our erstwhile philosophical conscience. The resolve was carried out in the form of a crit-

---

* F. Engels, *Outlines of a Critique of Political Economy* (see K. Marx, *Economic and Philosophic Manuscripts of 1844*, Moscow, 1959, pp. 175-209).—*Ed.*

icism of post-Hegelian philosophy.* The manuscript, two large
octavo volumes,· had long reached its place of publication in
Westphalia when we received the news that altered circumstances did not allow of its being printed. We abandoned the
manuscript to the gnawing criticism of the mice all the more
willingly as we had achieved our main purpose—self-clarification.
Of the scattered works in which we put our views before the public at that time, now from one aspect, now from another, I will
mention only the *Manifesto of the Communist Party,*** jointly written by Engels and myself, and *Discours sur le libre échange* published by me. The decisive points of our view were first scientifically, although only polemically, indicated in my work published
in 1847 and directed against Proudhon: *Misère de la Philosophie,*
etc. A dissertation written in German on *Wage Labour,**** in
which I put together my lectures on this subject delivered in the
Brussels German Workers' Society,[28] was interrupted, while being
printed, by the February Revolution[4] and my consequent forcible
removal from Belgium.

The editing of the *Neue Rheinische Zeitung*[27] in 1848 and 1849,
and the subsequent events, interrupted my economic studies which
could only be resumed in the year 1850 in London. The enormous
material for the history of political economy which is accumulated
in the British Museum, the favourable vantage point afforded by
London for the observation of bourgeois society, and finally the
new stage of development upon which the latter appeared to have
entered with the discovery of gold in California and Australia,
determined me to begin afresh from the very beginning and to
work through the new material critically. These studies led partly
of themselves into apparently quite remote subjects on which I
had to dwell for a shorter or longer period. Especially, however,
was the time at my disposal curtailed by the imperative necessity of
earning my living. My contributions, during eight years now, to
the first English-American newspaper, the *New York Tribune,*[118]
compelled an extraordinary scattering of my studies, since I occupy
myself with newspaper correspondence proper only in exceptional
cases. However, articles on striking economic events in England and
on the Continent constituted so considerable a part of my contributions that I was compelled to make myself familiar with practical
details which lie outside the sphere of the actual science of political
economy.

This sketch of the course of my studies in the sphere of political economy is intended only to show that my views, however they

---

* Marx and Engels, *The German Ideology.—Ed.*
** See pp. 35-63 of this volume.—*Ed.*
*** K. Marx, *Wage Labour and Capital* (see pp. 71-93 of this volume).—*Ed.*

may be judged and however little they coincide with the interested prejudices of the ruling classes, are the result of conscientious investigation lasting many years. But at the entrance to science, as at the entrance to hell, the demand must be posted:

Qui si convien lasciare ogni sospetto;
*Ogni viltà convien che qui sia morta.**

Karl Marx

London, January 1859

First published in the book
Zur Kritik der Politischen
Oekonomie von Karl Marx.
Erstes Heft, Berlin, 1859

Printed according to the text
of the book

Translated from the German

---

* Here all mistrust must be abandoned
And here must perish every craven thought.
[Dante, *The Divine Comedy*.]—*Ed.*

Karl Marx

WAGES, PRICE AND PROFIT[119]

[PRELIMINARY]

Citizens,

Before entering into the subject-matter, allow me to make a few preliminary remarks.

There reigns now on the Continent a real epidemic of strikes, and a general clamour for a rise of wages. The question will turn up at our Congress. You, as the head of the International Association,[120] ought to have settled convictions upon this paramount question. For my own part, I considered it, therefore, my duty to enter fully into the matter, even at the peril of putting your patience to a severe test.

Another preliminary remark I have to make in regard to Citizen Weston. He has not only proposed to you, but has publicly defended, in the interest of the working class, as he thinks, opinions he knows to be most unpopular with the working class. Such an exhibition of moral courage all of us must highly honour. I hope that, despite the unvarnished style of my paper, at its conclusion he will find me agreeing with what appears to me the just idea lying at the bottom of his theses, which, however, in their present form, I cannot but consider theoretically false and practically dangerous.

I shall now at once proceed to the business before us.

I [PRODUCTION AND WAGES]

Citizen Weston's argument rested, in fact, upon two premises: firstly, that the *amount of national production* is a *fixed thing*, a *constant* quantity or magnitude, as the mathematicians would say; secondly, that the *amount of real wages*, that is to say, of wages as measured by the quantity of the commodities they can buy, is a *fixed* amount, a *constant* magnitude.

Now, his first assertion is evidently erroneous. Year after year you will find that the value and mass of production increase, that the productive powers of the national labour increase, and that the amount of money necessary to circulate this increasing production continuously changes. What is true at the end of the year, and for different years compared with each other, is true for every average day of the year. The amount or magnitude of national production changes continuously. It is not a *constant* but a *variable* magnitude, and apart from changes in population it must be so, because of the continuous change in the *accumulation of capital* and the *productive powers of labour*. It is perfectly true that if a *rise in the general rate of wages* should take place today, that rise, whatever its ulterior effects might be, would, *by itself*, not *immediately* change the amount of production. It would, in the first instance, proceed from the existing state of things. But if *before* the rise of wages the national production was *variable*, and not *fixed*, it will continue to be variable and not fixed *after* the rise of wages.

But suppose the amount of national production to be *constant* instead of *variable*. Even then, what our friend Weston considers a logical conclusion would still remain a gratuitous assertion. If I have a given number, say eight, the *absolute* limits of this number do not prevent its parts from changing their *relative* limits. If profits were six and wages two, wages might increase to six and profits decrease to two, and still the total amount remain eight. Thus the fixed amount of production would by no means prove the fixed amount of wages. How then does our friend Weston prove this fixity? By asserting it.

But even conceding him his assertion, it would cut both ways, while he presses it only in one direction. If the amount of wages is a constant magnitude, then it can be neither increased nor diminished. If then, in enforcing a temporary rise of wages, the working men act foolishly, the capitalists, in enforcing a temporary fall of wages, would act not less foolishly. Our friend Weston does not deny that, under certain circumstances, the working men *can* enforce a rise of wages, but their amount being naturally fixed, there must follow a reaction. On the other hand, he knows also that the capitalists *can* enforce a fall of wages, and, indeed, continuously try to enforce it. According to the principle of the constancy of wages, a reaction ought to follow in this case not less than in the former. The working men, therefore, reacting against the attempt at, or the act of, lowering wages, would act rightly. They would, therefore, act rightly in enforcing *a rise of wages,* because every *reaction* against the lowering of wages is an *action* for raising wages. According to Citizen Weston's own principle of the *constancy of wages,* the working men ought, therefore, under certain circumstances, to combine and struggle for a rise of wages.

If he denies this conclusion, he must give up the premise from which it flows. He must not say that the amount of wages is a *constant quantity*, but that, although it cannot and must not *rise*, it can and must *fall*, whenever capital pleases to lower it. If the capitalist pleases to feed you upon potatoes instead of upon meat, and upon oats instead of upon wheat, you must accept his will as a law of political economy, and submit to it. If in one country the rate of wages is higher than in another, in the United States, for example, than in England, you must explain this difference in the rate of wages by difference between the will of the American capitalist and the will of the English capitalist, a method which would certainly very much simplify, not only the study of economic phenomena, but of all other phenomena.

But even then, we might ask, *why* the will of the American capitalist differs from the will of the English capitalist? And to answer the question you must go beyond the domain of *will*. A parson may tell me that God wills one thing in France, and another thing in England. If I summon him to explain this duality of will, he might have the brass to answer me that God wills to have one will in France and another will in England. But our friend Weston is certainly the last man to make an argument of such a complete negation of all reasoning.

The *will* of the capitalist is certainly to take as much as possible. What we have to do is not to talk about his *will*, but to inquire into his *power*, the *limits of that power*, and the *character of those limits*.

II [PRODUCTION, WAGES, PROFITS]

The address Citizen Weston read to us might have been compressed into a nutshell.

All his reasoning amounted to this: If the working class forces the capitalist class to pay five shillings instead of four shillings in the shape of money wages, the capitalist will return in the shape of commodities four shillings' worth instead of five shillings' worth. The working class would have to pay five shillings for what, before the rise of wages, they bought with four shillings. But why is this the case? Why does the capitalist only return four shillings' worth for five shillings? Because the amount of wages is fixed. But why is it fixed at four shillings' worth of commodities? Why not at three, or two, or any other sum? If the limit of the amount of wages is settled by an economic law, independent alike of the will of the capitalist and the will of the working man, the first thing Citizen Weston had to do was to state that law and prove it. He ought then, moreover, to have proved that the amount of wages actually paid at every given moment always corresponds exactly to the necessary amount of wages, and never deviates from it. If, on the other hand, the given limit of the amount of wages is founded on the *mere will* of the capitalist, or the limits of his avarice, it is an arbitrary limit. There is nothing necessary in it. It may be changed *by* the will of the capitalist, and may, therefore, be changed *against* his will.

Citizen Weston illustrated his theory by telling you that when a bowl contains a certain quantity of soup, to be eaten by a certain number of persons, an increase in the broadness of the spoons would not produce an increase in the amount of soup. He must allow me to find this illustration rather spoony. It reminded me somewhat of the simile employed by Menenius Agrippa. When the Roman plebeians struck against the Roman patricians, the patrician Agrippa told them that the patrician belly fed the plebeian members of the body politic. Agrippa failed to show that you feed the members of one man by filling the belly of another. Citizen Weston, on his part, has forgotten that the bowl from which the workmen eat is filled with the whole produce of the national labour, and that what prevents them fetching more out of it is neither the narrowness of the bowl nor the scantiness of its contents, but only the smallness of their spoons.

By what contrivance is the capitalist enabled to return four shillings' worth for five shillings? By raising the price of the commodity he sells. Now, does a rise and more generally a change in the prices of commodities, do the prices of commodities themselves, depend on the mere will of the capitalist? Or are, on the contrary, certain circumstances wanted to give effect to that will? If not, the ups and downs, the incessant fluctuations of market prices, become an insoluble riddle.

As we suppose that no change whatever has taken place either in the productive powers of labour, or in the amount of capital and labour employed, or in the value of the money wherein the values of products are estimated, but *only a change in the rate of wages*, how could that *rise of wages* affect the *prices of commodities*? Only by affecting the actual proportion between the demand for, and the supply of, these commodities.

It is perfectly true that, considered as a whole, the working class spends, and must spend, its income upon *necessaries*. A general rise in the rate of wages would, therefore, produce a rise in the demand for, and consequently in the *market prices of*, *necessaries*. The capitalists who produce these necessaries would be compensated for the risen wages by the rising market prices of their commodities. But how with the other capitalists, who do *not* produce necessaries? And you must not fancy them a small body. If you consider that two-thirds of the national produce are consumed by one-fifth of the population—a member of the House of Commons stated it recently to be but one-seventh of the population—you will understand what an immense proportion of the national produce must be produced in the shape of luxuries, or be *exchanged* for luxuries, and what an immense amount of the necessaries themselves must be wasted upon flunkeys, horses, cats, and so forth, a waste we know from experience to become always much limited with the rising prices of necessaries.

Well, what would be the position of those capitalists who do *not* produce necessaries? For the *fall in the rate of profit*, consequent upon the general rise of wages, they could not compensate themselves by a *rise in the price of their commodities*, because the demand for those commodities would not have increased. Their income would have decreased, and from this decreased income they would have to pay more for the same amount of higher-priced necessaries. But this would not be all. As their income had diminished they would have less to spend upon luxuries, and therefore their mutual demand for their respective commodities would diminish. Consequent upon this diminished demand the prices of their commodities would fall. In these branches of industry, therefore, *the rate of profit would fall*, not only in simple proportion to the general rise in the rate of wages, but in the compound ratio of the general rise of wages, the rise in the prices of necessaries, and the fall in the prices of luxuries.

What would be the consequence of *this difference in the rates of profit* for capitals employed in the different branches of industry? Why, the consequence that generally obtains whenever, from whatever reason, the *average rate of profit* comes to differ in the different spheres of production. Capital and labour would be transferred from the less remunerative to the more remunerative branches; and this process of transfer would go on until the supply in the one department of industry would have risen proportionately to the increased demand, and would have sunk in the other departments according to the decreased demand. This change effected, the general rate of profit would again be *equalised* in the different branches. As the whole derangement originally arose from a mere change in the proportion of the demand for, and the supply of, different commodities, the cause ceasing, the effect would cease, and *prices* would return to their former level and equilibrium. Instead of being limited to some branches of industry, *the fall in the rate of profit* consequent upon the rise of wages would have become general. According to our supposition, there would have taken place no change in the productive powers of labour, nor in the aggregate amount of production, but *that given amount of production would have changed its form*. A greater part of the produce would exist in the shape of necessaries, a lesser part in the shape of luxuries, or what comes to the same, a lesser part would be exchanged for foreign luxuries, and be consumed in its original form, or, what again comes to the same, a greater part of the native produce would be exchanged for foreign necessaries instead of for luxuries. The general rise in the rate of wages would, therefore, after a temporary disturbance of market prices, only result in a general fall of the rate of profit without any permanent change in the prices of commodities.

If I am told that in the previous argument I assume the whole surplus wages to be spent upon necessaries, I answer that I have made the supposition most advantageous to the opinion of Citizen Weston. If the surplus wages were spent upon articles formerly not entering into the consumption of the working men, the real increase of their purchasing power would need no proof. Being, however, only derived from an advance of wages, that increase of their purchasing power must exactly correspond to the decrease of the purchasing power of the capitalists. The *aggregate demand* for commodities would, therefore, not *increase*, but the constituent parts of that demand would *change*. The increasing demand on the one side would be counterbalanced by the decreasing demand on the other side. Thus the aggregate demand remaining stationary, no change whatever could take place in the market prices of commodities.

You arrive, therefore, at this dilemma: Either the surplus wages are equally spent upon all articles of consumption—then the expansion of demand on the part of the working class must be compensated by the contraction of demand on the part of the capitalist class—or the surplus wages are only spent upon some articles whose market prices will temporarily rise. Then the consequent rise in the rate of profit in some, and the consequent fall in the rate of profit in other branches of industry will produce a change in the distribution of capital and labour, going on·until the supply is brought up to the increased demand in the one department of industry, and brought down to the diminished demand in the other departments of industry. On the one supposition there will occur no change in the prices of commodities. On the other supposition, after some fluctuations of market prices, the exchangeable values of commodities will subside to the former level. On both suppositions the general rise in the rate of wages will ultimately result in nothing else but a general fall in the rate of profit.

To stir up your powers of imagination Citizen Weston requested you to think of the difficulties which a general rise of English agricultural wages from nine shillings to eighteen shillings would produce. Think, he exclaimed, of the immense rise in the demand for necessaries, and the consequent fearful rise in their prices! Now, all of you know that the average wages of the American agricultural labourer amount to more than double that of the English agricultural labourer, although the prices of agricultural produce are lower in the United States than in the United Kingdom, although the general relations of capital and labour obtain in the United States the same as in England, and although the annual amount of production is much smaller in the United States than in

England. Why, then, does our friend ring this alarum bell? Simply to shift the real question before us. A sudden rise of wages from nine shillings to eighteen shillings would be a sudden rise to the amount of 100 per cent. Now, we are not at all discussing the question whether the general rate of wages in England could be suddenly increased by 100 per cent. We have nothing at all to do with the *magnitude* of the rise, which in every practical instance must depend on, and be suited to, given circumstances. We have only to inquire how a general rise in the rate of wages, even if restricted to one per cent., will act.

Dismissing friend Weston's fancy rise of 100 per cent., I propose calling your attention to the real rise of wages that took place in Great Britain from 1849 to 1859.

You are all aware of the Ten Hours' Bill, or rather Ten-and-a-Half Hours' Bill,[121] introduced since 1848. This was one of the greatest economic changes we have witnessed. It was a sudden and compulsory rise of wages, not in some local trades, but in the leading industrial branches by which England sways the markets of the world. It was a rise of wages under circumstances singularly unpropitious. Dr. Ure, Professor Senior, and all the other official economical mouthpieces of the middle class, *proved*, and I must say upon much stronger grounds than those of our friend Weston, that it would sound the death-knell of English industry. They proved that it not only amounted to a simple rise of wages, but to a rise of wages initiated by, and based upon, a diminution of the quantity of labour employed. They asserted that the twelfth hour you wanted to take from the capitalist was exactly the only hour from which he derived his profit. They threatened a decrease of accumulation, rise of prices, loss of markets, stinting of production, consequent reaction upon wages, ultimate ruin. In fact, they declared Maximilien Robespierre's Maximum Laws[122] to be a small affair compared to it; and they were right in a certain sense. Well, what was the result? A rise in the money wages of the factory operatives, despite the curtailing of the working day, a great increase in the number of factory hands employed, a continuous fall in the prices of their products, a marvellous development in the productive powers of their labour, an unheard-of progressive expansion of the markets for their commodities. In Manchester, at the meeting, in 1860, of the Society for the Advancement of Science, I myself heard Mr. Newman confess that he, Dr. Ure, Senior, and all other official propounders of economic science had been wrong, while the instinct of the people had been right. I mention Mr. W. Newman,[123] not Professor Francis Newman, because he occupies an eminent position in economic science, as the contributor to, and editor of, Mr. Thomas Tooke's *History of Prices*, that magnificent work which traces the history of prices from 1793 to 1856. If our friend Weston's fixed idea of a fixed

amount of wages, a fixed amount of production, a fixed degree of
the productive power of labour, a fixed and permanent will of the
capitalists, and all his other fixedness and finality were correct,
Professor Senior's woeful forebodings would have been right, and
Robert Owen, who already in 1815 proclaimed a general limitation
of the working day the first preparatory step to the emancipation of
the working class[124] and actually in the teeth of the general prejudice
inaugurated it on his own hook in his cotton factory at New Lanark,
would have been wrong.

In the very same period during which the introduction of the Ten
Hours' Bill, and the rise of wages consequent upon it, occurred, there
took place in Great Britain, for reasons which it would be out of
place to enumerate here, *a general rise in agricultural wages*.

Although it is not required for my immediate purpose, in order not
to mislead you, I shall make some preliminary remarks.

If a man got two shillings weekly wages, and if his wages rose
to four shillings, the *rate of wages* would have risen by 100 per cent.
This would seem a very magnificent thing if expressed as a rise in
the *rate of wages*, although the *actual amount of wages,* four
shillings weekly, would still remain a wretchedly small, a starvation
pittance. You must not, therefore, allow yourselves to be carried
away by the high-sounding per cents in the *rate* of wages. You must
always ask, What was the *original* amount?

Moreover, you will understand, that if there were ten men
receiving each 2s. per week, five men receiving each 5s., and five
men receiving 11s. weekly, the twenty men together would receive
100s., or £5, weekly. If then a rise, say by 20 per cent., upon the
aggregate sum of their weekly wages took place, there would be
an advance from £5 to £6. Taking the average, we might say that
the *general rate of wages* had risen by 20 per cent., although, in
fact, the wages of the ten men had remained stationary, the wages
of the one lot of five men had risen from 5s. to 6s. only, and
the wages of the other lot of five men from 55s. to 70s. One-half
of the men would not have improved at all their position, one-quarter
would have improved it in an imperceptible degree, and only
one-quarter would have bettered it really. Still, reckoning by the
average, the total amount of the wages of those twenty men would
have increased by 20 per cent., and as far as the aggregate capital
that employs them, and the prices of the commodities they produce,
are concerned, it would be exactly the same as if all of them had
equally shared in the average rise of wages. In the case of agricultural
labour, the standard wages being very different in the different
counties of England and Scotland, the rise affected them very
unequally.

Lastly, during the period when that rise of wages took place
counteracting influences were at work, such as the new taxes

onsequent upon the Russian war,[125] the extensive demolition of the
welling-houses of the agricultural labourers,[126] and so forth.

Having premised so much, I proceed to state that from 1849 to
859 there took place a *rise of about 40 per cent.* in the average rate
f the agricultural wages of Great Britain. I could give you ample
letails in proof of my assertion, but for the present purpose think it
ufficient to refer you to the conscientious and critical paper read
n 1860 by the late Mr. John C. Morton at the London Society of
Arts[127] on *The Forces Used in Agriculture*. Mr. Morton gives the
returns, from bills and other authentic documents, which he had
collected from about one hundred farmers, residing in twelve Scotch
and thirty-five English counties.

According to our friend Weston's opinion, and taken together
with the simultaneous rise in the wages of the factory operatives,
here ought to have occurred a tremendous rise in the prices of
agricultural produce during the period 1849 to 1859. But what is
the fact? Despite the Russian war, and the consecutive unfavourable
harvests from 1854 to 1856, the average price of wheat, which is
the leading agricultural produce of England, fell from about £3
per quarter for the years 1838 to 1848 to about £2 10s. per quarter
for the years 1849 to 1859. This constitutes a fall in the price of
wheat of more than 16 per cent. simultaneously with an average rise
of agricultural wages of 40 per cent. During the same period, if we
compare its end with its beginning, 1859 with 1849, there was a
decrease of official pauperism from 934,419 to 860,470, the difference
being 73,949; a very small decrease, I grant, and which in the following years was again lost, but still a decrease.

It might be said that, consequent upon the abolition of the Corn
Laws,[128] the import of foreign corn was more than doubled during
the period from 1849 to 1859, as compared with the period from 1838
to 1848. And what of that? From Citizen Weston's standpoint one
would have expected that this sudden, immense, and continuously
increasing demand upon foreign markets must have sent up the
prices of agricultural produce there to a frightful height, the effect
of increased demand remaining the same, whether it comes from
without or from within. What was the fact? Apart from some years
of failing harvests, during all that period the ruinous fall in the
price of corn formed a standing theme of declamation in France; the
Americans were again and again compelled to burn their surplus of
produce; and Russia, if we are to believe Mr. Urquhart, prompted
the Civil War in the United States[129] because her agricultural
exports were crippled by the Yankee competition in the markets of
Europe.

Reduced to its abstract form, Citizen Weston's argument would
come to this: Every rise in demand occurs always on the basis of a
given amount of production. It can, therefore, *never increase the*

supply of the articles demanded, but can *only enhance their money prices*. Now the most common observation shows that an increase demand will, in some instances, leave the market prices of commodities altogether unchanged, and will, in other instances, cause temporary rise of market prices followed by an increased supply, followed by a reduction of the prices to their original level, and in many cases *below* their original level. Whether the rise of demand springs from surplus wages, or from any other cause, does not at all change the conditions of the problem. From Citizen Weston's standpoint the general phenomenon was as difficult to explain as the phenomenon occurring under the exceptional circumstances of a rise of wages. His argument had, therefore, no peculiar bearing whatever upon the subject we treat. It only expressed his perplexity at accounting for the laws by which an increase of demand produces an increase of supply, instead of an ultimate rise of market prices.

III [WAGES AND CURRENCY]

On the second day of the debate our friend Weston clothed his old assertions in new forms. He said: Consequent upon a general rise in money wages, more currency will be wanted to pay the same wages. The currency being *fixed*, how can you pay with this fixed currency increased money wages? First the difficulty arose from the fixed amount of commodities accruing to the working man, despite his increase of money wages; now it arises from the increased money wages, despite the fixed amount of commodities. Of course, if you reject his original dogma, his secondary grievance will disappear.

However, I shall show that this currency question has nothing at all to do with the subject before us.

In your country the mechanism of payments is much more perfected than in any other country of Europe. Thanks to the extent and concentration of the banking system, much less currency is wanted to circulate the same amount of values, and to transact the same or a greater amount of business. For example, as far as wages are concerned, the English factory operative pays his wages weekly to the shopkeeper, who sends them weekly to the banker, who returns them weekly to the manufacturer, who again pays them away to his working men, and so forth. By this contrivance the yearly wages of an operative, say of £52, may be paid by one single sovereign turning round every week in the same circle. Even in England the mechanism is less perfect than in Scotland, and is not everywhere equally perfect; and therefore we find, for example, that in some agricultural districts, as compared with the mere factory districts, much more currency is wanted to circulate a much smaller amount of values.

If you cross the Channel, you will find that the *money wages* are much lower than in England, but that they are circulated in Germany, Italy, Switzerland, and France by a *much larger amount of currency*. The same sovereign will not be so quickly intercepted by the banker or returned to the industrial capitalist; and, therefore, instead of one sovereign circulating £52 yearly, you want, perhaps, three sovereigns to circulate yearly wages to the amount of £25. Thus, by comparing continental countries with England, you will see at once that low money wages may require a much larger currency for their circulation than high money wages, and that this is, in fact, a merely technical point, quite foreign to our subject.

According to the best calculations I know, the yearly income of the working class of this country may be estimated at £250,000,000. This immense sum is circulated by about £3,000,000. Suppose a rise of wages of 50 per cent. to take place. Then, instead of £3,000,000 of currency, £4,500,000 would be wanted. As a very considerable part of the working man's daily expenses is laid out in silver and copper, that is to say, in mere tokens, whose relative value to gold is arbitrarily fixed by law, like that of inconvertible money paper, a rise of money wages by 50 per cent. would, in the extreme case, require an additional circulation of sovereigns, say to the amount of one million. One million, now dormant, in the shape of bullion or coin, in the cellars of the Bank of England, or of private bankers, would circulate. But even the trifling expense resulting from the additional minting or the additional wear and tear of that million might be spared, and would actually be spared, if any friction should arise from the want of the additional currency. All of you know that the currency of this country is divided into two great departments. One sort, supplied by bank-notes of different descriptions, is used in the transactions between dealers and dealers, and the larger payments from consumers to dealers, while another sort of currency, metallic coin, circulates in the retail trade. Although distinct, these two sorts of currency interwork with each other. Thus gold coin, to a very great extent, circulates even in larger payments for all the odd sums under £5. If tomorrow £4 notes, or £3 notes, or £2 notes were issued, the gold filling these channels of circulation would at once be driven out of them, and flow into those channels where it would be needed from the increase of money wages. Thus the additional million required by an advance of wages by 50 per cent. would be supplied without the addition of one single sovereign. The same effect might be produced, without one additional bank-note, by an additional bill circulation, as was the case in Lancashire for a very considerable time.

If a general rise in the rate of wages, for example, of 100 per cent., as Citizen Weston supposed it to take place in agricultural wages, would produce a great rise in the prices of necessaries, and,

according to his views, require an additional amount of currency
not to be procured, *a general fall in wages* must produce the same
effect, on the same scale, in an opposite direction. Well! All of you
know that the years 1858 to 1860 were the most prosperous years
for the cotton industry, and that peculiarly the year 1860 stands in
that respect unrivalled in the annals of commerce, while at the same
time all other branches of industry were most flourishing. The wages
of the cotton operatives and of all the other working men connected
with their trade stood, in 1860, higher than ever before. The American crisis came, and those aggregate wages were suddenly reduced
to about one-fourth of their former amount. This would have been
in the opposite direction a rise of 300 per cent. If wages rise from
five to twenty, we say that they rise by 300 per cent.; if they fall from
twenty to five, we say that they fall by 75 per cent., but the amount
of rise in the one and the amount of fall in the other case would be
the same, namely, fifteen shillings. This, then, was a sudden change
in the rate of wages unprecedented, and at the same time extending
over a number of operatives which, if we count all the operatives not
only directly engaged in but indirectly dependent upon the cotton
trade, was larger by one-half than the number of agricultural labourers. Did the price of wheat fall? It *rose* from the annual average of
47s. 8d. per quarter during the three years of 1858-60 to the annual
average of 55s. 10d. per quarter during the three years 1861-63. As
to the currency, there were coined in the mint in 1861 £8,673,232,
against £3,378,102 in 1860. That is to say, there were coined
£5,295,130 more in 1861 than in 1860. It is true the bank-note circulation was in 1861 less by £1,319,000 than in 1860. Take this off.
There remains still an overplus of currency for the year 1861, as
compared with the prosperity year, 1860, to the amount of £3,976,130,
or about £4,000,000; but the bullion reserve in the Bank of England
had simultaneously decreased, not quite to the same, but in an
approximating proportion.
Compare the year 1862 with 1842. Apart from the immense
increase in the value and amount of commodities circulated, in 1862
the capital paid in regular transactions for shares, loans, etc., for the
railways in England and Wales amounted alone to £320,000,000, a
sum that would have appeared fabulous in 1842. Still, the aggregate
amounts in currency in 1862 and 1842 were pretty nearly equal, and
generally you will find a tendency to a progressive diminution of
currency in the face of an enormously increasing value, not only of
commodities, but of monetary transactions generally. From our friend
Weston's standpoint this is an unsolvable riddle.
Looking somewhat deeper into this matter, he would have found
that, quite apart from wages, and supposing them to be fixed, the
value and mass of the commodities to be circulated, and generally the
amount of monetary transactions to be settled, vary daily; that the

amount of bank-notes issued varies daily; that the amount of payments realised without the intervention of any money, by the instrumentality of bills, checks, book-credits, clearing houses, varies daily; that, as far as actual metallic currency is required, the proportion between the coin in circulation and the coin and bullion in reserve or sleeping in the cellars of banks varies daily; that the amount of bullion absorbed by the national circulation and the amount being sent abroad for international circulation vary daily. He would have found that his dogma of a fixed currency is a monstrous error, incompatible with the everyday movement. He would have inquired into the laws which enable a currency to adapt itself to circumstances so continually changing, instead of turning his misconception of the laws of currency into an argument against a rise of wages.

IV [SUPPLY AND DEMAND]

Our friend Weston accepts the Latin proverb that *repetitio est mater studiorum,* that is to say, that repetition is the mother of study, and consequently he repeated his original dogma again under the new form that the contraction of currency, resulting from an enhancement of wages, would produce a diminution of capital, and so forth. Having already dealt with his currency crotchet, I consider it quite useless to enter upon the imaginary consequences he fancies to flow from his imaginary currency mishap. I shall proceed to at once reduce his *one and the same dogma,* repeated in so many different shapes, to its simplest theoretical form.

The uncritical way in which he has treated his subject will become evident from one single remark. He pleads against a rise of wages or against high wages as the result of such a rise. Now, I ask him, What are high wages and what are low wages? Why constitute, for example, five shillings weekly low, and twenty shillings weekly high wages? If five is low as compared with twenty, twenty is still lower as compared with two hundred. If a man was to lecture on the thermometer, and commenced by declaiming on high and low degrees, he would impart no knowledge whatever. He must first tell me how the freezing-point is found out, and how the boiling-point, and how these standard points are settled by natural laws, not by the fancy of the sellers or makers of thermometers. Now, in regard to wages and profits, Citizen Weston has not only failed to deduce such standard points from economical laws, but he has not even felt the necessity to look after them. He satisfied himself with the acceptance of the popular slang terms of low and high as something having a fixed meaning, although it is self-evident that wages can only be said to be high or low as compared with a standard by which to measure their magnitudes.

He will be unable to tell me why a certain amount of money is given for a certain amount of labour. If he should answer me, "This was settled by the law of supply and demand," I should ask him, in the first instance, by what law supply and demand are themselves regulated. And such an answer would at once put him out of court. The relations between the supply and demand of labour undergo perpetual change, and with them the market prices of labour. If the demand overshoots the supply wages rise; if the supply overshoots the demand wages sink, although it might in such circumstances be necessary to *test* the real state of demand and supply by a strike, for example, or any other method. But if you accept supply and demand as the law regulating wages, it would be as childish as useless to declaim against a rise of wages, because, according to the supreme law you appeal to, a periodical rise of wages is quite as necessary and legitimate as a periodical fall of wages. If you do *not* accept supply and demand as the law regulating wages, I again repeat the question, why a certain amount of money is given for a certain amount of labour?

But to consider matters more broadly: You would be altogether mistaken in fancying that the value of labour or any other commodity whatever is ultimately fixed by supply and demand. Supply and demand regulate nothing but the temporary *fluctuations* of market prices. They will explain to you why the market price of a commodity rises above or sinks below its *value*, but they can never account for that *value* itself. Suppose supply and demand to equilibrate, or, as the economists call it, to cover each other. Why, the very moment these opposite forces become equal they paralyse each other, and cease to work in the one or the other direction. At the moment when supply and demand equilibrate each other, and therefore cease to act, the *market* price of a commodity coincides with its *real value*, with the standard price round which its market prices oscillate. In inquiring into the nature of that *value*, we have, therefore, nothing at all to do with the temporary effects on market prices of supply and demand. The same holds true of wages and of the prices of all other commodities.

V [WAGES AND PRICES]

Reduced to their simplest theoretical expression, all our friend's arguments resolve themselves into this one single dogma: "*The prices of commodities are determined or regulated by wages.*"

I might appeal to practical observation to bear witness against this antiquated and exploded fallacy. I might tell you that the English factory operatives, miners, shipbuilders, and so forth, whose labour is relatively high-priced, undersell by the cheapness of their produce all other nations; while the English agricultural labourer, for example, whose labour is relatively low-priced, is undersold by almost every other nation because of the dearness of his produce. By comparing article with article in the same country, and the commodities of different countries, I might show, apart from some exceptions more apparent than real, that on an average the high-priced labour produces the low-priced, and the low-priced labour produces the high-priced commodities. This, of course, would not prove that the high price of labour in the one, and its low price in the other instance, are the respective causes of those diametrically opposed effects, but at all events it would prove that the prices of commodities are not ruled by the prices of labour. However, it is quite superfluous for us to employ this empirical method.

It might, perhaps, be denied that Citizen Weston has put forward the dogma: *"The prices of commodities are determined or regulated by wages."* In point of fact, he has never formulated it. He said, on the contrary, that profit and rent form also constituent parts of the prices of commodities, because it is out of the prices of commodities that not only the working man's wages, but also the capitalist's profits and the landlord's rents must be paid. But how, in his idea, are prices formed? First by wages. Then an additional percentage is joined to the price on behalf of the capitalist, and another additional percentage on behalf of the landlord. Suppose the wages of the labour employed in the production of a commodity to be ten. If the rate of profit was 100 per cent., to the wages advanced the capitalist would add ten, and if the rate of rent was also 100 per cent. upon the wages, there would be added ten more, and the aggregate price of the commodity would amount to thirty. But such a determination of prices would be simply their determination by wages. If wages in the above case rose to twenty, the price of the commodity would rise to sixty, and so forth. Consequently all the superannuated writers on political economy who propounded the dogma that wages regulate prices, have tried to prove it by treating profit and rent *as mere additional percentages upon wages*. None of them were, of course, able to reduce the limits of those percentages to any economic law. They seem, on the contrary, to think profits settled by tradition, custom, the will of the capitalist, or by some other equally arbitrary and inexplicable method. If they assert that they are settled by the competition between the capitalists, they say nothing. That competition is sure to equalise the different rates of profit in different trades, or reduce them to one average level, but it can never determine the level itself, or the general rate of profit.

What do we mean by saying that the prices of the commodities are determined by wages? Wages being but a name for the price of labour, we mean that the prices of commodities are regulated by the price of labour. As *"price"* is exchangeable value—and in speaking of value I speak always of exchangeable value—is exchangeable *value expressed in money*, the proposition comes to this, that "the *value of commodities* is determined by the value of labour," or that "the *value of labour is the general measure of value.*"

But how, then, is the "*value of labour*" itself determined? Here we come to a standstill. Of couse, to a standstill if we try reasoning logically. Yet the propounders of that doctrine make short work of logical scruples. Take our friend Weston, for example. First he told us that wages regulate the price of commodities and that consequently when wages rise prices must rise. Then he turned round to show us that a rise of wages will be no good because the prices of commodities had risen, and because wages were indeed measured by the prices of the commodities upon which they are spent. Thus we begin by saying that the value of labour determines the value of commodities, and we wind up by saying that the value of commodities determines the value of labour. Thus we move to and fro in the most vicious circle, and arrive at no conclusion at all.

On the whole it is evident that by making the value of one commodity, say labour, corn, or any other commodity, the general measure and regulator of value, we only shift the difficulty, since we determine one value by another, which on its side wants to be determined.

The dogma that "wages determine the prices of commodities," expressed in its most abstract 'terms, comes to this, that "value is determined by value," and this tautology means that, in fact, we know nothing at all about value. Accepting this premise, all reasoning about the general laws of political economy turns into mere twaddle. It was, therefore, the great merit of Ricardo that in his work on *The Principles of Political Economy*, published in 1817, he fundamentally destroyed the old, popular, and worn-out fallacy that "wages determine prices," a fallacy which Adam Smith and his French predecessors had spurned in the really scientific parts of their researches, but which they reproduced in their more exoterical and vulgarising chapters.

VI [VALUE AND LABOUR]

Citizens, I have now arrived at a point where I must enter upon the real development of the question. I cannot promise to do this in a very satisfactory way, because to do so I should be obliged to go over the whole field of political economy. I can, as the French would say, but effleurer la question, touch upon the main points.

The first question we have to put is: What is the *value* of a commodity? How is it determined?

At first sight it would seem that the value of a commodity is a thing quite *relative*, and not to be settled without considering one commodity in its relations to all other commodities. In fact, in speaking of the value, the value in exchange of a commodity, we mean the proportional quantities in which it exchanges with all other commodities. But then arises the question: How are the proportions in which commodities exchange with each other regulated?

We know from experience that these proportions vary infinitely. Taking one single commodity, wheat, for instance, we shall find that a quarter of wheat exchanges in almost countless variations of proportion with different commodities. Yet, *its value remaining always the same*, whether expressed in silk, gold, or any other commodity, it must be something distinct from, and independent of, these *different rates of exchange* with different articles. It must be possible to express, in a very different form, these various equations with various commodities.

Besides, if I say a quarter of wheat exchanges with iron in a certain proportion, or the value of a quarter of wheat is expressed in a certain amount of iron, I say that the value of wheat and its equivalent in iron are equal *to some third thing*, which is neither wheat nor iron, because I suppose them to express the same magnitude in two different shapes. Either of them, the wheat or the iron, must, therefore, independently of the other, be reducible to this third thing which is their common measure.

To elucidate this point I shall recur to a very simple geometrical illustration. In comparing the areas of triangles of all possible forms and magnitudes, or comparing triangles with rectangles, or any other rectilinear figure, how do we proceed? We reduce the area of any triangle whatever to an expression quite different from its visible form. Having found from the nature of the triangle that its area is equal to half the product of its base by its height, we can then compare the different values of all sorts of triangles, and of all rectilinear figures whatever, because all of them may be resolved into a certain number of triangles.

The same mode of procedure must obtain with the values of commodities. We must be able to reduce all of them to an expression common to all, distinguishing them only by the proportions in which they contain that identical measure.

As the *exchangeable values* of commodities are only *social functions* of those things, and have nothing at all to do with their *natural* qualities, we must first ask, What is the common *social substance* of all commodities? It is *Labour*. To produce a commodity a certain amount of labour must be bestowed upon it, or worked up in it. And I say not only *Labour*, but *social Labour*. A man who produces an article for his own immediate use, to consume it himself, creates a *product*, but not a commodity. As a self-sustaining producer he has nothing to do with society. But to produce a *commodity*, a man must not only produce an article satisfying some *social* want, but his labour itself must form part and parcel of the total sum of labour expended by society. It must be subordinate to the *Division of Labour within Society.* It is nothing without the other divisions of labour, and on its part is required to *integrate* them.

If we consider *commodities as values*, we consider them exclusively under the single aspect of *realised, fixed,* or, if you like, *crystallised social labour.* In this respect they can *differ* only by representing greater or smaller quantities of labour, as, for example, a greater amount of labour may be worked up in a silken handkerchief than in a brick. But how does one measure *quantities of labour*? By the *time the labour lasts,* in measuring the labour by the hour, the day, etc. Of course, to apply this measure, all sorts of labour are reduced to average or simple labour as their unit.

We arrive, therefore, at this conclusion. A commodity has a *value,* because it is a *crystallisation of social labour.* The *greatness* of its value, of its *relative* value, depends upon the greater or less amount of that social substance contained in it; that is to say, on the relative mass of labour necessary for its production. The *relative values of commodities* are, therefore, determined by the *respective quantities or amounts of labour, worked up, realised, fixed in them.* The *correlative* quantities of commodities which can be produced in the *same time of labour* are *equal.* Or the value of one commodity is to the value of another commodity as the quantity of labour fixed in the one is to the quantity of labour fixed in the other.

I suspect that many of you will ask, Does then, indeed, there exist such a vast, or any difference whatever, between determining the values of commodities by *wages,* and determining them by the *relative quantities of labour* necessary for their production? You must, however, be aware that the *reward* for labour, and *quantity* of labour, are quite disparate things. Suppose, for example, *equal quantities of labour* to be fixed in one quarter of wheat and one ounce of gold. I resort to the example because it was used by Benjamin Franklin in his first Essay published in 1729, and entitled, *A Modest Enquiry into the Nature and Necessity of a Paper Currency,* where he, one of the first, hit upon the true nature of value. Well. We suppose, then, that one quarter of wheat and one ounce of gold are *equal values* or *equivalents,* because they are *crystallisations of equal amounts of average labour,* of so many days' or so many weeks' labour respectively fixed in them. In thus determining the relative values of gold and corn, do we refer in any way whatever to the *wages* of the agricultural labourer and the miner? Not a bit. We leave it quite *indeterminate how* their day's or week's labour was paid, or even whether wages labour was employed at all. If it was, wages may have been very unequal. The labourer whose labour is realised in the quarter of wheat may receive two bushels only, and the labourer employed in mining may receive one-half of the ounce of gold. Or, supposing their wages to be equal, they may deviate in all possible proportions from the values of the commodities produced by them. They may amount to one-half, one-third, one-fourth, one-fifth, or any other proportional part of the one quarter of corn or the one ounce of gold. Their *wages* can, of course, not *exceed*, not be *more* than the values of the commodities they produced, but they can be *less* in every possible degree. Their *wages* will be *limited* by the *values* of the products, but the *values of their products* will not be limited by the wages. And above all, the values, the relative values of corn and gold, for example, will have been settled without any regard whatever to the value of the labour employed, that is to say, to *wages*. To determine the values of commodities by the *relative quantities of labour fixed in them*, is, therefore, a thing quite different from the tautological method of determining the values of commodities by the value of labour, or by *wages*. This point, however, will be further elucidated in the progress of our inquiry.

In calculating the exchangeable value of a commodity we must add to the quantity of labour *last* employed the quantity of labour *previously* worked up in the raw material of the commodity, and the labour bestowed on the implements, tools, machinery, and buildings, with which such labour is assisted. For example, the value of a certain amount of cotton-yarn is the crystallisation of the quantity of labour added to the cotton during the spinning process, the quantity of labour previously realised in the cotton itself, the quantity of labour realised in the coal, oil, and other auxiliary substances used, the quantity of labour fixed in the steam engine, the spindles, the factory building, and so forth. Instruments of production properly so-called, such as tools, machinery, buildings, serve again and again for a longer or shorter period during repeated processes of production. If they were used up at once, like the raw material, their whole value would at once be transferred to the commodities they assist in producing. But as a spindle, for example, is but gradually used up, an average calculation is made, based upon the average time it lasts, and its average waste of wear and tear during a certain period, say a day. In this way we calculate how much of the value of the spindle is transferred to the yarn daily spun, and how much, therefore, of the total amount of labour realised in a pound of yarn, for example, is due to the quantity of labour previously realised in the spindle. For our present purpose it is not necessary to dwell any longer upon this point.

It might seem that if the value of a commodity is determined by the *quantity of labour bestowed upon its production*, the lazier a man, or the clumsier a man, the more valuable his commodity, because the greater the time of labour required for finishing the commodity. This, however, would be a sad mistake. You will recollect that I used the word "*Social* labour," and many points are involved in this qualification of "*Social*." In saying that the value of a commodity is determined by the *quantity of labour* worked up or crystallised in it, we

mean *the quantity of labour necessary* for its production in a given
state of society, under certain social average conditions of production,
with a given social average intensity, and average skill of the labour
employed. When, in England, the power-loom came to compete with
the hand-loom, only one half of the former time of labour was wanted
to convert a given amount of yarn into a yard of cotton or cloth. The
poor hand-loom weaver now worked seventeen or eighteen hours
daily, instead of the nine or ten hours he had worked before. Still
the product of twenty hours of his labour represented now only ten
social hours of labour, or ten hours of labour socially necessary for
the conversion of a certain amount of yarn into textile stuffs. His
product of twenty hours had, therefore, no more value than his former
product of ten hours.

If then the quantity of socially necessary labour realised in commodities regulates their exchangeable values, every increase in the
quantity of labour wanted for the production of a commodity must
augment its value, as every diminution must lower it.

If the respective quantities of labour necessary for the production
of the respective commodities remained constant, their relative values
also would be constant. But such is not the case. The quantity of labour
necessary for the production of a commodity changes continuously
with the changes in the productive powers of the labour employed.
The greater the productive powers of labour, the more produce is
finished in a given time of labour: and the smaller the productive
powers of labour, the less produce is finished in the same time. If, for
example, in the progress of population it should become necessary to
cultivate less fertile soils, the same amount of produce would be only
attainable by a greater amount of labour spent, and the value of agricultural produce would consequently rise. On the other hand, if with
the modern means of production, a single spinner converts into yarn,
during one working day, many thousand times the amount of cotton
which he could have spun during the same time with the spinning
wheel, it is evident that every single pound of cotton will absorb many
thousand times less of spinning labour than it did before, and, consequently, the value added by spinning to every single pound of cotton
will be a thousand times less than before. The value of yarn will sink
accordingly.

Apart from the different natural energies and acquired working
abilities of different peoples, the productive powers of labour must
principally depend:

Firstly. Upon the *natural* conditions of labour, such as fertility of
soil, mines, and so forth;

Secondly. Upon the progressive improvement of the *Social Powers
of Labour*, such as are derived from production on a grand scale,
concentration of capital and combination of labour, subdivision of
labour, machinery, improved methods, appliance of chemical and

other natural agencies, shortening of time and space by means of communication and transport, and every other contrivance by which science presses natural agencies into the service of labour, and by which the social or co-operative character of labour is developed. The greater the productive powers of labour, the less labour is bestowed upon a given amount of produce; hence the smaller the value of this produce. The smaller the productive powers of labour, the more labour is bestowed upon the same amount of produce; hence the greater its value. As a general law we may, therefore, set it down that:—

The values of commodities are directly as the times of labour employed in their production, and are inversely as the productive powers of the labour employed.

Having till now only spoken of *Value*, I shall add a few words about *Price*, which is a peculiar form assumed by value.

Price, taken by itself, is nothing but the *monetary expression of value*. The values of all commodities of this country, for example, are expressed in gold prices, while on the Continent they are mainly expressed in silver prices. The value of gold or silver, like that of all other commodities, is regulated by the quantity of labour necessary for getting them. You exchange a certain amount of your national products, in which a certain amount of your national labour is crystallised, for the produce of the gold and silver producing countries, in which a certain quantity of *their* labour is crystallised. It is in this way, in fact by barter, that you learn to express in gold and silver the values of all commodities, that is, the respective quantities of labour bestowed upon them. Looking somewhat closer into the *monetary expression of value*, or what comes to the same, the conversion of value into price, you will find that it is a process by which you give to the *values* of all commodities an *independent* and *homogeneous form*, or by which you express them as quantities of equal social labour. So far as it is but the monetary expression of value, price has been called *natural price* by Adam Smith, "*prix nécessaire*" by the French physiocrats.[130]

What then is the relation between *value* and *market prices*, or between *natural prices* and *market prices*? You all know that the *market price* is the *same* for all commodities of the same kind, however the conditions of production may differ for the individual producers. The market price expresses only the *average amount of social labour* necessary, under the average conditions of production, to supply the market with a certain mass of a certain article. It is calculated upon the whole lot of a commodity of a certain description.

So far the *market price* of a commodity coincides with its *value*. On the other hand, the oscillations of market prices, rising now over, sinking now under the value or natural price, depend upon the fluctuations of supply and demand. The deviations of market prices from values are continual, but as Adam Smith says:

"The natural price ... is the central price, to which the prices of all commodities are continually gravitating. Different accidents may sometimes keep them suspended a good deal above it, and sometimes force them down even somewhat below it. But whatever may be the obstacles which hinder them from settling in this centre of repose and continuance they are constantly tending towards it."[131]

I cannot now sift this matter. It suffices to say that *if* supply and demand equilibrate each other, the market prices of commodities will correspond with their natural prices, that is to say, with their values, as determined by the respective quantities of labour required for their production. But supply and demand *must* constantly tend to equilibrate each other, although they do so only by compensating one fluctuation by another, a rise by a fall, and *vice versa*. If instead of considering only the daily fluctuations you analyse the movement of market prices for longer periods, as Mr. Tooke, for example, has done in his *History of Prices*, you will find that the fluctuations of market prices, their deviations from values, their ups and downs, paralyse and compensate each other; so that, apart from the effect of monopolies and some other modifications I must now pass by, all descriptions of commodities are, on the average, sold at their respective *values* or natural prices. The average periods during which the fluctuations of market prices compensate each other are different for different kinds of commodities, because with one kind it is easier to adapt supply to demand than with the other.

If then, speaking broadly, and embracing somewhat longer periods, all descriptions of commodities sell at their respective values, it is nonsense to suppose that profit, not in individual cases, but that the constant and usual profits of different trades spring from *surcharging* the prices of commodities, or selling them at a price over and above their *value*. The absurdity of this notion becomes evident if it is generalised. What a man would constantly win as a seller he would as constantly lose as a purchaser. It would not do to say that there are men who are buyers without being sellers, or consumers without being producers. What these people pay to the producers, they must first get from them for nothing. If a man first takes your money and afterwards returns that money in buying your commodities, you will never enrich yourselves by selling your commodities too dear to that same man. This sort of transaction might diminish a loss, but would never help in realising a profit.

To explain, therefore, the *general nature of profits*, you must start from the theorem that, on an average, commodities are *sold at their real value*, and *that profits are derived from selling them at their values*, that is, in proportion to the quantity of labour realised in them. If you cannot explain profit upon this supposition, you cannot explain it at all. This seems paradox and contrary to everyday observation. It is also paradox that the earth moves round the sun, and

:hat water consists of two highly inflammable gases. Scientific truth
s always paradox, if judged by everyday experience, which catches
)nly the delusive appearance of things.

VII LABOURING POWER

Having now, as far as it could be done in such a cursory manner,
analysed the nature of *Value*, of the *Value of any commodity whatever*, we must turn our attention to the specific *Value of Labour*. And
here, again, I must startle you by a seeming paradox. All of you feel
sure that what they daily sell is their Labour; that, therefore, Labour
has a Price, and that, the price of a commodity being only the
monetary expression of its value, there must certainly exist such a
thing as the *Value of Labour*. However, there exists no such thing as
the *Value of Labour* in the common acceptance of the word. We have
seen that the amount of necessary labour crystallised in a commodity
constitutes its value. Now, applying this notion of value, how could
we define, say, the value of a ten hours' working day? How much
labour is contained in that day? Ten hours' labour. To say that the
value of a ten hours' working day is equal to ten hours' labour, or the
quantity of labour contained in it, would be a tautological and, moreover, a nonsensical expression. Of course, having once found out the
true but hidden sense of the expression "*Value of Labour*," we shall
be able to interpret this irrational, and seemingly impossible application of value, in the same way that, having once made sure of the real
movement of the celestial bodies, we shall be able to explain their
apparent or merely phenomenal movements.

What the working man sells is not directly his *Labour*, but his
Labouring Power, the temporary disposal of which he makes over to
the capitalist. This is so much the case that I do not know whether
by the English laws, but certainly by some Continental Laws, the
maximum time is fixed for which a man is allowed to sell his labouring power. If allowed to do so for any indefinite period whatever,
slavery would be immediately restored. Such a sale, if it comprised
his lifetime, for example, would make him at once the lifelong slave
of his employer.

One of the oldest economists and most original philosophers of
England—Thomas Hobbes—has already, in his *Leviathan*, instinctively hit upon this point overlooked by all his successors. He says:

"*The value or worth of a man* is, as in all other things, his *price*: that is, so
much as would be given for the *Use of his Power*."

Proceeding from this basis, we shall be able to determine the *Value
of Labour* as that of all other commodities.

But before doing so, we might ask, how does this strange phenomenon arise, that we find on the market a set of buyers, possessed of land, machinery, raw material, and the means of subsistence all of them, save land in its crude state, the *products of labour*, and on the other hand, a set of sellers who have nothing to sell except their labouring power, their working arms and brains? That the one set buys continually in order to make a profit and enrich themselves while the other set continually sells in order to earn their livelihood? The inquiry into this question would be an inquiry into what the economists call *"Previous, or Original Accumulation,"* but which ought to be called *Original Expropriation*. We should find that this so-called *Original Accumulation* means nothing but a series of historical processes, resulting in a *Decomposition of the Original Union* existing between the Labouring Man and his Instruments of Labour. Such an inquiry, however, lies beyond the pale of my present subject. The *Separation* between the Man of Labour and the Instruments of Labour once established, such a state of things will maintain itself and reproduce itself upon a constantly increasing scale, until a new and fundamental revolution in the mode of production should again overturn it, and restore the original union in a new historical form.

What, then, is the *Value of Labouring Power*?

Like that of every other commodity, its value is determined by the quantity of labour necessary to produce it. The labouring power of a man exists only in his living individuality. A certain mass of necessaries must be consumed by a man to grow up and maintain his life. But the man, like the machine, will wear out, and must be replaced by another man. Beside the mass of necessaries required for *his own* maintenance, he wants another amount of necessaries to bring up a certain quota of children that are to replace him on the labour market and to perpetuate the race of labourers. Moreover, to develop his labouring power, and acquire a given skill, another amount of values must be spent. For our purpose it suffices to consider only *average* labour, the costs of whose education and development are vanishing magnitudes. Still I must seize upon this occasion to state that, as the costs of producing labouring powers of different quality differ, so must differ the values of the labouring powers employed in different trades. The cry for an *equality of wages* rests, therefore, upon a mistake, is an *insane* wish never to be fulfilled. It is an offspring of that false and superficial radicalism that accepts premises and tries to evade conclusions. Upon the basis of the wages system the value of labouring power is settled like that of every other commodity; and as different kinds of labouring power have different values, or require different quantities of labour for their production, they *must* fetch different prices in the labour market. To clamour for *equal or even equitable retribution* on the basis of the wages system is the same as to clamour for *freedom* on the basis of the slavery system. What you think just or equitable is out of the question. The question is: What is necessary and unavoidable with a given system of production?

After what has been said, it will be seen that the *value of labouring power* is determined by the *value of the necessaries* required to produce, develop, maintain, and perpetuate the labouring power.

VIII PRODUCTION OF SURPLUS VALUE

Now suppose that the average amount of the daily necessaries of a labouring man require *six hours of average labour* for their production. Suppose, moreover, six hours of average labour to be also realised in a quantity of gold equal to 3s. Then 3s. would be the *Price,* or the monetary expression of the *Daily Value* of that man's *Labouring Power.* If he worked daily six hours he would daily produce a value sufficient to buy the average amount of his daily necessaries, or to maintain himself as a labouring man.

But our man is a wages labourer. He must, therefore, sell his labouring power to a capitalist. If he sells it at 3s. daily, or 18s. weekly, he sells it at its value. Suppose him to be a spinner. If he works six hours daily he will add to the cotton a value of 3s. daily. This value, daily added by him, would be an exact equivalent for the wages, or the price of his labouring power, received daily. But in that case *no surplus value* or *surplus produce* whatever would go to the capitalist. Here, then, we come to the rub.

In buying the labouring power of the workman, and paying its value, the capitalist, like every other purchaser, has acquired the right to consume or use the commodity bought. You consume or use the labouring power of a man by making him work as you consume or use a machine by making it run. By paying the daily or weekly value of the labouring power of the workman, the capitalist has, therefore, acquired the right to use or make that labouring power work during the *whole day or week.* The working day or the working week has, of course, certain limits, but those we shall afterwards look more closely at.

For the present I want to turn your attention to one decisive point.

The *value* of the labouring power is determined by the quantity of labour necessary to maintain or reproduce it, but the *use* of that labouring power is only limited by the active energies and physical strength of the labourer. The daily or weekly *value* of the labouring power is quite distinct from the daily or weekly exercise of that power, the same as the food a horse wants and the time it can carry the horseman are quite distinct. The quantity of labour by which the *value*

of the workman's labouring power is limited forms by no means a
limit to the quantity of labour which his labouring power is apt to
perform. Take the example of our spinner. We have seen that, to daily
reproduce his labouring power, he must daily reproduce a value of
three shillings. which he will do by working six hours daily. But this
does not disable him from working ten or twelve or more hours a day.
But by paying the daily or weekly *value* of the spinner's labouring
power, the capitalist has acquired the right of using that labouring
power during *the whole day or week.* He will, therefore, make him
work say, daily, *twelve* hours. *Over and above* the six hours required
to replace his wages, or the value of his labouring power, he will,
therefore, have to work *six other hours*, which I shall call hours of
surplus labour, which surplus labour will realise itself in a *surplus
value* and a *surplus produce*. If our spinner, for example, by his daily
labour of six hours, added three shillings' value to the cotton, a value
forming an exact equivalent to his wages, he will, in twelve hours,
add six shillings' worth to the cotton, and produce *a proportional
surplus of yarn*. As he has sold his labouring power to the capitalist,
the whole value or produce created by him belongs to the capitalist,
the owner *pro tem.* of his labouring power. By advancing three
shillings, the capitalist will, therefore, realise a value of six shillings,
because, advancing a value in which six hours of labour are
crystallised, he will receive in return a value in which twelve hours
of labour are crystallised. By repeating this same process daily, the
capitalist will daily advance three shillings and daily pocket six
shillings, one-half of which will go to pay wages anew, and the other
half of which will form *surplus value*, for which the capitalist pays no
equivalent. It is this *sort of exchange between capital and labour*
upon which capitalistic production, or the wages system, is founded,
and which must constantly result in reproducing the working man as
a working man, and the capitalist as a capitalist.

The rate of surplus value, all other circumstances remaining the
same, will depend on the proportion between that part of the working day necessary to reproduce the value of the labouring power and
the *surplus time* or *surplus labour* performed for the capitalist. It
will, therefore, depend on the *ratio in which the working day is prolonged over and above that extent*, by working which the working
man would only reproduce the value of his labouring power, or
replace his wages.

IX VALUE OF LABOUR

We must now return to the expression, *"Value, or Price of Labour."*
We have seen that, in fact, it is only the value of the labouring
power, measured by the values of commodities necessary for its main-

tenance. But since the workman receives his wages *after* his labour is performed, and knows, moreover, that what he actually gives to the capitalist is his labour, the value or price of his labouring power necessarily appears to him as the *price* or *value of his labour itself.* If the price of his labouring power is three shillings, in which six hours of labour are realised, and if he works twelve hours, he necessarily considers these three shillings as the value or price of twelve hours of labour, although these twelve hours of labour realise themselves in a value of six shillings. A double consequence flows from this.

Firstly. *The value or price of the labouring power* takes the semblance of the *price or value of labour itself,* although, strictly speaking, value and price of labour are senseless terms.

Secondly. Although one part only of the workman's daily labour is *paid,* while the other part is *unpaid,* and while that unpaid or surplus labour constitutes exactly the fund out of which *surplus value* or *profit* is formed, it seems as if the aggregate labour was paid labour.

This false appearance distinguishes *wages labour* from other *historical* forms of labour. On the basis of the wages system even the *unpaid* labour seems to be *paid* labour. With the *slave,* on the contrary, even that part of his labour which is paid appears to be unpaid. Of course, in order to work the slave must live, and one part of his working day goes to replace the value of his own maintenance. But since no bargain is struck between him and his master, and no acts of selling and buying are going on between the two parties, all his labour seems to be given away for nothing.

Take, on the other hand, the peasant serf, such as he, I might say, until yesterday existed in the whole East of Europe. This peasant worked, for example, three days for himself on his own field or the field allotted to him, and the three subsequent days he performed compulsory and gratuitous labour on the estate of his lord. Here, then, the paid and unpaid parts of labour were sensibly separated, separated in time and space; and our Liberals overflowed with moral indignation at the preposterous notion of making a man work for nothing.

In point of fact, however, whether a man works three days of the week for himself on his own field and three days for nothing on the estate of his lord, or whether he works in the factory or the workshop six hours daily for himself and six for his employer, comes to the same, although in the latter case the paid and unpaid portions of labour are inseparably mixed up with each other, and the nature of the whole transaction is completely masked by the *intervention of a contract* and the *pay* received at the end of the week. The gratuitous labour appears to be voluntarily given in the one instance, and to be compulsory in the other. That makes all the difference.

In using the expression *"value of labour,"* I shall only use it as a popular slang term for *"value of labouring power."*

X PROFIT IS MADE BY SELLING A COMMODITY *AT* ITS VALUE

Suppose an average hour of labour to be realised in a value equal to sixpence, or twelve average hours of labour to be realised in six shillings. Suppose, further, the value of labour to be three shillings or the produce of six hours' labour. If, then, in the raw material, machinery, and so forth, used up in a commodity, twenty-four hours of average labour were realised, its value would amount to twelve shillings. If, moreover, the workman employed by the capitalist added twelve hours of labour to those means of production, these twelve hours would be realised in an additional value of six shillings. The *total value of the product* would, therefore, amount to thirty-six hours of realised labour, and be equal to eighteen shillings. But as the value of labour, or the wages paid to the workman, would be three shillings only, no equivalent would have been paid by the capitalist for the six hours of surplus labour worked by the workman, and realised in the value of the commodity. By selling this commodity at its value for eighteen shillings, the capitalist would, therefore, realise a value of three shillings, for which he had paid no equivalent. These three shillings would constitute the surplus value or profit pocketed by him. The capitalist would consequently realise the profit of three shillings, not by selling his commodity at a price *over and above* its value, but by selling it *at its real value*.

The value of a commodity is determined by the *total quantity of labour* contained in it. But part of that quantity of labour is realised in a value for which an equivalent has been paid in the form of wages; part of it is realised in a value for which *no* equivalent has been paid. Part of the labour contained in the commodity is *paid* labour; part is *unpaid* labour. By selling, therefore, the commodity *at its value*, that is, as the crystallisation of the *total quantity of labour* bestowed upon it, the capitalist must necessarily sell it at a profit. He sells not only what has cost him an equivalent, but he sells also what has cost him nothing, although it has cost his workman labour. The cost of the commodity to the capitalist and its real cost are different things. I repeat, therefore, that normal and average profits are made by selling commodities not *above* but *at their real values*.

XI THE DIFFERENT PARTS INTO WHICH
SURPLUS VALUE IS DECOMPOSED

The *surplus value*, or that part of the total value of the commodity in which the *surplus labour* or *unpaid labour* of the working man is realised, I call *Profit*. The whole of that profit is not pocketed by the employing capitalist. The monopoly of land enables the landlord to take one part of that *surplus value*, under the name of *rent*, whether the land is used for agriculture, buildings or railways, or for any other productive purpose. On the other hand, the very fact that the possession of the *instruments of labour* enables the employing capitalist to produce a *surplus value*, or, what comes to the same, to *appropriate to himself a certain amount of unpaid labour*, enables the owner of the means of labour, which he lends wholly or partly to the employing capitalist—enables, in one word, the money-lending capitalist to claim for himself under the name of *interest* another part of that surplus value, so that there remains to the employing capitalist *as such* only what is called *industrial* or *commercial profit*.

By what laws this division of the total amount of surplus value amongst the three categories of people is regulated is a question quite foreign to our subject. This much, however, results from what has been stated.

Rent, Interest, and Industrial Profit are only *different names for different parts* of the *surplus value* of the commodity, or the *unpaid labour enclosed in it*, and they are *equally derived from this source, and from this source alone*. They are not derived from *land* as such or from *capital* as such, but land and capital enable their owners to get their respective shares out of the surplus value extracted by the employing capitalist from the labourer. For the labourer himself it is a matter of subordinate importance whether that surplus value, the result of his surplus labour, or unpaid labour, is altogether pocketed by the employing capitalist, or whether the latter is obliged to pay portions of it, under the name of rent and interest, away to third parties. Suppose the employing capitalist to use only his own capital and to be his own landlord, then the whole surplus value would go into his pocket.

It is the employing capitalist who immediately extracts from the labourer this surplus value, whatever part of it he may ultimately be able to keep for himself. Upon this relation, therefore, between the employing capitalist and the wages labourer the whole wages system and the whole present system of production hinge. Some of the citizens who took part in our debate were, therefore, wrong in trying to mince matters, and to treat this fundamental relation between the employing capitalist and the working man as a secondary question, although they were right in stating that, under given circumstances, a rise of prices might affect in very unequal degrees the employing capitalist, the landlord, the moneyed capitalist, and, if you please the taxgatherer.

Another consequence follows from what has been stated.

That part of the value of the commodity which represents only the value of the raw materials, the machinery, in one word, the value of the means of production used up, forms *no revenue* at all, but replaces *only capital*. But, apart from this, it is false that the other part of the value of the commodity *which forms revenue*, or may be spent in the form of wages, profits, rent, interest, is *constituted* by the value of wages, the value of rent, the value of profits, and so forth. We shall, in the first instance, discard wages, and only treat industrial profits, interest, and rent. We have just seen that the *surplus value* contained in the commodity or that part of its value in which *unpaid labour* is realised, resolves itself into different fractions, bearing three different names. But it would be quite the reverse of the truth to say that its value is *composed* of, or *formed* by, the *addition* of the *independent values of these three constituents*.

If one hour of labour realises itself in a value of sixpence, if the working day of the labourer comprises twelve hours, if half of this time is unpaid labour, that surplus labour will add to the commodity a *surplus value* of three shillings, that is, a value for which no equivalent has been paid. This surplus value of three shillings constitutes the *whole fund* which the employing capitalist may divide, in whatever proportions, with the landlord and the money-lender. The value of these three shillings constitutes the limit of the value they have to divide amongst them. But it is not the employing capitalist who adds to the value of the commodity an arbitrary value for his profit, to which another value is added for the landlord, and so forth, so that the addition of these arbitrarily fixed values would constitute the total value. You see, therefore, the fallacy of the popular notion, which confounds the *decomposition of a given value* into three parts, with the *formation* of that value by the addition of three *independent* values, thus converting the aggregate value, from which rent, profit, and interest are derived, into an arbitrary magnitude.

If the total profit realised by a capitalist be equal to £100, we call this sum, considered as *absolute* magnitude, the *amount of profit*. But if we calculate the ratio which those £100 bear to the capital advanced, we call this *relative* magnitude, the *rate of profit*. It is evident that this rate of profit may be expressed in a double way.

Suppose £100 to be the capital *advanced in wages*. If the surplus value created is also £100—and this would show us that half the working day of the labourer consists of *unpaid* labour—and if we measured this profit by the value of the capital advanced in wages, we should say that the *rate of profit* amounted to one hundred per cent, because the value advanced would be one hundred and the value realised would be two hundred.

If, on the other hand, we should not only consider the *capital advanced in wages,* but the *total capital* advanced, say, for example, 500, of which £400 represented the value of raw materials, machinery, and so forth, we should say that the *rate of profit* amounted only to twenty per cent., because the profit of one hundred would be but the fifth part of the *total* capital advanced.

The first mode of expressing the rate of profit is the only one which shows you the real ratio between paid and unpaid labour, the real degree of the *exploitation* (you must allow me this French word) *of labour.* The other mode of expression is that in common use, and is, indeed, appropriate for certain purposes. At all events, it is very useful for concealing the degree in which the capitalist extracts gratuitous labour from the workman.

In the remarks I have still to make I shall use the word *Profit* for the whole amount of the surplus value extracted by the capitalist without any regard to the division of the surplus value between different parties, and in using the words *Rate of Profit,* I shall always measure profits by the value of the capital advanced in wages.

XII GENERAL RELATION OF PROFITS, WAGES AND PRICES

Deduct from the value of a commodity the value replacing the value of the raw materials and other means of production used upon it, that is to say, deduct the value representing the *past* labour contained in it, and the remainder of its value will resolve into the quantity of labour added by the working man *last* employed. If that working man works twelve hours daily, if twelve hours of average labour crystallise themselves in an amount of gold equal to six shillings, this additional value of six shillings is the *only* value his labour will have created. This given value, determined by the time of his labour, is the only fund from which both he and the capitalist have to draw their respective shares or dividends, the only value to be divided into wages and profits. It is evident that this value itself will not be altered by the variable proportions in which it may be divided amongst the two parties. There will also be nothing changed if in the place of one working man you put the whole working population, twelve million working days, for example, instead of one.

Since the capitalist and workman have only to divide this limited value, that is, the value measured by the total labour of the working man, the more the one gets the less will the other get, and *vice versa.* Whenever a quantity is given, one part of it will increase inversely as the other decreases. If the wages change, profits will change in an

opposite direction. If wages fall, profits will rise; and if wages ris
profits will fall. If the working man, on our former supposition, ge
three shillings, equal to one half of the value he has created, or if h
whole working day consists half of paid, half of unpaid labour, tl
rate of profit will be 100 per cent., because the capitalist would al:
get three shillings. If the working man receives only two shilling
or works only one-third of the whole day for himself, the capitali
will get four shillings, and the rate of profit will be 200 per cen
If the working man receives four shillings, the capitalist will onl
receive two, and the rate of profit would sink to 50 per cent, but a
these variations will not affect the value of the commodity. A gener:
rise of wages would, therefore, result in a fall of the general ra•
of profit, but not affect values.

But although the values of commodities, which must ultimatel
regulate their market prices, are exclusively determined by the tot:
quantities of labour fixed in them, and not by the division of tha
quantity into paid and unpaid labour, it by no means follows tha
the values of the single commodities, *or* lots of commodities, produce
during twelve hours, for example, will remain constant. The numbe
or mass of commodities produced in a given time of labour, or by
given quantity of labour, depends upon the *productive power* of th
labour employed, and not upon its *extent* or length. With one degre
of the productive power of spinning labour, for example, a workin
day of twelve hours may produce twelve pounds of yarn, with a lesse
degree of productive power only two pounds. If then twelve hour:
average labour were realised in the value of six shillings in the on
case, the twelve pounds of yarn would cost six shillings, in the othe
case the two pounds of yarn would also cost six shillings. One poun
of yarn would, therefore, cost sixpence in the one case, and thre•
shillings in the other. This difference of price would result fron
the difference in the productive powers of the labour employed
One hour of labour would be realised in one pound of yarn witl
the greater productive power, while with the smaller productive
power, six hours of labour would be realised in one pound of yarn
The price of a pound of yarn would, in the one instance, be onl\
sixpence, although wages were relatively high and the rate of profi•
low; it would be three shillings in the other instance, although wage:
were low and the rate of profit high. This would be so because the
price of the pound of yarn is regulated by the *total amount of labour
worked up in it*, and not by the *proportional division of that total*
amount into paid and unpaid labour. The fact I have before mentioned that high-priced labour may produce cheap, and low-priced
labour may produce dear commodities, loses, therefore, its paradoxi-
cal appearance. It is only the expression of the general law that the
value of a commodity is regulated by the quantity of labour worked
up in it, and that the quantity of labour worked up in it depends

together upon the productive powers of the labour employed, and will, therefore, vary with every variation in the productivity of labour.

XIII MAIN CASES OF ATTEMPTS AT RAISING WAGES OR RESISTING THEIR FALL

Let us now seriously consider the main cases in which a rise of wages is attempted or a reduction of wages resisted.

1. We have seen that the *value of the labouring power*, or in more popular parlance, the *value of labour*, is determined by the value of necessaries, or the quantity of labour required to produce them. If, then, in a given country the value of the daily average necessaries of the labourer represented six hours of labour expressed in three shillings, the labourer would have to work six hours daily to produce an equivalent for his daily maintenance. If the whole working day was twelve hours, the capitalist would pay him the value of his labour by paying him three shillings. Half the working day would be unpaid labour, and the rate of profit would amount to 100 per cent. But now suppose that, consequent upon a decrease of productivity, more labour should be wanted to produce, say, the same amount of agricultural produce, so that the price of the average daily necessaries should rise from three to four shillings. In that case the *value of labour* would rise by one third, or $33^1/_3$ per cent. Eight hours of the working day would be required to produce an equivalent for the daily maintenance of the labourer, according to his old standard of living. The surplus labour would therefore sink from six hours to four, and the rate of profit from 100 to 50 per cent. But in insisting upon a rise of wages, the labourer would only insist upon getting the *increased value of his labour*, like every other seller of a commodity, who, the costs of his commodities having increased, tries to get its increased value paid. If wages did not rise, or not sufficiently rise, to compensate for the increased values of necessaries, the *price* of labour would sink below the *value of labour*, and the labourer's standard of life would deteriorate.

But a change might also take place in an opposite direction. By virtue of the increased productivity of labour, the same amount of the average daily necessaries might sink from three to two shillings, or only four hours out of the working day, instead of six, be wanted to reproduce an equivalent for the value of the daily necessaries. The working man would now be able to buy with two shillings as many necessaries as he did before with three shillings. Indeed, the *value of labour* would have sunk, but that diminished value would command the same amount of commodities as before. Then profits would rise from three to four shillings, and the rate of profit from 100

to 200 per cent. Although the labourer's absolute standard of li
would have remained the same, his *relative* wages, and therewith l
relative social position, as compared with that of the capitalist, wou
have been lowered. If the working man should resist that reductic
of relative wages, he would only try to get some share in the i
creased productive powers of his own labour, and to maintain h
former relative position in the social scale. Thus, after the abolitic
of the Corn Laws,[128] and in flagrant violation of the most solem
pledges given during the anti-corn law agitation, the English facto
lords generally reduced wages ten per cent. The resistance of tl
workmen was at first baffled, but, consequent upon circumstances
cannot now enter upon, the ten per cent lost were afterwards regaine

2. The *values* of necessaries, and consequently the *value of labou*
might remain the same, but a change might occur in their *mone*
prices, consequent upon a previous change in the *value of mone*

By the discovery of more fertile mines and so forth, two ounce
of gold might, for example, cost no more labour to produce tha
one ounce did before. The *value* of gold would then be depreciate
by one half, or fifty per cent. As the *values* of all other commoditie
would then be expressed in twice their former *money prices*, so als
the same with the *value of labour*. Twelve hours of labour, formerl
expressed in six shillings, would now be expressed in twelve shilling:
If the working man's wages should remain three shillings, instead o
rising to six shillings, the *money price of his labour* would only b
equal to *half the value of his labour*, and his standard of life woul
fearfully deteriorate. This would also happen in a greater or lesse
degree if his wages should rise, but not proportionately to the fall ii
the value of gold. In such a case nothing would have been changed
either in the productive powers of labour, or in supply and demand
or in values. Nothing could have changed except the money *names* o
those values. To say that in such a case the workman ought not t
insist upon a proportionate rise of wages, is to say that he must be
content to be paid with names, instead of with things. All pas
history proves that whenever such a depreciation of money occurs
the capitalists are on the alert to seize this opportunity for defraud-
ing the workman. A very large school of political economists assert
that, consequent upon the new discoveries of gold lands, the better
working of silver mines, and the cheaper supply of quicksilver, the
value of precious metals has been again depreciated. This would
explain the general and simultaneous attempts on the Continent at a
rise of wages.

3. We have till now supposed that the *working day* has given
limits. The working day, however, has, by itself, no constant limits. It is the constant tendency of capital to stretch it to its utmost
physically possible length, because in the same degree surplus labour,
and consequently the profit resulting therefrom, will be increased.

he more capital succeeds in prolonging the working day, the greater
ie amount of other people's labour it will appropriate. During the
eventeenth and even the first two-thirds of the eighteenth century
ten hours' working day was the normal working day all over
ngland. During the anti-Jacobin war, which was in fact a war
aged by the British barons against the British working masses,[132]
apital celebrated its bacchanalia, and prolonged the working day
rom ten to twelve, fourteen, eighteen hours. Malthus, by no means
man whom you would suspect of a maudlin sentimentalism, declared
1 a pamphlet, published about 1815, that if this sort of thing was
o go on the life of the nation would be attacked at its very source.[133]
A few years before the general introduction of the newly-invented
nachinery, about 1765, a pamphlet appeared in England under the
itle, *An Essay on Trade.* The anonymous author, an avowed enemy
f the working classes, declaims on the necessity of expanding the
imits of the working day. Amongst other means to this end, he
roposes *working houses,*[134] which, he says, ought to be "Houses of
'error." And what is the length of the working day he prescribes for
hese "Houses of Terror"? *Twelve hours,* the very same time which
n 1832 was declared by capitalists, political economists, and min-
sters to be not only the existing but the necessary time of labour for
. child under twelve years.

By selling his labouring power, and he must do so under the
resent system, the working man makes over to the capitalist the
onsumption of that power, but within certain rational limits. He
ells his labouring power in order to maintain it, apart from its
iatural wear and tear, but not to destroy it. In selling his labouring
ower at its daily or weekly value, it is understood that in one day
r one week that labouring power shall not be submitted to two
lays' or two weeks' waste or wear and tear. Take a machine worth
1,000. If it is used up in ten years it will add to the value of the
ommodities in whose production it assists £100 yearly. If it be used
ip in five years it would add £200 yearly, or the value of its annual
vear and tear is in inverse ratio to the time in which it is consumed.
3ut this distinguishes the working man from the machine. Machinery
loes not wear out exactly in the same ratio in which it is used. Man,
in the contrary, decays in a greater ratio than would be visible from
he mere numerical addition of work.

In their attempts at reducing the working day to its former rational
limensions, or, where they cannot enforce a legal fixation of a nor-
nal working day, at checking overwork by a rise of wages, a rise
iot only in proportion to the surplus time exacted, but in a greater
iroportion, working men fulfil only a duty to themselves and their
ace. They only set limits to the tyrannical usurpations of capital.
Time is the room of human development. A man who has no free
time to dispose of, whose whole lifetime apart from the mere physi-

cal interruptions by sleep, meals, and so forth, is absorbed by h
labour for the capitalist, is less than a beast of burden. He is a mer
machine for producing Foreign Wealth, broken in body and brutalise
in mind. Yet the whole history of modern industry shows that capita
if not checked, will recklessly and ruthlessly work to cast down th
whole working class to the utmost state of degradation.

In prolonging the working day the capitalist may pay *higher wage*
and still lower the *value of labour*, if the rise of wages does not cor
respond to the greater amount of labour extracted, and the quicke
decay of the labouring power thus caused. This may be done ii
another way. Your middle-class statisticians will tell you, fo
instance, that the average wages of factory families in Lancashir
have risen. They forget that instead of the labour of the man, th
head of the family, his wife and perhaps three or four children ar
now thrown under the Juggernaut wheels[135] of capital, and that th
rise of the aggregate wages does not correspond to the aggregat
surplus labour extracted from the family.

Even with given limits of the working day, such as now exist ii
all branches of industry subjected to the factory laws, a rise of wage:
may become necessary, if only to keep up the old standard *value o:
labour*. By increasing the *intensity* of labour, a man may be made to
expend as much vital force in one hour as he formerly did in two
This has, to a certain degree, been effected in the trades, placed undei
the Factory Acts, by the acceleration of machinery, and the greater
number of working machines which a single individual has now to
superintend. If the increase in the intensity of labour or the mass of
labour spent in an hour keeps some fair proportion to the decrease in
the extent of the working day, the working man will still be the
winner. If this limit is overshot, he loses in one form what he has
gained in another, and ten hours of labour may then become as
ruinous as twelve hours were before. In checking this tendency of
capital, by struggling for a rise of wages corresponding to the rising
intensity of labour, the working man only resists the depreciation of
his labour and the deterioration of his race.

4. All of you know that, from reasons I have not now to explain,
capitalistic production moves through certain periodical cycles. It
moves through a state of quiescence, growing animation, prosperity,
overtrade, crisis, and stagnation. The market prices of commodities,
and the market rates of profit, follow these phases, now sinking
below their averages, now rising above them. Considering the whole
cycle, you will find that one deviation of the market price is being
compensated by the other, and that, taking the average of the cycle,
the market prices of commodities are regulated by their values. Well!
During the phase of sinking market prices and the phases of crisis
and stagnation, the working man, if not thrown out of employment
altogether, is sure to have his wages lowered. Not to be defrauded,

he must, even with such a fall of market prices, debate with the capitalist in what proportional degree a fall of wages has become necessary. If, during the phases of prosperity, when extra profits are made, he did not battle for a rise of wages, he would, taking the average of one industrial cycle, not even receive his *average wages*, or the *value* of his labour. It is the utmost height of folly to demand that while his wages are necessarily affected by the adverse phases of the cycle, he should exclude himself from compensation during the prosperous phases of the cycle. Generally, the *values* of all commodities are only realised by the compensation of the continuously changing market prices, springing from the continuous fluctuations of demand and supply. On the basis of the present system labour is only a commodity like others. It must, therefore, pass through the same fluctuations to fetch an average price corresponding to its value. It would be absurd to treat it on the one hand as a commodity, and to want on the other hand to exempt it from the laws which regulate the prices of commodities. The slave receives a permanent and fixed amount of maintenance; the wages labourer does not. He must try to get a rise of wages in the one instance, if only to compensate for a fall of wages in the other. If he resigned himself to accept the will, the dictates of the capitalist as a permanent economical law, he would share in all the miseries of the slave, without the security of the slave.

5. In all the cases I have considered, and they form ninety-nine out of a hundred, you have seen that a struggle for a rise of wages follows only in the track of *previous* changes, and is the necessary offspring of previous changes in the amount of production, the productive powers of labour, the value of labour, the value of money, the extent or the intensity of labour extracted, the fluctuations of market prices, dependent upon the fluctuations of demand and supply, and consistent with the different phases of the industrial cycle; in one word, as reactions of labour against the previous action of capital. By treating the struggle for a rise of wages independently of all these circumstances, by looking only upon the change of wages, and overlooking all the other changes from which they emanate, you proceed from a false premise in order to arrive at false conclusions.

XIV THE STRUGGLE BETWEEN CAPITAL AND LABOUR AND ITS RESULTS

1. Having shown that the periodical resistance on the part of the working men against a reduction of wages, and their periodical attempts at getting a rise of wages, are inseparable from the wages system, and dictated by the very fact of labour being assimilated to commodities, and therefore subject to the laws regulating the general

movement of prices; having, furthermore, shown that a general rise
of wages would result in a fall in the general rate of profit, but not
affect the average prices of commodities, or their values, the question
now ultimately arises, how far, in this incessant struggle between
capital and labour, the latter is likely to prove successful.

I might answer by a generalisation, and say that, as with all other
commodities, so with labour, its *market price* will, in the long run,
adapt itself to its *value*; that, therefore, despite all the ups and downs,
and do what he may, the working man will, on an average, only
receive the value of his labour, which resolves into the value of his
labouring power, which is determined by the value of the necessaries
required for its maintenance and reproduction, which value of necessaries finally is regulated by the quantity of labour wanted to produce
them.

But there are some peculiar features which distinguish the *value
of the labouring power, or the value of labour*, from the values of all
other commodities. The value of the labouring power is formed by
two elements—the one merely physical, the other historical or social.
Its *ultimate limit* is determined by the *physical* element, that is to say,
to maintain and reproduce itself, to perpetuate its physical existence,
the working class must receive the necessaries absolutely indispensable for living and multiplying. The *value* of those indispensable
necessaries forms, therefore, the ultimate limit of the *value of labour*.
On the other hand, the length of the working day is also limited by
ultimate, although very elastic boundaries. Its ultimate limit is given
by the physical force of the labouring man. If the daily exhaustion
of his vital forces exceeds a certain degree, it cannot be exerted anew,
day by day. However, as I said, this limit is very elastic. A quick
succession of unhealthy and short-lived generations will keep the
labour market as well supplied as a series of vigorous and long-lived
generations.

Besides this mere physical element, the value of labour is in every
country determined by a *traditional standard of life*. It is not mere
physical life, but it is the satisfaction of certain wants springing from
the social conditions in which people are placed and reared up. The
English standard of life may be reduced to the Irish standard; the
standard of life of a German peasant to that of a Livonian peasant.
The important part which historical tradition and social habitude
play in this respect, you may learn from Mr. Thornton's work on
Over-population, where he shows that the average wages in different
agricultural districts of England still nowadays differ more or less
according to the more or less favourable circumstances under which
the districts have emerged from the state of serfdom.

This historical or social element, entering into the value of labour,
may be expanded, or contracted, or altogether extinguished, so that
nothing remains but the *physical limit*. During the time of the anti-

Jacobin war, undertaken, as the incorrigible tax-eater and sinecurist, old George Rose, used to say, to save the comforts of our holy religion from the inroads of the French infidels, the honest English farmers, so tenderly handled in a former chapter of ours, depressed the wages of the agricultural labourers even beneath that *mere physical minimum*, but made up by Poor Laws[136] the remainder necessary for the physical perpetuation of the race. This was a glorious way to convert the wages labourer into a slave, and Shakespeare's proud yeoman into a pauper.

By comparing the standard wages or values of labour in different countries, and by comparing them in different historical epochs of the same country, you will find that the *value of labour* itself is not a fixed but a variable magnitude, even supposing the values of all other commodities to remain constant.

A similar comparison would prove that not only the *market rates* of profit change but its *average* rates.

But as to *profits*, there exists no law which determines their *minimum*. We cannot say what is the ultimate limit of their decrease. And why cannot we fix that limit? Because, although we can fix the *minimum* of wages, we cannot fix their *maximum*. We can only say that, the limits of the working day being given, the *maximum* of profit corresponds to the *physical minimum of wages*; and that wages being given, the *maximum of profit* corresponds to such a prolongation of the working day as is compatible with the physical forces of the labourer. The maximum of profit is, therefore, limited by the physical minimum of wages and the physical maximum of the working day. It is evident that between the two limits of this *maximum rate of profit* an immense scale of variations is possible. The fixation of its actual degree is only settled by the continuous struggle between capital and labour, the capitalist constantly tending to reduce wages to their physical minimum, and to extend the working day to its physical maximum, while the working man constantly presses in the opposite direction.

The matter resolves itself into a question of the respective powers of the combatants.

2. As to the *limitation of the working day* in England, as in all other countries, it has never been settled except by *legislative interference*. Without the working men's continuous pressure from without that interference would never have taken place. But at all events, the result was not to be attained by private settlement between the working men and the capitalists. This very necessity of *general political action* affords the proof that in its merely economic action capital is the stronger side.

As to the *limits* of the *value of labour*, its actual settlement always depends upon supply and demand, I mean the demand for labour on the part of capital, and the supply of labour by the working men. In colonial countries the law of supply and demand favours the working man. Hence the relatively high standard of wages in the United States. Capital may there try its utmost. It cannot prevent the labour market from being continuously emptied by the continuous conversion of wages labourers into independent, self-sustaining peasants. The position of wages labourer is for a very large part of the American people but a probational state, which they are sure to leave within a longer or shorter term. To mend this colonial state of things, the paternal British Government accepted for some time what is called the modern colonisation theory, which consists in putting an artificial high price upon colonial land, in order to prevent the too quick conversion of the wages labourer into the independent peasant.

But let us now come to old civilised countries, in which capital domineers over the whole process of production. Take, for example, the rise in England of agricultural wages from 1849 to 1859. What was its consequence? The farmers could not, as our friend Weston would have advised them, raise the value of wheat, nor even its market prices. They had, on the contrary, to submit to their fall. But during these eleven years they introduced machinery of all sorts, adopted more scientific methods, converted part of arable land into pasture, increased the size of farms, and with this the scale of production, and by these and other processes diminishing the demand for labour by increasing its productive power, made the agricultural population again relatively redundant. This is the general method in which a reaction, quicker or slower, of capital against a rise of wages takes place in old, settled countries. Ricardo has justly remarked that machinery is in constant competition with labour, and can often be only introduced when the price of labour has reached a certain height,[137] but the appliance of machinery is but one of the many methods for increasing the productive powers of labour. This very same development which makes common labour relatively redundant simplifies on the other hand skilled labour, and thus depreciates it.

The same law obtains in another form. With the development of the productive powers of labour the accumulation of capital will be accelerated, even despite a relatively high rate of wages. Hence, one might infer, as Adam Smith, in whose days modern industry was still in its infancy, did infer, that the accelerated accumulation of capital must turn the balance in favour of the working man, by securing a growing demand for his labour. From this same standpoint many contemporary writers have wondered that English capital having grown in the last twenty years so much quicker than English population, wages should not have been more enhanced. But simultaneously with the progress of accumulation there takes place a *progressive change* in the *composition of capital*. That part of the aggregate capital which consists of fixed capital, machinery, raw materials, means of production in all possible forms, progressively increases as compared with the other part of capital, which is laid out in wages or in the purchase of labour. This law has been stated in a more or less accurate manner by Mr. Barton, Ricardo, Sismondi, Professor Richard Jones, Professor Ramsay, Cherbuliez, and others.

If the proportion of these two elements of capital was originally one to one, it will, in the progress of industry, become five to one, and so forth. If of a total capital of 600, 300 is laid out in instruments, raw materials, and so forth, and 300 in wages, the total capital wants only to be doubled to create a demand for 600 working men instead of for 300. But if of a capital of 600, 500 is laid out in machinery, materials, and so forth, and 100 only in wages, the same capital must increase from 600 to 3,600 in ord r to create a demand for 600 workmen instead of 300. In the progress of industry the demand for labour keeps, therefore, no pace with accumulation of capital. It will still increase, but increase in a constantly diminishing ratio as compared with the increase of capital.

These few hints will suffice to show that the very development of modern industry must progressively turn the scale in favour of the capitalist against the working man, and that consequently the general tendency of capitalistic production is not to raise, but to sink the average standard of wages, or to push the *value of labour* more or less to its *minimum limit*. Such being the tendency of *things* in this system, is this saying that the working class ought to renounce their resistance against the encroachments of capital, and abandon their attempts at making the best of the occasional chances for their temporary improvement? If they did, they would be degraded to one level mass of broken wretches past salvation. I think I have shown that their struggles for the standard of wages are incidents inseparable from the whole wages system, that in 99 cases out of 100 their efforts at raising wages are only efforts at maintaining the given value of labour, and that the necessity of debating their price with the capitalist is inherent in their condition of having to sell themselves as commodities. By cowardly giving way in their everyday conflict with capital, they would certainly disqualify themselves for the initiating of any larger movement.

At the same time, and quite apart from the general servitude involved in the wages system, the working class ought not to exaggerate to themselves the ultimate working of these everyday struggles. They ought not to forget that they are fighting with effects, but not with the causes of those effects; that they are retarding the downward movement, but not changing its direction; that they are applying palliatives, not curing the malady. They ought, therefore, not to be exclusively absorbed in these unavoidable guerilla fights incessantly springing up from the never-ceasing encroachments of capital or changes of the market. They ought to understand that, with all the miseries it imposes pon them, the present system simultaneously engenders the *material conditions* and the *social forms* necessary for an economical reconstruction of society. Instead of the *conservative* motto, "*A fair day's wage for a fair day's work!*" they ought to inscribe on their banner the *revolutionary* watchword, "*Abolition of the wages system!*"

After this very long and, I fear, tedious exposition which I was obliged to enter into to do some justice to the subject-matter, I shall conclude by proposing the following resolutions:

Firstly. A general rise in the rate of wages would result in a fall of the general rate of profit, but, broadly speaking, not affect the prices of commodities.

Secondly. The general tendency of capitalist production is not to raise, but to sink the average standard of wages.

Thirdly. Trades Unions work well as centres of resistance against the encroachments of capital. They fail partially from an injudicious use of their power. They fail generally from limiting themselves to a guerilla war against the effects of the existing system, instead of simultaneously trying to change it, instead of using their organised forces as a lever for the final emancipation of the working class, that is to say, the ultimate abolition of the wages system.

Written by Marx between
the end of May and June
27, 1865

First published as a separate
pamphlet in London in 1898

Printed according to the
manuscript
Written in English

Karl Marx

PREFACE TO THE FIRST GERMAN EDITION OF THE FIRST VOLUME OF *CAPITAL*[138]

The work, the first volume of which I now submit to the public, forms the continuation of my *Zur Kritik der Politischen Ökonomie* (*A Contribution to the Critique of Political Economy*) published in 1859. The long pause between the first part and the continuation is due to an illness of many years' duration that again and again interrupted my work.

The substance of that earlier work is summarised in the first three chapters of this volume.[139] This is done not merely for the sake of connection and completeness. The presentation of the subject-matter is improved. As far as circumstances in any way permit, many points only hinted at in the earlier book are here worked out more fully, whilst, conversely, points worked out fully there are only touched upon in this volume. The sections on the history of the theories of value and of money are now, of course, left out altogether. The reader of the earlier work will find, however, in the notes to the first chapter additional sources of reference relative to the history of those theories.

Every beginning is difficult, holds in all sciences. To understand the first chapter, especially the section that contains the analysis of commodities, will, therefore, present the greatest difficulty. That which concerns more especially the analysis of the substance of value and the magnitude of value, I have, as much as it was possible, popularised.* The value-form, whose fully developed shape

---

This is the more necessary, as even the section of Ferdinand Lassalle's work against Schulze-Delitzsch, in which he professes to give "the intellectual quintessence" of my explanations on these subjects,[140] contains important mistakes. If Ferdinand Lassalle has borrowed almost literally from my writings, and without any acknowledgement, all the general theoretical propositions in his economic works, *e. g.*, those on the historical character of capital, on connection between the conditions of production and the mode of production. &c., &c., even to the terminology created by me, this may perhaps be due to purposes of propaganda. I am here, of course, not speaking of his detailed working-out and application of these propositions, with which I have nothing to do. [*Note by Marx.*]

is the money-form, is very elementary and simple. Nevertheless, the human mind has for more than 2.000 years sought in vain to get to the bottom of it, whilst on the other hand, to the successful analysis of much more composite and complex forms, there has been at least an approximation. Why? Because the body, as an organic whole, is more easy of study than are the cells of that body. In the analysis of economic forms, moreover, neither microscopes nor chemical reagents are of use. The force of abstraction must replace both. But in bourgeois society the commodity-form of the product of labour—or the value-form of the commodity—is the economic cell-form. To the superficial observer, the analysis of these forms seems to turn upon minutiae. It does in fact deal with minutiae, but they are of the same order as those dealt with in microscopic anatomy.

With the exception of the section on value-form, therefore, this volume cannot stand accused on the score of difficulty. I presuppose, of course, a reader who is willing to learn something new and therefore to think for himself.

The physicist either observes physical phenomena where they occur in their most typical form and most free from disturbing influence, or, wherever possible, he makes experiments under conditions that assure the occurrence of the phenomenon in its normality. In this work I have to examine the capitalist mode of production, and the conditions of production and exchange corresponding to that mode. Up to the present time, their classic ground is England. That is the reason why England is used as the chief illustration in the development of my theoretical ideas. If, however, the German reader shrugs his shoulders at the condition of the English industrial and agricultural labourers, or in optimist fashion comforts himself with the thought that in Germany things are not nearly so bad, I must plainly tell him: *"De te fabula narratur!"*[*]

Intrinsically, it is not a question of the higher or lower degree of development of the social antagonisms that result from the natural laws of capitalist production. It is a question of these laws themselves, of these tendencies working with iron necessity towards inevitable results. The country that is more developed industrially only shows, to the less developed, the image of its own future.

But apart from this. Where capitalist production is fully naturalised among the Germans (for instance, in the factories proper) the condition of things is much worse than in England,

---

* "It is of you that the story is told!" (Horace, *Satires*, Book One, Sat. I.)—*Ed.*

because the counterpoise of the Factory Acts is wanting. In all other spheres, we, like all the rest of Continental Western Europe, suffer not only from the development of capitalist production, but also from the incompleteness of that development. Alongside of modern evils, a whole series of inherited evils oppress us, arising from the passive survival of antiquated modes of production, with their inevitable train of social and political anachronisms. We suffer not only from the living, but from the dead. *Le mort saisit le vif!* *

The social statistics of Germany and the rest of Continental Western Europe are, in comparison with those of England, wretchedly compiled. But they raise the veil just enough to let us catch a glimpse of the Medusa head behind it. We should be appalled at the state of things at home, if, as in England, our governments and parliaments appointed periodically commissions of enquiry into economic conditions; if these commissions were armed with the same plenary powers to get at the truth; if it was possible to find for this purpose men as competent, as free from partisanship and respect of persons as are the English factory-inspectors, her medical reporters on public health, her commissioners of enquiry into the exploitation of women and children, into housing and food. Perseus wore a magic cap that the monsters he hunted down might not see him. We draw the magic cap down over eyes and ears as a make-believe that there are no monsters.

Let us not deceive ourselves on this. As in the 18th century, the American War of Independence[141] sounded the tocsin for the European middle class, so in the 19th century, the American civil war sounded it for the European working-class.[129] In England the progress of social disintegration is palpable. When it has reached a certain point, it must react on the continent. There it will take a form more brutal or more humane, according to the degree of development of the working-class itself. Apart from higher motives, therefore, their own most important interests dictate to the classes that are for the nonce the ruling ones, the removal of all legally removable hindrances to the free development of the working-class. For this reason, as well as others, I have given so large a space in this volume to the history, the details, and the results of English factory legislation. One nation can and should learn from others. And even when a society has got upon the right track for the discovery of the natural laws of its movement—and it is the ultimate aim of this work to lay bare the economic law of motion of modern society—it can neither clear by bold leaps, nor remove

---

* "The dead holds the living in his grasp!"—*Ed.*

by legal enactments, the obstacles offered by successive phases of
its normal development. But it can shorten and lessen the birth-
pangs.

To prevent possible misunderstanding, a word. I paint the
capitalist and the landlord in no sense *couleur de rose*. But here
individuals are dealt with only in so far as they are the personifications of economic categories, embodiments of particular class-
relations and class-interests. My standpoint, from which the evolution of the economic formation of society is viewed as a process of
natural history, can less than any other make the individual responsible for relations whose creature he socially remains, however
much he may subjectively raise himself above them.

In the domain of Political Economy, free scientific enquiry
meets not merely the same enemies as in all other domains. The
peculiar nature of the material it deals with, summons as foes into
the field of battle the most violent, mean and malignant passions
of the human breast, the Furies of private interest. The English
Established Church,*[142] *e.g.*, will more readily pardon an attack
on 38 of its 39 articles than on 1/39 of its income. Nowadays
atheism itself is *culpa levis*,** as compared with criticism of existing
property relations. Nevertheless, there is an unmistakable advance.
I refer, *e.g.*, to the Blue Book[143] published within the last few
weeks: "Correspondence with Her Majesty's Missions Abroad,
regarding Industrial Questions and Trades Unions." The representatives of the English Crown in foreign countries there declare
in so many words that in Germany, in France, to be brief, in all
the civilised states of the European continent, a radical change in
the existing relations between capital and labour is as evident and
inevitable as in England. At the same time, on the other side of the
Atlantic Ocean, Mr. Wade, Vice-President of the United States,
declared in public meetings that, after the abolition of slavery, a
radical change of the relations of capital and of property in land
is next upon the order of the day. These are signs of the times, not
to be hidden by purple mantles or black cassocks. They do not
signify that to-morrow a miracle will happen. They show that,
within the ruling-classes themselves, a foreboding is dawning, that
the present society is no solid crystal, but an organism capable of
change, and is constantly changing.

The second volume of this work will treat of the process of the
circulation of capital (Book II.), and of the varied forms assumed

---

* In the German original *Hochkirche*—High Church. It is a trend in the
Anglican Church which had followers mainly from among the aristocracy. It
preserved magnificent religious rites which underscored its continuity of Catholicism.—*Ed.*
** Light offence.—*Ed.*

by capital in the course of its development (Book III.), the third and last volume (Book IV.), the history of the theory.

Every opinion based on scientific criticism I welcome. As to the prejudices of so-called public opinion, to which I have never made concessions, now as aforetime the maxim of the great Florentine is mine:

*"Segui il tuo corso, e lascia dir le genti."**

Karl Marx

London, July 25, 1867

First published in the book:
K. Marx. *Das Kapital. Kritik der politischen Oekonomie.*
Erster Band. Hamburg, 1867

Printed according to the English edition,
London, 1887
Edited by Engels

---

* "Follow your own course, and let people talk" (Dante, *The Divine Comedy*, Purgatory, Canto V, paraphrased).—*Ed.*

Karl Marx

HISTORICAL TENDENCY OF CAPITALIST ACCUMULATION

CHAPTER XXXII OF THE FIRST VOLUME OF *CAPITAL*[138]

What does the prim tive accumulation of capital, *i.e.*, its historical genesis, resolve itself into? In so far as it is not immediate transformation of slaves and serfs into wage-labourers, and therefore a mere change of form, it only means the expropriation of the immediate producers, *i.e.*, the dissolution of private property based on the labour of its owner. Private property, as the antithesis to social, collective property, exists only where the means of labour and the external conditions of labour belong to private individuals. But according as these private individuals are labourers or not labourers, private property has a different character. The numberless shades, that it at first sight presents, correspond to the intermediate stages lying between these two extremes. The private property of the labourer in his means of production is the foundation of petty industry, whether agricultural, manufacturing, or both; petty industry, again, is an essential condition for the development of social production and of the free individuality of the labourer himself. Of course, this petty mode of production exists also under slavery, serfdom, and other states of dependence. But it flourishes, it lets loose its whole energy, it attains its adequate classical form, only where the labourer is the private owner of his own means of labour set in action by himself: the peasant of the land which he cultivates, the artisan of the tool which he handles as a virtuoso. This mode of production presupposes parcelling of the soil, and scattering of the other means of production. As it excludes the concentration of these means of production, so also it excludes co-operation, division of labour within each separate process of production, the control over, and the productive application of the forces of Nature by society, and the free development of the social productive powers. It is compatible only with a system of production, and a society, moving within narrow and more or less primitive bounds. To perpetuate it would be, as Pecqueur rightly says, "to decree universal mediocrity."[144] At a certain stage of development it brings forth the material agencies for its own dissolution. From that moment new forces and new passions spring up in the bosom of society; but the old social organisation fetters them and keeps them down. It must be annihilated; it is annihilated. Its annihilation, the transformation of the individualised and scattered means of production into socially concentrated ones, of the pigmy property of the many into the huge property of the few, the expropriation of the great mass of the people from the soil, from the means of subsistence, and from the means of labour, this fearful and painful expropriation of the mass of the people forms the prelude to the history of capital. It comprises a series of forcible methods, of which we have passed in review only those that have been epoch-making as methods of the primitive accumulation of capital. The expropriation of the immediate producers was accomplished with merciless Vandalism, and under the stimulus of passions the most infamous, the most sordid, the pettiest, the most meanly odious. Self-earned private property. that is based, so to say, on the fusing together of the isolated, independent labouring individual with the conditions of his labour, is supplanted by capitalistic private property, which rests on exploitation of the nominally free labour of others, i.e., on wages labour.*

As soon as this process of transformation has sufficiently decomposed the old society from top to bottom, as soon as the labourers are turned into proletarians, their means of labour into capital, as soon as the capitalist mode of production stands on its own feet, then the further socialisation of labour and further transformation of the land and other means of production into socially exploited and, therefore, common means of production, as well as the further expropriation of private proprietors, takes a new form. That which is now to be expropriated is no longer the labourer working for himself, but the capitalist exploiting many labourers. This expropriation is accomplished by the action of the immanent laws of capitalistic production itself, by the centralisation of capital. One capitalist always kills many. Hand in hand with this centralisation, or this expropriation of many capitalists by few, develop, on an ever-extending scale, the co-operative form of the labour-process, the conscious technical application of science, the methodical cultivation of the soil, the transformation of the instruments of labour into instruments of labour only usable in common, the economising of all means of production by their use as the means of production of combined, socialised labour, the entanglement of all peoples in the net of the world-market, and with this, the international character of the capitalistic régime. Along with the constantly diminishing number of the magnates of capital, who usurp and monopolise all advantages of this process of transformation,

---

* "We are in a situation that is entirely new for society ... we endeavour to separate every form of property from every form of labour." Sismondi, Nouveaux principes de l'économie politique, Vol. II, p. 434. [Note by Marx.]

Marx here refers to the second edition of the book, S. Sismondi, Nouveaux principes de l'économie politique, ou de la richesse dans ses rapports avec la population. [New Principles of Political Economy, or Wealth in Its Relations with the Population.] Vols. I-II, Paris 1827.—Ed.

grows the mass of misery, oppression, slavery, degradation, exploitation; but with this too grows the revolt of the working class, a class always increasing in numbers, and disciplined, united, organised by the very mechanism of the process of capitalist production itself. The monopoly of capital becomes a fetter upon the mode of production, which has sprung up and flourished along with, and under it. Centralisation of the means of production and socialisation of labour at last reach a point where they become incompatible with their capitalist integument. This integument is burst asunder. The knell of capitalist private property sounds. The expropriators are expropriated.

The capitalist mode of appropriation, the result of the capitalist mode of production, produces capitalist private property. This is the first negation of individual private property, as founded on the labour of the proprietor. But capitalist production begets, with the inexorability of a law of Nature, its own negation. It is the negation of negation. This does not re-establish private property for the producer, but gives him individual property based on the acquisitions of the capitalist era: *i.e.*, on co-operation and the possession in common of the land and of the means of production.

The transformation of scattered private property, arising from individual labour, into capitalist private property is, naturally, a process, incomparably more protracted, violent, and difficult, than the transformation of capitalistic private property, already practically resting on socialised production, into socialised property. In the former case, we had the expropriation of the mass of the people by a few usurpers; in the latter, we have the expropriation of a few usurpers by the mass of the people.*

First published in the book: Printed according to the
K. Marx. *Das Kapital. Kritik*   English edition,
der politischen Oekonomie.   London, 1887
Erster Band. Hamburg, 1867   Edited by Engels

---

* The advance of industry, whose involuntary promoter is the bourgeoisie, replaces the isolation of the labourers, due to competition, by their revolutionary combination, due to association. The development of Modern Industry, therefore, cuts from under its feet the very foundation on which the bourgeoisie produces and appropriates products. What the bourgeoisie, therefore, produces, above all, are its own grave-diggers. Its fall and the victory of the proletariat are equally inevitable.... Of all the classes that stand face to face with the bourgeoisie today, the proletariat alone is a really revolutionary class. The other classes perish and disappear in the face of Modern Industry, the proletariat is its special and essential product.... The lower middle classes, the small manufacturers, the shopkeepers, the artisan, the peasant, all these fight against the bourgeoisie, to save from extinction their existence as fractions of the middle class ... they are reactionary, for they try to roll back the wheel of history. [*Note by Marx.*]

Marx took this quotation from the *Manifesto of the Communist Party.*—See pp. 46 and 44 of this volume.—*Ed.*

Frederick Engels

PREFACE TO
THE PEASANT WAR IN GERMANY[145]

The following work was written in London in the summer of
1850, while the impression of the counter-revolution just then
completed was still fresh; it appeared in the fifth and sixth issues
of the *Neue Rheinische Zeitung. A Politico-Economic Review*,[146]
edited by Karl Marx, Hamburg, 1850. My political friends in Germany desire it to be reprinted, and I accede to their desire, because
to my regret, the work is still timely today.

It makes no claim to providing material derived from independent
research. On the contrary, the entire subject-matter on the peasant
risings and on Thomas Münzer is taken from Zimmermann.[147] His
book, despite gaps here and there, is still the best compilation of the
factual material. Moreover, old Zimmermann enjoyed his subject.
The same revolutionary instinct, which prompted him here to
champion the oppressed classes, made him later one of the best of
the extreme Left in Frankfurt.[148] It is true that since then he is said
to have aged somewhat.

If, nevertheless, Zimmermann's presentation lacks inner connections; if it does not succeed in showing the politico-religious controversies of the times as a reflection of the contemporary class
struggles; if it sees in these class struggles only oppressors and
oppressed, evil folk and good folk, and the ultimate victory of the
evil ones; if its exposition of the social conditions which determined
both the outbreak and the outcome of the struggle is extremely defective, it was the fault of the time in which the book came into
existence. On the contrary, for its time, it is written quite realistically
and is a laudable exception among the German idealist works on
history.

My presentation, while sketching the historic course of the
struggle only in its bare outlines, attempted to explain the origin
of the Peasant War, the position of the various parties that played
a part in it, the political and religious theories by which those
parties sought to clarify their position in their own minds, and
finally the result of the struggle itself as a necessary upshot of
the historically established conditions of the social life of these
classes; that is to say, it attempted to demonstrate the political
structure of the Germany of that time, the revolts against it and

the contemporary political and religious theories not as causes but as results of the stage of development of agriculture, industry, land and waterways, commerce in commodities and money then obtaining in Germany. This, the only materialist conception of history, originates not with myself but with Marx, and can also be found in his work on the French Revolution of 1848-49,* in the same *Review*, and in *The Eighteenth Brumaire of Louis Bonaparte.***

The parallel between the German Revolution of 1525 and that of 1848-49 was too obvious to be altogether rejected at that time. Nevertheless, despite the uniformity in the course of events, where various local revolts were crushed one after another by one and the same princely army, despite the often ludicrous similarity in the behaviour of the city burghers in both cases, the difference was clear and distinct.

"Who profited by the Revolution of 1525? The *princes*. Who profited by the Revolution of 1848? The *big* princes, Austria and Prussia. Behind the minor princes of 1525 stood the petty burghers, who chained the princes to themselves by taxes. Behind the big princes of 1850, behind Austria and Prussia, there stand the modern big bourgeois, rapidly getting them under their yoke by means of the national debt. And behind the big bourgeois stand the proletarians."***

I regret to have to say that in this paragraph much too much honour was done the German bourgeoisie. Both in Austria and Prussia it has indeed had the opportunity of "rapidly getting" the monarchy "under its yoke by means of the national debt," but nowhere did it ever make use of this opportunity.

The war of 1866[149] dropped Austria as a boon into the lap of the bourgeoisie. But it does not know how to rule, it is powerless and incapable of anything. It can do only one thing: savagely attack the workers as soon as they begin to stir. It is still at the helm solely because the *Hungarians* need it.

And in Prussia? True, the national debt has increased by leaps and bounds, the deficit has become a permanent feature, state expenditure grows from year to year, members of the bourgeoisie have a majority in the Chamber and without their consent taxes cannot be increased nor loans floated. But where is their power over the state? Only a few months ago, when there was again a deficit, the bourgeoisie occupied a most favourable position. By holding out only just *a little*, they could have forced far-reaching concessions. What do they do? They regard it as a sufficient concession that the government *allows them* to lay at its feet close on

---

* K. Marx, *The Class Struggles in France, 1848 to 1850.—Ed.*
** See pp. 96-179 of this volume.—*Ed.*
*** F. Engels, *The Peasant War in Germany*, Moscow, 1965, p. 127.—*Ed.*

nine millions, not for *one* year, oh no, but for *every* year, and for all time to come.

I do not want to blame the poor National-Liberals[150] in the Chamber more than they deserve. I know they have been left in the lurch by those who stand behind them, by the mass of the bourgeoisie. This mass does not *want* to rule. It still has 1848 in its bones.

Why the German bourgeoisie exhibits this astonishing cowardice will be discussed later.

In other respects the above statement has been fully confirmed. Beginning with 1850, the more and more definite recession into the background of the small states, serving now only as levers for Prussian or Austrian intrigues; the increasingly violent struggles for sole rule waged between Austria and Prussia; finally, the forcible settlement of 1866, after which Austria retains her own provinces, while Prussia subjugates directly or indirectly the whole of the North and the three states* of the Southwest are left out in the cold for the time being.

In all this grand performance of state nothing but the following is of importance for the German working class:

First, universal suffrage has given the workers the means of being directly represented in the legislative assembly.

Secondly, Prussia has set a good example by swallowing three other crowns held by the grace of God.** Even the National-Liberals do not believe that *after* this operation it still possesses the same immaculate crown, held by the grace of God, which it formerly ascribed to itself.

Thirdly, there is now only *one* serious adversary of the revolution in Germany—the Prussian government.

And fourthly, the German-Austrians will now at last have to make up their minds what they want to be, Germans or Austrians; whom they prefer to belong to—Germany or their extra-German transleithan appendages. It has been obvious for a long time that they have to give up one or the other, but this has been continually glossed over by the petty-bourgeois democrats.

As regards the other important controversial points relative to 1866, which since then have been thrashed out *ad nauseam* between the National-Liberals on the one hand, and the People's Party[151] on the other, the history of the next few years should prove that these two standpoints are so bitterly hostile to one another solely because they are the opposite poles of the same narrow-mindedness.

The year 1866 has changed almost nothing in the social pattern of Germany. The few bourgeois reforms—uniform weights and measures, freedom of movement, freedom of occupation, etc., all

---

* Bavaria, Baden, Württemberg.—*Ed.*

** Hanover, Hesse-Cassel, Nassau.—*Ed.*

within limits acceptable to the bureaucracy—do not even come
up to *what* the bourgeoisie of other West-European countries had
long possessed, and leave the main abuse, the system of bureaucratic tutelage,[152] untouched. For the proletariat all legislation concerning freedom of movement, the right of naturalisation, the
abolition of passports, *et cetera*, is anyhow made quite illusory by
the common police practices.

What is much more important than the grand performance of
1866 is the growth of German industry and commerce, of railways,
telegraphs and ocean shipping since 1848. However much this
progress lags behind that of England, or even of France, during the
same period, it is unprecedented for Germany and has accomplished
more in twenty years than previously in a whole century. Only
now has Germany been drawn, seriously and irrevocably, into
world commerce. The capital of the industrialists has multiplied
rapidly; the social position of the bourgeoisie has risen accordingly.
The surest sign of industrial prosperity—*swindling*—has established
itself abundantly and chained counts and dukes to its triumphal
chariot. German capital is now constructing Russian and Rumanian
railways—may it not come to grief!—whereas only fifteen years
ago, German railways went begging to English *entrepreneurs.*
How, then, is it possible that the bourgeoisie has not conquered
political power as well, that it behaves in so cowardly a manner
towards the government?

It is the misfortune of the German bourgeoisie to have arrived
too late, as is the favourite German manner. The period of its
florescence is occurring at a time when the bourgeoisie of the other
West-European countries is already politically in decline. In
England, the bourgeoisie could get its real representative, Bright,
into the government only by an extension of the franchise,[153] whose
consequences are bound to put an end to all bourgeois rule. In
France, where the bourgeoisie as such, as a class in its entirety,
held power for only two years, 1849 and 1850, under the republic,
it was able to continue its social existence only by abdicating its
political power to Louis Bonaparte and the army. And on account
of the enormously increased interaction of the three most advanced
European countries, it is today no longer possible for the bourgeoisie to settle down to comfortable political rule in Germany after
this rule has outlived its usefulness in England and France.

It is a peculiarity of the bourgeoisie, in contrast to all former
ruling classes, that there is a turning point in its development after
which every further expansion of its agencies of power, hence
primarily of its capital, only tends to make it more and more unfit
for political rule. "*Behind the big bourgeois stand the proletarians.*"
As the bourgeoisie develops its industry, commerce and means of
communication, it produces the proletariat. At a certain point—which

need not be reached everywhere at the same time or at the same stage of development—it begins to notice that its proletarian double is outgrowing it. From that moment on, it loses the strength required for exclusive political rule; it looks around for allies with whom to share its rule, or to whom to cede the whole of its rule, as circumstances may require.

In Germany this turning point came as early as 1848. To be sure, the German bourgeoisie was less frightened by the German proletariat than by the French. The June 1848 battle in Paris[6] showed the bourgeoisie what it ought to expect; the German proletariat was restless enough to prove to it that the seed that would yield the same crop had already been sown to German soil, too; from that day on the edge was taken off all bourgeois political action. The bourgeoisie looked round for allies, sold itself to them regardless of the price—and even today it has not advanced one step.

These allies are all reactionary by nature. There is the monarchy with its army and its bureaucracy; there is the big feudal nobility; there are the little cabbage-Junkers[19] and there are even the priests. With all of these the bourgeoisie made pacts and bargains, if only to save its dear skin, until at last it had nothing left to barter. And the more the proletariat developed, the more it felt as a class and acted as a class, the more faint-hearted did the bourgeois become. When the astonishingly bad strategy of the Prussians triumphed over the astonishingly worse strategy of the Austrians at Sadowa,[154] it was difficult to say who heaved a deeper sigh of relief—the Prussian bourgeois, who was also defeated at Sadowa, or the Austrian.

Our big bourgeois of 1870 still act exactly as the middle burghers of 1525 acted. As to the petty bourgeois, artisans and shopkeepers, they will always be the same. They hope to climb, to swindle their way into the big bourgeoisie; they are afraid of being thrown down into the proletariat. Hovering between fear and hope, they will during the struggle save their precious skin and join the victor when the struggle is over. Such is their nature.

The social and political activity of the proletariat has kept pace with the upsurgence of industry since 1848. The role that the German workers play today in their trade unions, co-operative societies, political associations and at meetings, elections and in the so-called Reichstag, is by itself sufficient proof of the transformation Germany has imperceptibly undergone in the last twenty years. It redounds to the credit of the German workers that *they alone* have succeeded in sending workers and workers' representatives into parliament—a feat which neither the French nor the English have so far accomplished.

But even the proletariat has not yet outgrown the parallel of 1525. The class exclusively dependent on wages all its life is still far from being the majority of the German people. It is, therefore, also compelled to seek allies. These are to be found only among the petty bourgeoisie, the lumpenproletariat of the cities, the small peasants and the agricultural labourers.

The *petty bourgeois* we have spoken of above. They are extremely unreliable except after a victory has been won, when their shouting in the beer houses knows no bounds. Nevertheless, there are very good elements among them, who join the workers of their own accord.

The *lumpenproletariat*, this scum of depraved elements from all classes, with headquarters in the big cities, is the worst of all the possible allies. This rabble is absolutely venal and absolutely brazen. If the French workers, in every revolution, inscribed on the houses: *Mort aux voleurs!* Death to thieves! and even shot some, they did it not out of reverence for property, but because they rightly considered it necessary above all to get rid of that gang. Every leader of the workers who uses these scoundrels as guards or relies on them for support proves himself by this action alone a traitor to the movement.

The *small peasants*—for the bigger peasants belong to the bourgeoisie—differ in kind.

They are either *feudal peasants* and still have to perform corvée services for their gracious lord. Now that the bourgeoisie has failed in its duty of freeing these people from serfdom, it will not be difficult to convince them that they can expect salvation only from the working class.

Or they are *tenant farmers*. In the latter case the situation is for the most part the same as in Ireland. Rents are pushed so high that in times of average crops the peasant and his family can barely make ends meet; when the crops are bad he is on the verge of starvation, is unable to pay his rent and is consequently entirely at the mercy of the landlord. The bourgeoisie never does anything for these people, unless it is compelled to. From whom then should they expect salvation if not from the workers?

There remain the peasants who cultivate their *own little patches of land*. In most cases they are so burdened with mortgages[155] that they are as dependent on the usurer as the tenant on the landlord. For them also there remains only a meagre wage, which, moreover, since there are good years and bad years, is highly uncertain. These people have least of all to expect anything from the bourgeoisie, because it is precisely the bourgeoisie, the capitalist usurers, who suck the lifeblood out of them. Still, most of these peasants cling to their property, though in reality it does not belong to them but to the usurer. It will have to be brought home to them all the same that they can be freed from the usurer only when a government dependent on the people has transformed all mortgages into debts to the state, and thereby lowered the interest rates. And this can be brought about only by the working class.

Wherever medium-sized and large estates prevail, *farm labourers* form the most numerous class in the countryside. This is the case throughout the North and East of Germany and it is *there* that the industrial workers of the towns find their *most numerous and most natural allies*. In the same way as the capitalist confronts the industrial worker, the landowner or large tenant confronts the farm labourer. The same measures that help the one must also help the other. The industrial workers can free themselves only by transforming the capital of the bourgeois, that is, the raw materials, machines and tools, and the means of subsistence they need to work in production, into the property of society, that is, into their own property, used by them in common. Similarly, the farm labourers can be rescued from their hideous misery only when, primarily, their chief object of labour, the land itself, is withdrawn from the private ownership of the big peasants and the still bigger feudal lords, transformed into public property and cultivated by cooperative associations of agricultural workers on their common account. Here we come to the famous decision of the International Working Men's Congress in Basle that it is in the interest of society to transform landed property into common, national property.[156] This resolution was adopted mainly for countries where there is big landed property, and where, consequently, these big estates are operated by one master and many labourers. This state of affairs, however, is still largely predominant in Germany, and therefore, next to England, the decision was most *timely precisely for Germany*. The agricultural proletariat, the farm labourers—that is the class from which the bulk of the armies of the princes is recruited. It is the class which, thanks to universal suffrage, sends into parliament the numerous feudal lords and Junkers; but it is also the class nearest to the industrial workers of the towns, which shares their living conditions and is steeped even more in misery than they. To galvanise and draw into the movement this class, impotent because split and scattered, is the immediate and most urgent task of the German labour movement. Its latent power is so well known to the government and nobility that they let the schools fall into decay deliberately in order to keep it ignorant. The day the farm labourers will have learned to understand their own interests, a reactionary, feudal, bureaucratic or bourgeois government will become impossible in Germany.

Written by Engels around
February 11, 1870

Published in the second edition
of *The Peasant War in Germany*.
Leipzig, October 1870

Printed according to the text
of the second edition
Translated from the German

SUPPLEMENT TO THE PREFACE OF 1870
FOR THE THIRD EDITION OF 1875[145]

The preceding passage was written over four years ago. It is still valid today. What was true after Sadowa[154] and the partition of Germany is being reconfirmed after Sedan[157] and the establishment of the Holy German Empire of the Prussian nation.[158] So little do "world-shaking" grand performances of state in the realm of so-called high politics change the direction of the historical movement!

What these grand performances of state are able to do, however, is to accelerate this movement. And in this respect, the authors of the above-mentioned "world-shaking events" have had involuntary successes, which they themselves surely find most undesirable but which, all the same, for better or for worse, they have to accept.

The war of 1866 shook the old Prussia to its foundations. After 1848 it had a hard time bringing the rebellious industrial element of the Western provinces, bourgeois as well as proletarian, under the old discipline again; still, this had been accomplished, and the interests of the Junkers of the Eastern provinces again became, next to those of the army, the dominant interests in the state. In 1866 almost all Northwest Germany became Prussian.[149] Apart from the irreparable moral injury the Prussian crown suffered by the grace of God owing to its having swallowed three other crowns by the grace of God,* the centre of gravity in the monarchy now shifted considerably to the west. The five million Rhinelanders and Westphalians were reinforced, first, by the four million Germans annexed directly, and then by the six million annexed indirectly, through the North-German Union.[159] And in 1870 there were further added the eight million Southwest Germans,[160] so that in the "New Reich," the fourteen and a half million old Prussians (from the six East Elbian provinces, including, besides, two million Poles) were confronted by some twenty-five million who had long outgrown the old Prussian Junker-feudalism. In this

---

* Hanover, Hesse-Cassel, Nassau.—Ed.

way the very victories of the Prussian army shifted the entire basis of the Prussian state structure; the Junker domination became intolerable even for the government. At the same time, however, the extremely rapid industrial development caused the struggle between bourgeois and worker to supersede the struggle between Junker and bourgeois, so that internally also the social foundations of the old state underwent a complete transformation. The basic precondition for the monarchy which had been slowly rotting since 1840, was the struggle between nobility and bourgeoisie, in which the monarchy held the balance. When the nobility no longer needed protection against the onrush of the bourgeoisie and it became necessary to protect all the propertied classes against the onrush of the working class, the old, absolute monarchy had to go over completely to the form of state expressly devised for this purpose: *the Bonapartist monarchy*. This transition of Prussia to Bonapartism I have already discussed elsewhere (*The Housing Question*, Part 2, pp. 26 et seq.*). What I did not have to stress there, but what is very essential here, is that this transition was the *greatest progress* made by Prussia since 1848, so much had Prussia lagged behind in modern development. It was, to be sure, still a semi-feudal state, whereas Bonapartism is, at any rate, a modern form of state which presupposes the abolition of feudalism. Hence, Prussia has had to begin to get rid of its numerous survivals of feudalism, to sacrifice Junkerdom as such. This, naturally, is being done in the mildest possible form and to the favourite tune of: *Immer langsam voran!*** Take the notorious District Ordinance. It abolishes the feudal privileges of the individual Junker in relation to his estate only to restore them as privileges of the totality of big landowners in relation to the entire district. The substance remains, being merely translated from the feudal into the bourgeois dialect. The old Prussian Junker is being forcibly transformed into something resembling an English squire, and need not have offered so much resistance because the one is as stupid as the other.

Thus it has been the peculiar fate of Prussia to complete its bourgeois revolution—begun in 1808 to 1813 and advanced to some extent in 1848—in the pleasant form of Bonapartism at the end of this century. If all goes well and the world remains nice and quiet, and all of us live long enough, we may see—perhaps in 1900 —that the government of Prussia will actually have abolished all feudal institutions and that Prussia will finally have arrived at the point where France stood in 1792.

---

* See Marx and Engels, *Selected Works*, Moscow, 1962, Vol. I, pp. 605-06.— *Ed.*

** "Always slowly forward!"—*Ed.*

The abolition of feudalism, expressed positively, means the establishment of bourgeois conditions. As the privileges of the nobility fall, legislation becomes more and more bourgeois. And here we come to the crux of the relation of the German bourgeoisie to the government. We have seen that the government is *compelled* to introduce these slow and petty reforms. However, in its dealings with the bourgeoisie it portrays each of these small concessions as a *sacrifice* made to the bourgeois, as a concession wrung from the crown with the greatest difficulty, for which the bourgeois ought in return to concede something to the government. And the bourgeois, though the true state of affairs is fairly clear to them, allow themselves to be fooled. This is the origin of the tacit agreement that forms the mute basis of all Reichstag and Prussian Chamber debates in Berlin. On the one hand, the government reforms the laws at a snail's pace in the interest of the bourgeoisie, removes the feudal obstacles to industry as well as those which arose from the multiplicity of small states, establishes uniform coinage, weights and measures, freedom of occupation, etc., puts Germany's labour power at the unrestricted disposal of capital by granting freedom of movement, and favours trade and swindling. On the other hand, the bourgeoisie leaves all actual political power in the hands of the government, votes taxes, loans and soldiers, and helps to frame all new reform laws in a way as to sustain the full force and effect of the old police power over undesirable elements. The bourgeoisie buys gradual social emancipation at the price of the immediate renunciation of political power. Naturally, the chief reason why such an agreement is acceptable to the bourgeoisie is not fear of the government but fear of the proletariat.

However wretched a figure our bourgeoisie may cut in the political field, it cannot be denied that as far as industry and commerce are concerned it is at last doing its duty. The impetuous growth of industry and commerce referred to in the introduction to the second edition* has since proceeded with still greater vigour. What has taken place in this respect since 1869 in the Rhine-Westphalian industrial region is quite unprecedented for Germany and reminds one of the upsurge in the English manufacturing districts at the beginning of this century. The same thing holds true for Saxony and Upper Silesia, Berlin, Hanover and the seaports. At last we have world trade, a really big industry, a really modern bourgeoisie. But in return we have also had a real crash, and have likewise got a real, powerful proletariat.

The future historian will attach much less importance in the history of Germany since 1869-74 to the roar of battle at Spichern,

---

* See pp. 235-41 of this volume.—*Ed.*

Mars-la-Tour[161] and Sedan, and everything connected therewith, than to the unpretentious, quiet but constantly progressing development of the German proletariat. As early as 1870, the German workers were subjected to a severe test: the Bonapartist war provocation and its natural effect, the general national enthusiasm in Germany. The German socialist workers did not allow themselves to be confused for a single moment. They did not show any hint of national chauvinism. They kept their heads in the midst of the wildest jubilation over the victory, demanding "an equitable peace with the French republic and no annexations". Not even martial law could silence them. No battle glory, no talk of German "imperial magnificence", produced any effect on them; liberation of the entire European proletariat was still their sole aim. We may say with assurance that in no other country have the workers hitherto been put to so hard a test and acquitted themselves so splendidly.

Martial law during the war was followed by trials for treason, for *lèse majesté*, for insulting officials, and by the ever increasing police chicanery of peacetime. The *Volksstaat*[162] usually had three or four editors in prison at one time and the other papers too. Every party speaker of any distinction had to stand trial at least once a year and was almost always convicted. Deportations, confiscations and the breaking-up of meetings proceeded in rapid succession, thick as hail. All in vain. The place of every man arrested or deported was at once filled by another; for every broken-up meeting two new ones were called, and thus the arbitrary power of the police was worn down in one place after the other by endurance and strict conformity to the law. All this persecution had the opposite effect to that intended. Far from breaking the workers' party or even bending it, it served only to enlist new recruits and consolidated the organisation. In their struggle with the authorities and also individual bourgeois, the workers showed themselves intellectually and morally superior, and proved, particularly in their conflicts with the so-called "providers of work", the employers, that they, the workers, were now the educated class and the capitalists were the ignoramuses. They conduct the fight for the most part with a sense of humour, which is the best proof of how sure they are of their cause and how conscious of their superiority. A struggle thus conducted on historically prepared soil must yield good results. The successes of the January elections stand unique in the history of the modern workers' movement[163] and the astonishment they caused throughout Europe was fully justified.

The German workers have two important advantages over those of the rest of Europe. First, they belong to the most theoretical people of Europe, and have retained the sense of theory which the

so-called "educated" classes of Germany have almost completely
lost. Without German philosophy, particularly that of Hegel,
German scientific socialism—the only scientific socialism that has
ever existed—would never have come into being. Without the
workers' sense of theory this scientific socialism would never
have entered their flesh and blood as much as is the case. What an
incalculable advantage this is may be seen, on the one hand, from
the indifference to theory which is one of the main reasons why
the English working-class movement crawls along so slowly in
spite of the splendid organisation of the individual trades, and on
the other hand, from the mischief and confusion wrought by Proudhonism in its original form among the French and Belgians, and
in the form further caricatured by Bakunin among the Spaniards
and Italians.

The second advantage is that, chronologically speaking, the
Germans were about the last to come into the workers' movement.
Just as German theoretical socialism will never forget that it rests
on the shoulders of Saint-Simon, Fourier and Owen—three men
who, in spite of all their fantastic notions and all their utopianism,
stand among the most eminent thinkers of all time and whose
genius anticipated innumerable things the correctness of which
is now being scientifically proved by us—so the practical workers'
movement in Germany ought never to forget that it developed on
the shoulders of the English and French movements, that it was
able simply to utilise their dearly paid experience and could now
avoid their mistakes, which were then mostly unavoidable. Where
would we be now without the precedent of the English trade
unions and French workers' political struggles, and especially
without the gigantic impulse of the Paris Commune[8]?

It must be said to the credit of the German workers that they
have exploited the advantages of their situation with rare understanding. For the first time since a workers' movement has existed, the struggle is being waged pursuant to its three sides—the
theoretical, the political and the economico-practical (resistance
to the capitalists)—in harmony and in its interconnections, and in
a systematic way. It is precisely in this, as it were concentric,
attack that the strength and invincibility of the German movement
lies.

Due to this advantageous situation, on the one hand, and to
the insular peculiarities of the English and the forcible suppression
of the French movement, on the other, the German workers stand
for the moment in the vanguard of the proletarian struggle. How
long events will allow them to occupy this place of honour, cannot
be foretold. But let us hope that as long as they occupy it they
will fill it fittingly. This demands redoubled efforts in every field
of struggle and agitation. In particular, it will be the duty of the

leaders to gain an ever clearer insight into all theoretical questions, to free themselves more and more from the influence of traditional phrases inherited from the old world outlook, and constantly to keep in mind that socialism, since it has become a science, demands that it be pursued as a science, that is, that it be studied. The task will be to spread with increased zeal among the masses of workers the ever more lucid understanding thus acquired and to knit together ever more strongly the organisation both of the party and of the trade unions. Even if the votes cast for the Socialists in January have formed quite a decent army, they are still far from constituting the majority of the working class; encouraging as are the successes of propaganda among the rural population, infinitely more remains to be done in this field. Hence, we must make it a point not to slacken the struggle, and to wrest from the enemy one town, one constituency after the other; the main point, however, is to safeguard the true international spirit, which allows no patriotic chauvinism to arise and which readily welcomes every new advance of the proletarian movement, no matter from which nation it comes. If the German workers progress in this way, they will not be marching exactly at the head of the movement—it is not at all in the interest of this movement that the workers of any particular country should march at its head—but will occupy an honourable place in the battle line; they will stand armed for battle when either unexpectedly grave trials or momentous events demand of them added courage, added determination and energy.

Frederick Engels

London, June 1, 1874

Published in the book:
Friedrich Engels, *Der Deutsche Bauernkrieg*. Leipzig, 1875

Printed according to the text
of the book
Translated from the German

Karl Marx

THE CIVIL WAR IN FRANCE[164]

INTRODUCTION BY FREDERICK ENGELS[165]

I did not anticipate that I would be asked to prepare a new edition of the Address of the General Council of the International on *The Civil War in France*, and to write an introduction to it. Therefore I can only touch briefly here on the most important points.

I am prefacing the longer work mentioned above by the two shorter Addresses of the General Council on the Franco-Prussian War.* In the first place, because the second of these, which itself cannot be fully understood without the first, is referred to in *The Civil War*. But also because these two Addresses, likewise drafted by Marx, are, no less than *The Civil War*, outstanding examples of the author's remarkable gift, first proved in *The Eighteenth Brumaire of Louis Bonaparte*,** for grasping clearly the character, the import and the necessary consequences of great historical events, at a time when these events are still in progress before our eyes or have only just taken place. And, finally, because today we in Germany are still having to endure the consequences which Marx predicted would follow from these events.

Has that which was declared in the first Address not come to pass: that if Germany's defensive war against Louis Bonaparte degenerated into a war of conquest against the French people, all the misfortunes which befell Germany after the so-called wars of liberation[166] would revive again with renewed intensity? Have we not had a further twenty years of Bismarck's rule, the Exceptional Law[167] and Socialist-baiting taking the place of the prosecutions of demagogues,[168] with the same arbitrary action of the police and with literally the same staggering interpretations of the law?

And has not the prediction been proved to the letter, that the annexation of Alsace-Lorraine would "force France into the arms of Russia," and that after this annexation Germany must either become the avowed servant of Russia, or must, after some short

---

* See pp. 260-63 and 264-70 of this volume.—*Ed.*
** See pp. 96-179 of this volume.—*Ed.*

respite, arm for a new war, and, moreover, "a race war against the combined Slavonic and Roman races"?* Has not the annexation of the French provinces driven France into the arms of Russia? Has not Bismarck for fully twenty years vainly wooed the favour of the tsar, wooed it with services even more lowly than those which little Prussia, before it became the "first Power in Europe," was wont to lay at Holy Russia's feet? And is there not every day still hanging over our heads the Damocles' sword of war, on the first day of which all the chartered covenants of princes will be scattered like chaff; a war of which nothing is certain but the absolute uncertainty of its outcome; a race war which will subject the whole of Europe to devastation by fifteen or twenty million armed men, and which is not raging already only because even the strongest of the great military states shrinks before the absolute incalculability of its final result?

All the more is it our duty to make again accessible to the German workers these brilliant proofs, now half-forgotten, of the farsightedness of international working-class policy in 1870.

What is true of these two Addresses is also true of *The Civil War in France*. On May 28, the last fighters of the Commune succumbed to superior forces on the slopes of Belleville; and only two days later, on May 30, Marx read to the General Council the work in which the historical significance of the Paris Commune is delineated in short, powerful strokes, but with such trenchancy, and above all such truth as has never again been attained in all the mass of literature on this subject.

Thanks to the economic and political development of France since 1789, Paris has been placed for the last fifty years in such a position that no revolution could break out there without assuming a proletarian character, that is to say, without the proletariat, which had bought victory with its blood, advancing its own demands after victory. These demands were more or less unclear and even confused, corresponding to the state of development reached by the workers of Paris at the particular period, but in the last resort they all amounted to the abolition of the class antagonism between capitalists and workers. It is true that no one knew how this was to be brought about. But the demand itself, however indefinitely it still was couched, contained a threat to the existing order of society; the workers who put it forward were still armed; therefore, the disarming of the workers was the first commandment for the bourgeois, who were at the helm of the state. Hence, after every revolution won by the workers, a new struggle, ending with the defeat of the workers.

---

* See p. 268 of this volume.—*Ed.*

This happened for the first time in 1848. The liberal bourgeois of the parliamentary opposition held banquets for securing a reform of the franchise, which was to ensure supremacy for their party. Forced more and more, in their struggle with the government, to appeal to the people, they had gradually to yield precedence to the radical and republican strata of the bourgeoisie and petty bourgeoisie. But behind these stood the revolutionary workers, and since 1830[86] these had acquired far more political independence than the bourgeois, and even the republicans, suspected. At the moment of the crisis between the government and the opposition, the workers began street-fighting; Louis Philippe vanished, and with him the franchise reform; and in its place arose the republic, and indeed one which the victorious workers themselves designated as a "social" republic. No one, however, was clear as to what this social republic was to imply; not even the workers themselves. But they now had arms and were a power in the state. Therefore, as soon as the bourgeois republicans in control felt something like firm ground under their feet, their first aim was to disarm the workers. This took place by driving them into the insurrection of June 1848[6] by direct breach of faith, by open defiance and the attempt to banish the unemployed to a distant province. The government had taken care to have an overwhelming superiority of force. After five days' heroic struggle, the workers were defeated. And then followed a blood-bath among the defenceless prisoners, the like of which has not been seen since the days of the civil wars which ushered in the downfall of the Roman republic. It was the first time that the bourgeoisie showed to what insane cruelties of revenge it will be goaded the moment the proletariat dares to take its stand against the bourgeoisie as a separate class, with its own interests and demands. And yet 1848 was only child's play compared with the frenzy of the bourgeoisie in 1871.

Punishment followed hard at heel. If the proletariat was .not yet able to rule France, the bourgeoisie could no longer do so. At least not at that period, when the greater part of it was still monarchically inclined, and it was divided into three dynastic parties[169] and a fourth, republican party. Its internal dissensions allowed the adventurer Louis Bonaparte to take possession of all the commanding points—army, police, administrative machinery —and, on December 2, 1851,[40] to explode the last stronghold of the bourgeoisie, the National Assembly. The Second Empire began— the exploitation of France by a gang of political and financial adventurers, but at the same time also an industrial development such as had never been possible under the narrow-minded and timorous system of Louis Philippe, with the exclusive domination of only a small section of the big bourgeoisie. Louis Bonaparte took the political power from the capitalists under the pretext of protecting them, the bourgeois, from the workers, and on the other hand the workers from them; but in return his rule encouraged speculation and industrial activity—in a word, the upsurgence and enrichment of the whole bourgeoisie to an extent hitherto unknown. To an even greater extent, it is true, corruption and mass thievery developed, clustering around the imperial court, and drawing their heavy percentages from this enrichment.

But the Second Empire was the appeal to French chauvinism, was the demand for the restoration of the frontiers of the First Empire, which had been lost in 1814, or at least those of the First Republic. A French empire within the frontiers of the old monarchy and, in fact, within the even more amputated frontiers of 1815—such a thing was impossible for any length of time. Hence the necessity for occasional wars and extensions of frontiers. But no extension of frontiers was so dazzling to the imagination of the French chauvinists as the extension to the German left bank of the Rhine. One square mile on the Rhine was more to them than ten in the Alps or anywhere else. Given the Second Empire, the demand for the restoration of the left bank of the Rhine, either all at once or piecemeal, was merely a question of time. The time came with the Austro-Prussian War of 1866[149]; cheated of the anticipated "territorial compensation" by Bismarck and by his own over-cunning, hesitant policy, there was now nothing left for Napoleon but war, which broke out in 1870 and drove him first to Sedan,[157] and thence to Wilhelmshöhe.

The necessary consequence was the Paris Revolution of September 4, 1870. The empire collapsed like a house of cards, and the republic was again proclaimed. But the enemy was standing at the gates; the armies of the empire were either hopelessly encircled at Metz or held captive in Germany. In this emergency the people allowed the Paris deputies to the former legislative body to constitute themselves into a "Government of National Defence." This was the more readily conceded, since, for the purposes of defence, all Parisians capable of bearing arms had enrolled in the National Guard and were armed, so that now the workers constituted a great majority. But very soon the antagonism between the almost completely bourgeois government and the armed proletariat broke into open conflict. On October 31, workers' battalions stormed the town hall and captured part of the membership of the government. Treachery, the government's direct breach of its undertakings, and the intervention of some petty-bourgeois battalions set them free again, and in order not to occasion the outbreak of civil war inside a city besieged by a foreign military power, the former government was left in office.

At last, on January 28, 1871, starved Paris capitulated. But with honours unprecedented in the history of war. The forts were surrendered, the city wall stripped of guns, the weapons of the regiments of the line and of the Mobile Guard were handed over and they themselves considered prisoners of war. But the National Guard kept its weapons and guns, and only entered into an armistice with the victors. And these did not dare enter Paris in triumph. They only dared to occupy a tiny corner of Paris, which into the bargain, consisted partly of public parks, and even this they only occupied for a few days! And during this time they, who had maintained their encirclement of Paris for 131 days, were themselves encircled by the armed workers of Paris, who kept a sharp watch that no "Prussian" should overstep the narrow bounds of the corner ceded to the foreign conqueror. Such was the respect which the Paris workers inspired in the army before which all the armies of the empire had laid down their arms; and the Prussian *Junkers*, who had come to take revenge at the home of the revolution, were compelled to stand by respectfully, and salute precisely this armed revolution!

During the war the Paris workers had confined themselves to demanding the vigorous prosecution of the fight. But now, when peace had come after the capitulation of Paris,[170] now Thiers, the new supreme head of the government, was compelled to realise that the rule of the propertied classes—big landowners and capitalists—was in constant danger so long as the workers of Paris had arms in their hands. His first action was an attempt to disarm them. On March 18, he sent troops of the line with orders to rob the National Guard of the artillery belonging to it, which had been constructed during the siege of Paris and had been paid for by public subscription. The attempt failed; Paris mobilised as one man for resistance, and war between Paris and the French Government sitting at Versailles was declared. On March 26 the Paris Commune was elected and on March 28 it was proclaimed. The Central Committee of the National Guard, which up to then had carried on the government, handed in its resignation to the Commune after it had first decreed the abolition of the scandalous Paris "Morality Police." On March 30 the Commune abolished conscription and the standing army, and declared the sole armed force to be the National Guard, in which all citizens capable of bearing arms were to be enrolled. It remitted all payments of rent for dwelling houses from October 1870 until April, the amounts already paid to be booked as future rent payments, and stopped all sales of articles pledged in the municipal loan office. On the same day the foreigners elected to the Commune were confirmed in office, because "the flag of the Commune is the flag of the World Republic." On April 1 it was decided that the highest salary to be received by any employee of the Commune, and therefore also by its members themselves, was not to exceed 6,000 francs (4,800 marks). On the following day the Commune decreed the separation of the church from the state, and the abolition of all state payments for religious purposes as well as the transformation of all church property into national property; as a result of which, on April 8, the exclusion from the schools of all religious symbols, pictures, dogmas, prayers—in a word, "of all that belongs to the sphere of the individual's conscience"—was ordered and gradually put into effect. On the 5th, in reply to the shooting, day after day, of captured Commune fighters by the Versailles troops, a decree was issued for the imprisonment of hostages, but it was never carried into execution. On the 6th, the guillotine was brought out by the 137th battalion of the National Guard, and publicly burnt, amid great popular rejoicing. On the 12th, the Commune decided that the Victory Column on the *Place Vendôme*, which had been cast from captured guns by Napoleon after the war of 1809, should be demolished as a symbol of chauvinism and incitement to national hatred. This was carried out on May 16. On April 16 it ordered a statistical tabulation of factories which had been closed down by the manufacturers, and the working out of plans for the operation of these factories by the workers formerly employed in them, who were to be organised in co-operative societies, and also plans for the organisation of these co-operatives in one great union. On the 20th it abolished night work for bakers, and also the employment offices, which since the Second Empire had been run as a monopoly by creatures appointed by the police—labour exploiters of the first rank; these offices were transferred to the mayoralties of the twenty *arrondissements* of Paris. On April 30 it ordered the closing of the pawnshops, on the ground that they were a private exploitation of the workers, and were in contradiction with the right of the workers to their instruments of labour and to credit. On May 5 it ordered the razing of the Chapel of Atonement, which had been built in expiation of the execution of Louis XVI.

Thus from March 18 onwards the class character of the Paris movement, which had previously been pushed into the background by the fight against the foreign invaders, emerged sharply and clearly. As almost only workers, or recognised representatives of the workers, sat in the Commune, its decisions bore a decidedly proletarian character. Either these decisions decreed reforms which the republican bourgeoisie had failed to pass solely out of cowardice, but which provided a necessary basis for the free activity of the working class—such as the realisation of the principle that *in relation to the state*, religion is a purely private matter— or the Commune promulgated decrees which were in the direct

interest of the working class and in part cut deeply into the old
order of society. In a beleaguered city, however, it was possible
to make at most a start in the realisation of all this. And from
the beginning of May onwards all their energies were taken up
by the fight against the armies assembled by the Versailles government in ever-growing numbers.

On April 7 the Versailles troops had captured the Seine crossing at Neuilly, on the western front of Paris; on the other hand,
in an attack on the southern front on the 11th they were repulsed
with heavy losses by General Eudes. Paris was continually bombarded and, moreover, by the very people who had stigmatised
as a sacrilege the bombardment of the same city by the Prussians.
These same people now begged the Prussian government for the
hasty return of the French soldiers taken prisoner at Sedan[157] and
Metz,[171] in order that they might recapture Paris for them. From
the beginning of May the gradual arrival of these troops gave the
Versailles forces a decided superiority. This already became evident when, on April 23, Thiers broke off the negotiations for the
exchange, proposed by the Commune, of the Archbishop of Paris*
and a whole number of other priests held as hostages in Paris,
for only one man, Blanqui, who had twice been elected to the
Commune but was a prisoner in Clairvaux. And even more from
the changed language of Thiers; previously procrastinating and
equivocal, he now suddenly became insolent, threatening, brutal.
The Versailles forces took the redoubt of Moulin Saquet on the
southern front, on May 3; on the 9th, Fort Issy, which had been
completely reduced to ruins by gunfire; on the 14th, Fort Vanves.
On the western front they advanced gradually, capturing the numerous villages and buildings which extended up to the city wall,
until they reached the main defences; on the 21st, thanks to
treachery and the carelessness of the National Guards stationed
there, they succeeded in forcing their way into the city. The Prussians, who held the northern and eastern forts, allowed the
Versailles troops to advance across the land north of the city,
which was forbidden ground to them under the armistice, and
thus to march forward, attacking on a wide front, which the
Parisians naturally thought covered by the armistice, and therefore held only weakly. As a result of this, only a weak resistance
was put up in the western half of Paris, in the luxury city proper;
it grew stronger and more tenacious the nearer the incoming
troops approached the eastern half, the working-class city proper.
It was only after eight days' fighting that the last defenders of
the Commune succumbed on the heights of Belleville and Menil-
montant; and then the massacre of defenceless men, women and

---

* Georges Darboy.—*Ed.*

children, which had been raging all through the week on an increasing scale, reached its zenith. The breechloaders could no longer kill fast enough; the vanquished were shot down in hundreds by *mitrailleuse* fire. The "Wall of the Federals"* at the Père Lachaise cemetery, where the final mass murder was consummated, is still standing today, a mute but eloquent testimony to the frenzy of which the ruling class is capable as soon as the working class dares to stand up for its rights. Then, when the slaughter of them all proved to be impossible, came the mass arrests, the shooting of victims arbitrarily selected from the prisoners' ranks, and the removal of the rest to great camps where they awaited trial by courts-martial. The Prussian troops surrounding the northeastern half of Paris had orders not to allow any fugitives to pass; but the officers often shut their eyes when the soldiers paid more obedience to the dictates of humanity than to those of the Supreme Command; particular honour is due to the Saxon army corps, which behaved very humanely and let through many who were obviously fighters for the Commune.

* * *

If today, after twenty years, we look back at the activity and historical significance of the Paris Commune of 1871, we shall find it necessary to make a few additions to the account given in *The Civil War in France*.

The members of the Commune were divided into a majority, the Blanquists, who had also been predominant in the Central Committee of the National Guard; and a minority, members of the International Working Men's Association,[120] chiefly consisting of adherents of the Proudhon school of socialism. The great majority of the Blanquists were at that time Socialists only by revolutionary, proletarian instinct; only a few had attained greater clarity on principles, through Vaillant, who was familiar with German scientific socialism. It is therefore comprehensible that in the economic sphere much was left undone which, according to our view today, the Commune ought to have done. The hardest thing to understand is certainly the holy awe with which they remained standing respectfully outside the gates of the Bank of France. This was also a serious political mistake. The bank in the hands of the Commune—this would have been worth more than ten thousand hostages. It would have meant the pressure of the whole of the French bourgeoisie on the Versailles government in favour of peace with the Commune. But what is still more won-

---

* Now usually called the Wall of the Communards —*Ed.*

derful is the correctness of much that nevertheless was done b·
the Commune, composed as it was of Blanquists and Proudhon
ists. Naturally, the Proudhonists were chiefly responsible for the
economic decrees of the Commune, both for their praiseworthy and
their unpraiseworthy aspects; as the Blanquists were for its political commissions and omissions. And in both cases the irony of
history willed—as is usual when doctrinaires come to the helm
—that both did the opposite of what the doctrines of their school
prescribed.

Proudhon, the Socialist of the small peasant and master-
craftsman, regarded association with positive hatred. He said of
it that there was more bad than good in it; that it was by nature
sterile, even harmful, because it was a fetter on the freedom of
the worker; that it was a pure dogma, unproductive and burden-
some, in conflict as much with the freedom of the worker as with
economy of labour; that its disadvantages multiplied more swiftly
than its advantages; that, as compared with it, competition, division of labour and private property were economic forces. Only
in the exceptional cases—as Proudhon called them—of large-scale
industry and large establishments, such as railways, was the association of workers in place. (See *General Idea of the Revolution*,[172] *3rd sketch.*)

By 1871, large-scale industry had already so much ceased to
be an exceptional case even in Paris, the centre of artistic handicrafts, that by far the most important decree of the Commune
instituted an organisation of large-scale industry and even of
manufacture which was not only to be based on the association
of the workers in each factory, but also to combine all these associations in one great union; in short, an organisation which, as
Marx quite rightly says in *The Civil War*, must necessarily have
led in the end to communism, that is to say, the direct opposite
of the Proudhon doctrine. And, therefore, the Commune was the
grave of the Proudhon school of socialism. Today this school has
vanished from French working-class circles; here, among the
Possibilists[173] no less than among the "Marxists," Marx's theory
now rules unchallenged. Only among the "radical" bourgeoisie are
there still Proudhonists.

The Blanquists fared no better. Brought up in the school of
conspiracy, and held together by the strict discipline which went
with it, they started out from the viewpoint that a relatively small
number of resolute, well-organised men would be able, at a given
favourable moment, not only to seize the helm of state, but also
by a display of great, ruthless energy, to maintain power until
they succeeded in sweeping the mass of the people into the revolution and ranging them round the small band of leaders. This
involved, above all, the strictest, dictatorial centralisation of all

power in the hands of the new revolutionary government. And what did the Commune, with its majority of these same Blanquists, actually do? In all its proclamations to the French in the provinces, it appealed to them to form a free federation of all French Communes with Paris, a national organisation which for the first time was really to be created by the nation itself. It was precisely the oppressing power of the former centralised government, army, political police, bureaucracy, which Napoleon had created in 1798 and which since then had been taken over by every new government as a welcome instrument and used against its opponents—it was precisely this power which was to fall everywhere, just as it had already fallen in Paris.

From the very outset the Commune was compelled to recognise that the working class, once come to power, could not go on managing with the old state machine; that in order not to lose again its only just conquered supremacy, this working class must, on the one hand, do away with all the old repressive machinery previously used against it itself, and, on the other, safeguard itself against its own deputies and officials, by declaring them all, without exception, subject to recall at any moment. What had been the characteristic attribute of the former state? Society had created its own organs to look after its common interests, originally through simple division of labour. But these organs, at whose head was the state power, had in the course of time, in pursuance of their own special interests, transformed themselves from the servants of society into the masters of society. This can be seen, for example, not only in the hereditary monarchy, but equally so in the democratic republic. Nowhere do "politicians" form a more separate and powerful section of the nation than precisely in North America. There, each of the two major parties which alternately succeed each other in power is itself in turn controlled by people who make a business of politics, who speculate on seats in the legislative assemblies of the Union as well as of the separate states, or who make a living by carrying on agitation for their party and on its victory are rewarded with positions. It is well known how the Americans have been trying for thirty years to shake off this yoke, which has become intolerable, and how in spite of it all they continue to sink ever deeper in this swamp of corruption. It is precisely in America that we see best how there takes place this process of the state power making itself independent in relation to society, whose mere instrument it was originally intended to be. Here there exists no dynasty, no nobility, no standing army, beyond the few men keeping watch on the Indians, no bureaucracy with permanent posts or the right to pensions. And nevertheless we find here two great gangs of political speculators, who alternately take possession of the state power and exploit it by the most corrupt means and for the most corrupt ends—and the nation is powerless against these two great cartels of politicians, who are ostensibly its servants, but in reality dominate and plunder it.

Against this transformation of the state and the organs of the state from servants of society into masters of society—an inevitable transformation in all previous states—the Commune made use of two infallible means. In the first place, it filled all posts—administrative, judicial and educational—by election on the basis of universal suffrage of all concerned, subject to the right of recall at any time by the same electors. And, in the second place, all officials, high or low, were paid only the wages received by other workers. The highest salary paid by the Commune to anyone was 6,000 francs. In this way an effective barrier to place-hunting and careerism was set up, even apart from the binding mandates to delegates to representative bodies which were added besides.

This shattering [*Sprengung*] of the former state power and its replacement by a new and truly democratic one is described in detail in the third section of *The Civil War*. But it was necessary to dwell briefly here once more on some of its features, because in Germany particularly the superstitious belief in the state has been carried over from philosophy into the general consciousness of the bourgeoisie and even of many workers. According to the philosophical conception, the state is the "realisation of the idea," or the Kingdom of God on earth, translated into philosophical terms, the sphere in which eternal truth and justice is or should be realised. And from this follows a superstitious reverence for the state and everything connected with it, which takes root the more readily since people are accustomed from childhood to imagine that the affairs and interests common to the whole of society could not be looked after otherwise than as they have been looked after in the past, that is, through the state and its lucratively positioned officials. And people think they have taken quite an extraordinarily bold step forward when they have rid themselves of belief in hereditary monarchy and swear by the democratic republic. In reality, however, the state is nothing but a machine for the oppression of one class by another, and indeed in the democratic republic no less than in the monarchy; and at best an evil inherited by the proletariat after its victorious struggle for class supremacy, whose worst sides the victorious proletariat, just like the Commune, cannot avoid having to lop off at once as much as possible until such time as a generation reared in new, free social conditions is able to throw the entire lumber of the state on the scrap heap.

Of late, the Social-Democratic philistine[174] has once more been filled with wholesome terror at the words: Dictatorship of the

Proletariat. Well and good, gentlemen, do you want to know
what this dictatorship looks like? Look at the Paris Commune.
That was the Dictatorship of the Proletariat.

F. Engels

London, on the twentieth anniversary
of the Paris Commune, March 18, 1891

Published in *Die Neuē Zeit*,
Bd. 2, No. 28, 1890-91, and in
the book: Marx. *Der Bürgerkrieg
in Frankreich*. Berlin, 1891

Printed according to the text
of the book
Translated from the German

FIRST ADDRESS OF THE GENERAL COUNCIL
OF THE INTERNATIONAL WORKING MEN'S
ASSOCIATION
ON THE FRANCO-PRUSSIAN WAR[175]

TO THE MEMBERS OF THE INTERNATIONAL WORKING MEN'S ASSOCIATION
IN EUROPE AND THE UNITED STATES

In the Inaugural Address of the *International Working Men's Association,* of November, 1864, we said:—"If the emancipation of the working classes requires their fraternal concurrence, how are they to fulfil that great mission with a foreign policy in pursuit of criminal designs, playing upon national prejudices and squandering in piratical wars the people's blood and treasure?" We defined the foreign policy aimed at by the International in these words: "Vindicate the simple laws of morals and justice, which ought to govern the relations of private individuals, as the laws paramount of the intercourse of nations."*

No wonder that Louis Bonaparte, who usurped his power by exploiting the war of classes in France, and perpetuated it by periodical wars abroad, should from the first have treated the International as a dangerous foe. On the eve of the plebiscite[176] he ordered a raid on the members of the Administrative Committees of the International Working Men's Association throughout France, at Paris, Lyons, Rouen, Marseilles, Brest, etc., on the pretext that the International was a secret society dabbling in a complot for his assassination, a pretext soon after exposed in its full absurdity by his own judges. What was the real crime of the French branches of the International? They told the French people publicly and emphatically that voting the plebiscite was voting despotism at home and war abroad. It has been, in fact, their work that in all the great towns, in all the industrial centres of France, the working class rose like one man to reject the plebiscite. Unfortunately the balance was turned by the heavy ignorance of the rural districts. The Stock Exchanges, the Cabinets, the ruling classes and the press of Europe celebrated the plebiscite as a signal victory of the French Emperor over the French working class; and it was the signal for the assassination, not of an individual, but of nations.

---

* Marx and Engels, *Selected Works,* Vol. I, Moscow, 1962, p. 385.—*Ed.*

The war plot of July, 1870,[177] is but an amended edition of the coup d'état of December, 1851.[40] At first view the thing seemed so absurd that France would not believe in its real good earnest. It rather believed the deputy* denouncing the ministerial war talk as a mere stock-jobbing trick. When, on July 15th, war was at last officially announced to the *Corps Législatif*, the whole opposition refused to vote the preliminary subsidies, even Thiers branded it as "detestable"; all the independent journals of Paris condemned it, and, wonderful to relate, the provincial press joined in almost unanimously.

Meanwhile, the Paris members of the International had again set to work. In the *Réveil*[178] of July 12th they published their manifesto "to the workmen of all nations," from which we extract the following few passages:

"Once more," they say, "on the pretext of the European equilibrium, of national honour, the peace of the world is menaced by political ambitions. French, German, Spanish workmen! let our voices unite in one cry of reprobation against war!... War for a question of preponderance or a dynasty, can, in the eyes of workmen, be nothing but a criminal absurdity. In answer to the warlike proclamations of those who exempt themselves from the impost of blood, and find in public misfortunes a source of fresh speculations, we protest, we who want peace, labour and liberty!... Brothers of Germany! Our division would only result in the complete triumph *of despotism* on both sides of the Rhine.... Workmen of all countries! whatever may for the present become of our common efforts, we, the members of the International Working Men's Association, who know of no frontiers, we send you as a pledge of indissoluble solidarity the good wishes and the salutations of the workmen of France."

This manifesto of our Paris section was followed by numerous similar French addresses, of which we can here only quote the declaration of Neuilly-sur-Seine, published in the *Marseillaise*[179] of July 22nd:

"The war, is it just?—No! The war, is it national?—No! It is merely dynastic. In the name of humanity, of democracy, and the true interests of France, we adhere completely and energetically to the protestation of the International against the war."

These protestations expressed the true sentiments of the French working people, as was soon shown by a curious incident. *The Band of the 10th of December*,[180] first organised under the presidency of Louis Bonaparte, having been masqueraded into *blouses* and let loose on the streets of Paris, there to perform the contortions of war fever, the real workmen of the Faubourgs came forward with public peace demonstrations so overwhelming that Pietri, the Prefect of Police, thought it prudent to at once stop all further street politics, on the plea that the real Paris people had

* Jules Favre.—*Ed.*

given sufficient vent to their pent-up patriotism and exuberant war enthusiasm.

Whatever may be the incidents of Louis Bonaparte's war with Prussia, the death knell of the Second Empire has already sounded at Paris. It will end as it began, by a parody. But let us not forget that it is the Governments and the ruling classes of Europe who enabled Louis Bonaparte to play during eighteen years the ferocious farce of the *Restored Empire*.

On the German side, the war is a war of defence, but who put Germany to the necessity of defending herself? Who enabled Louis Bonaparte to wage war upon her? *Prussia!* It was Bismarck who conspired with that very same Louis Bonaparte for the purpose of crushing popular opposition at home, and annexing Germany to the Hohenzollern dynasty. If the battle of Sadowa[154] had been lost instead of being won, French battalions would have overrun Germany as the allies of Prussia. After her victory did Prussia dream one moment of opposing a free Germany to an enslaved France? Just the contrary. While carefully preserving all the native beauties of her old system, she superadded all the tricks of the Second Empire, its real despotism and its mock democratism, its political shams and its financial jobs, its high-flown talk and its low *legerdemains*. The Bonapartist regime, which till then only flourished on one side of the Rhine, had now got its counterfeit on the other. From such a state of things, what else could result but *war*?

If the German working class allow the present war to lose its strictly defensive character and to degenerate into a war against the French people, victory or defeat will prove alike disastrous. All the miseries that befell Germany after her war of independence will revive with accumulated intensity.

The principles of the International are, however, too widely spread and too firmly rooted amongst the German working class to apprehend such a sad consummation. The voices of the French workmen have re-echoed from Germany. A mass meeting of workmen, held at Brunswick on July 16th, expressed its full concurrence with the Paris manifesto, spurned the idea of national antagonism to France, and wound up its resolutions with these words:—

"We are enemies of all wars, but above all of dynastic wars.... With deep sorrow and grief we are forced to undergo a defensive war as an unavoidable evil; but we call, at the same time, upon the whole German working class to render the recurrence of such an immense social misfortune impossible by vindicating for the peoples themselves the power to decide on peace and war, and making them masters of their own destinies."

At Chemnitz, a meeting of delegates representing 50,000 Saxon workers adopted unanimously a resolution to this effect:—

"In the name of the German Democracy, and especially of the workmen forming the Democratic Socialist party, we declare the present war to be exclusively dynastic.... We are happy to grasp the fraternal hand stretched out to us by the workmen of France.... Mindful of the watchword of the International Working Men's Association: *Proletarians of all countries, unite*, we shall never forget that the workmen of *all* countries are our *friends* and the despots of *all* countries our *enemies*."

The Berlin branch of the International has also replied to the Paris manifesto:—

"We," they say, "join with heart and hand your protestation.... Solemnly we promise that neither the sound of the trumpet, nor the roar of the cannon, neither victory nor defeat shall divert us from our common work for the union of the children of toil of all countries."

Be it so!

In the background of this suicidal strife looms the dark figure of Russia. It is an ominous sign that the signal for the present war should have been given at the moment when the Moscovite Government had just finished its strategical lines of railway and was already massing troops in the direction of the Pruth. Whatever sympathy the Germans may justly claim in a war of defence against Bonapartist aggression, they would forfeit at once by allowing the Prussian Government to call for, or accept, the help of the Cossacks. Let them remember that, after their war of independence against the first Napoleon,[166] Germany lay for generations prostrate at the feet of the Czar.

The English working class stretch the hand of fellowship to the French and German working people. They feel deeply convinced that whatever turn the impending horrid war may take, the alliance of the working classes of all countries will ultimately kill war. The very fact that while official France and Germany are rushing into a fratricidal feud, the workmen of France and Germany send each other messages of peace and goodwill; this great fact, unparalleled in the history of the past, opens the vista of a brighter future. It proves that in contrast to old society, with its economical miseries and its political delirium, a new society is springing up, whose International rule will be *Peace*, because its national ruler will be everywhere the same—*Labour*! The Pioneer of that new society is the International Working Men's Association.

256, High Holborn,
London, Western Central,
July 23, 1870

Written by Marx between
July 19 and 23, 1870
Published as a leaflet in English in
July 1870 and also as leaflets and
in the press in German, French and
Russian in August-September 1870

Printed according to the text
of the first English edition
of the leaflet, checked with
the text of the second English
edition of 1870 and the
authorised German edition
of 1870

SECOND ADDRESS OF THE GENERAL COUNCIL OF THE INTERNATIONAL WORKING MEN'S ASSOCIATION ON THE FRANCO-PRUSSIAN WAR[175]

TO THE MEMBERS OF THE INTERNATIONAL WORKING MEN'S ASSOCIATION IN EUROPE AND THE UNITED STATES

In our first Manifesto of the 23rd of July we said:—"The deat! knell of the Second Empire has already sounded at Paris. It wil end as it began, by a parody. But let us not forget that it is th Governments and the ruling classes of Europe who enabled Loui Napoleon to play during eighteen years the ferocious farce of th *Restored Empire.*"*

Thus, even before war operations had actually set in, we treate the Bonapartist bubble as a thing of the past.

If we were not mistaken as to the vitality of the Second Em pire, we were not wrong in our apprehension lest the German wa should "lose its strictly defensive character and degenerate int a war against the French people."** The war of defence ended, ir point of fact, with the surrender of Louis Bonaparte, the Sedan[15]
capitulation, and the proclamation of the Republic at Paris. Bu long before these events, the very moment that the utter rotten- ness of the Imperialist arms became evident, the Prussian mili- tary *camarilla* had resolved upon conquest. There lay an ugly obstacle in their way—*King William's own proclamations at the commencement of the war.* In his speech from the throne to the North German Diet, he had solemnly declared to make war upon the emperor of the French, and not upon the French people. On the 11th of August he had issued a manifesto to the French na- tion, where he said:

"The Emperor Napoleon having made, by land and sea, an attack on the Ger- man nation, which desired and still desires to live in peace with the French people, I have assumed the command of the German armies *to repel his aggression*, and I have been led by *military events to cross the frontiers of France.*"

Not content to assert the defensive character of the war by the statement that he only assumed the command of the German armies "*to repel aggression*," he added that he was only "led by

---

* See p. 262 of this volume.—*Ed.*
** Ibid.—*Ed.*

military events" to cross the frontiers of France. A defensive war does, of course, not exclude offensive operations, dictated by "military events."

Thus this pious king stood pledged before France and the world to a strictly defensive war. How to release him from his solemn pledge? The stage-managers had to exhibit him as giving, reluctantly, way to the irresistible behest of the German nation. They at once gave the cue to the liberal German middle class, with its professors, its capitalists, its aldermen, and its penmen. That middle class which in its struggle for civil liberty had, from 1846 to 1870, been exhibiting an unexampled spectacle of irresolution, incapacity, and cowardice, felt, of course, highly delighted to bestride the European scene as the roaring lion of German patriotism. It revindicated its civic independence by affecting to force upon the Prussian Government the secret designs of that same government. It does penance for its long-continued and almost religious faith in Louis Bonaparte's infallibility, by shouting for the dismemberment of the French Republic. Let us for a moment listen to the special pleadings of those stout-hearted patriots!

They dare not pretend that the people of Alsace and Lorraine pant for the German embrace; quite the contrary. To punish their French patriotism, Strasbourg, a town with an independent citadel commanding it, has for six days been wantonly and fiendishly bombarded by "German" explosive shells, setting it on fire, and killing great numbers of its defenceless inhabitants! Yet, the soil of those provinces once upon a time belonged to the whilom German Empire.[181] Hence, it seems, the soil and the human beings grown on it must be confiscated as imprescriptible German property. If the map of Europe is to be remade in the antiquary's vein, let us by no means forget that the Elector of Brandenburg, for his Prussian dominions, was the vassal of the Polish Republic.[182]

The more knowing patriots, however, require Alsace and the German-speaking part of Lorraine as a "material guarantee" against French aggression. As this contemptible plea has bewildered many weak-minded people, we are bound to enter more fully upon it.

There is no doubt that the general configuration of Alsace, as compared with the opposite bank of the Rhine, and the presence of a large fortified town like Strasbourg, about halfway between Basle and Germersheim, very much favour a French invasion of South Germany, while they offer peculiar difficulties to an invasion of France from South Germany. There is, further, no doubt that the addition of Alsace and German-speaking Lorraine would give South Germany a much stronger frontier, inasmuch as she would then be master of the crest of the Vosges mountains in

its whole length, and of the fortresses which cover its norther
passes. If Metz were annexed as well, France would certainly fo
the moment be deprived of her two principal bases of operatio
against Germany, but that would not prevent her from construct
ing a fresh one at Nancy or Verdun. While Germany owns Cob
lenz, Mainz, Germersheim, Rastadt, and Ulm, all bases of oper
ation against France, and plentifully made use of in this war
with what show of fair play can she begrudge France Strasbourg
and Metz, the only two fortresses of any importance she has or
that side? Moreover, Strasbourg endangers South Germany only
while South Germany is a separate power from North Germany
From 1792-95 South Germany was never invaded from that direc
tion, because Prussia was a party to the war against the French
Revolution; but as soon as Prussia made a peace of her own[183] in
1795, and left the South to shift for itself, the invasions of South
Germany, with Strasbourg for a base, began, and continued til
1809. The fact is, a *united* Germany can always render Strasbourg
and any French army in Alsace innocuous by concentrating al
her troops, as was done in the present war, between Saarloui
and Landau, and advancing, or accepting battle, on the line o
road between Mainz and Metz. While the mass of the German
troops is stationed there, any French army advancing from Stras
bourg into South Germany would be outflanked, and have its com
munications threatened. If the present campaign has proved any
thing, it is the facility of invading France from Germany.

But, in good faith, is it not altogether an absurdity and an
anachronism to make military considerations the principle by
which the boundaries of nations are to be fixed? If this rule wer
to prevail, Austria would still be entitled to Venetia and the lin
of the Mincio, and France to the line of the Rhine, in order t
protect Paris, which lies certainly more open to an attack from
the North East than Berlin does from the South West. If limit
are to be fixed by military interests, there will be no end to claims
because every military line is necessarily faulty, and may be im
proved by annexing some more outlying territory; and, moreover
they can never be fixed finally and fairly, because they alway
must be imposed by the conqueror upon the conquered, and con
sequently carry within them the seed of fresh wars.

Such is the lesson of all history. Thus with nations as wit
individuals. To deprive them of the power of offence, you mus
deprive them of the means of defence. You must not only garrott
but murder. If ever conqueror took "material guarantees" fo
breaking the sinews of a nation, the first Napoleon did so by th
Tilsit treaty,[184] and the way he executed it against Prussia an
the rest of Germany. Yet, a few years later, his gigantic powe
split like a rotten reed upon the German people. What are th

"material guarantees" Prussia, in her wildest dreams, can, or dare impose upon France, compared to the "material guarantees" the first Napoleon had wrenched from herself? The result will not prove the less disastrous. History will measure its retribution, not by the extent of the square miles conquered from France, but by the intensity of the crime of reviving, in the second half of the 19th century, *the policy of conquest!*

But, say the mouthpieces of Teutonic[185] patriotism, you must not confound Germans with Frenchmen. What we want is not glory, but safety. The Germans are an essentially peaceful people. In their sober guardianship, conquest itself changes from a condition of future war into a pledge of perpetual peace. Of course, it is not Germans that invaded France in 1792, for the sublime purpose of bayoneting the revolution of the 18th century. It is not Germans that befouled their hands by the subjugation of Italy, the oppression of Hungary, and the dismemberment of Poland. Their present military system, which divides the whole adult male population into two parts—one standing army on service, and another standing army on furlough, both equally bound in passive obedience to rulers by divine right—such a military system is, of course, a "material guarantee" for keeping the peace, and the ultimate goal of civilising tendencies! In Germany, as everywhere else, the sycophants of the powers that be poison the popular mind by the incense of mendacious self-praise.

Indignant as they pretend to be at the sight of French fortresses in Metz and Strasbourg, those German patriots see no harm in the vast system of Moscovite fortifications at Warsaw, Modlin, and Ivangorod. While gloating at the terrors of imperialist invasion, they blink at the infamy of autocratic tutelage.

As in 1865 promises were exchanged between Louis Bonaparte and Bismarck, so in 1870 promises have been exchanged between Gorchakov and Bismarck. As Louis Bonaparte flattered himself that the War of 1866, resulting in the common exhaustion of Austria and Prussia, would make him the supreme arbiter of Germany, so Alexander flattered himself that the War of 1870, resulting in the common exhaustion of Germany and France, would make him the supreme arbiter of the Western Continent. As the Second Empire thought the North-German Union[159] incompatible with its existence, so autocratic Russia must think herself endangered by a German empire under Prussian leadership. Such is the law of the old political system. Within its pale the gain of one state is the loss of the other. The Czar's paramount influence over Europe roots in his traditional hold on Germany. At a moment when in Russia herself volcanic social agencies threaten to shake the very base of autocracy, could the Czar afford to bear with such a loss of foreign prestige? Already the

Moscovite journals repeat the language of the Bonapartist journals after the war of 1866. Do the Teuton patriots really believe that liberty and peace will be guaranteed to Germany by forcing France into the arms of Russia? If the fortune of her arms, the arrogance of success, and dynastic intrigue lead Germany to a dismemberment of France, there will then only remain two courses open to her. She must at all risks become the *avowed* tool of Russian aggrandisement, or, after some short respite, make again ready for another "defensive" war, not one of those new-fangled "localised" wars, but a *war of races*—a war with the combined Slavonian and Roman races.

The German working class has resolutely supported the war, which it was not in their power to prevent, as a war for German independence and the liberation of France and Europe from that pestilential incubus, the Second Empire. It was the German workmen who, together with the rural labourers,. furnished the sinews and muscles of heroic hosts, leaving behind their half-starved families. Decimated by the battles abroad, they will be once more decimated by misery at home. In their turn they are now coming forward to ask for "guarantees,"—guarantees that their immense sacrifices have not been brought in vain, that they have conquered liberty, that the victory over the Imperialist armies will not, as in 1815, be turned into the defeat of the German people[186]; and, as the first of these guarantees, they claim an *honourable peace for France*, and the *recognition of the French Republic*.

The Central Committee of the German Socialist-Democratic Workmen's Party issued, on the 5th of September, a manifesto, energetically insisting upon these guarantees.

"We," they say, "we protest against the annexation of Alsace and Lorraine. And we are conscious of speaking in the name of the German working class. In the common interest of France and Germany, in the interest of peace and liberty, in the interest of Western civilisation against Eastern barbarism, the German workmen will not patiently tolerate the annexation of Alsace and Lorraine.... We shall faithfully stand by our fellow-workmen in all countries for the common international cause of the Proletariat!"

Unfortunately, we cannot feel sanguine of their immediate success. If the French workmen amidst peace failed to stop the aggressor, are the German workmen more likely to stop the victor amidst the clangour of arms? The German workmen's manifesto demands the extradition of Louis Bonaparte as a comman felon to the French Republic. Their rulers are, on the contrary, already trying hard to restore him to the Tuileries[187] as the best man to ruin France. However that may be, history will prove that the German working class are not made of the same malleable stuff as the German middle class. They will do their duty.

Like them, we hail the advent of the Republic in France, but at the same time we labour under misgivings which we hope will prove groundless. That Republic has not subverted the throne, but only taken its place become vacant. It has been proclaimed, not as a social conquest, but as a national measure of defence. It is in the hands of a Provisional Government composed partly of notorious Orleanists,[71] partly of middle-class Republicans, upon some of whom the insurrection of June, 1848,[6] has left its indelible stigma. The division of labour amongst the members of that Government looks awkward. The Orleanists have seized the strongholds of the army and the police, while to the professed Republicans have fallen the talking departments. Some of their first acts go far to show that they have inherited from the Empire, not only ruins, but also its dread of the working class. If eventual impossibilities are in wild phraseology demanded from the Republic, is it not with a view to prepare the cry for a "possible" government? Is the Republic, by some of its middle-class managers, not intended to serve as a mere stopgap and bridge over an Orleanist Restoration?

The French working class moves, therefore, under circumstances of extreme difficulty. Any attempt at upsetting the new Government in the present crisis, when the enemy is almost knocking at the doors of Paris, would be a desperate folly. The French workmen must perform their duties as citizens; but, at the same time, they must not allow themselves to be deluded by the national *souvenirs** of 1792, as the French peasants allowed themselves to be deluded by the national *souvenirs* of the First Empire. They have not to recapitulate the past, but to build up the future. Let them calmly and resolutely improve the opportunities of Republican liberty, for the work of their own class organisation. It will gift them with fresh Herculean powers for the regeneration of France, and our common task—the emancipation of labour. Upon their energies and wisdom hinges the fate of the Republic.

The English workmen have already taken measures to overcome, by a wholesome pressure from without, the reluctance of their Government to recognise the French Republic.[188] The present dilatoriness of the British Government is probably intended to atone for the Anti-Jacobin war and its former indecent haste in sanctioning the *coup d'état*.[189] The English workmen call also upon their Government to oppose by all its power the dismemberment of France, which part of the English press is so shameless enough to howl for. It is the same press that for twenty years deified Louis Bonaparte as the providence of Europe, that frantically cheered

---

* Remembrances.—*Ed.*

on the slaveholders' rebellion.[129] Now, as then, it drudges for the slaveholder.

Let the sections of the *International Working Men's Association* in every country stir the working classes to action. If they forsake their duty, if they remain passive, the present tremendous war will be but the harbinger of still deadlier international feuds, and lead in every nation to a renewed triumph over the workman by the lords of the sword, of the soil, and of capital.

Vive la République!

256, High Holborn,
London, Western Central,
September 9, 1870

Written by Marx between
September 6 and 9, 1870

Published as a leaflet in
English between September 11
and 13, 1870, and also as a
leaflet in German and in the
press in German and French in
September-December 1870

Printed according to the text
of the English leaflet

THE CIVIL WAR IN FRANCE[164]

ADDRESS OF THE GENERAL COUNCIL
OF THE INTERNATIONAL WORKING MEN'S
ASSOCIATION

TO ALL THE MEMBERS OF THE ASSOCIATION IN EUROPE AND THE UNITED STATES

I

On the 4th of September, 1870, when the working men of Paris proclaimed the Republic, which was almost instantaneously acclaimed throughout France, without a single voice of dissent, a cabal of place-hunting barristers, with Thiers for their statesman and Trochu for their general, took hold of the Hôtel de Ville. At that time they were imbued with so fanatical a faith in the mission of Paris to represent France in all epochs of historical crisis, that, to legitimate their usurped titles as governors of France, they thought it quite sufficient to produce their lapsed mandates as representatives of Paris. In our second address on the late war, five days after the rise of these men, we told you who they were.* Yet, in the turmoil of surprise, with the real leaders of the working class still shut up in Bonapartist prisons and the Prussians already marching upon Paris, Paris bore with their assumption of power, on the express condition that it was to be wielded for the single purpose of national defence. Paris, however, was not to be defended without arming its working class, organising them into an effective force, and training their ranks by the war itself. But Paris armed was the Revolution armed. A victory of Paris over the Prussian aggressor would have been a victory of the French workman over the French capitalist and his State parasites. In this conflict between national duty and class interest, the Government of National Defence did not hesitate one moment to turn into a Government of National Defection.

The first step they took was to send Thiers on a roving tour to all the courts of Europe, there to beg mediation by offering the barter of the Republic for a king. Four months after the commencement of the siege, when they thought the opportune moment come for breaking the first word of capitulation, Trochu, in the presence of Jules Favre and others of his colleagues, addressed the assembled mayors of Paris in these terms:

---

* See pp. 264-70 of this volume.—*Ed.*

"The first question put to me by my colleagues on the very evening of the 4th of September was this: Paris, can it with any chance of success stand a siege by the Prussian army? I did not hesitate to answer in the negative. Some of my colleagues here present will warrant the truth of my words and the persistence of my opinion. I told them, in these very terms, that, under the existing state of things, the attempt of Paris to hold out a siege by the Prussian army would be a folly. Without doubt, I added, it would be an heroic folly; but that would be all.... The events (managed by himself) have not given the lie to my prevision."

This nice little speech of Trochu was afterwards published by M. Corbon, one of the mayors present.

Thus, on the very evening of the proclamation of the republic, Trochu's "plan" was known to his colleagues to be the capitulation of Paris. If national defence had been more than a pretext for the personal government of Thiers, Favre, and Co., the upstarts of the 4th of September would have abdicated on the 5th— would have initiated the Paris people into Trochu's "plan," and called upon them to surrender at once, or to take their own fate into their own hands. Instead of this, the infamous impostors resolved upon curing the heroic folly of Paris by a regimen of famine and broken heads, and to dupe her in the meanwhile by ranting manifestoes, holding forth that Trochu, "the governor of Paris, will never capitulate," and Jules Favre, the foreign minister, will "not cede an inch of our territory, nor a stone of our fortresses." In a letter to Gambetta, that very same Jules Favre avows that what they were "defending" against were not the Prussian soldiers, but the working men of Paris. During the whole continuance of the siege the Bonapartist cut-throats, whom Trochu had wisely intrusted with the command of the Paris army, exchanged, in their intimate correspondence, ribald jokes at the well-understood mockery of defence. (See, for instance, the correspondence of Alphonse Simon Guiod, supreme commander of the artillery of the Army of Defence of Paris and Grand Cross of the Legion of Honour, to Susane, general of division of artillery, a correspondence published by the *Journal Officiel*[190] of the Commune.) The mask of imposture was at last dropped on the 28th of January, 1871.[191] With the true heroism of utter self-debasement, the Government of National Defence, in their capitulation, came out as the government of France by Bismarck's prisoners—a part so base that Louis Bonaparte himself had, at Sedan,[157] shrunk from accepting it. After the events of the 18th of March, on their wild flight to Versailles, the *capitulards*[192] left in the hands of Paris the documentary evidence of their treason, to destroy which, as the Commune says in its manifesto to the provinces,

"those men would not recoil from battering Paris into a heap of ruins washed by a sea of blood."

To be eagerly bent upon such a consummation, some of the leading members of the Government of Defence had, besides, most peculiar reasons of their own.

Shortly after the conclusion of the armistice, M. Millière, one of the representatives of Paris to the National Assembly, now shot by express order of Jules Favre, published a series of authentic legal documents in proof that Jules Favre, living in concubinage with the wife of a drunkard resident at Algiers, had, by a most daring concoction of forgeries, spread over many years, contrived to grasp, in the name of the children of his adultery, a large succession, which made him a rich man, and that, in a lawsuit undertaken by the legitimate heirs, he only escaped exposure by the connivance of the Bonapartist tribunals. As these dry legal documents were not to be got rid of by any amount of rhetorical horse-power, Jules Favre, for the first time in his life, held his tongue, quietly awaiting the outbreak of the civil war, in order, then, frantically to denounce the people of Paris as a band of escaped convicts in utter revolt against family, religion, order and property. This same forger had hardly got into power, after the 4th of September, when he sympathetically let loose upon society Pic and Taillefer, convicted, even under the empire, of forgery, in the scandalous affair of the *Étendard*.[193] One of these men, Taillefer, having dared to return to Paris under the Commune, was at once reinstated in prison ; and then Jules Favre exclaimed, from the tribune of the National Assembly, that Paris was setting free all her jailbirds!

Ernest Picard, the Joe Miller* of the government of National Defence, who appointed himself Finance Minister of the Republic after having in vain striven to become the Home Minister of the Empire, is the brother of one Arthur Picard, an individual expelled from the Paris *Bourse* as a blackleg (see report of the Prefecture of Police, dated the 13th of July, 1867), and convicted, on his own confession, of a theft of 300,000 francs, while manager of one of the branches of the *Société Générale*,[194] rue Palestro, No. 5 (see report of the Prefecture of Police, 11th December, 1868). This Arthur Picard was made by Ernest Picard the editor of his paper, *l'Electeur libre*.[195] While the common run of stockjobbers were led astray by the official lies of this Finance office paper, Arthur was running backwards and forwards, between the Finance office and the *Bourse*, there to discount the disasters of the French army. The whole financial correspondence of that worthy pair of brothers fell into the hands of the Commune.

Jules Ferry, a penniless barrister before the 4th of September, contrived, as Mayor of Paris during the siege, to job a fortune out of famine. The day on which he would have to give an account of his maladministration would be the day of his conviction.

---

* The German editions of 1871 and 1891 have Karl Vogt; the French edition of 1871, Falstaff.—*Ed.*

These men, then, could find, in the ruins of Paris only, their tickets-of-leave* : they were the very men Bismarck wanted. With the help of some shuffling of cards, Thiers, hitherto the secret prompter of the Government, now appeared at its head, with the ticket-of-leave-men for his Ministers.

Thiers, that monstrous gnome, has charmed the French bourgeoisie for almost half a century, because he is the most consummate intellectual expression of their own class-corruption. Before he became a statesman he had already proved his lying powers as an historian. The chronicle of his public life is the record of the misfortunes of France. Banded, before 1830, with the republicans, he slipped into office under Louis Philippe by betraying his protector Laffitte, ingratiating himself with the king by exciting mobriots against the clergy, during which the church of Saint Germain l'Auxerrois and the Archbishop's palace were plundered, and by acting the minister-spy upon, and the jail-*accoucheur* of, the Duchess de Berry.[196] The massacre of the republicans in the rue Transnonain, and the subsequent infamous laws of September against the press and the right of association, were his work.[197] Reappearing as the chief of the Cabinet in March, 1840, he astonished France with his plan of fortifying Paris.[198] To the Republicans, who denounced this plan as a sinister plot against the liberty of Paris, he replied from the tribune of the Chamber of Deputies:

"What! to fancy that any works of fortification could ever endanger liberty! And first of all you calumniate any possible Government in supposing that it could some day attempt to maintain itself by bombarding the capital; ... but that government would be a hundred times more impossible after its victory than before."

Indeed, no Government would ever have dared to bombard Paris from the forts, but that Government which had previously surrendered these forts to the Prussians.

When King Bomba[199] tried his hand at Palermo, in January, 1848, Thiers, then long since out of office, again rose in the Chamber of Deputies :

"You know, gentlemen, what is happening at Palermo. You, all of you, shake with horror (in the parliamentary sense) on hearing that during forty-eight hours a large town has been bombarded—by whom? Was it by a foreign enemy exercising the rights of war? No, gentlemen, it was by its own Government. And why? Because that unfortunate town demanded its rights. Well, then, for the demand of its rights it has got forty-eight hours of bombardment.... Allow me to appeal to the opinion of Europe. It is doing a service to mankind to arise, and

---

* In England common criminals are often discharged on parole after serving the greater part of their term, and are placed under police surveillance. On such discharge they receive a certificate called ticket-of-leave, their possessors being referred to as ticket-of-leave-men. [*Note by Engels to the German edition of 1871.*]

to make reverberate, from what is perhaps the greatest tribune in Europe, some words (indeed words) of indignation against such acts.... When the Regent Espartero, who had rendered services to his country (which M. Thiers never did), intended bombarding Barcelona, in order to suppress its insurrection, there arose from all parts of the world a general outcry of indignation."

Eighteen months afterwards, M. Thiers was amongst the fiercest defenders of the bombardment of Rome by a French army.[200] In fact, the fault of King Bomba seems to have consisted in this only, that he limited his bombardment to forty-eight hours.

A few days before the Revolution of February, fretting at the long exile from place and pelf to which Guizot had condemned him, and sniffing in the air the scent of an approaching popular commotion, Thiers, in that pseudo-heroic style which won him the nickname of *Mirabeau-mouche*,* declared to the Chamber of Deputies:

"I am of the party of Revolution, not only in France, but in Europe. I wish the Government of the Revolution to remain in the hands of moderate men ... but if that Government should fall into the hands of ardent minds, even into those of Radicals, I shall, for all that, not desert my cause. I shall always be of the party of the Revolution."

The Revolution of February came. Instead of displacing the Guizot Cabinet by the Thiers Cabinet, as the little man had dreamt, it superseded Louis Philippe by the Republic. On the first day of the popular victory he carefully hid himself, forgetting that the contempt of the working men screened him from their hatred. Still, with his legendary courage, he continued to shy the public stage, until the June massacres[6] had cleared it for his sort of action. Then he became the leading mind of the "Party of Order"[72] and its Parliamentary Republic, that anonymous interregnum, in which all the rival factions of the ruling class conspired together to crush the people, and conspired against each other to restore each of them its own monarchy. Then, as now, Thiers denounced the Republicans as the only obstacle to the consolidation of the Republic; then, as now, he spoke to the Republic as the hangman spoke to Don Carlos:—"I shall assassinate thee, but for thy own good." Now, as then, he will have to exclaim on the day after his victory: *"L'Empire est fait"*— the Empire is consummated. Despite his hypocritical homilies about necessary liberties and his personal grudge against Louis Bonaparte, who had made a dupe of him, and kicked out parliamentarism—and outside of its factitious atmosphere the little man is conscious of withering into nothingness—he had a hand in all the infamies of the Second Empire, from the occupation of Rome by French troops to the war with Prussia, which he incited by his fierce invective against German unity—not as a cloak of Prussian despotism, but as an

* Mirabeau the fly.—*Ed.*

encroachment upon the vested right of France in German disunion. Fond of brandishing, with his dwarfish arms, in the face of Europe the sword of the first Napoleon, whose historical shoe-black he had become, his foreign policy always culminated in the utter humiliation of France, from the London convention[201] of 1840 to the Paris capitulation of 1871, and the present civil war, where he hounds on the prisoners of Sedan and Metz[202] against Paris by special permission of Bismarck. Despite his versatility of talent and shiftness of purpose, this man has his whole lifetime been wedded to the most fossil routine. It is self-evident that to him the deeper under-currents of modern society remained forever hidden; but even the most palpable changes on its surface were abhorrent to a brain all the vitality of which had fled to the tongue. Thus he never tired of denouncing as a sacrilege any deviation from the old French protective system. When a minister of Louis Philippe, he railed at railways as a wild chimera; and when in opposition under Louis Bonaparte, he branded as a profanation every attempt to reform the rotten French army system. Never in his long political career has he been guilty of a single—even the smallest—measure of any practical use. Thiers was consistent only in his greed for wealth and his hatred of the men that produce it. Having entered his first ministry under Louis Philippe poor as Job, he left it a millionaire. His last ministry under the same king (of the 1st of March, 1840) exposed him to public taunts of peculation in the Chamber of Deputies, to which he was content to reply by tears—a commodity he deals in as freely as Jules Favre, or any other crocodile. At Bordeaux his first measure for saving France from impending financial ruin was to endow himself with three millions a year, the first and the last word of the "Economical Republic," the vista of which he had opened to his Paris electors in 1869. One of his former colleagues of the Chamber of Deputies of 1830, himself a capitalist and, nevertheless, a devoted member of the Paris Commune, M. Beslay, lately addressed Thiers thus in a public placard:

"The enslavement of labour by capital has always been the corner-stone of your policy, and from the very day you saw the Republic of Labour installed at the Hôtel de Ville, you have never ceased to cry out to France: 'These are criminals!' "

A master in small state roguery, a virtuoso in perjury and treason, a craftsman in all the petty stratagems, cunning devices, and base perfidies of parliamentary party-warfare; never scrupling, when out of office, to fan a revolution, and to stifle it in blood when at the helm of the state; with class prejudices standing him in the place of ideas, and vanity in the place of a heart; his private life as infamous as his public life is odious—even now, when playing the part of a French Sulla, he cannot help setting off the abomination of his deeds by the ridicule of his ostentation.

The capitulation of Paris, by surrendering to Prussia not only Paris, but all France, closed the long-continued intrigues of treason with the enemy, which the usurpers of the 4th of September had begun, as Trochu himself said, on that very same day. On the other hand, it initiated the civil war they were now to wage, with the assistance of Prussia, against the Republic and Paris. The trap was laid in the very terms of the capitulation. At that time above one-third of the territory was in the hands of the enemy, the capital was cut off from the provinces, all communications were disorganised. To elect under such circumstances a real representation of France was impossible, unless ample time were given for preparation. In view of this, the capitulation stipulated that a National Assembly must be elected within eight days; so that in many parts of France the news of the impending election arrived on its eve only. This assembly, moreover, was, by an express clause of the capitulation, to be elected for the sole purpose of deciding on peace or war, and, eventually, to conclude a treaty of peace. The population could not but feel that the terms of the armistice rendered the continuation of the war impossible, and that for sanctioning the peace imposed by Bismarck, the worst men in France were the best. But not content with these precautions, Thiers, even before the secret of the armistice had been broached to Paris, set out for an electioneering tour through the provinces, there to galvanise back into life the Legitimist party,[17] which now, along with the Orleanists,[71] had to take the place of the then impossible Bonapartists. He was not afraid of them. Impossible as a government of modern France, and, therefore, contemptible as rivals, what party were more eligible as tools of counter-revolution than the party whose action, in the words of Thiers himself (Chamber of Deputies, 5th January, 1833),

"had always been confined to the three resources of foreign invasion, civil war, and anarchy"?

They verily believed in the advent of their long-expected retrospective millennium. There were the heels of foreign invasion trampling upon France; there was the downfall of an empire, and the captivity of a Bonaparte; and there they were themselves. The wheel of history had evidently rolled back to stop at the "Chambre introuvable" of 1816.[203] In the assemblies of the republic, 1848 to 51, they had been represented by their educated and trained parliamentary champions; it was the rank-and-file of the party which now rushed in—all the Pourceaugnacs of France.

As soon as this Assembly of "Rurals"[204] had met at Bordeaux, Thiers made it clear to them that the peace preliminaries must be assented to at once, without even the honours of a Parliamentary debate, as the only condition on which Prussia would permit them to open the war against the Republic and Paris, its stronghold. The counter-revolution had, in fact, no time to lose. The Second Empire had more than doubled the national debt, and plunged all the large towns into heavy municipal debts. The war had fearfully swelled the liabilities, and mercilessly ravaged the resources of the nation. To complete the ruin, the Prussian Shylock was there with his bond for the keep of half a million of his soldiers on French soil, his indemnity of five milliards,[170] and interest at 5 per cent on the unpaid instalments thereof. Who was to pay the bill? It was only by the violent overthrow of the Republic that the appropriators of wealth could hope to shift on the shoulders of its producers the cost of a war which they, the appropriators, had themselves originated. Thus, the immense ruin of France spurred on these patriotic representatives of land and capital, under the very eyes and patronage of the invader, to graft upon the foreign war a civil war—a slaveholders' rebellion.

There stood in the way of this conspiracy one great obstacle—Paris. To disarm Paris was the first condition of success. Paris was therefore summoned by Thiers to surrender its arms. Then Paris was exasperated by the frantic anti-republican demonstrations of the "Rural" Assembly and by Thiers' own equivocations about the legal status of the Republic; by the threat to decapitate and decapitalise Paris; the appointment of Orleanist ambassadors; Dufaure's laws on over-due commercial bills and house-rents,[205] inflicting ruin on the commerce and industry of Paris; Pouyer-Quertier's tax of two centimes upon every copy of every imaginable publication; the sentences of death against Blanqui and Flourens; the suppression of the Republican journals; the transfer of the National Assembly to Versailles; the renewal of the state of siege declared by Palikao, and expired on the 4th of September; the appointment of Vinoy, the *Décembriseur*,[206] as governor of Paris—of Valentin, the imperialist *gendarme*, as its prefect of police—and of D'Aurelle de Paladines, the Jesuit general, as the commander-in-chief of its National Guard.

And now we have to address a question to M. Thiers and the men of national defence, his under-strappers. It is known that, through the agency of M. Pouyer-Quertier, his finance minister, Thiers had contracted a loan of two milliards. Now, is it true, or not,—

1. That the business was so managed that a consideration of several hundred millions was secured for the private benefit of Thiers, Jules Favre, Ernest Picard, Pouyer-Quertier, and Jules Simon? and—

2. That no money was to be paid down until after the "pacification" of Paris[207]?

At all events, there must have been something very pressing in the matter, for Thiers and Jules Favre, in the name of the majority of the Bordeaux Assembly, unblushingly solicited the immediate occupation of Paris by Prussian troops. Such, however, was not the game of Bismarck, as he sneeringly, and in public, told the admiring Frankfort philistines on his return to Germany.

II

Armed Paris was the only serious obstacle in the way of the counter-revolutionary conspiracy. Paris was, therefore, to be disarmed. On this point the Bordeaux Assembly was sincerity itself. If the roaring rant of its Rurals had not been audible enough, the surrender of Paris by Thiers to the tender mercies of the triumvirate of Vinoy the *Décembriseur*, Valentin the Bonapartist *gendarme*, and Aurelle de Paladines the Jesuit general, would have cut off even the last subterfuge of doubt. But while insultingly exhibiting the true purpose of the disarmament of Paris, the conspirators asked her to lay down her arms on a pretext which was the most glaring, the most barefaced of lies. The artillery of the Paris National Guard, said Thiers, belonged to the State, and to the State it must be returned. The fact was this: From the very day of the capitulation, by which Bismarck's prisoners had signed the surrender of France, but reserved to themselves a numerous body-guard for the express purpose of cowing Paris, Paris stood on the watch. The National Guard reorganised themselves and intrusted their supreme control to a Central Committee elected by their whole body, save some fragments of the old Bonapartist formations. On the eve of the entrance of the Prussians into Paris, the Central Committee took measures for the removal to Montmartre, Belleville, and La Villete of the cannon and *mitrailleuses* treacherously abandoned by the *capitulards* in and about the very quarters the Prussians were to occupy. That artillery had been furnished by the subscriptions of the National Guard. As their private property, it was officially recognised in the capitulation of the 28th of January, and on that very title exempted from the general surrender, into the hands of the conqueror, of arms belonging to the government. And Thiers was so utterly destitute of even the flimsiest pretext for initiating the war against Paris, that he had to resort to the flagrant lie of the artillery of the National Guard being State property!

The seizure of her artillery was evidently but to serve as the preliminary to the general disarmament of Paris, and, therefore, of the Revolution of the 4th of September. But that Revolution had become the legal status of France. The republic, its work, was recognised by the conqueror in the terms of the capitulation. After the capitulation, it was acknowledged by all the foreign Powers, and in its name the National Assembly had been summoned. The Paris working men's revolution of the 4th of September was the only legal title of the National Assembly seated at Bordeaux, and of its executive. Without it, the National Assembly would at once have to give way to the *Corps Législatif* elected in 1869 by universal suffrage under French, not under Prussian, rule, and forcibly dispersed by the arm of the Revolution. Thiers and his ticket-of-leave-men would have had to capitulate for safe conducts signed by Louis Bonaparte, to save them from a voyage to Cayenne.[208] The National Assembly, with its power of attorney to settle the terms of peace with Prussia, was but an incident of that Revolution, the true embodiment of which was still armed Paris, which had initiated it, undergone for it a five months' siege, with its horrors of famine, and made her prolonged resistance, despite Trochu's plan, the basis of an obstinate war of defence in the provinces. And Paris was now either to lay down her arms at the insulting behest of the rebellious slaveholders of Bordeaux, and acknowledge that her Revolution of the 4th of September meant nothing but a simple transfer of power from Louis Bonaparte to his Royal rivals; or she had to stand forward as the self-sacrificing champion of France, whose salvation from ruin, and whose regeneration were impossible, without the revolutionary overthrow of the political and social conditions that had engendered the Second Empire, and, under its fostering care, matured into utter rottenness. Paris, emaciated by a five months' famine, did not hesitate one moment. She heroically resolved to run all the hazards of a resistance against the French conspirators, even with Prussian cannon frowning upon her from her own forts. Still, in its abhorrence of the civil war into which Paris was to be goaded, the Central Committee continued to persist in a merely defensive attitude, despite the provocations of the Assembly, the usurpations of the Executive, and the menacing concentration of troops in and around Paris.

Thiers opened the civil war by sending Vinoy, at the head of a multitude of *sergents-de-ville* and some regiments of the line, upon a nocturnal expedition against Montmartre, there to seize, by surprise, the artillery of the National Guard. It is well known how this attempt broke down before the resistance of the National Guard and the fraternisation of the line with the people. Aurelle de Paladines had printed beforehand his bulletin of victory, and Thiers held ready the placards announcing his measures of *coup d'état*. Now these had to be replaced by Thiers' appeals, imparting his magnanimous resolve to leave the National Guard in the possession of their arms, with which, he said, he felt sure they would rally round the Government against the rebels. Out of 300,000 National Guards only 300 responded to this summons to rally round little Thiers against themselves. The glorious working men's Revolution of the 18th March took undisputed sway of Paris. The Central Committee was its provisional government. Europe seemed, for a moment, to doubt whether its recent sensational performances of state and war had any reality in them, or whether they were the dreams of a long bygone past.

From the 18th of March to the entrance of the Versailles troops into Paris, the proletarian revolution remained so free from the acts of violence in which the revolutions, and still more the counter-

revolutions, of the "better classes" abound, that no facts were left
to its opponents to cry out about but the execution of Generals
Lecomte and Clément Thomas, and the affair of the Place Vendôme.

One of the Bonapartist officers engaged in the nocturnal attempt
against Montmartre, General Lecomte, had four times ordered the
81st line regiment to fire at an unarmed gathering in the Place
Pigalle, and on their refusal fiercely insulted them. Instead of shooting women and children, his own men shot him. The inveterate
habits acquired by the soldiery under the training of the enemies
of the working class are, of course, not likely to change the very
moment these soldiers changed sides. The same men executed
Clément Thomas.

"General" Clément Thomas, a malcontent exquartermaster-
sergeant, had, in the latter times of Louis Philippe's reign, enlisted
at the office of the Republican newspaper *Le National*,[61] there to
serve in the double capacity of responsible man-of-straw (*gérant
résponsable*) and of duelling bully to that very combative journal.
After the revolution of February,[4] the men of the *National* having
got into power, they metamorphosed this old quartermaster-sergeant
into a general on the eve of the butchery of June,[6] of which he, like
Jules Favre, was one of the sinister plotters, and became one of the
most dastardly executioners. Then he and his generalship disappeared
for a long time, to again rise to the surface on the 1st November,
1870. The day before the Government of Defence, caught at the
Hôtel de Ville, had solemnly pledged their parole to Blanqui, Flourens, and other representatives of the working class, to abdicate
their usurped power into the hands of a commune to be freely elected
by Paris.[209] Instead of keeping their word, they let loose on Paris
the Bretons of Trochu, who now replaced the Corsicans of Bonaparte.[210] General Tamisier alone, refusing to sully his name by such
a breach of faith, resigned the commandership-in-chief of the
National Guard, and in his place Clément Thomas for once became again a general. During the whole of his tenure of command,
he made war, not upon the Prussians, but upon the Paris National
Guard. He prevented their general armament, pitted the bourgeois
battalions against the working men's battalions, weeded out the
officers hostile to Trochu's "plan," and disbanded, under the stigma
of cowardice, the very same proletarian battalions whose heroism
has now astonished their most inveterate enemies. Clément Thomas
felt quite proud of having reconquered his June pre-eminence as
the personal enemy of the working class of Paris. Only a few days
before the 18th of March, he laid before the War Minister, Le Flô,
a plan of his own for "finishing off *la fine fleur* [the cream] of the
Paris *canaille*." After Vinoy's rout, he must needs appear upon the
scene of action in the quality of an amateur spy. The Central Committee and the Paris working men were as much responsible for the

killing of Clément Thomas and Lecomte as the Princess of Wales
was for the fate of the people crushed to death on the day of her
entrance into London.

The massacre of unarmed citizens in the Place Vendôme is a
myth which M. Thiers and the Rurals persistently ignored in the
Assembly, intrusting its propagation exclusively to the servants'
hall of European journalism. "The men of order," the reactionists
of Paris, trembled at the victory of the 18th of March. To them it
was the signal of popular retribution at last arriving. The ghosts
of the victims assassinated at their hands from the days of June,
1848, down to the 22nd of January, 1871,[211] arose before their
faces. Their panic was their only punishment. Even the *sergents-de-
ville*, instead of being disarmed and locked up, as ought to have
been done, had the gates of Paris flung wide open for their safe
retreat to Versailles. The men of order were left not only unharmed,
but allowed to rally and quietly to seize more than one stronghold
in the very centre of Paris. This indulgence of the Central Committee—this magnanimity of the armed working men—so strangely
at variance with the habits of the "Party of Order," the latter
misinterpreted as mere symptoms of conscious weakness. Hence
their silly plan to try, under the cloak of an unarmed demonstration, what Vinoy had failed to perform with his cannon and *mitrailleuses*. On the 22nd of March a riotous mob of swells started from
the quarters of luxury, all the *petits crevés* in their ranks, and at
their head the notorious familiars of the Empire—the Heckeren,
Coëtlogon, Henri de Pène, etc. Under the cowardly pretence of a
pacific demonstration, this rabble, secretly armed with the weapons
of the bravo, fell into marching order, ill-treated and disarmed the
detached patrols and sentries of the National Guards they met with
on their progress, and, on debouching from the Rue de la Paix,
with the cry of "Down with the Central Committee! Down with
the assassins! The National Assembly for ever!" attempted to break
through the line drawn up there, and thus to carry by a surprise
the headquarters of the National Guard in the Place Vendôme. In
reply to their pistol-shots, the regular *sommations* (the French
equivalent of the English Riot Act)[212] were made, and, proving ineffective, fire was commanded by the general of the National
Guard.* One volley dispersed into wild flight the silly coxcombs,
who expected that the mere exhibition of their "respectability"
would have the same effect upon the Revolution of Paris as Joshua's
trumpets upon the wall of Jericho. The runaways left behind them
two National Guards killed, nine severely wounded (among them a
member of the Central Committee**), and the whole scene of their

---

* Bergeret.—*Ed.*
** Maljournal.—*Ed.*

exploit strewn with revolvers, daggers, and sword-canes, in evidence of the "unarmed" character of their "pacific" demonstration. When, on the 13th of June, 1849, the National Guard made a really pacific demonstration in protest against the felonious assault of French troops upon Rome,[200] Changarnier, then general of the Party of Order, was acclaimed by the National Assembly, and especially by M. Thiers, as the saviour of society, for having launched his troops from all sides upon these unarmed men, to shoot and sabre them down, and to trample them under their horses' feet. Paris, then, was placed under a state of siege. Dufaure hurried through the Assembly new laws of repression. New arrests, new proscriptions— a new reign of terror set in. But the lower orders manage these things otherwise. The Central Committee of 1871 simply ignored the heroes of the "pacific demonstration"; so much so that only two days later they were enabled to muster under Admiral Saisset for that *armed* demonstration, crowned by the famous stampede to Versailles. In their reluctance to continue the civil war opened by Thiers' burglarious attempt on Montmartre, the Central Committee made itself, this time, guilty of a decisive mistake in not at once marching upon Versailles, then completely helpless, and thus putting an end to the conspiracies of Thiers and his Rurals. Instead of this, the Party of Order was again allowed to try its strength at the ballot box, on the 26th of March, the day of the election of the Commune. Then, in the *mairies* of Paris, they exchanged bland words of conciliation with their too generous conquerors, muttering in their hearts solemn vows to exterminate them in due time.

Now look at the reverse of the medal. Thiers opened his second campaign against Paris in the beginning of April. The first batch of Parisian prisoners brought into Versailles was subjected to revolting atrocities, while Ernest Picard, with his hands in his trousers' pockets, strolled about jeering them, and while Mesdames Thiers and Favre, in the midst of their ladies of honour (?), applauded, from the balcony, the outrages of the Versailles mob. The captured soldiers of the line were massacred in cold blood; our brave friend, General Duval, the iron-founder, was shot without any form of trial. Galliffet, the kept man of his wife, so notorious for her shameless exhibitions at the orgies of the Second Empire, boasted in a proclamation of having commanded the murder of a small troop of National Guards, with their captain and lieutenant, surprised and disarmed by his Chasseurs. Vinoy, the runaway, was appointed by Thiers Grand Cross of the Legion of Honour, for his general order to shoot down every soldier of the line taken in the ranks of the Federals. Desmarêt, the gendarme, was decorated for the treacherous butcher-like chopping in pieces of the high-souled and chivalrous Flourens, who had saved the heads of the Government of Defence on the 31st of October, 1870.[213] "The encouraging particulars" of his assassination were triumphantly expatiated upon by Thiers in the National Assembly. With the elated vanity of a parliamentary Tom Thumb, permitted to play the part of a Tamerlane, he denied the rebels against his littleness every right of civilised warfare, up to the right of neutrality for ambulances. Nothing more horrid than that monkey, allowed for a time to give full fling to his tigerish instincts, as foreseen by Voltaire.* (See notes, p. 35.)**

After the decree of the Commune of the 7th April, ordering reprisals and declaring it to be its duty "to protect Paris against the cannibal exploits of the Versailles banditti, and to demand an eye for an eye, a tooth for a tooth,"[214] Thiers did not stop the barbarous treatment of prisoners, moreover insulting them in his bulletins as follows:—"Never have more degraded countenances of a degraded democracy met the afflicted gazes of honest men,"— honest like Thiers himself and his ministerial ticket-of-leave-men. Still the shooting of prisoners was suspended for a time. Hardly, however, had Thiers and his Decembrist generals[40] become aware that the Communal decree of reprisals was but an empty threat, that even their gendarme spies caught in Paris under the disguise of National Guards, that even *sergents-de-ville*, taken with incendiary shells upon them, were spared,—when the wholesale shooting of prisoners was resumed and carried on uninterruptedly to the end. Houses to which National Guards had fled were surrounded by gendarmes, inundated with petroleum (which here occurs for the first time in this war), and then set fire to, the charred corpses being afterwards brought out by the ambulance of the Press at the Ternes. Four National Guards having surrendered to a troop of mounted Chasseurs at Belle Epine, on the 25th of April, were afterwards shot down, one after another, by the captain, a worthy man of Galliffet's. One of his four victims, left for dead, Scheffer, crawled back to the Parisian outposts, and deposed to this fact before a commission of the Commune. When Tolain interpellated the War Minister upon the report of this commission, the Rurals drowned his voice and forbade Le Fl to answer. It would be an insult to their "glorious" army to speak of its deeds. The flippant tone in which Thiers' bulletins announced the bayoneting of the Federals surprised asleep at Moulin Saquet, and the wholesale fusillades at Clamart shocked the nerves even of the not over-sensitive London *Times*.[215] But it would be ludicrous today to attempt recounting the merely preliminary atrocities committed by the bombarders of Paris and the fomenters of a slaveholders' rebellion protected by foreign invasion. Amidst all these horrors, Thiers, forgetful of his parlia-

---

* Voltaire, *Candide*, Chapter 22.—*Ed.*
** See pp. 307-08 of this volume.—*Ed.*

mentary laments on the terrible responsibility weighing down his dwarfish shoulders, boasts in his bulletin that *l'Assemblée siège paisiblement* (the Assembly continues meeting in peace), and proves by his constant carousals, now with Decembrist generals, now with German princes, that his digestion is not troubled in the least, not even by the ghosts of Lecomte and Clément Thomas.

III

On the dawn of the 18th of March, Paris arose to the thunderburst of "Vive la Commune!" What is the Commune, that sphinx so tantalising to the bourgeois mind?

"The proletarians of Paris," said the Central Committee in its manifesto of the 18th March, "amidst the failures and treasons of the ruling classes, have understood that the hour has struck for them to save the situation by taking into their own hands the direction of public affairs.... They have understood that it is their imperious duty and their absolute right to render themselves masters of their own destinies, by seizing upon the governmental power."

But the working class cannot simply lay hold of the ready-made state machinery, and wield it for its own purposes.

The centralised State power, with its ubiquitous organs of standing army, police, bureaucracy, clergy, and judicature—organs wrought after the plan of a systematic and hierarchic division of labour,—originates from the days of absolute monarchy, serving nascent middle-class society as a mighty weapon in its struggles against feudalism. Still, its development remained clogged by all manner of mediaeval rubbish, seignorial rights, local privileges, municipal and guild monopolies and provincial constitutions. The gigantic broom of the French Revolution of the eighteenth century swept away all these relics of bygone times, thus clearing simultaneously the social soil of its last hindrances to the superstructure of the modern State edifice raised under the First Empire, itself the offspring of the coalition wars of old semi-feudal Europe against modern France. During the subsequent *régimes* the Government, placed under parliamentary control—that is, under the direct control of the propertied classes—became not only a hotbed of huge national debts and crushing taxes; with its irresistible allurements of place, pelf, and patronage, it became not only the bone of contention between the rival factions and adventurers of the ruling classes; but its political character changed simultaneously with the economic changes of society. At the same pace at which the progress of modern industry developed, widened, intensified the class antagonism between capital and labour, the State power assumed more and more the character of the national power of capital over labour, of a public force organised for social enslavement, of an engine of class despotism. After every revolution marking a progressive phase in the class struggle, the purely repressive character of the State power stands out in bolder and bolder relief. The Revolution of 1830, resulting in the transfer of Government from the landlords to the capitalists, transferred it from the more remote to the more direct antagonists of the working men. The bourgeois Republicans, who, in the name of the Revolution of February, took the State power, used it for the June massacres, in order to convince the working class that "social" republic meant the Republic ensuring their social subjection, and in order to convince the royalist bulk of the bourgeois and landlord class that they might safely leave the cares and emoluments of Government to the bourgeois "Republicans." However, after their one heroic exploit of June, the bourgeois Republicans had, from the front, to fall back to the rear of the "Party of Order"—a combination formed by all the rival fractions and factions of the appropriating class in their now openly declared antagonism to the producing classes. The proper form of their joint-stock Government was the *Parliamentary Republic*, with Louis Bonaparte for its President. Theirs was a *régime* of avowed class terrorism and deliberate insult toward the "vile multitude." If the Parliamentary Republic, as M. Thiers said, "divided them (the different fractions of the ruling class) least," it opened an abyss between that class and the whole body of society outside their spare ranks. The restraints by which their own divisions had under former *régimes* still checked the State power, were removed by their union; and in view of the threatening upheaval of the proletariat, they now used that State power mercilessly and ostentatiously as the national war-engine of capital against labour. In their uninterrupted crusade against the producing masses they were, however, bound not only to invest the executive with continually increased powers of repression, but at the same time to divest their own parliamentary stronghold—the National Assembly —one by one, of all its own means of defence against the Executive. The Executive, in the person of Louis Bonaparte, turned them out. The natural offspring of the "Party-of-Order" Republic was the Second Empire.

The empire, with the *coup d'état* for its certificate of birth, universal suffrage for its sanction, and the sword for its sceptre, professed to rest upon the peasantry, the large mass of producers not directly involved in the struggle of capital and labour. It professed to save the working class by breaking down Parliamentarism, and, with it, the undisguised subserviency of Government to the propertied classes. It professed to save the propertied classes by upholding their economic supremacy over the working class; and, finally, it professed to unite all classes by reviving for all the chimera of national glory. In reality, it was the only form of government possible at a time when the bourgeoisie had already lost, and the working class had not yet acquired, the faculty of ruling the nation. It was acclaimed throughout the world as the saviour of society. Under its sway, bourgeois society, freed from political cares, attained a development unexpected even by itself. Its industry and commerce expanded to colossal dimensions; financial swindling celebrated cosmopolitan orgies; the misery of the masses was set off by a shameless display of gorgeous, meretricious and debased luxury. The State power, apparently soaring high above society, was at the same time itself the greatest scandal of that society and the very hotbed of all its corruptions. Its own rottenness, and the rottenness of the society it had saved, were laid bare by the bayonet of Prussia, herself eagerly bent upon transferring the supreme seat of that *régime* from Paris to Berlin. Imperialism is, at the same time, the most prostitute and the ultimate form of the State power which nascent middle-class society had commenced to elaborate as a means of its own emancipation from feudalism, and which full-grown bourgeois society had finally transformed into a means for the enslavement of labour by capital.

The direct antithesis to the empire was the Commune. The cry of "social republic," with which the revolution of February was ushered in by the Paris proletariat, did but express a vague aspiration after a Republic that was not only to supersede the monarchical form of class-rule, but class-rule itself. The Commune was the positive form of that Republic.

Paris, the central seat of the old governmental power, and, at the same time, the social stronghold of the French working class, had risen in arms against the attempt of Thiers and the Rurals to restore and perpetuate that old governmental power bequeathed to them by the empire. Paris could resist only because, in consequence of the siege, it had got rid of the army, and replaced it by a National Guard, the bulk of which consisted of working men. This fact was now to be transformed into an institution. The first decree of the Commune, therefore, was the suppression of the standing army, and the substitution for it of the armed people.

The Commune was formed of the municipal councillors, chosen by universal suffrage in the various wards of the town, responsible and revocable at short terms. The majority of its members were naturally working men, or acknowledged representatives of the working class. The Commune was to be a working, not a parliamentary, body, executive and legislative at the same time. Instead of continuing to be the agent of the Central Government, the police was at once stripped of its political attributes, and turned into the responsible and at all times revocable agent of the Commune. So were the officials of all other branches of the Administration. From the members of the Commune downwards, the public service had to be done at *workmen's wages*. The vested interests and the representation allowances of the high dignitaries of State disappeared along with the high dignitaries themselves. Public functions ceased to be the private property of the tools of the Central Government. Not only municipal administration, but the whole initiative hitherto exercised by the State was laid into the hands of the Commune.

Having once got rid of the standing army and the police, the physical force elements of the old Government, the Commune was anxious to break the spiritual force of repression, the "parson-power," by the disestablishment and disendowment of all churches as proprietary bodies. The priests were sent back to the recesses of private life, there to feed upon the alms of the faithful in imitation of their predecessors, the Apostles. The whole of the educational institutions were opened to the people gratuitously, and at the same time cleared of all interference of Church and State. Thus, not only was education made accessible to all, but science itself freed from the fetters which class prejudice and governmental force had imposed upon it.

The judicial functionaries were to be divested of that sham independence which had but served to mask their abject subserviency to all succeeding governments to which, in turn, they had taken, and broken, the oaths of allegiance. Like the rest of public servants, magistrates and judges were to be elective, responsible, and revocable.

The Paris Commune was, of course, to serve as a model to all the great industrial centres of France. The communal *régime* once established in Paris and the secondary centres, the old centralised Government would in the provinces, too, have to give way to the self-government of the producers. In a rough sketch of national organisation which the Commune had no time to develop, it states clearly that the Commune was to be the political form of even the smallest country hamlet, and that in the rural districts the standing army was to be replaced by a national militia, with an extremely short term of service. The rural communes of every district were to administer their common affairs by an assembly of delegates in the central town, and these district assemblies were again to send deputies to the National Delegation in Paris, each delegate to be at any time revocable and bound by the *mandat impératif* (formal instructions) of his constituents. The few but important functions which still would remain for a central government were not to be suppressed, as has been intentionally mis-stated, but were to be discharged by Communal, and therefore strictly responsible agents. The unity of the nation was not to be broken, but, on the contrary, to be organised by the Communal Constitution and to become a reality by the destruction of the State power which claimed to be the embodiment of that unity independent of, and superior to, the nation itself, from which it was but a parasitic excrescence. While the merely repressive organs of the old governmental power were to be amputated, its legitimate functions were to be wrested from an authority usurping pre-eminence over society itself, and restored to the responsible agents of society. Instead of deciding once in three or six years which member of the ruling class was to misrepresent the people in Parliament, universal suffrage was to serve the people, constituted in Communes, as individual suffrage serves every other employer in the search for the workmen and managers in his business. And it is well known that companies, like individuals, in matters of real business generally know how to put the right man in the right place, and, if they for once make a mistake, to redress it promptly. On the other hand, nothing could be more foreign to the spirit of the Commune than to supersede universal suffrage by hierarchic investiture.[216]

It is generally the fate of completely new historical creations to be mistaken for the counterpart of older and even defunct forms of social life, to which they may bear a certain likeness. Thus, this new Commune, which breaks the modern State power, has been mistaken for a reproduction of the mediaeval Communes, which first preceded, and afterwards became the substratum of, that very State power. The Communal Constitution has been mistaken for an attempt to break up into a federation of small States, as dreamt of by Montesquieu and the Girondins,[76] that unity of great nations which, if originally brought about by political force, has now become a powerful coefficient of social production. The antagonism of the Commune against the State power has been mistaken for an exaggerated form of the ancient struggle against over-centralisation. Peculiar historical circumstances may have prevented the classical development, as in France, of the bourgeois form of government, and may have allowed, as in England, to complete the great central State organs by corrupt vestries, jobbing councillors, and ferocious poor-law guardians in the towns, and virtually hereditary magistrates in the counties. The Communal Constitution would have restored to the social body all the forces hitherto absorbed by the State parasite feeding upon, and clogging the free movement of, society. By this one act it would have initiated the regeneration of France. The provincial French middle class saw in the Commune an attempt to restore the sway their order had held over the country under Louis Philippe, and which, under Louis Napoleon, was supplanted by the pretended rule of the country over the towns. In reality, the Communal Constitution brought the rural producers under the intellectual lead of the central towns of their districts, and these secured to them, in the working men, the natural trustees of their interests. The very existence of the Commune involved, as a matter of course, local municipal liberty, but no longer as a check upon the, now superseded, State power. It could only enter into the head of a Bismarck, who, when not engaged in his intrigues of blood and iron, always likes to resume his old trade, so befitting his mental calibre, of contributor to *Kladderadatsch*[217] (the Berlin *Punch*), it could only enter into such a head, to ascribe to the Paris Commune aspirations after that caricature of the old French municipal organisation of 1791, the Prussian municipal constitution which degrades the town governments to mere secondary wheels in the police-machinery of the Prussian State. The Commune made that catchword of bourgeois revolutions, cheap government, a reality, by destroying the two greatest sources of expenditure—the standing army and State functionarism. Its very existence presupposed the non-existence of monarchy, which, in Europe at least, is the normal incumbrance and indispensable cloak of class-rule. It supplied the Republic with the basis of really democratic institutions. But neither cheap Government nor the "true Republic" was its ultimate aim; they were its mere concomitants.

The multiplicity of interpretations to which the Commune has been subjected, and the multiplicity of interests which construed it in their favour, show that it was a thoroughly expansive political form, while all previous forms of government had been emphatically repressive. Its true secret was this. It was essentially a working-class government, the produce of the struggle of the producing against the appropriating class, the political form at last discovered under which to work out the economic emancipation of labour.

Except on this last condition, the Communal Constitution would have been an impossibility and a delusion. The political rule of the producer cannot coexist with the perpetuation of his social slavery. The Commune was therefore to serve as a lever for uprooting the economical foundations upon which rests the existence of classes, and therefore of class-rule. With labour emancipated, every man becomes a working man, and productive labour ceases to be a class attribute.

It is a strange fact. In spite of all the tall talk and all the immense literature, for the last sixty years, about Emancipation of Labour, no sooner do the working men anywhere take the subject into their own hands with a will, than uprises at once all the apologetic phraseology of the mouthpieces of present society with its two poles of Capital and Wages Slavery (the landlord now is but the sleeping partner of the capitalist), as if capitalist society was still in its purest state of virgin innocence, with its antagonisms still undeveloped, with its delusions still unexploded, with its prostitute realities not yet laid bare. The Commune, they exclaim, intends to abolish property, the basis of all civilisation! Yes, gentlemen, the Commune intended to abolish that class-property which makes the labour of the many the wealth of the few. It aimed at the expropriation of the expropriators. It wanted to make individual property a truth by transforming the means of production, land and capital, now chiefly the means of enslaving and exploiting labour, into mere instruments of free and associated labour.—But this is Communism, "impossible" Communism! Why, those members of the ruling classes who are intelligent enough to perceive the impossibility of continuing the present system—and they are many—have become the obtrusive and full-mouthed apostles of co-operative production. If co-operative production is not to remain a sham and a snare; if it is to supersede the Capitalist system; if united co-operative societies are to regulate national production upon a common plan, thus taking it under their own control, and putting an end to the constant anarchy and periodical convulsions which are the fatality of Capitalist production—what else, gentlemen, would it be but Communism, "possible" Communism?

The working class did not expect miracles from the Commune. They have no ready-made utopias to introduce *par décret du peuple*. They know that in order to work out their own emancipation, and along with it that higher form to which present society is irresistibly tending by its own economical agencies, they will have to pass through long struggles, through a series of historic processes, transforming circumstances and men. They have no ideals to realise, but to set free the elements of the new society with which old collapsing bourgeois society itself is pregnant. In the full consciousness of their historic mission, and with the heroic resolve to act up to it, the working class can afford to smile at the coarse invective of the gentlemen's gentlemen with the pen and inkhorn, and at the didactic patronage of well-wishing bourgeois-doctrinaires, pouring forth their ignorant platitudes and sectarian crotchets in the oracular tone of scientific infallibility.

When the Paris Commune took the management of the revolution in its own hands; when plain working men for the first time dared to infringe upon the Governmental privilege of their "natural superiors," and, under circumstances of unexampled difficulty, performed their work modestly, conscientiously, and efficiently,— performed it at salaries the highest of which barely amounted to one-fifth of what, according to high scientific authority,* is the minimum required for a secretary to a certain metropolitan school board,—the old world writhed in convulsions of rage at the sight of the Red Flag, the symbol of the Republic of Labour, floating over the Hôtel de Ville

And yet, this was the first revolution in which the working class was openly acknowledged as the only class capable of social initiative, even by the great bulk of the Paris middle class—shopkeepers, tradesmen, merchants—the wealthy capitalists alone excepted. The Commune had saved them by a sagacious settlement of that ever-recurring cause of dispute among the middle classes themselves—

---

* Professor Huxley. [*Note to the German edition of 1871.*]

the debtor and creditor accounts.[218] The same portion of the middle class, after they had assisted in putting down the working men's insurrection of June, 1848, had been at once unceremoniously sacrificed to their creditors[219] by the then Constituent Assembly. But this was not their only motive for now rallying round the working class. They felt that there was but one alternative—the Commune, or the Empire—under whatever name it might reappear. The Empire had ruined them economically by the havoc it made of public wealth, by the wholesale financial swindling it fostered, by the props it lent to the artificially accelerated centralisation of capital, and the concomitant expropriation of their own ranks. It had suppressed them politically, it had shocked them morally by its orgies, it had insulted their Voltairianism by handing over the education of their children to the *frères Ignorantins*,[220] it had revolted their national feeling as Frenchmen by precipitating them headlong into a war which left only one equivalent for the ruins it made—the disappearance of the Empire. In fact, after the exodus from Paris of the high Bonapartist and capitalist *bohême*, the true middle-class Party of Order came out in the shape of the "Union Républicaine,"[221] enrolling themselves under the colours of the Commune and defending it against the wilful misconstruction of Thiers. Whether the gratitude of this great body of the middle class will stand the present severe trial,. time must show.

The Commune was perfectly right in telling the peasants that "its victory was their only hope." Of all the lies hatched at Versailles and re-echoed by the glorious European penny-a-liner, one of the most tremendous was that the Rurals represented the French peasantry. Think only of the love of the French peasant for the men to whom, after 1815, he had to pay the milliard of indemnity.[222] In the eyes of the French peasant, the very existence of a great landed proprietor is in itself an encroachment on his conquests of 1789. The bourgeois, in 1848, had burdened his plot of land with the additional tax of forty-five cents in the franc; but then he did so in the name of the revolution; while now he had fomented a civil war against the revolution, to shift on to the peasant's shoulders the chief load of the five milliards of indemnity to be paid to the Prussian. The Commune, on the other hand, in one of its first proclamations, declared that the true originators of the war would be made to pay its cost. The Commune would have delivered the peasant of the blood tax,—would have given him a cheap government,—transformed his present bloodsuckers, the notary, advocate, executor, and other judicial vampires, into salaried communal agents, elected by, and responsible to, himself. It would have freed him of the tyranny of the *garde champêtre*, the gendarme, and the prefect; would have put enlightenment by the schoolmaster in the place of stultification by the priest. And the French peasant is, above all, a man of reckoning. He would find it extremely reasonable that the pay of the priest, instead of being extorted by the taxgatherer, should only depend upon the spontaneous action of the parishioners' religious instincts. Such were the great immediate boons which the rule of the Commune—and that rule alone—held out to the French peasantry. It is, therefore, quite superfluous here to expatiate upon the more complicated but vital problems which the Commune alone was able, and at the same time compelled, to solve in favour of the peasant, *viz.*, the hypothecary debt, lying like an incubus upon his parcel of soil, the *prolétariat foncier* (the rural proletariat), daily growing upon it, and his expropriation from it enforced, at a more and more rapid rate, by the very development of modern agriculture and the competition of capitalist farming.

The French peasant had elected Louis Bonaparte president of the Republic; but the Party of Order[72] created the Empire. What the French peasant really wants he commenced to show in 1849 and 1850, by opposing his *maire* to the Government's prefect, his schoolmaster to the Government's priest, and himself to the Government's gendarme. All the laws made by the Party of Order in January and February, 1850, were avowed measures of repression against the peasant. The peasant was a Bonapartist, because the great Revolution, with all its benefits to him, was, in his eyes, personified in Napóleon. This delusion, rapidly breaking down under the Second Empire (and in its very nature hostile to the Rurals), this prejudice of the past, how could it have withstood the appeal of the Commune to the living interests and urgent wants of the peasantry?

The Rurals—this was, in fact, their chief apprehension—knew that three months' free communication of Communal Paris with the provinces would bring about a general rising of the peasants, and hence their anxiety to establish a police blockade around Paris, so as to stop the spread of the rinderpest.

If the Commune was thus the true representative of all the healthy elements of French society, and therefore the truly national Government, it was, at the same time, as a working men's Government, as the bold champion of the emancipation of labour, emphatically international. Within sight of the Prussian army, that had annexed to Germany two French provinces, the Commune annexed to France the working people all over the world.

The Second Empire had been the jubilee of cosmopolitan blacklegism, the rakes of all countries rushing in at its call for a share in its orgies and in the plunder of the French people. Even at this moment the right hand of Thiers is Ganesco, the foul Wallachian, and his left hand is Markovsky, the Russian spy. The Commune admitted all foreigners to the honour of dying for an immortal cause. Between the foreign war lost by their treason, and the civil war fomented by their conspiracy with the foreign invader, the bour-

geoisie had found the time to display their patriotism by organising
police-hunts upon the Germans in France. The Commune made a
German working man* its Minister of Labour. Thiers, the bourgeoisie, the Second Empire, had continually deluded Poland by loud
professions of sympathy, while in reality betraying her to, and doing
the dirty work of, Russia. The Commune honoured the heroic sons
of Poland** by placing them at the head of the defenders of Paris.
And, to broadly mark the new era of history it was conscious of
initiating, under the eyes of the conquering Prussians, on the one
side, and of the Bonapartist army, led by Bonapartist generals, on the
other, the Commune pulled down that colossal symbol of martial
glory, the Vendome column.[112]

The great social measure of the Commune was its own working
existence. Its special measures could but betoken the tendency of
a government of the people by the people. Such were the abolition
of the nightwork of journeymen bakers; the prohibition, under
penalty, of the employers' practice to reduce wages by levying upon
their work-people fines under manifold pretexts,—a process in
which the employer combines in his own person the parts of legislator, judge, and executor, and filches the money to boot. Another
measure of this class was the surrender, to associations of workmen,
under reserve of compensation, of all closed workshops and factories,
no matter whether the respective capitalists had absconded or preferred to strike work.

The financial measures of the Commune, remarkable for their
sagacity and moderation, could only be such as were compatible
with the state of a besieged town. Considering the colossal robberies
committed upon the city of Paris by the great financial companies
and contractors, under the protection of Haussmann,*** the Commune
would have had an incomparably better title to confiscate their
property than Louis Napoleon had against the Orleans family. The
Hohenzollern and the English oligarchs, who both have derived a
good deal of their estates from Church plunder, were, of course,
greatly shocked at the Commune clearing but 8,000 f. out of
secularisation.

While the Versailles Government, as soon as it had recovered
some spirit and strength, used the most violent means against the
Commune; while it put down the free expression of opinion all
over France, even to the forbidding of meetings of delegates from

---

* Leo Frankel.—*Ed.*
** J. Dąbrowski and W. Wróblewski.—*Ed.*
*** During the Second Empire, Baron Haussmann was Prefect of the Department of the Seine, that is, of the City of Paris. He introduced a number of
changes in the layout of the city for the purpose of facilitating the crushing of
workers' insurrections. [*Note to the Russian edition of 1905 edited by V. I. Lenin.*]
—*Ed.*

the large towns; while it subjected Versailles and the rest of France to an espionage far surpassing that of the Second Empire; while it burned by its gendarme inquisitors all papers printed at Paris, and sifted all correspondence from and to Paris; while in the National Assembly the most timid attempts to put in a word for Paris were howled down in a manner unknown even to the *Chambre introuvable*[203] of 1816; with the savage warfare of Versailles outside, and its attempts at corruption and conspiracy inside Paris—would the Commune not have shamefully betrayed its trust by affecting to keep up all the decencies and appearances of liberalism as in a time of profound peace? Had the Government of the Commune been akin to that of M. Thiers, there would have been no more occasion to suppress Party-of-Order papers at Paris than there was to suppress Communal papers at Versailles.

It was irritating indeed to the Rurals that at the very same time they declared the return to the church to be the only means of salvation for France, the infidel Commune unearthed the peculiar mysteries of the Picpus nunnery, and of the Church of Saint Laurent.[223] It was a satire upon M. Thiers that, while he showered grand crosses upon the Bonapartist generals in acknowledgement of their mastery in losing battles, signing capitulations, and turning cigarettes at Wilhelmshöhe, the Commune dismissed and arrested its generals whenever they were suspected of neglecting their duties. The expulsion from, and arrest by, the Commune of one of its members* who had slipped in under a false name, and had undergone at Lyons six days' imprisonment for simple bankruptcy, was it not a deliberate insult hurled at the forger, Jules Favre, then still the foreign minister of France, still selling France to Bismarck, and still dictating his orders to that paragon Government of Belgium? But indeed the Commune did not pretend to infallibility, the invariable attribute of all governments of the old stamp. It published its doings and sayings, it initiated the public into all its shortcomings.

In every revolution there intrude, at the side of its true agents, men of a different stamp; some of them survivors of and devotees to past revolutions, without insight into the present movement, but preserving popular influence by their known honesty and courage, or by the sheer force of tradition; others mere bawlers, who, by dint of repeating year after year the same set of stereotyped declamations against the Government of the day, have sneaked into the reputation of revolutionists of the first water. After the 18th of March, some such men did also turn up, and in some cases contrived to play pre-eminent parts. As far as their power went, they hampered the real action of the working class, exactly as men of that sort have hampered the full development of every previous

---

* Blanchet.—*Ed.*

revolution. They are an unavoidable evil: with time they are shaken off; but time was not allowed to the Commune.

Wonderful, indeed, was the change the Commune had wrought in Paris! No longer any trace of the meretricious Paris of the Second Empire. No longer was Paris the rendezvous of British landlords, Irish absentees,[224] American ex-slaveholders and shoddy men, Russian ex-serfowners, and Wallachian boyards. No more corpses at the morgue, no nocturnal burglaries, scarcely any robberies; in fact, for the first time since the days of February, 1848, the streets of Paris were safe, and that without any police of any kind.

"We," said a member of the Commune, "hear no longer of assassination, theft and personal assault; it seems indeed as if the police had dragged along with it to Versailles all its Conservative friends."

The *cocottes* had refound the scent of their protectors—the absconding men of family, religion, and, above all, of property. In their stead, the real women of Paris showed again at the surface —heroic, noble, and devoted, like the women of antiquity. Working, thinking, fighting, bleeding Paris—almost forgetful, in its incubation of a new society, of the cannibals at its gates—radiant in the enthusiasm of its historic initiative!

Opposed to this new world at Paris, behold the old world at Versailles—that assembly of the ghouls of all defunct *régimes*, Legitimists and Orleanists, eager to feed upon the carcass of the nation,— with a tail of antediluvian Republicans, sanctioning, by their presence in the Assembly, the slaveholders' rebellion, relying for the maintenance of their Parliamentary Republic upon the vanity of the senile mountebank at its head, and caricaturing 1789 by holding their ghastly meetings in the *Jeu de Paume*.* There it was, this Assembly, the representative of everything dead in France, propped up to the semblance of life by nothing but the swords of the generals of Louis Bonaparte. Paris all truth, Versailles all lie; and that lie vented through the mouth of Thiers.

Thiers tells a deputation of the mayors of the Seine-et-Oise,—

"You may rely upon my word, which I have *never* broken!"

He tells the Assembly itself that "it was the most freely elected and most Liberal Assembly France ever possessed"; he tells his motley soldiery that it was "the admiration of the world, and the finest army France ever possessed"; he tells the provinces that the bombardment of Paris by him was a myth:

"If some cannon-shots have been fired, it is not the deed of the army of Versailles, but of some insurgents trying to make believe that they are fighting, while they dare not show their faces."

---

* *Jeu de Paume*: The tennis court where the National Assembly of 1789 adopted its famous decisions.[225] [*Note to the German edition of 1871.*]

He again tells the provinces that

"the artillery of Versailles does not bombard Paris, but only cannonades it."

He tells the Archbishop of Paris that the pretended executions and reprisals (!) attributed to the Versailles troops were all moonshine. He tells Paris that he was only anxious "to free it from the hideous tyrants who oppress it," and that, in fact, the Paris of the Commune was "but a handful of criminals."

The Paris of M. Thiers was not the real Paris of the "vile multitude," but a phantom Paris, the Paris of the *francs-fileurs*,[226] the Paris of the Boulevards, male and female—the rich, the capitalist, the gilded, the idle Paris, now thronging with its lackeys, its blacklegs, its literary *bohême*, and its *cocottes* at Versailles, Saint-Denis, Rueil, and Saint-Germain; considering the civil war but an agreeable diversion, eyeing the battle going on through telescopes, counting the rounds of cannon, and swearing by their own honour and that of their prostitutes, that the performance was far better got up than it used to be at the Porte St. Martin. The men who fell were really dead; the cries of the wounded were cries in good earnest; and, besides, the whole thing was so intensely historical.

This is the Paris of M. Thiers, as the emigration of Coblenz was the France of M. de Calonne.[227]

IV

The first attempt of the slaveholders' conspiracy to put down Paris by getting the Prussians to occupy it, was frustrated by Bismarck's refusal. The second attempt, that of the 18th of March, ended in the rout of the army and the flight to Versailles of the Government, which ordered the whole administration to break up and follow in its track. By the semblance of peace-negotiations with Paris, Thiers found the time to prepare for war against it. But where to find an army? The remnants of the line regiments were weak in number and unsafe in character. His urgent appeal to the provinces to succour Versailles, by their National Guards and volunteers, met with a flat refusal. Brittany alone furnished a handful of *Chouans*[228] fighting under a white flag, every one of them wearing on his breast the heart of Jesus in white cloth, and shouting *"Vive le Roi!"* (Long live the King!) Thiers was, therefore, compelled to collect, in hot haste, a motley crew, composed of sailors, marines, Pontifical Zouaves,[229] Valentin's gendarmes, and Pietri's *sergents-de-ville* and *mouchards*. This army, however, would have been ridiculously ineffective without the instalments of imperialist war-prisoners, which Bismarck granted in numbers just sufficient to keep the civil war a-going, and keep the Versailles Government in abject dependence on Prussia. During the war itself, the Versailles police had to look after the Versailles army, while the gendarmes had to drag it on by exposing themselves at all posts of danger. The forts which fell were not taken, but bought. The heroism of the Federals convinced Thiers that the resistance of Paris was not to be broken by his own strategic genius and the bayonets at his disposal.

Meanwhile, his relations with the provinces became more and more difficult. Not one single address of approval came in to gladden Thiers and his Rurals. Quite the contrary. Deputations and addresses demanding, in a tone anything but respectful, conciliation with Paris on the basis of the unequivocal recognition of the Republic, the acknowledgement of the Communal liberties, and the dissolution of the National Assembly, whose mandate was extinct, poured in from all sides, and in such numbers that Dufaure, Thiers' Minister of Justice, in his circular of April 23 to the public prosecutors, commanded them to treat "the cry of conciliation" as a crime! In regard, however, of the hopeless prospect held out by his campaign, Thiers resolved to shift his tactics by ordering, all over the country, municipal elections to take place on the 30th of April, on the basis of the new municipal law dictated by himself to the National Assembly. What with the intrigues of his prefects, what with police intimidation, he felt quite sanguine of imparting, by the verdict of the provinces, to the National Assembly that moral power it had never possessed, and of getting at last from the provinces the physical force required for the conquest of Paris.

His banditti-warfare against Paris, exalted in his own bulletins, and the attempts of his ministers at the establishment, throughout France, of a reign of terror, Thiers was from the beginning anxious to accompany with a little by-play of conciliation, which had to serve more than one purpose. It was to dupe the provinces, to inveigle the middle-class element in Paris, and, above all, to afford the professed Republicans in the National Assembly the opportunity of hiding their treason against Paris behind their faith in Thiers. On the 21st of March, when still without an army, he had declared to the Assembly:

"Come what may, I will not send an army to Paris."

On the 27th March he rose again:

"I have found the Republic an accomplished fact, and I am firmly resolved to maintain it."

In reality, he put down the revolution at Lyons and Marseilles[230] in the name of the Republic, while the roars of his Rurals drowned the very mention of its name at Versailles. After this exploit, he toned down the "accomplished fact" into an hypothetical fact. The Orleans princes, whom he had cautiously warned off Bordeaux, were now, in flagrant breach of the law, permitted to intrigue at Dreux

The concessions held out by Thiers in his interminable interviews
with the delegates from Paris and the provinces, although constantly
varied in tone and colour, according to time and circumstances, did
in fact never come to more than the prospective restriction of
revenge to the

"handful of criminals implicated in the murder of Lecomte and Clément
Thomas,"

on the well-understood premise that Paris and France were un-
reservedly to accept M. Thiers himself as the best of possible Republics, as he, in 1830, had done with Louis Philippe. Even these concessions he not only took care to render doubtful by the official
comments put upon them in the Assembly through his Ministers.
He had his Dufaure to act. Dufaure, this old Orleanist lawyer, had
always been the justiciary of the state of siege, as now in 1871,
under Thiers, so in 1839 under Louis Philippe, and in 1849 under
Louis Bonaparte's presidency. While out of office he made a fortune
by pleading for the Paris capitalists, and made political capital by
pleading against the laws he had himself originated. He now hurried through the National Assembly not only a set of repressive laws
which were, after the fall of Paris, to extirpate the last remnants of
Republican liberty in France; he foreshadowed the fate of Paris by
abridging the, for him, too slow procedure of courts-martial,[231] and
by a newfangled, Draconic code of deportation. The Revolution of
1848, abolishing the penalty of death for political crimes, has
replaced it by deportation. Louis Bonaparte did not dare, at least not
in theory, to re-establish the *régime* of the guillotine. The Rural
Assembly, not yet bold enough even to hint that the Parisians were
not rebels, but assassins, had therefore to confine its prospective
vengeance against Paris to Dufaure's new code of deportation. Under
all these circumstances Thiers himself could not have gone on with
his comedy of conciliation, had it not, as he intended it to do, drawn
forth shrieks of rage from the Rurals, whose ruminating mind did
neither understand the play, nor its necessities of hypocrisy, tergi-
versation, and procrastination

In sight of the impending municipal elections of the 30th April,
Thiers enacted one of his great conciliation scenes on the 27th
April. Amidst a flood of sentimental rhetoric, he exclaimed from
the tribune of the Assembly:

"There exists no conspiracy against the Republic but that of Paris, which
compels us to shed French blood. I repeat it again and again. Let those impious
arms fall from the hands which hold them, and chastisement will be arrested at
once by an act of peace excluding only the small number of criminals."

To the violent interruption of the Rurals he replied:

"Gentlemen, tell me, I implore you, am I wrong? Do you really regret that I
could have stated the truth that the criminals are only a handful? Is it not for-

tunate in the midst of our misfortunes that those who have been capable to shed the blood of Clément Thomas and General Lecomte are but rare exceptions?"

France, however, turned a deaf ear to what Thiers flattered himself to be a parliamentary siren's song. Out of 700,000 municipal councillors returned by the 35,000 communes still left to France, the united Legitimists,[17] Orleanists[71] and Bonapartists did not carry 8,000. The supplementary elections which followed were still more decidedly hostile. Thus, instead of getting from the provinces the badly-needed physical force, the National Assembly lost even its last claim to moral force, that of being the expression of the universal suffrage of the country. To complete the discomfiture, the newly-chosen municipal councils of all the cities of France openly threatened the usurping Assembly at Versailles with a counter Assembly at Bordeaux.

Then the long-expected moment of decisive action had at last come for Bismarck. He peremptorily summoned Thiers to send to Frankfort plenipotentiaries for the definitive settlement of peace. In humble obedience to the call of his master, Thiers hastened to despatch his trusty Jules Favre, backed by Pouyer-Quertier. Pouyer-Quertier, an "eminent" Rouen cotton-spinner, a fervent and even servile partisan of the Second Empire, had never found any fault with it save its commercial treaty with England,[232] prejudicial to his own shop-interest. Hardly installed at Bordeaux as Thiers' Minister of Finance, he denounced that "unholy" treaty, hinted at its near abrogation, and had even the effrontery to try, although in vain (having counted without Bismarck), the immediate enforcement of the old protective duties against Alsace, where, he said, no previous international treaties stood in the way. This man, who considered counter-revolution as a means to put down wages at Rouen, and the surrender of French provinces as a means to bring up the price of his wares in France, was he not *the one* predestined to be picked out by Thiers as the helpmate of Jules Favre in his last and crowning treason?

On the arrival at Frankfort of this exquisite pair of plenipotentiaries, bully Bismarck at once met them with the imperious alternative: Either the restoration of the Empire, or the unconditional acceptance of my own peace terms! These terms included a shortening of the intervals in which the war indemnity was to be paid and the continued occupation of the Paris forts by Prussian troops until Bismarck should feel satisfied with the state of things in France; Prussia thus being recognised as the supreme arbiter in internal French politics! In return for this he offered to let loose, for the extermination of Paris, the captive Bonapartist army, and to lend them the direct assistance of Emperor William's troops. He pledged his good faith by making payment of the first instalment of the indemnity dependent on the "pacification" of Paris. Such a bait was, of course, eagerly swallowed by Thiers and his plenipotentiaries. They signed the treaty of peace on the 10th of May, and had it endorsed by the Versailles Assembly on the 18th.

In the interval between the conclusion of peace and the arrival of the Bonapartist prisoners, Thiers felt the more bound to resume his comedy of conciliation, as his Republican tools stood in sore need of a pretext for blinking their eyes at the preparations for the carnage of Paris. As late as the 8th of May he replied to a deputation of middle-class conciliators:

"Whenever the insurgents[233] will make up their minds for capitulation, the gates of Paris shall be flung wide open during a week for all except the murderers of Generals Clément Thomas and Lecomte."

A few days afterwards, when violently interpellated on these promises by the Rurals, he refused to enter into any explanations; not, however, without giving them this significant hint:

"I tell you there are impatient men amongst you, men who are in too great a hurry. They must have another eight days; at the end of these eight days there will be no more danger, and the task will be proportionate to their courage and to their capacities."

As soon as MacMahon was able to assure him that he could shortly enter Paris, Thiers declared to the Assembly that

"he would enter Paris with the *laws* in his hands, and demand a full expiation from the wretches who had sacrificed the lives of soldiers and destroyed public monuments."

As the moment of decision drew near he said—to the Assembly, "I shall be pitiless!"—to Paris, that it was doomed; and to his Bonapartist banditti, that they had State licence to wreak vengeance upon Paris to their hearts' content. At last, when treachery had opened the gates of Paris to General Douay, on the 21st of May, Thiers, on the 22nd, revealed to the Rurals the "goal" of his conciliation comedy, which they had so obstinately persisted in not understanding.

"I told you a few days ago that we were approaching *our goal*; today I come to tell you the *goal* is reached. The victory of order, justice and civilisation is at last won!"

So it was. The civilisation and justice of bourgeois order comes out in its lurid light whenever the slaves and drudges of that order rise against their masters. Then this civilisation and justice stand forth as undisguised savagery and lawless revenge. Each new crisis in the class struggle between the appropriator and the producer brings out this fact more glaringly. Even the atrocities of the bourgeois in June, 1848, vanish before the ineffable infamy of 1871. The self-sacrificing heroism with which the population of Paris—men,

women and children—fought for eight days after the entrance of the
Versaillese, reflects as much the grandeur of their cause, as the
infernal deeds of the soldiery reflect the innate spirit of that civilisation of which they are the mercenary vindicators. A glorious civilisation, indeed, the great problem of which is how to get rid of the
heaps of corpses it made after the battle was over!

To find a parallel for the conduct of Thiers and his bloodhounds
we must go back to the times of Sulla and the two Triumvirates[234]
of Rome. The same wholesale slaughter in cold blood; the same
disregard, in massacre, of age and sex; the same system of torturing
prisoners; the same proscriptions, but this time of a whole class; the
same savage hunt after concealed leaders, lest one might escape; the
same denunciations of political and private enemies; the same indifference for the butchery of entire strangers to the feud. There is
but this difference, that the Romans had no *mitrailleuses* for the
despatch, in the lump, of the proscribed, and that they had not "the
law in their hands," nor on their lips the cry of "civilisation."

And after those horrors, look upon the other, still more hideous,
face of that bourgeois civilisation as described by its own press!

"With stray shots," writes the Paris correspondent of a London Tory paper,
"still ringing in the distance, and untended wounded wretches dying amid the
tombstones of Père Lachaise—with 6,000 terror-stricken insurgents wandering in
an agony of despair in the labyrinth of the catacombs, and wretches hurried
through the streets to be shot down in scores by the *mitrailleuse*—it is revolting
to see the *cafés* filled with the votaries of absinthe, billiards, and dominoes; female profligacy perambulating the boulevards, and the sound of revelry disturbing the night from the *cabinets particuliers* of fashionable restaurants."

M. Edouard Hervé writes in the *Journal de Paris*,[235] a Versaillist
journal suppressed by the Commune:

"The way in which the population of Paris (!) manifested its satisfaction yesterday was rather more than frivolous, and we fear it will grow worse as time
progresses. Paris has now a *fête* day appearance, which is sadly out of place;
and, unless we are to be called the *Parisiens de la décadence*, this sort of thing
must come to an end."

And then he quotes the passage from Tacitus:

"Yet, on the morrow of that horrible struggle, even before it was completely
over, Rome—degraded and corrupt—began once more to wallow in the volup-
tuous slough which was destroying its body and polluting its soul—*alibi proelia
et vulnera; alibi balnea popinaeque* (here fights and wounds, there baths and
restaurants)."

M. Hervé only forgets to say that the "population of Paris" he
speaks of is but the population of the Paris of M. Thiers—the *francs-
fileurs* returning in throngs from Versailles, Saint-Denis, Rueil and
Saint-Germain—*the* Paris of the "Decline."

In all its bloody triumphs over the self-sacrificing champions of
a new and better society, that nefarious civilisation, based upon the

enslavement of labour, drowns the moans of its victims in a hue-
and-cry of calumny, reverberated by a worldwide echo. The serene
working men's Paris of the Commune is suddenly changed into a
pandemonium by the bloodhounds of "order." And what does this
tremendous change prove to the bourgeois mind of all countries?
Why, that the Commune has conspired against civilisation! The
Paris people die enthusiastically for the Commune in numbers
unequalled in any battle known to history. What does that prove?
Why, that the Commune was not the people's own government but
the usurpation of a handful of criminals! The women of Paris
joyfully give up their lives at the barricades and on the place of
execution. What does this prove? Why, that the demon of the Commune has changed them into Megaeras and Hecates! The moderation
of the Commune during two months of undisputed sway is equalled
only by the heroism of its defence. What does that prove? Why,
that for months the Commune carefully hid, under a mask of moderation and humanity, the blood-thirstiness of its fiendish instincts, to
be let loose in the hour of its agony!

The working men's Paris, in the act of its heroic self-holocaust,
involved in its flames buildings and monuments. While tearing to
pieces the living body of the proletariat, its rulers must·no longer
expect to return triumphantly into the intact architecture of their
abodes. The Government of Versailles cries, "Incendiarism!" and
whispers this cue to all its agents, down to the remotest hamlet, to
hunt up its enemies everywhere as suspect of professional incendiarism. The bourgeoisie of the whole world, which looks com-
placently upon the wholesale massacre after the battle, is convulsed
by horror at the desecration of brick and mortar!

When governments give state-licences to their navies to "kill,
burn and destroy," is that a licence for incendiarism? When the
British troops wantonly set fire to the Capitol at Washington and
to the summer palace of the Chinese Emperor,[236] was that incendiarism? When the Prussians, not for military reasons, but out of the
mere spite of revenge, burned down, by the help of petroleum,
towns like Châteaudun and innumerable villages, was that incendiarism? When Thiers, during six weeks, bombarded Paris, under
the pretext that he wanted to set fire to those houses only in which
there were people, was that incendiarism?—In war, fire is an arm
as legitimate as any. Buildings held by the enemy are shelled to set
them on fire. If their defenders have to retire, they themselves light
the flames to prevent the attack from making use of the buildings.
To be burnt down has always been the inevitable fate of all buildings situated in the front of battle of all the regular armies of the
world. But ir. the war of the enslaved against their enslavers, the
only justifiable war in history, this is by no means to hold good! The
Commune used fire strictly as a means of defence. They used it to

stop up to the Versailles troops those long, straight avenues which
Haussmann had expressly opened to artillery-fire; they used it to
cover their retreat, in the same way as the Versaillese, in their
advance, used their shells which destroyed at least as many buildings
as the fire of the Commune. It is a matter of dispute, even now,
which buildings were set fire to by the defence, and which by the
attack. And the defence resorted to fire only then, when the
Versaillese troops had already commenced their wholesale murdering
of prisoners. —Besides, the Commune had, long before, given full
public notice that, if driven to extremities, they would bury
themselves under the ruins of Paris, and make Paris a second
Moscow,[237] as the Government of Defence, but only as a cloak for
its treason, had promised to do. For this purpose Trochu had found
them the petroleum. The Commune knew that its opponents cared
nothing for the lives of the Paris people, but cared much for their
own Paris buildings. And Thiers, on the other hand, had given
them notice that he would be implacable in his vengeance. No sooner
had he got his army ready on one side, and the Prussians shutting
up the trap on the other, than he proclaimed: "I shall be pitiless!
The expiation will be complete, and justice will be stern!" If the
acts of the Paris working men were vandalism, it was the vandalism
of defence in despair, not the vandalism of triumph, like that which
the Christians perpetrated upon the really priceless art treasures of
heathen antiquity; and even that vandalism has been justified by
the historian as an unavoidable and comparatively trifling concomitant to the titanic struggle between a new society arising and
an old one breaking down. It was still less the vandalism of Haussmann, razing historic Paris to make place for the Paris of the
sightseer!
  But the execution by the Commune of the sixty-four hostages,
with the Archbishop of Paris at their head! The bourgeoisie and its
army in June, 1848, re-established a custom which had long disappeared from the practice of war—the shooting of their defenceless
prisoners. This brutal custom has since been more or less strictly
adhered to by the suppressors of all popular commotions in Europe
and India; thus proving that it constitutes a real "progress of
civilisation!" On the other hand, the Prussians, in France, had re-
established the practice of taking hostages—innocent men, who, with
their lives, were to answer to them for the acts of others. When
Thiers, as we have seen, from the very beginning of the conflict,
enforced the humane practice of shooting down the Communal
prisoners, the Commune, to protect their lives, was obliged to resort
to the Prussian practice of securing hostages. The lives of the
hostages had been forfeited over and over again by the continued
shooting of prisoners on the part of the Versaillese. How could they
be spared any longer after the carnage with which MacMahon's

raetorians[68] celebrated their entrance into Paris? Was even the last check upon the unscrupulous ferocity of bourgeois governments—the taking of hostages—to be made a mere sham of? The real murderer of Archbishop Darboy is Thiers. The Commune again and again had offered to exchange the archbishop, and ever so many priests in the bargain, against the single Blanqui, then in the hands of Thiers. Thiers obstinately refused. He knew that with Blanqui he would give to the Commune a head; while the archbishop would serve his purpose best in the shape of a corpse. Thiers acted upon the precedent of Cavaignac. How, in June 1848, did not Cavaignac and his men of order raise shouts of horror by stigmatising the insurgents as the assassins of Archbishop Affre! They knew perfectly well that the archbishop had been shot by the soldiers of order.[72] M. Jacquemet, the archbishop's vicar-general, present on the spot, had immediately afterwards handed them in his evidence to that effect.

All this chorus of calumny, which the party of Order never fail, in their orgies of blood, to raise against their victims, only proves that the bourgeois of our days considers himself the legitimate successor to the baron of old, who thought every weapon in his own hand fair against the plebeian, while in the hands of the plebeian a weapon of any kind constituted in itself a crime.

The conspiracy of the ruling class to break down the Revolution by a civil war carried on under the patronage of the foreign invader —a conspiracy which we have traced from the very 4th of September down to the entrance of MacMahon's praetorians through the gate of St. Cloud—culminated in the carnage of Paris. Bismarck gloats over the ruins of Paris, in which he saw perhaps the first instalment of that general destruction of great cities he had prayed for when still a simple Rural in the Prussian *Chambre introuvable* of 1849.[238] He gloats over the cadavers of the Paris proletariat. For him this is not only the extermination of revolution, but the extinction of France, now decapitated in reality, and by the French Government itself. With the shallowness characteristic of all successful statesmen, he sees but the surface of this tremendous historic event. Whenever before has history exhibited the spectacle of a conqueror crowning his victory by turning into, not only the gendarme, but the hired bravo of the conquered Government? There existed no war between Prussia and the Commune of Paris. On the contrary, the Commune had accepted the peace preliminaries, and Prussia had announced her neutrality. Prussia was, therefore, no belligerent. She acted the part of a bravo, a cowardly bravo, because incurring no danger; a hired bravo, because stipulating beforehand the payment of her blood-money of 500 millions on the fall of Paris. And thus, at last, came out the true character of the war, ordained by Providence as a chastisement of godless and debauched France by pious and moral

Germany! And this unparalleled breach of the law of nations, eve
as understood by the old-world lawyers, instead of arousing th
"civilised" Governments of Europe to declare the felonious Prussia
Government, the mere tool of the St. Petersburg Cabinet, an outlaw
amongst nations, only incites them to consider whether the fe
victims who escape the double cordon around Paris are not to b
given up to the hangman at Versailles!

That after the most tremendous war of modern times, the con
quering and the conquered hosts should fraternise for the commo
massacre of the proletariat—this unparalleled event does indicate
not, as Bismarck thinks, the final repression of a new society upheav
ing, but the crumbling into dust of bourgeois society. The highes
heroic effort of which old society is still capable is national war
and this is now proved to be a mere governmental humbug, intende
to defer the struggle of classes, and to be thrown aside as soon as tha
class struggle bursts out into civil war. Class rule is no longer able t
disguise itself in a national uniform; the national Governments ar
one as against the proletariat!

After Whit-Sunday, 1871, there can be neither peace nor truce
possible between the working men of France and the appropriators
of their produce. The iron hand of a mercenary soldiery may keep
for a time both classes tied down in common oppression. But the
battle must break out again and again in ever-growing dimensions, and
there can be no doubt as to who will be the victor in the end,—the
appropriating few, or the immense working majority. And the
French working class is only the advanced guard of the modern
proletariat.

While the European governments thus testify, before Paris, to
the international character of class-rule, they cry down the International Working Men's Association—the international counter-
organisation of labour against the cosmopolitan conspiracy of capital
—as the head fountain of all these disasters. Thiers denounced it as
the despot of labour, pretending to be its liberator. Picard ordered
that all communications between the French Internationals and those
abroad should be cut off; Count Jaubert, Thiers' mummified ac-
complice of 1835, declares it the great problem of all civilised
governments to weed it out. The Rurals roar against it, and the whole
European press joins the chorus. An honourable French writer,[*]
completely foreign to our Association, speaks as follows:—

"The members of the Central Committee of the National Guard, as well as
the greater part of the members of the Commune, are the most active, intelligent,
and energetic minds of the International Working Men's Association; ... men
who are thoroughly honest, sincere, intelligent, devoted, pure, and fanatical in
the *good* sense of the word."

---

[*] Evidently Robinet.—*Ed.*

The police-tinged bourgeois mind naturally figures to itself the International Working Men's Association as acting in the manner of a secret conspiracy, its central body ordering, from time to time, explosions in different countries. Our Association is, in fact, nothing but the international bond between the most advanced working men in the various countries of the civilised world. Wherever, in whatever shape, and under whatever conditions the class struggle obtains any consistency, it is but natural that members of our Association should stand in the foreground. The soil out of which it grows is modern society itself. It cannot be stamped out by any amount of carnage. To stamp it out, the Governments would have to stamp out the despotism of capital over labour—the condition of their own parasitical existence.

Working men's Paris, with its Commune, will be for ever celebrated as the glorious harbinger of a new society. Its martyrs are enshrined in the great heart of the working class. Its exterminators history has already nailed to that eternal pillory from which all the prayers of their priests will not avail to redeem them.

256, High Holborn, London,
Western Central, May 30, 1871

NOTES

I

"The column of prisoners halted in the Avenue Uhrich, and was drawn up, four or five deep, on the footway facing to the road. General Marquis de Galliffet and his staff dismounted and commenced an inspection from the left of the line. Walking down slowly and eyeing the ranks, the General stopped here and there, tapping a man on the shoulder or beckoning him out of the rear ranks. In most cases, without further parley, the individual thus selected was marched out into the centre of the road, where a small supplementary column was, thus, soon formed.... It was evident that there was considerable room for error. A mounted officer pointed out to General Galliffet a man and woman for some particular offence. The woman, rushing out of the ranks, threw herself on her knees, and, with outstretched arms, protested her innocence in passionate terms. The General waited for a pause, and then with most impassible face and unmoved demeanour, said, 'Madam, I have visited every theatre in Paris, your acting will have no effect on me' ('ce n'est pas la peine de jouer la comédie').... It was not a good thing on that day to be noticeably taller, dirtier, cleaner, older, or uglier than one's neighbours. One individual in particular struck me as probably owing his speedy release from the ills of this world to his having a broken nose.... Over a hundred being thus chosen, a firing party told off, and the column resumed its march, leaving them behind. A few minutes afterwards a dropping fire in our rear commenced, and continued for over a quarter of an hour. It was the execution of these summarily-convicted wretches."—Paris Correspondent Daily News,[239] June 8th.

—This Galliffet, "the kept man of his wife, so notorious for her shameless exhibitions at the orgies of the Second Empire," went, during the war, by the name of the French "Ensign Pistol."

"The *Temps*[240] which is a careful journal, and not given to sensation, tells dreadful story of people imperfectly shot and buried before life was extinct. great number were buried in the square round St. Jacques-la Bouchière; some them very superficially. In the daytime the roar of the busy streets prevented an notice being taken; but in the stillness of the night the inhabitants of the house in the neighbourhood were roused by distant moans, and in the morning clenched hand was seen protruding through the soil. In consequence of this, exhuma tions were ordered to take place.... That many wounded have been burie alive I have not the slightest doubt. One case I can vouch for. When Brunel wa shot with his mistress on the 24th ult. in the courtyard of a house in the Plac Vendôme, the bodies lay there until the afternoon of the 27th. When the buria party came to remove the corpses, they found the woman living still and took her t an ambulance. Though she had received four bullets she is now out of danger."— *Paris Correspondent Evening Standard*,[241] June 8th.

II

The following letter[242] appeared in the [London] *Times* of Jun 13th:

"To the Editor of the *Times:*

"Sir,—On June 6, 1871, M. Jules Favre issued a circular to all the European Powers, calling upon them to hunt down the International Working Men's Association. A few remarks will suffice to characterise that document.

"In the very preamble of our statutes it is stated that the International was founded 'September 28, 1864, at a public meeting held at St. Martin's Hall, Long Acre, London.'* For purposes of his own Jules Favre puts back the date of its origin behind 1862.

"In order to explain our principles, he professes to quote 'their (the International's) sheet of the 25th of March, 1869.' And then what does he quote? The sheet of a society which is not the International. This sort of manoeuvre he already recurred to when, still a comparatively young lawyer, he had to defend the *National*[61] newspaper, prosecuted for libel by Cabet. Then he pretended to read extracts from Cabet's pamphlets while reading interpolations of his own—a trick exposed while the Court was sitting, and which, but for the indulgence of Cabet, would have been punished by Jules Favre's expulsion from the Paris bar. Of all the documents quoted by him as documents of the International, not one belongs to the International. He says, for instance:

" 'The Alliance declares itself Atheist, says the General Council, constituted in London in July 1869.'

"The General Council never issued such a document. On the contrary, it issued a document** which quashed the original statutes of

---

* Marx/Engels, *Werke*, Band 16, Berlin, 1962, S. 13.—*Ed.*
** See K. Marx, "The International Working Men's Association and the Alliance of Socialist Democracy".—*Ed.*

he 'Alliance'—L'Alliance de la Démocratie Socialiste[243] at Geneva —quoted by Jules Favre.

"Throughout his circular, which pretends in part also to be directed against the Empire, Jules Favre repeats against the International but the police inventions of the public prosecutors of the Empire, which broke down miserably even before the law courts of that Empire.

"It is known that in its two addresses (of July and September last) on the late war,* the General Council of the International denounced the Prussian plans of conquest against France. Later on, Mr. Reitlinger, Jules Favre's private secretary, applied, though of course in vain, to some members of the General Council for getting up by the Council a demonstration against Bismarck, in favour of the Government of National Defence; they were particularly requested not to mention the republic. The preparations for a demonstration with regard to the expected arrival of Jules Favre in London were made —certainly with the best of intentions—in spite of the General Council, which, in its address of the 9th of September, had distinctly forewarned the Paris workmen against Jules Favre and his colleagues.

"What would Jules Favre say if, in its turn, the International were to send a circular on Jules Favre to all the Cabinets of Europe, drawing their particular attention to the documents published at Paris by the late M. Millière?

"I am, Sir, your obedient servant,

"John Hales,

"Secretary to the General Council of the International Working Men's Association."

256, High Holborn, London,
Western Central, June 12

In an article on "The International Society and its aims," that pious informer, the London *Spectator*[244] (June 24th), amongst other similar tricks, quotes, even more fully than Jules Favre has done, the above document of the "Alliance" as the work of the International, and that eleven days after the refutation had been published in the *Times*. We do not wonder at this. Frederick the Great used to say that of all Jesuits the worst are the Protestant ones.

Written by Marx in April-May 1871

Published as a pamphlet in London in mid-June 1871 and in several countries of Europe and the United States in 1871-72

Printed according to the third English edition of 1871, checked with the text of the German editions of 1871 and 1891

---

* See pp. 260-63 and 264-70 of this volume.—*Ed.*

Frederick Engels

APROPOS OF WORKING-CLASS POLITICAL ACTION

SPEECH MADE AT THE LONDON CONFERENCE OF THE
INTERNATIONAL WORKING MEN'S ASSOCIATION,
SEPTEMBER 21, 1871[245]

Complete abstention from political action is impossible. The abstentionist press participates in politics every day. It is only a question of how one does it, and of what politics one engages in. For the rest, to us abstention is impossible. The working-class party functions as a political party in most countries by now, and it is not for us to ruin it by preaching abstention. Living experience, the political oppression of the existing governments compels the workers to occupy themselves with politics whether they like it or not, be it for political or for social goals. To preach abstention to them is to throw them into the embrace of bourgeois politics. The morning after the Paris Commune,[8] which has made proletarian political action an order of the day, abstention is entirely out of the question.

We want the abolition of classes. What is the means of achieving it? The only means is political domination of the proletariat. For all this, now that it is acknowledged by one and all, we are told not to meddle with politics. The abstentionists say they are revolutionaries, even revolutionaries *par excellence*. Yet revolution is a supreme political act and those who want revolution must also want the means of achieving it, that is, political action, which prepares the ground for revolution and provides the workers with the revolutionary training without which they are sure to become the dupes of the Favres and Pyats the morning after the battle. However, our politics must be working-class politics. The workers' party must never be the tagtail of any bourgeois party; it must be independent and have its goal and its own policy.

The political freedoms, the right of assembly and association, and the freedom of the press—those are our weapons. Are we to sit back and abstain while somebody tries to rob us of them? It is said that a political act on our part implies that we accept the existing state of affairs. On the contrary, so long as this state of affairs offers us the means of protesting against it, our use of these means does not signify that we recognise the prevailing order.

First published in full in
the journal *The Communist
International* No. 29, .1934

Printed according to the
manuscript
Translated from the French

Karl Marx

CRITIQUE OF THE GOTHA PROGRAMME[246]

FOREWORD BY FREDERICK ENGELS[247]

The manuscript published here—the covering letter to Bracke as well as the critique of the draft programme—was sent in 1875, shortly before the Gotha Unity Congress,[248] to Bracke for communication to Geib, Auer, Bebel, and Liebknecht and subsequent return to Marx. Since the Halle Party Congress[249] has put the discussion of the Gotha Programme on the agenda of the Party, I think I would be guilty of suppression if I any longer withheld from publicity this important—perhaps the most important—document relevant to this discussion.

But the manuscript has yet another and more far-reaching significance. Here for the first time Marx's attitude to the line adopted by Lassalle in his agitation from the very beginning is clearly and firmly set forth, both as regards Lassalle's economic principles and his tactics.

The ruthless severity with which the draft programme is dissected here, the mercilessness with which the results obtained are enunciated and the shortcomings of the draft laid bare—all this today, after fifteen years, can no longer give offence. Specific Lassalleans now exist only abroad as isolated ruins, and in Halle the Gotha Programme was given up even by its creators as altogether inadequate.

Nevertheless, I have omitted a few sharp personal expressions and judgements where these were immaterial, and replaced them by dots. Marx himself would have done so if he had published the manuscript today. The violence of the language in some passages was provoked by two circumstances. In the first place, Marx and I had been more intimately connected with the German movement than with any other; we were, therefore, bound to be particularly perturbed by the decidedly retrograde step manifested by this draft programme. And secondly, we were at that time, hardly two years after the Hague Congress of the International,[250] engaged in the most violent struggle against Bakunin and his anarchists, who made us responsible for everything that happened in the labour movement in Germany; hence we had to expect that we would also be saddled with the secret paternity of this programme. These considerations do not now exist and so there is no necessity for the passages in question.

For reasons arising from the Press Law, also, a few sentences have been indicated only by dots. Where I have had to choose a milder expression this has been enclosed in square brackets. Otherwise the text has been reproduced word for word.

London, January 6, 1891

Published in the journal
Die Neue Zeit, Bd. 1, No. 18,
1890-91

Printed according to the text
of the journal
Translated from the German

Karl Marx

LETTER TO W. BRACKE

London, May 5, 1875

Dear Bracke,

When you have read the following critical marginal notes on the Unity Programme, would you be so good as to send them on to Geib and Auer, Bebel and Liebknecht for examination. I am exceedingly busy and have to overstep by far the limit of work allowed me by the doctors. Hence it was anything but a "pleasure" to write such a lengthy screed. It was however necessary so that the steps to be taken by me later on would not be misinterpreted by our friends in the Party for whom this communication is intended.

After the Unity Congress has been held, Engels and I will publish a short statement to the effect that our position is altogether remote from the said programme of principles and that we have nothing to do with it.

This is indispensable because the opinion—the entirely erroneous opinion—is held abroad and assiduously nurtured by enemies of the Party that we secretly guide from here the movement of the so-called Eisenach Party.[251] In a Russian book[252] that has recently appeared, Bakunin still makes me responsible, for example, not only for all the programmes, etc., of that Party but even for every step taken by Liebknecht from the day of his co-operation with the People's Party.[151]

Apart from this, it is my duty not to give recognition, even by diplomatic silence, to what in my opinion is a thoroughly objectionable programme that demoralises the Party.

Every step of real movement is more important than a dozen programmes. If, therefore, it was not possible—and the conditions of the time did not permit it—to go *beyond* the Eisenach programme, one should simply have concluded an agreement for action against the common enemy. But by drawing up a programme of principles (instead of postponing this until it has been prepared for by a considerable period of common activity) one sets up before the whole world landmarks by which it measures the level of the Party movement.

The Lassallean leaders came because circumstances forced them to. If they had been told in advance that there would be haggling about principles, they would *have had* to be content with a programme of action or a plan of organisation for common action. Instead of this, one permits them to arrive armed with mandates, recognises these mandates on one's part as binding, and thus surrenders unconditionally to those who are themselves in need of help. To crown the whole business, they are holding a congress *before the Congress of Compromise*, while one's own party is holding its congress *post festum*.[253] One had obviously had a desire to stifle all criticism and to give one's own party no opportunity for reflection. One knows that the mere fact of unification is satisfying to the workers, but it is a mistake to believe that this momentary success is not bought too dearly.

For the rest, the programme is no good, even apart from its sanctification of the Lassallean articles of faith.

I shall be sending you in the near future the last parts of the French edition of *Capital*. The printing was held up for a considerable time by a ban of the French Government. The thing will be ready this week or the beginning of next week. Have you received the previous six parts? Please let me have the address of Bernhard Becker, to whom I must also send the final parts.

The bookshop of the *Volksstaat*[162] has peculiar ways of doing things. Up to this moment, for example, I have not been sent a single copy of the *Cologne Communist Trial*.*

With best regards,

Yours,

Karl Marx

---

* K. Marx, *Enthüllungen über den Kommunisten-Prozess zu Köln* (Revelations about the Cologne Communist Trial) (see Marx/Engels, *Werke*, Band 8, Berlin, 1960, S. 405-70).—*Ed.*

Karl Marx

MARGINAL NOTES TO THE PROGRAMME OF THE GERMAN WORKERS' PARTY[246]

I

> 1. "Labour is the source of all wealth and all culture, *and since* useful labour is possible only in society and through society, the proceeds of labour belong undiminished with equal right to all members of society."

First Part of the Paragraph: "Labour is the source of all wealth and all culture."

Labour is *not the source* of all wealth. *Nature* is just as much the source of use values (and it is surely of such that material wealth consists!) as labour, which itself is only the manifestation of a force of nature, human labour power. The above phrase is to be found in all children's primers and is correct in so far as it is *implied* that labour is performed with the appurtenant subjects and instruments. But a socialist programme cannot allow such bourgeois phrases to pass over in silence the *conditions* that alone give them meaning. And in so far as man from the beginning behaves towards nature, the primary source of all instruments and subjects of labour, as an owner, treats her as belonging to him, his labour becomes the source of use values, therefore also of wealth. The bourgeois have very good grounds for falsely ascribing *supernatural creative power* to labour; since precisely from the fact that labour depends on nature it follows that the man who possesses no other property than his labour power must, in all conditions of society and culture, be the slave of other men who have made themselves the owners of the material conditions of labour. He can work only with their permission, hence live only with their permission.

Let us now leave the sentence as it stands, or rather limps. What would one have expected in conclusion? Obviously this:

"Since labour is the source of all wealth, no one in society can appropriate wealth except as the product of labour. Therefore, if he himself does not work, he lives by the labour of others and also acquires his culture at the expense of the labour of others."

Instead of this, by means of the verbal rivet *"and since"* a second proposition is added in order to draw a conclusion from this and not from the first one.

Second Part of the Paragraph: "Useful labour is possible only in society and through society."

According to the first proposition, labour was the source of all wealth and all culture; therefore no society is possible without labour. Now we learn, conversely, that no "useful" labour is possible without society.

One could just as well have said that only in society can useless and even socially harmful labour become a branch of gainful occupation, that only in society can one live by being idle, etc. etc.—in short, one could just as well have copied the whole of Rousseau.

And what is "useful" labour? Surely only labour which produces the intended useful result. A savage—and man was a savage after he had ceased to be an ape—who kills an animal with a stone, who collects fruits, etc., performs "useful" labour.

Thirdly. The Conclusion: "And since useful labour is possible only in society and through society, the proceeds of labour belong undiminished with equal right to all members of society."

A fine conclusion! If useful labour is possible only in society and through society, the proceeds of labour belong to society—and only so much therefrom accrues to the individual worker as is not required to maintain the "condition" of labour, society.

In fact, this proposition has at all times been made use of by the champions of the *state of society prevailing at any given time*. First come the claims of the government and everything that sticks to it, since it is the social organ for the maintenance of the social order; then come the claims of the various kinds of private property, for the various kinds of private property are the foundations of society, etc. One sees that such hollow phrases can be twisted and turned as desired.

The first and second parts of the paragraph have some intelligible connection only in the following wording:

"Labour becomes the source of wealth and culture only as social labour," or, what is the same thing, "in and through society."

This proposition is incontestably correct, for although isolated labour (its material conditions presupposed) can create use values, it can create neither wealth nor culture.

But equally incontestable is this other proposition:

"In proportion as labour develops socially, and becomes thereby a source of wealth and culture, poverty and destitution develop among the workers, and wealth and culture among the non-workers."

This is the law of all history hitherto. What, therefore, had to be done here, instead of setting down general phrases about "labour" and "society," was to prove concretely how in present capitalist society the material, etc., conditions have at last been created which enable and compel the workers to lift this social curse.

In fact, however, the whole paragraph, bungled in style and con-
nt, is only there in order to inscribe the Lassallean catchword of
e "undiminished proceeds of labour" as a slogan at the top of the
rty banner. I shall return later to the "proceeds of labour," "equal
ght," etc., since the same thing recurs in a somewhat different form
rther on.

> 2. "In present-day society, the instruments of
> labour are the monopoly of the capitalist class; the
> resulting dependence of the working class is the cause
> of misery and servitude in all its forms."

This sentence, borrowed from the Rules of the International, is
correct in this "improved" edition.
In present-day society the instruments of labour are the monopoly
 the landowners (the monopoly of property in land is even the
sis of the monopoly of capital) *and* the capitalists. In the passage
 question, the Rules of the International do not mention either the
e or the other class of monopolists. They speak of the "*monopoliser
 the means of labour*, that is, *the sources of life*." The addition,
ources of life," makes it sufficiently clear that land is included in
e instruments of labour.
The correction was introduced because Lassalle, for reasons now
nerally known, attacked *only* the capitalist class and not the
ndowners. In England, the capitalist is usually not even the owner
 the land on which his factory stands.

> 3. "The emancipation of labour demands the pro-
> motion of the instruments of labour to the common
> property of society and the co-operative regulation of
> the total labour with a fair distribution of the pro-
> ceeds of labour."

"Promotion of the instruments of labour to the common property"
ght obviously to read their "conversion into the common property";
t this only in passing.
What are "proceeds of labour"? The product of labour or its value?
nd in the latter case, is it the total value of the product or only that
rt of the value which labour has newly added to the value of the
eans of production consumed?
"Proceeds of labour" is a loose notion which Lassalle has put in
e place of definite economic conceptions.
What is "a fair distribution"?
Do not the bourgeois assert that the present-day distribution is
air"? And is it not, in fact, the only "fair" distribution on the
sis of the present-day mode of production? Are economic relations
gulated by legal conceptions or do not, on the contrary, legal

relations arise from economic ones? Have not also the social
sectarians the most varied notions about "fair" distribution?

To understand what is implied in this connection by the phra
"fair distribution," we must take the first paragraph and this o
together. The latter presupposes a society wherein "the instrumer
of labour are common property and the total labour is co-operative
regulated," and from the first paragraph we learn that "the procee
of labour belong undiminished with equal right to all members
society."

"To all members of society"? To those who do not work as wel
What remains then of the "undiminished proceeds of labour"? On
to those members of society who work? What remains then of tl
"equal right" of all members of society?

But "all members of society" and "equal right" are obvious
mere phrases. The kernel consists in this, that in this communi
society every worker must receive the "undiminished" Lassalle:
"proceeds of labour."

Let us take first of all the words "proceeds of labour" in the sen
of the product of labour; then the co-operative proceeds of labo
are the *total social product*.

From this must now be deducted:

First, cover for replacement of the means of production use
up.

Secondly, additional portion for expansion of production.

Thirdly, reserve or insurance funds to provide against accident
dislocations caused by natural calamities, etc.

These deductions from the "undiminished proceeds of labour" a
an economic necessity and their magnitude is to be determine
according to available means and forces, and partly by computatic
of probabilities, but they are in no way calculable by equity.

There remains the other part of the total product, intended
serve as means of consumption.

Before this is divided among the individuals, there has to l
deducted again, from it:

*First, the general costs of administration not belonging to prc
duction.*

This part will, from the outset, be very considerably restricte
in comparison with present-day society and it diminishes in prc
portion as the new society develops.

*Secondly, that which is intended for the common satisfaction o
needs*, such as schools, health services, etc.

From the outset this part grows considerably in comparison wit
present-day society and it grows in proportion as the new societ
develops.

Thirdly, funds for those unable to work, etc., in short, for what
included under so-called official poor relief today.

Only now do we come to the "distribution" which the programme, under Lassallean influence, alone has in view in its narrow fashion, namely, to that part of the means of consumption which is divided among the individual producers of the co-operative society.

The "undiminished proceeds of labour" have already unnoticeably become converted into the "diminished" proceeds, although what the producer is deprived of in his capacity as a private individual benefits him directly or indirectly in his capacity as a member of society.

Just as the phrase of the "undiminished proceeds of labour" has disappeared, so now does the phrase of the "proceeds of labour" disappear altogether.

Within the co-operative society based on common ownership of the means of production, the producers do not exchange their products; just as little does the labour employed on the products appear here *as the value* of these products, as a material quality possessed by them, since now, in contrast to capitalist society, individual labour no longer exists in an indirect fashion but directly as a component part of the total labour. The phrase "proceeds of labour," objectionable also today on account of its ambiguity, thus loses all meaning.

What we have to deal with here is a communist society, not as it has *developed* on its own foundations, but, on the contrary, just as it *emerges* from capitalist society; which is thus in every respect, economically, morally and intellectually, still stamped with the birth marks of the old society from whose womb it emerges. Accordingly, the individual producer receives back from society—after the deductions have been made—exactly what he gives to it. What he has given to it is his individual quantum of labour. For example, the social working day consists of the sum of the individual hours of work; the individual labour time of the individual producer is the part of the social working day contributed by him, his share in it. He receives a certificate from society that he has furnished such and such an amount of labour (after deducting his labour for the common funds), and with this certificate he draws from the social stock of means of consumption as much as costs the same amount of labour. The same amount of labour which he has given to society in one form he receives back in another.

Here obviously the same principle prevails as that which regulates the exchange of commodities, as far as this is exchange of equal values. Content and form are changed, because under the altered circumstances no one can give anything except his labour, and because, on the other hand, nothing can pass to the ownership of individuals except individual means of consumption. But, as far as the distribution of the latter among the individual producers is concerned, the same principle prevails as in the exchange of com-

modity-equivalents: a given amount of labour in one form
exchanged for an equal amount of labour in another form.

Hence, *equal right* here is still in principle—*bourgeois right*, ﹔
though principle and practice are no longer at loggerheads, whi
the exchange of equivalents in commodity exchange only exists ﹒
the average and not in the individual case.

In spite of this advance, this *equal right* is still constantly sti
matised by a bourgeois limitation. The right of the produce
is *proportional* to the labour they supply; the equality consis
in the fact that measurement is made with an *equal standar*
labour.

But one man is superior to another physically or mentally a﹔
so supplies more labour in the same time, or can labour for ﹔
longer time; and labour, to serve as a measure, must be defin﹔
by its duration or intensity, otherwise it ceases to be a standa﹔
of measurement. This *equal* right is an unequal right for unequ
labour. It recognises no class differences, because everyone is on
a worker like everyone else; but it tacitly recognises unequ
individual endowment and thus productive capacity as natur
privileges. *It is, therefore, a right of inequality, in its content, li﹔
every right.* Right by its very nature can consist only in the applic﹔
tion of an equal standard; but unequal individuals (and they wou﹔
not be different individuals if they were not unequal) are measu﹔
able only by an equal standard in so far as they are brought und﹔
an equal point of view, are taken from one *definite* side only, f﹔
instance, in the present case, are regarded *only as workers* an﹔
nothing more is seen in them, everything else being ignore﹔
Further, one worker is married, another not; one has mo﹔
children than another, and so on and so forth. Thus, with a﹔
equal performance of labour, and hence an equal share in th﹔
social consumption fund, one will in fact receive more tha﹔
another, one will be richer than another, and so on. To avo﹔
all these defects, right instead of being equal would have to b﹔
unequal.

But these defects are inevitable in the first phase of communi﹔
society as it is when it has just emerged after prolonged birth pan﹔
from capitalist society. Right can never be higher than the econom﹔
structure of society and its cultural development conditioned thereb﹔

In a higher phase of communist society, after the enslavin﹔
subordination of the individual to the division of labour, an﹔
therewith also the antithesis between mental and physical labou﹔
has vanished; after labour has become not only a means of lif﹔
but life's prime want; after the productive forces have also in﹔
creased with the all-round development of the individual, and a﹔
the springs of co-operative wealth flow more abundantly—only the﹔
can the narrow horizon of bourgeois right be crossed in its entiret﹔

and society inscribe on its banners: From each according to his ability, to each according to his needs!

I have dealt more at length with the "undiminished proceeds of labour," on the one hand, and with "equal right" and "fair distribution," on the other, in order to show what a crime it is to attempt, on the one hand, to force on our Party again, as dogmas, ideas which in a certain period had some meaning but have now become obsolete verbal rubbish, while again perverting, on the other, the realistic outlook, which it cost so much effort to instil into the Party but which has now taken root in it, by means of ideological nonsense about right and other trash so common among the democrats and French Socialists.

Quite apart from the analysis so far given, it was in general a mistake to make a fuss about so-called *distribution* and put the principal stress on it.

Any distribution whatever of the means of consumption is only a consequence of the distribution of the conditions of production themselves. The latter distribution, however, is a feature of the mode of production itself. The capitalist mode of production, for example, rests on the fact that the material conditions of production are in the hands of non-workers in the form of property in capital and land, while the masses are only owners of the personal condition of production, of labour power. If the elements of production are so distributed, then the present-day distribution of the means of consumption results automatically. If the material conditions of production are the co-operative property of the workers themselves, then there likewise results a distribution of the means of consumption different from the present one. Vulgar socialism (and from it in turn a section of the democracy) has taken over from the bourgeois economists the consideration and treatment of distribution as independent of the mode of production and hence the presentation of socialism as turning principally on distribution. After the real relation has long been made clear, why retrogress again?

> 4. "The emancipation of labour must be the work of the working class, relatively to which all other classes are *only one reactionary mass*."

The first strophe is taken from the introductory words of the Rules of the International, but "improved." There it is said: "The emancipation of the working class must be the act of the workers themselves"*; here, on the contrary, the "working class" has to emancipate—what? "Labour." Let him understand who can.

---

* See K. Marx, *General Rules of the International Working Men's Association* (Marx and Engels, *Selected Works*, Vol. I, Moscow, 1962, p. 386).—*Ed.*

In compensation, the antistrophe, on the other hand, is a Las-sallean quotation of the first water: "relatively to which (the work-ing class) all other classes are *only one reactionary mass.*"

In the *Communist Manifesto* it is said: "Of all the classes that stand face to face with the bourgeoisie today, the proletariat alone is a *really revolutionary class.* The other classes decay and finally disappear in the face of Modern Industry; the proletariat is its special and essential product."*

The bourgeoisie is here conceived as a revolutionary class—as the bearer of large-scale industry—relatively to the feudal lords and the lower middle class, who desire to maintain all social posi-tions that are the creation of obsolete modes of production. Thus they do not form *together* with the *bourgeoisie* only one reaction-ary mass.

On the other hand, the proletariat is revolutionary relatively to the bourgeoisie because, having itself grown up on the basis of large-scale industry, it strives to strip off from production the capitalist character that the bourgeoisie seeks to perpetuate. But the *Manifesto* adds that the "lower middle class" is becoming revolutionary "in view of [its] impending transfer into the prole-tariat."

From this point of view, therefore, it is again nonsense to say that it, together with the bourgeoisie, and with the feudal lords into the bargain, "form only one reactionary mass" relatively to the working class.

Has one proclaimed to the artisans, small manufacturers, etc., and *peasants* during the last elections: Relatively to us you, together with the bourgeoisie and feudal lords, form only one reactionary mass?

Lassalle knew the *Communist Manifesto* by heart, as his faith-ful followers know the gospels written by him. If, therefore, he has falsified it so grossly, this has occurred only to put a good colour on his alliance with absolutist and feudal opponents against the bourgeoisie.

In the above paragraph, moreover, his oracular saying is dragged in by main force without any connection with the botched quotation from the Rules of the International. Thus is it here simply an impertinence, and indeed not at all displeasing to Herr Bismarck, one of those cheap pieces of insolence in which the Marat of Berlin** deals.

---

* See p. 44 of this volume.—*Ed.*
** The "Marat of Berlin" is obviously an ironical reference to Hasselmann, the chief editor of the *Neuer Social-Demokrat*, the central organ of the Lassalle-ans.—*Ed.*

> 5. "The working class strives for its emancipation
> first of all *within the framework of the present-day
> national state*, conscious that the necessary result of
> its efforts, which are common to the workers of all
> civilised countries, will be the international brother-
> hood of peoples."

Lassalle, in opposition to the *Communist Manifesto* and to all earlier socialism, conceived the workers' movement from the narrowest national standpoint. He is being followed in this—and that after the work of the International!

It is altogether self-evident that, to be able to fight at all, the working class must organise itself at home *as a class* and that its own country is the immediate arena of its struggle. In so far its class struggle is national, not in substance, but, as the *Communist Manifesto* says, "in form." But the "framework of the present-day national state," for instance, the German Empire, is itself in its turn economically "within the framework" of the world market, politically "within the framework" of the system of states. Every businessman knows that German trade is at the same time foreign trade, and the greatness of Herr Bismarck consists, to be sure, precisely in his pursuing a kind of *international* policy.

And to what does the German workers' party reduce its internationalism? To the consciousness that the result of its efforts will be *"the international brotherhood of peoples"*—a phrase borrowed from the bourgeois League of Peace and Freedom,[254] which is intended to pass as equivalent to the international brotherhood of the working classes in the joint struggle against the ruling classes and their governments. Not a word, therefore, *about the international functions* of the German working class! And it is thus that it is to challenge its own bourgeoisie—which is already linked up in brotherhood against it with the bourgeois of all other countries—and Herr Bismarck's international policy of conspiracy!

In fact, the internationalism of the programme stands *even infinitely below* that of the Free Trade Party. The latter also asserts that the result of its efforts will be "the international brotherhood of peoples." But it also *does* something to make trade international and by no means contents itself with the consciousness—that all peoples are carrying on trade at home.

The international activity of the working classes does not in any way depend on the existence of the *International Working Men's Association*. This was only the first attempt to create a central organ for that activity; an attempt which was a lasting success on account of the impulse which it gave but which was no longer realisable in its *first historical form* after the fall of the Paris Commune.[8]

Bismarck's *Norddeutsche* was absolutely right when it announced, to the satisfaction of its master, that the German workers' party had sworn off internationalism in the new programme.[255]

II

> "Starting from these basic principles, the German
> workers' party strives by all legal means for the *free
> state—and—*socialist society: the abolition of the
> wage system *together with* the *iron law of wages*
> —and—exploitation in every form; the elimination
> of all social and political inequality."

I shall return to the "free" state later.

So, in future, the German workers' party has got to believe in
Lassalle's "iron law of wages"! That this may not be lost, the
nonsense is perpetrated of speaking of the "abolition of the wage
system" (it should read: system of wage labour) "*together with*
the iron law of wages." If I abolish wage labour, then naturally
I abolish its laws also, whether they are of "iron" or sponge. But
Lassalle's attack on wage labour turns almost solely on this so-called
law. In order, therefore, to prove that Lassalle's sect has conquered,
the "wage system" must be abolished "*together with*" the iron law
of wages" and not without it.

It is well known that nothing of the "iron law of wages" is Lassalle's except the word "iron" borrowed from Goethe's "great,
eternal iron laws." The word *iron* is a label by which the true
believers recognise one another. But if I take the law with Lassalle's
stamp on it and, consequently, in his sense, then I must also take
it with his substantiation for it. And what is that? As Lange already
showed, shortly after Lassalle's death, it is the Malthusian theory
of population[256] (preached by Lange himself). But if this theory is
correct, then again I *cannot* abolish the law even if I abolish wage
labour a hundred times over, because the law then governs not only
the system of wage labour but *every* social system. Basing themselves
directly on this, the economists have been proving for fifty years
and more that socialism cannot abolish poverty, *which has its basis
in nature*, but can only make it *general*, distribute it simultaneously
over the whole surface of society!

But all this is not the main thing. *Quite apart* from the *false*
Lassallean formulation of the law, the truly outrageous retrogression consists in the following:

Since Lassalle's death there has asserted itself in *our* Party the
scientific understanding that wages are not what they *appear* to
be, namely, the *value*, or *price*, *of labour*, but only a masked form
for the *value*, or *price*, *of labour power*. Thereby the whole bourgeois conception of wages hitherto, as well as all the criticism
hitherto directed against this conception, was thrown overboard
once for all and it was made clear that the wage-worker has permission to work for his own subsistence, that is, *to live*, only in so
far as he works for a certain time gratis for the capitalist (and

hence also for the latter's co-consumers of surplus value); that the whole capitalist system of production turns on the increase of this gratis labour by extending the working day or by developing the productivity, that is, increasing the intensity of labour power, etc.; that, consequently, the system of wage labour is a system of slavery, and indeed of a slavery which becomes more severe in proportion as the social productive forces of labour develop, whether the worker receives better or worse payment. And after this understanding has gained more and more ground in our Party, one returns to Lassalle's dogmas although one must have known that Lassalle *did not know* what wages were, but following in the wake of the bourgeois economists took the appearance for the essence of the matter.

It is as if, among slaves who have at last got behind the secret of slavery and broken out in rebellion, a slave still in thrall to obsolete notions were to inscribe on the programme of the rebellion: Slavery must be abolished because the feeding of slaves in the system of slavery cannot exceed a certain low maximum!

Does not the mere fact that the representatives of our Party were capable of perpetrating such a monstrous attack on the understanding that has spread among the mass of our Party prove by itself with what criminal levity and with what lack of conscience they set to work in drawing up this compromise programme!

Instead of the indefinite concluding phrase of the paragraph, "the elimination of all social and political inequality," it ought to have been said that with the abolition of class distinctions all social and political inequality arising from them would disappear of itself.

III

> "The German workers' party, in order to *pave the way to the solution of the social question,* demands the establishment of producers' co-operative societies *with state aid under the democratic control of the toiling people.* The producers' co-operative societies *are to be called into being* for industry and agriculture on such a scale *that the socialist organisation of the total labour will arise from them.*"

After the Lassallean "iron law of wages," the physic of the prophet. The way to it is "paved" in worthy fashion. In place of the existing class struggle appears a newspaper scribbler's phrase: "the social *question,*" to the "*solution*" of which one "paves the way." Instead of arising from the revolutionary process of transformation of society, the "socialist organisation of the total labour" "arises" from the "state aid" that the state gives to the producers' co-operative societies and which the *state*, not the worker, *"calls into being."* It is worthy of Lassalle's imagination that with state loans one can build a new society just as well as a new railway!

From the remnants of a sense of shame, "state aid" has been put—under the democratic control of the "toiling people."

In the first place, the majority of the "toiling people" in Germany consists of peasants, and not of proletarians.

Secondly, "democratic" means in German *"volksherrschaftlich"* ["by the rule of the people"]. But what does "control by the rule of the people of the toiling people" mean? And particularly in the case of a toiling people which, through these demands that it puts to the state, expresses its full consciousness that it neither rules nor is ripe for ruling!

It would be superfluous to deal here with the criticism of the recipe prescribed by Buchez in the reign of Louis Philippe in *opposition* to the French Socialists and accepted by the reactionary workers of the *Atelier*.[257] The chief offence does not lie in having inscribed this specific nostrum in the programme, but in taking, in general, a retrograde step from the standpoint of a class movement to that of a sectarian movement.

That the workers desire to establish the conditions for co-operative production on a social scale, and first of all on a national scale, in their own country, only means that they are working to revolutionise the present conditions of production, and it has nothing in common with the foundation of co-operative societies with state aid. But as far as the present co-operative societies are concerned, they are of value *only* in so far as they are the independent creations of the workers and not protégés either of the governments or of the bourgeois.

IV

I come now to the democratic section.

A. *"The free basis of the state."*

First of all, according to II, the German workers' party strives for "the free state."

Free state—what is this?

It is by no means the aim of the workers, who have got rid of the narrow mentality of humble subjects, to set the state free. In the German Empire the "state" is almost as "free" as in Russia. Freedom consists in converting the state from an organ superimposed upon society into one completely subordinate to it, and today, too, the forms of state are more free or less free to the extent that they restrict the "freedom of the state."

The German workers' party—at least if it adopts the programme —shows that its socialist ideas are not even skin-deep; in that, instead of treating existing society (and this holds good for any future one) as the *basis* of the existing state (or of the future state in the case of future society), it treats the state rather as an independent entity that possesses its own *intellectual, ethical and libertarian bases*.

And what of the riotous misuse which the programme makes of the words *"present-day state," "present-day society,"* and of the still more riotous misconception it creates in regard to the state to which it addresses its demands?

"Present-day society" is capitalist society, which exists in all civilised countries, more or less free from medieval admixture, more or less modified by the particular historical development of each country, more or less developed. On the other hand, the "present-day state" changes with a country's frontier. It is different in the Prusso-German Empire from what it is in Switzerland, and different in England from what it is in the United States. "The present-day state" is, therefore, a fiction.

Nevertheless, the different states of the different civilised countries, in spite of their motley diversity of form, all have this in common, that they are based on modern bourgeois society, only one more or less capitalistically developed. They have, therefore, also certain essential characteristics in common. In this sense it is possible to speak of the "present-day states," in contrast with the future, in which its present root, bourgeois society, will have died off.

The question then arises: what transformation will the state undergo in communist society? In other words, what social functions will remain in existence there that are analogous to present state functions? This question can only be answered scientifically, and one does not get a flea-hop nearer to the problem by a thousandfold combination of the word people with the word state.

Between capitalist and communist society lies the period of the revolutionary transformation of the one into the other. Corresponding to this is also a political transition period in which the state can be nothing but *the revolutionary dictatorship of the proletariat*.

Now the programme does not deal with this nor with the future state of communist society.

Its political demands contain nothing beyond the old democratic litany familiar to all: universal suffrage, direct legislation, popular rights, a people's militia, etc. They are a mere echo of the bourgeois People's Party,[151] of the League of Peace and Freedom. They are all demands which, in so far as they are not exaggerated in fantastic

presentation, have already been *realised*. Only the state to which
they belong does not lie within the borders of the German Empire,
but in Switzerland, the United States, etc. This sort of "state of the
future" is a present-day state, although existing outside the
"framework" of the German Empire.

But one thing has been forgotten. Since the German workers'
party expressly declares that it acts within "the present-day national state," hence within *its own* state, the Prusso-German Empire—its demands would indeed otherwise be largely meaningless,
since one only demands what one has not got—it should not have
forgotten the chief thing, namely, that all those pretty little gewgaws
rest on the recognition of the so-called sovereignty of the people
and hence are appropriate only in a *democratic republic*.

Since one has not the courage—and wisely so, for the circumstances demand caution—to demand the democratic republic, as
the French workers' programmes under Louis Philippe and under
Louis Napoleon did, one should not have resorted, either, to the
subterfuge, neither "honest"* nor decent, of demanding things
which have meaning only in a democratic republic from a state
which is nothing but a police-guarded military despotism, embellished with parliamentary forms, alloyed with a feudal admixture,
already influenced by the bourgeoisie and bureaucratically carpent-
ered, and then to assure this state into the bargain that one
imagines one will be able to force such things upon it "by legal
means."

Even vulgar democracy, which sees the millennium in the democratic republic and has no suspicion that it is precisely in this last
form of state of bourgeois society that the class struggle has to be
fought out to a conclusion—even it towers mountains above this kind
of democratism which keeps within the limits of what is permitted
by the police and not permitted by logic.

That, in fact, by the word "state" is meant the government
machine, or the state in so far as it forms a special organism separated from society through division of labour, is shown by the
words "the German workers' party demands *as the economic basis
of the state*: a single progressive income tax," etc. Taxes are the
economic basis of the government machinery and of nothing else.
In the state of the future, existing in Switzerland, this demand has
been pretty well fulfilled. Income tax presupposes various sources
of income of the various social classes, and hence capitalist society.
It is, therefore, nothing remarkable that the Liverpool financial
reformers, bourgeois headed by Gladstone's brother, are putting
forward the same demand as the programme.

---

* "*Honest*" was the epithet applied to the Eisenachers. Here a play upon
words.—*Ed.*

B. "The German workers' party demands as the intellectual and ethical basis of the state:
"1. Universal and *equal elementary education* by the state. Universal compulsory school attendance. Free instruction."

Equal elementary education? What idea lies behind these words? Is it believed that in present-day society (and it is only with this one has to deal) education can be *equal* for all classes? Or is it demanded that the upper classes also shall be compulsorily reduced to the modicum of education—the elementary school—that alone is compatible with the economic conditions not only of the wage-workers but of the peasants as well?

"Universal compulsory school attendance. Free instruction." The former exists even in Germany, the second in Switzerland and in the United States in the case of elementary schools. If in some states of the latter country higher educational institutions are also "free" that only means in fact defraying the cost of the education of the upper classes from the general tax receipts. Incidentally, the same holds good for "free administration of justice" demanded under A, 5. The administration of criminal justice is to be had free everywhere; that of civil justice is concerned almost exclusively with conflicts over property and hence affects almost exclusively the possessing classes. Are they to carry on their litigation at the expense of the national coffers?

The paragraph on the schools should at least have demanded technical schools (theoretical and practical) in combination with the elementary school.

"*Elementary education by the state*" is altogether objectionable. Defining by a general law the expenditures on the elementary schools, the qualifications of the teaching staff, the branches of instruction, etc., and, as is done in the United States, supervising the fulfilment of these legal specifications by state inspectors, is a very different thing from appointing the state as the educator of the people! Government and Church should rather be equally excluded from any influence on the school. Particularly, indeed, in the Prusso-German Empire (and one should not take refuge in the rotten subterfuge that one is speaking of a "state of the future"; we have seen how matters stand in this respect) the state has need, on the contrary, of a very stern education by the people.

But the whole programme, for all its democratic clang, is tainted through and through by the Lassallean sect's servile belief in the state, or, what is no better, by a democratic belief in miracles, or rather it is a compromise between these two kinds of belief in miracles, both equally remote from socialism.

"*Freedom of science*" says a paragraph of the Prussian Constitution. Why, then, here?

"Freedom of conscience"! If one desired at this time of the *Kulturkampf*[258] to remind liberalism of its old catchwords, it surely could have been done only in the following form: Everyone should be able to attend to his religious as well as his bodily needs without the police sticking their noses in. But the workers' party ought at any rate in this connection to have expressed its awareness of the fact that bourgeois "freedom of conscience" is nothing but the toleration of all possible kinds of *religious freedom of conscience*, and that for its part it endeavours rather to liberate the conscience from the witchery of religion. But one chooses not to transgress the "bourgeois" level.

I have now come to the end, for the appendix that now follows in the programme does not constitute a characteristic component part of it. Hence I can be very brief here.

2. *"Normal working day."*

In no other country has the workers' party limited itself to such an indefinite demand, but has always fixed the length of the working day that it considers normal under the given circumstances.

3. "Restriction of female labour and prohibition of child labour."

The standardisation of the working day must include the restriction of female labour, in so far as it relates to the duration, intermissions, etc., of the working day; otherwise it could only mean the exclusion of female labour from branches of industry that are especially unhealthy for the female body or are objectionable morally for the female sex. If that is what was meant, it should have been said so.

"Prohibition of child labour." Here it was absolutely essential to state the age limit.

A *general prohibition* of child labour is incompatible with the existence of large-scale industry and hence an empty, pious wish. Its realisation—if it were possible—would be reactionary, since, with a strict regulation of the working time according to the different age groups and other safety measures for the protection of children, an early combination of productive labour with education is one of the most potent means for the transformation of present-day society

4. "State supervision of factory, workshop and domestic industry."

In consideration of the Prusso-German state it should definitely have been demanded that the inspectors are to be removable only by a court of law; that any worker can have them prosecuted for neglect of duty; that they must belong to the medical profession.

5. "Regulation of prison labour."

A petty demand in a general workers' programme. In any case, it should have been clearly stated that there is no intention from fear of competition to allow ordinary criminals to be treated like beasts, and especially that there is no desire to deprive them of their sole means of betterment, productive labour. This was surely the least one might have expected from Socialists.

6. "An effective liability law."

It should have been stated what is meant by an "effective" liability law.

Be it noted, incidentally, that in speaking of the normal working day the part of factory legislation that deals with health regulations and safety measures, etc., has been overlooked. The liability law only comes into operation when these regulations are infringed.

In short, this appendix also is distinguished by slovenly editing. *Dixi et salvavi animam meam.**

Written by Marx in April
or early May 1875

Abridged version published in   Printed according to the
the journal *Die Neue Zeit*,   manuscript
Bd. 1, No. 18, 1890-91   Translated from the German

---

* I have spoken and saved my soul.—*Ed.*

Frederick Engels

LETTER TO A. BEBEL[259]

London, March 18-28, 1875

Dear Bebel,

I received your letter of February 23 and am glad you are in such good health.

You ask me what we think of the unification business. Unfortunately we have fared the same as you. Neither Liebknecht nor anyone else has sent us any information and we too, therefore, know only what is in the papers, and there was nothing in them until the draft programme appeared about a week ago! This draft has certainly astonished us not a little.

Our Party has so frequently made offers of reconciliation or at least of co-operation to the Lassalleans and has been so frequently and contemptuously repulsed by the Hasenclevers, Hasselmanns, and Tölckes that any child must have drawn the conclusion: if these gentlemen are now coming and offering reconciliation themselves they must be in a damned tight fix. But considering the well-known character of these people it is our duty to utilise their fix in order to stipulate for every possible guarantee, so that they shall not reestablish their shaken position in the opinion of the workers at the expense of our Party. They should have been received with extreme coolness and mistrust, and union made dependent on the extent to which they were willing to drop their sectarian slogans and their state aid and to accept in its essentials the Eisenach programme of 1869[251] or a revised edition of it adapted to the present day. Our Party has *absolutely nothing to learn* from the Lassalleans in the theoretical sphere and therefore in what is decisive for the programme, but the Lassalleans certainly have something to learn from our Party; the first condition of union should be that they cease to be sectarians, Lassalleans, and above all that the universal panacea of state aid should be, if not entirely relinquished, at any rate recognised by them as a subordinate transitional measure, one among and alongside of many other possible ones. The draft programme shows that our people are a hundred times superior theoretically to the Lassallean leaders—but to the same extent inferior to them in political cunning; the "honest" have been once more cruelly gypped by the dishonest.

In the first place Lassalle's high-sounding but historically false phrase is accepted: in relation to the working class all other classes are only one reactionary mass. This proposition is true only in a few exceptional cases: for instance, in a revolution of the proletariat, like the Commune, or in a country where not only the bourgeoisie has moulded state and society in its own image but where in its wake the democratic petty bourgeoisie, too, has already carried out this remoulding down to its final consequences. If in Germany, for instance, the democratic petty bourgeoisie belonged to this reactionary mass, how could the Social-Democratic Workers' Party have gone hand in hand with it—with the People's Party[151]—for years? How can the *Volksstaat*[162] take almost the whole of its political contents from the petty-bourgeois-democratic *Frankfurter Zeitung*[260]? And how comes it that no less than seven demands are included in this programme which directly and literally coincide with the programme of the People's Party and the petty-bourgeois democracy? I mean the seven political demands, 1 to 5 and 1 to 2, of which there is not a single one that is not *bourgeois*-democratic.[261]

Secondly, the principle that the workers' movement is an international movement is, to all intents and purposes, completely disavowed for the present day, and at that by people who have upheld this principle most gloriously for five whole years under the most difficult conditions. The German workers' position at the head of the European movement reposes *essentially* on their genuinely international attitude during the war[262]; no other proletariat would have behaved so well. And now this principle is to be disavowed by them at the very moment when the workers everywhere abroad are emphasising it in the same degree as the governments are striving to suppress every attempted manifestation of it in any organisation! And what is left of the internationalism of the workers' movement then? The faint prospect—not even of a future co-operation of the European workers for their emancipation—no, but of a future "international brotherhood of peoples," of the "United States of Europe" of the bourgeois of the Peace League![254]

It was of course quite unnecessary to speak of the International as such. But surely the very least would have been to make no retreat from the programme of 1869 and to say about the following: *although* the German workers' party is operating *first of all* within the state boundaries laid down for it (it has no right to speak in the name of the European proletariat and especially no right to say something false), it is conscious of its solidarity with the workers of all countries and will always be ready hereafter, as it has been hitherto, to fulfil the obligations imposed upon it by this solidarity. Obligations of that kind exist even without directly proclaiming or regarding oneself as a part of the International; for instance, help and abstention from blacklegging in strikes; care taken that the

Party organs keep the German workers informed about the movement abroad; agitation against the threat or the outbreak of dynastic wars, behaviour during such wars similar to that carried out in model fashion in 1870 and 1871, etc.

Thirdly, our people have allowed the Lassallean "iron law of wages" to be foisted upon them, a law based on a quite antiquated economic view, namely, that the worker receives on the average only the *minimum* of the wage, because, according to Malthus's theory of population, there are always too many workers (this was Lassalle's argument). Now Marx has proved in detail in *Capital* that the laws regulating wages are very complicated, that sometimes one predominates and sometimes another, according to circumstances, that therefore they are in no sense iron but on the contrary very elastic, and that the matter can by no means be dismissed in a few words, as Lassalle imagined. The Malthusian argument in support of the law, which Lassalle copied from Malthus and Ricardo (with a distortion of the latter), as it is to be found, for instance, in the *Arbeiterlesebuch*, page 5, quoted from another pamphlet of Lassalle's, has been refuted in detail by Marx in the section on the "Accumulation of Capital."* Thus by adopting Lassalle's "iron law" we commit ourselves to a false thesis with a false substantiation.

Fourthly, the programme puts forward as its *sole social* demand —Lassalle's state aid in its most naked form, as Lassalle stole it from Buchez. And this after Bracke has very well exposed the utter futility of this demand[263] and after almost all, if not all, our Party speakers have been obliged to come out against this "state aid" in fighting the Lassalleans! Lower than this our Party could not humiliate itself. Internationalism brought down to Amand Gögg and socialism to the bourgeois republican Buchez, who put forward this demand *in opposition to the Socialists*, in order to get the better of them!

At the most, however, "state aid" in the Lassallean sense is only a *single* measure among many others designed to attain the end here lamely described as "paving the way to the solution of the social question"—as if a theoretically *unsolved* social *question* still existed for us! So if one says: the German workers' party strives for the abolition of wage labour, and with it of class distinctions, by the establishment of co-operative production in industry and agriculture and on a national scale; it supports every measure appropriate for the attainment of this end!—then no Lassallean can have anything against it.

Fifthly, there is not a word about the organisation of the working class as a class by means of the trade unions. And that is a very

---

* K. Marx, *Capital*, Vol. I, Moscow, 1965, pp. 564-712.—*Ed.*

essential point, for this is the real class organisation of the proletariat, in which it carries on its daily struggles with capital, in which
it trains itself, and which nowadays even amid the worst reaction
(as in Paris at present) can simply no longer be smashed. Considering the importance which this organisation has attained also in
Germany, it would be absolutely necessary in our opinion to mention it in the programme and if possible to leave open a place for it
in the Party organisation.

All this has been done by our people to please the Lassalleans.
And what has the other side conceded? That a heap of rather confused *purely democratic demands* should figure in the programme,
of which several are a mere matter of fashion, as, for instance, the
"legislation by the people" which exists in Switzerland and does
more harm than good if it does anything at all. *Administration* by
the people, that would be something. Equally lacking is the first condition of all freedom: that all officials should be responsible for all
their official acts to every citizen before the ordinary courts and
according to common law. Of the fact that such demands as freedom
of science and freedom of conscience figure in every liberal bourgeois programme and appear somewhat strange here, I shall say
nothing more.

The free people's state is transformed into the free state. Taken
in its grammatical sense, a free state is one where the state is free
in relation to its citizens, hence a state with a despotic government.
The whole talk about the state should be dropped, especially since
the Commune, which was no longer a state in the proper sense of
the word. The "people's state" has been thrown in our faces by the
Anarchists to the point of disgust, although already Marx's book
against Proudhon* and later the *Communist Manifesto*** directly
declare that with the introduction of the socialist order of society
the state will dissolve of itself and disappear. As, therefore, the state
is only a transitional institution which is used in the struggle, in the
revolution, to hold down one's adversaries by force, it is pure nonsense to talk of a free people's state: so long as the proletariat still
uses the state, it does not use it in the interests of freedom but in
order to hold down its adversaries, and as soon as it becomes possible to speak of freedom the state as such ceases to exist. We
would therefore propose to replace *state* everywhere by *Gemein-
wesen*, a good old German word which can very well convey the
meaning of the French word *"commune."*

"The elimination of all social and political inequality" is also a
very questionable phrase in place of "the abolition of all class distinctions." Between one country and another, one province and

---

* K. Marx, *The Poverty of Philosophy.—Ed.*
** See pp. 35-63 of this volume.—*Ed.*

another and even one locality and another there will always exist
a *certain* inequality in the conditions of life, which it will be possible
to reduce to a minimum but never entirely remove. Alpine dwellers
will always have different conditions of life from those of people
living on plains. The idea of socialist society as the realm of *equality* is a one-sided French idea resting upon the old "liberty, equality, fraternity"—an idea which was justified as a *stage of development* in its own time and place but which, like all the one-sided
ideas of the earlier socialist schools, should now be overcome, for
it only produces confusion in people's heads and more precise modes
of presentation of the matter have been found.

I shall stop, although almost every word in this programme, which
has, moreover, been composed in a flat and flaccid style, could be
criticised. It is of such a character that if adopted Marx and I shall
never be able to give our adherence to the *new* party established
on this basis, and shall have very seriously to consider what our
attitude towards it—in public as well—should be. You must remember that abroad *we* are made responsible for any and every utterance and action of the German Social-Democratic Workers' Party.
Thus Bakunin in his work *Statehood and Anarchy*, where we have
to answer for every thoughtless word spoken or written by Liebknecht since the *Demokratisches Wochenblatt*[264] was started. People like to imagine that we run the whole show from here, while
you know as well as I that we have hardly ever interfered in any
way in internal Party affairs, and when we did, then only in order
to make good, as far as possible, blunders, and *only theoretical*
blunders, which have in our opinion been committed. But you will
realise for yourself that this programme marks a turning point which
may very easily compel us to refuse any and every responsibility
for the party which accepts it.

In general, the official programme of a party is of less importance
than what the party does. But *a new* programme is after all a
banner publicly raised, and the outside world judges the party by
it. It should, therefore, on no account take a step backwards, as this
one does in comparison with the Eisenach programme. One should
also take into consideration what the workers of other countries
will say to this programme, what impression will be produced by
this bending of the knee to Lassalleanism on the part of the whole
German socialist proletariat.

At the same time I am convinced that a union on *this* basis will
not last a year. Are the best minds in our Party to lend themselves
to grinding out repetitions, learnt by rote, of the Lassallean precepts
on the iron law of wages and state aid? I should like to see you
doing it, for instance! And if they did do this they would be hissed
down by their audiences. And I am sure the Lassalleans will insist
on just *these* points of the programme like the Jew Shylock on his

ɔound of flesh.* The separation will come; but we shall have made
Hasselmann, Hasenclever, Tölcke and Co. "honest" again; we shall
come out of the separation weaker and the Lassalleans stronger;
ɔur Party will have lost its political virginity and will never again
ɔe able to come out wholeheartedly against the Lassallean phrases
which it will have inscribed for a time on its own banner; and if the
Lassalleans then once more say that they are the most genuine, the
only workers' party, while our people are bourgeois, the programme
will be there to prove it. All the socialist measures in it are *theirs*,
and all *our* Party has put into it are the demands of the petty-
bourgeois democracy, which is nevertheless described *also by it*
in the same programme as a part of the "reactionary mass."

I had let this letter lie here as you are to be freed only on April 1,
in honour of Bismarck's birthday, and I did not want to expose it
to the chance of being intercepted in any attempt to smuggle it in.
And now a letter has just come from Bracke, who has also his grave
doubts about the programme and wants to know our opinion. I
am therefore sending this letter to him to be forwarded, so that
he can read it and I need not write all this stuff over again. Moreover, I have also told the unvarnished truth to Ramm; to Liebknecht
I wrote only briefly. I will not forgive him for never telling us a
single word about the whole thing (while Ramm and others thought
he had given us exact information) until it was too late, so to speak.
But this is what he has always done—hence the large amount of
disagreeable correspondence which we, both Marx and I, have had
with him; but this time it is really too bad and *we are certainly not
going along with him.*

See that you manage to come here in the summer. You will, of
course, stay with me, and if the weather is good we can go sea-
bathing for a couple of days, from which you will derive a lot of
benefit after your long spell in jail.

Friendly greetings!

Yours, *F. E.*

Marx has recently moved to a new flat. Now his address is: 41
Maitlend Park, Crescent, North-West, London.

First published in the book:
A. Bebel, *Aus meinem Leben.*
Vol. II, Stuttgart, 1911

Printed according to the text
of the book
Translated from the German

---

* Shakespeare, *The Merchant of Venice*, Act I, Scene 3.—*Ed.*

Frederick Engels

INTRODUCTION TO *DIALECTICS OF NATURE*[265]

Modern natural science, which alone has achieved a scientific, systematic, all-round development, as contrasted with the brilliant natural-philosophical intuitions of antiquity and the extremely important but sporadic discoveries of the Arabs, which for the most part vanished without results—this modern natural science dates, like all more recent history, from that mighty epoch which we Germans term the Reformation after the national calamity that overtook us at that time, and which the French term the *Renaissance* and the Italians the *Cinquecento*,* although it is not fully expressed by any of these names. It is the epoch which had its rise in the last half of the fifteenth century. Royalty, with the support of the burghers of the towns, broke the power of the feudal nobility and established the great monarchies, based essentially on nationality, within which the modern European nations and modern bourgeois society came to development; and while the burghers and nobles were still grappling with one another, the peasant war in Germany pointed prophetically to future class struggles, by bringing on to the stage not only the peasants in revolt—that was no longer anything new—but, behind them, the beginnings of the modern proletariat, with the red flag in their hands and the demand for common ownership of property on their lips. In the manuscripts saved from the fall of Byzantium, in the antique statues dug out of the ruins of Rome, a new world was revealed to the astonished West, that of ancient Greece; the ghosts of the Middle Ages vanished before its shining forms; Italy rose to an undreamt-of flowering of art, which seemed like a reflection of classical antiquity and was never attained again. In Italy, France and Germany a new literature arose, the first modern literature; shortly afterwards came the classical epochs of English and Spanish literature. The bounds of the old *orbis terrarum*** were pierced; only now was the world really discovered and the basis

---

* Literally, the five-hundreds, that is, the sixteenth century.—*Ed.*
** *Orbis terrarum*: Literally, orb of lands, the term used by the ancient Romans for *the earth.—Ed.*

laid for subsequent world trade and the transition of handicraft to manufacture, which in its turn formed the starting-point for modern large-scale industry. The spiritual dictatorship of the Church was shattered; it was directly cast off by the majority of the Germanic peoples, who adopted Protestantism, while among the Latins a cheerful spirit of free thought, taken over from the Arabs and nourished by the newly-discovered Greek philosophy, took root more and more and prepared the way for the materialism of the eighteenth century.

It was the greatest progressive revolution that mankind had so far experienced, a time which called for giants and produced giants—giants in power of thought, passion and character, in universality and learning. The men who founded the modern rule of the bourgeoisie had anything but bourgeois limitations. On the contrary, the adventurous character of the time imbued them to a greater or less degree. There was hardly any man of importance then living who had not travelled extensively, who did not command four or five languages, who did not shine in a number of fields. Leonardo da Vinci was not only a great painter but also a great mathematician, mechanician and engineer, to whom the most diverse branches of physics are indebted for important discoveries; Albrecht Dürer was painter, engraver, sculptor, architect, and in addition invented a system of fortification embodying many of the ideas that much later were again taken up by Montalembert and the modern German science of fortification. Machiavelli was statesman, historian, poet, and at the same time the first notable military author of modern times. Luther not only cleansed the Augean stable[266] of the Church but also that of the German language; he created modern German prose and composed the text and melody of that triumphal hymn which became the *Marseillaise* of the sixteenth century.[267] For the heroes of that time had not yet come under the servitude of the division of labour, the restricting effects of which, with their production of one-sidedness, we so often notice in their successors. But what is especially characteristic of them is that they almost all pursue their lives and activities in the midst of the contemporary movements, in the practical struggle; they take sides and join in the fight, one by speaking and writing, another with the sword, many with both. Hence the fullness and force of character that makes them complete men. Men of the study are the exception: either persons of second or third rank or cautious philistines who do not want to burn their fingers.

At that time natural science too was moving in the midst of the general revolution and was itself thoroughly revolutionary; for it had to fight for and win its right of existence. Side by side with the great Italians from whom modern philosophy dates, it

provided its martyrs for the stake and the prisons of the Inquisition. And it is characteristic that Protestants outdid Catholics in
persecuting the free investigation of nature. Calvin burnt Servetus
when the latter was on the point of discovering the course of the
circulation of the blood, and indeed he kept him roasting alive during two hours; for the Inquisition at least it sufficed to simply burn
Giordano Bruno.

The revolutionary act by which natural science declared its
independence and, as it were, repeated Luther's burning of the
Bull was the publication of the immortal work by which Copernicus, though timidly and, so to speak, only from his deathbed,
threw down the gauntlet to ecclesiastical authority in the affairs
of nature.[268] The emancipation of natural science from theology
dates from that time, although the fighting out of the particular
reciprocal claims has dragged out up to our day and in some
minds is still far from completion. Thenceforward, however, the
development of the sciences proceeded with giant strides, and,
it might be said, gained in force in proportion to the square of
the distance (in time) from its point of departure. It was as if the
world were to be shown that henceforth the law of motion valid
for the highest product of organic matter, the human mind, is the
converse of that for inorganic substance.

The main work in the first period of natural science that now
opened lay in mastering the material immediately at hand. In
most fields a start had to be made from the very beginning. Antiquity had bequeathed Euclid and the Ptolemaic solar system;
the Arabs had left behind the decimal notation, the beginnings
of algebra, the modern numerals, and alchemy; the Christian
Middle Ages nothing at all. Of necessity, in this situation the most
elementary natural science, the mechanics of terrestrial and heavenly bodies, occupied first place, and alongside of it, as hand-
maiden to it, the discovery and perfecting of mathematical methods. Great work was achieved here. At the end of the period,
characterised by Newton and Linnaeus, we find these branches of
science brought to a certain conclusion. The basic features of the
most essential mathematical methods were established: analytical
geometry chiefly by Descartes, logarithms by Napier, and differen-
tial and integral calculus by Leibniz and perhaps Newton. The
same holds good of the mechanics of solid bodies, the main laws
of which were made clear once for all. Finally, in the astronomy
of the solar system Kepler discovered the laws of planetary movement and Newton formulated them from the point of view of general laws of motion of matter. The other branches of natural
science were far from arriving at even this preliminary conclusion.
Only towards the end of the period did the mechanics of fluid and

gaseous bodies receive further treatment.* Physics proper had still not gone beyond its first beginnings, with the exception of optics, the exceptional progress of which was due to the practical needs of astronomy. By the phlogistic theory,[269] chemistry was only just emancipating itself from alchemy. Geology had not yet gone beyond the embryonic stage of mineralogy; hence palaeontology could not yet exist at all. Finally, in the field of biology, the essential preoccupation was still with the collection and first sifting of the immense material, not only botanical and zoological but also anatomical and physiological proper. There could as yet be hardly any talk of the comparison of the various forms of life among themselves, of the investigation of their geographical distribution and their climatological, etc., living conditions. Here only botany and zoology arrived at an approximate conclusion owing to Linnaeus.

But what especially characterised this period is the elaboration of a peculiar general outlook, in which the central point is the view of the *absolute immutability of nature*. In whatever way nature itself might have come into being, once present it remained as it was as long as it existed. The planets and their satellites, once set in motion by the mysterious "first impulse," circled on and on in their prescribed ellipses for all eternity or at any rate until the end of all things. The stars remained for ever fixed and immovable in their places, keeping one another therein by "universal gravitation." The earth had persisted without alteration from all eternity or, if you prefer, from the day of its creation. The "five continents" of the present day had always existed, and they had always had the same mountains, valleys and rivers, the same climate, the same flora and fauna, except in so far as change or transplantation had taken place at the hand of man. The species of plants and animals had been established once for all when they came into existence; like continually produced like, and it was a good deal for Linnaeus to have conceded that possibly here and there new species might have arisen by crossing. In contrast to the history of mankind, which develops in·time, there was ascribed to the history of nature only an unfolding in space. All change, all development in nature, was negated. Natural science, so revolutionary at the outset, suddenly found itself confronted by an out-and-out conservative nature, in which even today everything was as it had been at the beginning and in which—to the end of the world or for all eternity—everything was to remain as it had been since the beginning.

High as the natural science of the first half of the eighteenth century stood above Greek antiquity in knowledge and even in

---

* In the margin of the manuscript Engels noted in pencil: "Torricelli in connection with the control of Alpine rivers."—*Ed.*

the sifting of its material, it stood just as low beneath it in the
ideological mastery of this material, in the general outlook on
nature. For the Greek philosophers the world was essentially
something that had emerged from chaos, something that had
developed, something that had become. For the natural scientists
of the period that we are dealing with it was something ossified,
something unalterable, and for most of them something that had
been made at one stroke. Science was still deeply enmeshed in
theology. Everywhere it sought and found as the ultimate thing
an impulse from outside that was not to be explained from nature
itself. Even if attraction, by Newton pompously baptised universal gravitation, was conceived as an essential property of matter,
whence came the unexplained tangential force which gave rise to
the orbits of the planets? How did the innumerable species of
animals and plants come into being? And how, above all, did
man arise, since after all it was certain that he did not exist
from all eternity? To such questions natural science only too
frequently answered by making the creator of all things responsible. Copernicus, at the beginning of the period, dismisses all
theology[270]; Newton closes the period with the postulate of a divine
first impulse. The highest general idea to which this natural science
attained was that of the purposiveness of the arrangements of
nature, the shallow teleology of Wolff,[271] according to which cats
were created to eat mice, mice to be eaten by cats, and the whole
of nature to testify to the wisdom of the creator. It is to the highest
credit of the philosophy of the time that it did not let itself be led
astray by the limited state of contemporary natural knowledge, that
—from Spinoza to the great French materialists—it insisted on
explaining the world from the world itself and left the justification
in detail to the natural science of the future.

I include the materialists of the eighteenth century in this period
because no natural scientific material was available to them other
than that above described. Kant's epoch-making work remained
a secret to them, and Laplace came long after them.[272] We should
not forget that this obsolete outlook on nature, although riddled
through and through by the progress of science, dominated the
entire first half of the nineteenth century,* and in substance is even
now still taught in all schools.**

---

* In the margin of the manuscript is a note in pencil: "The rigidity of the
old outlook on nature provided the basis for the general comprehension of all
natural science as a single whole. The French encyclopaedists,[273] still purely
mechanically—alongside of one another; and then simultaneously St. Simon and
German philosophy of nature, perfected by Hegel."—Ed.
** How tenaciously even in 1861 this view could be held by a man whose
scientific achievements had provided highly important material for abolishing it
is shown by the following classic words:

The first breach in this petrified outlook on nature was made
not by a natural scientist but by a philosopher. In 1755 appeared
Kant's *General Natural History and Theory of the Heavens*. The
question of the first impulse was eliminated; the earth and the
whole solar system appeared as something that had *become* in
the course of time. If the great majority of the natural scientists
had had a little less of the repugnance to thinking that Newton
expressed in the warning: "Physics, beware of metaphysics!"[274]
they would have been compelled from this single brilliant discovery of Kant's to draw conclusions that would have spared them
endless deviations and immeasurable amounts of time and labour
wasted in false directions. For Kant's discovery contained the point
of departure for all further progress. If the earth was something
that had become, then its present geological, geographical and
climatic state, and its plants and animals likewise must be something that had become; it must have a history not only of co-existence in space but also of succession in time. If at once further
investigations had been resolutely pursued in this direction, natural
science would now be considerably further advanced than it is.
But what good could come of philosophy? Kant's work remained
without immediate results, until many years later Laplace and
Herschel expounded its content and substantiated it in greater
detail, thereby gradually securing recognition for the "nebular hypothesis." Further discoveries finally brought it victory; the most
important of these were: the proper motion of the fixed stars, the
demonstration of a resistant medium in cosmic space, the proof
furnished by spectral analysis of the chemical identity of cosmic
matter and the existence of such incandescent nebular masses as
Kant had postulated.*

It is, however, permissible to doubt whether the majority of
natural scientists would so soon have become conscious of the
contradiction of a changing earth that supposedly bore immutable
organisms, had not the dawning conception that nature does not

"All the arrangements of our solar system, so far as we are capable of
comprehending them, aim at preservation of what exists and at unchanging continuance. Just as since the most ancient times no animal and no plant on earth
has become more perfect or in general different, just as we find in all organisms
only stages *alongside of* one another and not *following* one another, just as our
own race has always remained the same in corporeal respects—so even the greatest diversity in the co-existing cosmic bodies will not justify us in assuming that
these forms are merely different stages of development; on the contrary, everything created is equally perfect in itself." (Mädler, *Popular Astronomy*, Berlin
1861, 5th edition, p. 316.) [*Note by Engels.*]
    The book referred to is, in full, J. H. Mädler, *Der Wunderbau des Weltalls
oder populäre Astronomie* [*The Marvellous Edifice of the Cosmos, or Popular
Astronomy*], 5 Aufl., Berlin 1861.—*Ed.*
    * A note in the margin of the manuscript: "Retardation of rotation by the
tides, also from Kant, only now understood."—*Ed.*

just *exist*, but *comes into being* and *goes out of being*, derived support from another quarter. Geology arose and pointed out, not only the terrestrial strata formed one after another and deposited one upon another, but also the shells and skeletons of extinct animals and the trunks, leaves and fruits of no longer existing plants contained in these strata. One had to make up one's mind to acknowledge that not only the earth as a whole but also its present surface and the plants and animals living on it possessed a history in time. At first the acknowledgement occurred reluctantly enough. Cuvier's theory of the revolutions of the earth was revolutionary in phrase and reactionary in substance. In place of a single divine creation it put a whole series of repeated acts of creation, made the miracle an essential lever of nature. Lyell first brought sense into geology by substituting for the sudden revolutions due to the moods of the creator the gradual effects of a slow transformation of the earth.*

Lyell's theory was even more incompatible than any of its predecessors with the assumption of constant organic species. Gradual transformation of the earth's surface and of all conditions of life led directly to gradual transformation of the organisms and their adaptation to the changing environment, to the variability of species. But tradition is a power not only in the Catholic Church but also in natural science. For years Lyell himself did not see the contradiction, and his pupils still less. This is only to be explained by the division of labour that had meanwhile become dominant in natural science, which more or less restricted each person to his special sphere, there being only a few whom it did not rob of a comprehensive view.

Meanwhile physics had made mighty advances, the results of which were summed up almost simultaneously by three different persons in the year 1842, which was epoch-making for this branch of natural science. Mayer in Heilbronn and Joule in Manchester demonstrated the transformation of heat into mechanical energy and of mechanical energy into heat. The determination of the mechanical equivalent of heat put this result beyond question. Simultaneously, by simply working up the separate physical results already arrived at, Grove—not a natural scientist by profession but an English lawyer—proved that all so-called physical energy, mechanical energy, heat, light, electricity, magnetism, indeed even so-called chemical energy, become transformed into one another under definite conditions without any loss of energy occurring, and

---

* The defect of Lyell's view—at least in its first form—lay in conceiving the forces at work on the earth as constant, constant in quality and quantity. The cooling off of the earth does not exist for him; the earth does not develop in a definite direction but merely changes in an inconsequent, fortuitous manner. [*Note by Engels.*]

so proved subsequently, along physical lines, Descartes's principle that the quantity of motion present in the world is constant. With that the special physical energies, the as it were invariable "species" of physics, were resolved into variously differentiated forms of motion of matter, passing into one another according to definite laws. The fortuitousness of the existence of so and so much physical energy was eliminated from science by the proof of their inter-connections and transitions. Physics, like astronomy before it, had arrived at a result that necessarily pointed to the eternal cycle of matter in motion as the ultimate conclusion.

The wonderfully rapid development of chemistry, since Lavoisier, and especially since Dalton, attacked the old conceptions of nature from another aspect. The preparation by inorganic means of compounds that hitherto had been produced only in the living organism proved that the laws of chemistry have the same validity for organic as for inorganic bodies, and to a large extent bridged the gulf between inorganic and organic nature, a gulf that Kant still regarded as for ever impassable.

Finally, in the sphere of biological research also, mainly the scientific journeys and expeditions that had been systematically organised since the middle of the previous century, the more thorough exploration of the European colonies in all parts of the world by specialists living there, and further the progress of palaeontology, anatomy, and physiology in general, particularly since the systematic use of the microscope and the discovery of the cell, had accumulated so much material that the application of the comparative method became possible and at the same time necessary.* On the one hand, the conditions of life of the various floras and faunas were determined by means of comparative physical geography; on the other hand, the various organisms were compared with one another according to their homologous organs, and this not only in their mature condition but at all stages of their development. The more deeply and exactly this research was carried on, the more did the rigid system of an unchangeably fixed organic nature crumble away at its touch. Not only did separate species of plants and animals become more and more indistinguishably blended, but animals turned up, such as the *amphioxus* and *lepidosiren*,[275] that made a mockery of all previous classification**; and finally organisms were encountered of which it was not even possible to say whether they belonged to the vegetable or animal kingdom. More and more the gaps in the palaeontological record were filled up, compelling even the most reluctant to acknowledge the

---

* A note in the margin of the manuscript: "Embryology."—*Ed.*
** A note in the margin of the manuscript: "Ceratodus. Ditto archaeopteryx,[276] etc."—*Ed.*

striking parallelism between the evolutionary history of the organic world as a whole and that of the individual organism, the Ariadne' thread that was to lead the way out of the labyrinth in which botany and zoology appeared to have become more and more deeply lost. It was characteristic that, almost simultaneously with Kant' attack on the eternity of the solar system, C.F. Wolff in 1759 launched the first attack on the fixity of species and proclaimed the theory of descent.[277] But what in his case was still only a brilliant anticipation took firm shape in the hands of Oken, Lamarck, Baer and was victoriously carried through by Darwin[278] in 1859, exactly a hundred years later. Almost simultaneously it was established that protoplasm and the cell, which had already been shown to be the ultimate morphological constituents of all organisms, occurred as the lowest organic forms living independently. This not only reduced the gulf between inorganic and organic nature to a minimum but removed one of the most essential difficulties that had previously stood in the way of the theory of descent of organisms. The new conception of nature was complete in its main features: all rigidity was dissolved, all fixity dissipated, all particularity that had been regarded as eternal became transient, the whole of nature shown as moving in eternal flux and cycles.

* * *

Thus we have once again returned to the mode of contemplation of the great founders of Greek philosophy: that all nature, from the smallest thing to the biggest, from grains of sand to suns, from protista[279] to man, has its existence in eternal coming into being and going out of being, in ceaseless flux, in unresting motion and change. Only with the essential difference that what for the Greeks was a brilliant intuition is in our case the result of strictly scientific research in accordance with experience, and hence appears in much more definite and clearer form. To be sure, the empirical proof of this cyclical motion is not wholly free from gaps, but these are insignificant in comparison with what has already been firmly established, and with each year they become more and more filled up. And how could the proof in detail be otherwise than incomplete when one bears in mind that the most essential branches of science —transplanetary astronomy, chemistry, geology—have a scientific existence of barely a hundred years, and the comparative method in physiology one of barely fifty years, and that the basic form of almost all vital development, the cell, is a discovery not yet forty years old!

* * *

The innumerable suns and solar systems of our cosmic island, bounded by the outermost stellar rings of the Milky Way, developed by contraction and cooling from swirling, glowing masses of vapour, the laws of motion of which will perhaps be disclosed after the observations of some centuries have given us an insight into the proper motion of the stars. Obviously, this development did not proceed everywhere at the same rate. The existence of dark, not merely planetary bodies, hence extinct suns in our stellar system, suggests itself more and more to astronomy (Mädler); on the other hand (according to Secchi), a part of the vaporous nebular patches belong to our stellar system as suns not yet completed, whereby it is not excluded that other nebulae, as Mädler maintains, are distant independent cosmic islands, the relative stage of development of which must be determined by the spectroscope.

How a solar system develops from a separate nebular mass has been shown in detail by Laplace in a manner still unsurpassed; subsequent science has more and more confirmed him.

On the separate bodies so formed—suns as well as planets and satellites—the form of motion of matter at first prevailing is that which we call heat. There can be no question of chemical compounds of the elements even at a temperature like that still possessed by the sun; the extent to which heat is transformed into electricity or magnetism under such conditions continued solar observations will show; it is already as good as proved that the mechanical motion taking place on the sun arises solely from the conflict of heat with gravity.

The smaller the separate bodies, the quicker they cool off. Satellites, asteroids and meteors first of all, just as our moon has long been extinct. The planets more slowly, the central body slowest of all.

With progressive cooling the interplay of the physical forms of motion which become transformed into one another comes more and more to the forefront, until finally a point is reached at which chemical affinity begins to make itself felt, the previously chemically indifferent elements become differentiated, chemically, one after another, obtain chemical properties, and enter into combinations with one another. These combinations change continually with the decreasing temperature, which affects differently not only each element but also each separate combination of elements, changing also with the consequent passage of part of the gaseous matter first to the liquid and then the solid state, and with the new conditions thus created.

The period when the planet has a firm shell and accumulations of water on its surface coincides with that when its intrinsic heat diminishes more and more in comparison with the heat emitted to it from the central body. Its atmosphere becomes the arena of meteorological phenomena in the sense in which we now understand the word; its surface becomes the arena of geological changes in which the deposits resulting from atmospheric precipitation gain increasing preponderance over the slowly decreasing external effects of the incandescent fluid interior.

If, finally, the temperature becomes so far equalised that over a considerable portion of the surface at least it does not exceed the limits within which albumen is capable of life, then, if other chemical preconditions are favourable, living protoplasm forms. What these preconditions are we do not yet know, which is not to be wondered at since so far not even the chemical formula of albumen has been established—we do not even know how many chemically different albuminous bodies there are—and since only about ten years ago the fact became known that completely structureless albumen exercises all the essential functions of life: digestion, excretion, movement, contraction, reaction to stimuli, and reproduction.

Thousands of years may have passed before the conditions arose in which the next advance could take place and this formless albumen produce the first cell by formation of nucleus and membrane. But this first cell also provided the foundation for the morphological development of the whole organic world; the first to develop, as it is permissible to assume from the whole analogy of the palaeontological record, were innumerable species of noncellular and cellular protista, of which the *Eozoon canadense*[280] alone has come down to us, and of which some gradually differentiated into the first plants and others into the first animals. And from the first animals there developed, essentially by further differentiation, the numerous classes, orders, families, genera and species of animals; and lastly vertebrates, the form in which the nervous system attains its fullest development; and among these again lastly that vertebrate animal in which nature attains consciousness of itself—man.

Man, too, arises by differentiation. Not only individually, differentiated out of a single egg cell to the most complicated organism that nature produces—no, also historically. When after thousands of years of struggle the differentiation of hand from foot, and erect gait, were finally established, man became distinct from the ape and the basis was laid for the development of articulate speech and the mighty development of the brain that has since made the gulf between man and ape unbridgeable. The specialisation of the hand—this implies the *tool*, and the tool implies specifically human activity, the transforming reaction of man on nature, production. Animals in the narrower sense also have tools, but only as limbs of their bodies: the ant, the bee, the beaver; animals also produce, but their productive effect on surrounding nature in relation to the latter amounts to nothing at all. Man alone has succeeded in impressing his stamp on nature, not only by shifting plants and animals from one place to another, but also by so altering the aspect and climate of his dwelling place, and even the plants and animals

hemselves, that the consequences of his activity can disappear only
vith the general extinction of the terrestrial globe. And he has
ccomplished this primarily and essentially by means of the *hand*.
:ven the steam engine, so far his most powerful tool for the trans-
ormation of nature, depends, because it is a tool, in the last resort
n the hand. But step by step with the development of the hand
vent that of the brain; came consciousness, first of all of the con-
litions for producing separate practically useful results, and later,
.mong the more favoured peoples and arising from the preceding,
nsight into the natural laws governing them. And with the rapidly
;rowing knowledge of the laws of nature the means for reacting
n nature also grew; the hand alone would never have achieved the
team engine if the brain of man had not developed correlatively
vith and alongside of it, and partly owing to it.

With man we enter *history*. Animals also have a history, that of
heir derivation and gradual evolution to their present state. This
iistory, however, is made for them, and in so far as they them-
elves take part in it, this occurs without their knowledge or desire.
On the other hand, the further human beings become removed
from animals in the narrower sense of the word, the more they
make their history themselves, consciously, the less becomes the
influence of unforeseen effects and uncontrolled forces on this history, and the more accurately does the historical result correspond
to the aim laid down in advance. If, however, we apply this measure to human history, to that of even the most developed peoples
of the present day, we find that there still exists here a colossal
discrepancy between the proposed aims and the results arrived at,
that unforeseen effects predominate, and that the uncontrolled
forces are far more powerful than those set into motion according to
plan. And this cannot be otherwise as long as the most essential
historical activity of men, the one which has raised them from
bestiality to humanity and which forms the material foundation of
all their other activities, namely, the production of their means of
subsistence, that is, today, social production, is particularly subject to the interplay of unintended effects of uncontrolled forces and
achieves its desired end only by way of exception and, much more
frequently, the exact opposite. In the most advanced industrial
countries we have subdued the forces of nature and pressed them
into the service of mankind; we have thereby infinitely multiplied
production, so that a child now produces more than a hundred adults
previously. And what is the consequence? Increasing overwork and
increasing misery of the masses, and every ten years a great crash.
Darwin did not know what a bitter satire he wrote on mankind, and
especially on his countrymen, when he showed that free competition,
the struggle for existence, which the economists celebrate as the
highest historical achievement, is the normal state of the *animal*

kingdom. Only conscious organisation of social production, in whic
production and distribution are carried on in a planned way, ca
elevate mankind above the rest of the animal world socially in th
same way that production in general has done this for men specific
ally. Historical development makes such an organisation daily mor
indispensable, but also with every day more possible. From it wi}
date a new epoch of history, in which mankind itself, and witl
mankind all branches of its activity, and especially natural scienc
will experience an advance before which everything preceding it wi}
pale into insignificance.

Nevertheless, all that comes into being deserves to perish.* Mil
lions of years may elapse, hundreds of thousands of generation
be born and die, but inexorably the time will come when the failin{
warmth of the sun will no longer suffice to melt the ice thrustin{
itself forward from the poles; when the human race, crowdin{
more and more about the equator, will finally no longer find eve}
there enough heat for life; when gradually even the last trace o}
organic life will vanish; and the earth, an extinct frozen globe lik{
the moon, will circle in deepest darkness and in an ever narrowe}
orbit about the equally extinct sun, and at last fall into it. Othe}
planets will have preceded it, others will follow it; instead of th{
bright, warm solar system with its harmonious arrangement o}
members, only a cold, dead sphere will still pursue its lonely path
through cosmic space. And what will happen to our solar system wil}
happen sooner or later to all the other systems of our cosmic island,
will happen to those of all the other innumerable cosmic islands,
even to those the light of which will never reach the earth while
there is a living human eye to receive it.

And when such a solar system has completed its life history and
succumbs to the fate of all that is finite, death, what then? Will the
sun's corpse roll on for all eternity as a corpse through infinite space,
and all the once infinitely diversely differentiated natural forces
pass for ever into one single form of motion, attraction? "Or"—as
Secchi asks (p. 810)—"do forces exist in nature which can reconvert
the dead system into its original state of an incandescent nebula and
reawake it to new life? We do not know."

At all events we do not know in the sense that we know that
$2 \times 2 = 4$ or that the attraction of matter increases and decreases
according to the square of the distance. In theoretical natural science, however, which as far as possible builds up its view of nature
into a harmonious whole, and without which nowadays even the
most thoughtless empiricist cannot get anywhere, we have very often
to reckon with incompletely known magnitudes; and logical consistency of thought has had to help at all times to get over

---

* Mephistopheles's words in Goethe's *Faust*, Part I, Scene 3.—*Ed.*

lefective knowledge. Modern natural science has had to take over rom philosophy the principle of the indestructibility of motion; it an no longer exist without this principle. But the motion of matter s not merely crude mechanical motion, mere change of place; it s heat and light, electric and magnetic stress, chemical combination and dissociation, life and, finally, consciousness. To say that matter luring the whole unlimited time of its existence has only once, and or what is an infinitesimally short period in comparison with its eternity, found itself able to differentiate its motion and thereby o unfold the whole wealth of this motion, and that before and after his remains restricted for all eternity to mere change of place— his is equivalent to maintaining that matter is mortal and motion transitory. The indestructibility of motion cannot be merely quantitative, it must also be conceived qualitatively; matter whose purely mechanical change of place includes indeed the possibility of being transformed under favourable conditions into heat, electricity, chemical action, life, but which is not capable of producing these conditions from out of itself, such matter has *forfeited motion*; motion which has lost the capacity of being transformed into the various forms appropriate to it may indeed still have *dynamis** but no longer *energia,*** and so has become partially destroyed. Both, however, are unthinkable.

This much is certain: there was a time when the matter of our cosmic island had transformed such a quantity of motion—of what kind we do not yet know—into heat that there could be developed from it the solar systems appertaining to (according to Mädler) at least twenty million stars, the gradual extinction of which is likewise certain. How did this transformation take place? We know that just as little as Father Secchi knows whether the future *caput mortuum**** of our solar system will ever again be converted into the raw material for new solar systems. But here either we must have recourse to a creator or we are forced to the conclusion that the incandescent raw material for the solar systems of our cosmic island was produced in a natural way by transformations of motion which are *by nature inherent* in moving matter, and the conditions of which, therefore, must be reproduced by matter, even if only after millions and millions of years, more or less accidentally, but with the necessity that is also inherent in accident.

The possibility of such a transformation is more and more being conceded. The view is being arrived at that the heavenly bodies are ultimately destined to plunge into one another, and one even calculates the amount of heat which must be developed on such

---

* *Dynamis*: Potentiality.—*Ed.*
** *Energia*: Effectiveness.—*Ed.*
*** *Caput mortuum*: Literally—dead head; here in the sense of dead remnants.—*Ed.*

collisions. The sudden flaring up of new stars, and the equall
sudden increase in brightness of familiar ones, of which we ar
informed by astronomy, is most easily explained by such collision:
Not only does our group of planets move about the sun, and ou
sun within our cosmic island, but our whole cosmic island als
moves in space in temporary, relative equilibrium with the othe
cosmic islands, for even the relative equilibrium of freely floatin;
bodies can only exist where the motion is reciprocally conditioned
and it is assumed by many that the temperature in cosmic spac
is not everywhere the same. Finally, we know that, with th
exception of an infinitesimal portion, the heat of the innumerabl
suns of our cosmic island vanishes into space and fails to raise th
temperature of cosmic space even by a millionth of a degree cen
tigrade. What becomes of all this enormous quantity of heat? Is i
for ever dissipated in the attempt to heat cosmic space, has it cease
to exist practically, and does it continue to exist only theoretically
in the fact that cosmic space has become warmer by a decima
fraction of a degree beginning with ten or more noughts? Such ar
assumption denies the indestructibility of motion; it admits of th
possibility that by the cosmic bodies successively plunging into on
another all existing mechanical motion will be converted into hea
and the latter radiated into cosmic space, so that in spite of al
"indestructibility of force" all motion in general would have ceased.
(Incidentally it is seen here how inaccurate is the term: indestructibility of force, instead of: indestructibility of motion.) Hence we
arrive at the conclusion that in some way, which it will some time
later be the task of natural science to demonstrate, the heat radiated
into cosmic space must be able to become transformed into another
form of motion, in which it can once more be stored up and rendered active. Thereby the chief difficulty in the way of the recon-
version of extinct suns into incandescent vapour disappears.

For the rest, the eternally repeated succession of worlds in infinite
time is only the logical complement to the co-existence of innumerable worlds in infinite space—a principle the necessity of which even
the anti-theoretical Yankee brain of Draper was forced to admit.*

It is an eternal cycle in which matter moves, a cycle that certainly only completes its orbit in periods of time for which our terrestrial year is no adequate measure, a cycle in which the time
of highest development, the time of organic life, and still more that
of the life of beings conscious of themselves and of nature, is just as
scantily meted out as the space in which life and self-consciousness
come into operation; a cycle in which every finite mode of existence

---

* "The multiplicity of worlds in infinite space leads to the conception of a
succession of worlds in infinite time." (J. W. Draper, *History of the Intellectual
Development of Europe*, Vol. 2, p. [325].) [*Note by Engels.*]

of matter, whether it be sun or nebular vapour, single animal or genus of animals, chemical combination or dissociation, is equally transient, and wherein nothing is eternal but eternally changing, eternally moving matter and the laws according to which it moves and changes. But however often, and however relentlessly, this cycle is completed in time and space, however many millions of suns and earths may come into being and go out of being, however long it may take before the conditions for organic life are brought about in a solar system even on a single planet, however innumerable the organic beings that have to precede and first pass away before animals with a brain capable of thought develop from their midst, and for a short span of time find conditions suitable for life, only to be exterminated later without mercy, we have the certainty that matter remains eternally the same in all its transformations, that none of its attributes can ever be lost, and therefore, also, that with the same iron necessity with which it will again exterminate on the earth its highest creation, the thinking mind, it must somewhere else and at another time again engender it.

Written by Engels in 1875-76

First published in German and
Russian in *Marx-Engels Archive*,
Book II, 1925

Printed according to the
manuscript
Translated from the
German

Frederick Engels

THE PART PLAYED BY LABOUR
IN THE TRANSITION FROM APE TO MAN[281]

Labour is the source of all wealth, the political economists assert. And it really is the source—next to nature, which supplies it with the material that it converts into wealth. But it is even infinitely more than this. It is the prime basic condition for all human existence, and this to such an extent that, in a sense, we have to say that labour created man himself.

Many hundreds of thousands of years ago, during an epoch, not yet definitely determinable, of that period of the earth's history known to geologists as the Tertiary period, most likely towards the end of it, a particularly highly-developed race of anthropoid apes lived somewhere in the tropical zone—probably on a great continent that has now sunk to the bottom of the Indian Ocean. Darwin has given us an approximate description of these ancestors of ours. They were completely covered with hair, they had beards and pointed ears, and they lived in bands in the trees.[282]

Climbing assigns different functions to the hands and the feet, and when their mode of life involved locomotion on level ground, these apes gradually got out of the habit of using their hands [in walking—*Tr.*] and adopted a more and more erect posture. This was *the decisive step in the transition from ape to man*.

All extant anthropoid apes can stand erect and move about on their feet alone, but only in case of urgent need and in a very clumsy way. Their natural gait is in a half-erect posture and includes the use of the hands. The majority rest the knuckles of the fist on the ground and, with legs drawn up, swing the body through their long arms, much as a cripple moves on crutches. In general, all the transition stages from walking on all fours to walking on two legs are still to be observed among the apes today. The latter gait, however, has never become more than a makeshift for any of them.

It stands to reason that if erect gait among our hairy ancestors became first the rule and then, in time, a necessity, other diverse functions must, in the meantime, have devolved upon the hands. Already among the apes there is some difference in the way the hands and the feet are employed. In climbing, as mentioned above, the hands and feet have different uses. The hands are used mainly for gathering and holding food in the same way as the forepaws of the lower mammals are used. Many apes use their hands to build themselves nests in the trees or even to construct roofs between the branches to protect themselves against the weather, as the chimpanzee, for example, does. With their hands they grasp sticks to defend themselves against enemies, and with their hands they bombard their enemies with fruits and stones. In captivity they use their hands for a number of simple operations copied from human beings. It is in this that one sees the great gulf between the undeveloped hand of even the most man-like apes and the human hand that has been highly perfected by hundreds of thousands of years of labour. The number and general arrangement of the bones and muscles are the same in both hands, but the hand of the lowest savage can perform hundreds of operations that no simian hand can imitate—no simian hand has ever fashioned even the crudest stone knife.

The first operations for which our ancestors gradually learned to adapt their hands during the many thousands of years of transition from ape to man could have been only very simple ones. The lowest savages, even those in whom regression to a more animal-like condition with a simultaneous physical degeneration can be assumed, are nevertheless far superior to these transitional beings. Before the first flint could be fashioned into a knife by human hands, a period of time probably elapsed in comparison with which the historical period known to us appears insignificant. But the decisive step had been taken, *the hand had become free* and could henceforth attain ever greater dexterity; the greater flexibility thus acquired was inherited and increased from generation to generation.

Thus the hand is not only the organ of labour, *it is also the product of labour*. Labour, adaptation to ever new operations, the inheritance of muscles, ligaments, and, over longer periods of time, bones that had undergone special development and the ever-renewed employment of this inherited finesse in new, more and more complicated operations, have given the human hand the high degree of perfection required to conjure into being the pictures of a Raphael, the statues of a Thorwaldsen, the music of a Paganini.

But the hand did not exist alone, it was only one member of an integral, highly complex organism. And what benefited the hand, benefited also the whole body it served; and this in two ways.

In the first place, the body benefited from the law of correlation of growth, as Darwin called it. This law states that the specialised forms of separate parts of an organic being are always bound up with certain forms of other parts that apparently have no connection with them. Thus all animals that have red blood cells without cell nuclei, and in which the head is attached to the first vertebra by means of a double articulation (condyles), also without exception possess lacteal glands for suckling their young. Similarly, cloven hoofs in mammals are regularly associated with the possession of a multiple stomach for rumination. Changes in certain forms involve changes in the form of other parts of the body, although we cannot explain the connection. Perfectly white cats with blue eyes are always, or almost always, deaf. The gradually increasing perfection of the human hand, and the commensurate adaptation of the feet for erect gait, have undoubtedly, by virtue of such correlation, reacted on other parts of the organism. However, this action has not as yet been sufficiently investigated for us to be able to do more here than to state the fact in general terms.

Much more important is the direct, demonstrable influence of the development of the hand on the rest of the organism. It has already been noted that our simian ancestors were gregarious; it is obviously impossible to seek the derivation of man, the most social of all animals, from non-gregarious immediate ancestors. Mastery over nature began with the development of the hand, with labour, and widened man's horizon at every new advance. He was continually discovering new, hitherto unknown, properties in natural objects. On the other hand, the development of labour necessarily helped to bring the members of society closer together by increasing cases of mutual support and joint activity, and by making clear the advantage of this joint activity to each individual. In short, men in the making arrived at the point where *they had something to say* to each other. Necessity created the organ; the undeveloped larynx of the ape was slowly but surely transformed by modulation to produce constantly more developed modulation, and the organs of the mouth gradually learned to pronounce one articulate sound after another.

Comparison with animals proves that this explanation of the origin of language from and in the process of labour is the only correct one. The little that even the most highly-developed animals need to communicate to each other does not require articulate speech. In a state of nature, no animal feels handicapped by its inability to speak or to understand human speech. It is quite different when it has been tamed by man. The dog and the horse, by association with man, have developed such a good ear for articulate speech that they easily learn to understand any language within their range of concept. Moreover they have acquired the capacity for feelings such as affection for man, gratitude, etc., which were previously foreign to them. Anyone who has had much to do with such animals will hardly be able to escape the conviction that in many cases they *now* feel their inability to speak as a defect, although, unfortunately, it is one that can no longer be remedied because their vocal organs are too specialised in a definite direction. However, where vocal organs exist, within certain limits even this inability disappears. The buccal organs of birds are as different from those of man as they can be, yet birds are the only animals that can learn to speak; and it is the bird with the most hideous voice, the parrot, that speaks best of all. Let no one object that the parrot does not understand what it says. It is true that for the sheer pleasure of talking and associating with human beings, the parrot will chatter for hours at a stretch, continually repeating its whole vocabulary. But within the limits of its range of concepts it can also learn to understand what it is saying. Teach a parrot swear words in such a way that it gets an idea of their meaning (one of the great amusements of sailors returning from the tropics); tease it and you will soon discover that it knows how to use its swear words just as correctly as a Berlin costermonger. The same is true of begging for titbits.

First labour, after it and then with it, speech—these were the two most essential stimuli under the influence of which the brain of the ape gradually changed into that of man, which for all its similarity is far larger and more perfect. Hand in hand with the development of the brain went the development of its most immediate instruments—the senses. Just as the gradual development of speech is inevitably accompanied by a corresponding refinement of the organ of hearing, so the development of the brain as a whole is accompanied by a refinement of all the senses. The eagle sees much farther than man, but the human eye discerns considerably more in things than does the eye of the eagle. The dog has a far keener sense of smell than man, but it does not distinguish a hundredth part of the odours that for man are definite signs denoting different things. And the sense of touch, which the ape hardly possesses in its crudest initial form, has been developed only side by side with the development of the human hand itself, through the medium of labour.

The reaction on labour and speech of the development of the brain and its attendant senses, of the increasing clarity of consciousness, power of abstraction and of judgement, gave both labour and speech an ever-renewed impulse to further development. This development did not reach its conclusion when man finally became distinct from the ape, but on the whole made further powerful progress, its degree and direction varying among different peoples and at different times, and here and there even being interrupted by local or temporary regression. This further development has been strongly urged forward, on the one hand, and guided along more definite directions, on the other, by a new element which came into play with the appearance of fully-fledged man, namely, *society*.

Hundreds of thousands of years—of no greater significance in the history of the earth than one second in the life of man*—certainly elapsed before human society arose out of a troupe of tree-climbing monkeys. Yet it did finally appear. And what do we find once more as the characteristic difference between the troupe of monkeys and human society? *Labour*. The ape herd was satisfied to browse over the feeding area determined for it by geographical conditions or the resistance of neighbouring herds; it undertook migrations and struggles to win new feeding grounds, but it was incapable of extracting from them more than they offered in their natural state, except that it unconsciously fertilised the soil with its own excrement. As soon as all possible feeding grounds were occupied, there could be no further increase in the ape population; the number of animals could at best remain stationary. But all animals waste a great deal of food, and, in addition, destroy in the germ the next generation of the food supply. Unlike the hunter, the wolf does not spare the doe which would provide it with the young the next year; the goats in Greece, that eat away the young bushes before they grow to maturity, have eaten bare all the mountains of the country. This "predatory economy" of animals plays an important part in the gradual transformation of species by forcing them to adapt themselves to other than the usual food, thanks to which their blood acquires a different chemical composition and the whole physical constitution gradually alters, while species that have remained unadapted die out. There is no doubt that this predatory economy contributed powerfully to the transition of our ancestors from ape to man. In a race of apes that far surpassed all others in intelligence and adaptability, this predatory economy must have led to a continual increase in the number of plants used for food and to the consumption of more and more edible parts of food plants. In short, food became more and more varied, as did also the substances entering the body with it, substances that were the chemical premises for the transition to man. But all that was not yet labour in the proper sense of the word. Labour begins with the making of tools. And what are the most ancient tools that we find—the most ancient judging by the heirlooms of prehistoric man that have been discovered, and by the mode of life of the earliest historical peoples and of the rawest of contemporary savages? They are hunting and fishing implements, the former at the same time serving as weapons. But hunting and fishing presuppose the transition from an exclusively vegetable diet to the concomitant use of meat, and this is another important step in the process of transition from ape to man. A *meat diet* contained in

---

* A leading authority in this respect, Sir William Thomson, has calculated that *little more than a hundred million years* could have elapsed since the time when the earth had cooled sufficiently for plants and animals to be able to live on it. [*Note by Engels.*]

an almost ready state the most essential ingredients required by the organism for its metabolism. By shortening the time required for digestion, it also shortened the other vegetative bodily processes that correspond to those of plant life, and thus gained further time, material and desire for the active manifestation of animal life proper. And the farther man in the making moved from the vegetable kingdom the higher he rose above the animal. Just as becoming accustomed to a vegetable diet side by side with meat converted wild cats and dogs into the servants of man, so also adaptation to a meat diet, side by side with a vegetable diet, greatly contributed towards giving bodily strength and independence to man in the making. The meat diet, however, had its greatest effect on the brain, which now received a far richer flow of the materials necessary for its nourishment and development, and which, therefore, could develop more rapidly and perfectly from generation to generation. With all due respect to the vegetarians man did not come into existence without a meat diet, and if the latter, among all peoples known to us, has led to cannibalism at some time or other (the forefathers of the Berliners, the Weletabians or Wilzians, used to eat their parents as late as the tenth century), that is of no consequence to us today.

The meat diet led to two new advances of decisive importance—the harnessing of fire and the domestication of animals. The first still further shortened the digestive process, as it provided the mouth with food already, as it were, half-digested; the second made meat more copious by opening up a new, more regular source of supply in addition to hunting, and moreover provided, in milk and its products, a new article of food at least as valuable as meat in its composition. Thus both these advances were, in themselves, new means for the emancipation of man. It would lead us too far afield to dwell here in detail on their indirect effects notwithstanding the great importance they have had for the development of man and society.

Just as man learned to consume everything edible, he also learned to live in any climate. He spread over the whole of the habitable world, being the only animal fully able to do so of its own accord. The other animals that have become accustomed to all climates—domestic animals and vermin—did not become so independently, but only in the wake of man. And the transition from the uniformly hot climate of the original home of man to colder regions, where the year was divided into summer and winter, created new requirements—shelter and clothing as protection against cold and damp, and hence new spheres of labour, new forms of activity, which further and further separated man from the animal.

By the combined functioning of hands, speech organs and brain, not only in each individual but also in society, men became capable

of executing more and more complicated operations, and were able
to set themselves, and achieve, higher and higher aims. The work
of each generation itself became different, more perfect and more
diversified. Agriculture was added to hunting and cattle raising
then came spinning, weaving, metalworking, pottery and navigation. Along with trade and industry, art and science finally appeared
Tribes developed into nations and states. Law and politics arose
and with them that fantastic reflection of human things in the
human mind—religion. In the face of all these images, which
appeared in the first place to be products of the mind and seemed
to dominate human societies, the more modest productions of the
working hand retreated into the background, the more so since the
mind that planned the labour was able, at a very early stage in the
development of society (for example, already in the primitive family),
to have the labour that had been planned carried out by other hands
than its own. All merit for the swift advance of civilisation was
ascribed to the mind, to the development and activity of the brain.
Men became accustomed to explain their actions as arising out of
thoughts instead of their needs (which in any case are reflected and
perceived in the mind); and so in the course of time there emerged
that idealistic world outlook which, especially since the fall of the
world of antiquity, has dominated men's minds. It still rules them
to such a degree that even the most materialistic natural scientists
of the Darwinian school are still unable to form any clear idea of the
origin of man, because under this ideological influence they do not
recognise the part that has been played therein by labour.

Animals, as has already been pointed out, change the environment by their activities in the same way, even if not to the same
extent, as man does, and these changes, as we have seen, in turn
react upon and change those who made them. In nature nothing
takes place in isolation. Everything affects and is affected by every
other thing, and it is mostly because this manifold motion and interaction is forgotten that our natural scientists are prevented from
gaining a clear insight into the simplest things. We have seen how
goats have prevented the regeneration of forests in Greece; on the
island of St. Helena, goats and pigs brought by the first arrivals
have succeeded in exterminating its old vegetation almost completely, and so have prepared the ground for the spreading of plants
brought by later sailors and colonists. But animals exert a lasting
effect on their environment unintentionally and, as far as the
animals themselves are concerned, accidentally. The further removed men are from animals, however, the more their effect on
nature assumes the character of premeditated, planned action
directed towards definite preconceived ends. The animal destroys
the vegetation of a locality without realising what it is doing. Man
destroys it in order to sow field crops on the soil thus released, or

to plant trees or vines which he knows will yield many times the amount planted. He transfers useful plants and domestic animals from one country to another and thus changes the flora and fauna of whole continents. More than this. Through artificial breeding both plants and animals are so changed by the hand of man that they become unrecognisable. The wild plants from which our grain varieties originated are still being sought in vain. There is still some dispute about the wild animals from which our very different breeds of dogs or our equally numerous breeds of horses are descended.

It goes without saying that it would not occur to us to dispute the ability of animals to act in a planned, premeditated fashion. On the contrary, a planned mode of action exists in embryo wherever protoplasm, living albumen, exists and reacts, that is, carries out definite, even if extremely simple, movements as a result of definite external stimuli. Such reaction takes place even where there is yet no cell at all, far less a nerve cell. There is something of the planned action in the way insect-eating plants capture their prey, although they do it quite unconsciously. In animals the capacity for conscious, planned action is proportional to the development of the nervous system, and among mammals it attains a fairly high level. While fox hunting in England one can daily observe how unerringly the fox makes use of its excellent knowledge of the locality in order to elude its pursuers, and how well it knows and turns to account all favourable features of the ground that cause the scent to be lost. Among our domestic animals, more highly developed thanks to association with man, one can constantly observe acts of cunning on exactly the same level as those of children. For, just as the developmental history of the human embryo in the mother's womb is only an abbreviated repetition of the history, extending over millions of years, of the bodily evolution of our animal ancestors, starting from the worm, so the mental development of the human child is only a still more abbreviated repetition of the intellectual development of these same ancestors, at least of the later ones. But all the planned action of all animals has never succeeded in impressing the stamp of their will upon the earth. That was left for man.

In short, the animal merely *uses* its environment, and brings about changes in it simply by his presence; man by his changes makes it serve his ends, *masters* it. This is the final, essential distinction between man and other animals, and once again it is labour that brings about this distinction.*

Let us not, however, flatter ourselves overmuch on account of our human victories over nature. For each such victory nature takes its revenge on us. Each victory, it is true, in the first place

---

* A note in the margin of the manuscript: "Veredlung" (Improvement).—*Ed.*

brings about the results we expected, but in the second and third places it has quite different, unforeseen effects which only too often cancel the first. The people who, in Mesopotamia, Greece, Asia Minor and elsewhere, destroyed the forests to obtain cultivable land, never dreamed that by removing along with the forests the collecting centres and reservoirs of moisture they were laying the basis for the present forlorn state of those countries. When the Italians of the Alps used up the pine forests on the southern slopes, so carefully cherished on the northern slopes, they had no inkling that by doing so they were cutting at the roots of the dairy industry in their region; they had still less inkling that they were thereby depriving their mountain springs of water for the greater part of the year, and making it possible for them to pour still more furious torrents on the plains during the rainy seasons. Those who spread the potato in Europe were not aware that with these farinaceous tubers they were at the same time spreading scrofula. Thus at every step we are reminded that we by no means rule over nature like a conqueror over a foreign people, like someone standing outside nature—but that we, with flesh, blood and brain, belong to nature, and exist in its midst, and that all our mastery of it consists in the fact that we have the advantage over all other creatures of being able to learn its laws and apply them correctly.

And, in fact, with every day that passes we are acquiring a better understanding of these laws and getting to perceive both the more immediate and the more remote consequences of our interference with the traditional course of nature. In particular, after the mighty advances made by the natural sciences in the present century, we are more than ever in a position to realise and hence to control even the more remote natural consequences of at least our day-to-day production activities. But the more this progresses the more will men not only feel but also know their oneness with nature, and the more impossible will become the senseless and unnatural idea of a contrast between mind and matter, man and nature, soul and body, such as arose after the decline of classical antiquity in Europe and obtained its highest elaboration in Christianity.

It required the labour of thousands of years for us to learn a little of how to calculate the more remote *natural* effects of our actions in the field of production, but it has been still more difficult in regard to the more remote *social* effects of these actions. We mentioned the potato and the resulting spread of scrofula. But what is scrofula compared to the effect which the reduction of the workers to a potato diet had on the living conditions of the masses of the people in whole countries, or compared to the famine the potato blight brought to Ireland in 1847, which consigned to the grave a million Irishmen, nourished solely or almost exclusively on potatoes, and forced the emigration overseas of two million more?

When the Arabs learned to distil spirits, it never entered their heads that by so doing they were creating one of the chief weapons for the annihilation of the aborigines of the then still undiscovered American continent. And when afterwards Columbus discovered this America, he did not know that by doing so he was laying the basis for the Negro slave trade and giving a new lease of life to slavery, which in Europe had long ago been done away with. The men who in the seventeenth and eighteenth centuries laboured to create the steam engine had no idea that they were preparing the instrument which more than any other was to revolutionise social relations throughout the world. Especially in Europe, by concentrating wealth in the hands of a minority and dispossessing the huge majority, this instrument was destined at first to give social and political domination to the bourgeoisie, but later, to give rise to a class struggle between bourgeoisie and proletariat which can end only in the overthrow of the bourgeoisie and the abolition of all class antagonisms. But in this sphere, too, by long and often cruel experience and by collecting and analysing historical material, we are gradually learning to get a clear view of the indirect, more remote, social effects of our production activity, and so are afforded an opportunity to control and regulate these effects as well.

This regulation, however, requires something more than mere knowledge. It requires a complete revolution in our hitherto existing mode of production, and simultaneously a revolution in our whole contemporary social order.

All hitherto existing modes of production have aimed merely at achieving the most immediately and directly useful effect of labour. The further consequences, which appear only later and become effective through gradual repetition and accumulation, were totally neglected. The original common ownership of land corresponded, on the one hand, to a level of development of human beings in which their horizon was restricted in general to what lay immediately available, and presupposed, on the other hand, a certain superfluity of land that would allow some latitude for correcting the possible bad results of this primeval type of economy. When this surplus land was exhausted, common ownership also declined. All higher forms of production, however, led to the division of the population into different classes and thereby to the antagonism of ruling and oppressed classes. Thus the interests of the ruling class became the driving factor of production, since production was no longer restricted to providing the barest means of subsistence for the oppressed people. This has been put into effect most completely in the capitalist mode of production prevailing today in Western Europe. The individual capitalists, who dominate production and exchange, are able to concern themselves only with the most immediate useful effect of their actions. Indeed, even this useful effect

—inasmuch as it is a question of the usefulness of the article that is produced or exchanged—retreats far into the background, and the sole incentive becomes the profit to be made on selling.

* * *

Classical political economy, the social science of the bourgeoisie, examines mainly only social effects of human actions in the fields of production and exchange that are actually intended. This fully corresponds to the social organisation of which it is the theoretical expression. As individual capitalists are engaged in production and exchange for the sake of the immediate profit, only the nearest, most immediate results must first be taken into account. As long as the individual manufacturer or merchant sells a manufactured or purchased commodity with the usual coveted profit, he is satisfied and does not concern himself with what afterwards becomes of the commodity and its purchasers. The same thing applies to the natural effects of the same actions. What cared the Spanish planters in Cuba, who burned down forests on the slopes of the mountains and obtained from the ashes sufficient fertiliser for *one* generation of very highly profitable coffee trees—what cared they that the heavy tropical rainfall afterwards washed away the unprotected upper stratum of the soil, leaving behind only bare rock! In relation to nature, as to society, the present mode of production is predominantly concerned only about the immediate, the most tangible result; and then surprise is expressed that the more remote effects of actions directed to this end turn out to be quite different, are mostly quite the opposite in cnaracter; that the harmony of supply and demand is transformed into the very reverse opposite, as shown by the course of each ten years' industrial cycle—even Germany has had a little preliminary experience of it in the "crash"[283]; that private ownership based on one's own labour must of necessity develop into the expropriation of the workers, while all wealth becomes more and more concentrated in the hands of non-workers; that [...]*

Written by Engels in 1876

First published in the journal *Die Neue Zeit*, Bd. 2, No. 44, 1895-96

Printed according to the manuscript
Translated from the German

* Here the manuscript breaks off.—*Ed.*

Frederick Engels

KARL MARX

Karl Marx, the man who was the first to give socialism, and thereby the whole labour movement of our day, a scientific foundation, was born at Treves in 1818. He studied in Bonn and Berlin, at first taking up law, but he soon devoted himself exclusively to the study of history and philosophy, and in 1842 was on the point of establishing himself as an assistant professor in philosophy when the political movement which had arisen since the death of Frederick William III directed his life into a different channel. With his collaboration, the leaders of the Rhenish liberal bourgeoisie, the Camphausens, Hansemanns, etc., had founded, in Cologne, the *Rheinische Zeitung*[115] and in the autumn of 1842, Marx, whose criticism of the proceedings of the Rhenish *Landtag* had excited very great attention, was put at the head of the paper. The *Rheinische Zeitung* naturally appeared under censorship, but the censorship could not cope with it.* The *Rheinische Zeitung* almost always got through the articles which mattered; the censor was first supplied with insignificant fodder for him to strike out, until he either gave way of himself or was compelled to give way by the threat that then the paper would not appear the next day. Ten newspapers with the same courage as the *Rheinische Zeitung* and whose publishers would have allowed a few hundred thalers extra to be expended on typesetting—and the censorship would have been made impossible in Germany as early as 1843. But the German newspaper owners were petty-minded, timid Philistines and the *Rheinische Zeitung* carried on the struggle alone. It wore out one censor after another; finally it came under a double censorship; after the first censorship the *Regierungspräsident*** had once more and finally to censor it. That also was of no avail. In the beginning

---

* The first censor of the *Rheinische Zeitung* was Police Councillor Dolleschall, the same man who once struck out an advertisement in the *Kölnische Zeitung*[284] of the translation of Dante's *Divine Comedy* by Philalethes (later King John of Saxony) with the remark: One must not make a comedy of divine affairs. [*Note by Engels.*]

** *Regierungspräsident*: In Prussia, regional representative of the central executive.—*Ed.*

of 1843, the government declared that it was impossible to keep this newspaper in check and suppressed it without more ado.

Marx, who in the meanwhile had married the sister of von Westphalen, later minister of the reaction, removed to Paris, and there, in conjunction with A. Ruge, published the *German-French Annuals*,[117] in which he opened the series of his socialist writings with a *Criticism of the Hegelian Philosophy of Law*. Further, together with F. Engels, *The Holy Family. Against Bruno Bauer and Co.*, a satirical criticism of one of the latest forms blunderingly assumed by the German philosophical idealism of the time.

The study of political economy and of the history of the Great French Revolution still allowed Marx time enough for occasional attacks on the Prussian government; the latter revenged itself in the spring of 1845 by securing from the Guizot ministry—Herr Alexander von Humboldt is said to have acted as intermediary— his expulsion from France.[285] Marx shifted his domicile to Brussels and published there in French in 1847: *The Poverty of Philosophy*, a criticism of Proudhon's *Philosophy of Poverty*, and in 1848 *Discourse on Free Trade*. At the same time he made use of the opportunity to found a German workers' society[28] in Brussels and so commenced practical agitation. The latter became still more important for him when he and his political friends in 1847 entered the secret *Communist League*, which had already been in existence for a number of years. Its whole structure was now radically changed; this association, which previously was more or less conspiratorial, was transformed into a simple organisation of communist propaganda, which was only secret because necessity compelled it to be so, the *first* organisation of the German Social-Democratic Party. The League existed wherever German workers' unions were to be found; in almost all of these unions in England, Belgium, France and Switzerland, and in very many of the unions in Germany, the leading members belonged to the League and the share of the League in the incipient German labour movement was very considerable. Moreover, our League was the first which emphasised the international character of the whole labour movement and realised it in practice, which had Englishmen, Belgians, Hungarians, Poles, etc., as members and which organised international labour meetings, especially in London.

The transformation of the League took place at two congresses held in 1847, the second of which resolved on the elaboration and publication of the fundamental principles of the Party in a manifesto to be drawn up by Marx and Engels. Thus arose the *Manifesto of the Communist Party*,* which first appeared in 1848, shortly

---

* See pp. 35-63 of this volume.—*Ed.*

before the February Revolution, and has since been translated into almost all European languages.

The *Deutsche Brüsseler Zeitung,*[286] in which Marx participated and which mercilessly exposed the blessings of the police regime of the fatherland, caused the Prussian government to try to effect Marx's expulsion once more, but in vain. When, however, the February Revolution resulted in popular movements also in Brussels, and a radical change appeared to be imminent in Belgium, the Belgian government arrested Marx without ceremony and deported him. In the meanwhile, the French Provisional Government had sent him through Flocon an invitation to return to Paris, and he accepted this call.

In Paris he came out especially against the swindle, widespread among the Germans there, of wanting to form the German workers in France into armed legions in order to carry the revolution and the republic into Germany. On the one hand, Germany had to make her revolution herself, and, on the other hand, every revolutionary foreign legion formed in France was betrayed in advance by the Lamartines of the Provisional Government to the government which was to be overthrown, as occurred in Belgium and Baden.

After the March Revolution, Marx went to Cologne and founded there the *Neue Rheinische Zeitung,*[27] which was in existence from June 1, 1848, to May 19, 1849—the only paper which represented the standpoint of the proletariat within the democratic movement of the time, as shown in its unreserved championship of the Paris June insurgents of 1848,[6] which cost the paper the defection of almost all its shareholders. In vain the *Kreuzzeitung*[287] pointed to the "Chimborazo* impudence" with which the *Neue Rheinische Zeitung*[146] attacked everything sacred, from the king and vice-regent of the realm down to the gendarme, and that, too, in a Prussian fortress with a garrison of 8,000 at that time. In vain was the rage of the Rhenish liberal Philistines, who had suddenly become reactionary. In vain was the paper suspended by martial law in Cologne for a lengthy period in the autumn of 1848. In vain the Reich Ministry of Justice in Frankfort denounced article after article to the Cologne Public Prosecutor in order that judicial proceedings should be taken. Under the very eyes of the police the paper calmly went on being edited and printed, and its distribution and reputation increased with the vehemence of its attacks on the government and the bourgeoisie. When the Prussian *coup d'état*[36] took place in November 1848, the *Neue Rheinische Zeitung* called at the head of each issue upon the peo-

---

* *Chimborazo*: one of the highest peaks of the Andes Mountains in South America.—*Ed.*

ple to refuse to pay taxes and to meet violence with violence. In the spring of 1849, both on this account and because of another article, it was made to face a jury, but on both occasions was acquitted. Finally, when the May risings of 1848 in Dresden and the Rhine province[30] had been suppressed, and the Prussian campaign against the Baden-Palatinate rising had been inaugurated by the concentration and mobilisation of considerable masses of troops, the government believed itself strong enough to suppress the *Neue Rheinische Zeitung* by force. The last number—printed in red ink—appeared on May 19.

Marx again went to Paris, but only a few weeks after the demonstration of June 13, 1849,[288] he was faced by the French government with the choice of either shifting his residence to Brittany or leaving France. He preferred the latter and moved to London, where he has lived uninterruptedly ever since.

An attempt to continue to issue the *Neue Rheinische Zeitung* in the form of a review (in Hamburg 1850) had to be given up after a while in view of the ever-increasing violence of the reaction. Immediately after the *coup d'état* in France in December 1851, Marx published: *The Eighteenth Brumaire of Louis Bonaparte** (Boston 1852; second edition, Hamburg 1869, shortly before the war). In 1853 he wrote *Revelations about the Cologne Communist Trial* (first printed in Basle, later in Boston, and again recently in Leipzig).

After the condemnation of the members of the Communist League in Cologne,[9] Marx withdrew from political agitation and for ten years devoted himself, on the one hand, to the study of the rich treasures offered by the library of the British Museum in the sphere of political economy, and, on the other hand, to writing for the *New York Tribune*,[118] which up to the outbreak of the American Civil War[129] published not only contributions signed by him but also numerous leading articles on conditions in Europe and Asia from his pen. His attacks on Lord Palmerston, based on an exhaustive study of British official documents, were reprinted in London in pamphlet form.

As the first fruit of his many years of study of economics, there appeared in 1859 *A Contribution to the Critique of Political Economy*, Part I (Berlin, Duncker). This work contains the first coherent exposition of the Marxian theory of value, including the doctrine of money. During the Italian War[289] Marx, in the German newspaper *Das Volk*,[290] appearing in London, attacked Bonapartism, which at that time posed as liberal and playing the part of liberator of the oppressed nationalities, and also the Prussian policy of the day, which under the cover of neutrality was seeking

---

* See pp. 96-179 of this volume. —*Ed.*

o fish in troubled waters. In this connection it was necessary to attack also Herr Karl Vogt, who at that time, on the commission of Prince Napoleon (Plon-Plon) and in the pay of Louis Napoleon, was carrying on agitation for the neutrality, and indeed the sympathy, of Germany. When Vogt heaped upon him the most abominable and deliberately false calumnies, Marx answered with *Herr Vogt* (London 1860), in which Vogt and the other gentlemen of the imperialist sham-democratic gang were exposed, and Vogt himself on the basis of both external and internal evidence was convicted of receiving bribes from the December Empire. The confirmation came just ten years later: in the list of the Bonaparte hirelings, found in the Tuileries[187] in 1870 and published by the September government,[291] there was the following entry under the letter V: "Vogt—in August 1859 there were remitted to him —Frs. 40,000."

Finally, in 1867 there appeared in Hamburg: *Capital, a Critical Analysis of Capitalist Production*, Volume I, Marx's chief work, which expounds the foundations of his economic-socialist conceptions and the main features of his criticism of existing society, the capitalist mode of production and its consequences. The second edition of this epoch-making work appeared in 1872; the author is engaged in the elaboration of the second volume.

Meanwhile the labour movement in various countries of Europe had so far regained strength that Marx could entertain the idea of realising a long-cherished wish: the foundation of a Workers' Association embracing the most advanced countries of Europe and America, which would demonstrate bodily, so to speak, the international character of the socialist movement both to the workers themselves and to the bourgeois and the governments—for the encouragement and strengthening of the proletariat, for striking fear into the hearts of its enemies. A mass meeting in favour of Poland, which had just then again been crushed by Russia, held on September 28, 1864, in St. Martin's Hall in London, provided the occasion for bringing forward the matter, which was enthusiastically taken up. The *International Working Men's Association* was founded; a Provisional General Council, with its seat in London, was elected at the meeting, and Marx was the soul of this as of all subsequent General Councils up to the Hague Congress.[250] He drafted almost every one of the documents issued by the General Council of the International, from the *Inaugural Address*, 1864, to the *Address on the Civil War in France*,* 1871. To describe Marx's activity in the International is to write

---

* K. Marx, *Inaugural Address of the Working Men's International Association* (Marx and Engels, *Selected Works*, Vol. I, Moscow 1962, pp. 377-85) and *The Civil War in France* (see pp. 271-307 of this volume).—*Ed.*

the history of this Association, which in any case still lives in th memory of European workers.

The fall of the Paris Commune[8] put the International in an im possible position. It was thrust into the forefront of European his tory at a moment when it had everywhere been deprived of al possibility of successful practical action. The events which raisec it to the position of the seventh Great Power simultaneously for bade it to mobilise its fighting forces and employ them in action on pain of inevitable defeat and the setting back of the labour movement for decades. In addition, from various sides elements were pushing themselves forward that sought to exploit the sud denly enhanced fame of the Association for the purpose of gratify ing personal vanity or personal ambition, without understanding the real position of the International or without regard for it. A heroic decision had to be taken, and it was again Marx who took it and who carried it through at the Hague Congress. In a solemn resolution, the International disclaimed all responsibility for the doings of the Bakuninists, who formed the centre of those unreasonable and unsavoury elements. Then, in view of the impossibility of also meeting, in the face of the general reaction, the increased demands which were being imposed upon it, and of maintaining its complete efficacy other than by a series of sacrifices which would have drained the labour movement of its life-blood—in view of this situation, the International withdrew from the stage for the time being by transferring the General Council to America. The results have proved how correct was this decision—which was at the time, and has been since, so often censured. On the one hand, it put a stop then and since to all attempts to make useless *putsches* in the name of the International, while, on the other hand, the continuing close intercourse between the socialist workers' parties of the various countries proved that the consciousness of the identity of interests and of the solidarity of the proletariat of all countries evoked by the International is able to assert itself even without the bond of a formal international association, which for the moment had become a fetter.

After the Hague Congress, Marx at last found peace and leisure again for resuming his theoretical work, and it is to be hoped he will be able before long to have the second volume of *Capital* ready for the press.

Of the many important discoveries through which Marx has inscribed his name in the annals of science, we can here dwell on only two.

The first is the revolution brought about by him in the whole conception of world history. The whole previous view of history was based on the conception that the ultimate causes of all historical changes are to be looked for in the changing ideas of human

>eings, and that of all historical changes political changes are
he most important and dominate the whole of history. But the
question was not asked as to whence the ideas come into men's
minds and what the driving causes of the political changes are.
Only upon the newer school of French, and partly also of English,
historians had the conviction forced itself that, since the Middle
Ages at least, the driving force in European history was the struggle of the developing bourgeoisie with the feudal aristocracy for
social and political domination. Now Marx has proved that the
whole of previous history is a history of class struggles, that in all
the manifold and complicated political struggles the only thing
at issue has been the social and political rule of social classes, the
maintenance of domination by older classes and the conquest of
domination by newly arising classes. To what, however, do these
classes owe their origin and their continued existence? They owe
it to the particular material, physically sensible conditions in
which society at a given period produces and exchanges its means
of subsistence. The feudal rule of the Middle Ages rested on the
self-sufficient economy of small peasant communities, which themselves produced almost all their requirements, in which there was
almost no exchange and which received from the arms-bearing
nobility protection from without and national or at least political
cohesion. When the towns arose and with them separate handicraft industry and trade intercourse, at first internal and later
international, the urban bourgeoisie developed, and already during the Middle Ages achieved, in struggle with the nobility, its
inclusion in the feudal order as likewise a privileged estate. But
with the discovery of the extra-European world, from the middle
of the fifteenth century onwards, this bourgeoisie acquired a far
more extensive sphere of trade and therewith a new spur for its
industry; in the most important branches handicrafts were supplanted by manufacture, now on a factory scale, and this again
was supplanted by large-scale industry, become possible owing to
the discoveries of the previous century, especially that of the
steam engine. Large-scale industry, in its turn, reacted on trade
by driving out the old manual labour in backward countries, and
creating the present-day new means of communication: steam en-
gines, railways, electric telegraphy, in the more developed ones.
Thus the bourgeoisie came more and more to combine social
wealth and social power in its hands, while it still for a long
period remained excluded from political power, which was in the
hands of the nobility and the monarchy supported by the nobility.
But at a certain stage—in France since the Great Revolution—it
also conquered political power, and now in turn became the ruling
class over the proletariat and small peasants. From this point of
view all the historical phenomena are explicable in the simplest

possible way—with sufficient knowledge of the particular economic condition of society, which it is true is totally lacking in our
professional historians, and in the same way the conceptions and
ideas of each historical period are most simply to be explained
from the economic conditions of life and from the social and political relations of the period, which are in turn determined by these
economic conditions. History was for the first time placed on its
real basis; the palpable but previously totally overlooked fact that
men must first of all eat, drink, have shelter and clothing, therefore must *work*, before they can fight for domination, pursue politics, religion, philosophy, etc.—this palpable fact at last came
into its historical rights.

This new conception of history, however, was of supreme significance for the socialist outlook. It showed that all previous history moved in class antagonisms and class struggles, that there
have always existed ruling and ruled, exploiting and exploited
classes, and that the great majority of mankind has always been
condemned to arduous labour and little enjoyment. Why is this?
Simply because in all earlier stages of development of mankind
production was so little developed that the historical development
could proceed only in this antagonistic form, that historical progress as a whole was assigned to the activity of a small privileged
minority, while the great mass remained condemned to . producing by their labour their own meagre means of subsistence
and also the increasingly rich means of the privileged. But the
same investigation of history, which in this way provides a natural and reasonable explanation of the previous class rule, otherwise only explicable from the wickedness of man, also leads to
the realisation that, in consequence of the so tremendously increased productive forces of the present time, even the last pretext
has vanished for a division of mankind into rulers and ruled, exploiters and exploited, at least in the most advanced countries;
that the ruling big bourgeoisie has fulfilled its historic mission,
that it is no longer capable of the leadership of society and has
even become a hindrance to the development of production, as the
trade crises, and especially the last great collapse,[283] and the depressed condition of industry in all countries have proved; that
historical leadership has passed to the proletariat, a class which,
owing to its whole position in society, can only free itself by
abolishing altogether all class rule, all servitude and all exploitation; and that the social productive forces, which have outgrown
the control of the bourgeoisie, are only waiting for the associated
proletariat to take possession of them in order to bring about a
state of things in which every member of society will be enabled
to participate not only in production but also in the distribution
and administration of social wealth, and which so increases the

social productive forces and their yield by planned operation of the whole of production that the satisfaction of all reasonable needs will be assured to everyone in an ever-increasing measure.

The second important discovery of Marx is the final elucidation of the relation between capital and labour, in other words, the demonstration how, within present society and under the existing capitalist mode of production, the exploitation of the worker by the capitalist takes place. Ever since political economy had put forward the proposition that labour is the source of all wealth and of all value, the question became inevitable: How is this then to be reconciled with the fact that the wage-worker does not receive the whole sum of value created by his labour but has to surrender a part of it to the capitalist? Both the bourgeois economists and the Socialists exerted themselves to give a scientifically valid answer to this question, but in vain, until at last Marx came forward with the solution. This solution is as follows: The present-day capitalist mode of production presupposes the existence of two social classes—on the one hand, that of the capitalists, who are in possession of the means of production and subsistence, and, on the other hand, that of the proletarians, who, being excluded from this possession, have only a single commodity for sale, their labour power, and who therefore have to sell this labour power of theirs in order to obtain possession of means of subsistence. The value of a commodity is, however, determined by the socially necessary quantity of labour embodied in its production, and, therefore, also in its reproduction; the value of the labour power of an average human being during a day, month or year is determined, therefore, by the quantity of labour embodied in the quantity of means of subsistence necessary for the maintenance of this labour power during a day, month or year. Let us assume that the means of subsistence of a worker for one day require six hours of labour for their production, or, what is the same thing, that the labour contained in them represents a quantity of labour of six hours; then the value of labour power for one day will be expressed in a sum of money which also embodies six hours of labour. Let us assume further that the capitalist who employs our worker pays him this sum in return, pays him, therefore, the full value of his labour power. If now the worker works six hours of the day for the capitalist, he has completely replaced the latter's outlay—six hours' labour for six hours' labour. But then there would be nothing in it for the capitalist, and the latter therefore looks at the matter quite differently. He says: I have bought the labour power of this worker not for six hours but for a whole day, and accordingly he makes the worker work 8, 10, 12, 14 or more hours, according to circumstances, so that the product of the seventh, eighth and following hours is a product of unpaid labour and wanders, to begin with, into the pocket of the capitalist. Thus the worker in the service of the capitalist not only reproduces the value of his labour power, for which he receives pay, but over and above that he also produces a *surplus value* which, appropriated in the first place by the capitalist, is in its further course divided according to definite economic laws among the whole capitalist class and forms the basic stock from which arise ground rent, profit, accumulation of capital, in short, all the wealth consumed or accumulated by the non-labouring classes. But this proved that the acquisition of riches by the present-day capitalists consists just as much in the appropriation of the unpaid labour of others as that of the slave-owner or the feudal lord exploiting serf labour, and that all these forms of exploitation are only to be distinguished by the difference in manner and method by which the unpaid labour is appropriated. This, however, also removed the last justification for all the hypocritical phrases of the possessing classes to the effect that in the present social order right and justice, equality of rights and duties and a general harmony of interests prevail, and present-day bourgeois society, no less than its predecessors, was exposed as a grandiose institution for the exploitation of the huge majority of the people by a small, ever-diminishing minority.

Modern, scientific socialism is based on these two important facts. In the second volume of *Capital* these and other hardly less important scientific discoveries concerning the capitalist system of society will be further developed, and thereby those aspects also of political economy not touched upon in the first volume will undergo revolutionisation. May it be vouchsafed to Marx to be able soon to have it ready for the press.

Written by Engels in mid-June, 1877

Published in the *Volkskalender*,
an almanac which appeared in
Brunswick in 1878

Printed according to the
almanac text
Translated from the
German

Frederick Engels

SOCIALISM: UTOPIAN AND SCIENTIFIC[292]

SPECIAL INTRODUCTION TO THE ENGLISH EDITION
OF 1892

The present little book is, originally, a part of a larger whole. About 1875, Dr. E. Dühring, *privatdocent* at Berlin University, suddenly and rather clamorously announced his conversion to socialism, and presented the German public not only with an elaborate socialist theory, but also with a complete practical plan for the reorganisation of society. As a matter of course, he fell foul of his predecessors; above all, he honoured Marx by pouring out upon him the full vials of his wrath.

This took place about the time when the two sections of the Socialist Party in Germany—Eisenachers and Lassalleans[248]—had just effected their fusion, and thus obtained not only an immense increase of strength, but, what was more, the faculty of employing the whole of this strength against the common enemy. The Socialist Party in Germany was fast becoming a power. But to make it a power, the first condition was that the newly-conquered unity should not be imperilled. And Dr. Dühring openly proceeded to form around himself a sect, the nucleus of a future separate party. It thus became necessary to take up the gauntlet thrown down to us, and to fight out the struggle whether we liked it or not.

This, however, though it might not be an over-difficult, was evidently a long-winded business. As is well known, we Germans are of a terribly ponderous *Gründlichkeit*, radical profundity or profound radicality, whatever you may like to call it. Whenever anyone of us expounds what he considers a new doctrine, he has first to elaborate it into an all-comprising system. He has to prove that both the first principles of logic and the fundamental laws of the universe had existed from all eternity for no other purpose than to ultimately lead to this newly-discovered, crowning theory. And Dr. Dühring, in this respect, was quite up to the national mark. Nothing less than a complete *System of Philosophy*, mental, moral, natural, and historical; a complete *System of Political Economy and Socialism*; and, finally, a *Critical History of Political Economy*—three big volumes in octavo, heavy extrinsically and intrinsically, three army corps of arguments mobilised

against all previous philosophers and economists in general, and
against Marx in particular—in fact, an attempt at a complete
"revolution in science"—these were what I should have to tackle.
I had to treat of all and every possible subject, from the concepts
of time and space to Bimetallism[293]; from the eternity of matter
and motion to the perishable nature of moral ideas; from Darwin's
natural selection to the education of youth in a future society.
Anyhow, the systematic comprehensiveness of my opponent gave
me the opportunity of developing, in opposition to him, and in a
more connected form than had previously been done, the views
held by Marx and myself on this great variety of subjects. And
that was the principal reason which made me undertake this otherwise ungrateful task.

My reply was first published in a series of articles in the Leipzig *Vorwärts*,[294] the chief organ of the Socialist Party, and later
on as a book: *Herrn Eugen Dührings Umwälzung der Wissenschaft*
(*Mr. E. Dühring's Revolution in Science*), a second edition of
which appeared in Zurich, 1886.

At .the request of my friend, Paul Lafargue, now representative of Lille in the French Chamber of Deputies, I arranged three
chapters of this book as a pamphlet, which he translated and
published in 1880, under the title: *Socialisme utopique.et socialisme
scientifique*. From this French text a Polish and a Spanish edition
were prepared. In 1883, our German friends brought out the
pamphlet in the original language. Italian, Russian, Danish, Dutch,
and Roumanian translations, based upon the German text, have
since been published. Thus, with the present English edition, this
little book circulates in ten languages. I am not aware that any
other socialist work, not even our *Communist Manifesto**[*] of 1848
or Marx's *Capital*, has been so often translated. In Germany it has
had four editions of about 20,000 copies in all.

The appendix, "The Mark,"[295] was written with the intention of
spreading among the German Socialist Party some elementary
knowledge of the history and development of landed property
in Germany. This seemed all the more necessary at a time when
the assimilation by that party of the working people of the towns
was in a fair way of completion, and when the agricultural
labourers and peasants had to be taken in hand. This appendix
has been included in the translation, as the original forms of
tenure of land common to all Teutonic tribes, and the history of
their decay, are even less known in England than in Germany.
I have left the text as it stands in the original, without alluding to
the hypothesis recently started by Maxim Kovalevsky, according
to which the partition of the arable and meadow lands[296] among

---

* See pp. 35-63 of this volume.—*Ed.*

the members of the Mark was preceded by their being cultivated for joint-account by a large patriarchal family community embracing several generations (as exemplified by the still existing South Slavonian Zadruga), and that the partition, later on, took place when the community had increased, so as to become too unwieldy for joint-account management. Kovalevsky is probably quite right, but the matter is still *sub judice*.*

The economic terms used in this work, as far as they are new, agree with those used in the English edition of Marx's *Capital*. We call "production of commodities" that economic phase where articles are produced not only for the use of the producers, but also for purposes of exchange; that is, *as commodities*, not as use values. This phase extends from the first beginnings of production for exchange down to our present time; it attains its full development under capitalist production only, that is, under conditions where the capitalist, the owner of the means of production, employs, for wages, labourers, people deprived of all means of production except their own labour-power, and pockets the excess of the selling price of the products over his outlay. We divide the history of industrial production since the Middle Ages into three periods: (1) handicraft, small master craftsmen with a few journeymen and apprentices, where each labourer produces the complete article; (2) manufacture, where greater numbers of workmen, grouped in one large establishment, produce the complete article on the principle of division of labour, each workman performing only one partial operation, so that the product is complete only after having passed successively through the hands of all; (3) modern industry, where the product is produced by machinery driven by power, and where the work of the labourer is limited to superintending and correcting the performances of the mechanical agent.

I am perfectly aware that the contents of this work will meet with objection from a considerable portion of the British public. But if we Continentals had taken the slightest notice of the prejudices of British "respectability," we should be even worse off than we are. This book defends what we call "historical materialism," and the word materialism grates upon the ears of the immense majority of British readers. "Agnosticism"[297] might be tolerated, but materialism is utterly inadmissible.

And yet the original home of all modern materialism, from the seventeenth century onwards, is England.

"Materialism is the natural-born son of Great Britain. Already the British schoolman,[298] Duns Scotus, asked, 'whether it was impossible for matter to think?'

* *Sub judice*—under consideration.—*Ed.*

"In order to effect this miracle, he took refuge in God's omnipotence, *i.e.*, he made theology[270] preach materialism. Moreover, he was a nominalist.[299] Nominalism, the first form of materialism, is chiefly found among the English schoolmen.

"The real progenitor of English materialism is Bacon. To him natural philosophy is the only true philosophy, and physics based upon the experience of the senses is the chiefest part of natural philosophy. Anaxagoras and his homoiomeriae,[300] Democritus and his atoms, he often quotes as his authorities. According to him the senses are infallible and the source of all knowledge. All science is based on experience, and consists in subjecting the data furnished by the senses to a rational method of investigation. Induction, analysis, comparison, observation, experiment, are the principal forms of such a rational method. Among the qualities inherent in matter, motion is the first and foremost, not only in the form of mechanical and mathematical motion, but chiefly in the form of an impulse, a vital spirit, a tension—or a 'qual,' to use a term of Jakob Böhme's*—of matter.

"In Bacon, its first creator, materialism still occludes within itself the germs of a many-sided development. On the one hand, matter, surrounded by a sensuous, poetic glamour, seems to attract man's whole entity by winning smiles. On the other, the aphoristically formulated doctrine pullulates with inconsistencies imported from theology.

"In its further evolution, materialism becomes one-sided. Hobbes is the man who systematises Baconian materialism. Knowledge based upon the senses loses its poetic blossom, it passes into the abstract experience of the mathematician; geometry is proclaimed as the queen of sciences. Materialism takes to misanthropy. If it is to overcome its opponent, misanthropic, fleshless spiritualism, and that on the latter's own ground, materialism has to chastise its own flesh and turn ascetic. Thus, from a sensual, it passes into an intellectual, entity; but thus, too, it evolves all the consistency, regardless of consequences, characteristic of the intellect.

"Hobbes, as Bacon's continuator, argues thus: if all human knowledge is furnished by the senses, then our concepts and ideas are but the phantoms, divested of their sensual forms, of the real world. Philosophy can but give names to these phantoms. One

---

* "Qual" is a philosophical play upon words. Qual literally means torture, a pain which drives to action of some kind; at the same time the mystic Böhme puts into the German word something of the meaning of the Latin *qualitas*; his "qual" was the activating principle arising from, and promoting in its turn, the spontaneous development of the thing, relation, or person subject to it, in contradistinction to a pain inflicted from without. [*Note by Engels to the English edition.*]

name may be applied to more than one of them. There may even be names of names. It would imply a contradiction if, on the one hand, we maintained that all ideas had their origin in the world of sensation, and, on the other, that a word was more than a word; that besides the beings known to us by our senses, beings which are one and all individuals, there existed also beings of a general, not individual, nature. An unbodily substance is the same absurdity as an unbodily body. Body, being, substance, are but different terms for the same reality. *It is impossible to separate thought from matter that thinks.* This matter is the substratum of all changes going on in the world. The word infinite is meaningless, unless it states that our mind is capable of performing an endless process of addition. Only material things being perceptible to us, we cannot know anything about the existence of God. My own existence alone is certain. Every human passion is a mechanical movement which has a beginning and an end. The objects of impulse are what we call good. Man is subject to the same laws as nature. Power and freedom are identical.

"Hobbes had systematised Bacon, without, however, furnishing a proof for Bacon's fundamental principle, the origin of all human knowledge from the world of sensation. It was Locke who, in his *Essay on the Human Understanding*, supplied this proof.[301]

"Hobbes had shattered the theistic[302] prejudices of Baconian materialism; Collins, Dodwell, Coward, Hartley, Priestley, similarly shattered the last theological bars that still hemmed in Locke's sensationalism.[303] At all events, for practical materialists, deism[304] is but an easy-going way of getting rid of religion."*

Thus Karl Marx wrote about the British origin of modern materialism. If Englishmen nowadays do not exactly relish the compliment he paid their ancestors, more's the pity. It is none the less undeniable that Bacon, Hobbes and Locke are the fathers of that brilliant school of French materialists which made the eighteenth century, in spite of all battles on land and sea won over Frenchmen by Germans and Englishmen, a pre-eminently French century, even before that crowning French Revolution, the results of which we outsiders, in England as well as in Germany, are still trying to acclimatise.

There is no denying it. About the middle of this century, what struck every cultivated foreigner who set up his residence in England, was what he was then bound to consider the religious bigotry and stupidity of the English respectable middle class. We, at that time, were all materialists, or, at least, very advanced

---

* Marx and Engels, *Die heilige Familie*, Frankfurt a. M., 1845, pp. 201-04. [See Marx and Engels, *The Holy Family*, Chapter VI, 3. Absolute Criticism's Third Campaign, (d), Moscow, 1956.—*Ed.*]

freethinkers, and to us it appeared inconceivable that almost al educated people in England should believe in all sorts of impossible miracles, and that even geologists like Buckland and Mantell should contort the facts of their science so as not to clash too much with the myths of the book of Genesis; while, in order to find people who dared to use their own intellectual faculties with regard to religious matters, you had to go amongst the uneducated, the "great unwashed," as they were then called, the working people, especially the Owenite Socialists.

But England has been "civilised" since then. The exhibition of 1851[102] sounded the knell of English insular exclusiveness. England became gradually internationalised—in diet, in manners, in ideas; so much so that I begin to wish that some English manners and customs had made as much headway on the Continent as other Continental habits have made here. Anyhow, the introduction and spread of salad-oil (before 1851 known only to the aristocracy) has been accompanied by a fatal spread of Continental scepticism in matters religious, and it has come to this, that agnosticism, though not yet considered "the thing" quite as much as the Church of England, is yet very nearly on a par, as far as respectability goes, with Baptism, and decidedly ranks above the Salvation Army.[305] And I cannot help believing that under these circumstances it will be consoling to many who sincerely regret and condemn this progress of infidelity to learn that these "new-fangled notions" are not of foreign origin, are not "made in Germany," like so many other articles of daily use, but are undoubtedly Old English, and that their British originators two hundred years ago went a good deal further than their descendants now dare to venture.

What, indeed, is agnosticism but, to use an expressive Lancashire term, "shamefaced" materialism? The agnostic's conception of Nature is materialistic throughout. The entire natural world is governed by law, and absolutely excludes the intervention of action from without. But, he adds, we have no means either of ascertaining or of disproving the existence of some Supreme Being beyond the known universe. Now, this might hold good at the time when Laplace, to Napoleon's question, why in the great astronomer's *Mécanique céleste* the Creator was not even mentioned, proudly replied: "*Je n'avais pas besoin de cette hypothèse.*"* But nowadays, in our evolutionary conception of the universe, there is absolutely no room for either a Creator or a Ruler; and to talk of a Supreme Being shut out from the whole existing world, implies a contradiction in terms, and, as it seems to me, a gratuitous insult to the feelings of religious people.

---

* "I had no need of this hypothesis."—*Ed.*

Again, our agnostic admits that all our knowledge is based
upon the information imparted to us by our senses. But, he adds,
how do we know that our senses give us correct representations
of the objects we perceive through them? And he proceeds to in-
form us that, whenever he speaks of objects or their qualities, he
does in reality not mean these objects and qualities, of which he
cannot know anything for certain, but merely the impressions
which they have produced on his senses. Now, this line of reasoning seems undoubtedly hard to beat by mere argumentation. But
before there was argumentation there was action. *Im Anfang war
die Tat.** And human action had solved the difficulty long before
human ingenuity invented it. The proof of the pudding is in the
eating. From the moment we turn to our own use these objects,
according to the qualities we perceive in them, we put to an infallible test the correctness or otherwise of our sense-perceptions. If
these perceptions have been wrong, then our estimate of the use
to which an object can be turned must also be wrong, and our attempt must fail. But if we succeed in accomplishing our aim, if
we find that the object does agree with our idea of it, and does
answer the purpose we intended it for, then that is positive proof
that our perceptions of it and of its qualities, *so far*, agree with
reality outside ourselves. And whenever we find ourselves face to
face with a failure, then we generally are not long in making out
the cause that made us fail; we find that the perception upon
which we acted was either incomplete and superficial, or combined with the results of other perceptions in a way not war-
ranted by them—what we call defective reasoning. So long as we
take care to train and to use our senses properly, and to keep our
action within the limits prescribed by perceptions properly made
and properly used, so long we shall find that the result of our action proves the conformity of our perceptions with the objective
nature of the things perceived. Not in one single instance, so far,
have we been led to the conclusion that our sense-perceptions,
scientifically controlled, induce in our minds ideas respecting the
outer world that are, by their very nature, at variance with reality, or that there is an inherent incompatibility between the outer
world and our sense-perceptions of it.

But then come the Neo-Kantian agnostics and say: We may
correctly perceive the qualities of a thing, but we cannot by any
sensible or mental process grasp the thing-in-itself. This "thing-
in-itself" is beyond our ken. To this Hegel, long since, has replied:
If you know all the qualities of a thing, you know the thing itself;
nothing remains but the fact that the said thing exists without us;
and when your senses have taught you that fact, you have

---

* In the beginning was the deed. From Goethe's *Faust.—Ed.*

grasped the last remnant of the thing-in-itself, Kant's celebrated unknowable *Ding an sich*. To which it may be added that in Kant's time our knowledge of natural objects was indeed so fragmentary that he might well suspect, behind the little we knew about each of them, a mysterious "thing-in-itself." But one after another these ungraspable things have been grasped, analysed and, what is more, *reproduced* by the giant progress of science and what we can produce we certainly cannot consider as unknowable. To the chemistry of the first half of this century organic substances were such mysterious objects; now we learn to build them up one after another from their chemical elements without the aid of organic processes. Modern chemists declare that as soon as the chemical constitution of no matter what body is known, it can be built up from its elements. We are still far from knowing the constitution of the highest organic substances, the albuminous bodies; but there is no reason why we should not, if only after centuries, arrive at the knowledge and, armed with it, produce artificial albumen. But if we arrive at that, we shall at the same time have produced organic life, for life, from its lowest to its highest forms, is but the normal mode of existence of albuminous bodies.

As soon, however, as our agnostic has made these formal mental reservations, he talks and acts as the rank materialist he at bottom is. He may say that, as far as *we* know, matter and motion, or as it is now called, energy, can neither be created nor destroyed, but that we have no proof of their not having been created at some time or other. But if you try to use this admission against him in any particular case, he will quickly put you out of court. If he admits the possibility of spiritualism[306] *in abstracto*, he will have none of it *in concreto*. As far as we know and can know, he will tell you, there is no Creator and no Ruler of the universe; as far as we are concerned, matter and energy can neither be created nor annihilated; for us, mind is a mode of energy, a function of the brain; all we know is that the material world is governed by immutable laws, and so forth. Thus, as far as he is a scientific man, as far as he *knows* anything, he is a materialist; outside his science, in spheres about which he knows nothing, he translates his ignorance into Greek and calls it agnosticism.

At all events, one thing seems clear: even if I was an agnostic, it is evident that I could not describe the conception of history sketched out in this little book as "historical agnosticism." Religious people would laugh at me, agnostics would indignantly ask, was I going to make fun of them? And thus I hope even British respectability will not be overshocked if I use, in English as well as in so many other languages, the term "historical materialism," to designate that view of the course of history which seeks the ultimate cause and the great moving power of all important historic events in the economic development of society, in the changes in the modes of production and exchange, in the consequent division of society into distinct classes, and in the struggles of these classes against one another.

This indulgence will perhaps be accorded to me all the sooner if I show that historical materialism may be of advantage even to British respectability. I have mentioned the fact that, about forty or fifty years ago, any cultivated foreigner settling in England was struck by what he was then bound to consider the religious bigotry and stupidity of the English respectable middle class. I am now going to prove that the respectable English middle class of that time was not quite as stupid as it looked to the intelligent foreigner. Its religious leanings can be explained.

When Europe emerged from the Middle Ages, the rising middle class of the towns constituted its revolutionary element. It had conquered a recognised position within mediaeval feudal organisation, but this position, also, had become too narrow for its expansive power. The development of the middle class, the *bourgeoisie*, became incompatible with the maintenance of the feudal system; the feudal system, therefore, had to fall.

But the great international centre of feudalism was the Roman Catholic Church. It united the whole of feudalised Western Europe, in spite of all internal wars, into one grand political system, opposed as much to the schismatic[307] Greeks as to the Mohammedan countries. It surrounded feudal institutions with the halo of divine consecration. It had organised its own hierarchy on the feudal model, and, lastly, it was itself by far the most powerful feudal lord, holding, as it did, fully one-third of the soil of the Catholic world. Before profane feudalism could be successfully attacked in each country and in detail, this, its sacred central organisation, had to be destroyed.

Moreover, parallel with the rise of the middle class went on the great revival of science; astronomy, mechanics, physics, anatomy, physiology, were again cultivated. And the bourgeoisie, for the development of its industrial production, required a science which ascertained the physical properties of natural objects and the modes of action of the forces of Nature. Now up to then science had but been the humble handmaid of the Church, had not been allowed to overstep the limits set by faith, and for that reason had been no science at all. Science rebelled against the Church; the bourgeoisie could not do without science, and, therefore, had to join in the rebellion.

The above, though touching but two of the points where the rising middle class was bound to come into collision with the established religion, will be sufficient to show, first, that the class most directly interested in the struggle against the pretensions of the Roman Church was the bourgeoisie; and second, that every struggle against

feudalism, at that time, had to take on a religious disguise, had to b
directed against the Church in the first instance. But if the universi
ties and the traders of the cities started the cry, it was sure to finc
and did find, a strong echo in the masses of the country people, th
peasants, who everywhere had to struggle for their very existenc
with their feudal lords, spiritual and temporal.

The long fight of the bourgeoisie against feudalism culminate
in three great, decisive battles.

The first was what is called the Protestant Reformation in Ger
many. The war cry raised against the Church by Luther was res
ponded to by two insurrections of a political nature: first, that of th
lower nobility under Franz von Sickingen, 1523, then the great Pea
sants' War, 1525. Both were defeated, chiefly in consequence of th
indecision of the parties most interested, the burghers of the towns—
an indecision into the causes of which we cannot here enter. From
that moment the struggle degenerated into a fight between the local
princes and the central power, and ended by blotting out Germany
for two hundred years, from the politically active nations of Europe
The Lutheran Reformation produced a new creed indeed, a religion
adapted to absolute monarchy. No sooner were the peasants of North-
East Germany converted to Lutheranism than they were from freemen reduced to serfs.

But where Luther failed, Calvin won the day. Calvin's creed was
one fit for the boldest of the bourgeoisie of his time. His predestina-
tion doctrine was the religious expression of the fact that in the commercial world of competition success or failure does not depend
upon a man's activity or cleverness, but upon circumstances uncontrollable by him. It is not of him that willeth or of him that runneth,
but of the mercy of unknown superior economic powers; and this was
especially true at a period of economic revolution, when all old commercial routes and centres were replaced by new ones, when India
and America were opened to the world, and when even the most
sacred economic articles of faith—the value of gold and silver—began to totter and to break down. Calvin's church constitution was
thoroughly democratic and republican; and where the kingdom of
God was republicanised, could the kingdoms of this world remain
subject to monarchs, bishops and lords? While German Lutheranism
became a willing tool in the hands of princes, Calvinism founded a
republic in Holland, and active republican parties in England, and,
above all, Scotland.

In Calvinism, the second great bourgeois upheaval found its
doctrine ready cut and dried. This upheaval took place in England.
The middle class of the towns brought it on, and the yeomanry of
the country districts fought it out. Curiously enough, in all the three
great bourgeois risings, the peasantry furnishes the army that has
to do the fighting; and the peasantry is just the class that, the victory

once gained, is most surely ruined by the economic consequences of that victory. A hundred years after Cromwell, the yeomanry of England had almost disappeared. Anyhow, had it not been for that yeomanry and for the *plebeian* element in the towns, the bourgeoisie alone would never have fought the matter out to the bitter end, and would never have brought Charles I to the scaffold. In order to secure even those conquests of the bourgeoisie that were ripe for gathering at the time, the revolution had to be carried considerably further —exactly as in 1793 in France and 1848 in Germany. This seems, in fact, to be one of the laws of evolution of bourgeois society.

Well, upon this excess of revolutionary activity there necessarily followed the inevitable reaction which in its turn went beyond the point where it might have maintained itself. After a series of oscillations, the new centre of gravity was at last attained and became a new starting-point. The grand period of English history, known to respectability under the name of "the Great Rebellion," and the struggles succeeding it, were brought to a close by the comparatively puny event entitled by Liberal historians "the Glorious Revolution."[308]

The new starting-point was a compromise between the rising middle class and the ex-feudal landowners. The latter, though called, as now, the aristocracy, had been long since on the way which led them to become what Louis Philippe in France became at a much later period, "the first bourgeois of the kingdom." Fortunately for England, the old feudal barons had killed one another during the Wars of the Roses.[309] Their successors, though mostly scions of the old families, had been so much out of the direct line of descent that they constituted quite a new body, with habits and tendencies far more bourgeois than feudal. They fully understood the value of money, and at once began to increase their rents by turning hundreds of small farmers out and replacing them by sheep. Henry VIII, while squandering the Church lands, created fresh bourgeois landlords by wholesale; the innumerable confiscations of estates, regranted to absolute or relative upstarts, and continued during the whole of the seventeenth century, had the same result. Consequently, ever since Henry VII, the English "aristocracy," far from counteracting the development of industrial production, had, on the contrary, sought to indirectly profit thereby; and there had always been a section of the great landowners willing, from economical or political reasons, to co-operate with the leading men of the financial and industrial bourgeoisie. The compromise of 1689 was, therefore, easily accomplished. The political spoils of "pelf and place" were left to the great landowning families, provided the economic interests of the financial, manufacturing and commercial middle class were sufficiently attended to. And these economic interests were at that time powerful enough to determine the general policy of the nation. There might

be squabbles about matters of detail, but, on the whole, the aristocratic oligarchy knew too well that its own economic prosperity was irretrievably bound up with that of the industrial and commercial
middle class.

From that time, the bourgeoisie was a humble, but still a recognised
component of the ruling classes of England. With the rest of them,
it had a common interest in keeping in subjection the great working
mass of the nation. The merchant or manufacturer himself stood in
the position of master, or, as it was until lately called, of "natural
superior" to his clerks, his workpeople, his domestic servants. His
interest was to get as much and as good work out of them as he could;
for this end they had to be trained to proper submission. He was himself religious; his religion had supplied the standard under which
he had fought the king and the lords; he was not long in discovering
the opportunities this same religion offered him for working upon
the minds of his natural inferiors, and making them submissive to the
behests of the masters it had pleased God to place over them. In short,
the English bourgeoisie now had to take a part in keeping down the
"lower orders," the great producing mass of the nation, and one of
the means employed for that purpose was the influence of religion.

There was another fact that contributed to strengthening the religious leanings of the bourgeoisie. That was the rise of materialism
in England. This new doctrine not only shocked the pious feelings
of the middle class; it announced itself as a philosophy only fit for
scholars and cultivated men of the world, in contrast to religion,
which was good enough for the uneducated masses, including the
bourgeoisie. With Hobbes it stepped on the stage as a defender of
royal prerogative and omnipotence; it called upon absolute monarchy to keep down that *puer robustus sed malitiosus*,* to wit, the people. Similarly, with the successors of Hobbes, with Bolingbroke,
Shaftesbury, etc., the new deistic form of materialism remained an
aristocratic, esoteric doctrine, and, therefore, hateful to the middle
class both for its religious heresy and for its anti-bourgeois political
connections. Accordingly, in opposition to the materialism and deism
of the aristocracy, those Protestant sects which had furnished the
flag and the fighting contingent against the Stuarts continued to
furnish the main strength of the progressive middle class, and form
even today the backbone of "the Great Liberal Party."

In the meantime materialism passed from England to France,
where it met and coalesced with another materialistic school of philosophers, a branch of Cartesianism.[310] In France, too, it remained at
first an exclusively aristocratic doctrine. But soon its revolutionary
character asserted itself. The French materialists did not limit their
criticism to matters of religious belief; they extended it to whatever

---

* Robust but malicious boy.—*Ed.*

scientific tradition or political institution they met with; and to prove the claim of their doctrine to universal application, they took the shortest cut, and boldly applied it to all subjects of knowledge in the giant work after which they were named—the *Encyclopédie.* Thus, in one or the other of its two forms—avowed materialism or deism—it became the creed of the whole cultured youth of France; so much so that, when the Great Revolution broke out, the doctrine hatched by English Royalists gave a theoretical flag to French Republicans and Terrorists, and furnished the text for the Declaration of the Rights of Man[311].

The Great French Revolution was the third uprising of the bourgeoisie, but the first that had entirely cast off the religious cloak, and was fought out on undisguised political lines; it was the first, too, that was really fought out up to the destruction of one of the combatants, the aristocracy, and the complete triumph of the other, the bourgeoisie. In England the continuity of prerevolutionary and postrevolutionary institutions, and the compromise between landlords and capitalists, found its expression in the continuity of judicial precedents and in the religious preservation of the feudal forms of the law. In France the Revolution constituted a complete breach with the traditions of the past; it cleared out the very last vestiges of feudalism, and created in the *Code Civil*[312] a masterly adaptation of the old Roman law—that almost perfect expression of the juridical relations corresponding to the economic stage called by Marx the production of commodities—to modern capitalistic conditions; so masterly that this French revolutionary code still serves as a model for reforms of the law of property in all other countries, not excepting England. Let us, however, not forget that if English law continues to express the economic relations of capitalistic society in that barbarous feudal language which corresponds to the thing expressed, just as English spelling corresponds to English pronunciation—*vous écrivez Londres et vous prononcez Constantinople,** said a Frenchman—that same English law is the only one which has preserved through ages, and transmitted to America and the Colonies, the best part of that old Germanic personal freedom, local self-government and independence from all interference but that of the law courts which on the Continent has been lost during the period of absolute monarchy, and has nowhere been as yet fully recovered.

To return to our British bourgeois. The French Revolution gave him a splendid opportunity, with the help of the Continental monarchies, to destroy French maritime commerce, to annex French colonies, and to crush the last French pretensions to maritime rivalry. That was one reason why he fought it. Another was that the ways of this revolution went very much against his grain. Not only its

---

* *You write London, but pronounce Constantinople.—Ed.*

"execrable" terrorism, but the very attempt to carry bourgeois rule to extremes. What should the British bourgeois do without his aristocracy, that taught him manners, such as they were, and invented fashions for him—that furnished officers of the army, which kept order at home, and the navy, which conquered colonial possessions and new markets abroad? There was indeed a progressive minority of the bourgeoisie, that minority whose interests were not so well attended to under the compromise; this section, composed chiefly of the less wealthy middle class, did sympathise with the Revolution, but it was powerless in Parliament.

Thus, if materialism became the creed of the French Revolution, the God-fearing English bourgeois held all the faster to his religion. Had not the reign of terror[313] in Paris proved what was the upshot, if the religious instincts of the masses were lost? The more materialism spread from France to neighbouring countries, and was reinforced by similar doctrinal currents, notably by German philosophy, the more, in fact, materialism and free thought generally became on the Continent the necessary qualifications of a cultivated man, the more stubbornly the English middle class stuck to its manifold religious creeds. These creeds might differ from one another, but they were, all of them, distinctly religious, Christian creeds.

While the Revolution ensured the political triumph of the bourgeoisie in France, in England Watt, Arkwright, Cartwright, and others initiated an industrial revolution, which completely shifted the centre of gravity of economic power. The wealth of the bourgeoisie increased considerably faster than that of the landed aristocracy. Within the bourgeoisie itself, the financial aristocracy, the bankers, etc., were more and more pushed into the background by the manufacturers. The compromise of 1689, even after the gradual changes it had undergone in favour of the bourgeoisie, no longer corresponded to the relative position of the parties to it. The character of these parties, too, had changed; the bourgeoisie of 1830 was very different from that of the preceding century. The political power still left to the aristocracy, and used by them to resist the pretensions of the new industrial bourgeoisie, became incompatible with the new economic interests. A fresh struggle with the aristocracy was necessary; it could end only in a victory of the new economic power. First, the Reform Act[15] was pushed through, in spite of all resistance, under the impulse of the French Revolution of 1830. It gave to the bourgeoisie a recognised and powerful place in Parliament. Then the repeal of the Corn Laws, which settled, once for all, the supremacy of the bourgeoisie, and especially of its most active portion, the manufacturers, over the landed aristocracy. This was the greatest victory of the bourgeoisie; it was, however, also the last it gained in its own exclusive interest. Whatever triumphs it obtained later on, it had to share with a new social power, first its ally, but soon its rival.

The industrial revolution had created a class of large manufacturing capitalists, but also a class—and a far more numerous one—of manufacturing workpeople. This class gradually increased in numbers, in proportion as the industrial revolution seized upon one branch of manufacture after another, and in the same proportion it increased in power. This power it proved as early as 1824, by forcing a reluctant Parliament to repeal the acts forbidding combinations of workmen.[314] During the Reform agitation, the working men constituted the Radical wing of the Reform party; the Act of 1832 having excluded them from the suffrage, they formulated their demands in the People's Charter, and constituted themselves, in opposition to the great bourgeois Anti-Corn Law party,[315] into an independent party, the Chartists,[22] the first working men's party of modern times.

Then came the Continental revolutions of February and March 1848, in which the working people played such a prominent part, and, at least in Paris, put forward demands which were certainly inadmissible from the point of view of capitalist society. And then came the general reaction. First the defeat of the Chartists on the 10th April, 1848,[316] then the crushing of the Paris working men's insurrection in June of the same year,[6] then the disasters of 1849 in Italy, Hungary, South Germany, and at last the victory of Louis Bonaparte over Paris, 2nd December, 1851.[40] For a time, at least, the bugbear of working-class pretensions was put down, but at what cost! If the British bourgeois had been convinced before of the necessity of maintaining the common people in a religious mood, how much more must he feel that necessity after all these experiences? Regardless of the sneers of his Continental compeers, he continued to spend thousands and tens of thousands, year after year, upon the evangelisation of the lower orders; not content with his own native religious machinery, he appealed to Brother Jonathan, the greatest organiser in existence of religion as a trade, and imported from America revivalism, Moody and Sankey, and the like[317]; and, finally, he accepted the dangerous aid of the Salvation Army, which revives the propaganda of early Christianity, appeals to the poor as the elect, fights capitalism in a religious way, and thus fosters an element of early Christian class antagonism, which one day may become troublesome to the well-to-do people who now find the ready money for it.

It seems a law of historical development that the bourgeoisie can in no European country get hold of political power—at least for any length of time—in the same exclusive way in which the feudal aristocracy kept hold of it during the Middle Ages. Even in France, where feudalism was completely extinguished, the bourgeoisie, as a whole, has held full possession of the Government for very short periods only. During Louis Philippe's reign, 1830-48, a very small

portion of the bourgeoisie ruled the kingdom; by far the larger par
were excluded from the suffrage by the high qualification. Under
the Second Republic, 1848-51, the whole bourgeoisie ruled, but for
three years only; their incapacity brought on the Second Empire. It
is only now, in the Third Republic, that the bourgeoisie as a whole
have kept possession of the helm for more than twenty years; and
they are already showing lively signs of decadence. A durable reign
of the bourgeoisie has been possible only in countries like America
where feudalism was unknown, and society at the very beginning
started from a bourgeois basis. And even in France and America
the successors of the bourgeoisie, the working people, are already
knocking at the door.

In England, the bourgeoisie never held undivided sway. Even the
victory of 1832[15] left the landed aristocracy in almost exclusive possession of all the leading Government offices. The meekness with
which the wealthy middle class submitted to this remained inconceivable to me until the great Liberal manufacturer, Mr. W. A. Forster, in a public speech implored the young men of Bradford to learn
French, as a means to get on in the world, and quoted from his own
experience how sheepish he looked when, as a Cabinet Minister, he
had to move in society where French was, at least, as necessary as
English! The fact was, the English middle class of that time were, as
a rule, quite uneducated upstarts, and could not help leaving to the
aristocracy those superior Government places where other qualifications were required than mere insular narrowness and insular conceit, seasoned by business sharpness.* Even now the endless newspaper debates about middle-class education show that the English
middle class does not yet consider itself good enough for the best education, and looks to something more modest. Thus, even after the
repeal of the Corn Laws, it appeared a matter of course that the men

---

* And even in business matters, the conceit of national chauvinism is but a
sorry adviser. Up to quite recently, the average English manufacturer considered
it derogatory for an Englishman to speak any language but his own, and felt
rather proud than otherwise of the fact that "poor devils" of foreigners settled in
England and took off his hands the trouble of disposing of his products abroad.
He never noticed that these foreigners, mostly Germans, thus got command of
a very large part of British foreign trade, imports and exports, and that the
direct foreign trade of Englishmen became limited, almost entirely, to the colonies, China, the United States and South America. Nor did he notice that these
Germans traded with other Germans abroad, who gradually organised a complete network of commercial colonies all over the world. But when Germany, about
forty years ago, seriously began manufacturing for export, this network served
her admirably in her transformation, in so short a time, from a corn-exporting
into a first-rate manufacturing country. Then, about ten years ago, the British
manufacturer got frightened, and asked his ambassadors and consuls how it was
that he could no longer keep his customers together. The unanimous answer was:
(1) You don't learn your customer's language but expect him to speak your own;
(2) You don't even try to suit your customer's wants, habits, and tastes, but expect
him to conform to your English ones. [Note by Engels.]

·ho had carried the day, the Cobdens, Brights, Forsters, etc., should ·emain excluded from a share in the official government of the coun-·y, until twenty years afterwards a new Reform Act[318] opened to ·hem the door of the Cabinet. The English bourgeoisie are, up to the ·resent day, so deeply penetrated by a sense of their social inferi-·rity that they keep up, at their own expense and that of the nation, ·n ornamental caste of drones to represent the nation worthily at all ·tate functions; and they consider themselves highly honoured when-·ver one of themselves is found worthy of admission into this select ·nd privileged body, manufactured, after all, by themselves.

The industrial and commercial middle class had, therefore, not ·et succeeded in driving the landed aristocracy completely from poli-·ical power when another competitor, the working class, appeared ·n the stage. The reaction after the Chartist movement and the Con-·inental revolutions, as well as the unparalleled extension of English ·trade from 1848 to 1866 (ascribed vulgarly to Free Trade alone, but due far more to the colossal development of railways, ocean steamers and means of intercourse generally), had again driven the working class into the dependency of the Liberal Party, of which they formed, as in pre-Chartist times, the Radical wing. Their claims to the fran-chise, however, gradually became irresistible; while the Whig[319] leaders of the Liberals "funked," Disraeli showed his superiority by making the Tories[81] seize the favourable moment and introduce household suffrage in the boroughs, along with a redistribution of seats. Then followed the ballot; then in 1884 the extension of household suffrage to the counties and a fresh redistribution of seats, by which electoral districts were to some extent equalised. All these measures considerably increased the electoral power of the working class, so much so that in at least 150 to 200 constituencies that class now furnishes the majority of voters. But parliamentary govern-ment is a capital school for teaching respect for tradition; if the middle class look with awe and veneration upon what Lord John Manners playfully called "our old nobility," the mass of the working people then looked up with respect and deference to what used to be designated as "their betters," the middle class. Indeed, the British workman, some fifteen years ago, was the model work-man, whose respectful regard for the position of his master, and whose self-restraining modesty in claiming rights for himself, consoled our German economists of the *Katheder-Socialist*[320] school for the incurable communistic and revolutionary tendencies of their own working-men at home.

But the English middle class—good men of business as they are—saw farther than the German professors. They had shared their power but reluctantly with the working class. They had learnt, during the Chartist years, what that *puer robustus sed malitiosus*, the people, is capable of. And since that time, they had

been compelled to incorporate the better part of the People'
Charter in the Statutes of the United Kingdom. Now, if ever
the people must be kept in order by moral means, and the first and
foremost of all moral means of action upon the masses is and
remains—religion. Hence the parsons' majorities on the school
boards, hence the increasing self-taxation of the bourgeoisie for the
support of all sorts of revivalism, from ritualism[321] to the Salvation
Army.

And now came the triumph of British respectability over the
free thought and religious laxity of the Continental bourgeois.
The workmen of France and Germany had become rebellious.
They were thoroughly infected with socialism, and, for very good
reasons, were not at all particular as to the legality of the means
by which to secure their own ascendency. The *puer robustus*, here
turned from day to day more *malitiosus*. Nothing remained to
the French and German bourgeoisie as a last resource but to
silently drop their free thought, as a youngster, when sea-sickness
creeps upon him, quietly drops the burning cigar he brought
swaggeringly on board; one by one, the scoffers turned pious in
outward behaviour, spoke with respect of the Church, its dogmas
and rites, and even conformed with the latter as far as could
not be helped. French bourgeois dined *maigre* on Fridays, and
German ones sat out long Protestant sermons in their pews on
Sundays. They had come to grief with materialism. *"Die Religion
muss dem Volk erhalten werden,"*—religion must be kept alive
for the people—that was the only and the last means to save
society from utter ruin. Unfortunately for themselves, they did not
find this out until they had done their level best to break up
religion for ever. And now it was the turn of the British bourgeois to sneer and to say: "Why, you fools, I could have told you
that two hundred years ago!"

However, I am afraid neither the religious stolidity of the
British, nor the *post festum* conversion of the Continental bourgeois will stem the rising proletarian tide. Tradition is a great
retarding force, is the *vis inertiae* of history, but, being merely
passive, is sure to be broken down; and thus religion will be no
lasting safeguard to capitalist society. If our juridical, philosophical, and religious ideas are the more or less remote offshoots of
the economical relations prevailing in a given society, such ideas
cannot, in the long run, withstand the effects of a complete change
in these relations. And, unless we believe in supernatural revelation, we must admit that no religious tenets will ever suffice to prop
up a tottering society.

In fact, in England too, the working people have begun to move
again. They are, no doubt, shackled by traditions of various kinds.
Bourgeois traditions, such as the widespread belief that there

can be but two parties, Conservatives and Liberals, and that the working class must work out its salvation by and through the great Liberal Party. Working-men's traditions, inherited from their first tentative efforts at independent action, such as the exclusion, from ever so many old Trade Unions, of all applicants who have not gone through a regular apprenticeship; which means the breeding, by every such union, of its own blacklegs. But for all that the English working class is moving, as even Professor Brentano has sorrowfully had to report to his brother Katheder-Socialists. It moves, like all things in England, with a slow and measured step, with hesitation here, with more or less unfruitful, tentative attempts there; it moves now and then with an overcautious mistrust of the name of socialism, while it gradually absorbs the substance; and the movement spreads and seizes one layer of the workers after another. It has now shaken out of their torpor the unskilled labourers of the East End[322] of London, and we all know what a splendid impulse these fresh forces have given it in return. And if the pace of the movement is not up to the impatience of some people, let them not forget that it is the working class which keeps alive the finest qualities of the English character, and that, if a step in advance is once gained in England, it is, as a rule, never lost afterwards. If the sons of the old Chartists, for reasons explained above, were not quite up to the mark, the grandsons bid fair to be worthy of their forefathers.

But the triumph of the European working class does not depend upon England alone. It can only be secured by the co-operation of, at least, England, France, and Germany.[323] In both the latter countries the working-class movement is well ahead of England. In Germany it is even within measurable distance of success. The progress it has there made during the last twenty-five years is unparalleled. It advances with ever-increasing velocity. If the German middle class have shown themselves lamentably deficient in political capacity, discipline, courage, energy, and perseverance, the German working class have given ample proof of all these qualities. Four hundred years ago, Germany was the starting-point of the first upheaval of the European middle class; as things are now, is it outside the limits of possibility that Germany will be the scene, too, of the first great victory of the European proletariat?

F. Engels

April 20th, 1892

Published in the book: Frederick Engels, *Socialism: Utopian and Scientific*, London, 1892, and authorised abridged German translation in the journal *Die Neue Zeit*, Bd. 1, Nos. 1 and 2, 1892-93

Printed according to the text of the book
Written in English

SOCIALISM: UTOPIAN AND SCIENTIFIC[292]

I

Modern socialism is, in its essence, the direct product of the recognition, on the one hand, of the class antagonisms existing in the society of today between proprietors and non-proprietors, between capitalists and wage-workers; on the other hand, of the anarchy existing in production. But, in its theoretical form, modern socialism originally appears ostensibly as a more logical extension of the principles laid down by the great French philosophers of the eighteenth century. Like every new theory, modern socialism had, at first, to connect itself with the intellectual stock-in-trade ready to its hand, however deeply its roots lay in material economic facts.

The great men, who in France prepared men's minds for the coming revolution, were themselves extreme revolutionists. They recognised no external authority of any kind whatever. Religion, natural science, society, political institutions—everything was subjected to the most unsparing criticism: everything must justify its existence before the judgement-seat of reason or give up existence. Reason became the sole measure of everything. It was the time when, as Hegel says, the world stood upon its head*; first in the sense that the human head, and the principles arrived at by its thought, claimed to be the basis of all human action and association; but by and by, also, in the wider sense that the

---

* This is a passage on the French Revolution: "Thought, the concept of law, all at once made itself felt, and against this the old scaffolding of wrong could make no stand. In this conception of law, therefore, a constitution has now been established, and henceforth everything must be based upon this. Since the sun had been in the firmament, and the planets circled round him, the sight had never been seen of man standing upon his head—i.e., on the Idea—and building reality after this image. Anaxagoras first said that the Nous, reason, rules the world; but now, for the first time, had man come to recognise that the Idea must rule the mental reality. And this was a magnificent sunrise. All thinking beings have participated in celebrating this holy day. A sublime emotion swayed men at that time, an enthusiasm of reason pervaded the world, as if now had come the reconciliation of the Divine Principle with the world." [Hegel: *Philosophy of History*, 1840, p. 535.] Is it not high time to set the anti-Socialist law[168] in action against such teachings, subversive and to the common danger, by the late Professor Hegel? [*Note by Engels.*]

reality which was in contradiction to these principles had, in fact, to be turned upside down. Every form of society and government then existing, every old traditional notion was flung into the lumber-room as irrational; the world had hitherto allowed itself to be led solely by prejudices; everything in the past deserved only pity and contempt. Now, for the first time, appeared the light of day, the kingdom of reason; henceforth superstition, injustice, privilege, oppression, were to be superseded by eternal truth, eternal Right, equality based on Nature and the inalienable rights of man.

We know today that this kingdom of reason was nothing more than the idealised kingdom of the bourgeoisie; that this eternal Right found its realisation in bourgeois justice; that this equality reduced itself to bourgeois equality before the law; that bourgeois property was proclaimed as one of the essential rights of man; and that the government of reason, the Contrat Social of Rousseau,[324] came into being, and only could come into being, as a democratic bourgeois republic. The great thinkers of the eighteenth century could, no more than their predecessors, go beyond the limits imposed upon them by their epoch.

But, side by side with the antagonism of the feudal nobility and the burghers, who claimed to represent all the rest of society, was the general antagonism of exploiters and exploited, of rich idlers and poor workers. It was this very circumstance that made it possible for the representatives of the bourgeoisie to put themselves forward as representing not one special class, but the whole of suffering humanity. Still further. From its origin the bourgeoisie was saddled with its antithesis: capitalists cannot exist without wage-workers, and, in the same proportion as the mediaeval burgher of the guild developed into the modern bourgeois, the guild journeyman and the day-labourer, outside the guilds, developed into the proletarian. And although, upon the whole, the bourgeoisie, in their struggle with the nobility, could claim to represent at the same time the interests of the different working classes of that period, yet in every great bourgeois movement there were independent outbursts of that class which was the forerunner, more or less developed, of the modern proletariat. For example, at the time of the German Reformation and the Peasants' War, the Anabaptists[325] and Thomas Münzer; in the great English Revolution, the Levellers;[326] in the great French Revolution, Babeuf.

There were theoretical enunciations corresponding with these revolutionary uprisings of a class not yet developed; in the sixteenth and seventeenth centuries, Utopian pictures of ideal social conditions[327]; in the eighteenth, actual communistic theories (Morelly and Mably). The demand for equality was no longer limit-

ed to political rights; it was extended also to the social conditions of individuals. It was not simply class privileges that wer
to be abolished, but class distinctions themselves. A communism
ascetic, denouncing all the pleasures of life, Spartan, was th
first form of the new teaching. Then came the three great Utopians: Saint-Simon, to whom the middle-class movement, side b-
side with the proletarian, still had a certain significance; Fourier
and Owen, who in the country where capitalist production was mos
developed, and under the influence of the antagonisms begotten o
this, worked out his proposals for the removal of class distinctior
systematically and in direct relation to French materialism.

One thing is common to all three. Not one of them appears a
a representative of the interests of that proletariat which his
torical development had, in the meantime, produced. Like th-
French philosophers, they do not claim to emancipate a partic
ular class to begin with, but all humanity at once. Like them, the-
wish to bring in the kingdom of reason and eternal justice, bu
this kingdom, as they see it, is as far as heaven from earth, fron
that of the French philosophers.

For, to our three social reformers, the bourgeois world, based
upon the principles of these philosophers, is quite as irrational
and unjust, and, therefore, finds its way to the dust-hole quit
as readily as feudalism and all the earlier stages of society. I
pure reason and justice have not, hitherto, ruled the world, thi
has been the case only because men have not rightly understood
them. What was wanted was the individual man of genius, who
has now arisen and who understands the truth. That he has now
arisen, that the truth has now been clearly understood, is not
an inevitable event, following of necessity in the chain of historical development, but a mere happy accident. He might just as
well have been born 500 years earlier, and might then have spared
humanity 500 years of error, strife, and suffering.

We saw how the French philosophers of the eighteenth century,
the forerunners of the Revolution, appealed to reason as the sole
judge of all that is. A rational government, rational society, were
to be founded; everything that ran counter to eternal reason was
to be remorselessly done away with. We saw also that this eternal
reason was in reality nothing but the idealised understanding of
the eighteenth century citizen, just then evolving into the bourgeois.
The French Revolution had realised this rational society and
government.

But the new order of things, rational enough as compared with
earlier conditions, turned out to be by no means absolutely rational.
The state based upon reason completely collapsed. Rousseau's
Contrat Social had found its realisation in the Reign of Terror,[313]
from which the bourgeoisie, who had lost confidence in their

own political capacity, had taken refuge first in the corruption of the Directorate,[328] and, finally, under the wing of the Napoleonic despotism. The promised eternal peace was turned into an endless war of conquest. The society based upon reason had fared no better. The antagonism between rich and poor, instead of dissolving into general prosperity, had become intensified by the removal of the guild and other privileges, which had to some extent bridged it over, and by the removal of the charitable institutions of the Church. The "freedom of property" from feudal fetters, now veritably accomplished, turned out to be, for the small capitalists and small proprietors, the freedom to sell their small property, crushed under the overmastering competition of the large capitalists and landlords, to these great lords, and thus, as far as the small capitalists and peasant proprietors were concerned, became "freedom *from* property." The development of industry upon a capitalistic basis made poverty and misery of the working masses conditions of existence of society. Cash payment became more and more, in Carlyle's phrase, the sole nexus between man and man. The number of crimes increased from year to year. Formerly, the feudal vices had openly stalked about in broad daylight; though not eradicated, they were now at any rate thrust into the background. In their stead, the bourgeois vices, hitherto practised in secret, began to blossom all the more luxuriantly. Trade became to a greater and greater extent cheating. The "fraternity" of the revolutionary motto[329] was realised in the chicanery and rivalries of the battle of competition. Oppression by force was replaced by corruption; the sword, as the first social lever, by gold. The right of the first night was transferred from the feudal lords to the bourgeois manufacturers. Prostitution increased to an extent never heard of. Marriage itself remained, as before, the legally recognised form, the official cloak of prostitution, and, moreover, was supplemented by rich crops of adultery.

In a word, compared with the splendid promises of the philosophers, the social and political institutions born of the "triumph of reason" were bitterly disappointing caricatures. All that was wanting was the men to formulate this disappointment, and they came with the turn of the century. In 1802 Saint-Simon's Geneva letters appeared; in 1808 appeared Fourier's first work, although the groundwork of his theory dated from 1799; on January 1, 1800, Robert Owen undertook the direction of New Lanark.[330]

At this time, however, the capitalist mode of production, and with it the antagonism between the bourgeoisie and the proletariat, was still very incompletely developed. Modern industry, which had just arisen in England, was still unknown in France. But modern industry develops, on the one hand, the conflicts which make absolutely necessary a revolution in the mode of production, and the doing away with its capitalistic character—conflict not only between the classes begotten of it, but also between the very productive forces and the forms of exchange created by it. And, on the other hand, it develops, in these very gigantic productive forces, the means of ending these conflicts. If, therefore about the year 1800, the conflicts arising from the new social order were only just beginning to take shape, this holds still more fully as to the means of ending them. The "have-nothing" masses of Paris, during the Reign of Terror, were able for a moment to gain the mastery, and thus to lead the bourgeois revolution to victory in spite of the bourgeoisie themselves. But, in doing so, they only proved how impossible it was for their domination to last under the conditions then obtaining. The proletariat, which then for the first ·time evolved itself from these "have-nothing" masses as the nucleus of a new class, as yet quite incapable of independent political action, appeared as an oppressed, suffering order, to whom, in its incapacity to help itself, help could, at best, be brought in from without or down from above.

This historical situation also dominated the founders of socialism. To the crude conditions of capitalistic production and the crude class conditions corresponded crude theories. The solution of the social problems, which as yet lay hidden in undeveloped economic conditions, the Utopians attempted to evolve out of the human brain. Society presented nothing but wrongs; to remove these was the task of reason. It was necessary, then, to discover a new and more perfect system of social order and to impose this upon society from without by propaganda, and, wherever it was possible, by the example of model experiments. These new social systems were foredoomed as Utopian; the more completely they were worked out in detail, the more they could not avoid drifting off into pure phantasies.

These facts once established, we need not dwell a moment longer upon this side of the question, now wholly belonging to the past. We can leave it to the literary small fry to solemnly quibble over these phantasies, which today only make us smile, and to crow over the superiority of their own bald reasoning, as compared with such "insanity." For ourselves, we delight in the stupendously grand thoughts and germs of thought that everywhere break out through their phantastic covering, and to which these Philistines are blind.

Saint-Simon was a son of the great French Revolution, at the outbreak of which he was not yet thirty. The Revolution was the victory of the third estate,[331] i.e., of the great masses of the nation, *working* in production and in trade, over the privileged *idle* classes, the nobles and the priests. But the victory of the third estate soon revealed itself as exclusively the victory of a small part of this "estate," as the conquest of political power by the socially privileged section of it, i.e., the propertied bourgeoisie. And the bourgeoisie

had certainly developed rapidly during the Revolution, partly by
speculation in the lands of the nobility and of the Church,
confiscated and afterwards put up for sale, and partly by frauds
upon the nation by means of army contracts. It was the domination
of these swindlers that, under the Directorate, brought France to the
verge of ruin, and thus gave Napoleon the pretext for his *coup
d'état.*

Hence, to Saint-Simon the antagonism between the third estate
and the privileged classes took the form of an antagonism between
"workers" and "idlers." The idlers were not merely the old
privileged classes, but also all who, without taking any part in
production or distribution, lived on their incomes. And the workers
were not only the wage-workers, but also the manufacturers, the
merchants, the bankers. That the idlers had lost the capacity for
intellectual leadership and political supremacy had been proved,
and was by the Revolution finally settled. That the non-possessing
classes had not this capacity seemed to Saint-Simon proved by the
experiences of the Reign of Terror. Then, who was to lead and
command? According to Saint-Simon, science and industry, both
united by a new religious bond, destined to restore that unity of
religious ideas which had been lost since the time of the Reformation—a necessarily mystic and rigidly hierarchic "new Christianity."
But science, that was the scholars; and industry, that was, in the
first place, the working bourgeois, manufacturers, merchants, bankers.
These bourgeois were, certainly, intended by Saint-Simon to transform themselves into a kind of public officials, of social trustees;
but they were still to hold, *vis-à-vis* of the workers, a commanding
and economically privileged position. The bankers especially were
to be called upon to direct the whole of social production by the
regulation of credit. This conception was in exact keeping with a
time in which modern industry in France and, with it, the chasm
between bourgeoisie and proletariat was only just coming into
existence. But what Saint-Simon especially lays stress upon is this:
what interests him first, and above all other things, is the lot of the
class that is the most numerous and the most poor (*"la classe la plus
nombreuse et la plus pauvre"*).

Already in his Geneva letters, Saint-Simon lays down the proposition that

"all men ought to work."

In the same work he recognises also that the Reign of Terror was
the reign of the non-possessing masses.

"See," says he to them, "what happened in France at the time when your
comrades held sway there: they brought about a famine."

But to recognise the French Revolution as a class war, and not
simply one between nobility and bourgeoisie, but between nobility,

bourgeoisie, and the non-possessors, was, in the year 1802, a most pregnant discovery. In 1816, he declares that politics is the science of production, and foretells the complete absorption of politics by economics. The knowledge that economic conditions are the basis of political institutions appears here only in embryo. Yet what is here already very plainly expressed is the idea of the future conversion of political rule over men into an administration of things and a direction of processes of production—that is to say, the "abolition of the state," about which recently there has been so much noise.

Saint-Simon shows the same superiority over his contemporaries, when in 1814, immediately after the entry of the allies into Paris,* and again in 1815, during the Hundred Days' War,[332] he proclaims the alliance of France with England, and then of both these countries with Germany, as the only guarantee for the prosperous development and peace of Europe. To preach to the French in 1815 an alliance with the victors of Waterloo[333] required as much courage as historical foresight.

If in Saint-Simon we find a comprehensive breadth of view, by virtue of which almost all the ideas of later Socialists that are not strictly economic are found in him in embryo, we find in Fourier a criticism of the existing conditions of society, genuinely French and witty, but not upon that account any the less thorough. Fourier takes the bourgeoisie, their inspired prophets before the Revolution, and their interested eulogists after it, at their own word. He lays bare remorselessly the material and moral misery of the bourgeois world. He confronts it with the earlier philosophers' dazzling promises of a society in which reason alone should reign, of a civilisation in which happiness should be universal, of an illimitable human perfectibility, and with the rose-coloured phraseology of the bourgeois ideologists of his time. He points out how everywhere the most pitiful reality corresponds with the most high-sounding phrases, and he overwhelms this hopeless fiasco of phrases with his mordant sarcasm.

Fourier is not only a critic; his imperturbably serene nature makes him a satirist, and assuredly one of the greatest satirists of all time. He depicts, with equal power and charm, the swindling speculations that blossomed out upon the downfall of the Revolution, and the shopkeeping spirit prevalent in, and characteristic of, French commerce at that time. Still more masterly is his criticism of the bourgeois form of the relations between the sexes, and the position of woman in bourgeois society. He was the first to declare that in any given society the degree of woman's emancipation is the natural measure of the general emancipation.

---

* On March 31, 1814.—Ed.

But Fourier is at his greatest in his conception of the history of society. He divides its whole course, thus far, into four stages of evolution—savagery, barbarism, the patriarchate, civilisation. This last is identical with the so-called civil, or bourgeois, society of today—*i.e.*, with the social order that came in with the sixteenth century. He proves

"that the civilised stage raises every vice practised by barbarism in a simple fashion into a form of existence, complex, ambiguous, equivocal, hypocritical"—

that civilisation moves in "a vicious circle," in contradictions which it constantly reproduces without being able to solve them; hence it constantly arrives at the very opposite to that which it wants to attain, or pretends to want to attain, so that, e.g.,

"under civilisation poverty is born of super-abundance itself."

Fourier, as we see, uses the dialectic method in the same masterly way as his contemporary, Hegel. Using these same dialectics, he argues against the talk about illimitable human perfectibility, that every historical phase has its period of ascent and also its period of descent, and he applies this observation to the future of the whole human race. As Kant introduced into natural science the idea of the ultimate destruction of the earth, Fourier introduced into historical science that of the ultimate destruction of the human race.

Whilst in France the hurricane of the Revolution swept over the land, in England a quieter, but not on that account less tremendous, revolution was going on. Steam and the new toolmaking machinery were transforming manufacture into modern industry, and thus revolutionising the whole foundation of bourgeois society. The sluggish march of development of the manufacturing period changed into a veritable storm and stress period of production. With constantly increasing swiftness the splitting-up of society into large capitalists and non-possessing proletarians went on. Between these, instead of the former stable middle class, an unstable mass of artisans and small shopkeepers, the most fluctuating portion of the population, now led a precarious existence.

The new mode of production was, as yet, only at the beginning of its period of ascent; as yet it was the normal, regular method of production—the only one possible under existing conditions. Nevertheless, even then it was producing crying social abuses—the herding together of a homeless population in the worst quarters of the large towns; the loosening of all traditional moral bonds, of patriarchal subordination, of family relations; overwork, especially of women and children, to a frightful extent; complete demoralisation of the working class, suddenly flung into altogether new conditions, from the country into the town, from agriculture into modern industry, from stable conditions of existence into insecure ones that changed from day to day.

At this juncture there came forward as a reformer a manufacturer 29 years old—a man of almost sublime, childlike simplicity of character, and at the same time one of the few born leaders of men. Robert Owen had adopted the teaching of the materialistic philosophers: that man's character is the product, on the one hand, of heredity; on the other, of the environment of the individual during his lifetime, and especially during his period of development. In the industrial revolution most of his class saw only chaos and confusion, and the opportunity of fishing in these troubled waters and making large fortunes quickly. He saw in it the opportunity of putting into practice his favourite theory, and so of bringing order out of chaos. He had already tried it with success, as superintendent of more than five hundred men in a Manchester factory. From 1800 to 1829, he directed the great cotton mill at New Lanark, in Scotland, as managing partner, along the same lines, but with greater freedom of action and with a success that made him a European reputation. A population, originally consisting of the most diverse and, for the most part, very demoralised elements, a population that gradually grew to 2,500, he turned into a model colony, in which drunkenness, police, magistrates, lawsuits, poor laws, charity, were unknown. And all this simply by placing the people in conditions worthy of human beings, and especially by carefully bringing up the rising generation. He was the founder of infant schools, and introduced them first at New Lanark. At the age of two the children came to school, where they enjoyed themselves so much that they could scarcely be got home again. Whilst his competitors worked their people thirteen or fourteen hours a day, in New Lanark the working-day was only ten and a half hours. When a crisis in cotton stopped work for four months, his workers received their full wages all the time. And with all this the business more than doubled in value, and to the last yielded large profits to its proprietors.

In spite of all this, Owen was not content. The existence which he secured for his workers was, in his eyes, still far from being worthy of human beings.

"The people were slaves at my mercy."

The relatively favourable conditions in which he had placed them were still far from allowing a rational development of the character and of the intellect in all directions, much less of the free exercise of all their faculties.

"And yet, the working part of this population of 2,500 persons was daily producing as much real wealth for society as less than half a century before, it would have required the working part of a population of 600,000 to create. I asked myself, what became of the difference between the wealth consumed by 2,500 persons and that which would have been consumed by 600,000?"*

The answer was clear. It had been used to pay the proprietors of the establishment 5 per cent on the capital they had laid out, in addition to over £300,000 clear profit. And that which held for New Lanark held to a still greater extent for all the factories in England.

"If this new wealth had not been created by machinery, imperfectly as it has been applied, the wars of Europe, in opposition to Napoleon, and to support the aristocratic principles of society, could not have been maintained. And yet this new power was the creation of the working class."**

To them, therefore, the fruits of this new power belonged. The newly-created gigantic productive forces, hitherto used only to enrich individuals and to enslave the masses, offered to Owen the foundations for a reconstruction of society; they were destined, as the common property of all, to be worked for the common good of all. Owen's communism was based upon this purely business foundation, the outcome, so to say, of commercial calculation. Throughout, it maintained this practical character. Thus, in 1823, Owen proposed the relief of the distress in Ireland by communist colonies, and drew up complete estimates of costs of founding them, yearly expenditure, and probable revenue. And in his definite plan for the future, the technical working out of details is managed with such practical knowledge—ground plan, front and side and bird's-eye views all included—that the Owen method of social reform once accepted, there is from the practical point of view little to be said against the actual arrangement of details.

His advance in the direction of communism was the turning-point in Owen's life. As long as he was simply a philanthropist, he was rewarded with nothing but wealth, applause, honour, and glory. He was the most popular man in Europe. Not only men of his own class, but statesmen and princes listened to him approvingly. But when he came out with his communist theories that was quite another thing. Three great obstacles seemed to him especially to block the path to social reform: private property, religion, the present form of marriage. He knew what confronted him if he attacked these—outlawry, excommunication from official society, the loss of his whole social position. But nothing of this prevented him from attacking them without fear of consequences, and what he had foreseen happened. Banished from official society, with a conspiracy of silence against him in the press, ruined by his unsuccessful

* From "The Revolution in Mind and Practice," p. 21, a memorial addressed to all the "red Republicans, Communists and Socialists of Europe," and sent to the provisional government of France, 1848, and also "to Queen Victoria and her responsible advisers." [Note by Engels.]
** Note, l.c., p. 22. [Note by Engels.]

communist experiments in America, in which he sacrificed all his fortune, he turned directly to the working class and continued working in their midst for thirty years. Every social movement, every real advance in England on behalf of the workers links itself on to the name of Robert Owen. He forced through in 1819, after five years' fighting, the first law limiting the hours of labour of women and children in factories. He was president of the first Congress at which all the Trade Unions of England united in a single great trade association.[334] He introduced as transition measures to the complete communistic organisation of society, on the one hand, co-operative societies for retail trade and production. These have since that time, at least, given practical proof that the merchant and the manufacturer are socially quite unnecessary. On the other hand, he introduced labour bazaars for the exchange of the products of labour through the medium of labour-notes, whose unit was a single hour of work[335]; institutions necessarily doomed to failure, but completely anticipating Proudhon's bank of exchange[336] of a much later period, and differing entirely from this in that it did not claim to be the panacea for all social ills, but only a first step towards a much more radical revolution of society.

The Utopians' mode of thought has for a long time governed the socialist ideas of the nineteenth century, and still governs some of them. Until very recently all French and English Socialists did homage to it. The earlier German communism, including that of Weitling, was of the same school. To all these socialism is the expression of absolute truth, reason and justice, and has only to be discovered to conquer all the world by virtue of its own power. And as absolute truth is independent of time, space, and of the historical development of man, it is a mere accident when and where it is discovered. With all this, absolute truth, reason, and justice are different with the founder of each different school. And as each one's special kind of absolute truth, reason, and justice is again conditioned by his subjective understanding, his conditions of existence, the measure of his knowledge and his intellectual training, there is no other ending possible in this conflict of absolute truths than that they shall be mutually exclusive one of the other. Hence, from this nothing could come but a kind of eclectic, average socialism, which, as a matter of fact, has up to the present time dominated the minds of most of the socialist workers in France and England. Hence, a mish-mash allowing of the most manifold shades of opinion; a mish-mach of such critical statements, economic theories, pictures of future society by the founders of different sects, as excite a minimum of opposition; a mish-mash which is the more easily brewed the more the definite sharp edges of the individual constituents are rubbed down in the stream of debate, like rounded pebbles in a brook.

To make a science of socialism, it had first to be placed upon a real basis.

II

In the meantime, along with and after the French philosophy of the eighteenth century had arisen the new German philosophy, culminating in Hegel. Its greatest merit was the taking up again of dialectics as the highest form of reasoning. The old Greek philosophers were all born natural dialecticians, and Aristotle, the most encyclopaedic intellect of them, had already analysed the most essential forms of dialectic thought. The newer philosophy, on the other hand, although in it also dialectics had brilliant exponents (e.g., Descartes and Spinoza), had especially through English influence, become more and more rigidly fixed in the so-called metaphysical mode of reasoning, by which also the French of the eighteenth century were almost wholly dominated, at all events in their special philosophical work. Outside philosophy in the restricted sense, the French nevertheless produced masterpieces of dialectics. We need only call to mind Diderot's *Le Neveu de Rameau* and Rousseau's *Discours sur l'origine et les fondements de l'inégalité parmi les hommes.* We give here, in brief, the essential character of these two modes of thought.

When we consider and reflect upon Nature at large or the history of mankind or our own intellectual activity, at first we see the picture of an endless entanglement of relations and reactions, permutations and combinations, in which nothing remains what, where and as it was, but everything moves, changes, comes into being and passes away. We see, therefore, at first the picture as a whole, with its individual parts still more or less kept in the background; we observe the movements, transitions, connections, rather than the things that move, combine and are connected. This primitive, naïve but intrinsically correct conception of the world is that of ancient Greek philosophy, and was first clearly formulated by Heraclitus: everything is and is not, for everything is fluid, is constantly changing, constantly coming into being and passing away.

But this conception, correctly as it expresses the general character of the picture of appearances as a whole, does not suffice to explain the details of which this picture is made up, and so long as we do not understand these, we have not a clear idea of the whole picture. In order to understand these details we must detach them from their natural or historical connection and examine each one separately, its nature, special causes, effects, etc. This is, primarily the task of natural science and historical research: branches of science which the Greeks of classical times, on very good grounds, relegated to a subordinate position, because they had first of all to collect materials for these sciences to work upon. A certain amount of natural and historical material must be collected before there can be any critical analysis, comparison, and arrangement in classes, orders, and species. The foundations of the exact natural sciences were, therefore, first worked out by the Greeks of the Alexandrian period,[337] and later on, in the Middle Ages, by the Arabs. Real natural science dates from the second half of the fifteenth century, and thence onward it had advanced with constantly increasing rapidity. The analysis of Nature into its individual parts, the grouping of the different natural processes and objects in definite classes, the study of the internal anatomy of organic bodies in their manifold forms—these were the fundamental conditions of the gigantic strides in our knowledge of Nature that have been made during the last four hundred years. But this method of work has also left us as legacy the habit of observing natural objects and processes in isolation, apart from their connection with the vast whole; of observing them in repose, not in motion; as constants, not as essentially variables; in their death, not in their life. And when this way of looking at things was transferred by Bacon and Locke from natural science to philosophy, it begot the narrow, metaphysical mode of thought peculiar to the last century.

To the metaphysician, things and their mental reflexes, ideas, are isolated, are to be considered one after the other and apart from each other, are objects of investigation fixed, rigid, given once for all. He thinks in absolutely irreconcilable antitheses. "His communication is 'yea, yea; nay, nay'; for whatsoever is more than these cometh of evil."* For him a thing either exists or does not exist; a thing cannot at the same time be itself and something else. Positive and negative absolutely exclude one another; cause and effect stand in a rigid antithesis one to the other.

At first sight this mode of thinking seems to us very luminous, because it is that of so-called sound common sense. Only sound common sense, respectable fellow that he is, in the homely realm of his own four walls, has very wonderful adventures directly he ventures out into the wide world of research. And the metaphysical mode of thought, justifiable and necessary as it is in a number of domains whose extent varies according to the nature of the particular object of investigation, sooner or later reaches a limit, beyond which it becomes one-sided, restricted, abstract, lost in insoluble contradictions. In the contemplation of individual things, it forgets the connection between them; in the contemplation of their existence, it forgets the beginning and end of that existence; of their repose, it forgets their motion. It cannot see the wood for the trees.

For everyday purposes we know and can say, e.g., whether an

* The Bible, Matthew, Chapter 5, Verse 37.—*Ed.*

animal is alive or not. But, upon closer inquiry, we find that this is, in many cases, a very complex question, as the jurists know very well. They have cudgelled their brains in vain to discover a rational limit beyond which the killing of the child in its mother's womb is murder. It is just as impossible to determine absolutely the moment of death, for physiology proves that death is not an instantaneous, momentary phenomenon, but a very protracted process.

In like manner, every organic being is every moment the same and not the same; every moment it assimilates matter supplied from without, and gets rid of other matter; every moment some cells of its body die and others build themselves anew; in a longer or shorter time the matter of its body is completely renewed, and is replaced by other molecules of matter, so that every organic being is always itself, and yet something other than itself.

Further, we find upon closer investigation that the two poles of an antithesis, positive and negative, e.g., are as inseparable as they are opposed, and that despite all their opposition, they mutually interpenetrate. And we find, in like manner, that cause and effect are conceptions which only hold good in their application to individual cases; but as soon as we consider the individual cases in their general connection with the universe as a whole, they run into each other, and they become confounded when we contemplate that universal action and reaction in which causes and effects are eternally changing places, so that what is effect here and now will be cause there and then, and *vice versa*.

None of these processes and modes of thought enters into the framework of metaphysical reasoning. Dialectics, on the other hand, comprehends things and their representations, ideas, in their essential connection, concatenation, motion, origin, and ending. Such processes as those mentioned above are, therefore, so many corroborations of its own method of procedure.

Nature is the proof of dialectics, and it must be said for modern science that it has furnished this proof with very rich materials increasing daily, and thus has shown that, in the last resort, Nature works dialectically and not metaphysically; that she does not move in the eternal oneness of a perpetually recurring circle, but goes through a real historical evolution. In this connection Darwin must be named before all others. He dealt the metaphysical conception of Nature the heaviest blow by his proof that all organic beings, plants, animals, and man himself, are the products of a process of evolution going on through millions of years. But the naturalists who have learned to think dialectically are few and far between, and this conflict of the results of discovery with preconceived modes of thinking explains the endless confusion now reigning in theoretical natural science the despair of teachers as well as learners, of authors and readers alike.

An exact representation of the universe, of its evolution, of the development of mankind, and of the reflection of this evolution in the minds of men, can therefore only be obtained by the methods of dialectics with its constant regard to the innumerable actions and reactions of life and death, of progressive or retrogressive changes. And in this spirit the new German philosophy has worked. Kant began his career by resolving the stable solar system of Newton and its eternal duration, after the famous initial impulse had once been given, into the result of a historic process, the formation of the sun and all the planets out of a rotating nebulous mass. From this he at the same time drew the conclusion that, given this origin of the solar system, its future death followed of necessity. His theory half a century later was established mathematically by Laplace, and half a century after that the spectroscope proved the existence in space of such incandescent masses of gas in various stages of condensation.

This new German philosophy culminated in the Hegelian system. In this system—and herein is its great merit—for the first time the whole world, natural, historical, intellectual, is represented as a process, i.e., in constant motion, change, transformation, development; and the attempt is made to trace out the internal connection that makes a continuous whole of all this movement and development. From this point of view the history of mankind no longer appeared as a wild whirl of senseless deeds of violence, all equally condemnable at the judgement-seat of mature philosophic reason and which are best forgotten as quickly as possible, but as the process of evolution of man himself. It was now the task of the intellect to follow the gradual march of this process through all its devious ways, and to trace out the inner law running through all its apparently accidental phenomena.

That the Hegelian system did not solve the problem it propounded is here immaterial. Its epoch-making merit was that it propounded the problem. This problem is one that no single individual will ever be able to solve. Although Hegel was—with Saint-Simon—the most encyclopaedic mind of his time, yet he was limited, first, by the necessarily limited extent of his own knowledge and, second, by the limited extent and depth of the knowledge and conceptions of his age. To these limits a third must be added. Hegel was an idealist. To him the thoughts within his brain were not the more or less abstract pictures of actual things and processes, but, conversely, things and their evolution were only the realised pictures of the "Idea," existing somewhere from eternity before the world was. This way of thinking turned everything upside down, and completely reversed the actual connection of things in the world. Correctly and ingeniously as many individual groups of facts were grasped by Hegel, yet, for the reasons just given, there is much that is botched, artificial, laboured, in a word, wrong in point of detail. The Hegelian system, in itself, was a colossal miscarriage—but it was also the last of its kind. It was suffering, in fact, from an internal and incurable contradiction. Upon the one hand, its essential proposition was the conception that human history is a process of evolution, which, by its very nature, cannot find its intellectual final term in the discovery of any so-called absolute truth. But, on the other hand, it laid claim to being the very essence of this absolute truth. A system of natural and historical knowledge, embracing everything, and final for all time, is a contradiction to the fundamental law of dialectic reasoning. This law, indeed, by no means excludes, but, on the contrary, includes the idea that the systematic knowledge of the external universe can make giant strides from age to age.

The perception of the fundamental contradiction in German idealism led necessarily back to materialism, but, *nota bene*, not to the simply metaphysical, exclusively mechanical materialism of the eighteenth century. Old materialism looked upon all previous history as a crude heap of irrationality and violence; modern materialism sees in it the process of evolution of humanity, and aims at discovering the laws thereof. With the French of the eighteenth century, and even with Hegel, the conception obtained of Nature as a whole, moving in narrow circles, and for ever immutable, with its eternal celestial bodies, as Newton, and unalterable organic species, as Linnaeus, taught. Modern materialism embraces the more recent discoveries of natural science, according to which Nature also has its history in time, the celestial bodies, like the organic species that, under favourable conditions, people them, being born and perishing. And even if Nature, as a whole, must still be said to move in recurrent cycles, these cycles assume infinitely larger dimensions. In both aspects, modern materialism is essentially dialectic, and no longer requires the assistance of that sort of philosophy which, queen-like, pretended to rule the remaining mob of sciences. As soon as each special science is bound to make clear its position in the great totality of things and of our knowledge of things, a special science dealing with this totality is superfluous or unnecessary. That which still survives of all earlier philosophy is the science of thought and its laws—formal logic and dialectics. Everything else is subsumed in the positive science of Nature and history.

Whilst, however, the revolution in the conception of Nature could only be made in proportion to the corresponding positive materials furnished by research, already much earlier certain historical facts had occurred which led to a decisive change in the conception of history. In 1831, the first working-class rising took place in Lyons; between 1838 and 1842, the first national working-class movement, that of the English Chartists, reached its height. The class struggle between proletariat and bourgeoisie came to the front in the history of the most advanced countries in Europe, in proportion to the development, upon the one hand, of modern industry, upon the other, of the newly-acquired political supremacy of the bourgeoisie. Facts more and more strenuously gave the lie to the teachings of bourgeois economy as to the identity of the interests of capital and labour, as to the universal harmony and universal prosperity that would be the consequence of unbridled competition. All these things could no longer be ignored, any more than the French and English socialism, which was their theoretical, though very imperfect, expression. But the old idealist conception of history, which was not yet dislodged, knew nothing of class struggles based upon economic interests, knew nothing of economic interests; production and all economic relations appeared in it only as incidental, subordinate elements in the "history of civilisation."

The new facts made imperative a new examination of all past history. Then it was seen that *all* past history, with the exception of its primitive stages, was the history of class struggles; that these warring classes of society are always the products of the modes of production and of exchange—in a word, of the *economic* conditions of their time; that the economic structure of society always furnishes the real basis, starting from which we can alone work out the ultimate explanation of the whole superstructure of juridical and political institutions as well as of the religious, philosophical, and other ideas of a given historical period. Hegel had freed history from metaphysics—he had made it dialectic; but his conception of history was essentially idealistic. But now idealism was driven from its last refuge, the philosophy of history; now a materialistic treatment of history was propounded, and a method found of explaining man's "knowing" by his "being," instead of, as heretofore, his "being" by his "knowing."

From that time forward socialism was no longer an accidental discovery of this or that ingenious brain, but the necessary outcome of the struggle between two historically developed classes—the proletariat and the bourgeoisie. Its task was no longer to manufacture a system of society as perfect as possible, but to examine the historico-economic succession of events from which these classes, and their antagonism had of necessity sprung, and to discover in the economic conditions thus created the means of ending the conflict. But the socialism of earlier days was as incompatible with this materialistic conception as the conception of Nature of the French materialists was with dialectics and modern natural science. The socialism of earlier days certainly criticised the existing capitalistic mode of producton and its consequences. But it could not explain them, and, therefore, could not get the mastery of them. It could only simply reject them as bad. The more strongly this earlier socialism denounced the exploitation of the working class, inevitable under capitalism, the less able was it clearly to show in what this exploitation consisted and how it arose. But for this it was necessary —(1) to present the capitalistic method of production in its historical connection and its inevitableness during a particular historical period, and therefore, also, to present its inevitable downfall; and (2) to lay bare its essential character, which was still a secret. This was done by the discovery of *surplus value*. It was shown that the appropriation of unpaid labour is the basis of the capitalist mode of production and of the exploitation of the worker that occurs under it; that even if the capitalist buys the labour power of his labourer at its full value as a commodity on the market, he yet extracts more value from it than he paid for; and that in the ultimate analysis this surplus value forms those sums of value from which are heaped up the constantly increasing masses of capital in the hands of the possessing classes. The genesis of capitalist production and the production of capital were both explained.

These two great discoveries, the materialistic conception of history and the revelation of the secret of capitalistic production through surplus value, we owe to Marx. With these discoveries socialism became a science. The next thing was to work out all its details and relations.

III

The materialist conception of history starts from the proposition that the production of the means to support human life and, next to production, the exchange of things produced, is the basis of all social structure; that in every society that has appeared in history, the manner in which wealth is distributed and society divided into classes or orders is dependent upon what is produced, how it is produced, and how the products are exchanged. From this point of view the final causes of all social changes and political revolutions are to be sought, not in men's brains, not in men's better insight into eternal truth and justice, but in changes in the modes of production and exchange. They are to be sought not in the *philosophy*, but in the *economics* of each particular epoch. The growing perception that existing social institutions are unreasonable and unjust, that reason has become unreason and right wrong,* is only proof that in the modes of production and exchange changes have silently taken place with which the social order, adapted to earlier economic conditions, is no longer in keeping. From this it also follows that the means of getting rid of the incongruities that have been brought to light must also be present, in a more or less developed condition, within the changed modes of production themselves. These means

---

* Mephistopheles in Goethe's *Faust*, Part I, Scene 4 (Faust's study).—*Ed.*

are not to be invented by deduction from fundamental principles, but are to be discovered in the stubborn facts of the existing system of production.

What is, then, the position of modern socialism in this connection?

The present structure of society—this is now pretty generally conceded—is the creation of the ruling class of today, of the bourgeoisie. The mode of production peculiar to the bourgeoisie, known, since Marx, as the capitalist mode of production, was incompatible with the feudal system, with the privileges it conferred upon individuals, entire social ranks and local corporations, as well as with the hereditary ties of subordination which constituted the framework of its social organisation. The bourgeoisie broke up the feudal system and built upon its ruins the capitalist order of society, the kingdom of free competition, of personal liberty, of the equality, before the law, of all commodity owners, of all the rest of the capitalist blessings. Thenceforward the capitalist mode of production could develop in freedom. Since steam, machinery, and the making of machines by machinery transformed the older manufacture into modern industry, the productive forces evolved under the guidance of the bourgeoisie developed with a rapidity and in a degree unheard of before. But just as the older manufacture, in its time, and handicraft, becoming more developed under its influence, had come into collision with the feudal trammels of the guilds, so now modern industry, in its more complete development, comes into collision with the bounds within which the capitalistic mode of production holds it confined. The new productive forces have already outgrown the capitalistic mode of using them. And this conflict between productive forces and modes of production is not a conflict engendered in the mind of man, like that between original sin and divine justice. It exists, in fact, objectively, outside us, independently of the will and actions even of the men that have brought it on. Modern socialism is nothing but the reflex, in thought, of this conflict in fact; its ideal reflection in the minds, first, of the class directly suffering under it, the working class.

Now, in what does this conflict consist?

Before capitalistic production, i.e., in the Middle Ages, the system of petty industry obtained generally, based upon the private property of the labourers in their means of production; in the country, the agriculture of the small peasant, freeman or serf; in the towns the handicrafts organised in guilds. The instruments of labour—land, agricultural implements, the workshop, the tool—were the instruments of labour of single individuals, adapted for the use of one worker, and, therefore, of necessity, small, dwarfish, circumscribed. But, for this very reason they belonged, as a rule, to the producer himself. To concentrate these scattered, limited means of production, to enlarge them, to turn them into the powerful levers of production of the present day— this was precisely the historic role of capitalist production and of its upholder, the bourgeoisie. In the fourth section of *Capital* Marx has explained in detail, how since the fifteenth century this has been historically worked out through the three phases of simple co-operation, manufacture and modern industry. But the bourgeoisie, as is also shown there, could not transform these puny means of production into mighty productive forces without transforming them, at the same time, from means of production of the individual into *social* means of production only workable by a collectivity of men. The spinning-wheel, the hand-loom, the blacksmith's hammer, were replaced by the spinning-machine, the power-loom, the steam-hammer; the individual workshop, by the factory implying the co-operation of hundreds and thousands of workmen. In like manner, production itself changed from a series of individual into a series of social acts, and the products from individual to social products. The yarn, the cloth, the metal articles that now came out of the factory, were the joint product of many workers, through whose hands they had successively to pass before they were ready. No one person could say of them: "I made that; this is *my* product."

But where, in a given society, the fundamental form of pro- duction is that spontaneous division of labour which creeps in gradually and not upon any preconceived plan, there the prod- ucts take on the form of *commodities*, whose mutual exchange, buying and selling, enable the individual producers to satisfy their manifold wants. And this was the case in the Middle Ages. The peasant, e.g., sold to the artisan agricultural products and bought from him the products of handicraft. Into this society of individual producers, of commodity producers, the new mode of production thrust itself. In the midst of the old division of labour, grown up spontaneously and upon *no definite plan*, which had governed the whole of society, now arose division of labour upon a *definite plan*, as organised in the factory; side by side with *individual* production appeared *social* production. The products of both were sold in the same market, and, therefore, at prices at least approximately equal. But organisation upon a definite plan was stronger than spontaneous division of labour. The factories working with the combined social forces of a collectivity of in- dividuals produced their commodities far more cheaply than the individual small producers. Individual production succumbed in one department after another. Socialised production revolution- ised all the old methods of production. But its revolutionary char- acter was, at the same time, so little recognised that it was, on

the contrary, introduced as a means of increasing and developing the production of commodities. When it arose, it found ready-
made, and made liberal use of, certain machinery for the production and exchange of commodities: merchants' capital, handicraft,
wage-labour. Socialised production thus introducing itself as a
new form of the production of commodities, it was a matter of
course that under it the old forms of appropriation remained in
full swing, and were applied to its products as well.

In the mediaeval stage of evolution of the production of commodities, the question as to the owner of the product of labour
could not arise. The individual producer, as a rule, had, from
raw material belonging to himself, and generally his own handi-
work, produced it with his own tools, by the labour of his own
hands or of his family. There was no need for him to appropriate
the new product. It belonged wholly to him, as a matter of course.
His property in the product was, therefore, based *upon his own
labour*. Even where external help was used, this was, as a rule,
of little importance, and very generally was compensated by
something other than wages. The apprentices and journeymen of
the guilds worked less for board and wages than for education,
in order that they might become master craftsmen themselves.

Then came the concentration of the means of production and
of the producers in large workshops and manufactories, their
transformation into actual socialised means of production and socialised producers. But the socialised producers and means of
production and their products were still treated, after this change,
just as they had been before, i.e., as the means of production and
the products of individuals. Hitherto, the owner of the instruments
of labour had himself appropriated the product, because, as a
rule, it was his own product and the assistance of others was the
exception. Now the owner of the instruments of labour always
appropriated to himself the product, although it was no longer
his product but exclusively the product of the *labour of others*.
Thus, the products now produced socially were not appropriated
by those who had actually set in motion the means of production
and actually produced the commodities, but by the *capitalists*.
The means of production, and production itself, had become in
essence socialised. But they were subjected to a form of appropriation which presupposes the private production of individuals, under which, therefore, everyone owns his own product and
brings it to market. The mode of production is subjected to this
form of appropriation, although it abolishes the conditions upon
which the latter rests.*

---

* It is hardly necessary in this connection to point out that, even if the *form*
of appropriation remains the same, the *character* of the appropriation is just as

This contradiction, which gives to the new mode of production its capitalistic character, *contains the germ of the whole of the social antagonisms of today*. The greater the mastery obtained by the new mode of production over all important fields of production and in all manufacturing countries, the more it reduced individual production to an insignificant residuum, *the more clearly was brought out the incompatibility of socialised production with capitalistic appropriation*.

The first capitalists found, as we have said, alongside of other forms of labour, wage-labour ready-made for them on the market. But it was exceptional, complementary, accessory, transitory wage-labour. The agricultural labourer, though, upon occasion, he hired himself out by the day, had a few acres of his own land on which he could at all events live at a pinch. The guilds were so organised that the journeyman of today became the master of tomorrow. But all this changed, as soon as the means of production became socialised and concentrated in the hands of capitalists. The means of production, as well as the product, of the individual producer became more and more worthless; there was nothing left for him but to turn wage-worker under the capitalist. Wage-labour, aforetime the exception and accessory, now became the rule and basis of all production; aforetime complementary, it now became the sole remaining function of the worker. The wage-worker for a time became a wage-worker for life. The number of these permanent wage-workers was further enormously increased by the breaking-up of the feudal system that occurred at the same time, by the disbanding of the retainers of the feudal lords, the eviction of the peasants from their homesteads, etc. The separation was made complete between the means of production concentrated in the hands of the capitalists, on the one side, and the producers, possessing nothing but their labour-power, on the other. *The contradiction between socialised production and capitalistic appropriation manifested itself as the antagonism of proletariat and bourgeoisie.*

We have seen that the capitalistic mode of production thrust its way into a society of commodity-producers, of individual producers, whose social bond was the exchange of their products. But every society based upon the production of commodities has this peculiarity: that the producers have lost control over their

---

much revolutionised as production is by the changes described above. It is, of course, a very different matter whether I appropriate to myself my own product or that of another. Note in passing that wage-labour, which contains the whole capitalistic mode of production in embryo, is very ancient; in a sporadic, scattered form it existed for centuries alongside of slave-labour. But the embryo could duly develop into the capitalistic mode of production only when the necessary historical preconditions had been furnished. [*Note by Engels.*]

own social interrelations. Each man produces for himself with such means of production as he may happen to have, and for such exchange as he may require to satisfy his remaining wants. No one knows how much of his particular article is coming on the market, nor how much of it will be wanted. No one knows whether his individual product will meet an actual demand, whether he will be able to make good his costs of production or even to sell his commodity at all. Anarchy reigns in socialised production.

But the production of commodities, like every other form of production, has its peculiar, inherent laws inseparable from it; and these laws work, despite anarchy, in and through anarchy. They reveal themselves in the only persistent form of social inter-relations, i.e., in exchange, and here they affect the individual producers as compulsory laws of competition. They are, at first, unknown to these producers themselves, and have to be discovered by them gradually and as the result of experience. They work themselves out, therefore, independently of the producers, and in antagonism to them, as inexorable natural laws of their particular form of production. The product governs the producers.

In mediaeval society, especially in the earlier centuries, production was essentially directed towards satisfying the wants of the individual. It satisfied, in the main, only the wants of the producer and his family. Where relations of personal dependence existed, as in the country, it also helped to satisfy the wants of the feudal lord. In all this there was, therefore, no exchange; the products, consequently, did not assume the character of commodities. The family of the peasant produced almost everything they wanted: clothes and furniture, as well as means of subsistence. Only when it began to produce more than was sufficient to supply its own wants and the payments in kind to the feudal lord, only then did it also produce commodities. This surplus, thrown into socialised exchange and offered for sale, became commodities.

The artisans of the towns, it is true, had from the first to produce for exchange. But they, also, themselves supplied the greatest part of their own individual wants. They had gardens and plots of land. They turned their cattle out into the communal forest, which, also, yielded them timber and firing. The women spun flax, wool, and so forth. Production for the purpose of exchange, production of commodities, was only in its infancy. Hence, exchange was restricted, the market narrow, the methods of production stable; there was local exclusiveness without, local unity within; the Mark* in the country; in the town, the guild.

---

* See Appendix. [*Note by Engels.*]—Here Engels refers to his work *The Mark.* —*Ed.*

But with the extension of the production of commodities, and especially with the introduction of the capitalist mode of production, the laws of commodity production, hitherto latent, came into action more openly and with greater force. The old bonds were loosened, the old exclusive limits broken through, the producers were more and more turned into independent, isolated producers of commodities. It became apparent that the production of society at large was ruled by absence of plan, by accident, by anarchy; and this anarchy grew to greater and greater height. But the chief means by aid of which the capitalist mode of production intensified this anarchy of socialised production was the exact opposite of anarchy. It was the increasing organisation of production, upon a social basis, in every individual productive establishment. By this, the old, peaceful, stable condition of things was ended. Wherever this organisation of production was introduced into a branch of industry, it brooked no other method of production by its side. The field of labour became a battle-ground. The great geographical discoveries,[338] and the colonisation following upon them, multiplied markets and quickened the transformation of handicraft into manufacture. The war did not simply break out between the individual producers of particular localities. The local struggles begot in their turn national conflicts, the commercial wars of the seventeenth and the eighteenth centuries.[339]

Finally, modern industry and the opening of the world market made the struggle universal, and at the same time gave it an unheard-of virulence. Advantages in natural or artificial conditions of production now decide the existence or non-existence of individual capitalists, as well as of whole industries and countries. He that falls is remorselessly cast aside. It is the Darwinian struggle of the individual for existence transferred from Nature to society with intensified violence. The conditions of existence natural to the animal appear as the final term of human development. The contradiction between socialised production and capitalistic appropriation now presents itself as *an antagonism between the organisation of production in the individual workshop and the anarchy of production in society generally.*

The capitalistic mode of production moves in these two forms of the antagonism immanent to it from its very origin. It is never able to get out of that "vicious circle" which Fourier had already discovered. What Fourier could not, indeed, see in his time is that this circle is gradually narrowing; that the movement becomes more and more a spiral, and must come to an end, like the movement of the planets, by collision with the centre. It is the compelling force of anarchy in the production of society at large that more and more completely turns the great majority of men into proletarians; and it is the masses of the proletariat again who will finally put an end to anarchy in production. It is the compelling force of anarchy in social production that turns the limitless perfectibility of machinery under modern industry into a compulsory law by which every individual industrial capitalist must perfect his machinery more and more, under penalty of ruin.

But the perfecting of machinery is making human labour superfluous. If the introduction and increase of machinery means the displacement of millions of manual by a few machine-workers, improvement in machinery means the displacement of more and more of the machine-workers themselves. It means, in the last instance, the production of a number of available wage-workers in excess of the average needs of capital, the formation of a complete industrial reserve army, as I called it in 1845,* available at the times when industry is working at high pressure, to be cast out upon the street when the inevitable crash comes, a constant dead weight upon the limbs of the working class in its struggle for existence with capital, a regulator for the keeping of wages down to the low level that suits the interests of capital. Thus it comes about, to quote Marx, that machinery becomes the most powerful weapon in the war of capital against the working class; that the instruments of labour constantly tear the means of subsistence out of the hands of the labourer; that the very product of the worker is turned into an instrument for his subjugation.** Thus it comes about that the economising of the instruments of labour becomes at the same time, from the outset, the most reckless waste of labour power, and robbery based upon the normal conditions under which labour functions***; that machinery, the most powerful instrument for shortening labour time, becomes the most unfailing means for placing every moment of the labourer's time and that of his family at the disposal of the capitalist for the purpose of expanding the value of his capital. Thus it comes about that the overwork of some becomes the preliminary condition for the idleness of others, and that modern industry, which hunts after new consumers over the whole world, forces the consumption of the masses at home down to a starvation minimum, and in doing thus destroys its own home market. "The law that always equilibrates the relative surplus population, or industrial reserve army, to the extent and energy of accumulation, this law rivets the labourer to capital more firmly than the wedges of Vulcan did Prometheus to the rock. It establishes an accumulation of misery, corresponding with accumulation of

---

* *The Condition of the Working Class in England*, p. 109. [*Note by Engels.*] See Marx and Engels, *On Britain*, Moscow, 1962, p. 119.—*Ed.*
** Karl Marx, *Capital*, Vol. I, Moscow, 1965, pp. 435-87.—*Ed.*
*** Ibid., p. 462.—*Ed.*

capital. Accumulation of wealth at one pole is, therefore, at the same time, accumulation of misery, agony of toil, slavery, ignorance, brutality, mental degradation, at the opposite pole, i.e., on the side of the class that produces *its own product in the form of capital*." (Marx's *Capital*, p. 671.)* And to expect any other division of the products from the capitalistic mode of production is the same as expecting the electrodes of a battery not to decompose acidulated water, not to liberate oxygen at the positive, hydrogen at the negative pole, so long as they are connected with the battery.

We have seen that the ever-increasing perfectibility of modern machinery is, by the anarchy of social production, turned into a compulsory law that forces the individual industrial capitalist always to improve his machinery, always to increase its productive force. The bare possibility of extending the field of production is transformed for him into a similar compulsory law. The enormous expansive force of modern industry, compared with which that of gases is mere child's play, appears to us now as a *necessity* for expansion, both qualitative and quantitative, that laughs at all resistance. Such resistance is offered by consumption, by sales, by the markets for the products of modern industry. But the capacity for extension, extensive and intensive, of the markets is primarily governed by quite different laws that work much less energetically. The extension of the markets cannot keep pace with the extension of production. The collision becomes inevitable, and as this cannot produce any real solution so long as it does not break in pieces the capitalist mode of production, the collisions become periodic. Capitalist production has begotten another "vicious circle."

As a matter of fact, since 1825, when the first general crisis broke out, the whole industrial and commercial world, production and exchange among all civilised peoples and their more or less barbaric hangers-on, are thrown out of joint about once every ten years. Commerce is at a standstill, the markets are glutted, products accumulate, as multitudinous as they are unsaleable, hard cash disappears, credit vanishes, factories are closed, the mass of the workers are in want of the means of subsistence, because they have produced too much of the means of subsistence; bankruptcy follows upon bankruptcy, execution upon execution. The stagnation lasts for years; productive forces and products are wasted and destroyed wholesale, until the accumulated mass of commodities finally filters off, more or less depreciated in value, until production and exchange gradually begin to move again Little by little the pace quickens. It becomes a trot. The industrial trot breaks into a canter, the canter in turn grows into the headlong gallop of a perfect steeplechase of

---

* Ibid., p. 645.—*Ed.*

industry, commercial credit, and speculation which finally, after breakneck leaps, ends where it began—in the ditch of a crisis. And so over and over again. We have now, since the year 1825, gone through this five times, and at the present moment (1877) we are going through it for the sixth time. And the character of these crises is so clearly defined that Fourier hit all of them off when he described the first as "*crise pléthorique*," a crisis from plethora.

In these crises, the contradiction between socialised production and capitalist appropriation ends in a violent explosion. The circulation of commodities is, for the time being, stopped. Money, the means of circulation, becomes a hindrance to circulation. All the laws of production and circulation of commodities are turned upside down. The economic collision has reached its apogee. *The mode of production is in rebellion against the mode of exchange.*

The fact that the socialised organisation of production within the factory has developed so far that it has become incompatible with the anarchy of production in society, which exists side by side with and dominates it, is brought home to the capitalists themselves by the violent concentration of capital that occurs during crises, through the ruin of many large, and a still greater number of small, capitalists. The whole mechanism of the capitalist mode of production breaks down under the pressure of the productive forces, its own creations. It is no longer able to turn all this mass of means of production into capital. They lie fallow, and for that very reason the industrial reserve army must also lie fallow. Means of production, means of subsistence, available labourers, all the elements of production and of general wealth, are present in abundance. But "abundance becomes the source of distress and want" (Fourier), because it is the very thing that prevents the transformation of the means of production and subsistence into capital. For in capitalistic society the means of production can only function when they have undergone a preliminary transformation into capital, into the means of exploiting human labour power. The necessity of this transformation into capital of the means of production and subsistence stands like a ghost between these and the workers. It alone prevents the coming together of the material and personal levers of production; it alone forbids the means of production to function, the workers to work and live. On the one hand, therefore, the capitalistic mode of production stands convicted of its own incapacity to further direct these productive forces. On the other, these productive forces themselves, with increasing energy, press forward to the removal of the existing contradiction, to the abolition of their quality as capital, to the *practical recognition of their character as social productive forces.*

This rebellion of the productive forces, as they grow more and more powerful, against their quality as capital, this stronger and stronger command that their social character shall be recognised, forces the capitalist class itself to treat them more and more as social productive forces, so far as this is possible under capitalist conditions. The period of industrial high pressure, with its unbounded inflation of credit, not less than the crash itself, by the collapse of great capitalist establishments, tends to bring about that form of the socialisation of great masses of means of production which we meet with in the different kinds of joint-stock companies. Many of these means of production and of distribution are, from the outset, so colossal that, like the railways, they exclude all other forms of capitalistic exploitation. At a further stage of evolution this form also becomes insufficient. The producers on a large scale in a particular branch of industry in a particular country unite in a trust, a union for the purpose of regulating production. They determine the total amount to be produced, parcel it out among themselves, and thus enforce the selling price fixed beforehand. But trusts of this kind, as soon as business becomes bad, are generally liable to break up, and on this very account compel a yet greater concentration of association. The whole of the particular industry is turned into one gigantic joint-stock company; internal competition gives place to the internal monopoly of this one company. This has happened in 1890 with the English alkali production, which is now, after the fusion of 48 large works, in the hands of one company, conducted upon a single plan, and with a capital of £6,000,000.

In the trusts, freedom of competition changes into its very opposite—into monopoly; and the production without any definite plan of capitalistic society capitulates to the production upon a definite plan of the invading socialistic society. Certainly this is so far still to the benefit and advantage of the capitalists. But in this case the exploitation is so palpable that it must break down. No nation will put up with production conducted by trusts, with so barefaced an exploitation of the community by a small band of dividend-mongers.

In any case, with trusts or without, the official representative of capitalist society—the state—will ultimately have to undertake the direction of production.* This necessity for conversion into state

* I say "have to." For only when the means of production and distribution have *actually* outgrown the form of management by joint-stock companies, and when, therefore, the taking them over by the state has become *economically* inevitable, only then—even if it is the state of today that effects this—is there an economic advance, the attainment of another step preliminary to the taking over of all productive forces by society itself. But of late, since Bismarck went in for state ownership of industrial establishments, a kind of spurious socialism has arisen, degenerating, now and again, into something of flunkeyism, that without more ado declares *all* state ownership, even of the Bismarckian sort, to be socialistic. Certainly, if the taking over by the state of the tobacco industry is socialistic, then Napoleon and Metternich must be numbered among the founders of socialism. If the Belgian state, for quite ordinary political and financial reasons, itself constructed its chief railway lines; if Bismarck, not under any economic compulsion, took over for the state the chief Prussian lines, simply to be the

property is felt first in the great institutions for intercourse and communication—the post office, the telegraphs, the railways.

If the crises demonstrate the incapacity of the bourgeoisie for managing any longer modern productive forces, the transformation of the great establishments for production and distribution into joint-stock companies, trusts and state property shows how unnecessary the bourgeoisie are for that purpose. All the social functions of the capitalist are now performed by salaried employees. The capitalist has no further social function than that of pocketing dividends, tearing off coupons, and gambling on the Stock Exchange, where the different capitalists despoil one another of their capital. At first the capitalistic mode of production forces out the workers. Now it forces out the capitalists, and reduces them, just as it reduced the workers, to the ranks of the surplus population, although not immediately into those of the industrial reserve army.

But the transformation, either into joint-stock companies and trusts, or into state ownership, does not do away with the capitalistic nature of the productive forces. In the joint-stock companies and trusts this is obvious. And the modern state, again, is only the organisation that bourgeois society takes on in order to support the external conditions of the capitalist mode of production against the encroachments as well of the workers as of individual capitalists. The modern state, no matter what its form, is essentially a capitalist machine, the state of the capitalists, the ideal personification of the total national capital. The more it proceeds to the taking over of productive forces, the more does it actually become the national capitalist, the more citizens does it exploit. The workers remain wage-workers—proletarians. The capitalist relation is not done away with. It is rather brought to a head. But, brought to a head, it topples over. State ownership of the productive forces is not the solution of the conflict, but concealed within it are the technical conditions that form the elements of that solution.

This solution can only consist in the practical recognition of the social nature of the modern forces of production, and therefore in the harmonising of the modes of production, appropriation, and exchange with the socialised character of the means of production. And this can only come about by society openly and directly taking possession of the productive forces which have outgrown all control

better able to have them in hand in case of war, to bring up the railway employees as voting cattle for the government, and especially to create for himself a new source of income independent of parliamentary votes—this was, in no sense, a socialistic measure, directly or indirectly, consciously or unconsciously. Otherwise, the Royal Maritime Company,[340] the Royal porcelain manufacture, and even the regimental tailor shops of the Army would also be socialistic institutions, or even, as was seriously proposed by a sly dog in Frederick William III's reign, the taking over by the state of the brothels. [Note by Engels.]

except that of society as a whole. The social character of the means of production and of the products today reacts against the producers, periodically disrupts all production and exchange, acts only like a law of Nature working blindly, forcibly, destructively. But with the taking over by society of the productive forces, the social character of the means of production and of the products will be utilised by the producers with a perfect understanding of its nature, and instead of being a source of disturbance and periodical collapse, will become the most powerful lever of production itself.

Active social forces work exactly like natural forces: blindly, forcibly, destructively, so long as we do not understand, and reckon with, them. But when once we understand them, when once we grasp their action, their direction, their effects, it depends only upon ourselves to subject them more and more to our own will, and by means of them to reach our own ends. And this holds quite especially of the mighty productive forces of today. As long as we obstinately refuse to understand the nature and the character of these social means of action—and this understanding goes against the grain of the capitalist mode of production and its defenders—so long these forces are at work in spite of us, in opposition to us, so long they master us, as we have shown above in detail.

But when once their nature is understood, they can, in the hands of the producers working together, be transformed from master demons into willing servants. The difference is as that between the destructive force of electricity in the lightning of the storm, and electricity under command in the telegraph and the voltaic arc; the difference between a conflagration, and fire working in the service of man. With this recognition, at last, of the real nature of the productive forces of today, the social anarchy of production gives place to a social regulation of production upon a definite plan, according to the needs of the community and of each individual. Then the capitalist mode of appropriation, in which the product enslaves first the producer and then the appropriator, is replaced by the mode of appropriation of the products that is based upon the nature of the modern means of production; upon the one hand, direct social appropriation, as means to the maintenance and extension of production—on the other, direct individual appropriation, as means of subsistence and of enjoyment.

Whilst the capitalist mode of production more and more completely transforms the great majority of the population into proletarians, it creates the power which, under penalty of its own destruction, is forced to accomplish this revolution. Whilst it forces on more and more the transformation of the vast means of production, already socialised, into state property, it shows itself the way to accomplishing this revolution. *The proletariat seizes political power and turns the means of production into state property.*

But, in doing this, it abolishes itself as proletariat, abolishes all class distinctions and class antagonisms, abolishes also the state as state. Society thus far, based upon class antagonisms, had need of the state. That is, of an organisation of the particular class which was *pro tempore* the exploiting class, an organisation for the purpose of preventing any interference from without with the existing conditions of production, and, therefore, especially, for the purpose of forcibly keeping the exploited classes in the condition of oppression corresponding with the given mode of production (slavery, serfdom, wage-labour). The state was the official representative of society as a whole; the gathering of it together into a visible embodiment. But it was this only in so far as it was the state of that class which itself represented, for the time being, society as a whole: in ancient times, the state of slave-owning citizens; in the Middle Ages, the feudal lords; in our own time, the bourgeoisie. When at last it becomes the real representative of the whole of society, it renders itself unnecessary. As soon as there is no longer any social class to be held in subjection; as soon as class rule, and the individual struggle for existence based upon our present anarchy in production, with the collisions and excesses arising from these, are removed, nothing more remains to be repressed, and a special repressive force, a state, is no longer necessary. The first act by virtue of which the state really constitutes itself the representative of the whole of society—the taking possession of the means of production in the name of society—this is, at the same time, its last independent act as a state. State interference in social relations becomes, in one domain after another, superfluous, and then dies out of itself; the government of persons is replaced by the administration of things, and by the conduct of processes of production. The state is not "abolished." *It dies out.* This gives the measure of the value of the phrase "*a free state*,"* both as to its justifiable use at times by agitators, and as to its ultimate scientific insufficiency; and also of the demands of the so-called anarchists for the abolition of the state out of hand.

Since the historical appearance of the capitalist mode of production, the appropriation by society of all the means of production has often been dreamed of, more or less vaguely, by individuals, as well as by sects, as the ideal of the future. But it could become possible, could become a historical necessity, only when the actual conditions for its realisation were there. Like every other social advance, it becomes practicable, not by men understanding that the existence of classes is in contradiction to justice, equality, etc., not by the mere willingness to abolish these classes, but by virtue of certain new economic conditions. The separation of society into an exploiting and an exploited class, a ruling and an oppressed class, was the necessary

---

* See pp. 326-30 and 334-35 of this volume.—*Ed.*

consequence of the deficient and restricted development of production in former times. So long as the total social labour only yields a produce which but slightly exceeds that barely necessary for the existence of all; so long, therefore, as labour engages all or almost all the time of the great majority of the members of society—so long, of necessity, this society is divided into classes. Side by side with the great majority, exclusively bond slaves to labour, arises a class freed from directly productive labour, which looks after the general affairs of society: the direction of labour, state business, law, science, art, etc. It is, therefore, the law of division of labour that lies at the basis of the division into classes. But this does not prevent this division into classes from being carried out by means of violence and robbery, trickery and fraud. It does not prevent the ruling class, once having the upper hand, from consolidating its power at the expense of the working class, from turning its social leadership into an intensified exploitation of the masses.

But if, upon this showing, division into classes has a certain historical justification, it has this only for a given period, only under given social conditions. It was based upon the insufficiency of production. It will be swept away by the complete development of modern productive forces. And, in fact, the abolition of classes in society presupposes a degree of historical evolution at which the existence, not simply of this or that particular ruling class, but of any ruling class at all, and, therefore, the existence of class distinction itself has become an obsolete anachronism. It presupposes, therefore, the development of production carried out to a degree at which appropriation of the means of production and of the products, and, with this, of political domination, of the monopoly of culture, and of intellectual leadership by a particular class of society, has become not only superfluous but economically, politically, intellectually, a hindrance to development.

This point is now reached. Their political and intellectual bankruptcy is scarcely any longer a secret to the bourgeoisie themselves. Their economic bankruptcy recurs regularly every ten years. In every crisis, society is suffocated beneath the weight of its own productive forces and products, which it cannot use, and stands helpless, face to face with the absurd contradiction that the producers have nothing to consume, because consumers are wanting. The expansive force of the means of production bursts the bonds that the capitalist mode of production had imposed upon them. Their deliverance from these bonds is the one precondition for an unbroken, constantly accelerated development of the productive forces, and therewith for a practically unlimited increase of production itself. Nor is this all. The socialised appropriation of the means of production does away, not only with the present artificial restrictions upon production, but also with the positive waste and devastation of productive forces and products that are at the present time the inevitable concomitants of production, and that reach their height in the crises. Further, it sets free for the community at large a mass of means of production and of products, by doing away with the senseless extravagance of the ruling classes of today and their political representatives. The possibility of securing for every member of society, by means of socialised production, an existence not only fully sufficient materially, and becoming day by day more full, but an existence guaranteeing to all the free development and exercise of their physical and mental faculties—this possibility is now for the first time here, but *it is here.**

With the seizing of the means of production by society, production of commodities is done away with, and, simultaneously, the mastery of the product over the producer. Anarchy in social production is replaced by systematic, definite organisation. The struggle for individual existence disappears. Then for the first time man, in a certain sense, is finally marked off from the rest of the animal kingdom, and emerges from mere animal conditions of existence into really human ones. The whole sphere of the conditions of life which environ man, and which have hitherto ruled man, now comes under the dominion and control of man, who for the first time becomes the real, conscious lord of Nature, because he has now become master of his own social organisation. The laws of his own social action, hitherto standing face to face with man as laws of Nature foreign to, and dominating him, will then be used with full understanding, and so mastered by him. Man's own social organisation, hitherto confronting him as a necessity imposed by Nature and history, now becomes the result of his own free action. The extraneous objective forces that have hitherto governed history pass under the control of man himself. Only from that time will man himself, more and more consciously, make his own history—only from that time will the social causes set in movement by him have, in the main and in a constantly growing measure, the results intended by him. It is the ascent of man from the kingdom of necessity to the kingdom of freedom.

Let us briefly sum up our sketch of historical evolution.

---

* A few figures may serve to give an approximate idea of the enormous expansive force of the modern means of production, even under capitalist pressure. According to Mr. Giffen, the total wealth of Great Britain and Ireland amounted, in round numbers in

1814 to £2,200,000,000.
1865 to £6,100,000,000.
1875 to £8,500,000,000.

As an instance of the squandering of means of production and of products during a crisis, the total loss in the German iron industry alone, in the crisis 1873-78, was given at the second German Industrial Congress (Berlin, February 21, 1878) as £22,750,000. [*Note by Engels.*]

I. *Mediaeval Society*—Individual production on a small scale. Means of production adapted for individual use; hence primitive, ungainly, petty, dwarfed in action. Production for immediate consumption, either of the producer himself or of his feudal lord. Only where an excess of production over this consumption occurs is such excess offered for sale, enters into exchange. Production of commodities, therefore, only in its infancy. But already it contains within itself, in embryo, *anarchy in the production of society at large.*

II. *Capitalist Revolution*—Transformation of industry, at first by means of simple co-operation and manufacture. Concentration of the means of production, hitherto scattered, into great workshops. As a consequence, their transformation from individual to social means of production—a transformation which does not, on the whole, affect the form of exchange. The old forms of appropriation remain in force. The capitalist appears. In his capacity as owner of the means of production, he also appropriates the products and turns them into commodities. Production has become a *social* act. Exchange and appropriation continue to be *individual* acts, the acts of individuals. *The social product is appropriated by the individual capitalist.* Fundamental contradiction, whence arise all the contradictions in which our present-day society moves, and which modern industry brings to light.

A. Severance of the producer from the means of production. Condemnation of the worker to wage-labour for life. *Antagonism between the proletariat and the bourgeoisie.*

B. Growing predominance and increasing effectiveness of the laws governing the production of commodities. Unbridled competition. *Contradiction between socialised organisation in the individual factory and social anarchy in production as a whole.*

C. On the one hand, perfecting of machinery, made by competition compulsory for each individual manufacturer, and complemented by a constantly growing displacement of labourers. *Industrial reserve army.* On the other hand, unlimited extension of production, also compulsory under competition, for every manufacturer. On both sides, unheard-of development of productive forces, excess of supply over demand, over-production, glutting of the markets, crises every ten years, the vicious circle: excess here, of means of production and products—excess there, of labourers, without employment and without means of existence. But these two levers of production and of social well-being are unable to work together, because the capitalist form of production prevents the productive forces from working and the products from circulating, unless they are first turned into capital—which their very superabundance prevents. The contradiction has grown into an absurdity. *The mode of production rises in rebellion against the form of exchange*. The bourgeoisie are convicted of incapacity further to manage their own social productive forces.

D. Partial recognition of the social character of the productive forces forced upon the capitalists themselves. Taking over of the great institutions for production and communication, first by joint-stock companies, later on by trusts, then by the state. The bourgeoisie demonstrated to be a superfluous class. All its social functions are now performed by salaried employees.

III. *Proletarian Revolution*—Solution of the contradictions. The proletariat seizes the public power, and by means of this transforms the socialised means of production, slipping from the hands of the bourgeoisie, into public property. By this act, the proletariat frees the means of production from the character of capital they have thus far borne, and gives their socialised character complete freedom to work itself out. Socialised production upon a predetermined plan becomes henceforth possible. The development of production makes the existence of different classes of society thenceforth an anachronism. In proportion as anarchy in social production vanishes, the political authority of the state dies out. Man, at last the master of his own form of social organisation, becomes at the same time the lord over Nature, his own master—free.

To accomplish this act of universal emancipation is the historical mission of the modern proletariat. To thoroughly comprehend the historical conditions and thus the very nature of this act, to impart to the now oppressed proletarian class a full knowledge of the conditions and of the meaning of the momentous act it is called upon to accomplish, this is the task of the theoretical expression of the proletarian movement, scientific socialism.

Written by Engels between January and the first half of March 1880

Published in the journal *La Revue socialiste* Nos. 3, 4 and 5, March 20, April 20 and May 5, 1880, and as a separate pamphlet in French: F. Engels, *Socialisme utopique et socialisme scientifique*, Paris, 1880

Printed according to the text of the authorised English edition of 1892

Frederick Engels

SPEECH AT THE GRAVESIDE OF KARL MARX

On the 14th of March, at a quarter to three in the afternoon, the greatest living thinker ceased to think. He had been left alone for scarcely two minutes, and when we came back we found him in his armchair, peacefully gone to sleep—but for ever.

An immeasurable loss has been sustained both by the militant proletariat of Europe and America, and by historical science, in the death of this man. The gap that has been left by the departure of this mighty spirit will soon enough make itself felt.

Just as Darwin discovered the law of development of organic nature, so Marx discovered the law of development of human history: the simple fact, hitherto concealed by an overgrowth of ideology, that mankind must first of all eat, drink, have shelter and clothing, before it can pursue politics, science, art, religion, etc.; that therefore the production of the immediate material means of subsistence and consequently the degree of economic development attained by a given people or during a given epoch form the foundation upon which the state institutions, the legal conceptions, art, and even the ideas on religion, of the people concerned have been evolved, and in the light of which they must, therefore, be explained, instead of *vice versa*, as had hitherto been the case.

But that is not all. Marx also discovered the special law of motion governing the present-day capitalist mode of production and the bourgeois society that this mode of production has created. The discovery of surplus value suddenly threw light on the problem, in trying to solve which all previous investigations, of both bourgeois economists and socialist critics, had been groping in the dark.

Two such discoveries would be enough for one lifetime. Happy the man to whom it is granted to make even one such discovery. But in every single field which Marx investigated—and he investigated very many fields, none of them superficially—in every field, even in that of mathematics, he made independent discoveries.

Such was the man of science. But this was not even half the man. Science was for Marx a historically dynamic, revolutionary force. However great the joy with which he welcomed a new discovery in some theoretical science whose practical application perhaps it was as yet quite impossible to envisage, he experienced quite another kind of joy when the discovery involved immediate revolutionary changes in industry, and in historical development in general. For example, he followed closely the development of the discoveries made in the field of electricity and recently those of Marcel Deprez.

For Marx was before all else a revolutionist. His real mission in life was to contribute, in one way or another, to the overthrow of capitalist society and of the state institutions which it had brought into being, to contribute to the liberation of the modern proletariat, which *he* was the first to make conscious of its own position and its needs, conscious of the conditions of its emancipation. Fighting was his element. And he fought with a passion, a tenacity and a success such as few could rival. His work on the first *Rheinische Zeitung* (1842),[115] the Paris *Vorwärts* (1844),[341] the *Deutsche Brüsseler Zeitung*,[286] (1847), the *Neue Rheinische Zeitung* (1848-49),[27] the *New York Tribune* (1852-61),[118] and in addition to these a host of militant pamphlets, work in organisations in Paris, Brussels and London, and finally, crowning all, the formation of the great International Working Men's Association[120]—this was indeed an achievement of which its founder might well have been proud even if he had done nothing else.

And, consequently, Marx was the best hated and most calumniated man of his time. Governments, both absolutist and republican, deported him from their territories. Bourgeois, whether conservative or ultra-democratic, vied with one another in heaping slanders upon him. All this he brushed aside as though it were cobweb, ignoring it, answering only when extreme necessity compelled him. And he died beloved, revered and mourned by millions of revolutionary fellow workers—from the mines of Siberia to California, in all parts of Europe and America—and I make bold to say that though he may have had many opponents he had hardly one personal enemy.

His name will endure through the ages, and so also will his work!

Speech delivered in English by
Engels at Highgate Cemetery,
London, on March 17, 1883

Published in German in the
newspaper *Der Sozialdemokrat*
No. 13, March 22, 1883

Printed according to the
newspaper text
Translated from the German

Frederick Engels

ON THE HISTORY OF THE COMMUNIST LEAGUE[342]

With the sentence of the Cologne Communists in 1852,[9] the curtain falls on the first period of the independent German workers' movement. Today this period is almost forgotten. Yet it lasted from 1836 to 1852 and, with the spread of German workers abroad, the movement developed in almost all civilised countries. Nor is that all. The present-day international workers' movement is in substance a direct continuation of the German workers' movement of that time, which was the *first international workers' movement* of all time, and which brought forth many of those who took the leading role in the International Working Men's Association.[120] And the theoretical principles that the Communist League had inscribed on its banner in the *Communist Manifesto** of 1847 constitute today the strongest international bond of the entire proletarian movement of both Europe and America.

Up to now there has been only one main source for a coherent history of that movement. This is the so-called Black Book, *The Communist Conspiracies of the Nineteenth Century*, by Wermuth and Stieber, Berlin, two parts, 1853 and 1854. This crude compilation, which bristles with deliberate falsifications, fabricated by two of the most contemptible police scoundrels of our century, today still serves as the final source for all non-communist writings about that period.

What I am able to give here is only a sketch, and even this only in so far as the League itself is concerned; only what is absolutely necessary to understand the *Revelations*. I hope that some day I shall have the opportunity to work up the rich material collected by Marx and myself on the history of that glorious period of the youth of the international workers' movement.

* * *

In 1836 the most extreme, chiefly proletarian elements of the secret democratic-republican Outlaws' League, which was founded by German refugees in Paris in 1834, split off and formed the

---

* See pp. 35-63 of this volume.—*Ed.*

new secret *League of the Just.* The parent League, in which only
sleepy-headed elements *à la* Jakobus Venedey were left, soon fell
asleep altogether: when in 1840 the police scented out a few sections in Germany, it was hardly even a shadow of its former self.
The new League, on the contrary, developed comparatively rapidly. Originally it was a German outlier of the French worker-
communism, reminiscent of Babouvism[343] and taking shape in Paris
at about this time; community of goods was demanded as the
necessary consequence of "equality." The aims were those of the
Parisian secret societies of the time: half propaganda association,
half conspiracy, Paris, however, being always regarded as the
central point of revolutionary action, although the preparation of
occasional *putsches* in Germany was by no means excluded. But
as Paris remained the decisive battleground, the League was at
that time actually not much more than the German branch of the
French secret societies, especially the *Société des saisons* led
by Blanqui and Barbès, with which a close connection was maintained. The French went into action on May 12, 1839; the sections
of the League marched with them and thus were involved in the
common defeat.[344]

Among the Germans arrested were *Karl Schapper* and *Heinrich
Bauer*; Louis Philippe's government contented itself with deport-
ing them after a fairly long imprisonment. Both went to London.
Schapper came from Weilburg in Nassau and while a student of
forestry at Giessen in 1832 was a member of the conspiracy organised by Georg Büchner; he took part in the storming of the
Frankfort constable station on April 3, 1833,[345] escaped abroad and
in February 1834 joined Mazzini's march on Savoy.[346] Of gigantic
stature, resolute and energetic, always ready to risk civil existence and life, he was a model of the professional revolutionist that
played a certain role in the thirties. In spite of a certain sluggish-
ness of thought, he was by no means incapable of profound theoretical understanding, as is proved by his development from
"demagogue"[168] to Communist, and he held then all the more rigidly to what he had once come to recognise. Precisely on that account his revolutionary passion sometimes got the better of his
understanding, but he always afterwards realised his mistake and
openly acknowledged it. He was fully a man and what he did for
the founding of the German workers' movement will not be forgotten.

Heinrich Bauer, from Franconia, was a shoemaker; a lively,
alert, witty little fellow, whose little body, however, also contained
much shrewdness and determination.

Arrived in London, where Schapper, who had been a compositor in Paris, now tried to earn his living as a teacher of languages, they both set to work gathering up the broken threads

nd made London the centre of the League. They were joined
ver here, if not already earlier in Paris, by *Joseph Moll*, a watch-
naker from Cologne, a medium-sized Hercules—how often did
chapper and he victoriously defend the entrance to a hall
gainst hundreds of onrushing opponents—a man who was at
east the equal of his two comrades in energy and determination,
nd intellectually superior to both of them. Not only was he a
oorn diplomat, as the success of his numerous trips on various
nissions proved; he was also more capable of theoretical insight.
came to know all three of them in London in 1843. They were
he first revolutionary proletarians whom I met, and however far
npart our views were at that time in details—for I still owned, as
igainst their narrow-minded equalitarian communism,* a goodly
dose of just as narrow-minded philosophical arrogance—I shall
never forget the deep impression that these three real men made
upon me, who was then still only wanting to become a man.

In London, as in a lesser degree in Switzerland, they had the
benefit of freedom of association and assembly. As early as February 7, 1840, the legally functioning German Workers' Educational Association, which still exists, was founded.[347] The Association served the League as a recruiting ground for new members,
and since, as always, the Communists were the most active and
intelligent members of the Association, it was a matter of course
that its leadership lay entirely in the hands of the League. The
League soon had several communities, or, as they were then still
called, "lodges," in London. The same obvious tactics were followed in Switzerland and elsewhere. Where workers' associations
could be founded, they were utilised in like manner. Where this
was forbidden by law, one joined choral societies, athletic clubs,
and the like. Connections were to a large extent maintained by
members who were continually travelling back and forth; they
also, when required, served as emissaries. In both respects the
League obtained lively support through the wisdom of the governments which, by resorting to deportation, converted any objectionable worker—and in nine cases out of ten he was a member
of the League—into an emissary.

The extent to which the restored League spread was considerable. Notably in Switzerland, *Weitling, August Becker* (a highly
gifted man who, however, like so many Germans, came to grief
because of innate instability of character) and others created a
strong organisation more or less pledged to Weitling's communist system. This is not the place to criticise the communism of

---

* By equalitarian communism I understand, as stated, only that communism
which bases itself exclusively or predominantly on the demand for equality.
[*Note by Engels.*]

Weitling. But as regards its significance as the first independen theoretical stirring of the German proletariat, I still today sub scribe to Marx's words in the Paris *Vorwärts*[341] of 1844: "Wher could the (German) bourgeoisie—including its philosophers and learned scribes—point to a work *relating to the emancipation of the bourgeoisie*—its political emancipation—comparable to Weit ling's *Guarantees of Harmony and Freedom*? If one compares the drab mealy-mouthed mediocrity of German political literature with this immeasurable and brilliant debut of the German workers, i one compares these *gigantic children's shoes of the proletariat* with the dwarf proportions of the worn-out political shoes of the bourgeoisie, one must prophesy an athlete's figure for this Cinderella."* This athlete's figure confronts us today, although still far from being fully grown.

Numerous sections existed also in Germany; in the nature of things they were of a transient character, but those coming into existence more than made up for those passing away. Only after seven years, at the end of 1846, did the police discover traces of the League in Berlin (Mentel) and Magdebourg (Beck), without being in a position to follow them further.

In Paris, Weitling, who was still there in 1840, likewise gathered the scattered elements together again before he left for Switzerland.

The tailors formed the central force of the League. German tailors were everywhere: in Switzerland, in London, in Paris. In the last-named city, German was so much the prevailing tongue in this trade that I was acquainted there in 1846 with a Norwegian tailor who had travelled directly by sea from Trondhjem to France and in the space of eighteen months had learned hardly a word of French but had acquired an excellent knowledge of German. Two of the Paris communities in 1847 consisted predominantly of tailors, one of cabinetmakers.

After the centre of gravity had shifted from Paris to London, a new feature grew conspicuous: from being German, the League gradually became *international*. In the workers' society there were to be found, besides Germans and Swiss, also members of all those nationalities for whom German served as the chief means of communication with foreigners, notably, therefore, Scandinavians, Dutch, Hungarians, Czechs, Southern Slavs, and also Russians and Alsatians. In 1847 the regular frequenters included a British grenadier of the Guards in uniform. The society soon called itself the *Communist* Workers' Educational Association, and the member-

---

* See Karl Marx, "Kritische Randglossen zu dem Artikel 'Der König von Preussen und die Sozialreform. Von einem Preussen'" (Marx/Engels, *Werke*, Bd. 1, Dietz Verlag, Berlin, 1958, S. 392-409).—*Ed.*

ip cards bore the inscription "All Men Are Brothers," in at least
enty languages, even if not without mistakes here and there. Like
e open Association, so also the secret League soon took on a more
ternational character; at first in a restricted sense, practically
rough the varied nationalities of its members, theoretically through
e realisation that any revolution to be victorious must be a
uropean one. One did not go any further as yet; but the founda-
ons were there.

Close connections were maintained with the French revolutionists
rough the London refugees, comrades-in-arms of May 12, 1839.
milarly with the more radical Poles. The official Polish *émigrés*,
s also Mazzini, were, of course, opponents rather than allies. The
nglish Chartists,[22] on account of the specific English character of
eir movement, were disregarded as not revolutionary. The London
aders of the League came in touch with them only later, through
e.

In other ways, too, the character of the League had altered with
vents. Although Paris was still—and at that time quite rightly—
oked upon as the mother city of the revolution, one had never-
eless emerged from the state of dependence on the Paris con-
pirators. The spread of the League raised its self-consciousness.
t was felt that roots were being struck more and more in the Ger-
an working class and that these German workers were historically
alled upon to be the standard-bearers of the workers of the North
nd East of Europe. In Weitling was to be found a communist
heoretician who could be boldly placed at the side of his con-
emporary French rivals. Finally, the experience of May 12 had
aught us that for the time being there was nothing to be gained by
ttempts at *putsches*. And if one still continued to explain every
vent as a sign of the approaching storm, if one still preserved
ntact the old, semi-conspiratorial rules, that was mainly the fault of
he old revolutionary defiance, which had already begun to collide
with the sounder views that were gaining headway.

However, the social doctrine of the League, indefinite as it was
ontained a very great defect, but one that had its roots in the con-
litions themselves. The members, in so far as they were workers at
ll, were almost exclusively artisans. Even in the big metropolises,
the man who exploited them was usually only a small master. The
exploitation of tailoring on a large scale, what is now called the
manufacture of ready-made clothes, by the conversion of handicraft
tailoring into a domestic industry working for a big capitalist, was
at that time even in London only just making its appearance. On
the one hand, the exploiter of these artisans was a small master; on
the other hand, they all hoped ultimately to become small masters
themselves. In addition, a mass of inherited guild notions still clung
to the German artisan at that time. The greatest honour is due to

them, in that they, who were themselves not yet full proletarians b
only an appendage of the petty bourgeoisie, an appendage which w;
passing into the modern proletariat and which did not yet stand ;
direct opposition to the bourgeoisie, that is, to big capital—in th;
these artisans were capable of instinctively anticipating their futur
development and of constituting themselves, even if not yet wit
full consciousness, the party of the proletariat. But it was also in
evitable that their old handicraft prejudices should be a stumblin
block to them at every moment, whenever it was a question o
criticising existing society in detail, that is, of investigating eco
nomic facts. And I do not believe there was a single man in th
whole League at that time who had ever read a book on politica
economy. But that mattered little; for the time being "equality,
"brotherhood" and "justice" helped them to surmount every theo
retical obstacle.

Meanwhile a second, essentially different communism wa
developing alongside that of the League and of Weitling. Whil
I was in Manchester, it was tangibly brought home to me that th
economic facts, which have so far played no role or only a con
temptible one in the writing of history, are, at least in the moderr
world, a decisive historical force; that they form the basis of th
origination of the present-day class antagonisms; that these class
antagonisms, in the countries where they have become fully
developed, thanks to large-scale industry, hence especially in Eng
land, are in their turn the basis of the formation of political parties
and of party struggles, and thus of all political history. Marx had
not only arrived at the same view, but had already, in the German-
French Annals (1844),[117] generalised it to the effect that, speaking
generally, it is not the state which conditions and regulates civil
society, but civil society which conditions and regulates the state,
and, consequently, that policy and its history are to be explained
from the economic relations and their development, and not vice
versa. When I visited Marx in Paris in the summer of 1844, our
complete agreement in all theoretical fields became evident and our
joint work dates from that time. When, in the spring of 1845, we
met again in Brussels, Marx had already fully developed his
materialist theory of history in its main features from the above-
mentioned basis and we now applied ourselves to the detailed
elaboration of the newly-won mode of outlook in the most varied
directions.

This discovery, which revolutionised the science of history and,
as we have seen, is essentially the work of Marx—a discovery in
which I can claim for myself only a very insignificant share—was,
however, of immediate importance for the contemporary workers'
movement. Communism among the French and Germans, Chartism
among the English, now no longer appeared as something accidental

hich could just as well not have occurred. These movements now
esented themselves as a movement of the modern oppressed class,
e proletariat, as the more or less developed forms of its historically
cessary struggle against the ruling class, the bourgeoisie; as forms
f the class struggle, but distinguished from all earlier class struggles
y this one thing, that the present-day oppressed class, the proletariat,
annot achieve its emancipation without at the same time emancipat-
g society as a whole from division into classes and, therefore,
om class struggles. And communism now no longer meant the
oncoction, by means of the imagination, of an ideal society as
erfect as possible, but insight into the nature, the conditions and
e consequent general aims of the struggle waged by the prole-
ariat.

Now, we were by no means of the opinion that the new scientific
esults should be confided in large tomes exclusively to the "learned"
vorld. Quite the contrary. We were both of us already deeply in-
olved in the political movement, and possessed a certain following
i the educated world, especially of Western Germany, and
bundant contact with the organised proletariat. It was our duty to
rovide a scientific foundation for our view, but it was equally im-
ortant for us to win over the European and in the first place the
3erman proletariat to our conviction. As soon as we had become
lear in our own minds, we set about the task. We founded a German
vorkers' society in Brussels[28] and took over the *Deutsche Brüsseler
Zeitung*,[286] which served us as an organ up to the February Revolu-
ion.[4] We kept in touch with the revolutionary section of the English
Chartists through Julian Harney, the editor of the central organ of
he movement, *The Northern Star*,[348] to which I was a contributor.
We entered likewise into a sort of cartel with the Brussels democrats
Marx was vice-president of the Democratic Society[349]) and with the
'rench Social-Democrats of the *Réforme*,[23] which I furnished with
iews of the English and German movements. In short, our connec-
ions with the radical and proletarian organisations and press organs
vere quite what one could wish.

Our relations with the League of the Just were as follows: The
:xistence of the League was, of course, known to us; in 1843
Schapper had suggested that I join it, which I at that time naturally
refused to do. But we not only kept up our continuous correspondence
with the Londoners but remained on still closer terms with
Dr. Everbeck, then the leader of the Paris communities. Without
3oing into the League's internal affairs, we learnt of every important
happening. On the other hand, we influenced the theoretical views
of the most important members of the League by word of mouth,
oy letter and through the press. For this purpose we also made use
of various lithographed circulars, which we dispatched to our friends
and correspondents throughout the world on particular occasions,

when it was a question of the internal affairs of the Communis
Party in process of formation. In these, the League itself sometime
came to be dealt with. Thus, a young Westphalian student, Herman
Kriege, who went to America, came forward there as an emissar
of the League and associated himself with the crazy Harro Harrin
for the purpose of using the League to turn South America upsid
down. He founded a paper* in which, in the name of the Leagu
he preached an extravagant communism of love dreaming, based o
"love" and overflowing with love. Against this we let fly with
circular that did not fail of its effect.** Kriege vanished from th
League scene.

   Later, Weitling came to Brussels. But he was no longer the naïv
young journeyman-tailor who, astonished at his own talents, wa
trying to clarify in his own mind just what a communist societ
would look like. He was now the great man, persecuted by th
envious on account of his superiority, who scented rivals, secre
enemies and traps everywhere—the prophet, driven from countr
to country, who carried a recipe for the realisation of heaven o
earth ready-made in his pocket, and who was possessed with th
idea that everybody intended to steal it from him. He had alread
fallen out with the members of the League in London; and i
Brussels, where Marx and his wife welcomed him with almos
superhuman forbearance, he also could not get along with anyone
So he soon afterwards went to America to try out his role of prophe
there.

   All these circumstances contributed to the quiet revolution tha
was taking place in the League, and especially among the leader
in London. The inadequacy of the previous conception of commu
nism, both the simple French equalitarian communism and that o
Weitling, became more and more clear to them. The tracing o
communism back to primitive Christianity introduced by Weitling—
no matter how brilliant certain passages to be found in his *Gospel o*
Poor Sinners—had resulted in delivering the movement in Switzer
land to a large extent into the hands, first of fools like Albrecht, and
then of exploiting fake prophets like Kuhlmann. The "true socialism"
dealt in by a few literary writers—a translation of French socialist
phraseology into corrupt Hegelian German, and sentimental love
dreaming (see the section on German or "True" Socialism in the
*Communist Manifesto***)—that Kriege and the study of the cor
responding literature introduced in the League was found soon to
disgust the old revolutionists of the League, if only because of its

---

   * *Der Volks-Tribun.*[350]—*Ed.*
   ** Karl Marx/Friedrich Engels, "Zirkular gegen Kriege" (see Marx/Engels,
Werke, Bd. 4, Dietz Verlag, Berlin, 1959, S. 3-17).—*Ed.*
   *** See pp. 56-58 of this volume.—*Ed.*

bbering feebleness. As against the untenability of the previous
eoretical views, and as against the practical aberrations resulting
erefrom, it was realised more and more in London that Marx and
were right in our new theory. This understanding was undoubtedly
omoted by the fact that among the London leaders there were now
o men who were considerably superior to those previously men-
ned in capacity for theoretical knowledge: the miniature painter
arl Pfänder from Heilbronn and the tailor Georg Eccarius from
huringia.*

It suffices to say that in the spring of 1847 Moll visited Marx in
ussels and immediately afterwards me in Paris, and invited us
peatedly, in the name of his comrades, to enter the League. He
ported that they were as much convinced of the general correctness
our mode of outlook as of the necessity of freeing the League
om the old conspiratorial traditions and forms. Should we enter,
e would be given an opportunity of expounding our critical com-
unism before a congress of the League in a manifesto, which would
en be published as the manifesto of the League; we would likewise
: able to contribute our quota towards the replacement of the
solete League organisation by one in keeping with the new times
d aims.

We entertained no doubt that an organisation within the German
orking class was necessary, if only for propaganda purposes, and
at this organisation, in so far as it would not be merely local in
aracter, could only be a secret one, even outside Germany. Now,
ere already existed exactly such an organisation in the shape of
e League. What we previously objected to in this League was
ow relinquished as erroneous by the representatives of the League
emselves; we were even invited to co-operate in the work of
organisation. Could we say no? Certainly not. Therefore, we
ntered the League; Marx founded a League community in Brussels
om among our close friends, while I attended the three Paris
ommunities.

In the summer of 1847, the first League Congress took place in
ondon, at which W. Wolff represented the Brussels and I the
aris communities. At this congress the reorganisation of the League
as carried through first of all. Whatever remained of the old
ystical names dating back to the conspiratorial period was now
bolished; the League now consisted of communities, circles, lead-

---

* Pfänder died about eight years ago in London. He was a man of peculiarly
ne intelligence, witty, ironical and dialectical. Eccarius, as we know, was later
or many years Secretary of the General Council of the International Working
Men's Association, in the General Council of which the following old League
members were to be found, among others: Eccarius, Pfänder, Lessner, Lochner,
Marx and myself. Eccarius subsequently devoted himself exclusively to the
English trade-union movement. [Note by Engels.]

ing circles, a Central Committee and a Congress, and hencefor
called itself the "Communist League." "The aim of the League
the overthrow of the bourgeoisie, the rule of the proletariat, tl
abolition of the old, bourgeois society based on class antagonisr
and the foundation of a new society without classes and witho
private property"—thus ran the first article.* The organisation itse
was thoroughly democratic, with elective and always removab
boards. This alone barred all hankering after conspiracy, whi
requires dictatorship, and the League was converted—for ordina
peace times at least—into a pure propaganda society. These ne
Rules were submitted to the communities for discussion—so dem
cratic was the procedure now followed—then once again debate
at the Second Congress and finally adopted by the latter
December 8, 1847. They are to be found reprinted in Wermu
and Stieber, Vol. I, p. 239, Appendix X.

The Second Congress took place during the end of November ar
beginning of December of the same year. Marx also attended th
time and expounded the new theory in a fairly long debate—tl
congress lasted at least ten days. All contradiction and doubt we
finally set at rest, the new basic principles were unanimously adopte
and Marx and I were commissioned to draw up the Manifesto.*
This was done immediately afterwards. A few weeks before tl
February Revolution it was sent to London to be printed. Since the
it has travelled round the world, has been translated into almost a
languages and today still serves in numerous countries as a guide fc
the proletarian movement. In place of the old League motto, "A
Men Are Brothers," appeared the new battle cry, "Working Me
of All Countries, Unite!" which openly proclaimed the internation
character of the struggle. Seventeen years later this battle cr
resounded throughout the world as the watchword of the Interna
tional Working Men's Association, and today the militant proletari
of all countries has inscribed it on its banner.

The February Revolution broke out. The London Central Com
mittee functioning hitherto immediately transferred its powers t
the Brussels leading circle. But this decision came at a time whe
an actual state of siege already existed in Brussels, and the German
in particular could no longer assemble anywhere. We were all of u
just on the point of going to Paris, and so the new Central Com
mittee decided likewise to dissolve, to hand over all its powers t
Marx and to empower him immediately to constitute a new Centra
Committee in Paris. Hardly had the five persons who adopted thi
decision (March 3, 1848) separated, before the police forced thei

* See Marx/Engels, *Werke*, Bd. 4, Dietz Verlag, Berlin, 1959, S. 596-60
("Statuten des Bundes der Kommunisten").—*Ed.*
** See pp. 35-63 of this volume.—*Ed.*

ιy into Marx's house, arrested him and compelled him to leave
ιr France on the following day, which was just where he was want-
g to go.

In Paris we all soon came together again. There the following
ιcument was drawn up and signed by all the members of the new
εntral Committee. It was distributed throughout Germany and
ιany a one can still learn something from it even today:

DEMANDS OF THE COMMUNIST PARTY IN GERMANY[351]

1. The whole of Germany shall be declared a single indivisible
εpublic.

3. Representatives of the people shall be paid so that workers also
ιn sit in the parliament of the German people.

4. Universal arming of the people.

7. The estates of the princes and other feudal estates, all mines,
ιts, etc., shall be transformed into state property. On these estates,
ιgriculture is to be conducted on a large scale and with the most
ιodern scientific means for the benefit of all society.

8. Mortgages on peasant holdings shall be declared state property;
ιterest on such mortgages shall be paid by the peasants to the
ιate.

9. In the districts where tenant farming is developed, land rent
ιr farming dues shall be paid to the state as a tax.

11. All means of transport: railways, canals, steamships, roads,
ιost, etc., shall be taken over by the state. They are to be converted
ιnto state property and put at the disposal of the non-possessing
ιlass.

14. Limitation of the right of inheritance.

15. Introduction of a steeply graded progressive taxation and
ιbolition of taxes on consumer goods.

16. Establishment of national workshops. The state shall guar-
ιntee a living to all workers and provide for those unable to work.

17. Universal free elementary education.

It is in the interest of the German proletariat, of the petty bourgeoisie and peasantry, to work with all possible energy to put the
above measures through. For only by their realisation can the millions in Germany, who up to now have been exploited by a small
number of people and whom it will be attempted to keep in further
subjection, get their rights and the power that are their due as the
producers of all wealth.

> The Committee: *Karl Marx, Karl Schapper,*
> *H. Bauer, F. Engels, F. Moll, W. Wolff*

At that time the craze for revolutionary legions prevailed
Paris. Spaniards, Italians, Belgians, Dutch, Poles and Germa
flocked together in crowds to liberate their respective fatherlan
The German legion was led by Herwegh, Bornsted, Börnstein. Sir
immediately after the revolution all foreign workers not only l
their jobs but in addition were harassed by the public, the inf
into these legions was very great. The new government saw in th
a means of getting rid of foreign workers and granted them *l'éta*
du soldat, that is, quarters along their line of march and a marchi
allowance of fifty centimes per day up to the frontier, whereaft
the eloquent Lamartine, the Foreign Minister who was so readi
moved to tears, quickly found an opportunity of betraying them
their respective governments.

We opposed this playing with revolution in the most decisi
fashion. To carry an invasion, which was to import the revoluti
forcibly from outside, into the midst of the ferment then goi
on in Germany, meant to undermine the revolution in Germa
itself, to strengthen the governments and to deliver the legionaries
Lamartine guaranteed for that—defenceless into the hands of t
German troops. When subsequently the revolution was victorious
Vienna and Berlin, the legion became all the more purposeless; b
once begun, the game was continued.

We founded a German communist club,[352] in which we advise
the workers to keep away from the legion and to return instea
to their homes singly and work there for the movement. Our o
friend Flocon, who had a seat in the Provisional Governmen
obtained for the workers sent by us the same travel facilities a
had been granted to the legionaries. In this way we returned thre
or four hundred workers to Germany, including the great majorit
of the League members.

As could easily be foreseen, the League proved to be much to
weak a lever as against the popular mass movement that had no
broken out. Three-quarters of the League members who had previ
ously lived abroad had changed their domicile by returning to thei
homeland; their previous communities were thus to a great exten
dissolved and they lost all contact with the League. One part, th
more ambitious among them, did not even try to resume this contact
but each one began a small separate movement on his own account i
his own locality. Finally, the conditions in each separate petty state
each province and each town were so different that the League woulc
have been incapable of giving more than the most general directives
such directives were, however, much better disseminated through
the press. In short, from the moment when the causes which had
made the secret League necessary ceased to exist, the secret League
as such ceased to mean anything. But this could least of all surprise

e persons who had just stripped this same secret League of the last
estige of its conspiratorial character.

That, however, the League had been an excellent school for
volutionary activity was now demonstrated. On the Rhine, where
the *Neue Rheinische Zeitung*[27] provided a firm centre, in Nassau,
n Rhenish Hesse, etc., everywhere members of the League stood at
the head of the extreme democratic movement. The same was the
ase in Hamburg. In South Germany the predominance of petty-
bourgeois democracy stood in the way. In Breslau, Wilhelm Wolff
was active with great success until the summer of 1848; in addition
he received a Silesian mandate as an alternate representative in the
Frankfort parliament.[148] Finally, the compositor Stephan Born, who
had worked in Brussels and Paris as an active member of the League,
founded a Workers' Brotherhood in Berlin which became fairy
widespread and existed until 1850. Born, a very talented young man,
who, however, was a bit too much in a hurry to become a political
figure, "fraternised" with the most miscellaneous ragtag and bobtail
in order to get a crowd together, and was not at all the man who
could bring unity into the conflicting tendencies, light into the chaos.
Consequently, in the official publications of the association the views
represented in the *Communist Manifesto* were mingled hodge-podge
with guild recollections and guild aspirations, fragments of Louis
Blanc and Proudhon, protectionism, etc.; in short, they wanted to
please everybody. In particular, strikes, trade unions and producers'
co-operatives were set going and it was forgotten that above all it
was a question of first conquering, by means of political victories,
the field in which alone such things could be realised on a lasting
basis. When, afterwards, the victories of the reaction made the
leaders of the Brotherhood realise the necessity of taking a direct
part in the revolutionary struggle, they were naturally left in the
lurch by the confused mass which they had grouped around themselves. Born took part in the Dresden uprising in May 1849[30] and
had a lucky escape. But, in contrast to the great political movement
of the proletariat, the Workers' Brotherhood proved to be a pure
Sonderbund [separate league], which to a large extent existed only
on paper and played such a subordinate role that the reaction did
not find it necessary to suppress it until 1850, and its surviving
branches until several years later. Born, whose real name was Buttermilch, has not become a big political figure but a petty Swiss
professor, who no longer translates Marx into guild language but
the meek Renan into his own fulsome German.

With June 13, 1849, in Paris,[288] the defeat of the May insurrections in Germany and the suppression of the Hungarian revolution
by the Russians, a great period of the 1848 Revolution came to a
close. But the victory of the reaction was as yet by no means final.
A reorganisation of the scattered revolutionary forces was required,

and hence also of the League. The situation again forbade, as
1848, any open organisation of the proletariat; hence one had
organise again in secret.

In the autumn of 1849 most of the members of the previous centr
committees and congresses gathered again in London. The only on
still missing were Schapper, who was jailed in Wiesbaden but can
after his acquittal, in the spring of 1850, and Moll, who, after he ha
accomplished a series of most dangerous missions and agitation
journeys—in the end he recruited mounted gunners for the Palatina
artillery* right in the midst of the Prussian army in the Rhir
Province—joined the Besançon workers' company of Willich
corps and was killed by a shot in the head during the encounter
the Murg in front of the Rotenfels Bridge. On the other hand Willic
now entered upon the scene. Willich was one of those sentiment:
Communists so common in Western Germany since 1845, who o
that account alone was instinctively, furtively antagonistic to ou
critical tendency. More than that, he was entirely the prophet, cor
vinced of his personal mission as the predestined liberator of th
German proletariat and as such a direct claimant as much to politic:
as to military dictatorship. Thus, to the primitive Christian com
munism previously preached by Weitling was added a kind of com
munist Islam. However, the propaganda of this new religion wa
for the time being restricted to the refugee barracks under Willich
command.

Hence, the League was organised afresh; the Address of Marc
1850** was published in an appendix (Bd. IX, No. 1),[353] an
Heinrich Bauer sent as an emissary to Germany. The Address
composed by Marx and myself, is still of interest today, becaus
petty-bourgeois democracy is even now the party which must cer
tainly be the first to come to power in Germany as the saviour o
society from the communist workers on the occasion of the nex
European upheaval now soon due (the European revolutions, 1815
1830, 1848-52, 1870, have occurred at intervals of fifteen to eighteer
years in our century). Much of what is said there is, therefore, stil
applicable today. Heinrich Bauer's mission was crowned with
complete success. The trusty little shoemaker was a born diplomat
He brought the former members of the League, who had partly
become laggards and partly were acting on their own account, back
into the active organisation, and particularly also the then leaders

---

* The reference is to the artillery of the revolutionary army that fought against
the Prussian government troops in the Baden-Palatinate insurrection of May-
June 1849.—*Ed.*

** K. Marx and F. Engels, "Address of the Central Committee to the Communist League," March 1850 (see Marx and Engels, *Selected Works*, Vol. I,
Moscow, 1962, pp. 106-17).—*Ed.*

the Workers' Brotherhood. The League began to play the
ominant role in the workers', peasants' and athletic associations to
far greater extent than before 1848, so that the next quarterly
address to the communities, in June 1850,* could already report
at the student Schurz from Bonn (later on American ex-minister),
who was touring Germany in the interest of petty-bourgeois democracy, "had found all fit forces already in the hands of the League."
he League was undoubtedly the only revolutionary organisation
that had any significance in Germany.

But what purpose this organisation should serve depended very
substantially on whether the prospects of a renewed upsurge of the
revolution were realised. And in the course of the year 1850 this
became more and more improbable, indeed impossible. The industrial crisis of 1847, which had paved the way for the Revolution
of 1848, had been overcome: a new, unprecedented period of industrial prosperity had set in; whoever had eyes to see and used
them must have clearly realised that the revolutionary storm of 1848
was gradually spending itself.

"With this general prosperity, in which the productive forces
of bourgeois society develop as luxuriantly as is at all possible within
bourgeois relationships, *there can be no talk of a real revolution.
Such a revolution is only possible in the periods when both these
factors, the modern productive forces and the bourgeois productive
forms, come in collision with each other. The various quarrels in
which the representatives of the individual factions of the continental
party of order now indulge and mutually compromise themselves,
far from providing the occasion for new revolutions are, on the
contrary, possible only because the basis of the relationships is
momentarily so secure and, what the reaction does not know, so
bourgeois. From it all attempts of the reaction to hold up bourgeois
development will rebound just as certainly as all moral indignation
and all enthusiastic proclamations of the democrats.*" Thus Marx
and I wrote in the "Revue of May to October 1850" in the *Neue
Rheinische Zeitung. Politisch-ökonomische Revue*,[146] Nos. V and VI,
Hamburg 1850, p. 153.**

This cool estimation of the situation, however, was regarded as
heresy by many persons, at a time when Ledru-Rollin, Louis Blanc,
Mazzini, Kossuth and, among the lesser German lights, Ruge, Kinkel,
Gögg and the rest of them crowded in London to form provisional
governments of the future not only for their respective fatherlands

---

* Karl Marx/Friedrich Engels, "Ansprache der Zentralbehörde an den Bund
om Juni 1850" (see Marx/Engels, *Werke*, Bd. 7, Dietz Verlag, Berlin, 1960,
3. 306-12).—*Ed.*
** Karl Marx/Friedrich Engels, "Revue. Mai bis Oktober [1850]" (see
Marx/Engels, *Werke*, Bd. 7, Dietz Verlag, Berlin, 1960, S. 440).—*Ed.*

but for the whole of Europe, and when the only thing still necessa
was to obtain the requisite money from America as a loan for t
revolution to realise at a moment's notice the European revoluti
and the various republics which went with it as a matter of cour
Can anyone be surprised that a man like Willich was taken in
this, that Schapper, acting on his old revolutionary impulse, a
allowed himself to be fooled, and that the majority of the Lond
workers, to a large extent refugees themselves, followed them in
the camp of the bourgeois-democratic artificers of revolution? Suff
it to say that the reserve maintained by us was not to the mind
these people; one was to enter into the game of making revolutio
We most decisively refused to do so. A split ensued; more about tl
is to be read in the *Revelations*.* Then came the arrest of Nothjun
followed by that of Haupt, in Hamburg. The latter turned trait
by divulging the names of the Cologne Central Committee and bei
slated as the chief witness in the trial; but his relatives had no desi
to be thus disgraced and bundled him off to Rio de Janeiro, whe
he later established himself as a businessman and in recognition
his services was appointed first Prussian and then German Cons
General. He is now again in Europe.**

For a better understanding of the *Revelations*, I give the list (
the Cologne accused: 1) P. G. Röser, cigarmaker; 2) Heinricl
Bürgers, who later died, a progressive[354] deputy to the Landta;
3) Peter Nothjung, tailor, who died a few years ago a photographe
in Breslau; 4) W. J. Reiff; 5) Dr. Hermann Becker, now chief burg
master of Cologne and member of the Upper House; 6) Dr. Rolan
Daniels, physician, who died a few years after the trial as a resu
of tuberculosis contracted in prison; 7) Karl Otto, chemist; 8) D
Abraham Jacoby, now physician in New York; 9) Dr. I. J. Klei;
now physician and town councillor in Cologne; 10) Ferdinand Freili
grath, who, however, was at that time already in London; 11) I. I
Ehrhard, clerk; 12) Friedrich Lessner, tailor, now in London. Afte
a public trial before a jury lasting from October 4 to November 1!
1852, the following were sentenced for attempted high treason
Röser, Bürgers and Nothjung to six, Reiff, Otto and Becker to fiv
and Lessner to three years' confinement in a fortress; Daniels, Klei
Jacoby and Ehrhard were acquitted.

With the Cologne trial the first period of the German communi

---

* K. Marx, "Enthüllungen über den Kommunisten-Prozeß zu Köln" (Marx
Engels, *Werke*, Bd. 8, Dietz Verlag, Berlin, 1960, S. 405-70).—*Ed.*
** Schapper died in London at the end of the sixties. Willich took part in th
American Civil War[129] with distinction; he became Brigadier-General and wa
shot in the chest during the battle of Murfreesboro (Tennessee) but recovere
and died about ten years ago in America. Of the other persons mentioned above
I will only remark that Heinrich Bauer was lost track of in Australia, and tha
Weitling and Everbeck died in America. [*Note by Engels.*]

orkers' movement comes to an end. Immediately after the sentence
e dissolved our League; a few months later the Willich-Schapper
parate league[355] was also laid to eternal rest.

* * *

A whole generation lies between then and now At that time
ermany was a country of handicraft and of domestic industry
ased on hand labour; now it is a big industrial country still
ndergoing continual industrial transformation. At that time one had
 seek out one by one the workers who had an understanding of
eir position as workers and of their historico-economic antagonism
 capital, because this antagonism itself was only just beginning to
evelop. Today the entire German proletariat has to be placed under
xceptional laws,[167] merely in order to slow down a little the process
f its development to full consciousness of its position as an op-
ressed class. At that time the few persons whose minds had
enetrated to the point of realising the historical role of the pro-
tariat had to foregather in secret, to assemble clandestinely in
nall communities of 3 to 20 persons. Today the German proletariat
o longer needs any official organisation, either public or secret.*
he simple self-evident interconnection of like-minded class com-
ades suffices, without any rules, boards, resolutions or other tangible
orms, to shake the whole German Empire to its foundations.
ismarck is the arbiter of Europe beyond the frontiers of Germany,
ut within them there grows daily more threateningly the athletic
igure of the German proletariat that Marx foresaw already in 1844,
he giant for whom the cramped imperial edifice designed to fit the
hilistine is even now becoming inadequate and whose mighty
tature and broad shoulders are growing until the moment comes
vhen by merely rising from his seat he will shatter the whole
tructure of the imperial constitution into fragments. And still more.
he international movement of the European and American pro-
etariat has become so much strengthened that not merely its first
arrow form—the secret League—but even its second, infinitely
vider form—the open International Working Men's Association—
as become a fetter for it, and that the simple feeling of solidarity
ased on the understanding of the identity of class position suffices
o create and to hold together one and the same great party of the
roletariat among the workers of all countries and tongues. The
loctrine which the League represented from 1847 to 1852, and which
t that time could be treated by the wise Philistines with a shrug of
he shoulders as the hallucinations of utter madcaps, as the secret

---

* These words of Engels's are an ironic challenge of Bismarck's policy to pro-
iibit the proletarian party and strangle the workers' movement.—*Ed.*

doctrine of a few scattered sectarians, has now innumerable adheren
in all civilised countries of the world, among those condemned
the Siberian mines as much as among the gold diggers of Californi
and the founder of this doctrine, the most hated, most slandered ma
of his time, *Karl Marx*, was, when he died, the ever-sought-for an
ever-willing counsellor of the proletariat of both the old and th
new world.

Frederick Enge

Published in the book:
Karl Marx. *Enthüllungen
über den Kommunisten-Prozeß
zu Köln.* Hottingen-Zürich,
1885, and in the newspaper
Der Sozialdemokrat Nos. 46-48
November 12, 19 and 26, 1885

Printed according to the
text of the book
Translated from the Germ

Frederick Engels

THE ORIGIN OF THE FAMILY, PRIVATE PROPERTY AND THE STATE[356]

PREFACE TO THE FIRST EDITION 1884

The following chapters constitute, in a sense, the fulfilment of a bequest. It was no less a person than Karl Marx who had planned to present the results of Morgan's researches in connection with the conclusions arrived at by his own—within certain limits I might say our own—materialist investigation of history and thus to make clear their whole significance. For Morgan rediscovered in America, in his own way, the materialist conception of history that had been discovered by Marx forty years ago, and in his comparison of barbarism and civilisation was led by this conception to the same conclusions, in the main points, as Marx had arrived at. And just as *Capital* was for years both zealously plagiarised and persistently hushed up on the part of the official economists in Germany, so was Morgan's *Ancient Society** treated by the spokesmen of "prehistoric" science in England. My work can offer but a meagre substitute for that which my departed friend was not destined to accomplish. However, I have before me, in his extensive extracts from Morgan,** critical notes which I reproduce here wherever this is at all possible.

According to the materialistic conception, the determining factor in history is, in the last resort, the production and reproduction of immediate life. But this itself is of a twofold character. On the one hand, the production of the means of subsistence, of food, clothing and shelter and the tools requisite therefore; on the other, the production of human beings themselves, the propagation of the species. The social institutions under which men of a definite historical epoch and of a definite country live are conditioned by both kinds of production: by the stage of development of labour, on the one hand, and of the family, on the other. The less the development of labour, and the more limited its

---

* *Ancient Society, or Researches in the Lines of Human Progress from Savagery Through Barbarism to Civilisation.* By Lewis H. Morgan, London, MacMillan & Co., 1877. This book was printed in America, and is remarkably difficult to obtain in London. The author died a few years ago. [*Note by Engels.*]
** The reference is to Karl Marx's *Abstract of Morgan's "Ancient Society"* (see *Marx-Engels Archive*, Vol. IX, 1941, pp. 1-192).—*Ed.*

volume of production and, therefore, the wealth of society, the more preponderatingly does the social order appear to be dominated by ties of sex. However, within this structure of society based on ties of sex, the productivity of labour develops more and more; with it, private property and exchange, differences in wealth, the possibility of utilising the labour power of others, and thereby the basis of class antagonisms: new social elements, which strive in the course of generations to adapt the old structure of society to the new conditions, until, finally, the incompatibility of the two leads to a complete revolution. The old society, built on groups based on ties of sex, bursts asunder in the collision of the newly-developed social classes; in its place a new society appears, constituted in a state, the lower units of which are no longer groups based on ties of sex but territorial groups, a society in which the family system is entirely dominated by the property system, and in which the class antagonisms and class struggles, which make up the content of all hitherto *written* history, now freely develop.

Morgan's great merit lies in having discovered and reconstructed this prehistoric foundation of our written history in its main features, and in having found in the groups based on ties of sex of the North American Indians the key to the most important, hitherto insoluble, riddles of the earliest Greek, Roman and German history. His book, however, was not the work of one day. He grappled with his material for nearly forty years until he completely mastered it. That is why his book is one of the few epoch-making works of our time.

In the following exposition the reader will, on the whole, easily be able to distinguish between what has been taken from Morgan and what I have added myself. In the historical sections dealing with Greece and Rome I have not limited myself to Morgan's data, but have added what I had at my disposal. The sections dealing with the Celts and the Germans are substantially my own; here Morgan had at his disposal almost exclusively second-hand sources, and, as far as German conditions were concerned—with the exception of Tacitus—only the wretched liberal falsifications of Mr. Freeman. The economic arguments, sufficient for Morgan's purpose but wholly inadequate for my own, have all been elaborated afresh by myself. And, finally, I of course am responsible for all conclusions wherever Morgan is not expressly quoted.

Written around May 26, 1884

Published in the book: F. Engels, *Der Ursprung der Familie, des Privateigenthums und des Staats.* Hottingen-Zürich, 1884

Printed according to the text of the fourth German edition, of the book, 1891

Translated from the German

PREFACE TO THE FOURTH EDITION 1891

The previous large editions of this work have been out of print now for almost six months and the publisher* has for some time past desired me to prepare a new edition. More urgent tasks have hitherto prevented me from doing so. Seven years have elapsed since the first edition appeared, and during this period our knowledge of the original forms of the family has made important progress. It was, therefore, necessary diligently to apply the hand to the work of amplification and improvement, particularly in view of the fact that the proposed stereotyping of the present text will make further changes on my part impossible for some time to come.

I have, therefore, submitted the whole text to a careful revision, and have made a number of additions, in which, I hope, due regard has been paid to the present state of science. Further, in the course of this preface, I give a brief review of the development of the history of the family from Bachofen to Morgan, principally because the English prehistoric school, which is tinged with chauvinism, continues to do its utmost to kill by silence the revolution Morgan's discoveries have made in conceptions of the history of primitive society, although it does not hesitate in the least to appropriate his results. Elsewhere, too, this English example is followed only too often.

My work has been translated into various languages. First into Italian: *L'origine della famiglia, della proprietà privata e dello stato, versione riveduta dall'autore, di Pasquale Martignetti*; Benevento 1885. Then Rumanian: *Origina familiei, proprietatei private si a statului, traducere de Joan Nadejde*, in the Yassy periodical *Contemporanul*,[357] September 1885 to May 1886. Further into Danish: *Familjens, Privatejendommens og Statens Oprindelse, Dansk, af Forfatteren gennemgaaet Udgave, besorget af Gerson Trier*, Köbenhavn 1888. A French translation by Henri Ravé based on the present German edition is in the press.

* * *

Until the beginning of the sixties there was no such thing as a history of the family. In this sphere historical science was still completely under the influence of the Five Books of Moses. The patriarchal form of the family, described there in greater detail than anywhere else, was not only implicitly accepted as the oldest form of the family, but also—after excluding polygamy—identified with the present-day bourgeois family, as if the family had really undergone no historical development at all. At most it was admitted that a period of promiscuous sexual relationships might have existed

---

* J. Dietz.—*Ed.*

in primeval times. To be sure, in addition to monogamy, Oriental
polygamy and Indo-Tibetan polyandry were also known, but these
three forms could not be arranged in any historical sequence and
appeared disconnectedly alongside of each other. That among certain
peoples of ancient times, and among some still existing savages, the
line of descent was reckoned not from the father but from the mother
and, therefore, the female lineage alone was regarded as valid; that
among many peoples of today marriage within definite larger groups
—not subjected to closer investigation at that time—is prohibited
and that this custom is to be met with in all parts of the world—these
facts were indeed known and new examples were constantly being
brought to light. But nobody knew what to do with them, and even
in E.B. Tylor's *Researches into the Early History of Mankind*, etc.
(1865), they figure merely as "strange customs" along with the taboo
in force among some savages against the touching of burning wood
with iron tools, and similar religious bosh and nonsense.

The study of the history of the family dates from 1861, from the
publication of Bachofen's *Mother Right*. In this work the author
advances the following propositions: 1) that in the beginning humanity lived in a state of sexual promiscuity, which the author unhap-
pily designates as "hetaerism"; 2) that such promiscuity excludes
all certainty as regards paternity, that lineage, therefore, could be
reckoned only through the female line—according to mother right—
and that originally this was the case among all the peoples of antiquity; 3) that consequently women, who, as mothers, were the only
definitely ascertainable parents of the younger generation, were treated with a high degree of consideration and respect, which, according to Bachofen's conception, was enhanced to the complete rule
of women (gynaecocracy); 4) that the transition to monogamy,
where the woman belongs exclusively to one man, implied the violation of a primeval religious injunction (that is, in actual fact, the
violation of the ancient traditional right of the other men to the
same woman), a violation which had to be atoned for, or the toleration of which had to be purchased, by surrendering the woman for a
limited period of time.

Bachofen finds evidence in support of these propositions in
countless passages of ancient classical literature, which he had
assembled with extraordinary diligence. According to him, the
evolution from "hetaerism" to monogamy, and from mother right
to father right, takes place, particularly among the Greeks, as a
consequence of the evolution of religious ideas, the intrusion of
new deities, representatives of the new outlook, into the old traditional pantheon representing the old outlook, so that the latter is more
and more driven into the background by the former. Thus, according to Bachofen, it is not the development of the actual conditions
under which men live, but the religious reflection of these conditions

of life in the minds of men that brought about the historical changes in the mutual social position of man and woman. Bachofen accordingly points to the *Oresteia* of Aeschylus as a dramatic depiction of the struggle between declining mother right and rising and victorious father right in the Heroic Age. Clytemnestra has slain her husband Agamemnon, just returned from the Trojan War, for the sake of her lover Aegisthus; but Orestes, her son by Agamemnon, avenges his father's murder by slaying his mother. For this he is pursued by the Erinyes, the demonic defenders of mother right, according to which matricide is the most heinous and inexpiable of crimes. But Apollo, who through his oracle has incited Orestes to commit this deed, and Athena, who is called in as arbiter—the two deities which here represent the new order, based on father right—protect him. Athena hears both sides. The whole controversy is briefly summarised in the debate which now ensues between Orestes and the Erinyes. Orestes declares that Clytemnestra is guilty of a double outrage; for in killing *her* husband she also killed *his* father. Why then have the Erinyes persecuted him and not Clytemnestra, who is much the greater culprit? The reply is striking:

"*Unrelated by blood* was she to the man that she slew."*

The murder of a man not related by blood, even though he be the husband of the murderess, is expiable and does not concern the Erinyes. Their function is to avenge only murders among blood-relatives, and the most heinous of all these, according to mother right, is matricide. Apollo now intervenes in defence of Orestes. Athena calls upon the Areopagites—the Athenian jurors—to vote on the question. The votes for acquittal and for the conviction are equal. Then Athena, as President of the Court, casts her vote in favour of Orestes and acquits him. Father right has gained the day over mother right. The "gods of junior lineage," as they are described by the Erinyes themselves, are victorious over the Erinyes, and the latter allow themselves finally to be persuaded to assume a new office in the service of the new order.

This new but absolutely correct interpretation of the *Oresteia* is one of the best and most beautiful passages in the whole book, but it shows at the same time that Bachofen himself believes in the Erinyes, Apollo and Athena at least as much as Aeschylus did in his day; he, in fact, believes that in the Heroic Age of Greece they performed the miracle of overthrowing mother right and replacing it by father right. Clearly, such a conception—which regards religion as the decisive lever in world history—must finally end in sheer mysticism. It is, therefore, an arduous and by no means always profitable task to wade through Bachofen's bulky

* Aeschylus, *Oresteia. Eumenides.—Ed.*

quarto volume. But all this does not detract from his merit as a pioneer, for he was the first to substitute for mere phrases about an unknown primitive condition of promiscuous sexual intercourse proof that ancient classical literature teems with tràces of a condition that had in fact existed before monogamy among the Greeks and the Asiatics, in which not only a man had sexual intercourse with more than one woman, but a woman had sexual intercourse with more than one man, without violating the established custom; that this custom did not disappear without leaving traces in the form of the limited surrender by which women were compelled to purchase their right to monogamian marriage; that descent, therefore, could orginally be reckoned only in the female line, from mother to mother, that this exclusive validity of the female line persisted far into the time of monogamy with assured, or at least recognised, paternity; and that this original position of the mother as the sole certain parent of her children assured her, and thus women in general, a higher social status than they have ever enjoyed since. Bachofen did not express these propositions as clearly as this—his mystical outlook prevented him from doing so; but he proved that they were correct, and this, in 1861, meant a complete revolution.

Bachofen's bulky tome was written in German, that is, in the language of the nation which, at that time, interested itself less than any other in the prehistory of the present-day family. He, therefore, remained unknown. His immediate successor in this field appeared in 1865, without ever having heard of Bachofen.

This successor was J. F. McLennan, the direct opposite of his predecessor. Instead of the talented mystic, we have here the dry-as-dust lawyer; instead of exuberant poetic fancy, we have the plausible arguments of the advocate pleading his case. McLennan finds among many savage, barbarian and even civilised peoples of ancient and modern times a form of marriage in which the bridegroom, alone or accompanied by friends, has to feign to carry off the bride from her relatives by force. This custom must be the survival of a previous custom, whereby the men of one tribe acquired their wives from outside, from other tribes, by actually abducting them by force. How then did this "marriage by abduction" originate? As long as men could find sufficient women in their own tribe there was no occasion for it whatsoever. But quite as often we find that among undeveloped peoples certain groups exist (which round about 1865 were still often identified with the tribes themselves) within which marriage is forbidden, so that the men are obliged to secure their wives, and the women their husbands, from outside the group; while among others the custom prevails that the men of a certain group are compelled to find their wives only within their own group. McLennan calls the first type of group exogamous, and the second endogamous, and without further ado establishes a rigid antithesis between exogamous and endogamous "tribes." And although his own researches into exogamy bring under his very nose the fact that in many, if not most, or even all cases this antithesis exists only in his own imagination, he nevertheless makes it the foundation of his entire theory. Accordingly, exogamous tribes may procure their wives only from other tribes; and in the state of permanent inter-tribal warfare that is characteristic of savagery, this, he believes, could be done only by abduction.

McLennan argues further: Whence this custom of exogamy? The conceptions of consanguinity and incest have nothing to do with it, for these are things which developed only much later. But the custom, widespread among savages, of killing female children immediately after birth, might. This custom created a superfluity of men in each individual tribe, the necessary and immediate sequel of which was the common possession of a woman by a number of men—polyandry. The consequence of this again was that the mother of a child was known, but the father was not, hence kinship was reckoned only in the female line to the exclusion of the male—mother right. And another consequence of the dearth of women within a tribe—a dearth mitigated but not overcome by polyandry—was precisely the system-atic, forcible abduction of women of other tribes.

"As exogamy and polyandry are referable to one and the same cause—a want of balance between the sexes—we are forced *to regard all the exogamous races as having originally been polyandrous....* Therefore, we must hold it to be beyond dispute that among exogamous races the first system of kinship was that which recognised blood ties through mothers only." (McLennan, *Studies in Ancient History*, 1886. *Primitive Marriage*, p. 124.)

McLennan's merit lies in having drawn attention to the general prevalence and great importance of what he terms exogamy. But he by no means *discovered* the existence of exogamous groups, and still less did he understand it. Apart from the earlier, isolated notes of many observers which served as McLennan's sources, Latham (*Descriptive Ethnology*, 1859) exactly and correctly described this institu-tion among the Indian Magars[358] and declared that it was generally prevalent and existed in all parts of the world—a passage which McLennan himself quotes. And our Morgan, too, as far back as 1847, in his letters on the Iroquois (in the *American Review*), and in 1851 in *The League of the Iroquois* proved that it existed in this tribe, and described it correctly, whereas, as we shall see, McLennan's lawyer's mentality caused far greater confusion on this subject than Bachofen's mystical fantasy did in the sphere of mother right. It is also to McLennan's credit that he recognised the system of tracing descent through mothers as the original one, although, as he himself admitted later, Bachofen anticipated him in this. But here again he is far from clear; he speaks continually of "kinship through females only" and constantly applies this expression—correct for an earlier stage—also to later stages of development, where, although descent and inheritance are still exclusively reckoned in the female line, kinship is also recognised and expressed in the male line. This is the restricted outlook of the jurist, who creates a rigid legal term for himself and continues to apply it without modification to conditions which in the meantime have rendered it inapplicable.

In spite of its plausibility, McLennan's theory evidently did not seem to be too well founded even to the author himself. At least, he himself is struck by the fact that

"it is observable that the form of [mock] capture is now most distinctly marked and impressive just among those races which have *male* kinship [meaning descent through the male line]" (p. 140).

And, again:

"It is a curious fact that nowhere now, that we are aware of, is infanticide *a system* where exogamy and the earliest form of kinship co-exist" (p. 146).

Both these facts directly refute his interpretation, and he can oppose to them only new, still more intricate, hypotheses.

Nevertheless, in England his theory met with great approbation and evoked great response. McLennan was generally accepted there as the founder of the history of the family, and the most eminent authority in this field. His antithesis between exogamous and endogamous "tribes," notwithstanding the few exceptions and modifications admitted, remained nevertheless the recognised foundation of the prevailing view, and was the blinker which made any free survey of the field under investigation and, consequently, any definite progress, impossible. The overrating of McLennan, which became the vogue in England and, following the English fashion, elsewhere as well, makes it a duty to point out in contrast that the harm he caused with his completely erroneous antithesis between exogamous and endogamous "tribes" outweighs the good done by his researches.

Meanwhile, more and more facts soon came to light, which did not fit into his neat scheme. McLennan knew only three forms of marriage—polygamy, polyandry and monogamy. But once attention had been directed to this point, more and more proofs were discovered of the fact that among undeveloped peoples forms of marriage existed in which a group of men possessed a group of women in common; and Lubbock (in his *The Origin of Civilisation*, 1870) acknowledged this group marriage ("communal marriage") to be a historical fact.

Immediately after, in 1871, *Morgan* appeared with new and, in many respects, conclusive material. He had become convinced that the peculiar system of kinship prevailing among the Iroquois was common to all the aborigines of the United States and was thus spread over a whole continent, although it conflicted directly with the degrees of kinship actually arising from the connubial system in force there. He thereupon prevailed on the American Federal Government to collect information about the kinship systems of the other peoples, on the basis of questionnaires and tables drawn up by himself; and he discovered from the answers: 1) that the American Indian system of kinship prevailed also among numerous tribes in Asia, and, in a somewhat modified form, in Africa and Australia; 2) that it was completely explained by a form of group marriage, now approaching extinction, in Hawaii and in other Australian islands; and 3) that, however, alongside this marriage form, a system of kinship prevailed in these same islands which could only be explained by a still earlier but now extinct form of group marriage. He published the collected data and his conclusions from them in his *Systems of Consanguinity and Affinity*, 1871 and thereby carried the discussion on to an infinitely wider field. Taking the systems of kinship as his starting-point, he reconstructed the forms of the family corresponding to them, and thereby opened up a new avenue of investigation and a more far-reaching retrospect into the prehistory of mankind. Were this method to be recognised as valid, McLennan's neat construction would be resolved into thin air.

McLennan defended his theory in a new edition of *Primitive Marriage (Studies in Ancient History*, 1876). While he himself very artificially constructs a history of the family out of sheer hypotheses, he demands of Lubbock and Morgan not only proofs for every one of their statements, but proofs of incontestable validity such as alone would be admitted in a Scottish court of law. And this is done by the man who, from the close relationship between one's mother's brother and one's sister's son among the Germans (Tacitus, *Germania*, c. 20), from Caesar's report that the Britons in groups of ten or twelve possessed their wives in common, and from all the other reports of ancient writers concerning community of women among the barbarians, unhesitatingly concludes that polyandry was the rule among all these peoples! It is like listening to counsel for the prosecution, who permits himself every license in preparing his own case, but demands the most formal and legally most valid proof for every word of counsel for the defence.

Group marriage is a pure figment of the imagination, he asserts, and thus falls back far behind Bachofen. Morgan's systems of kinship, he says, are nothing more than mere precepts on social politeness, proved by the fact that the Indians also address strangers, white men, as "brother," or "father." It is as if one were to argue that the terms father, mother, brother, sister are merely empty forms of address because Catholic priests and abbesses are likewise addressed as father and mother, and because monks and nuns, and even freemasons and members of English craft unions, in solemn session assembled, are addressed as brother and sister. In short, McLennan's defence was miserably weak.

One point, however, remained on which he had not been challenged. The antithesis between exogamous and endogamous tribes on which his whole system was founded not only remained unshaken, but was even generally accepted as the cornerstone of the entire history of the family. It was admitted that McLennan's attempt to explain this antithesis was inadequate and contradicted the very facts he himself had enumerated. But the antithesis itself, the existence of two mutually exclusive types of separate and independent tribes, one of which took its wives from within the tribe, while this was absolutely forbidden to the other—this passed as incontrovertible gospel truth. Compare, for example, Giraud-Teulon's *Origin of the Family* (1874) and even Lubbock's *Origin of Civilisation* (Fourth Edition, 1882).

This is the point at which Morgan's chief work enters: *Ancient Society* (1877), the book upon which the present work is based. What Morgan only dimly surmised in 1871 is here developed with full comprehension. Endogamy and exogamy constitute no antithesis; up to the present no exogamous "tribes" have been brought to light anywhere. But at the time when group marriage still prevailed—and in all probability it existed everywhere at one time or other—the tribe consisted of a number of groups related by blood on the mother's side, gentes, within which marriage was strictly prohibited, so that although the men of a gens could, and as a rule did, take their wives from within their tribe, they had, however, to take them from outside their gens. Thus, while the gens itself was strictly exogamous, the tribe, embracing all the gentes, was as strictly endogamous. With this, the last remnants of McLennan's artificial structure definitely collapsed.

Morgan, however, did not rest content with this. The gens of the American Indians served him further as a means of making the second decisive advance in the field 'of investigation he had entered upon. He discovered that the gens, organised according to mother right, was the original form out of which developed the later gens, organised according to father right, the gens as we find it among the civilised peoples of antiquity. The Greek and Roman gens, an enigma to all previous historians, was now explained by the Indian gens, and thus a new basis was found for the whole history of primitive society.

The rediscovery of the original mother-right gens as the stage preliminary to the father-right gens of the civilised peoples has the same significance for the history of primitive society as Darwin's theory of evolution has for biology, and Marx's theory of surplus value for political economy. It enabled Morgan to outline for the first time a history of the family, wherein at least the classical stages of development are, on the whole, provisionally established, as far as the material at present available permits. Clearly, this opens a new era in the treatment of the history of primitive society. The mother-right gens has become the pivot around which this entire science turns; since its discovery we know in which direction to conduct our researches, what to investigate and how to classify the results of our investigations. As a consequence, progress in this field is now much more rapid than before Morgan's book appeared.

Morgan's discoveries are now generally recognised, or rather appropriated, by prehistorians in England, too. But scarcely one of them will openly acknowledge that it is to Morgan that we owe this revolution in outlook. In England his book is hushed up as far as possible, and Morgan himself is dismissed with condescending praise for his *previous* work; the details of his exposition are eagerly picked on for criticism, while an obstinate silence reigns with regard to his really great discoveries. The original edition of *Ancient Society* is now out of print; in America there is no profitable market for books of this sort; in England, it would seem, the book was systematically suppressed, and the only edition of this epoch-making work still available in the book trade is—the German translation.

Whence this reserve, which it is difficult not to regard as a conspiracy of silence, particularly in view of the host of quotations given merely for politeness' sake and of other evidences of camaraderie, in which the writings of our recognised prehistorians abound? Is it perhaps because Morgan is an American, and it is very hard for English prehistorians, despite their highly commendable diligence in the collection of material, to have to depend for the general viewpoint which determines the arrangement and grouping of this material, in short, for their ideas, upon two talented foreigners—Bachofen and Morgan? A German might be tolerated, but an American? Every Englishman waxes patriotic when faced with an American, amusing examples of which I have come across while I was in the United States.[359] To this must be added that McLennan was, so to speak, the officially proclaimed founder and leader of the English prehistoric school; that it was, in a sense, good form among prehistorians to refer only with the greatest reverence to his artificially constructed historical theory leading from infanticide, through polyandry and marriage by abduction, to the mother-right family; that the slightest doubt cast upon the existence of mutually wholly exclusive exogamous and endogamous "tribes" was regarded as rank heresy; so that Morgan, in thus resolving all these hallowed dogmas into thin air, was guilty of a kind of sacrilege. Moreover, he resolved them in such a way that he had only to state his case for it to become obvious at once; and the McLennan worshippers, hitherto confusedly staggering about between exogamy and endogamy, were almost driven to beating their foreheads and exclaiming: How could we have been so stupid as not to have discovered all this for ourselves long ago!

And, as though this were not crime enough to prohibit the official school from treating him with anything else but cold indifference, Morgan filled the cup to overflowing not only by criticising civilisation, the society of commodity production, the basic form of our present-day society, after a fashion reminiscent of Fourier, but also by speaking of a future transformation of society in words which Karl Marx might have used. He received his deserts, therefore, when McLennan indignantly charged him with having "a profound antipathy to the historical method," and when Professor Giraud-Teulon endorsed this view in Geneva as late as 1884. Was it not this same M. Giraud-Teulon, who, in 1874 (*Origines de la famille*), was still wandering helplessly in the maze of McLennan's exogamy, from which it took Morgan to liberate him?

It is not necessary for me to deal here with the other advances which the history of primitive society owes to Morgan; a reference to what is needed will be found in the course of this book. During the fourteen years that have elapsed since the publication of his chief work our material relating to the history of primitive human societies has been greatly augmented. In addition to anthropologists, travellers and professional prehistorians, students of comparative law have taken the field and have contributed new material and new points of view. As a consequence, some of Morgan's hypotheses pertaining to particular points have been shaken, or even become untenable. But nowhere have the newly-collected data led to the supplanting of his principal conceptions by others. In its main features, the order he introduced into the study of the history of primitive society holds good to this day. We can even say that it is finding increasingly general acceptance in the same measure as his authorship of this great advance is being concealed.*

Frederick Engels

London, June 16, 1891

Published in the journal
Die Neue Zeit, Bd. 2,
No. 41, 1890-91, and in the
book: Friedrich Engels. *Der
Ursprung der Familie,
des Privateigenthums und
des Staats.* Stuttgart, 1891

Printed according to the
text of the book checked
with the text of the journal
Translated from the German

---

* On my return voyage from New York in September 1888 I met an ex-Congressman for Rochester who had known Lewis Morgan. Unfortunately, he could tell me little about him. Morgan, he said, had lived in Rochester as a private citizen occupying himself only with his studies. His brother was a colonel in the army, and held a post in the War Department at Washington. Through the good offices of his brother, he had succeeded in interesting the government in his researches and in publishing a number of his works at public cost. This ex-Congressman said that he himself had also assisted in this while in Congress. [*Note by Engels.*]

THE ORIGIN OF THE FAMILY, PRIVATE PROPERTY AND THE STATE

IN THE LIGHT OF THE RESEARCHES OF LEWIS H. MORGAN[356]

I

PREHISTORIC STAGES OF CULTURE

Morgan was the first person with expert knowledge to attempt to introduce a definite order into the prehistory of man; unless important additional material necessitates alterations, his classification may be expected to remain in force.

Of the three main epochs, savagery, barbarism and civilisation, he is naturally concerned only with the first two, and with the transition to the third. He subdivides each of these two epochs into a lower, middle and upper stage, according to the progress made in the production of the means of subsistence; for, as he says:

"Upon their skill in this direction, the whole question of human supremacy on the earth depended. Mankind are the only beings who may be said to have gained an absolute control over the production of food. The great epochs of human progress have been indentified, more or less directly, with the enlargement of the sources of subsistence."*

The evolution of the family proceeds concurrently, but does not offer such conclusive criteria for the delimitation of the periods.

1. SAVAGERY

1. *Lower Stage.* Infancy of the human race. Man still lived in his original habitat, tropical or subtropical forests, dwelling, at least partially, in trees; this alone explains his continued survival in face of the large beasts of prey. Fruits, nuts and roots served him as food; the formation of articulate speech was the main achievement of this period. None of the peoples that became known during the historical period were any longer in this primeval state. Although this period may have lasted for many thousands of years, we have no direct evidence of its existence; but once we admit the descent of man from the animal kingdom, the acceptance of this transitional stage is inevitable.

2. *Middle Stage.* Begins with the utilisation of fish (under which head we also include crabs, shellfish and other aquatic animals) for food and with the employment of fire. These two are complemen-

---

* See also *Marx-Engels Archive*, Vol. IX, p. 4.—*Ed.*

tary, since fish food becomes fully available only by the use of fire.
This new food, however, made man independent of climate and
locality. By following the rivers and coasts man was able, even in
his savage state, to spread over the greater part of the earth's surface.
The crude, unpolished stone implements of the earlier Stone Age—
the so-called palaeolithic—which belong wholly, or predominantly,
to this period, and are scattered over all the continents, are evidence
of these migrations. The newly-occupied territories as well as the un-
ceasingly active urge for discovery, linked with their command of
the art of producing fire by friction, made available new foodstuffs,
such as farinaceous roots and tubers, baked in hot ashes or in baking
pits (ground ovens), and game, which was occasionally added to the
diet after the invention of the first weapons—the club and the spear.
Exclusively hunting peoples, such as figure in books, that is, peoples
subsisting *solely* by hunting, have never existed, for the fruits of the
chase are much too precarious to make that possible. As a consequence
of the continued uncertainty with regard to sources of foodstuffs
cannibalism appears to have arisen at this stage, and continued for a
long time. The Australians and many Polynesians are to this day in
this middle stage of savagery.

3. *Upper Stage.* Begins with the invention of the bow and arrow,
whereby wild game became a regular item of food, and hunting one
of the normal occupations. Bow, string and arrow constitute a very
composite instrument, the invention of which presupposes long accumulated experience and sharpened mental powers, and, consequently,
a simultaneous acquaintance with a host of other inventions. If we
compare the peoples which, although familiar with the bow and
arrow, are not yet acquainted with the art of pottery (from which
point Morgan dates the transition to barbarism), we find, even at
this early stage, beginnings of settlement in villages, a certain mastery of the production of means of subsistence: wooden vessels and
utensils, finger weaving (without looms) with filaments of bast, baskets woven from bast or rushes, and polished (neolithic) stone implements. For the most part, also, fire and the stone axe have already
provided the dug-out canoe and, in places, timber and planks for
house-building. All these advances are to be found, for example,
among the Indians of North-Western America, who, although
familiar with the bow and arrow, know nothing of pottery
The bow and arrow was for savagery what the iron sword was
for barbarism and firearms for civilisation, namely, the decisive
weapon.

2. BARBARISM

1. *Lower Stage.* Dates from the introduction of pottery. This
latter had its origin, demonstrably in many cases and probably

everywhere, in the coating of baskets or wooden vessels with clay in order to render them fire-proof; whereby it was soon discovered that moulded clay also served the purpose without the inner vessel.

Up to this point we could regard the course of evolution as being generally valid for a definite period among all peoples, irrespective of locality. With the advent of barbarism, however, we reach a stage where the difference in natural endowment of the two great continents begins to assert itself. The characteristic feature of the period of barbarism is the domestication and breeding of animals and the cultivation of plants. Now the Eastern Continent, the so-called Old World, contained almost all the animals suitable for domestication and all the cultivable cereals with one exception; while the Western America contained only one domesticable mammal, the llama, and this only in a part of the South; and only one cereal fit for cultivation, but that the best, maize. The effect of these different natural conditions was that from now on the population of each hemisphere went its own special way, and the landmarks on the border lines between the various stages are different in each of the two cases.

2. *Middle Stage.* Begins, in the East, with the domestication of animals; in the West, with the cultivation of edible plants by means of irrigation, and with the use of adobes (bricks dried in the sun) and stone for buildings.

We shall commence with the West, because there this stage was nowhere outgrown until the European Conquest.

At the time of their discovery the Indians in the lower stage of barbarism (to which all those found east of the Mississippi belonged) already engaged to a certain extent in the garden cultivation of maize and perhaps also of pumpkins, melons and other garden produce, which supplied a very substantial part of their food. They lived in wooden houses, in villages surrounded by stockades. The tribes of the North-West, particularly those living in the region of the Columbia River, still remained in the upper stage of savagery and were familiar neither with pottery nor with any kind of plant cultivation. On the other hand, the so-called Pueblo Indians of New Mexico,[360] the Mexicans, Central Americans and Peruvians were in the middle stage of barbarism at the time of the Conquest. They lived in fort-like houses built of adobe or stone; they cultivated, in artificially irrigated gardens, maize and other edible plants, varying according to location and climate, which constituted their chief source of food, and they had even domesticated a few animals—the Mexicans the turkey and other birds, and the Peruvians the llama. They were furthermore acquainted with the working up of metals—except iron, which was the reason why they could not yet dispense with the use of stone weapons and stone implements. The Spanish Conquest cut short all further independent development.

In the East, the middle stage of barbarism commenced with the domestication of milk and meat-yielding animals, while plant cultivation appears to have remained unknown until very late in this period. The domestication and breeding of cattle and the formation of large herds seem to have been the cause of the differentiation of the Aryans and the Semites from the remaining mass of barbarians. Names of cattle are still common to the European and the Asiatic Aryans, the names of cultivable plants hardly at all.

In suitable places the formation of herds led to pastoral life; among the Semites, on the grassy plains of the Euphrates and the Tigris; among the Aryans, on those of India, of the Oxus and the Jaxartes,[361] of the Don and the Dnieper. The domestication of animals must have been first accomplished on the borders of such pasture lands. It thus appears to later generations that the pastoral peoples originated in areas which, far from being the cradle of mankind, were, on the contrary, almost uninhabitable for their savage forebears and even for people in the lower stage of barbarism. Conversely, once these barbarians of the middle stage had taken to pastoral life, it would never have occurred to them to leave the grassy watered plains of their own accord and return to the forest regions which had been the home of their ancestors. Even when the Aryans and Semites were driven farther north and west, they found it impossible to settle in the forest regions of Western Asia and Europe until they had been enabled, by the cultivation of cereals, to feed their cattle on this less favourable soil, and particularly to pass the winter there. It is more than probable that the cultivation of cereals was introduced here primarily because of the necessity of providing fodder for cattle and only later became important for human nourishment.

The plentiful meat and milk diet among the Aryans and the Semites, and particularly the beneficial effects of these foods on the development of children, may, perhaps, explain the superior development of these two races. In fact, the Pueblo Indians of New Mexico, who are reduced to an almost exclusively vegetarian diet, have a smaller brain than the more meat- and fish-eating Indians in the lower stage of barbarism. At any rate, cannibalism gradually disappears at this stage, and survives only as a religious rite or, what is almost identical in this instance, sorcery.

3. *Upper Stage.* Begins with the smelting of iron ore and passes into civilisation through the invention of alphabetic writing and its utilisation for literary records. At this stage, which, as we have already noted, was traversed independently only in the eastern hemisphere, more progress was made in production than in all the

previous stages put together. To it belong the Greeks of the Heroic Age, the Italian tribes shortly before the foundation of Rome, the Germans of Tacitus and the Normans of the days of the Vikings.[362]

Above all, we here encounter for the first time the iron plough-share drawn by cattle, making possible land cultivation on a wide scale—tillage—and, in the conditions then prevailing, a prac-tically unlimited increase in the means of subsistence; in connec-tion with this we find also the clearing of forests and their trans-formation into arable and pasture land—which, again, would have been impossible on a wide scale without the iron axe and spade. But with this there also came a rapid increase of the population and dense populations in small areas. Prior to tillage only very exceptional circumstances could have brought together half a million people under one central leadership; in all probability this never happened.

In the poems of Homer, particularly the *Iliad*, we find the up-per stage of barbarism at its zenith. Improved iron tools, the bel-lows, the handmill, the potter's wheel, the making of oil and wine, the working up of metals developing into an art, waggons and war chariots, shipbuilding with planks and beams, the beginnings of architecture as an art, walled towns with towers and battle-ments, the Homeric epic and the entire mythology—these are the chief heritages carried over by the Greeks in their transition from barbarism to civilisation. If we compare with this Caesar's and even Tacitus' descriptions of the Germans, who were on the threshold of that stage of culture from which the Homeric Greeks were preparing to advance to a higher one, we will see how rich was the development of production in the upper stage of barbarism.

The picture of the evolution of mankind through savagery and barbarism to the beginnings of civilisation that I have here sketched after Morgan is already rich enough in new and, what is more, incontestable features, incontestable because they are taken straight from production; nevertheless it will appear faint and meagre compared with the picture which will unfold itself at the end of our journey. Only then will it be possible to give a full view of the transition from barbarism to civilisation and the striking contrast between the two. For the time being we can generalise Morgan's periodisation as follows: Savagery—the period in which the appropriation of natural products, ready for use, predominated; the things produced by man were, in the main, instruments that facilitated this appropriation. Barbarism—the period in which knowledge of cattle breeding and land cultivation was acquired, in which methods of increasing the productivity of nature through human activity were learnt. Civilisation—the period in which knowledge of the further working up of natural products, of in-dustry proper, and of art was acquired.

II

THE FAMILY

Morgan, who spent the greater part of his life among the Iroquois—who still inhabit the State of New York—and was adopted by one of their tribes (the Senecas), found a system of consanguinity prevailing among them that stood in contradiction to their actual family relationships. Marriage between single pairs, with easy dissolution by either side, which Morgan termed the "pairing family," was the rule among them. The offspring of such a married couple was known and recognised by all, and no doubt could arise as to the person to whom the designation father, mother, son, daughter, brother, sister should be applied. But the actual use of these terms was to the contrary. The Iroquois calls not only his own children sons and daughters, but those of his brothers also; and they call him father. On the other hand, he calls his sisters' children his nephews and nieces; and they call him uncle. Inversely, the Iroquois woman calls her sisters' children her sons and daughters along with her own; and they call her mother. On the other hand, she addresses her brothers' children as her nephews and nieces; and she is called their aunt. In the same way, the children of brothers call one another brothers and sisters, and so do the children of sisters. Contrariwise, the children of a woman and those of her brother call each other cousins. And these are no mere empty terms, but expressions of ideas actually in force concerning nearness and collateralness, equality and inequality of blood relationship; and these ideas serve as the foundation of a completely worked-out system of consanguinity, capable of expressing some hundreds of different relationships of a single individual. Furthermore, this system not only exists in full force among all American Indians (no exceptions have as yet been discovered), but also prevails almost unchanged among the aborigines of India, among the Dravidian tribes in the Deccan and the Gaura tribes[363] in Hindustan. The terms of kinship current among the Tamils of South India and the Seneca Iroquois in the State of New York are identical even at the present day for more than two hundred different relationships. And among these tribes in India, also, as among all the American Indians, the relationships arising out of the prevailing form of the family stand in contradiction to the system of consanguinity.

How is this to be explained? In view of the decisive role which kinship plays in the social order of all peoples in the stage of savagery and barbarism, the significance of so widespread a system cannot be explained away by mere phrases. A system which is generally prevalent throughout America, which likewise exists in Asia among peoples of an entirely different race, and more or

less modified forms of which abound everywhere throughout
Africa and Australia, requires to be historically explained; it
cannot be explained away, as McLennan, for example, attempted
to do. The terms father, child, brother and sister are no mere
honorific titles, but carry with them absolutely definite and very
serious mutual obligations, the totality of which forms an essential
part of the social constitution of these peoples. And the explanation was found. In the Sandwich Islands (Hawaii) there existed
as late as the first half of the present century a form of the family
which yielded just such fathers and mothers, brothers and sisters,
sons and daughters, uncles and aunts, nephews and nieces, as are
demanded by the American and ancient Indian system of consanguinity. But strangely enough, the system of consanguinity
prevalent in Hawaii again clashed with the actual form of the
family existing there. There, all first cousins, without exception,
are regarded as brothers and sisters and as the common children,
not only of their mother and her sisters, or of their father and his
brothers, but of all the brothers and sisters of their parents without distinction. Thus, if the American system of consanguinity
presupposes a more primitive form of the family, no longer existing in America itself, but actually still found in Hawaii, the Hawaiian system of consanguinity, on the other hand, points to an
even more aboriginal form of the family, which, although not
provable as still extant anywhere, *must* nevertheless have existed,
for otherwise the system of consanguinity corresponding to it could
not have arisen.

"The family," says Morgan, "represents an active principle. It is never stationary, but advances from a lower to a higher form as society advances from a
lower to a higher condition. Systems of consanguinity, on the contrary, are passive,
recording the progress made by the family at long intervals apart, and only
changing radically when the family has radically changed."

"And," adds Marx, "the same applies to political, juridical,
religious and philosophical systems generally."* While the family
continues to live, the system of consanguinity becomes ossified,
and while this latter continues to exist in the customary form, the
family outgrows it. However, just as Cuvier could with certainty
conclude, from the pouch bones of an animal skeleton found near
Paris, that this belonged to a marsupial and that now extinct
marsupials had once lived there, so we, with the same certainty,
can conclude, from a historically transmitted system of consanguinity, that an extinct form of the family corresponding to it had
once existed.

The systems of consanguinity and forms of the family just
referred to differ from those which prevail today in that each child

---

* See *Marx-Engels Archive*, Vol. IX, p. 21.—*Ed.*

has several fathers and mothers. According to the American system of consanguinity, to which the Hawaiian family corresponds, brother and sister cannot be the father and the mother of one and the same child; the Hawaiian system of consanguinity, on the contrary, presupposes a family in which this was the rule. We are confronted with a series of forms of the family which directly contradict the forms hitherto generally accepted as being the only ones prevailing. The traditional conception knows monogamy only, along with polygamy on the part of individual men, and even, perhaps, polyandry on the part of individual women, and hushes up the fact—as is the way with moralising Philistines—that in practice these bounds imposed by official society are silently but unblushingly transgressed. The study of the history of primitive society, on the contrary, reveals to us conditions in which men live in polygamy and their wives simultaneously in polyandry, and the common children are, therefore, regarded as being common to them all; in their turn, these conditions undergo a whole series of modifications until they are ultimately dissolved in monogamy. These modifications are of such a character that the circle of people embraced by the tie of common marriage— very wide originally—becomes narrower and narrower, until, finally, only the single couple is left, which predominates today.

In thus constructing retrospectively the history of the family, Morgan, in agreement with the majority of his colleagues, arrived at a primitive stage at which promiscuous intercourse prevailed within a tribe, so that every woman belonged equally to every man and, similarly, every man to every woman. There had been talk about such a primitive condition ever since the last century, but only in a most general way; Bachofen was the first—and this was one of his great services—to take this condition seriously and to search for traces of it in historical and religious traditions. We know today that the traces he discovered do not at all lead back to a social stage of sexual promiscuity, but to a much later form, group marriage. That primitive social stage, if it really existed, belongs to so remote an epoch that we can scarcely expect to find *direct* evidence of its former existence in social fossils, among backward savages. It is precisely to Bachofen's credit that he placed this question in the forefront of investigation.*

---

* How little Bachofen understood what he had discovered, or rather guessed, is proved by his description of this primitive condition as *hetaerism*. This word was used by the Greeks, when they introduced it, to describe intercourse between unmarried men, or those living in monogamy, and unmarried women; it always presupposes the existence of a definite form of marriage outside of which this intercourse takes place, and includes prostitution, at least as an already existing possibility. The word was never used in any other sense and I use it in this sense with Morgan. Bachofen's highly important discoveries are everywhere incredibly mystified by his fantastic belief that the historically arisen relations be-

It has become the fashion of late to deny the existence of this
initial stage in the sexual life of mankind. The aim is to spare
humanity this "shame." Apart from pointing to the absence of any
direct evidence, reference is particularly made to the example of the
rest of the animal world; wherefrom Letourneau (*Evolution of
Marriage and Family*, 1888) collected numerous facts purporting to
show that here, too, complete sexual promiscuity belongs to a lower
stage. The only conclusion I can draw from all these facts, however,
is that they prove absolutely nothing as far as man and his primeval
conditions of life are concerned. Mating for lengthy periods of time
among vertebrate animals can be sufficiently explained on physiological grounds; for example, among birds, the need of help by the
female during brooding time; the examples of faithful monogamy
among birds prove nothing whatsoever for human beings, since these
are not descended from birds. And if strict monogamy is to be
regarded as the acme of all virtue, then the palm must be given to the
tapeworm, which possesses a complete male and female sexual apparatus in every one of its 50 to 200 proglottids or segments of the body,
and passes the whole of its life in cohabiting with itself in every one
of these segments. If, however, we limit ourselves to mammals, we
find all forms of sexual life among them: promiscuity, suggestions
of group marriage, polygamy and monogamy. Only polyandry is
absent. This could only be achieved by humans. Even our nearest
relatives, the *quadrumana*, exhibit the utmost possible diversity in
the grouping of male and female; and, if we want to draw the line
closer and consider only the four anthropoid apes, Letourneau can
tell us only that they are sometimes monogamous and sometimes
polygamous, while Saussure, quoted by Giraud-Teulon, asserts that
they are monogamous. The recent assertions of Westermarck in his
The History of Human Marriage (London 1891) regarding monogamy
among anthropoid apes are also no proof by far. In short, the reports
are of such a character that the honest Letourneau admits:

"For the rest, there exists among the mammals absolutely no strict relation
betwen the degree of intellectual development and the form of sexual union."

And Espinas (*Animal Societies*, 1877) says point-blank:

"The horde is the highest social group observable among animals. It *seems*
to be composed of families, but right from the outset *the family and the horde
stand in antagonism to each other*, they develop in inverse ratio."

As is evident from the above, we know next to nothing conclusively about the family and other social groupings of the anthropoid apes. The reports directly contradict one another. Nor is
this to be wondered at. How contradictory, how much in need of

tween man and woman sprang from men's religious ideas of the given period and
not from their actual conditions of life. [*Note by Engels.*]

critical examination and sifting are the reports in our possessio
concerning even savage human tribes! But ape societies are still mo
difficult to observe than human societies. We must, therefore, fo
the present reject every conclusion drawn from such absolutely unre
liable reports.

The passage from Espinas, quoted above, however, provides u
with a better clue. Among the higher animals the horde and th
family are not complementary, but antagonistic to each other. Espina
describes very neatly how jealousy amongst the males at mating tim
loosens, or temporarily dissolves, every gregarious horde.

"Where the family is closely bound together hordes are rare exceptions. On th
other hand, the horde arises almost naturally where free sexual intercourse o
polygamy is the rule.... For a horde to arise the family ties must have bec
loosened and the individual freed again. That is why we so rarely meet with o
ganised flocks among birds.... Among mammals, on the other hand, more o
less organised societies are to be found, precisely because the individual in th
case is not merged in the family.... Thus, at its inception, the collective feelin
[conscience collective] of the horde can have no greater enemy than the collectiv
feeling of the family. Let us not hesitate to say: if a higher social form than th
family has evolved, it can have been due solely to the fact that it incorporate
within itself families which had undergone a fundamental transformation; whic
does not exclude the possibility that, precisely for this reason, these familie
were later able to reconstitute themselves under infinitely more favourable circum
stances." (Espinas, op, cit. [Ch.I], quoted by Giraud-Teulon in his Origin of Mar
riage and Family, 1884, pp. 518-20.)

From this it becomes apparent that animal societies have, to b
sure, a certain value in drawing conclusions regarding human socie
ties—but only in a negative sense. As far as we have ascertained, th
higher vertebrates know only two forms of the family: polygamy o
the single pair. In both cases only one adult male, only one husband
is permissible. The jealousy of the male, representing both tie and
limits of the family, brings the animal family into conflict with th
horde. The horde, the higher social form, is rendered impossible here
loosened there, or dissolved altogether during the mating season; a
best, its continued development is hindered by the jealousy of the
male. This alone suffices to prove that the animal family and primitive human society are incompatible things; that primitive man, working his way up out of the animal stage, either knew no family whatsoever, or at the most knew a family that is non-existent among animals.
So weaponless an animal as the creature that was becoming man
could survive in small numbers also in isolation, with the single pair
as the highest form of gregariousness, as is ascribed by Westermarck
to the gorilla and chimpanzee on the basis of hunters' reports. For
evolution out of the animal stage, for the accomplishment of the
greatest advance known to nature, an additional element was needed:
the replacement of the individual's inadequate power of defence by
the united strength and joint effort of the horde. The transition to

ιe human stage out of conditions such as those under which the
ιnthropoid apes live today would be absolutely inexplicable. These
ιpes rather give the impression of being stray sidelines gradually
ιpproaching extinction, and, at any rate, in process of decline. This
ιlone is sufficient reason for rejecting all conclusions that are based
ιn parallels drawn between their family forms and those of primitive
ιan. Mutual toleration among the adult males, freedom from jeal-
ιusy, was, however, the first condition for the building of those large
ιnd enduring groups in the midst of which alone the transition from
ιnimal to man could be achieved. And indeed, what do we find as
ιhe oldest, most primitive form of the family, of which undeniable
ιvidence can be found in history, and which even today can be studied
ιere and there? Group marriage, the form in which whole groups of
ιnen and whole groups of women belong to one another, and which
ιeaves but little scope for jealousy. And further, we find at a later
ιtage of development the exceptional form of polyandry, which still
ιmore militates against all feeling of jealousy, and is, therefore, un-
ιknown to animals. Since, however, the forms of group marriage
ιknown to us are accompanied by such peculiarly complicated condi-
ιtions that they necessarily point to earlier, simpler forms of sexual
relations and thus, in the last analysis, to a period of promiscuous
intercourse corresponding to the period of transition from animality
to humanity, references to the forms of marriage among animals bring
us back again to the very point from which they were supposed to
have led us once and for all.

What, then, does promiscuous sexual intercourse mean? That the
restrictions in force at present or in earlier times did not exist. We
have already witnessed the collapse of the barrier of jealousy.
If anything is certain, it is that jealousy is an emotion of comparatively late development. The same applies to the conception of
incest. Not only did brother and sister live as man and wife originally, but sexual relations between parents and children are permitted
among many peoples to this day. Bancroft (*The Native Races of the
Pacific States of North America*, 1875, Vol. I) testifies to the existence of this among the Kaviats of the Bering Strait, the Kadiaks near
Alaska and the Tinnehs in the interior of British North America.
Letourneau has collected reports of the same fact among the Chippe-
wa Indians, the Cucus in Chile, the Caribbeans[364] and the Karens of
Indo-China, not to mention the accounts of the ancient Greeks and
Romans concerning the Parthians, Persians, Scythians, Huns, etc.
Prior to the invention of incest (and it *is* an invention, and one of the
utmost value), sexual intercourse between parents and children could
be no more disgusting than between other persons belonging to
different generations—such as indeed occurs today even in the most
Philistine countries without exciting great horror; in fact, even old
"maids" of over sixty, if they are rich enough, occasionally marry

young men of about thirty. However, if we eliminate from the most primitive forms of the family known to us the conceptions of incest that are associated with them—conceptions totally different from our own and often in direct contradiction to them—we arrive at a form of sexual intercourse which can only be described as promiscuous—promiscuous in so far as the restrictions later established by custom did not yet exist. It by no means necessarily follows from this that a higgledy-piggledy promiscuity was in daily practice. Separate pairings for a limited time are by no means excluded; in fact, even in group marriage they now constitute the majority of cases. And if Westermarck, the latest to deny this original state, defines as marriage every case where the two sexes remain mated until the birth of offspring, then it may be said that this kind of marriage could very well occur under the conditions of promiscuous sexual intercourse without in any way contradicting promiscuity, that is, the absence of barriers to sexual intercourse set up by custom. Westermarck, to be sure, starts out from the viewpoint that

"promiscuity involves a suppression of individual inclinations," so that "prostitution is its most genuine form."

To me it rather seems that all understanding of primitive conditions remains impossible so long as we regard them through brothel spectacles. We shall return to this point again when dealing with group marriage.

According to Morgan, there developed out of this original condition of promiscuous intercourse, probably at a very early stage:

1. The *Consanguine Family,* the first stage of the family. Here the marriage groups are ranged according to generations: all the grandfathers and grandmothers within the limits of the family are all mutual husbands and wives, the same being the case with their children, the fathers and mothers, whose children will again form a third circle of common mates, their children—the great grandchildren of the first—in turn, forming a fourth circle. Thus, in this form of the family, only ancestors and descendants, parents and children, are excluded from the rights and obligations (as we would say) of marriage with one another. Brothers and sisters, male and female cousins of the first, second and more remote degrees are all mutually brothers and sisters, and *precisely because of this* are all mutually husbands and wives. At this stage the relation of brother and sister includes the exercise of sexual intercourse with one another as a matter of course.* In its typical form, such a family would consist of

---

* Marx, in a letter written in the spring of 1882,[365] expresses himself in the strongest possible terms about the utter falsification of primeval times appearing in Wagner's *Nibelung* text. "Whoever heard of a brother embracing his sister as his bride?"[366] To these "lewd gods" of Wagner's, who in quite modern style, spiced their love affairs with a little incest, Marx gave the answer: "In primeval

e descendants of a pair, among whom, again, the descendants of
ach degree are all brothers and sisters, and, precisely for that reason,
ll mutual husbands and wives.

The consanguine family has become extinct. Even the rawest
eoples known to history furnish no verifiable examples of this form
f the faimly. The conclusion that it *must* have existed, however, is
orced upon us by the Hawaiian system of consanguinity, still preva-
ent throughout Polynesia, which expresses degrees of consanguinity
uch as can arise only under such a form of the family; and we are
orced to the same conclusion by the entire further development of
he family, which postulates this form as a necessary preliminary
tage.

2. The *Punaluan Family.* If the first advance in organisation was
he exclusion of parents and children from mutual sexual relations,
he second was the exclusion of brothers and sisters. In view of the
greater similarity in the ages of the participants, this step forward
was infinitely more important, but also more difficult, than the first.
If was accomplished gradually, commencing most probably with the
exclusion of natural brothers and sisters (that is, on the maternal side)
from sexual relations, at first in isolated cases, then gradually becoming the rule (in Hawaii exceptions to this rule still existed in the
present century), and ending with the prohibition of marriage even
between collateral brothers and sisters, or, as we would call them,
between first, second and third cousins. According to Morgan it

"affords a good illustration of the operation of the principle of natural selection".

---

times the sister *was* the wife, *and that was moral.*" [*Note by Engels to the 1884
edition.*]

A French friend [Bonnier] and admirer of Wagner does not agree with this
note, and points out that already in the *Ogisdrecka*, the earlier *Edda*,[367] which
Wagner took as his model, Loki reproaches Freya thus: "Thine own brother has
thou embraced before the gods." Marriage between brother and sister, he claimed
was proscribed already at that time. The *Ogisdrecka* is the expression of a time
when belief in the ancient myths was completely shattered; it is a truly Lucianian
satire on the gods. If Loki, as Mephistopheles, thus reproaches Freya, it argues
rather against Wagner. A few verses later, Loki also says to Njord: "You begat
[such] a son by our sister" [*Uidh systur thinni gaztu slikan mög*]. Now, Njord is
not an Asa but a Vana, and says, in the Ynglinga saga,[368] that marriages between
brothers and sisters are customary in Vanaland, which is not the case amongst
the Asas. This would seem to indicate that the Vanas were older gods than the
Asas. At any rate, Njord lived among the Asas as their equal, and the *Ogisdrecka*
is thus rather a proof that intermarriage between brothers and sisters, at least
among the gods, did not yet arouse any revulsion at the time the Norwegian
Sagas of the gods originated. If one wants to excuse Wagner, one would do better
to cite Goethe instead of the *Edda*, for Goethe, in his Ballad of God and the
Bayadere, makes a similar mistake regarding the religious surrender of women,
which he likens far too closely to modern prostitution. [*Note by Engels to the
fourth edition, 1891.*]

It is beyond question that tribes among whom inbreeding was re stricted by this advance were bound to develop more rapidly an fully than those among whom intermarriage between brothers an sisters remained both rule and duty. And how powerfully the effec of this advance was felt is proved by the institution of the *gens*, whic arose directly from it and shot far beyond the mark. The gens was th foundation of the social order of most, if not all, the barbarian people of the world, and in Greece and Rome we pass directly from it int civilisation.

Every primeval family had to split up after a couple of generations at the latest. The original communistic common household, whicl prevailed without exception until the late middle stage of barbarism determined a certain maximum size of the family community, varyinş according to circumstances but fairly definite in each locality. A: soon as the conception of the impropriety of sexual intercourse be tween the children of a common mother arose, it was bound to have an effect upon such divisions of old and the foundation of new house hold communities [*Hausgemeinden*] (which, however, did not necessa rily coincide with the family group). One or more groups of sisters became the nucleus of one household, their natural brothers the nu cleus of the other. In this or some similar way the form of the family which Morgan calls the punaluan family developed out of the con sanguine family. According to the Hawaiian custom, a number of sisters, either natural or collateral (that is, first, second or more distant cousins), were the common wives of their common husbands, from which relation, however, their brothers were excluded. These hus bands no longer addressed one another as brothers—which indeed they no longer had to be—but as punalua, that is, intimate com panion, partner, as it were. In the same way, a group of natural or collateral brothers held in common marriage a number of women, who were *not* their sisters, and these women addressed one another as punalua. This is the classical form of family structure [*Familien formation*] which later admitted of a series of variations, and the essential characteristic feature of which was: mutual community of husbands and wives within a definite family circle, from which, however, the brothers of the wives—first the natural brothers, and later the collateral brothers also—were excluded, the same applying conversely to the sisters of the husbands.

This form of the family now furnishes us with the most complete accuracy the degrees of kinship as expressed in the American system. The children of my mother's sisters still remain her children, the children of my father's brothers being likewise his children, and all of them are my brothers and sisters; but the children of my mother's brothers are now her nephews and nieces, the children of my father's sisters are his nephews and nieces, and they all are my cousins. For while my mother's sisters' husbands still remain her husbands, and

y father's brothers' wives likewise still remain his wives—by right,
not always in actual fact—the social proscription of sexual intercourse between brothers and sisters now divided the first cousins,
itherto indiscriminately regarded as brothers and sisters, into two
lasses: some remain (collateral) brothers and sisters as before; the
thers, the children of brothers on the one hand and of sisters on the
ther, *can* no longer be brothers and sisters, can no longer have com-
1on parents, whether father, mother, or both, and therefore the class
f nephews and nieces, male and female cousins—which would have
een senseless in the previous family system—becomes necessary for
he first time. The American system of consanguinity, which appears
o be utterly absurd in every family form based on some kind of individual marriage, is rationally explained and naturally justified, down
o its minutest details, by the punaluan family. To the extent that this
system of consanguinity was prevalent, to exactly the same extent, at
east, must the punaluan family, or a form similar to it, have existed.

This form of the family, proved actually to have existed in Hawaii,
would probably have been demonstrable throughout Polynesia, had
the pious missionaries—like the quondam Spanish monks in America
—been able to perceive in these unchristian relations something more
than mere "abomination."* When Caesar tells us of the Britons, who
at that time were in the middle stage of barbarism, that "by tens and
by twelves they possessed their wives in common; and it was mostly
brothers with brothers and parents with their children," this is best
explained as group marriage. Barbarian mothers have not ten or twelve
sons old enough to be able to keep wives in common, but the American system of consanguinity, which corresponds to the punaluan family, provides many brothers, since all a man's near and distant
cousins are his brothers. The expression "parents with their children"
may conceivably be a misunderstanding on Caesar's part; this system, however, does not absolutely exclude the presence of father and
son, or mother and daughter, in the same marriage group, though it
does exclude the presence of father and daughter, or mother and son.
In the same way, this or a similar form of group marriage provides
the simplest explanation of the reports of Herodotus and other ancient writers, concerning community of wives among savage and
barbarian peoples. This also applies to the description of the Tikurs
of Oudh (north of the Ganges) given by Watson and Kaye in their
book *The People of India:*

---

* There can no longer be any doubt that the traces of indiscriminate sexual
intercourse, his so-called *"Sumpfzeugung"* which Bachofen believes he has discovered, lead back to group marriage. "If Bachofen regards these punaluan marriages
as 'lawless,' a man of that period would likewise regard most present-day marriages between near and distant cousins on the father's or the mother's side as inces-
tuous, that is, as marriages between consanguineous brothers and sisters." (Marx.)—
[*Note by Engels.*]

"They live together (that is, sexually) almost indiscriminately in large co-
munities, and when two people are regarded as married, the tie is but nomina-

In by far the majority of cases the institution of the *gens* see-
to have originated directly from the punaluan family. To be sur-
the Australian class system also offers a starting-point for it[369]: t-
Australians have gentes; but they have not yet the punaluan famil-
they have a cruder form of group marriage.

In all forms of the group family it is uncertain who the father -
a child is, but it is certain who the mother is. Although she calls *a-*
the children of the aggregate family her children and is charged wit-
the duties of a mother towards them, she, nevertheless, knows h-
natural children from the others. It is thus clear that, wherever grou-
marriage exists, descent is traceable only on the *maternal* side, an-
thus the *female line* alone is recognised. This, in fact, is the cas-
among all savage peoples and among those belonging to the lowe-
stage of barbarism; and it is Bachofen's second great achievement t-
have been the first to discover this. He terms this exclusive recognition of lineage through the mother, and the inheritance relations tha-
arose out of it in the course of time, mother right. I retain this term-
for the sake of brevity. It is, however, an unhappy choice, for at thi-
social stage, there is as yet no such thing as right in the legal sense-

Now if we take from the punaluan family one of the two typica-
groups—namely, that consisting of a number of natural and collatera-
sisters (that is, those descendant from natural sisters in the first, second or more remote degree), together with their children and thei-
natural or collateral brothers on their mother's side (who according t-
our premise are *not* their husbands), we obtain exactly that circle o-
persons who later appear as members of a gens, in the original form-
of this institution. They have all a common ancestress, whose female-
descendants, generation by generation, are sisters by virtue-
of descent from her. These sisters' husbands, however, can no-
longer be their brothers, that is, cannot be descended from-
this ancestress, and, therefore, do not belong to the consanguineous-
group, the later gens; but their children do belong to this group,
since descent on the mother's side is alone decisive, because it alone-
is certain. Once the proscription of sexual intercourse between all-
brothers and sisters, including even the most remote collateral relations on the mother's side, becomes established, the above group is-
transformed into a gens—that is, constitutes itself as a rigidly limited-
circle of blood relatives in the female line, who are not allowed to-
marry one another; from now on it increasingly consolidates itself by-
other common institutions of a social and religious character, and-
differentiates itself from the other gentes of the same tribe. We shall-
deal with this in greater detail later. If, however, we find that the-
gens not only necessarily, but even obviously, evolved out of the punaluan family, then there is ground for assuming almost as a certainty-

that this form of the family existed formerly among all peoples to whom gentile institutions are traceable—that is, nearly all barbarian and civilised peoples.

At the time Morgan wrote his book our knowledge of group marriage was still very limited. A little was known about the group marriages current among the Australians, who were organised in classes, and, in addition, Morgan, as early as 1871, published the information that reached him concerning the Hawaiian punaluan family. On the one hand, the punaluan family furnished the complete explanation of the system of consanguinity prevalent among the American Indians—the system which was the starting-point of all of Morgan's investigations; on the other hand, it constituted a ready point of departure for the derivation of the mother-right gens; and, finally, it represented a far higher stage of development than the Australian classes. It is, therefore, comprehensible that Morgan should conceive the punaluan family as a stage of development necessarily preceding the pairing family, and assume that it was generally prevalent in earlier times. Since then we have learned of a series of other forms of group marriage and now know that Morgan went too far in this respect. Nevertheless, in his punaluan family, he had the good fortune to come across the highest, the classical form of group marriage, the form from which the transition to a higher stage is most easily explained.

We are indebted to the English missionary Lorimer Fison for the most essential enrichment of our knowledge of group marriage, for he studied this form of the family for years in its classical home, Australia. He found the lowest stage of development among the Australian Negroes of Mount Gambier in South Australia. The whole tribe is here divided into two great classes—Kroki and Kumite. Sexual intercourse within each of these classes is strictly proscribed; on the other hand, every man of one class is the born husband of every woman of the other class, and she is his born wife. Not individuals, but entire groups are married to one another; class to class. And be it noted, no reservations at all are made here concerning difference of age, or special blood relationship, other than those determined by the division into two exogamous classes. A Kroki legitimately has every Kumite woman for his wife; since, however, his own daughter by a Kumite woman is, according to mother right, also a Kumite, she is thereby the born wife of every Kroki, including her father. At all events, the class organisation, as we know it, imposes no restriction here. Hence, this organisation either arose at a time when, despite all dim impulses to limit inbreeding, sexual intercourse between parents and children was not yet regarded with any particular horror, in which case the class system would have arisen directly out of a condition of promiscuous sexual intercourse; or intercourse between parents and children *had already been* proscribed by custom when the classes arose, in which case the present 'position points back to the consanguine family, and is the first advance beyond it. The latter assumption is the more probable. Cases of marital connections between parents and children have not, as far as I am aware, been reported from Australia; and the later form of exogamy the mother-right gens, also as a rule tacitly presupposes the prohibition of such converse as something already existing upon its establishment.

Apart from Mount Gambier, in South Australia, the two-class system is likewise to be found along the Darling River, farther East and in Queensland, in the North-East, thus being very widespread. This system excludes only marriage between brothers and sisters between the children of brothers and between the children of sisters on the mother's side, because these belong to the same class; on the other hand, the children of brother and sister are permitted to marry. A further step towards the prevention of inbreeding is to be found among the Kamilaroi, along the Darling River, in New South Wales. where the two original classes are split into four, and each one of these four classes is likewise married bodily to another definite class. The first two classes are the born spouses of each other; the children become members of the third or the fourth class according to whether the mother belongs to the first or the second class; and the children of the third and fourth classes, which are likewise married to each other, belong again to the first and second classes. So that one generation always belongs to the first and second classes, the next belongs to the third and fourth, and the next again to the first and second. According to this system, the children of brothers and sisters (on the mother's side) may not become man and wife—their grandchildren, however, may. This strangely complicated system is made even more intricate by the grafting on of mother-right gentes, at any rate, later; but we cannot go into this here. We see, then, how the impulse towards the prevention of inbreeding asserts itself time and again, but in a groping, spontaneous way, without clear consciousness of purpose.

Group marriage, which in the case of Australia is still class marriage, the state of marriage of a whole class of men, often scattered over the whole breadth of the continent, with a similarly widely distributed class of women—this group marriage, when observed more closely, is not quite so horrible as is fancied by the Philistine in his brothel-tainted imagination. On the contrary, long years passed before its existence was even suspected, and indeed, it has been again disputed only quite recently. To the superficial observer it appears to be a kind of loose monogamy and, in places, polygamy, accompanied by occasional infidelity. One must spend years, as Fison and Howitt did, on the task of discovering the law that regulates these conditions of marriage—which in practice rather remind the average European of his own marital customs—the law according to which ᴉn Australian Negro, even when a stranger thousands of miles away ᴉrom his home, among people whose very language he does not ᴉnderstand, nevertheless, quite often, in roaming from camp to camp, ᴉrom tribe to tribe, finds women who guilelessly, without resistance, ᴉive themselves to him; and according to which he who has sever- ᴉl wives offers one of them to his guest for the night. Where the ᴉuropean can see only immorality and lawlessness, strict law actu- ᴉlly reigns. The women belong to the stranger's marriage class, and ᴉre therefore his born wives; the same moral law which assigns one ᴉo the other, prohibits, on pain of banishment, all intercourse outside ᴉhe marriage classes that belong to each other. Even where women are ᴉbducted, which is frequently the case, and in some areas the rule, ᴉhe class law is scrupulously observed.

The abduction of women already reveals even here a trace of the transition to individual marriage—at least in the form of the pairing marriage: After the young man has abducted, or eloped with, the girl with the assistance of his friends, all of them have sexual intercourse with her one after the other, whereupon, however, she is regarded the wife of the young man who initiated the abduction. And, conversely, should the abducted woman run away from the man and be captured by another, she becomes the latter's wife, and the first man loses his privilege. Thus, exclusive relations, pairing for longer or shorter periods, and also polygamy, establish themselves alongside of and within the system of group marriage, which, in general, continues to exist; so that here also group marriage is gradually dying out, the only question being which will first disappear from the scene as a result of European influence—group marriage or the Australian Negroes who indulge in it.

In any case, marriage in whole classes, such as prevails in Australia, is a very low and primitive form of group marriage; whereas the punaluan family is, as far as we know, its highest stage of development. The former would seem to be the form corresponding to the social status of roving savages, while the latter presupposes relatively stable settlements of communistic communities and leads directly to the next and higher stage of development. Some intermediate stages will assuredly be found between these two; here an only just opened and barely trodden field of investigation lies before us.

3. The *Pairing Family*. A certain pairing for longer or shorter periods took place already under group marriage, or even earlier. Among his numerous wives, the man had a principal wife (one can scarcely yet call her his favourite wife) and he was her principal husband, among the others. This situation contributed in no small degree to the confusion among the missionaries, who see in group marriage, now promiscuous community of wives, now wanton adultery. Such habitual pairing, however, necessarily became more and more established as the gens developed and as the numbers of classes

of "brothers" and "sisters" between which marriage was now impos
sible increased. The impetus given by the gens to prevent marriage
between blood relatives drove things still further. Thus we find tha
among the Iroquois and most other Indian tribes in the lower stage
of barbarism, marriage is prohibited between *all* relatives recognised
by their system, and these are of several hundred kinds. This growing
complexity of marriage prohibitions rendered group marriages
more and more impossible; they were supplanted by the *pairing
family*. At this stage one man lives with one woman, yet in such
manner that polygamy and occasional infidelity remain men's
privileges, even though the former is seldom practised for economic reasons; at the same time, the strictest fidelity is demanded
of the woman during the period of cohabitation, adultery on her
part being cruelly punished. The marriage tie can, however, be
easily dissolved by either side, and the children belong solely to
the mother, as previously.

In this ever widening exclusion of blood relatives from marriage, natural selection also continues to have its effect. In Morgan's words,

marriage between non-consanguineous gentes "tended to create a more vigorous
stock physically and mentally. When two advancing tribes are blended into one
people ... the new skull and brain would widen and lengthen to the sum of the
capabilities of both."*

Tribes constituted according to gentes were bound, therefore, to
gain the upper hand over the more backward ones, or carry them
along by force of their example.

Thus, the evolution of the family in prehistoric times consisted
in the continual narrowing of the circle—originally embracing
the whole tribe—within which marital community between the
two sexes prevailed. By the successive exclusion, first of closer,
then of ever remoter relatives, and finally even of those merely
related by marriage; every kind of group marriage was ultimately rendered practically impossible; and in the end there
remained only the one, for the moment still loosely united, couple,
the molecule, with the dissolution of which marriage itself completely ceases. This fact alone shows how little individual sex
love, in the modern sense of the word, had to do with the origin
of monogamy. The practice of all peoples in this stage affords
still further proof of this. Whereas under previous forms of the
family men were never in want of women but, on the contrary,
had a surfeit of them, women now became scarce and were sought
after. Consequently, with pairing marriage begins the abduction
and purchase of women—widespread *symptoms*, but nothing

---

* See also *Marx-Engels Archive*, Vol. IX, p. 28.—*Ed.*

more, of a much more deeply-rooted change that had set in. These symptoms, mere methods of obtaining women, McLennan, the pedantic Scot, nevertheless metamorphosed into special classes of families which he called "marriage by abduction" and "marriage by purchase." Moreover, among the American Indians, and also among other tribes (at the same stage), the arrangement of a marriage is not the affair of the two parties to the same, who indeed, are often not even consulted, but of their respective mothers. Two complete strangers are thus often betrothed and only learn of the conclusion of the deal when the marriage day approaches. Prior to the marriage, presents are made by the bridegroom to the gentile relatives of the bride (that is, to her relatives on her mother's side, not to the father and his relatives), these presents serving as purchase gifts for the ceded girl. The marriage may be dissolved at the pleasure of either of the two spouses. Nevertheless, among many tribes, for example, the Iroquois, public sentiment gradually developed against such separations. When conflicts arise, the gentile relatives of both parties intervene and attempt a reconciliation, and separation takes place only after such efforts prove fruitless, the children remaining with the mother and each party being free to marry again.

The pairing family, itself too weak and unstable to make an independent household necessary, or even desirable, did not by any means dissolve the communistic household transmitted from earlier times. But the communistic household implies the supremacy of women in the house, just as the exclusive recognition of a natural mother, because of the impossibility of determining the natural father with certainty, signifies high esteem for the women, that is, for the mothers. That woman was the slave of man at the commencement of society is one of the most absurd notions that have come down to us from the period of Enlightenment of the eighteenth century. Woman occupied not only a free but also a highly respected position among all savages and all barbarians of the lower and middle stages and partly even of the upper stage. Let Arthur Wright, missionary for many years among the Seneca Iroquois, testify what her place still was in the pairing family:

"As to their family system, when occupying the old long houses [communistic households embracing several families] ... it is probable that some one clan [gens] predominated, the women taking in husbands from other clans [gentes].... Usually the female portion ruled the house; the stores were in common; but woe to the luckless husband or lover who was too shiftless to do his share of the providing. No matter how many children or whatever goods he might have in the house, he might at any time be ordered to pack up his blanket and budge; and after such orders it would not be healthful for him to attempt to disobey. The house would be too hot for him; and he had to retreat to his own clan [gens]; or, as was often done, go and start a new matrimonial alliance in some other.

The women were the great power among the clans [gentes], as everywhere else
They did not hesitate, when occasion required, to knock off the horns, as it wa
technically called, from the head of the chief and send him back to the rank
of the warriors."*

The communistic household, in which most of the women o
even all the women belong to one and the same gens, while the
men come from various other gentes, is the material foundation of
that predominancy of women which generally obtained in primitive times; and Bachofen's discovery of this constitutes the third
great service he has rendered. I may add, furthermore, that the
reports of travellers and missionaries about women among savages
and barbarians being burdened with excessive toil in no way conflict with what has been said above. The division of labour between
the two sexes is determined by causes entirely different from those
that determine the status of women in society. Peoples whose
women have to work much harder than we would consider proper
often have far more real respect for women than our Europeans
have for theirs. The social status of the lady of civilisation, surrounded by sham homage and estranged from all real work, is
socially infinitely lower than that of the hard-working woman of
barbarism, who was regarded among her people as a real lady
(lady, *frowa*, *Frau*=mistress [*Herrin*]) and was such by the nature
of her position.

Whether or not the pairing family has totally supplanted
group marriage in America today must be decided by closer investigation among the North-Western and particularly among
the South American peoples who are still in the higher stage of
savagery. So very many instances of sexual freedom are reported
with regard to these latter that the complete suppression of the
old group marriage can scarcely be assumed. At any rate, not
all traces of it have as yet disappeared. Among at least forty
North American tribes, the man who marries the eldest sister in
a family is entitled to all her sisters as wives as soon as they
reach the requisite age—a survival of the community of husbands
for a whole group of sisters. And Bancroft relates that the tribes
of the Californian peninsula (in the upper stage of savagery)
have certain festivities, during which several "tribes" congregate
for the purpose of indiscriminate sexual intercourse. These are
manifestly gentes for whom these festivities represent dim memories of the times when the women of one gens had all the men
of another for their common husbands, and *vice versa*. The same
custom still prevails in Australia. Among a few peoples it happens that the older men, the chiefs and sorcerer-priests, exploit
the community of wives for their own ends and monopolise most

---

* See also *Marx-Engels Archive*, Vol. IX, pp. 26-27.—*Ed.*

of the women for themselves; but they, in their turn, have to allow the old common possession to be restored during certain feasts and great popular gatherings and permit their wives to enjoy themselves with the young men. Westermarck (pp. 28 and 29) adduces a whole series of examples of such periodical Saturnalian feasts[370] during which the old free sexual intercourse comes into force again for a short period, as, for example, among the Hos, the Santals, the Panjas and Kotars of India, among some African peoples, etc. Curiously enough, Westermarck concludes from this that they are relics, not of group marriage, which he rejects, but—of the mating season common alike to primitive man and the other animals.

We now come to Bachofen's fourth great discovery, that of the widespread form of transition from group marriage to pairing. What Bachofen construes as a penance for infringing the ancient commandments of the gods, the penance with which the woman buys her right to chastity, is in fact nothing more than a mystical expression for the penance by means of which the woman purchases her redemption from the ancient community of husbands and acquires the right to give herself to *one* man only. This penance takes the form of limited surrender: the Babylonian women had to surrender themselves once a year in the temple of Mylitta. Other Middle Eastern peoples sent their girls for years to the Temple of Anaitis, where they had to practise free love with favourites of their own choice before they were allowed to marry. Similar customs bearing a religious guise are common to nearly all Asiatic peoples between the Mediterranean and the Ganges. The propitiatory sacrifice for the purpose of redemption becomes gradually lighter in the course of time, as Bachofen notes:

"The annually repeated offering yields place to the single performance; the hetaerism of the matrons is succeeded by that of the maidens, its practice during marriage by practice before marriage, the indiscriminate surrender to all by surrender to certain persons" (*Mother Right*, p. XIX).

Among other peoples, the religious guise is absent; among some—the Thracians, Celts, etc., of antiquity, and many aboriginal inhabitants of India, the Malay peoples, South Sea Islanders and many American Indians even to this day—the girls enjoy the greatest sexual freedom until their marriage. Particularly is this the case throughout almost the whole of South America, as anybody who has penetrated a little into the interior can testify. Thus, Agassiz (*A Journey in Brazil*, Boston and New York, 1886, p. 266) relates the following about a rich family of Indian descent. When he was introduced to the daughter and enquired after her father, who, he supposed, was the mother's husband, an officer on active service in the war against Paraguay, the mother answered smilingly: "*naõ tem pai, é filha da fortuna*"—she has no father, she is the daughter of chance.

"It is the way the Indian or half-breed women here always speak of their illegitimate children, unconscious of any wrong or shame. So far is this from being an unusual case that the opposite seems the exception. Children [often] know [only] about their mother, for all the care and responsibility falls upon her; but they have no knowledge of their father, nor does it seem to occur to the woman that she or her children have any claim upon him."

What here appears to be so strange to the civilised man is simply the rule according to mother right and in group marriage.

Among still other peoples, the bridegroom's friends and relatives, or the wedding guests, exercise their old traditional right to the bride at the wedding itself, and the bridegroom has his turn last of all; for instance, on the Balearic Islands and among the African Augilas of antiquity, and among the Bareas of Abyssinia even now. In the case of still other peoples, again, an official person—the chief of the tribe or of the gens, the cacique, shaman, priest, prince or whatever his title—represents the community and exercises the right of first night with the bride. Despite all neoromantic whitewashing, this *jus primae noctis** persists to this day as a relic of group marriage among most of the natives of the Alaska territory (Bancroft, *Native Races*, I, p. 81), among the Tahus in North Mexico (*ibid.*, p. 584) and among other peoples; and it existed throughout the Middle Ages at least in the originally Celtic countries, where it was directly transmitted from group marriage; for instance, in Aragon. While the peasant in Castile was never a serf, in Aragon the most ignominious serfdom prevailed until abolished by the decree issued by Ferdinand the Catholic in 1486. This public act states:

"We pass judgement and declare that the aforementioned lords (señors, barons)... also shall not sleep the first night with the woman taken in wedlock by a peasant, nor on the wedding night, after she has gone to bed, stride over it and over the woman as a sign of their authority; nor shall the aforementioned lords avail themselves of the services of the sons or daughters of the peasant, with or without payment, against their will." (Quoted in the Catalonian original by Sugenheim, *Serfdom*, Petersburg 1861, p. 355.)

Bachofen is again absolutely right when he contends throughout that the transition from what he terms "hetaerism" or "*Sumpfzeugung*" to monogamy was brought about essentially by the women. The more the old traditional sexual relations lost their naïve, primitive jungle character, as a result of the development of the economic conditions of life, that is, with the undermining of the old communism and the growing density of the popula-

---

* Right of the first night.—*Ed.*

tion, the more degrading and oppressive must they have appeared to the women; the more fervently must they have longed for the right to chastity, to temporary or permanent marriage with one man only, as a deliverance. This advance could not have originated from the men, if only for the reason that they have never—not even to the present day—dreamed of renouncing the pleasures of actual group marriage. Only after the transition to pairing marriage had been effected by the women could the men introduce strict monogamy—for the women only, of course.

The pairing family arose on the border line between savagery and barbarism, mainly at the upper stage of savagery, and here and there only at the lower stage of barbarism. It is the form of the family characteristic of barbarism, in the same way as group marriage is characteristic of savagery and monogamy of civilisation. For its further development to stable monogamy, causes different from those we have hitherto found operating were required. In the pairing family, the group was already reduced to its last unit, its two-atom molecule—to one man and one woman. Natural selection had completed its work by constantly reducing the circle of community marriage; there was nothing more left for it to do in this direction. If no new, *social* driving forces had come into operation, there would have been no reason why a new form of the family should arise out of the pairing family. But these driving forces did commence to operate.

We now leave America, the classical soil of the pairing family. There is no evidence to enable us to conclude that a higher form of the family developed there, or that strict monogamy existed in any part of it at any time before its discovery and conquest. It was otherwise in the Old World.

Here the domestication of animals and the breeding of herds had developed a hitherto unsuspected source of wealth and created entirely new social relationships. Until the lower stage of barbarism, fixed wealth consisted almost entirely of the house, clothing, crude ornaments and the implements for procuring and preparing food: boats, weapons and household utensils of the simplest kind. Food had to be won anew day by day. Now, with herds of horses, camels, donkeys, oxen, sheep, goats and pigs, the advancing pastoral peoples—the Aryans in the Indian land of the five rivers and the Ganges area, as well as in the then much more richly watered steppes of the Oxus and the Jaxartes, and the Semites on the Euphrates and the Tigris—acquired possessions demanding merely supervision and most elementary care in order to propagate in ever-increasing numbers and to yield the richest nutriment in milk and meat. All previous means of procuring food now sank into the background. Hunting, once a necessity, now became a luxury.

But to whom did this new wealth belong? Originally, undoubtedly, to the gens. But private property in herds must have developed at a very early stage. It is hard to say whether Father Abraham appeared to the author of the so-called First Book of Moses as the owner of his herds and flocks in his own right as head of a family community or by virtue of his status as actual hereditary chief of a gens. One thing, however, is certain, and that is that we must not regard him as a property owner in the modern sense of the term. Equally certain is it that on the threshold of authenticated history we find that everywhere the herds are already the separate property of the family chiefs, in exactly the same way as were the artistic products of barbarism, metal utensils, articles of luxury and, finally, human cattle—the slaves.

For now slavery also was invented. The slave was useless to the barbarian of the lower stage. It was for this reason that the American Indians treated their vanquished foes quite differently from the way they were treated in the upper stage. The men were either killed or adopted as brothers by the tribe of the victors. The women were either taken in marriage or likewise just adopted along with their surviving children. Human labour power at this stage yielded no noticeable surplus as yet over the cost of its maintenance. With the introduction of cattle breeding, of the working up of metals, of weaving and, finally, of field cultivation, this changed. Just as the once so easily obtainable wives had now acquired an exchange value and were bought, so it happened with labour power, especially after the herds had finally been converted into family possessions. The family did not increase as rapidly as the cattle. More people were required to tend them; the captives taken in war were useful for just this purpose, and, furthermore, they could be bred like the cattle itself.

Such riches, once they had passed into the private possession of families and there rapidly multiplied, struck a powerful blow at a society founded on pairing marriage and mother-right gens. Pairing marriage had introduced a new element into the family. By the side of the natural mother it had placed the authenticated natural father—who was probably better authenticated than many a "father" of the present day. According to the division of labour then prevailing in the family, the procuring of food and the implements necessary thereto, and therefore, also, the ownership of the latter, fell to the man; he took them with him in case of separation, just as the woman retained the household goods. Thus, according to the custom of society at that time, the man was also the owner of the new sources of foodstuffs—the cattle—and later, of the new instrument of labour—the slaves. According to the custom of the same society, however, his children could not inherit from him, for the position in this respect was as follows:

According to mother right, that is, as long as descent was reckoned solely through the female line, and according to the original custom of inheritance in the gens, it was the gentile relatives that at first inherited from a deceased member of the gens. The property had to remain within the gens. At first, in view of the insignificance of the chattels in question, it may, in practice, have passed to the nearest gentile relatives—that is, to the blood relatives on the mother's side. The children of the deceased, however, belonged not to his gens, but to that of their mother. In the beginning, they inherited from their mother, along with the rest of their mother's blood relatives, and later, perhaps, had first claim upon her property; but they could not inherit from their father, because they did not belong to his gens, and his property had to remain in the latter. On the death of the herd owner, therefore, his herds passed, first of all, to his brothers and sisters and to his sisters' children or to the descendants of his mother's sisters. His own children, however, were disinherited.

Thus, as wealth increased, it, on the one hand, gave the man a more important status in the family than the woman, and, on the other hand, created a stimulus to utilise this strengthened position in order to overthrow the traditional order of inheritance in favour of his children. But this was impossible as long as descent according to mother right prevailed. This had, therefore, to be overthrown, and it was overthrown; and it was not so difficult to do this as it appears to us now. For this revolution—one of the most decisive ever experienced by mankind—need not have disturbed one single living member of a gens. All the members could remain what they were previously. The simple decision sufficed that in future the descendants of the male members should remain in the gens, but that those of the females were to be excluded from the gens and transferred to that of their father. The reckoning of descent through the female line and the right of inheritance through the mother were hereby overthrown and male lineage and right of inheritance from the father instituted. We know nothing as to how and when this revolution was effected among the civilised peoples. It falls entirely within prehistoric times. That it was actually *effected* is more than proved by the abundant traces of mother right which have been collected, especially by Bachofen. How easily it is accomplished can be seen from a whole number of Indian tribes, among whom it has only recently taken place and is still proceeding, partly under the influence of increasing wealth and changed methods of life (transplantation from the forests to the prairies), and partly under the moral influence of civilisation and the missionaries. Of eight Missouri tribes, six have male and two still retain the female lineage and female inheritance line. Among the Shawnees, Miamis and Delawares it has become the custom to transfer the children to the father's gens by giving them one of the gentile names obtaining therein, in order that they may inherit from him. "Innate human casuistry to seek to change things by changing their names! And to find loopholes for breaking through tradition within tradition itself, wherever a direct interest provided a sufficient motive!" (Marx.)* As a consequence, hopeless confusion arose; and matters could only be straightened out, and partly were straightened out, by the transition to father right. "This appears altogether to be the most natural transition." (Marx.)** As for what the experts on comparative law have to tell us regarding the ways and means by which this transition was effected among the civilised peoples of the Old World—almost mere hypotheses, of course—see M. Kovalevsky, *Outline of the Origin and Evolution of the Family and Property*, Stockholm 1890.

The overthrow of mother right was the *world-historic defeat of the female sex*. The man seized the reins in the house also, the woman was degraded, enthralled, the slave of the man's lust, a mere instrument for breeding children. This lowered position of women, especially manifest among the Greeks of the Heroic and still more of the Classical Age, has become gradually embellished and dissembled and, in part, clothed in a milder form, but by no means abolished.

The first effect of the sole rule of the men that was now established is shown in the intermediate form of the family which now emerges, the patriarchal family. Its chief attribute is not polygamy —of which more anon—but

"the organisation of a number of persons, bond and free, into a family, under the paternal power of the head of the family. In the Semitic form, this family chief lives in polygamy, the bondsman has a wife and children, and the purpose of the whole organisation is the care of flocks and herds over a limited area."[371]

The essential features are the incorporation of bondsmen and the paternal power; the Roman family, accordingly, constitutes the perfected type of this form of the family. The word *familia* did not originally signify the ideal of our modern Philistine, which is a compound of sentimentality and domestic discord. Among the Romans, in the beginning, it did not even refer to the married couple and their children, but to the slaves alone. *Famulus* means a household slave and *familia* signifies the totality of slaves belonging to one individual. Even in the time of Gaius the *familia, id*

---

* See *Marx-Engels Archive*, Vol. IX, p. 111.—*Ed.*
** Ibid., p. 112.—*Ed.*

est patrimonium (that is, the inheritance) was bequeathed by will.
The expression was invented by the Romans to describe a new
social organism, the head of which had under him wife and children and a number of slaves, under Roman paternal power, with
power of life and death over them all.

"The term, therefore, is no older than the ironclad family system of the Latin
tribes, which came in after field agriculture and after legalised servitude, as
well as after the separation of the Greeks and (Aryan) Latins."[372]

To which Marx adds: "The modern family contains in embryo
not only slavery (*servitus*) but serfdom also, since from the very
beginning it is connected with agricultural services. It contains
within itself in *miniature* all the antagonisms which later develop
on a wide scale within society and its state."[*]

Such a form of the family shows the transition of the pairing
family to monogamy. In order to guarantee the fidelity of the wife,
that is, the paternity of the children, the woman is placed in the
man's absolute power; if he kills her, he is but exercising his right

With the patriarchal family we enter the field of written history and, therewith, a field in which the science of comparative law
can render us important assistance. And in fact it has here procured
us considerable progress. We are indebted to Maxim Kovalevsky
(*Outline of the Origin and Evolution of the Family and Property*,
Stockholm 1890, pp. 60-100) for the proof that the patriarchal
household community (*Hausgenossenschaft*), such as we still find it
today among the Serbs and the Bulgars under the designations of
Zadruga (meaning something like fraternity) or *Bratstvo* (brotherhood), and among the Oriental peoples in a modified form, constituted the transition stage between the mother-right family which
evolved out of group marriage and the individual family known
to the modern world. This appears to be proved at least as far
as the civilised peoples of the Old World, the Aryans and Semites,
are concerned.

The South-Slavic *Zadruga* provides the best existing example of
such a family community. It embraces several generations of the descendants of one father and their wives, who all live together in one
household, till their fields in common, feed and clothe themselves
from the common store and communally own all surplus products.
The community is under the supreme management of the master of
the house (*domàcin*), who represents it in external affairs, may dispose of smaller objects, and manages the finances, being responsible for the latter as well as for the regular conduct of business. He
is elected and does not by any means need to be the eldest. The
women and their work are under the direction of the mistress of the
house (*domàcica*), who is usually the *domàcin*'s wife. In the choice of

See *Marx-Engels Archive*, Vol. IX, p. 31.—*Ed.*

husbands for the girls she has an important, often the decisive voice. Supreme power, however, is vested in the Family Council, the assembly of all adult members, women as well as men. To this assembly the master of the house renders his account; it makes all the important decisions, administers justice among the members, decides on purchases and sales of any importance, especially of landed property, etc.

It was only about ten years ago that the existence of such large family communities in Russia also was proved[373]; they are now generally recognised as being just as firmly rooted in the popular customs of the Russians as the *obščina*, or village community. They figure in the most ancient Russian law code—the *Pravda* of Yaroslav—under the same name (*verv*) as in the Dalmatian laws,[374] and references to them may be found also in Polish and Czech historical sources.

According to Heusler (*Institutes of German Right*) the economic unit among the Germans also was not originally the individual family in the modern sense, but the "house community" [*Hausgenossenschaft*], consisting of several generations, or individual families, and more often than not including plenty of bondsmen. The Roman family, too, has been traced back to this type, and in consequence the absolute power of the head of the house, as also the lack of rights of the remaining members of the family in relation to him, has recently been strongly questioned. Similar family communities are likewise supposed to have existed among the Celts in Ireland; in France they continued to exist in Nivernais under the name of *parçonneries* right up to the French Revolution, while in Franche-Comté they are not quite extinct even today. In the district of Louhans (Saône et Loire) may be seen large peasant houses with a lofty communal central hall reaching up to the roof, surrounded by sleeping rooms, to which access is had by staircases of from six to eight steps, and in which dwell several generations of the same family.

In India, the household community with common tillage of the soil was already mentioned by Nearchus, in the time of Alexander the Great, and exists to this day in the same area, in the Punjab and the entire North-Western part of the country. Kovalevsky himself was able to testify to its existence in the Caucasus. It still exists in Algeria among the Kabyles. It is said to have existed even in America; attempts are being made to identify it with the *calpullis*[375] in ancient Mexico, described by Zurita; Cunow, on the other hand, has proved fairly clearly (in *Ausland*,[376] 1890, Nos 42-44) that a kind of Mark constitution existed in Peru (where, peculiarly enough, the Mark was called *marca*) at the time of the Conquest, with periodical allotment of the cultivated land, that is, individual tillage.

At any rate, the patriarchal household community with common land ownership and common tillage now assumes quite another significance than hitherto. We can no longer doubt the important transitional role which it played among the civilised and many other peoples of the Old World between the mother-right family and the monogamian family. We shall return later on to the further conclusion drawn by Kovalevsky, namely, that it was likewise the transition stage out of which developed the village, or Mark, community with individual cultivation and at first periodical, then permanent allotment of arable and pasture lands.

As regards family life within these household communities, it should be noted that in Russia, at least, the head of the house is reputed to be strongly abusing his position as far as the younger women, particularly his daughters-in-law, are concerned, and to be very often converting them into a harem; these conditions are rather eloquently reflected in the Russian folk songs.

A few words more about polygamy and polyandry before we deal with monogamy, which developed rapidly following the overthrow of mother right. Both these marriage forms can only be exceptions, historical luxury products, so to speak, unless they appeared side by side in any country, which, as is well known, is not the case. As, therefore, the men, excluded from polygamy, could not console themselves with the women left over from polyandry, the numerical strength of men and women without regard to social institutions having been fairly equal hitherto, it is evident that neither the one nor the other form of marriage could rise to general prevalence. Actually, polygamy on the part of a man was clearly a product of slavery and limited to a few exceptional cases. In the Semitic patriarchal family, only the patriarch himself and, at most, a couple of his sons lived in polygamy; the others had to be content with one wife each. It remains the same today throughout the entire Orient. Polygamy is a privilege of the rich and the grandees, the wives being recruited chiefly by the purchase of female slaves; the mass of the people live in monogamy. Just such an exception is provided by polyandry in India and Tibet, the certainly not uninteresting origin of which from group marriage requires closer investigation. In its practice, at any rate, it appears to be much more tolerable than the jealous harem establishments of the Mohammedans. At least, among the Nairs in India, the men, in groups of three, four or more, have, to be sure, one wife in common; but each of them can simultaneously have a second wife in common with three or more other men, and, in the same way, a third wife, a fourth and so on. It is a wonder that McLennan did not discover a new class—that of *club marriage*— in these marriage clubs, membership of several of which at a time was open to the men, and which he himself described. This marriage club business, however, is by no means real polyandry; on the contrary, as has been noted by Giraud-Teulon, it is a specialised form of group marriage, the men living in polygamy, the women in polyandry.

4. The *Monogamian Family*. As already indicated, this arises out of the pairing family in the transition period from the middle to the

upper stage of barbarism, its final victory being one of the signs of the beginning of civilisation. It is based on the supremacy of the man; its express aim is the begetting of children of undisputed paternity, this paternity being required in order that these children may in due time inherit their father's wealth as his natural heirs. The monogamian family differs from pairing marriage in the far greater rigidity of the marriage tie, which can now no longer be dissolved at the pleasure of either party. Now, as a rule, only the man can dissolve it and cast off his wife. The right of conjugal infidelity remains his even now, sanctioned, at least, by custom (the *Code Napoléon*[312] expressly concedes this right to the husband as long as he does not bring his concubine into the conjugal home[377]), and is exercised more and more with the growing development of society. Should the wife recall the ancient sexual practice and desire to revive it, she is punished more severely than ever before.

We are confronted with this new form of the family in all its severity among the Greeks. While, as Marx observes,* the position of the goddesses in mythology represents an earlier period, when women still occupied a freer and more respected place, in the Heroic Age we already find women degraded owing to the predominance of the man and the competition of female slaves. One may read in the *Odyssey* how Telemachus cuts his mother short and enjoins silence upon her.** In Homer the young female captives become the objects of the sensual lust of the victors; the military chiefs, one after the other, according to rank, choose the most beautiful ones for themselves. The whole of the *Iliad*, as we know, revolves around the quarrel between Achilles and Agamemnon over such a female slave. In connection with each Homeric hero of importance mention is made of a captive maiden with whom he shares tent and bed. These maidens are taken back home, to the conjugal house, as was Cassandra by Agamemnon in Aeschylus.*** Sons born of these slaves receive a small share of their father's estate and are regarded as freemen. Teukros was such an illegitimate son of Telamon and was permitted to adopt his father's name. The wedded wife is expected to tolerate all this, but to maintain strict chastity and conjugal fidelity herself. True, in the Heroic Age the Greek wife is more respected than in the period of civilisation; for the husband, however, she is, in reality, merely the mother of his legitimate heirs, his chief housekeeper, and the superintendent of the female slaves, whom he may make, and does make, his concubines at will. It is the existence of slavery side by side with monogamy, the existence of beautiful young slaves who belong to the *man* with all they have, that from the very beginning stamped on mon-

---

* See *Marx-Engels Archive*, Vol. IX, p. 32.—*Ed.*
** Homer, *Odyssey*, Ode I.—*Ed.*
*** Aeschylus, *Oresteia. Agamemnon.—Ed.*

ogamy its specific character as monogamy *only for the woman*, but not for the man. And it retains this character to this day.

As regards the Greeks of later times, we must differentiate between the Dorians and the Ionians. The former, of whom Sparta was the classical example, had in many respects more ancient marriage relationships than even Homer indicates. In Sparta we find a form of pairing marriage—modified by the state in accordance with the conceptions there prevailing—which still retains many vestiges of group marriage. Childless marriages were dissolved: King Anaxandridas (about 560 B.C.) took another wife in addition to his first, childless one, and maintained two households; King Aristones of the same period added a third to two previous wives who were barren, one of whom he, however, let go. On the other hand, several brothers could have a wife in common. A person having a preference for his friend's wife could share her with him; and it was regarded as proper to place one's wife at the disposal of a lusty "stallion," as Bismarck would say, even when this person was not a citizen. A passage in Plutarch, where a Spartan woman sends a lover who is pursuing her with his attentions to interview her husband, would indicate, according to Schömann, still greater sexual freedom. Real adultery, the infidelity of the wife behind the back of her husband, was thus unheard of. On the other hand, domestic slavery was unknown in Sparta, at least in its heyday; the Helot serfs lived segregated on the estates and thus there was less temptation for the Spartiates[378] to have intercourse with their women. That in all these circumstances the women of Sparta enjoyed a very much more respected position than all other Greek women was quite natural. The Spartan women and the *élite* of the Athenian *hetaerae* are the only Greek women of whom the ancients speak with respect, and whose remarks they consider as being worthy of record.

Among the Ionians—of whom Athens is characteristic—things were quite different. Girls learned only spinning, weaving and sewing, at best a little reading and writing. They were practically kept in seclusion and consorted only with other women. The women's quarter was a separate and distinct part of the house, on the upper floor, or in the rear building, not easily accessible to men, particularly strangers; to this the women retired when men visitors came. The women did not go out unless accompanied by a female slave; at home they were virtually kept under guard; Aristophanes speaks of Molossian hounds kept to frighten off adulterers,[379] while in Asiatic towns, at least, eunuchs were maintained to keep guard over the women; they were manufactured for the trade in Chios as early as Herodotus' day, and according to Wachsmuth, not merely for the barbarians. In Euripides, the wife is described as *oikurema*,* a thing for housekeeping (the word is in the neuter gender), and apart from the business of

---

* Euripides, *Orestes.—Ed.*

bearing children, she was nothing more to the Athenian than the chief
housemaid. The husband had his gymnastic exercises, his public
affairs, from which the wife was excluded; in addition, he often had
female slaves at his disposal and, in the hey-day of Athens, extensive
prostitution, which was viewed with favour by the state, to say the
least. It was precisely on the basis of this prostitution that the sole
outstanding Greek women developed, who by their *esprit* and artistic taste towered as much above the general level of ancient woman-
hood as the Spartiate women did by virtue of their character. That
one had first to become a *hetaera* in order to become a woman is the
strongest indictment of the Athenian family.

In the course of time, this Athenian family became the model upon
which not only the rest of the Ionians, but also all the Greeks of the
mainland and of the colonies increasingly moulded their domestic
relationships. But despite all seclusion and surveillance the Greek
women found opportunities often enough for deceiving their husbands. The latter, who would have been ashamed to evince any love
for their own wives, amused themselves with *hetaerae* in all kinds of
amours. But the degradation of the women recoiled on the men
themselves and degraded them too, until they sank into the perversion
of boy-love, degrading both themselves and their gods by the myth
of Ganymede.

This was the origin of monogamy, as far as we can trace it among
the most civilised and highly-developed people of antiquity. It was
not in any way the fruit of individual sex love, with which it had
absolutely nothing in common, for the marriages remained marriages of convenience, as before. It was the first form of the family
based not on natural but on economic conditions, namely, on the victory of private property over original, naturally developed, common
ownership. The rule of the man in the family, the procreation of
children who could only be his, destined to be the heirs of his wealth
—these alone were frankly avowed by the Greeks as the exclusive
aims of monogamy. For the rest, it was a burden, a duty to the gods,
to the state and to their ancestors, which just had to be fulfilled. In
Athens the law made not only marriage compulsory, but also the fulfilment by the man of a minimum of the so-called conjugal duties.

Thus, monogamy does not by any means make its appearance in
history as the reconciliation of man and woman, still less as the highest form of such a reconciliation. On the contrary, it appears as
the subjection of one sex by the other, as the proclamation of a conflict between the sexes entirely unknown hitherto in prehistoric times.
In an old unpublished manuscript, the work of Marx and myself in
1846, I find the following: "The first division of labour is that between man and woman for child breeding."* And today I can add:

* Marx and Engels, *The German Ideology*, Moscow, 1964, pp. 42-43.—*Ed.*

The first class antagonism which appears in history coincides with the development of the antagonism between man and woman in monogamian marriage, and the first class oppression with that of the female sex by the male. Monogamy was a great historical advance, but at the same time it inaugurated, along with slavery and private wealth, that epoch, lasting until today, in which every advance is likewise a relative regression, in which the well-being and development of the one group are attained by the misery and repression of the other. It is the cellular form of civilised society, in which we can already study the nature of the antagonisms and contradictions which develop fully in the latter.

The old relative freedom of sexual intercourse by no means disappeared with the victory of the pairing family, or even of monogamy.

"The old conjugal system, now reduced to narrower limits by the gradual disappearance of the punaluan groups, still environed the advancing family, which it was to follow to the verge of civilisation.... It finally disappeared in the new form of hetaerism, which still follows mankind in civilisation as a dark shadow upon the family."

By hetaerism Morgan means that extramarital sexual intercourse between men and unmarried women which exists *alongside of monogamy*, and, as is well known, has flourished in the most diverse forms during the whole period of civilisation and is steadily developing into open prostitution. This hetaerism is directly traceable to group marriage, to the sacrificial surrender of the women, whereby they purchased their right to chastity. The surrender for money was at first a religious act, taking place in the temple of the Goddess of Love, and the money originally flowed into the coffers of the temple. The hierodules[380] of Anaitis in Armenia, of Aphrodite in Corinth, as well as the religious dancing girls attached to the temples in India—the so-called bayaders (the word is a corruption of the Portuguese *bailadeira*, a female dancer)—were the first prostitutes. This sacrificial surrender, originally obligatory for all women, was later practised vicariously by these priestesses alone on behalf of all other women. Hetaerism among other peoples grows out of the sexual freedom permitted to girls before marriage—hence likewise a survival of group marriage, only transmitted to us by another route. With the rise of property differentiation—that is, as far back as the upper stage of barbarism—wage labour appears sporadically alongside of slave labour; and simultaneously, as its necessary correlate, the professional prostitution of free women appears side by side with the forced surrender of the female slave. Thus, the heritage bequeathed to civilisation by group marriage is double-sided, just as everything engendered by civilisation is double-sided, double-tongued, self-contradictory and antagonistic: on the one hand, monogamy, on the other, hetaerism, including its most extreme form, prostitution. Hetaerism is as much a social institution as any other; it is a continuation of the old sexual freedom—in favour of the men. Although, in reality, it is not only tolerated but even practised with gusto, particularly by the ruling classes, it is condemned in words. In reality, however, this condemnation by no means hits the men who indulge in it, it hits only the women: they are ostracised and cast out in order to proclaim once again the absolute domination of the male over the female sex as the fundamental law of society.

A second contradiction, however, is hereby developed within monogamy itself. By the side of the husband, whose life is embellished by hetaerism, stands the neglected wife. And it is just as impossible to have one side of a contradiction without the other as it is to retain the whole of an apple in one's hand after half has been eaten. Nevertheless, the men appear to have thought differently, until their wives taught them to know better. Two permanent social figures, previously unknown, appear on the scene along with monogamy—the wife's paramour and the cuckold. The men had gained the victory over the women, but the act of crowning the victor was magnanimously undertaken by the vanquished. Adultery—proscribed, severely penalised, but irrepressible—became an unavoidable social institution alongside of monogamy and hetaerism. The assured paternity of children was now, as before, based, at best, on moral conviction; and in order to solve the insoluble contradiction, Article 312 of the *Code Napoléon* decreed:

"*L'enfant conçu pendant le mariage a pour père le mari,*" "a child conceived during marriage has for its father the husband".

This is the final outcome of three thousand years of monogamy.

Thus, in the monogamian family, in those cases that faithfully reflect its historical origin and that clearly bring out the sharp conflict between man and woman resulting from the exclusive domination of the male, we have a picture in miniature of the very antagonisms and contradictions in which society, split up into classes since the commencement of civilisation, moves, without being able to resolve and overcome them. Naturally, I refer here only to those cases of monogamy where matrimonial life really takes its course according to the rules governing the original character of the whole institution, but where the wife rebels against the domination of the husband. That this is not the case with all marriages no one knows better than the German Philistine, who is no more capable of ruling in the home than in the state, and whose wife, therefore, with full justification, wears the breeches of which he is unworthy. But in consolation he imagines himself to be far superior to his French companion in misfortune, who, more often than he, fares far worse.

The monogamian family, however, did not by any means appear

verywhere and always in the classically harsh form which it as-
umed among the Greeks. Among the Romans, who as future world
conquerors took a longer, if less refined, view than the Greeks, woman was more free and respected. The Roman believed the conjugal
fidelity of his wife to be adequately safeguarded by his power of life
and death over her. Besides, the wife, just as well as the husband,
could dissolve the marriage voluntarily. But the greatest advance in
the development of monogamy definitely occurred with the entry of
the Germans into history, because, probably owing to their poverty,
monogamy does not yet appear to have completely evolved among
them out of the pairing marriage. This we conclude from three circumstances mentioned by Tacitus. Firstly, despite their firm belief in
the sanctity of marriage—"each man is contented with a single wife,
and the women lived fenced around with chastity"—polygamy existed
for men of rank and the tribal chiefs, a situation similar to that of the
Americans among whom pairing marriage prevailed. Secondly, the
transition from mother right to father right could only have been
accomplished a short time previously, for the mother's brother—the
closest male gentile relative according to mother right—was still
regarded as being an almost closer relative than one's own father,
which likewise corresponds to the standpoint of the American Indians, among whom Marx found the key to the understanding of our
own prehistoric past, as he often used to say. And thirdly, women
among the Germans were highly respected and were influential in
public affairs also—which directly conflicts with the domination of
the male characteristic of monogamy. Nearly all these are points on
which the Germans are in accord with the Spartans, among whom,
likewise, as we have already seen, pairing marriage had not completely disappeared. Thus, in this connection also, an entirely new
element acquired world supremacy with emergence of the Germans.
The new monogamy which now developed out of the mingling of
races on the ruins of the Roman world clothed the domination of
the men in milder forms and permitted women to occupy, at least with
regard to externals, a far freer and more respected position than
classical antiquity had ever known. This, for the first time, created
the possibility for the greatest moral advance which we derive from
and owe to monogamy—a development taking place within it, parallel with it, or in opposition to it, as the case might be, namely,
modern individual sex love, previously unknown to the whole world.

This advance, however, definitely arose out of the circumstance
that the Germans still lived in the pairing family, and as far as
possible, grafted the position of woman corresponding thereto on to
monogamy. It by no means arose as a result of the legendary, wonderful moral purity of temperament of the Germans, which was limited to the fact that, in practice, the pairing family did not reveal the
same glaring moral antagonisms as monogamy. On the contrary, the

Germans, in their migrations, particularly South-East, to the nomad
of the steppes on the Black Sea, suffered considerable moral degener
ation and, apart from their horsemanship, acquired serious un
natural vices from them, as is attested to explicitly by Ammianu
about the Taifali, and by Procopius about the Heruli.[381]

Although monogamy was the only known form of the family ou
of which modern sex love could develop, it does not follow that thi
love developed within it exclusively, or even predominantly, as the
mutual love of man and wife. The whole nature of strict monogamian marriage under male domination ruled this out. Among all historically active classes, that is, among all ruling classes, matrimony
remained what it had been since pairing marriage—a matter of convenience arranged by the parents. And the first form of sex love that
historically emerges as a passion, and as a passion in which any person (at least of the ruling classes) has a right to indulge, as the highest form of the sexual impulse—which is precisely its specific feature—this, its first form, the chivalrous love of the Middle Ages, was
by no means conjugal love. On the contrary, in its classical form,
among the Provençals, it steers under full sail towards adultery, the
praises of which are sung by their poets. The *"Albas,"* in German
Tagelieder [Songs of the Dawn], are the flower of Provençal love
poetry. They describe in glowing colours how the knight lies with his
love—the wife of another—while the watchman stands guard outside, calling him at the first faint streaks of dawn (*alba*) so that he
may escape unobserved. The parting scene then constitutes the climax.
The Northern French as well as the worthy Germans, likewise adopted this style of poetry, along with the manners of chivalrous love
which corresponded to it; and on this same suggestive theme our own
old Wolfram von Eschenbach has left us three exquisite Songs of
the Dawn, which I prefer to his three long heroic poems.

Bourgeois marriage of our own times is of two kinds. In Catholic
countries the parents, as heretofore, still provide a suitable wife for
their young bourgeois son, and the consequence is naturally the fullest unfolding of the contradiction inherent in monogamy—flourishing hetaerism on the part of the husband, and flourishing adultery on the part of the wife. The Catholic Church doubtless abolished divorce only because it was convinced that for adultery, as for
death, there is no cure whatsoever. In Protestant countries, on the
other hand, it is the rule that the bourgeois son is allowed to seek a
wife for himself from his own class, more or less freely. Consequently, marriage can be based on a certain degree of love which, for
decency's sake, is always assumed, in accordance with Protestant hypocrisy. In this case, hetaerism on the part of the men is less actively
pursued and adultery on the woman's part is not so much the rule.
Since, in every kind of marriage, however, people remain what they
were before they married, and since the citizens of Protestant coun-

ries are mostly Philistines, this Protestant monogamy leads merely, f we take the average of the best cases, to a wedded life of leaden boredom, which is described as domestic bliss. The best mirror of these two ways of marriage is the novel; the French novel for the Catholic style, and the German novel for the Protestant. In both cases "he gets it": in the German novel the young man gets the girl; in the French, the husband gets the cuckold's horns. Which of the two is in the worse plight is not always easy to make out. For the dullness of the German novel excites the same horror in the French bourgeois as the "immorality" of the French novel excites in the German Philistine, although lately, since "Berlin is becoming a metropolis," the German novel has begun to deal a little less timidly with hetaerism and adultery, long known to exist there.

In both cases, however, marriage is determined by the class position of the participants, and to that extent always remains marriage of convenience. In both cases, this marriage of convenience often enough turns into the crassest prostitution—sometimes on both sides, but much more generally on the part of the wife, who differs from the ordinary courtesan only in that she does not hire out her body, like a wage-worker, on piece-work, but sells it into slavery once for all. And Fourier's words hold good for all marriages of convenience:

"Just as in grammer two negatives make a positive, so in the morals of marriage, two prostitutions make one virtue."

Sex love in the relation of husband and wife is and can become the rule only among the oppressed classes, that is, at the present day, among the proletariat, no matter whether this relationship is officially sanctioned or not. But here all the foundations of classical monogamy are removed. Here, there is a complete absence of all property, for the safeguarding and inheritance of which monogamy and male domination were established. Therefore, there is no stimulus whatever here to assert male domination. What is more, the means, too, are absent; bourgeois law, which protects this domination, exists only for the propertied classes and their dealings with the proletarians. It costs money, and therefore, owing to the worker's poverty, has no validity in his attitude towards his wife. Personal and social relations of quite a different sort are the decisive factors here. Moreover, since large-scale industry has transferred the woman from the house to the labour market and the factory, and makes her, often enough, the bread-winner of the family, the last remnants of male domination in the proletarian home have lost all foundation—except, perhaps, for some of that brutality towards women which became firmly rooted with the establishment of monogamy. Thus, the proletarian family is no longer monogamian in the strict sense, even in cases of the most passionate love and strictest faithfulness of the two parties, and despite all spiritual and worldly benedictions which may have been received. The two eternal adjuncts of monogamy—hetae rism and adultery—therefore, play an almost negligible role here the woman has regained, in fact, the right of separation, and wher the man and woman cannot get along they prefer to part. In short proletarian marriage is monogamian in the etymological sense o the word, but by no means in the historical sense.

Our jurists, to be sure, hold that the progress of legislation to ar increasing degree removes all cause for complaint on the part of the woman. Modern civilised systems of law are recognising more and more, first, that, in order to be effective, marriage must be an agreement voluntarily entered into by both parties; and secondly, that during marriage, too, both parties must be on an equal footing in respect to rights and obligations. If, however, these two demands were consistently carried into effect, women would have all that they could ask for.

This typical lawyer's reasoning is exactly the same as that with which the radical republican bourgeois dismisses the proletarian. The labour contract is supposed to be voluntarily entered into by both parties. But it is taken to be voluntarily entered into as soon as the law has put both parties on an equal footing *on paper*. The power given to one party by its different class position, the pressure it exercises on the other—the real economic position of both—all this is no concern of the law. And both parties, again, are supposed to have equal rights for the duration of the labour contract, unless one or the other of the parties expressly waived them. That the concrete economic situation compels the worker to forego even the slightest semblance of equal rights—this again is something the law cannot help.

As far as marriage is concerned, even the most progressive law is fully satisfied as soon as the parties formally register their voluntary desire to get married. What happens behind the legal curtains, where real life is enacted, how this voluntary agreement is arrived at—is no concern of the law and the jurist. And yet the simplest comparison of laws should serve to show the jurist what this voluntary agreement really amounts to. In countries where the children are legally assured of an obligatory share of their parents' property and thus cannot be disinherited—in Germany, in the countries under French law, etc.—the children must obtain their parents' consent in the question of marriage. In countries under English law, where parental consent to marriage is not legally requisite, the parents have full testatory freedom over their property and can, if they so desire, cut their children off with a shilling. It is clear, therefore, that despite this, or rather just because of this, among those classes which have something to inherit, freedom to marry is not one whit greater in England and America than in France or Germany.

The position is no better with regard to the juridical equality of man and woman in marriage. The inequality of the two before the law, which is a legacy of previous social conditions, is not the cause but the effect of the economic oppression of women. In the old communistic household, which embraced numerous couples and their children, the administration of the household, entrusted to the women, was just as much a public, a socially necessary industry as the providing of food by the men. This situation changed with the patriarchal family, and even more with the monogamian individual family. The administration of the household lost its public character. It was no longer the concern of society. It became a *private service*. The wife became the first domestic servant, pushed out of participation in social production. Only modern large-scale industry again threw open to her—and only to the proletarian woman at that—the avenue to social production; but in such a way that, when she fulfils her duties in the private service of her family, she remains excluded from public production and cannot earn anything; and when she wishes to take part in public industry and earn her living independently, she is not in a position to fulfil her family duties. What applies to the woman in the factory applies to her in all the professions, right up to medicine and law. The modern individual family is based on the open or disguised domestic enslavement of the woman; and modern society is a mass composed solely of individual families as its molecules. Today, in the great majority of cases, the man has to be the earner, the bread-winner of the family, at least among the propertied classes, and this gives him a dominating position which requires no special legal privileges. In the family, he is the bourgeois; the wife represents the proletariat. In the industrial world, however, the specific character of the economic oppression that weighs down the proletariat stands out in all its sharpness only after all the special legal privileges of the capitalist class have been set aside and the complete juridical equality of both classes is established. The democratic republic does not abolish the antagonism between the two classes; on the contrary, it provides the field on which it is fought out. And, similarly, the peculiar character of man's domination over woman in the modern family, and the necessity, as well as the manner, of establishing real social equality between the two, will be brought out into full relief only when both are completely equal before the law. It will then become evident that the first premise for the emancipation of women is the reintroduction of the entire female sex into public industry; and that this again demands that the quality possessed by the individual family of being the economic unit of society be abolished.

* * *

We have, then, three chief forms of marriage, which, by ar large, conform to the three main stages of human developmen For savagery—group marriage; for barbarism—pairing marriag for civilisation—monogamy, supplemented by adultery and prost tution. In the upper stage of barbarism, between pairing marriag and monogamy, there is wedged in the dominion exercised by me over female slaves, and polygamy.

As our whole exposition has shown, the advance to be noted i this sequence is linked with the peculiar fact that while women ar more and more deprived of the sexual freedom of group marriag the men are not. Actually, for men, group marriage exists to th day. What for a woman is a crime entailing dire legal and soci consequences, is regarded in the case of man as being honourabl or, at most, as a slight moral stain that one bears with pleasure. Th more the old traditional hetaerism is changed in our day by capital ist commodity production and adapted to it, and the more it transformed into unconcealed prostitution, the more demoralisin are its effects. And it demoralises the men far more than it do the women. Among women, prostitution degrades only those un fortunates who fall into its clutches; and even these are not de graded to the degree that is generally believed. On the other han it degrades the character of the entire male world. Thus, in nin cases out of ten, a long engagement is practically a preparator school for conjugal infidelity.

We are now approaching a social revolution in which th hitherto existing economic foundations of monogamy will dis appear just as certainly as will those of its supplement—prostitu tion. Monogamy arose out of the concentration of considerabl wealth in the hands of one person—and that a man—and out o the desire to bequeath this wealth to this man's children and to n one else's. For this purpose monogamy was essential on the woman' part, but not on the man's; so that this monogamy of the woma in no way hindered the overt or covert polygamy of the man The impending social revolution, however, by transforming a least the far greater part of permanent inheritable wealth— the means of production—into social property, will reduce al this anxiety about inheritance to a minimum. Since monogamy arose from economic causes, will it disappear when these causes disappear?

One might not unjustly answer: far from disappearing, it wil only begin to be completely realised. For with the conversion o the means of production into social property, wage labour, the proletariat, also disappears, and therewith, also, the necessity for a certain—statistically calculable—number of women to surrender themselves for money. Prostitution disappears; monogamy, instead of declining, finally becomes a reality—for the men as well.

At all events, the position of the men thus undergoes considerable change. But that of the women, of *all* women, also undergoes important alteration. With the passage of the means of production into common property, the individual family ceases to be the economic unit of society. Private housekeeping is transformed into a social industry. The care and education of the children becomes a public matter. Society takes care of all children equally, irrespective of whether they are born in wedlock or not. Thus, the anxiety about the "consequences," which is today the most important social factor—both moral and economic—that hinders a girl from giving herself freely to the man she loves, disappears. Will this not be cause enough for a gradual rise of more unrestrained sexual intercourse, and along with it, a more lenient public opinion regarding virginal honour and feminine shame? And finally, have we not seen that monogamy and prostitution in the modern world, although opposites, are nevertheless inseparable opposites, poles of the same social conditions? Can prostitution disappear without dragging monogamy with it into the abyss?

Here a new factor comes into operation, a factor that, at most, existed in embryo at the time when monogamy developed, namely, individual sex love.

No such thing as individual sex love existed before the Middle Ages. That personal beauty, intimate association, similarity in inclinations, etc., aroused desire for sexual intercourse among people of opposite sexes, that men as well as women were not totally indifferent to the question of with whom they entered into this most intimate relation is obvious. But this is still a far cry from the sex love of our day. Throughout antiquity marriages were arranged by the parents; the parties quietly acquiesced. The little conjugal love that was known to antiquity was not in any way a subjective inclination, but an objective duty; not a reason for but a correlate of marriage. In antiquity, love affairs in the modern sense occur only outside official society. The shepherds, whose joys and sorrows in love are sung by Theocritus and Moschus, or by Longus's *Daphnis and Chloë*, are mere slaves, who have no share in the state, the sphere of the free citizen. Except among the slaves, however, we find love affairs only as disintegration products of the declining ancient world; and with women who are also beyond the pale of official society, with *hetaerae,* that is, with alien or freed women: in Athens beginning with the eve of its decline, in Rome at the time of the emperors. If love affairs really occurred between free male and female citizens, it was only in the form of adultery. And sex love in our sense of the term was so immaterial to that classical love poet of antiquity, old Anacreon, that even the sex of the beloved one was a matter of complete indifference to him.

Our sex love differs materially from the simple sexual desire, th eros, of the ancients. First, it presupposes reciprocal love on th part of the loved one; in this respect, the woman stands on a pa with the man; whereas in the ancient eros, the woman was by n means always consulted. Secondly, sex love attains a degree c intensity and permanency where the two parties regard non-posses sion or separation as a great, if not the greatest, misfortune; i order to possess each other they take great hazards, even riskin life itself—what in antiquity happened at best, only in cases o adultery. And finally, a new moral standard arises for judgin sexual intercourse. The question asked is not only whether suc intercourse was legitimate or illicit, but also whether it arose fror mutual love or not? It goes without saying that in feudal or bour geois practice this new standard fares no better than all the othe moral standards—it is simply ignored. But it fares no worse, eithe It is recognised in theory, on paper, like all the rest. And mor than this cannot be expected for the present.

Where antiquity broke off with its start towards sex love, th Middle Ages began, namely, with adultery. We have alread described chivalrous love, which gave rise to the Songs of the Dawn There is still a wide gulf between this kind of love, which aimec at breaking up matrimony, and the love destined to be its foun dation, a gulf never completely bridged by the age of chivalry Even when we pass from the frivolous Latins to the virtuous Ger mans, we find, in the *Nibelungenlied*, that Kriemhild—althoug secretly in love with Siegfried every whit as much as he is witl her—nevertheless, in reply to Gunther's intimation that he ha plighted her to a knight whom he does not name, answers simply:

"You have no need to ask; as you command, so will I be for ever. He whom you, my lord, choose for my husband, to him will I gladly plight my troth."*

It never even occurs to her that her love could possibly be considered in this matter. Gunther seeks the hand of Brunhild without ever having seen her, and Etzel does the same with Kriemhild. The same occurs in the *Gudrun*,[382] where Sigebant of Ireland seeks the hand of Ute the Norwegian, Hettel of Hegelingen that of Hilde of Ireland; and lastly, Siegfried of Morland, Hartmut of Ormany and Herwing of Seeland seek the hand of Gudrun; and here for the first time it happens that Gudrun, of her own free will, decides in favour of the last named. As a rule, the bride of a young prince is selected by his parents; if these are no longer alive, he chooses her himself with the counsel of his highest vassal chiefs, whose word carries great weight in all cases. Nor can it be otherwise. For the knight, or baron, just as for the prince

* See *Nibelungenlied*, Song X.—*Ed.*

mself, marriage is a political act, an opportunity for the acces-
on of power through new alliances; the interest of the *House*
ad not individual inclination are the decisive factor. How can
ve here hope to have the last word regarding marriage?

It was the same for the guildsman of the medieval towns. The
ery privileges which protected him—the guild charters with their
ecial stipulations, the artificial lines of demarcation which legally
parated him from other guilds, from his own fellow guildsmen
ad from his journeymen and apprentices—considerably restricted
ae circle in which he could hope to secure a suitable spouse. And
ae question as to who was the most suitable was definitely decided
ader this complicated system, not by individual inclination, but
y family interest.

Up to the end of the Middle Ages, therefore, marriage, in the
verwhelming majority of cases, remained what it had been from
ae commencement, an affair that was not decided by the two prin-
ipal parties. In the beginning one came into the world married,
aarried to a whole group of the opposite sex. A similar relation pro-
ably existed in the later forms of group marriage, only with an ever
acreasing narrowing of the group. In the pairing family it is the rule
aat the mothers arrange their children's marriages; and here also,
onsiderations of new ties of relationship that are to strengthen the
oung couple's position in the gens and tribe are the decisive factor.
And when, with the predominance of private property over common
roperty, and with the interest in inheritance, father right and mon-
gamy gain the ascendancy, marriage becomes more than ever de-
endent on economic considerations. The *form* of marriage by pur-
hase disappears, the transaction itself is to an ever increasing degree
arried out in such a way that not only the woman but the man also
s appraised, not by his personal qualities but by his possessions. The
dea that the mutual inclinations of the principal parties should be
he overriding reason for matrimony had been unheard of in the
ractice of the ruling classes from the very beginning. Such things
ook place, at best, in romance only, or—among the oppressed clas-
es, which did not count.

This was the situation found by capitalist production when, follow-
ng the era of geographical discoveries, it set out to conquer the
vorld through world trade and manufacture. One would think that
his mode of matrimony should have suited it exceedingly, and such
was actually the case. And yet—the irony of world history is unfath-
omable—it was capitalist production that had to make the decisive
reach in it. By transforming all things into commodities, it dis-
olved all ancient traditional relations, and for inherited customs and
historical rights it substituted purchase and sale, "free" contract. And
H. S. Maine, the English jurist, believed that he made a colossal discovery when he said that our entire progress in comparison with pre-

vious epochs consists in our having evolved from status to contra
from an inherited state of affairs to one voluntarily contracted–
statement which, in so far as it is correct, was contained long ago
the *Communist Manifesto.**

But the closing of contracts presupposes people who can free
dispose of their persons, actions and possessions, and who meet ea
other on equal terms. To create such "free" and "equal" people w
precisely one of the chief tasks of capitalist production. Although
the beginning this took place only in a semi-conscious manner, and
religious guise to boot, nevertheless, from the time of the Luthera
and Calvinistic Reformation it became a firm principle that a pe
son was completely responsible for his actions only if he possesse
full fredom of the will when performing them, and that it was a
ethical duty to resist all compulsion to commit unethical acts. B
how does this fit in with the previous practice of matrimony? A
cording to bourgeois conceptions, matrimony was a contract, a leg
affair, indeed the most important of all, since it disposed of the bod
and mind of two persons for life. True enough, formally the bargai
was struck voluntarily; it was not done without the consent of th
parties; but how this consent was obtained, and who really arrange
the marriage was known only too well. But if real freedom to decid
was demanded for all other contracts, why not for this one? Had nc
the two young people about to be paired the right freely to dispose o
themselves, their bodies and organs? Did not sex love become th
fashion as a consequence of chivalry, and was not the love of hus
band and wife its correct bourgeois form, as against the adulterou
love of the knights? But if it was the duty of married people to lov
each other, was it not just as much the duty of lovers to marry eacl
other and nobody else? And did not the right of these lovers stanc
higher than that of parents, relatives and other traditional marriag
brokers and match-makers? If the right of free personal investigatio
unceremoniously forced its way into church and religion, how coulc
it halt at the intolerable claim of the older generation to dispose o
body and soul, the property, the happiness and unhappiness of the
younger generation?

These questions were bound to arise in a period which loosened
all the old social ties and which shook the foundations of all traditional conceptions. At one stroke the size of the world had increased
nearly tenfold. Instead of only a quadrant of a hemisphere the whole
globe was now open to the gaze of the West Europeans who hastened
to take possession of the other seven quadrants. And the thousand-
year-old barriers set up by the medieval prescribed mode of thought
vanished in the same way as did the old, narrow barriers of the
homeland. An infinitely wider horizon opened up both to man's outer

* See pp. 35-63 of this volume.—*Ed.*

 d inner eye. Of what avail were the good intentions of respecta-
lity, the honoured guild privileges handed down through the gener-
 ions, to the young man who was allured by India's riches, by the
 old and silver mines of Mexico and Potosi? It was the knight-errant
 eriod of the bourgeoisie; it had its romance also, and its love dreams,
 at on a bourgeois basis and in the last analysis, with bourgeois ends
 view.

Thus it happened that the rising bourgeoisie, particularly in the
 rotestant countries, where the existing order was shaken up most
 all, increasingly recognised freedom of contract for marriage also
 nd carried it through in the manner described above. Marriage re-
 ained class marriage, but, within the confines of the class, the par-
 es were accorded a certain degree of freedom of choice. And on
 aper, in moral theory as in poetic description, nothing was more un-
 akably established than that every marriage not based on mutual
 ex love and on the really free agreement of man and wife was im-
 oral. In short, love marriage was proclaimed a human right; not
 nly as man's right (droit de l'homme) but also, by way of exception,
 s woman's right (droit de la femme).

But in one respect this human right differed from all other so-
 alled human rights. While, in practice, the latter remained limited
 o the ruling class, the bourgeoisie—the oppressed class, the prole-
 ariat, being directly or indirectly deprived of them—the irony of
 istory asserts itself here once again. The ruling class continues to be
 ominated by the familiar economic influences and, therefore, only
 a exceptional cases can it show really voluntary marriages; whereas,
 s we have seen, these are the rule among the dominated class.

Thus, full freedom in marriage can become generally operative
 nly when the abolition of capitalist production, and of the property
 elations created by it, has removed all those secondary economic
 onsiderations which still exert so powerful an influence on the
 hoice of a partner. Then, no other motive remains than mutual
 ffection.

Since sex love is by its very nature exclusive—although this ex-
 lusiveness is fully realised today only in the woman—then marriage
 ased on sex love is by its very nature monogamy. We have seen how
 ight Bachofen was when he regarded the advance from group mariage to individual marriage chiefly as the work of the women; only
 he advance from pairing marriage to monogamy can be placed to
 he men's account, and, historically, this consisted essentially in a
 vorsening of the position of women and in facilitating infidelity on
 he part of the men. With the disappearance of the economic considerations which compelled women to tolerate the customary infide-
 ity of the men—the anxiety about their own livelihood and even
 nore about the future of their children—the equality of woman thus
 achieved will, judging from all previous experience, result far more

effectively in the men becoming really monogamous than in t
women becoming polyandrous.

What will most definitely disappear from monogamy, however,
all the characteristics stamped on it in consequence of its havi
arisen out of property relationships. These are, first, the dominan
of the man, and secondly, the indissolubility of marriage. The pred
minance of the man in marriage is simply a consequence of his ec
nomic predominance and will vanish with it automatically. T
indissolubility of marriage is partly the result of the economic co
ditions under which monogamy arose, and partly a tradition fro
the time when the connection between these economic conditions an
monogamy was not yet correctly understood and was exaggerate
by religion. Today it has been breached a thousandfold. If on
marriages that are based on love are moral, then, also only those a
moral in which love continues. The duration of the urge of indiv
dual sex love differs very much according to the individual, particu
larly among men; and a definite cessation of affection, or its di
placement by a new passionate love, makes separation a blessing f
both parties as well as for society. People will only be spared th
experience of wading through the useless mire of divorce proceeding:

Thus, what we can conjecture at present about the regulation o
sex relationships after the impending effacement of capitalist pro
duction is, in the main, of a negative character, limited mostly t
what will vanish. But what will be added? That will be settled afte
a new generation has grown up: a generation of men who never i
all their lives have had occasion to purchase a woman's surrende
either with money or with any other means of social power, and o
women who have never been obliged to surrender to any man out o
any consideration other than that of real love, or to refrain fron
giving themselves to their beloved for fear of the economic conse
quences. Once such people appear, they will not care a rap abou
what we today think they should do. They will establish their own
practice and their own public opinion, conformable therewith, on the
practice of each individual—and that's the end of it.

In the meantime, let us return to Morgan, from whom we have
strayed quite considerably. The historical investigation of the social
institutions which developed during the period of civilisation lies out
side the scope of his book. Consequently, he concerns himself only
briefly with the fate of monogamy during this period. He, too, regards
the development of the monogamian family as an advance, as an ap
proximation to the complete equality of the sexes, without, however,
considering that this goal has been reached. But, he says,

"when the fact is accepted that the family has passed through four successive
forms, and is now in a fifth, the question at once arises whether this form can
be permanent in the future. The only answer that can be given is that it must
advance as society advances, and change as society changes, even as it has done

in the past. It is the creation of the social system, and will reflect its culture. As the monogamian family has improved greatly since the commencement of civilisation, and very sensibly in modern times, it is at least supposable that it is capable of still further improvement until the equality of the sexes is attained. Should the monogamian family in the distant future fail to answer the requirements of society it is impossible to predict the nature of its successor."

III

THE IROQUOIS GENS

We now come to a further discovery of Morgan's, which is at least as important as the reconstruction of the primitive form of the family out of the systems of consanguinity. The demonstration of the fact that the bodies of *consanguinei* within the American-Indian tribe, designated by the names of animals, are in essence identical with the *genea* of the Greeks and the *gentes* of the Romans; that the American was the original form of the gens and the Greek and Roman the later, derivative form; that the entire social organisation of the Greeks and Romans of primitive times in gens, phratry and tribe finds its faithful parallel in that of the American Indians; that (as far as our present sources of information go) the gens is an institution common to all barbarians up to their entry into civilisation, and even afterwards—this demonstration cleared up at one stroke the most difficult parts of the earliest Greek and Roman history. At the same time it has thrown unexpected light on the fundamental features of the social constitution of primitive times—before the introduction of the *state*. Simple as this may seem when one knows it—nevertheless, Morgan discovered it only very recently. In his previous work, published in 1871,* he had not yet hit upon the secret, the discovery of which since reduced for a time the usually so confident English prehistorians to a mouse-like silence.

The Latin word *gens*, which Morgan employs as a general designation for this body of *consanguinei*, is, like its Greek equivalent, *genos*, derived from the common Aryan root *gan* (in German, where the Aryan g is, according to rule, replaced by *k*, it is *kan*), which means to beget. *Gens, genos*, the Sanscrit *janas*, the Gothic *kuni* (in accordance with the above-mentioned rule), the ancient Nordic and Anglo-Saxon *kyn*, the English *kin*, the Middle High German *künne*, all equally signify kinship, descent. However, *gens* in the Latin and *genos* in the Greek are specially used for those bodies of *consanguinei* which boast a common descent (in this case from a common male ancestor) and which, through certain social and religious institutions, are linked together into a special community, whose origin

---

* See pp. 456-57 of this volume.—*Ed.*

and nature had hitherto, nevertheless, remained obscure to all our historians.

We have already seen above, in connection with the punaluan family, how a gens in its original form is constituted. It consists of all persons who, by virtue of punaluan marriage and in accordance with the conceptions necessarily predominating therein, constitute the recognised descendants of a definite individual ancestress, the founder of the gens. Since paternity is uncertain in this form of the family female lineage alone is valid. Since the brothers may not marry their sisters, but only women of different descent, the children born of such women fall, according to mother right, outside the gens. Thus, only the offspring of the *daughters* of each generation remain in the kinship group, while the offspring of the sons go over into the gentes of their mothers. What, then, becomes of this consanguine group once it constitutes itself as a separate group, as against similar groups within the tribe?

Morgan takes the gens of the Iroquois, particularly that of the Seneca tribe, as the classical form of the original gens. They have eight gentes, named after the following animals: 1) Wolf; 2) Bear; 3) Turtle; 4) Beaver; 5) Deer; 6) Snipe; 7) Heron; 8) Hawk. The following usages prevail in each gens:

1. It elects its sachem (headman in times of peace) and its chief (leader in war). The sachem had to be elected from within the gens itself and his office was hereditary in the gens, in the sense that it had to be immediately filled whenever a vacancy occurred. The war chief could be elected also outside the gens and the office could at times remain vacant. The son of the previous sachem never succeeded to the office, since mother right prevailed among the Iroquois, and the son, therefore, belonged to a different gens. The brother or the sister's son, however, was often elected. All voted at the election—both men and women. The choice, however, had to be confirmed by the remaining seven gentes and only then was the elected person ceremonially installed, this being carried out by the general council of the entire Iroquois Confederacy. The significance of this will be seen later. The sachem's authority within the gens was of a paternal and purely moral character. He had no means of coercion at his command. He was by virtue of his office a member also of the tribal council of the Senecas, as well as of the Council of the Confederacy of all the Iroquois. The war chief could give orders only in military expeditions.

2. The gens can depose the sachem and war chief at will. This again is carried through jointly by the men and women. Thereafter, the deposed rank as simple warriors and private persons like the rest. The council of the tribe can also depose the sachems, even against the wishes of the gens.

3. No member is permitted to marry within the gens. This is the fundamental rule of the gens, the bond which keeps it together; it is

he negative expression of the very positive blood relationship by
virtue of which the individuals associated in it really become a gens.
By the discovery of this simple fact Morgan, for the first time, revealed
the nature of the gens. How little the gens had been understood
until then is proved by the earlier reports concerning savages and barbarians, in which the various bodies constituting the gentile organisa-
ion are ignorantly and indiscriminately referred to as tribe, clan,
chum, etc.; and regarding these it is sometimes asserted that marriage
within any such body is prohibited. This gave rise to the hopeless confusion in which Mr. McLennan could intervene as a Napoleon, creating order by his fiat: All tribes are divided into those within which
marriage is forbidden (exogamous) and those within which it is permitted (endogamous). And after having thus thoroughly muddled
matters he could indulge in most profound investigations as to which
of his two absurd classes was the older, exogamy or endogamy. This
nonsense ceased automatically with the discovery of the gens based
on blood relationship and the consequent impossibility of marriage
between its members. Obviously, at the stage at which we find the
Iroquois, the rule forbidding marriage within the gens is inflexibly
adhered to.

4. The property of deceased persons was distributed among the
remaining members of the gens—it had to remain in the gens. In
view of the insignificance of the effects which an Iroquois could leave,
the heritage was divided among the nearest relatives in the gens;
when a man died, among his natural brothers and sisters and his
maternal uncle; when a woman died, then among her children and
natural sisters, but not her brothers. That is precisely the reason why
it was impossible for man and wife to inherit from each other, and
why children could not inherit from their father.

5. The members of the gens were bound to give one another
assistance, protection and particularly support in avenging injuries
inflicted by outsiders. The individual depended and could depend
for his security on the protection of the gens. Whoever injured him
injured the whole gens. From this—the blood ties of the gens—arose
the obligation of blood revenge, which was unconditionally recognised by the Iroquois. If a non-member of a gens slew a member of
the gens the whole gens to which the slain person belonged was
pledged to blood revenge. First mediation was tried. A council of
the slayer's gens was held and propositions were made to the council
of the victim's gens for a composition of the matter—mostly in the
form of expressions of regret and presents of considerable value. If
these were accepted, the affair was settled. If not, the injured gens
appointed one or more avengers, whose duty it was to pursue
and slay the murderer. If this was accomplished the gens of
the latter had no right to complain; the matter was regarded as
adjusted.

6. The gens has definite names or series of names which it alone in the whole tribe, is entitled to use, so that an individual's name also indicates the gens to which he belongs. A gentile name carrie gentile rights with it as a matter of course.

7. The gens can adopt strangers and thereby admit them int the tribe as a whole. Prisoners of war that were not slain becam members of the Seneca tribe by adoption into a gens and thereb obtained the full tribal and gentile rights. The adoption took plac at the request of individual members of the gens—men placed th stranger in the relation of a brother or sister, women in that of ; child. For confirmation, ceremonial acceptance into the gens wa necessary. Gentes exceptionally shrunk in numbers were often re plenished by mass adoption from another gens, with the latter' consent. Among the Iroquois, the ceremony of adoption into th gens was performed at a public meeting of the council of the tribe which turned it practically into a religious ceremony.

8. It would be difficult to prove special religious rites among the Indian gentes—and yet the religious ceremonies of the Indian are more or less connected with the gentes. Among the Iroquois at their six annual religious ceremonies, the sachems and wa chiefs of the individual gentes were reckoned among the "Keeper of the Faith" *ex officio* and exercised priestly functions.

9. The gens has a common burial place. That of the Iroquois o New York State, who have been hemmed in by the whites, has now disappeared, but it formerly existed. It still survives amongs other Indian tribes, as, for instance, amongst the Tuscaroras, a tribe closely related to the Iroquois, who, although Christian, still retain in their cemetery a special row for each gens, so that the mother is buried in the same row as her children, but not the father. And among the Iroquois also, all the members of the gens are mourners at the funeral, prepare the grave, deliver funeral orations and so forth.

10. The gens has a council, the democratic assembly of all adult male and female members of the gens, all with equal voice. This council elected and deposed the sachems and war chiefs and, like- wise, the remaining "Keepers of the Faith." It decided about pen- ance gifts (*wergild*) or blood revenge, for murdered gentiles. It adopted strangers into the gens. In short, it was the sovereign power in the gens.

These are the powers of a typical Indian gens.

"All the members of an Iroquois gens were personally free, and they were bound to defend each other's freedom; they were equal in privileges and in per- sonal rights, the sachems and chiefs claiming no superiority; and they were a brotherhood bound together by the ties of kin. Liberty, equality, and fraternity, though never formulated, were cardinal principles of the gens. The gens was the unit of a social system, the foundation upon which Indian society was organised. [This] serves to explain that sense of independence and personal dignity universally an attribute of Indian character."*

At the time of their discovery the Indians in all North America were organised in gentes in accordance with mother right. Only in a few tribes, as amongst the Dakotas, the gentes had fallen into decay, while in some others, such as the Ojibwas and Omahas, they were organised in accordance with father right.

Among numerous Indian tribes having more than five or six gentes, we find three, four and more gentes united in a special group which Morgan—faithfully translating the Indian term by its Greek counterpart—calls the phratry (brotherhood). Thus, the Senecas have two phratries, the first embracing the gentes 1 to 4, and the second the gentes 5 to 8. Closer investigation shows that these phratries, in the main, represent those original gentes into which the tribe split at the outset; for with the prohibition of marriage within the gens, each tribe had necessarily to consist of at least two gentes in order to be capable of independent existence. As the tribe increased, each gens again subdivided into two or more gentes, each of which now appears as a separate gens, while the original gens, which embraces all the daughter gentes, lives on as the phratry. Among the Senecas and most other Indian tribes, the gentes in one phratry are brother gentes, while those in others are their cousin gentes—designations which, as we have seen, have a very real and expressive significance in the American system of consanguinity. Originally, indeed, no Seneca could marry within his phratry; but this prohibition has long since lapsed and is limited only to the gens. The Senecas had a tradition that the Bear and the Deer were the two original gentes, of which the others were offshoots. Once this new institution had become firmly rooted, it was modified according to need. In order to maintain equilibrium, whole gentes out of other phratries were occasionally transferred to those in which gentes had died out. This explains why we find gentes of the same name variously grouped among the phratries in different tribes.

Among the Iroquois the fuctions of the phratry are partly social and partly religious. 1) The ball game is played by phratries, one against the other; each phratry puts forward its best players, the remaining members of the phratry being spectators arranged according to phratry, who bet against each other on the success of their respective sides. 2) At the council of the tribe the sachems and war chiefs of each phratry sit together, the two groups facing each other, and each speaker addresses the representatives of each phratry as a separate body. 3) If a murder was committed in the tribe and the victim and the slayer did not belong to the same

* See also *Marx-Engels Archive*, Vol. IX, p. 71.—*Ed.*

phratry, the aggrieved gens often appealed to its brother gentes; these held a phratry council and addressed themselves to the other phratry, as a body, asking it also to summon a council for the adjustment of the matter. Here again the phratry appears as the original gens and with greater prospects of success than the weaker individual gens, its offspring. 4) On the death of persons of consequence, the opposite phratry undertook the arrangement of the funeral and the burial rites, while the phratry of the deceased went along as mourners. If a sachem died the opposite phratry notified the federal council of the Iroquois of the vacancy in the office. 5) The council of the phratry again appeared on the scene at the election of a sachem. Confirmation by the brother gentes was regarded as rather a matter of course, but the gentes of the other phratry might be opposed. In such a case the council of this phratry met and, if it upheld the opposition, the election was null and void. 6) Formerly, the Iroquois had special religious mysteries, which white men called "medicine lodges." Among the Senecas those were celebrated by two religious fraternities, one for each phratry, with a regular initiation ritual for new members. 7) If, as is almost certain, the four lineages (kinship groups) that occupied the four quarters of Tlascalá at the time of the Conquest[383] were four phratries, this proves that the phratries, as among the Greeks, and similar bodies of *consanguinei* among the Germans, served also as military units. These four lineages went into battle, each one as a separate host, with its own uniform and flag, and a leader of its own.

Just as several gentes constitute a phratry, so, in the classical form, several phratries constitute a tribe. In many cases the middle link, the phratry, is missing among greatly weakened tribes. What are the distinctive features of the Indian tribe in America?

1. The possession of its own territory and its own name. In addition to the area of actual settlement, each tribe possessed considerable territory for hunting and fishing. Beyond this there was a wide stretch of neutral land reaching to the territory of the next tribe; the extent of this neutral territory was relatively small where the languages of the two tribes were related, and large where not. Such neutral ground was the border forest of the Germans, the wasteland which Caesar's Suevi created around their territory, the *îsarnholt* (Danish *jarnved, limes Danicus*) between the Danes and the Germans, the Saxon forest and the *branibor* (defence forest in Slavic)—from which Brandenburg derives its name—between Germans and Slavs. The territory thus marked out by imperfectly defined boundaries was the common land of the tribe, recognised as such by neighbouring tribes, and defended by the tribe against any encroachment. In most cases, the uncertainty of the boundaries became a practical inconvenience only when the population had

greatly increased. The tribal names appear to have been the result more of accident than of deliberate choice. As time passed it frequently happened that neighbouring tribes designated a tribe by a name different from that which it itself used, like the case of the Germans [*die Deutschen*], whose first comprehensive historical name—*Germani* [*Germanen*]—was bestowed on them by the Celts.

2. A special *dialect* peculiar to this tribe only. In fact, tribe and dialect are substantially co-extensive. The establishment of new tribes and dialects through subdivision was in progress in America until quite recently, and can hardly have ceased altogether even now. Where two weakened tribes have amalgamated into one, it happens, by way of exception, that two closely related dialects are spoken in the same tribe. The average strength of American tribes is under 2,000. The Cherokees, however, are nearly 26,000 strong—being the largest number of Indians in the United States that speak the same dialect.

3. The right of investing the sachems and war chiefs elected by the gentes, and

4. The right to depose them again, even against the wishes of their gens. As these sachems and war chiefs are members of the tribal council, these rights of the tribe in relation to them are self-explanatory. Wherever a confederacy of tribes was established and all the tribes were represented in a federal council, the above rights were transferred to this latter body.

5. The possession of common religious ideas (mythology) and rites of worship.

"After the fashion of barbarians the American Indians were a religious people."[384]

Their mythology has not yet been critically investigated by any means. They already personified their religious ideas—spirits of all kinds—but in the lower stage of barbarism in which they lived there was as yet no plastic representation, no so-called idols. It is a nature and element worship evolving towards polytheism. The various tribes had their regular festivals with definite forms to worship, particularly dancing and games. Dancing especially was an essential part of all religious ceremonies, each tribe performing its own separately.

6. A tribal council for common affairs. It consisted of all the sachems and war chiefs of the individual gentes—the real representatives of the latter, because they could always be deposed. The council sat in public, surrounded by the other members of the tribe, who had the right to join in the discussion and to secure a hearing for their opinions, and the council made the decision. As a rule it was open to everyone present to address the council;

even the women could express their views through a spokesman of their own choice. Among the Iroquois the final decisions had to be adopted unanimously, as was also the case with many of the decisions of the German Mark communities. In particular, the regulation of relations with other tribes devolved upon the tribal council. It received and sent embassies, it declared war and concluded peace. When war broke out it was carried on mainly by volunteers. In principle each tribe was in a state of war with every other tribe with which it had not expressly concluded a treaty of peace. Military expeditions against such enemies were for the most part organised by a few outstanding warriors. They gave a war dance; whoever joined in the dance thereby declared his intention to participate in the expedition. A detachment was immediately formed and it set out forthwith. When the tribal territory was attacked, its defence was in the same manner conducted mainly by volunteers. The departure and return of such detachments were always made the occasion for public festivities. The sanction of the tribal council for such expeditions was not necessary. It was neither sought nor given. They were exactly like the private war expeditions of the German retainers, as Tacitus has described them, except that among the Germans the body of retainers had already assumed a more permanent character, and constituted a strong nucleus, organised in times of peace, around which the remaining volunteers grouped themselves in the event of war. Such military detachments were seldom numerically strong. The most important expeditions of the Indians, even those covering great distances, were carried through by insignificant fighting forces. When several such retinues gathered for an important engagement, each group obeyed its own leader only. The unity of the plan of campaign was ensured, more or less, by a council of these leaders. It was the method of war adopted by the Alamanni of the Upper Rhine in the fourth century, as described by Ammianus Marcellinus.

7. In some tribes we find a head-chief [Oberhäuptling], whose powers, however, are very slight. He is one of the sachems, who in cases demanding speedy action has to take provisional measures until such time as the council can assemble and make the final decision. This is a feeble but, as further development showed, generally fruitless inchoate attempt to create an official with executive authority; actually, as will be seen, it was the highest military commander [oberster Heerführer] who, in most cases, if not in all, developed into such an official.

The great majority of American Indians never got beyond the stage of tribal integration. Constituting numerically small tribes, separated from one another by wide border-lands, and enfeebled by perpetual warfare, they occupied an enormous territory with but few people. Alliances arising out of temporary emergencies were concluded here and there between kindred tribes and dissolved again with the passing of the emergency. But in certain areas originally kindred but subsequently disunited tribes reunited in lasting confederacies, and so took the first step towards the formation of nations. In the United States we find the most advanced form of such a confederacy among the Iroquois. Emigrating from their original home west of the Mississippi, where they probably constituted a branch of the great Dakota family, they settled down after protracted wanderings in what is today the State of New York. They were divided into five tribes: Senecas, Cayugas, Onondagas, Oneidas and Mohawks. Subsisting on fish, game and the produce of a crude horticulture, they lived in villages protected mostly by palisades. Never more than 20,000 strong, they had a number of gentes common to all the five tribes; they spoke closely-related dialects of the same language and occupied a continuous tract of territory that was divided among the five tribes. Since this area had been newly conquered, habitual cooperation among these tribes against those they displaced was only natural. At the beginning of the fifteenth century at the latest, this developed into a regular "permanent league," a confederacy, which, conscious of its new-found strength, immediately assumed an aggressive character and at the height of its power—about 1675 —had conquered large stretches of the surrounding country, expelling some of the inhabitants and forcing others to pay tribute. The Iroquois Confederacy was the most advanced social organisation attained by the Indians who had not emerged from the lower stage of barbarism (that is, excepting the Mexicans, New Mexicans and Peruvians). The fundamental features of the Confederacy were as follows:

1. Perpetual alliance of the five consanguine tribes on the basis of complete equality and independence in all internal tribal affairs. This blood relationship constituted the true basis of the Confederacy. Of the five tribes, three were called the father tribes and were brothers one to another; the other two were called son tribes and were likewise brother tribes to each other. Three gentes—the oldest—still had living representatives in all the five tribes, while another three had in three tribes. The members of each of these gentes were all brothers throughout the five tribes. The common language, with mere dialectal differences, was the expression and the proof of common descent.

2. The organ of the Confederacy was a Federal Council comprised of fifty sachems, all of equal rank and dignity; this council passed finally on all matters pertaining to the Confederacy.

3. At the time the Confederacy was constituted these fifty sachems were distributed among the tribes and gentes as the bearers

of new offices, especially created to suit the aims of the Confederacy. They were elected anew by the gentes concerned whenever
a vacancy arose, and could always be removed by them. The right
to invest them with office belonged, however, to the Federal Council.

4. These federal sachems were also sachems in their own respective tribes, and each had a seat and a vote in the tribal council.

5. All decisions of the Federal Council had to be unanimous.

6. Voting was by tribes, so that each tribe and all the council
members in each tribe had to agree before a binding decision
could be made.

7. Each of the five tribal councils could convene the Federal
Council, but the latter had no power to convene itself.

8. Its meetings took place before the assembled people. Every
Iroquois had the right to speak; the council alone decided.

9. The Confederacy had no official head, no chief executive.

10. It did, however, have two supreme war chiefs, enjoying
equal authority and equal power (the two "kings" of the Spartans,
the two consuls in Rome).

This was the whole social constitution under which the Iroquois
lived for over four hundred years, and still do live. I have given
Morgan's account of it in some detail because it gives us the opportunity of studying the organisation of a society which as yet
knows no *state*. The state presupposes a special public authority
separated from the totality of those concerned in each case; and
Maurer with true instinct recognises the German Mark constitution
as *per se* a purely social institution differing essentially from the
state, although it largely served as its foundation later on. In all
his writings, therefore, Maurer investigates the gradual rise of
public authority out of and side by side with the original constitutions of the Marks, villages, manors and towns. The North American Indians show how an originally united tribe gradually spread
over an immense continent; how tribes, through fission, became
peoples, whole groups of tribes; how the languages changed not
only until they became mutually unintelligible, but until nearly
every trace of original unity disappeared; and how at the same
time individual gentes within the tribes broke up into several; how
the old mother gentes persisted as phratries, and the names of
these oldest gentes still remain the same among widely remote and
long-separated tribes—the Wolf and the Bear are still gentile names
among a majority of Indian tribes. Generally speaking, the constitution described above applies to them all—except that many of
them did not get as far as a confederation of kindred tribes.

But we also see that once the gens as a social unit was given,
the entire system of gentes, phratries and tribe developed with
almost compelling necessity—because naturally—out of this unit.

All three are groups of various degrees of consanguinity, each complete in itself and managing its own affairs, but each also supplementing the rest. And the sphere of affairs devolving on them comprised the totality of the public affairs of the barbarians in the lower stage. Wherever, therefore, we discover the gens as the social unit of a people, we may look for an organisation of the tribe similar to that described above; and where sufficient sources are available, as, for example, amongst the Greeks and the Romans, we shall not only find them, but we shall also convince ourselves that, where the sources fail us, a comparison with the American social constitution will help us out of the most difficult doubts and enigmas.

And this gentile constitution is wonderful in all its childlike simplicity! Everything runs smoothly without soldiers, gendarmes or police; without nobles, kings, governors, prefects or judges; without prisons; without trials. All quarrels and disputes are settled by the whole body of those concerned—the gens or the tribe or the individual gentes among themselves. Blood revenge threatens only as an extreme or rarely applied measure, of which our capital punishment is only the civilised form, possessed of all the advantages and drawbacks of civilisation. Although there are many more affairs in common than at present—the household is run in common and communistically by a number of families, the land is tribal property, only the small gardens being temporarily assigned to the households—still, not a bit of our extensive and complicated machinery of administration is required. Those concerned decide, and in most cases century-old custom has already regulated everything. There can be no poor and needy—the communistic household and the gens know their obligations towards the aged, the sick and those disabled in war. All are free and equal—including the women. There is as yet no room for slaves, nor, as a rule, for the subjugation of alien tribes. When the Iroquois conquered the Eries and the "Neutral Nations"[385] about the year 1651, they invited them to join the Confederacy as equal members; only when the vanquished refused were they driven out of their territory. And the kind of the men and women that are produced by such a society is indicated by the admiration felt by all white men who came into contact with uncorrupted Indians, admiration of the personal dignity, straightforwardness, strength of character and bravery of these barbarians.

We have witnessed quite recently examples of this bravery in Africa. The Zulu Kaffirs a few years ago, like the Nubians a couple of months ago*—in both of which tribes gentile institutions have

---

* The reference is to the war between the British and the Zulus in 1879 and between the British and the Nubians in 1883.—*Ed.*

not yet died out—did what no European army can do.[386] Armed only
with pikes and spears and without firearms, they advanced, under
a hail of bullets from the breech loaders, right up to the bayonets
of the English infantry—acknowledged as the best in the world
for fighting in close formation—throwing them into disorder and
even beating them back more than once; and this, despite the
colossal disparity in arms and despite the fact that they have no
such thing as military service, and do not know what military
exercises are. Their capacity and endurance are best proved by
the complaint of the English that a Kaffir can move faster and
cover a longer distance in twenty-four hours than a horse. As an
English painter says, their smallest muscle stands out, hard and
steely, like whipcord.

This is what mankind and human society were like before class
divisions arose. And if we compare their condition with that of
the overwhelming majority of civilised people today, we will find
an enormous gulf between the present-day proletarian and small
peasant and the ancient free member of a gens.

This is one side of the picture. Let us not forget, however, that
this organisation was doomed to extinction. It never developed
beyond the tribe; the confederacy of tribes already signified the
commencement of its downfall, as we shall see later, and as the
attempts of the Iroquois to subjugate others have shown. What
was outside the tribe was outside the law. Where no express treaty
of peace existed, war raged between tribe and tribe; and war was
waged with the cruelty that distinguishes man from all other
animals and which was abated only later in self-interest. The gentile constitution in full bloom, as we have seen it in America, presupposed an extremely undeveloped form of production, that is,
an extremely sparse population spread over a wide territory, and
therefore the almost complete domination of man by external
nature, alien, opposed, incomprehensible to him, a domination reflected in his childish religious ideas. The tribe remained the bound-
ary for man, in relation to himself as well as to outsiders: the tribe,
the gens and their institutions were sacred and inviolable, a
superior power, instituted by nature, to which the individual
remained absolutely subject in feeling, thought and deed. Impressive
as the people of this epoch may appear to us, they differ in no
way one from another, they are still bound, as Marx says, to the
umbilical cord of the primordial community. The power of these
primordial communities had to be broken, and it was broken. But
it. was broken by influences which from the outset appear to us
as a degradation, a fall from the simple moral grandeur of the
ancient gentile society. The lowest interests—base greed, brutal
sensuality, sordid avarice, selfish plunder of common possessions—
usher in the new, civilised society, class society; the most

outrageous means—theft, rape, deceit and treachery—undermine and topple the old, classless, gentile society. And the new society, during all the 2,500 years of its existence, has never been anything but the development of the small minority at the expense of the exploited and oppressed great majority; and it is so today more than ever before.

IV

THE GRECIAN GENS

Greeks as well as Pelasgians and other peoples of the same tribal origin were constituted since prehistoric times in the same organic series as the Americans: gens, phratry, tribe, confederacy of tribes. The phratry might be missing, as, for example, among the Dorians; the confederacy of tribes might not be fully developed yet in every case; but the gens was everywhere the unit. At the time the Greeks entered into history, they were on the threshold of civilisation. Almost two entire great periods of development lie between the Greeks and the above-mentioned American tribes, the Greeks of the Heroic Age being by so much ahead of the Iroquois. For this reason the Grecian gens no longer bore the archaic character of the Iroquois gens; the stamp of group marriage was becoming considerably blurred. Mother right had given way to father right; thereby rising private wealth made the first breach in the gentile constitution. A second breach naturally followed the first: after the introduction of father right, the fortune of a wealthy heiress would, by virtue of her marriage, fall to her husband, that is to say, to another gens; and so the foundation of all gentile law was broken, and in such cases the girl was not only permitted, but *obliged* to marry within the gens, in order that the latter might retain the fortune.

According to Grote's *History of Greece*, the Athenian gens in particular was held together by:

1. Common religious ceremonies, and exclusive privilege of the priesthood in honour of a definite god, supposed to be the primitive ancestor of the gens, and characterised in this capacity by a special surname.

2. A common burial place. (Compare Demosthenes' *Eubulides*.)

3. Mutual rights of inheritance.

4. Reciprocal obligation to afford help, defence and support against the use of force.

5. Mutual right and obligation to marry in the gens in certain cases, especially for orphaned daughters or heiresses.

6. Possession, in some cases at least, of common property, and of an archon (magistrate) and treasurer of its own.

The phratry, binding together several gentes, was less intimate,

but here too we find mutual rights and duties of similar charac
ter, especially a communion of particular religious rites and the
right of prosecution in the event of a phrator being slain. Again
all the phratries of a tribe performed periodically certain common
sacred ceremonies under the presidency of a magistrate called the
phylobasileus (tribal magistrate) selected from among the noble.
(*eupatrides*).

Thus Grote. And Marx adds: "In the Grecian gens the savage
(for example, the Iroquois) is unmistakably discerned."[*] He
becomes still more unmistakable when we investigate somewhat
further.

For the Grecian gens has also the following attributes:

7. Descent according to father right.

8. Prohibition of intermarrying in the gens except in the case
of heiresses. This exception and its formulation as an injunction
clearly proves the validity of the old rule. This follows also from
the universally accepted rule that when a woman married she
renounced the religious rites of her gens and acquired those of
the gens of her husband, in whose phratry she was enrolled. This,
and a famous passage in Dicaearchus, go to prove that marriage
outside of the gens was the rule. Becker in *Charicles* directly
assumes that nobody was permitted to marry in his or her own gens.

9. The right of adoption into the gens; it was practised by
adoption into the family, but with public formalities, and only in
exceptional cases.

10. The right to elect and depose the chiefs. We know that
every gens had its archon; but nowhere is it stated that this office
was hereditary in certain families. Until the end of barbarism,
the probability is always against strict heredity, which would be
totally incompatible with conditions where rich and poor had
absolutely equal rights in the gens.

Not only Grote, but also Niebuhr, Mommsen and all other
previous historians of classical antiquity failed to solve the problem of the gens. Although they correctly noted many of its distinguishing features, they always regarded it as a *group of families*
and thus made it impossible for themselves to understand the
nature and origin of the gens. Under the gentile constitution,
the family was never a unit of organisation, nor could it be, for
man and wife necessarily belonged to two different gentes. The
gens as a whole belonged to the phratry, the phratry to the tribe;
but in the case of the family, it half belonged to the gens of the
husband and half to that of the wife. The state, too, does not
recognise the family in public law; to this day it exists only in
civil law. Nevertheless, all written history so far takes as its point

---

[*] See *Marx-Engels Archive*, Vol. IX, p. 134.—*Ed.*

of departure the absurd assumption, which became inviolable in the eighteenth century, that the monogamian individual family, an institution scarcely older than civilisation, is the nucleus around which society and the state gradually crystallised.

"Mr. Grote will also please note," adds Marx, "that although the Greeks traced their gentes to mythology, the gentes are older than mythology with its gods and demigods, which *they themselves* had created."*

Grote is quoted with preference by Morgan as a prominent and quite unsuspicious witness. He relates further that every Athenian gens had a name derived from its reputed ancestor; that before Solon's time as a general rule, and afterwards if a man died intestate, his gentiles (*gennêtes*) inherited his property; and that if a man was murdered, first his relatives, next his *gennêtes*, and finally the phrators of the slain had the right and duty to prosecute the criminal in the courts:

"all that we hear of the most ancient Athenian laws is based upon the gentile and phratric divisions."

The descent of the gentes from common ancestors has been a brain-racking puzzle to the "school-taught Philistines" (Marx.)** Naturally, since they claim that these ancestors are purely mythical, they are at a loss to explain how the gentes developed out of separate and distinct, originally totally unrelated families; yet they must accomplish this somehow, if only to explain the existence of the gentes. So they circle round in a whirlpool of words and do not get beyond the phrase: the genealogy is indeed mythical, but the gens is real. And finally, Grote says—the bracketed remarks being by Marx—:

"We hear of this genealogy but rarely, because it is only brought before the public in certain cases pre-eminent and venerable. But the humbler gentes had their common rites [rather peculiar, Mr. Grote!] and common superhuman ancestor and genealogy, as well as the more celebrated [how very peculiar this, Mr. Grote, in *humbler* gentes!]: the scheme and ideal basis [my dear sir! Not *ideal*, but carnal—*germanice**** *fleischlich*!] was the same in all."*)

Marx sums up Morgan's reply to this as follows: "The system of consanguinity corresponding to the gens in its original form— the Greeks once possessed it like other mortals—preserved the knowledge of the mutual relation of all members of the gens. They learned this for them decisively important fact by practice from early childhood. With the advent of the monogamian family this dropped into oblivion. The gentile name created a genealogy

* See *Marx-Engels Archive*, Vol. IX, p. 136.—*Ed.*
** Ibid., p. 137.—*Ed.*
*** In plain German.—*Ed.*
*) See *Marx-Engels Archive*, Vol. IX, p. 138.—*Ed.*

compared with which that of the monogamian family seemed insignificant. This name was now to attest to its bearers the fact of
their common ancestry. But the genealogy of the gens went so far
back that its members could no longer prove their mutual real kinship, except in a limited number of cases of more recent common
ancestors. The name itself was the proof of a common ancestry, and
conclusive proof, except in cases of adoption. The actual denial of
all kinship between gentiles à la Grote* and Niebuhr, which transforms the gens into a purely fictitious, fanciful creation of the brain,
is, on the other hand, worthy of 'ideal' scientists, that is, of cloistered
bookworms. Because the concatenation of the generations, especially
with the incipience of monogamy, is removed into the distance, and
the reality of the past seems reflected in mythological fantasy, the
good old Philistines concluded, and still conclude, that the fancied
genealogy created real gentes!"**

As among the Americans, the *phratry* was a mother gens, split
up into several daughter gentes, and at the same time uniting them,
often tracing them all to a common ancestor. Thus, according to
Grote,

"all the contemporary members of the phratry of Hekataeus had a common
god for their ancestor at the sixteenth degree."

Hence, all the gentes of this phratry were literally brother gentes.
The phratry is still mentioned by Homer as a military unit in that
famous passage where Nestor advises Agamemnon: Draw up the
troops by tribes and by phratries so that phratry may support phratry,
and tribe tribe.***

The phratry also has the right and the duty to prosecute the murderer of a phrator, indicating that in former times it had the duty of
blood revenge. Furthermore, it has common sanctuaries and festivals;
for the development of the entire Grecian mythology from the traditional old Aryan cult of nature was essentially due to the gentes and
phratries and took place within them. The phratry also had a chief
(*phratriarchos*) and, in the opinion of de Coulanges, assemblies which
would make binding decisions, a tribunal and an administration. Even
the state of a later period, while ignoring the gens, left certain public
functions to the phratry.

A number of kindred phratries constituted a tribe. In Attica there
were four tribes of three phratries each, each phratry consisting of
thirty gentes. This meticulous division of the groups presupposes a
conscious and planned interference with the order of things that had

---

* Marx's manuscript says Pollux, a 2nd-century Greek scholar to whom Grote
has frequent references.—*Ed.*
** See *Marx-Engels Archive*, Vol. IX, pp. 138-39.—*Ed.*
*** Homer, *Iliad*, Ode II.—*Ed.*

taken shape spontaneously. How, when and why this was done Grecian history does not disclose, for the Greeks themselves preserved memories that did not reach beyond the Heroic Age.

Closely packed in a comparatively small territory as the Greeks were, their differences in dialect were less conspicuous than those that developed in the extensive American forests. Nevertheless, even here we find only tribes of the same main dialect united in a larger aggregate; and even little Attica had its own dialect, which later on became the prevailing language in Greek prose.

In the epics of Homer we generally find the Greek tribes already combined into small peoples, within which, however, the gentes, phratries and tribes still retained their full independence. They already lived in walled cities. The population increased with the growth of the herds, with field agriculture and the beginnings of the handicrafts. With this came increased differences in wealth, which gave rise to an aristocratic element within the old natural-grown democracy. The various small peoples engaged in constant warfare for the possession of the best land and also for the sake of loot. The enslavement of prisoners of war was already a recognised institution.

The constitution of these tribes and small peoples was as follows:

1. The permanent authority was the *council* (*boulê*), originally composed, most likely, of the chiefs of the gentes, but later on, when their number became too large, selected, which created the opportunity to develop and strengthen the aristocratic element. Dionysius definitely speaks of the council of the Heroic Age as being composed of notables (*kratistoi*). The council had the final decision in important matters. In Aeschylus, the council of Thebes passes a decision binding in the given case that the body of Eteocles be buried with full honours, and that the body of Polyneices be thrown out to be devoured by the dogs.* Later, with the rise of the state, this council was transformed into a senate.

2. The *popular assembly* (*agora*). Among the Iroquois we saw that the people, men and women, stood in a circle around the council meetings, taking an orderly part in the discussions and thus influencing its decisions. Among the Homeric Greek, this *Umstand*,** to use an old German legal expression, had developed into a complete popular assembly, as was also the case with the ancient Germans. The assembly was convened by the council to decide important matters; every man had the right to speak. The decision was made by a show of hands (Aeschylus in *The Suppliants*), or by acclamation. It was sovereign and final, for, as Schömann says in his *Antiquities of Greece*:

---

* Aeschylus, *Seven Against Thebes.—Ed.*
** *Umstand*: Those standing around.—*Ed.*

"Whenever a matter is discussed that requires the co-operation of the people for its execution, Homer gives us no indication of any means by which the people could be forced to it against their will."

At this time, when every adult male member of the tribe was a warrior, there was as yet no public authority separated from the people that could have been set up against it. Primitive democracy was still in full bloom, and this must remain the point of departure in judging power and the status of the council and of the *basileus*.

3. The *military commander* (*basileus*). On this point, Marx makes the following comment: "The European savants, most of them born servants of princes, represent the *basileus* as a monarch in the modern sense. The Yankee republican Morgan objects to this. Very ironically, but truthfully, he says of the oily Gladstone and his *Juventus Mundi:*

" 'Mr. Gladstone, who presents to his readers the Grecian chiefs of the Heroic Age as kings and princes, with the superadded qualities of gentlemen, is forced to admit that on the whole we seem to have the custom or law of primogeniture sufficiently but not oversharply defined.' "*

As a matter of fact, Mr. Gladstone himself must have realised that such a contingent system of primogeniture sufficiently but not oversharply defined is as good as none at all.

What the position as regards heredity was in the case of the offices of chiefs among the Iroquois and also other Indians we have already seen. In so far as all officials were elected, mostly within the gens, they were, to that extent, hereditary in the gens. Gradually, a vacancy came to be filled preferably by the next gentile relative—the brother or the sister's son—unless good reasons existed for passing him over. The fact that in Greece, under father right, the office of *basileus* was generally transmitted to the son, or one of the sons, only indicates that the probability of succession by public election was in favour of the sons; but it by no means implies legal succession without public election. Here we perceive, among the Iroquois and Greeks, the first rudiments of special aristocratic families within the gentes, and among the Greeks also the first rudiments of the future hereditary chieftainship or monarchy. Hence it is to be supposed that among the Greeks the *basileus* was either elected by the people or, at least, had to be confirmed by its recognised organ—the council or the *agora*—as was the case with the Roman "king" (*rex*).

In the *Iliad* the ruler of men, Agamemnon, appears, not as the supreme king of the Greeks, but as supreme commander of a federal army before a besieged city. And when dissension broke out among the Greeks, it is to this quality of his that Odysseus points in the famous passage: the commanding of many is not a good thing: let us have one commander, etc. (to which the popular verse about the

---

* See *Marx-Engels Archive*, Vol. IX, p. 143.—*Ed*

sceptre was added later).* "Odysseus is not here lecturing on the form of government, but is demanding obedience to the supreme commander of the army in the field. For the Greeks, who appear before Troy only as an army, the proceedings in the *agora* are sufficiently democratic. When speaking of gifts, that is, the division of the spoils, Achilles never makes Agamemnon or some other *basileus* the divider, but always the 'sons of the Achaeans,' that is to say, the people. The attributes 'begotten of Zeus,' 'nourished by Zeus,' do not prove anything, because *every* gens is descended from some god, and the gens of the tribal chief from a 'prominent' god, in this case Zeus. Even bondsmen, such as the swineherd Eumeaus and others, are 'divine' (*dioi* or *theioi*), even in the *Odyssey*, and hence in a much later period than the *Iliad*. Likewise in the *Odyssey*, we find the name of *heros* given to the herald Mulios as well as to the blind bard Demodocus.** In short, the word *basileia*, which the Greek writers apply to Homer's so-called kingship (because military leadership is its chief distinguishing mark), with the council and popular assembly alongside of it, means merely—military democracy." (Marx.)***

Besides military functions, the *basileus* had also sacerdotal and judicial functions; the latter were not clearly specified, but the former he exercised in his capacity of highest representative of the tribe, or of the confederacy of tribes. There is no reference anywhere to civil, administrative functions; but it seems that he was *ex officio* a member of the council. Etymologically, it is quite correct to translate *basileus* as king, because king *(kuning)* is derived from *kuni, künne*, and signifies chief of a gens. But the old-Greek *basileus* in nowise corresponds to the modern meaning of the word king. Thucydides expressly refers to the old *basileia* as *patrikê*, that is, derived from the gens, and states that it had specified, hence restricted, functions. And Aristotle says that the *basileia* of the Heroic Age was a leadership over freemen, and that the *basileus* was a military chief, judge and high priest. Hence, the *basileus* had no governmental power in the later sense.*)

* Homer, *Iliad*, Ode II.—*Ed.*
** In Marx's manuscript here follows the following phrase omitted by Engels: "just as *basileus*, the term *choiranos* (χοίρανος), which Odysseus uses in reference to Agamemnon, also means only a military chief."—*Ed.*
*** See *Marx-Engels Archive*, Vol. IX, pp. 144-45.—*Ed.*
*) Like the Grecian *basileus*, the Aztec military chief has been wrongly presented as a prince in the modern sense. Morgan was the first to subject to historical criticism the reports of the Spaniards, who at first misunderstood and exaggerated, and later deliberately misrepresented things; he showed that the Mexicans were in the middle stage of barbarism, but on a higher plane than the New Mexican Pueblo Indians, and that their constitution, so far as the garbled accounts enable us to judge, corresponded to the following: a confederacy of three tribes, which had made a number of others tributary, and which was governed by a Federal Council and a federal military chief, whom the Spaniards had made into an "emperor." [*Note by Engels.*]

Thus, in the Grecian constitution of the Heroic Age, we still find the old gentile system full of vigour; but we also see the beginning of its decay: father right and the inheritance of property by the children, which favoured the accumulation of wealth in the family and gave the latter power as against the gens; differentiation in wealth affecting in turn the social constitution by creating first rudiments of a hereditary nobility and monarchy; slavery, first limited to prisoners of war, but already paving the way to the enslavement of fellow members of the tribe and even of the gens; the degeneration of the old intertribal warfare to systematic raids, on land and sea, for the purpose of capturing cattle, slaves, and treasure as a regular means of gaining a livelihood. In short, wealth is praised and respected as the highest treasure, and the old gentile institutions are perverted in order to justify forcible robbery of wealth. Only one thing was missing: an institution that would not only safeguard the newly-acquired property of private individuals against the communistic traditions of the gentile order, would not only sanctify private property, formerly held in such light esteem, and pronounce this sanctification the highest purpose of human society, but would also stamp the gradually developing new forms of acquiring property, and consequently, of constantly accelerating increase in wealth, with the seal of general public recognition; an institution that would perpetuate, not only the newly-rising class division of society, but also the right of the possessing class to exploit the non-possessing classes and the rule of the former over the latter.

And this institution arrived. The *state* was invented.

V

THE RISE OF THE ATHENIAN STATE

How the state developed, some of the organs of the gentile constitution being transformed, some displaced, by the intrusion of new organs, and, finally, all superseded by real governmental authorities—while the place of the actual "people in arms" defending itself through its gentes, phratries and tribes was taken by an armed "public power" at the service of these authorities and, therefore, also available against the people—all this can nowhere be traced better, at least in its initial stage, than in ancient Athens. The forms of the changes are, in the main, described by Morgan; the economic content which gave rise to them I had largely to add myself.

In the Heroic Age, the four tribes of the Athenians were still installed in separate parts of Attica. Even the twelve phratries comprising them seem still to have had separate seats in the twelve towns of Cecrops. The constitution was that of the Heroic Age: a popular assembly, a popular council, a *basileus*. As far back as written history

es we find the land already divided up and transformed into pri-
te property, which corresponds with the relatively developed state
commodity production and a commensurate commodity trade
wards the end of the higher stage of barbarism. In addition to
reals, wine and oil were cultivated. Commerce on the Aegean Sea
ssed more and more from Phoenician into Attic hands. As a result
the purchase and sale of land and the continued division of labour
tween agriculture and handicrafts, trade and navigation, the mem-
rs of gentes, phratries and tribes very soon intermingled. The dis-
icts of the phratry and the tribe received inhabitants who, although
ey were fellow countrymen, did not belong to these bodies and,
erefore, were strangers in their own places of residence. For in time
peace, every phratry and every tribe administered its own affairs
ithout consulting the popular council or the *basileus* in Athens. But
habitants of the area of the phratry or tribe not belonging to either
turally could not take part in the administration.

This so disturbed the regulated functioning of the organs of the
ntile constitution that a remedy was already needed in the Heroic
ge. A constitution, attributed to Theseus, was introduced. The main
ature of this change was the institution of a central administration
Athens, that is to say, some of the affairs that hitherto had been
nducted independently by the tribes were declared to be common
fairs and transferred to a general council sitting in Athens. There-
y, the Athenians went a step further than any ever taken by any
digenous people in America: the simple federation of neighbouring
ibes was now supplanted by the coalescence of all the tribes into one
ngle people. This gave rise to a system of general Athenian popular
w, which stood above the legal usages of the tribes and gentes. It
estowed on the citizens of Athens, as such, certain rights and addi-
onal legal protection even in territory that was not their own tribe's.
his, however, was the first step towards undermining the gen-
le constitution; for it was the first step towards the subsequent ad-
ission of citizens who were alien to all the Attic tribes and were and
emained entirely outside the pale of the Athenian gentile constitu-
on. A second institution attributed to Theseus was the division of
he entire people, irrespective of gentes, phratries and tribes, into
hree classes: *eupatrides,* or nobles; *geomoroi*, or tillers of the land;
nd *demiurgi*, or artisans, and the granting to the nobles of the ex-
lusive right to public office. True, apart from reserving to the nobles
he right to hold public office, this division remained inoperative, as
t created no other legal distinctions between the classes. It is im-
ortant, however, because it reveals to us the new social elements that
ad quietly developed. It shows that the customary holding of office
n the gens by certain families had already developed into a priv-
lege of these families that was little contested; that these families,
lready powerful owing to their wealth, began to unite outside of

their gentes into a privileged class: and that the nascent state sanctio
ed this usurpation. It shows, furthermore, that the division of labo
between husbandmen and artisans had become strong enough to co
test the superiority, socially, of the old division into gentes and trib
And finally, it proclaimed the irreconcilable antagonism betwe
gentile society and the state. The first attempt to form a state consis
ed in breaking up the gentes by dividing the members of each in
a privileged and an inferior class, and the latter again into two voc
tional classes, thus setting one against the other.

The ensuing political history of Athens up to the time of Sol
is only incompletely known. The office of *basileus* fell into disus
archons, elected from among the nobility, became the heads of tl
state. The rule of the nobility steadily increased until, round abo
600 B.C., it became unbearable. The principal means for stifling tl
liberty of the commonalty were—money and usury. The nobility live
mainly in and around Athens, where maritime commerce, wi
occasional piracy still as a sideline, enriched it and concentrated mo
etary wealth in its hands. From this point the developing mone
system penetrated like a corroding acid into the traditional life
the rural communities founded on natural economy. The genti
constitution is absolutely incompatible with the money system. Tl
ruin of the Attic small-holding peasants coincided with the looser
ing of the old gentile bonds that protected them. Creditor's bills an
mortgage bonds—for by then the Athenians had also invented tl
mortgage[155]—respected neither the gens nor the phratry. But tl
old gentile constitution knew nothing of money, credit and mone
ary debt. Hence the constantly expanding money rule of the nobilit
gave rise to a new law, that of custom, to protect the creditor again
the debtor and sanction the exploitation of the small peasant by th
money owner. All the rural districts of Attica bristled with mortgag
posts bearing the legend that the lot on which they stood was mor
gaged to so and so for so and so much. The fields that were not s
designated had for the most part been sold on account of overdu
mortgages or non-payment of interest and had become the propert
of the noble-born usurers; the peasant was glad if he was permitte
to remain as a tenant and live on *one-sixth* of the product of hi
labour while paying *five-sixths* to his new master as rent. More thar
that: if the sum obtained from the sale of the lot did not cover th
debt, or if such a debt was not secured by a pledge, the debtor had t
sell his children into slavery abroad in order to satisfy the creditor'
claim. The sale of his children by the father—such was the first frui
of father right and monogamy! And if the blood-sucker was stil
unsatisfied, he could sell the debtor himself into slavery. Such was the
pleasant dawn of civilisation among the Athenian people.

Formerly, when the conditions of life of the people were still in
keeping with the gentile constitution, such a revolution would have

een impossible; but here it had come about nobody knew how. Let
s return for a moment to the Iroquois. Among them a state of things
ke that which had now imposed itself on theAthenians without their
wn doing, so to say, and certainly against their will, was inconceiv-
ble. There the mode of production of the means of subsistence,
hich, year in and year out, remained unchanged, could never give
se to such conflicts, imposed from without, as it were; to antagonism
etween rich and poor, between exploiters and exploited. The Iro-
uois were still far from controlling the forces of nature; but within
he limits set for them by nature they were masters of their produc-
ion. Apart from bad harvests in their little gardens, the exhaustion
f the fish supply in their lakes and rivers, or of game in their forests,
hey knew what the outcome would be of their mode of gaining a live-
ihood. The outcome would be: means of sustenance, meagre or abun-
lant; but it could never be unpremiditated social upheavals, the se-
ering of gentile bonds, or the splitting of the members of gentes and
ribes into antagonistic classes fighting each other. Production was
arried on within the most restricted limits, but—the producers
xercised control over their own product. This was the immense
dvantage of barbarian production that was lost with the advent
f civilisation; and to win it back on the basis of the enormous
ontrol man now exercises over the forces of nature, and of the
ree association that is now possible, will be the task of the next
enerations.

Not so among the Greeks. The appearance of private property in
erds of cattle and articles of luxury led to exchange between indi-
iduals, to the transformation of products into *commodities*. Here
ies the root of the entire revolution that followed. When the producers no longer directly consumed their product, but let it go out
f their hands in the course of exchange, they lost control over it.
They no longer knew what became of it, and the possibility arose
that the product might some day be turned against the producers,
used as a means of exploiting and oppressing them. Hence, no society can for any length of time remain master of its own production
and continue to control the social effects of its process of production,
unless it abolishes exchange between individuals.

The Athenians were soon to learn, however, how quickly after
individual exchange is established and products are converted into
commodities, the product manifests its rule over the producer. With
the production of commodities came the tilling of the soil by individual cultivators for their own account, soon followed by individual
ownership of the land. Then came money, that universal commodity
for which all others could be exchanged. But when men invented
money they little suspected that they were creating a new social power, the one universal power to which the whole of society must
bow. It was this new power, suddenly sprung into existence without

the will or knowledge of its own creators, that the Athenians felt i
all the brutality of its youth.

What was to be done? The old.gentile organisation had not onl
proved impotent against the triumphant march of money; it wa
also absolutely incapable of providing a place within its framewor
for such things as money, creditors, debtors and the forcible collec
tion of debts. But the new social power was there, and neither piou
wishes nor a longing for the return of the good old times could driv
money and usury out of existence. Moreover, a number of othe
minor breaches had been made in the gentile constitution. The indis
criminate mingling of the gentiles and phrators throughout the whol
of Attica, and especially in the city of Athens, increased from gen
eration to generation, in spite of the fact that an Athenian, whil
allowed to sell plots of land out of his gens, was still prohibited fron
thus selling his dwelling house. The division of labour between th
different branches of production—agriculture, handicraft, numerou
skills within the various crafts, trade, navigation, etc.—had deve
loped more fully with the progress of industry and commerce. The
population was now divided according to occupation into rather well-
defined groups, each of which had a number of new, common interests that found no place in the gens or phratry and, therefore, necessitated the creation of new offices to attend to them. The number
of slaves had increased considerably and must have far exceeded
that of the free Athenians even at this early stage. The gentile constitution originally knew no slavery and was, therefore, ignorant of
any means of holding this mass of bondsmen in check. And finally,
commerce had attracted a great many strangers who settled in
Athens because it was easier to make money there, and according to
the old constitution these strangers enjoyed neither rights nor the
protection of the law. In spite of traditional toleration, they remained a disturbing and foreign element among the people.

In short, the gentile constitution was coming to an end. Society
was daily growing more and more out of it; it was powerless to
check or ally even the most distressing evils that were arising under
its very eyes. In the meantime, however, the state had quietly developed. The new groups formed by division of labour, first between
town and country, then between the various branches of urban industry, had created new organs to protect their interests. Public officers of every description were instituted. And then the young state
needed, above all, its own fighting forces, which among the seafaring
Athenians could at first be only naval forces, to be used for occasional small wars and to protect merchant vessels. At some uncertain time before Solon, the naucraries were instituted, small territorial districts, twelve in each tribe. Every naucrary had to furnish,
equip and man a war vessel and, in addition, detail two horsemen.
This arrangement was a twofold attack on the gentile constitution.

irst, it created a public power which was no longer simply identi-
al with the armed people in its totality; secondly, it for the first time
ivided the people for public purposes, not according to kinship
roups, but territorially, according to *common domicile*. We shall
ee what this signified.

As the gentile constitution could not come to the assistance of the
xploited people, they could look only to the rising state. And the
tate brought help in the form of the constitution of Solon, while at
ie same time strengthening itself anew at the expense of the old
onstitution. Solon—the manner in which his reform of 594 B. C.
vas brought about does not concern us here—started the series of
o-called political revolutions by an encroachment on property. All
evolutions until now have been revolutions for the protection of one
ind of property against another kind of property. They cannot pro-
ect one kind without violating another. In the Great French Revolu-
ion feudal property was sacrificed in order to save bourgeois pro-
erty; in Solon's revolution, creditors' property had to suffer for the
enefit of debtors' property. The debts were simply annulled. We
ire not acquainted with the exact details, but Solon boasts in his
oems that he removed the mortgage posts from the encumbered
ands and enabled all who had fled or had been sold abroad for debt
o return home. This could have been done only by openly violating
property rights. And indeed, the object of all so-called political revo-
utions, from first to last, was to protect *one* kind of property by
:onfiscating—also called stealing—*another* kind of property. It is
:hus absolutely true that for 2,500 years private property could be
protected only by violating property rights.

But now a way had to be found to prevent such re-enslavement
of the free Athenians. This was first achieved by general measures;
for example, the prohibition of contracts which involved the personal hypothecation of the debtor. Furthermore, a maximum was fixed
for the amount of land any one individual could own, in order to
put some curb, at least, on the craving of the nobility for the peasants' land. Then followed constitutional amendments, of which the
most important for us are the following:

The council was increased to four hundred members, one hundred from each tribe. Here, then, the tribe still served as a basis.
But this was the only side of the old constitution that was incorporated in the new body politic. For the rest, Solon divided the citizens
into four classes, according to the amount of land owned and its yield.
Five hundred, three hundred and one hundred and fifty medimni of
grain (1 medimnus equals appr. 41 litres) were the minimum yields
for the first three classes; whoever had less land or none at all
belonged to the fourth class. Only members of the first three classes
could hold office; the highest offices were filled by the first class. The
fourth class had only the right to speak and vote in the popular

assembly. But here all officials were elected, here they had to giv
account of their actions, here all the laws were made, and here th
fourth class was in the majority. The aristocratic privileges wer
partly renewed in the form of privileges of wealth, but the peopl
retained the decisive power. The four classes also formed the basi
for the reorganisation of the fighting forces. The first two classes fur
nished the cavalry; the third had to serve as heavy infantry; th
fourth served as light infantry, without armour, or in the navy, anc
probably were paid.

Thus, an entirely new element was introduced into the constitu
tion: private ownership. The rights and duties of the citizens were
graduated according to the amount of land they owned; and as the
propertied classes gained influence the old consanguine groups were
driven into the background. The gentile constitution suffered another
defeat.

The gradation of political rights according to property, however
was not an indispensable institution for the state. Important as it
may have been in the constitutional history of states, nevertheless, a
good many states, and the most completely developed at that, did
without it. Even in Athens it played only a transient role. Since the
time of Aristides, all offices were open to all the citizens.

During the next eighty years Athenian society gradually took the
course along which it further developed in subsequent centuries.
Usurious land operations, rampant in the pre-Solon period, were
checked, as was the unlimited concentration of landed property.
Commerce and the handicrafts and useful arts conducted on an ever-
increasing scale with slave labour became the predominating branches
of occupation. Enlightenment made progress. Instead of exploiting their own fellow-citizens in the old brutal manner, the Athenians
now exploited mainly the slaves and non-Athenian clients. Movable
property, wealth in money, slaves and ships, increased more and
more; but instead of being simply a means for purchasing land, as
in the first period with its limitations, it became an end in itself. This,
on the one hand, gave rise to the successful competition of the new,
wealthy industrial and commercial class with the old power of the
nobility, but, on the other hand, it deprived the old gentile constitution of its last foothold. The gentes, phratries and tribes, whose
members were now scattered all over Attica and lived completely
intermingled, thus became entirely useless as political bodies. A large
number of Athenian citizens did not belong to any gens; they were
immigrants who had been adopted into citizenship, but not into any
of the old bodies of *consanguinei*. Besides, there was a steadily increasing number of foreign immigrants who only enjoyed protection.[387]

Meanwhile, the struggles of the parties proceeded. The nobility
tried to regain its former privileges and for a short time recovered

its supremacy, until the revolution of Cleisthenes (509 B.C.) brought about its final downfall; and with them fell the last remnants of the gentile constitution.

In his new constitution, Cleisthenes ignored the four old tribes based on the gentes and phratries. Their place was taken by an entirely new organisation based exclusively on the division of the citizens according to place of domicile, already attempted in the naucraries. Not membership of a body of *consanguinei,* but place of domicile was now the deciding factor. Not people, but territory was now divided; politically, the inhabitants became mere attachments of the territory.

The whole of Attica was divided into one hundred self-governing townships, or demes. The citizens (demots) of a deme elected their official head (demarch), a treasurer and thirty judges with jurisdiction in minor cases. They also received their own temple and a tutelary deity, or *heros,* whose priests they elected. The supreme power in the deme was the assembly of the demots. This, as Morgan correctly remarks, is the prototype of the self-governing American municipality. The modern state in its highest development ends with the very unit with which the rising state in Athens began.

Ten of these units (demes) formed a tribe, which, however, as distinct from the old gentile tribe [*Geschlechtsstamm*], was now called a local tribe [*Ortsstamm*]. The local tribe was not only a self-governing political body, but also a military body. It elected a phylarch or tribal head, who commanded the cavalry, a taxiarch, who commanded the infantry, and a *strategos,* who was in command of the entire contingent raised in the tribal territory. Furthermore, it furnished five war vessels with crews and commander; and it received an Attic *heros,* by whose name it was known, as its guardian saint. Finally, it elected fifty councillors to the council of Athens.

The consummation was the Athenian state, governed by a council of five hundred—elected by the ten tribes—and, in the last instance by the popular assembly, which every Athenian citizen could attend and vote in. Archons and other officials attended to the different departments of administration and the courts. In Athens there was no official possessing supreme executive authority.

By this new constitution and by the admission of a large number of dependents [*Schutzverwandter*], partly immigrants and partly freed slaves, the organs of the gentile constitution were eliminated from public affairs. They sank to the position of private associations and religious societies. But their moral influence, the traditional conceptions and views of the old gentile period, survived for a long time and expired only gradually. This became evident in a subsequent state institution.

We have seen that an essential feature of the state is a public pow-

er distinct from the mass of the people. At that time Athens possessed only a militia and a navy equipped and manned directly by the
people. These afforded protection against external enemies and held
the slaves in check, who at that time already constituted the great
majority of the population. For the citizens, this public power at first
existed only in the shape of the police force, which is as old as the
state, and that is why the naïve Frenchmen of the eighteenth century
spoke, not of civilised, but of policed nations (*nations policées*).* Thus,
simultaneously with their state, the Athenians established a police
force, a veritable gendarmerie of foot and mounted bowmen—
Landjäger, as they say in South Germany and Switzerland. This
gendarmerie consisted—of *slaves*. The free Athenian regarded this
police duty as being so degrading that he preferred being arrested by
an armed slave rather than perform such ignominious duties himself. This was still an expression of the old gentile mentality. The
state could not exist without a police force, but it was still young
and did not yet command sufficient moral respect to give prestige to
an occupation that necessarily appeared infamous to the old gentiles.

How well this state, now completed in its main outlines, suited the
new social condition of the Athenians was apparent from the rapid
growth of wealth, commerce and industry. The class antagonism on
which the social and political institutions rested was no longer that
between the nobles and the common people, but that between slaves
and freemen, dependents and citizens. When Athens was at the
height of prosperity the total number of free Athenian citizens, wom-
en and children included, amounted to about 90,000; the slaves of
both sexes numbered 365,000, and the dependents—immigrants and
freed slaves—45,000. Thus, for every adult male citizen there were
at least eighteen slaves and more than two dependents. The large
number of slaves is explained by the fact that many of them worked
together in manufactories with large rooms under overseers. With
the development of commerce and industry came the accumulation
and concentration of wealth in a few hands; the mass of the free
citizens was impoverished and had to choose between going into
handicrafts and competing with slave labour, which was considered ignoble and base and, moreover, promised little success—and
complete pauperisation. Under the prevailing circumstances what
happened was the latter, and being in the majority they dragged
the whole Athenian state down with them. It was not democracy that
caused the downfall of Athens, as the European schoolmasters who
cringe before royalty would have us believe, but slavery, which
brought the labour of the free citizen into contempt.

---

* A play on words: *policé*—civilised, *police*—police —*Ed.*

The rise of the state among the Athenians presents a very typical example of state building in general; because, on the one hand, it took place in a pure form, without the interference of violence, external or internal (the short period of usurpation by Pisistratus left no trace behind it); because, on the other hand, it represented the rise of a highly-developed form of state, the democratic republic, emerging directly out of gentile society; and lastly, because we are sufficiently acquainted with all the essential details.

VI

THE GENS AND THE STATE IN ROME

According to the legend about the foundation of Rome, the first settlement was undertaken by a number of Latin gentes (one hundred, the legend says) united into one tribe. A Sabellian tribe, also said to consist of one hundred gentes, soon followed, and finally a third tribe of various elements, again numbering one hundred gentes, joined them. The whole story reveals at the very first glance that here hardly anything except the gens was a natural product, and that the gens itself, in many cases, was only an offshoot of a mother gens still existing in the old habitat. The tribes bear the mark of having been artificially constituted; nevertheless, they consisted mostly of kindred elements and were formed on the model of the old, naturally grown, not artificially constituted, tribe; and it is not improbable that a genuine old tribe formed the nucleus of each of these three tribes. The connecting link, the phratry, contained ten gentes and was called the *curia*. Hence, there were thirty of them.

That the Roman gens was an institution identical with the Grecian gens is a recognised fact; if the Grecian gens was a continuation of the social unit the primitive form of which is presented by the American Redskins, then the same, naturally, holds good for the Roman gens. Hence, we can be more brief in its treatment.

At least during the earliest times of the city, the Roman gens had the following constitution:

1. Mutual right of inheritance of the property of deceased gentiles; the property remained in the gens. Since father right was already in force in the Roman gens, as it was in the Grecian gens, the offspring of female lineage were excluded. According to the law of the Twelve Tables, the oldest written law of Rome known to us,[388] the natural children had the first title to the estate; in case no natural children existed, the *agnates* (kin of *male* lineage) took their place; and in their absence came the gentiles. In all cases the property remained in the gens. Here we observe the gradual infiltration into gentile practice of new legal provisions, caused by increased

wealth and monogamy: the originally equal right of inheritance o¹
the gentiles was first limited in practice to the *agnates*, probably a
a very remote date as mentioned above, and afterwards to the chil
dren and their offspring in the male line. Of course, in the Twelve
Tables this appears in reverse order.

2. Possession of a common burial place. The patrician gens Clau-
dia, on immigrating into Rome from Regilli, received a plot and also
a common burial place in the city. Even under Augustus, the head
of Varus, who had fallen in the Teutoburg Forest, was brought to
Rome and interred in the *gentilitius tumulus**; hence, his gens
(Quinctilia) still had its own tomb.

3. Common religious celebrations. These, the *sacra gentilitia*,**
are well known.

4. Obligation not to marry within the gens. In Rome this does
not appear to have ever become a written law, but the custom
remained. Of the innumerable names of Roman married couples
that have come down to our day there is not a single case where
husband and wife have the same gentile name. The law of inheritance also proves this rule. A woman by her marriage forfeited her
agnatic rights, left her gens, and neither she nor her children
could inherit her father's property, or that of his brothers, for
otherwise the father's gens would lose the property. This rule has
a meaning only on the assumption that the woman was not permitted to marry a member of her own gens.

5. Possession of land in common. In primeval times this always
obtained when the tribal territory was first divided. Among the
Latin tribes we find the land partly in the possession of the tribe,
partly of the gens, and partly of households that could hardly
have represented single families at that time. Romulus is credited
with having been the first to assign land to single individuals,
about a hectare (two *jugera*) to each. Nevertheless, even later we
still find land in the hands of the gentes, not to mention state
lands, around which the whole internal history of the republic
turned.

6. Reciprocal obligation of members of the gens to assist and
help redress injuries. Written history records only paltry remnants
of this; from the outset the Roman state manifested such superior
power that the duty of redress of injury devolved upon it. When
Appius Claudius was arrested, his whole gens, including his
personal enemies, put on mourning. At the time of the second
Punic War[389] the gentes united to ransom their fellow gentiles
who were in captivity; they were *forbidden* to do this by the
senate.

---

* Mound of the gens.—*Ed.*
** Sacred celebrations of the gens.—*Ed.*

7. Right to bear the gentile name. This was in force until the time of the emperors. Freed slaves were permitted to assume the gentile names of their former masters, although without gentile rights.

8. Right of adopting strangers into the gens. This was done by adoption into a family (as among the Red Indians), which brought with it adoption into the gens.

9. The right to elect and depose chiefs is nowhere mentioned. Inasmuch, however, as during the first period of Rome's existence all offices, from the elective king downward, were filled by election or appointment, and as the *curiae* elected also their own priests, we are justified in assuming that the same existed in regard to the gentile chiefs (*principes*)—no matter how well-established the rule of choosing the candidates from the same family may have been already.

Such were the powers of a Roman gens. With the exception of the complete transition to father right, they are the true image of the rights and duties of an Iroquois gens. Here, too "the Iroquois is plainly discerned."*

The confusion that still reigns even among our most authoritative historians on the question of the Roman gentile order is shown by the following example: In his treatise on Roman proper names of the Republican and Augustinian era (*Roman Researches*, Berlin 1864, Vol. I), Mommsen writes:

"The gentile name is not only borne by all male gentiles, including adopted persons and wards, except, of course, the slaves, but also by the women.... The tribe [*Stamm*] (as Mommsen here translates *gens*) is ... a community derived from a common—actual, assumed or even invented—ancestor and united by common rites, burial places and inheritance. All personally free individuals, hence women also, may and must be registered in them. But determining the gentile name of a married woman offers some difficulty. This indeed did not exist as long as women were prohibited from marrying anyone but members of their own gens; and evidently for a long time the women found it much more difficult to marry outside the gens than in it. This right, the *gentis enuptio*,** was still bestowed as a personal privilege and reward during the sixth century.... But wherever such outside marriages occurred the woman in primeval times must have been transferred to the tribe of her husband. Nothing is more certain than that by the old religious marriage the woman fully joined the legal and sacramental community of her husband and left her own. Who does not know that the married woman forfeits her active and passive right of inheritance in respect to her gentiles, but enters the inheritance group of her husband, her children and his gentiles? And if her husband adopts her as his child and brings her into his family, how can she remain separated from his gens?" (Pp. 8-11.)

Thus, Mommsen asserts that Roman women belonging to a certain gens were originally free to marry only *within* their gens; according to him, the Roman gens, therefore, was endogamous,

---

* See *Marx-Engels Archive*, Vol. IX, p. 134.—*Ed.*
** Of marrying outside the gens.—*Ed.*

not exogamous. This opinion, which contradicts the experien
of all other peoples, is principally, if not exclusively, based on
single, disputed passage in Livy (Book xxxix, ch. 19) accordi
to which the senate decreed in the year 568 of the City, that
186 B. C.,

> *uti Feceniae Hispalae datio, deminutio, gentis enuptio, tutoris optio item ess*
> *quasi ei vir testamento dedisset; utique ei ingenuo nubere liceret, neu quid ei q*
> *eam duxisset, ob id fraudi ignominiaeve esset*—that Fecenia Hispalla shall ha
> the right to dispose of her property, to diminish it, to marry outside of the gen
> to choose a guardian, just as if her (deceased) husband had conferred this right o
> her by testament; that she shall be permitted to marry a freeman and that f
> the man who marries her this shall not constitute a misdemeanour or disgrace

Undoubtedly, Fecenia, a freed slave, here obtained permissio
to marry outside of the gens. And it is equally doubtless, accord
ing to this, that the husband had the right to confer on his wif
by testament the right to marry outside of the gens after his deatl
But outside of *which* gens?

If a woman had to marry in her gens, as Mommsen assume:
then she remained in this gens after her marriage. In the firs
place, however, this assertion that the gens was endogamous
the very thing to be proved. In the second place, if the woman ha
to marry in the gens, then naturally the man had to do the same
otherwise he could never get a wife. Then we arrive at a stat
where a man could by testament confer on his wife a right whicl
he did not possess himself for his own enjoyment, which bring
us to a legal absurdity. Mommsen realises this, and therefore
conjectures:

> "marriage outside of the gens most probably required in law not only the
> consent of the person authorised, but of all members of the gens." (P. 10, note.

First this is a very bold assumption; and secondly, it contradicts
the clear wording of the passage. The senate gives her this right as
her *husband's proxy*; it expressly gives her no more and no less
than her husband could have given her; but what it does give is an
absolute right, free from all restriction, so that, if she should make
use of it, her new husband shall not suffer in consequence. The
senate even instructs the present and future consuls and praetors
to see that she suffers no inconvenience from the use of this right.
Mommsen's supposition, therefore, appears to be absolutely inadmissible.

Then again: suppose a woman married a man from another
gens, but remained in her own gens. According to the passage
quoted above, her husband would then have the right to permit
his wife to marry outside of her own gens. That is, he would
have the right to make provisions in regard to the affairs of a
gens to which he did not belong at all. The thing is so utterly
unreasonable that we need say no more about it.

Nothing remains but to assume that in her first marriage the woman wedded a man from another gens and thereby became without more ado a member of her husband's gens, which Mommsen himself admits for such cases. Then the whole matter at once explains itself. The woman, torn from her old gens by her marriage, and adopted into her husband's gentile group, occupies a special position in the new gens. She is now a gentile, but not a kin by blood; the manner in which she was adopted excludes from the outset all prohibition of marrying in the gens into which she has entered by marriage. She has, moreover, been adopted into the marriage group of the gens and on her husband's death inherits some of his property, that is to say, the property of a fellow member of the gens. What is more natural than that this property should remain in the gens and that she should be obliged to marry a member of her first husband's gens and no other? If, however, an exception is to be made, who is more competent to authorise this than the man who bequeathed this property to her, her first husband? At the time he bequeathed a part of his property to her and simultaneously gave her permission to transfer this property to another gens by marriage, or as a result of marriage, he was still the owner of this property; hence he was literally only disposing of his own property. As for the woman and her relation to her husband's gens, it was the husband who, by an act of his own free will—the marriage—introduced her into his gens. Thus, it appears quite natural, too, that he should be the proper person to authorise her to leave this gens by another marriage. In short, the matter appears simple and obvious as soon as we discard the strange conception of an endogamous Roman gens and, with Morgan, regard it as having originally been exogamous.

Finally, there is still another view, which has probably found the largest number of advocates, namely, that the passage in Livy only means

"that freed slave girls (*libertae*) cannot, without special permission, *e gente nubere* (marry outside of the gens) or take any step which, being connected with *capitis deminutio minima*,* would result in the *liberta* leaving the gentile group." Lange, *Roman Antiquities*, Berlin 1856, Vol. I, p. 195, where the passage we have taken from Livy is commented on in a reference to Huschke.)

If this assumption is correct, the passage proves still less as regards the status of free Roman women, and there is so much less ground for speaking of their obligation to marry in the gens.

The expression *enuptio gentis* occurs only in this single passage and is not found anywhere else in the entire Roman literature. The word *enubere*, to marry outside, is found only three times, also in Livy, and not in reference to the gens. The fantastic

---

* Slightest loss of family rights.—*Ed.*

idea that Roman women were permitted to marry only in the
gens owes its existence solely to this single passage. But it ca·
not be sustained in the least; for either the passage refers
special restrictions for freed slave women, in which case it prov·
nothing for free-born women (*ingenuae*); or it applies also
free-born women, in which case it rather proves that the wom·
as a rule married outside of the gens and were by their marria;
transferred to their husbands' gens. Hence it speaks against Momn·
sen and for Morgan.

Almost three hundred years after the foundation of Rome tl
gentile bonds were still so strong that a patrician gens, the F·
bians, with permission from the senate could undertake by itse
an expedition against the neighbouring town of Veii. Three hundr·
and six Fabians are said to have marched out and to have be·
killed in an ambuscade. A single boy, left behind, propagat·
the gens.

As we have said, ten gentes formed a phratry, which here w·
called a *curia*, and was endowed with more important functio;
than the Grecian phratry. Every *curia* had its own religious pra·
tices, sacred relics and priests. The latter in a body formed o·
of the Roman colleges of priests. Ten *curiae* formed a tribe, whi·
probably had originally its own elected chief—leader in war a·
high priest—like the rest of the Latin tribes. The three trib·
together formed the Roman people, the *populus Romanus*.

Thus, only those could belong to the Roman people who we;
members of a gens, and hence of a *curia* and tribe. The first co·
stitution of this people was as follows. Public affairs were co·
ducted by the senate composed, as Niebuhr was the first to sta·
correctly, of the chiefs of the three hundred gentes; as the elde·
of the gentes they were called fathers, *patres*, and as a body sena·
(council of elders, from *senex*, old). Here too the customary choi·
of men from the same family in each gens brought into being tl
first hereditary nobility. These families called themselves patr·
cians and claimed the exclusive right to the seats in the senat·
and to all other offices. The fact that in the course of time tl
people allowed this claim so that it became an actual right
expressed in the legend that Romulus bestowed the rank of patr·
cian and its privileges on the first senators and their descendant·
The senate, like the Athenian *boulê*, had power to decide in man·
affairs and to undertake the preliminary discussion of more impo·
tant measures, especially of new laws. These were decided by th·
popular assembly, called *comitia curiata* (assembly of *curiae*
The assembled people are grouped by *curiae*, in each *curia* prob·
ably by gentes, and in deciding questions each of the thirty *curia*
had one vote. The assembly of *curiae* adopted or rejected law·
elected all higher officials including the *rex* (so-called king), de·

red war (but the senate concluded peace), and decided as a
supreme court, on appeal of the parties, all cases involving capital
punishment for Roman citizens. Finally, by the side of the senate
and the popular assembly stood the *rex*, corresponding exactly to
the Grecian *basileus*, and by no means such an almost absolute
monarch as Mommsen represents him to have been.* The *rex*
also was military commander, high priest and presiding officer
of certain courts. He had no civil functions, or any power over
life, liberty and property of the citizens whatever, except such as
resulted from his disciplinary power as military commander or
from his power to execute sentence as presiding officer of the
court. The office of *rex* was not hereditary; on the contrary, he
was first elected, probably on the nomination of his predecessor,
by the assembly of *curiae* and then solemnly invested by a second
assembly. That he could also be deposed is proved by the fate of
Tarquinius Superbus.

Like the Greeks in the Heroic Age, the Romans at the time
of the so-called kings lived in a military democracy based on
gentes, phratries and tribes, from which it developed. Even though
the *curiae* and tribes may have been partly artificial formations,
they were moulded after the genuine and natural models of the
society in which they originated and which still surrounded them
on all sides. And though the naturally developed patrician nobility
had already gained ground, though the *reges* attempted gradually
to enlarge the scope of their powers—this does not change the
original and fundamental character of the constitution and this
alone matters.

Meanwhile, the population of the city of Rome and of the Roman territory, enlarged by conquest, increased, partly by immigration, partly through the inhabitants of the subjugated, mostly
Latin, districts. All these new subjects (we leave out the question
of the clients for the moment) were outside of the old gentes,
curiae and tribes, and so were not part of the *populus Romanus*,
the Roman people proper. They were personally free, could own
land, had to pay taxes and were liable to military service. But
they were not eligible for office and could neither participate in
the assembly of *curiae* nor in the distribution of conquered state
lands. They constituted the plebs, excluded from all public rights.

---

* The Latin *rex* is equivalent to the Celtic-Irish *righ* (tribal chief) and the
Gothic *reiks*. That this, like our *Fürst* (English first and Danish förste), originally
signified gentile or tribal chief is evident from the fact that the Goths in the fourth
century already had a special term for the king of later times, the military chief
of a whole people, namely, *thiudans*. In Ulfila's translation of the Bible Artaxer-
es and Herod are never called *reiks* but *thiudans*, and the realm of the Emperor Tiberius not *reiki*, but *thiudinassus*. In the name of the Gothic *thiudans*, or
king, as we inaccurately translate it, Thiudareiks, Theodorich, that is, Dietrich,
both names flow together. [*Note by Engels.*]

Owing to their continually increasing numbers, their milita training and armament, they became a menace to the old popu. who had now closed their ranks hermetically against all increa The land, moreover, seems to have been fairly evenly divided b tween *populus* and plebs, while the mercantile and industr wealth, though as yet not very considerable, may have been main in the hands of the plebs.

In view of the utter darkness that enshrouds the whole le endary origin of Rome's historical beginning—a darkness inte sified by the rationalistic-pragmatic attempts at interpretation an reports of later legally trained authors whose works serve us source material—it is impossible to make any definite statemen about the time, the course and the causes of the revolution th put an end to the old gentile constitution. The only thing we a certain of is that its causes lay in the conflicts between the pleb and the *populus*.

The new constitution, attributed to *rex* Servius Tullius an based on the Grecian model, more especially that of Solon, create a new popular assembly including or excluding all, *populus* an plebeians alike, according to whether they rendered military serv ice or not. The whole male population liable to military servic was divided into six classes, according to wealth. The minimun property qualifications in the first five classes were, respectively: I 100,000 asses; II, 75,000 asses; III, 50,000 asses; IV, 25,000 asses V, 11,000 asses; which, according to Dureau de la Malle, i equal to about 14,000, 10,500, 7,000, 3,600 and 1,570 marks, re spectively. The sixth class, the proletarians, consisted of thos who possessed less and were exempt from military service and taxation. In the new assembly of *centuriae* (*comitia centuriata* the citizens formed ranks after the manner of soldiers, in com panies of one hundred (*centuria*), and each *centuria* had one vote The first class placed 80 *centuriae* in the field; the second 22, the third 20, the fourth 22, the fifth 30 and the sixth, for propriety' sake, one. To these were added 18 *centuriae* of horsemen com posed of the most wealthy; altogether 193. For a majority 97 votes were required. But the horsemen and the first class alone had together 98 votes, thus being in the majority; when they were united valid decisions were made without even asking the other classes.

Upon this new assembly of *centuriae* now devolved all the political rights of the former assembly of *curiae* (a few nominal ones excepted); the *curiae* and the gentes composing them were thereby, as was the case in Athens, degraded to the position of mere private and religious associations and as such they still vegetated for a long time, while the assembly of *curiae* soon fell into oblivion. In order to eliminate the three old gentile tribes, too, from the state, four territorial tribes were introduced, each tribe inhabiting one quarter of the city and receiving certain political rights.

Thus, in Rome also, the old social order based on personal ties of blood was destroyed even before the abolition of the so-called kingdom, and a new constitution, based on territorial division and distinction of wealth, a real state constitution, took its place. The public power here consisted of the citizenry liable to military service, and was directed not only against the slaves, but also against the so-called proletarians, who were excluded from military service and the right to carry arms.

The new constitution was merely further developed upon the expulsion of the last *rex*, Tarquinius Superbus, who had usurped real royal power, and the institution, in place of the *rex*, of two military commanders (consuls) with equal powers (as among the Iroquois). Within this constitution moved the whole history of the Roman republic with all its struggles between patricians and plebeians for admission to office and a share in the state lands; and the final dissolution of the patrician nobility in the new class of big land and money owners, who gradually absorbed all the land of the peasants ruined by military service, cultivated with the aid of slaves the enormous new tracts thus created, depopulated Italy, and thus opened the gates not only to imperial rule, but also to its successors, the German barbarians.

VII

THE GENS AMONG THE CELTS AND GERMANS

Space prevents us from going into the gentile institutions still found in a more or less pure form among the most diverse savage and barbarian peoples of the present day; or into the traces of such institutions found in the ancient history of civilised nations in Asia. One or the other is met with everywhere. A few illustrations may suffice: Even before the gens had been recognised it was pointed out and accurately described in its main outlines by the man who took the greatest pains to misunderstand it. McLennan, who wrote of this institution among the Kalmucks, the Circassians, the Samoyeds[*] and three Indian peoples: the Waralis, the Magars and the Munniporees. Recently it was described by Maxim Kovalevsky, who discovered it among the Pshavs, Khevsurs, Svanetians and other Caucasian tribes. Here we shall confine ourselves to a few brief notes on the existence of the gens among Celts and Germans.

---

[*] Old name for Nentsi.—*Ed.*

The oldest Celtic laws that have come down to our day show the gens still in full vitality. In Ireland it is alive, at least instinctively, in the popular mind to this day, after the English forcibly blew it up. It was still in full bloom in Scotland in the middle of the last century, and here, too, it succumbed only to the arms, laws and courts of the English.

The old Welsh laws, written several centuries before the English Conquest,[390] not later than the eleventh century, still show communal field agriculture of whole villages, although only as exceptions and as the survival of a former universal custom. Every family had five acres for its own cultivation; another plot was at the same time cultivated in common and its yield divided. Judging by the Irish and Scotch analogies there cannot be any doubt that these village communities represent gentes or subdivisions of gentes, even though a reinvestigation of the Welsh laws, which I cannot undertake for lack of time (my notes are from 1869[391]), should not directly corroborate this. The thing, however, that the Welsh sources, and the Irish, do prove directly is that among the Celts the pairing family had not yet given way by far to monogamy in the eleventh century. In Wales, marriage did not become indissoluble, or rather did not cease to be subject to notice of dissolution, until after seven years. Even if only three nights were wanting to make up the seven years, a married couple could still separate. Then their property was divided between them: the woman divided, the man made his choice. The furniture was divided according to certain very funny rules. If the marriage was dissolved by the man, he had to return the woman's dowry and a few other articles; if the woman desired a separation, she received less. Of the children the man was given two, the woman one, namely, the middle child. If the woman married again after her divorce, and her first husband fetched her back, she was obliged to follow him, even if she already had *one* foot in her new husband's bed. But if two people had lived together for seven years, they were considered man and wife, even without the preliminaries of a formal marriage. Chastity among girls before marriage was by no means strictly observed, nor was it demanded; the regulations governing this subject are of an extremely frivolous nature and run counter to all bourgeois morals. When a woman committed adultery, her husband had a right to beat her—this was one of three cases when he could do so without incurring a penalty—but after that he could not demand any other redress, for

"the same offence shall either be atoned for or avenged, but not both."[392]

The reasons that entitled a woman to a divorce without detriment to her rights at the settlement were of a very diverse nature: the man's foul breath was a sufficient reason. The redemption money to be paid to the tribal chief or king for the right of the first night (*gobr merch*, hence the medieval name *marcheta*, French *marquette*) plays a conspicuous part in the legal code. The women had the right to vote at the popular assemblies. Add to this that similar conditions are shown to have existed in Ireland; that time marriages were also quite the custom there, and that the women were assured of liberal and well-defined privileges in case of separation, even to the point of remuneration for domestic services; that a "first wife" existed by the side of others, and in dividing a decedent's property no distinction was made between legitimate and illegitimate children—and we have a picture of the pairing family compared with which the form of marriage valid in North America seems strict; but this is not surprising in the eleventh century for a people which in Caesar's time was still living in group marriage.

The Irish gens (*sept*; the tribe was called *clainne*, clan) is confirmed and described not only by the ancient law-books, but also by the English jurists of the seventeenth century who were sent across for the purpose of transforming the clan lands into domains of the King of England. Up to this time, the land had been the common property of the clan or gens, except where the chiefs had already converted it into their private domain. When a gentile died, and a household was thus dissolved, the gentile chief (called *caput cognationis* by the English jurists) redistributed the whole gentile land among the other households. This distribution must in general have taken place according to rules such as were observed in Germany. We still find a few villages—very numerous forty or fifty years ago— with fields held in so-called rundale. Each of the peasants, individual tenants on the soil that once was the common property of the gens but had been seized by the English conquerors, pays rent for his particular plot, but all the arable and meadow land is combined and shared out, according to situation and quality, in strips, or "*Gewanne*," as they are called on the Mosel, and each one receives a share of each *Gewann*. Moorland and pastures are used in common. As recently as fifty years ago, redivision was still practised occasionally, sometimes annually. The map of such a rundale village looks exactly like that of a German community of farming households [*Gehöferschaft*] on the Mosel or in the Hochwald. The gens also survives in the "factions." The Irish peasants often form parties that seem to be founded on absolutely absurd and senseless distinctions and are quite incomprehensible to Englishmen. The only purpose of these factions is apparently to rally for the popular sport of solemnly beating the life out of one another. They are artificial reincarnations, later substitutes for the blasted gentes that in their own peculiar way demonstrate the continuation of the inherited gentile instinct. Incidentally, in some localities members of the same gens still live together on what is practically their old territory. During the thirties,

for instance, the great majority of the inhabitants of the country o
Monaghan had only four family names, that is, were descended from
four gentes, or clans.*

The downfall of the gentile order in Scotland dates from the
suppression of the rebellion of 1745.[394] Precisely what link in this
order the Scotch clan represents remains to be investigated; no
doubt it is a link. Walter Scott's novels bring the clan in the
Highlands of Scotland vividly before our eyes. It is, as Morgan
says,

> "an excellent type of the gens in organisation and in spirit, and an extraor-
> dinary illustration of the power of the gentile life over its members.... We find
> in their feuds and blood revenge, in their localisation by gentes, in their use of
> lands in common, in the fidelity of the clansman to his chief and of the members
> of the clan to each other, the usual and persistent features of gentile society....
> Descent was in the male line, the children of the males remaining members of
> the clan, while the children of its female members belonged to the clans of their
> respective fathers."[395]

The fact that mother right was formerly in force in Scotland is
proved by the royal family of the Picts, in which, according to
Bede, inheritance in the female line prevailed. We even see evidences of the punaluan family preserved among the Scots as well
as the Welsh until the Middle Ages in the right of the first night,
which the chief of the clan or the king, the last representative of
the former common husbands, could claim with every bride, unless redeemed.

*   *   *

That the Germans were organised in gentes up to the time
of the migration of peoples is an indisputable fact. Evidently they
settled in the territory between the Danube, the Rhine, the Vis-

---

* During a few days that I spent in Ireland[393] I again realised to what extent
the rural population there is still living in the conceptions of the gentile period.
The landlord, whose tenant the peasant is, is still considered by the latter as a
sort of clan chief who supervises the cultivation of the soil in the interest of all,
is entitled to tribute from the peasant in the form of rent, but also has to assist the
peasant in cases of need. Likewise, everyone in comfortable circumstances is considered under obligation to help his poorer neighbours whenever they are in
distress.
Such assistance is not charity; it is what the poor clansman is entitled to by
right from his rich fellow clansman or clan chief. This explains why political economists and jurists complain of the impossibility of inculcating the modern idea
of bourgeois property into the minds of the Irish peasants. Property that has only
rights, but no duties, is absolutely beyond the ken of the Irishman. No wonder so
many Irishmen with such naïve gentile conceptions, who are suddenly cast into
the modern great cities of England and America, among a population with entirely different moral and legal standards, become utterly confused in their views
of morals and justice, lose all hold and often are bound to succumb to demoralisation in masses. [Note by Engels to the fourth edition, 1891.]

tula and the northern seas only a few centuries before our era; the Cimbri and Teutoni were still in full migration, and the Suevi did not settle down until Caesar's time. Caesar expressly states that they settled down in gentes and kinships (*gentibus cognationibusque*), and in the mouth of a Roman of the Julia gens the word *gentibus* has a definite meaning that cannot possibly be misconstrued. This holds good for all Germans; even the settling of the conquered Roman provinces appears to have proceeded still in gentes. The Alamannian Law confirms the fact that the people settled on the conquered land south of the Danube in gentes (*genealogiae*)[396]; *genealogia* is used in exactly the same sense as *Mark* or *Dorfgenossenschaft** was used later. Recently Kovalevsky has expressed the view that these *genealogiae* were large household communities among which the land was divided, and from which the village communities developed later on. The same may be true of the *fara*, the term which the Burgundians and Langobards—a Gothic and a Herminonian, or High German, tribe—applied to nearly, if not exactly, the same thing that in the Alamannian book of laws is called *genealogia*. Whether this really represents the gens or the household community is a matter that must be further investigated.

The language records leave us in doubt as to whether all the Germans had a common term for gens, and if so, what term. Etymologically, the Greek *genos*, the Latin *gens*, corresponds to the Gothic *kuni*, Middle High German *künne*, and is used in the same sense. We are led back to the time of mother right by the fact that the terms for "woman" are derived from the same root: Greek *gynê*, Slav *zena*, Gothic *qvino*, Old Norse *kona*, *kuna*. Among Langobards and Burgundians we find, as stated, the term, *fara*, which Grimm derives from the hypothetical root *fisan*, to beget. I should prefer to trace it to the more obvious root *faran*, *fahren*, to wander, a term which designates a certain well-defined section of the nomadic train, composed, it almost goes without saying, of relatives; a term, which, in the course of centuries of wandering, first to the East and then to the West, was gradually applied to the gentile community itself. Further, there is the Gothic *sibja*, Anglo-Saxon *sib*, Old High German *sippia, sippa, Sippe.*** Old Norse has only the plural *sifjar*, relatives; the singular occurs only as the name of a goddess, *Sif*. Finally, another expression occurs in the Hildebrand, Song,[397] where Hildebrand asks Hadubrand

"who is your father among the men of the people ... or what is your kin?" (*eddo huêlihhes cnuosles du sis*).

---

* Village community.—*Ed.*
** Kinsfolk.—*Ed.*

If there was a common German term for gens, it might well have been the Gothic *kuni*, this is not only indicated by its identity with the corresponding term in kindred languages, but also by the fact that the word *kuning*, *König*, which originally signified chief of gens or tribe, is derived from it. *Sibja*, *Sippe*, does not appear worthy of consideration; in Old Norse, at least, *sifjar* signified not only relatives by blood, but also by marriage; hence it comprises the members of at least *two gentes*; thus the term *sif* cannot have been the term for gens.

Among the Germans, as among the Mexicans and Greeks, the horsemen as well as the wedge-like columns of infantry were grouped in battle array by gentes. When Tacitus says: by families and kinships, the indefinite expression he uses is explained by the fact that in his time the gens had long ceased to be a living association in Rome.

Of decisive significance is a passage in Tacitus where he says: The mother's brother regards his nephew as his son; some even hold that the blood tie between the maternal uncle and the nephew is more sacred and close than that between father and son, so that when hostages are demanded the sister's son is considered a better pledge than the natural son of the man whom they desire to place under bond. Here we have a living survival of the mother right, and hence original, gens, and it is described as something which particularly distinguishes the Germans.* If a member of such a gens gave his own son as a pledge for an obligation he had undertaken, and if this son became the victim of his father's breach of faith, that was the concern of the father alone. When the son of a sister was sacrificed, however, then the most sacred gentile law was violated. The next of kin, who was bound above all others to protect the boy or young man, was responsible for his death; he should either have refrained from giving the boy as a pledge, or have kept the contract. If we had no other trace of gentile organisation among the Germans, this one passage would be sufficient proof.

---

* The Greeks know only in the mythology of the Heroic Age the special intimacy of the bond between the maternal uncle and his nephew, a relic of mother right found among many peoples. According to Diodorus, IV, 34, Meleager kills the sons of Thestius, the brothers of his mother Althaea. The latter regards this deed as such a heinous crime that she curses the murderer, her own son, and prays for his death. It is related that "the gods fulfilled her wish and ended Meleager's life." According to the same author (Diodorus, IV, 44), the Argonauts under Heracles landed in Thracia and there found that Phineus, at the instigation of his second wife, shamefully maltreats his two sons by his first, deserted wife, Cleopatra, the Boread. But among the Argonauts there are also some Boreades, the brothers of Cleopatra, the maternal uncles, therefore, of the maltreated boys. They at once come to their nephews' aid, set them free and kill their guards. [*Note by Engels*.]

Still more decisive, as it comes about eight hundred years later, is a passage in the Old Norse song about the twilight of the gods and the end of the world, the *Völuspâ*. In this "Vision of the Seeress," in which, as Bang and Bugge have now shown, also elements of Christianity are interwoven, the description of the period of universal depravity and corruption preceding the cataclysm contains this passage:

> Broedhr munu berjask ok at bönum verdask, munu *systrungar* sifjum spilla.
> "Brothers will wage war against one another and become each other's slayers, and *sisters' children* will break the bonds of kinship."

Systrungar means son of the mother's sister, and in the poet's eyes, the repudiation by such of blood relationship caps the climax of the crime of fratricide. The climax lies in *systrungar*, which emphasises the kinship on the maternal side. If the term *syskina-börn*, brother's and sister's children, or *syskina-synir*, brother's and sister's sons, had been used, the second line would not have been a crescendo as against the first but a weakening diminuendo. Thus, even in the time of the Vikings,[362] when the *Völuspâ* was composed, the memory of mother right was not yet obliterated in Scandinavia.

For the rest, in Tacitus' time, at least among the Germans with whom he was more familiar, mother right had already given way to father right: the children were the heirs of the father; in the absence of children, the brothers and the paternal and maternal uncles were the heirs. The admission of the mother's brother to inheritance is connected with the preservation of the above-mentioned custom, and also proves how recent father right was among the Germans at that time. We find traces of mother right even late in the Middle Ages. In this period fatherhood was still a matter of doubt, especially among serfs, and when a feudal lord demanded the return of a fugitive serf from a city, it was required, for instance, in Augsburg, Basel and Kaiserslautern, that the fact of his serfdom should be established by the oaths of six of his immediate blood relatives, exclusively on his mother's side. (Maurer, *Urban Constitution*, I, p. 381.)

Another relic of mother right, then beginning to fall into decay, was the, from the Roman standpoint almost inexplicable, respect the Germans had for the female sex. Girls of noble family were regarded as the best hostages guaranteeing the keeping of contracts with Germans. In battle, nothing stimulated their courage so much as the horrible thought that their wives and daughters might be captured and carried into slavery. They regarded the woman as being holy and something of a prophetess, and they heeded her advice in the most important matters. Veleda, the Bructerian priestess on the Lippe River, was the moving spirit of the whole Batavian insurrection, in which Civilis, at the head of Germans and Belgians, shook the foundations of Roman rule in Gaul.[398] The women appear to have held undisputed sway in the house. Tacitus says that they, with the old men and children, had, of course, to do all the work, for the men went hunting, drank and loafed; but he does not say who cultivated the fields, and as according to his explicit statement the slaves only paid dues and performed no compulsory labour, it would appear that what little agricultural work was required had to be performed by the bulk of the adult men.

As was stated above, the form of marriage was the pairing family gradually approximating to monogamy. It was not yet strict monogamy, for polygamy was permitted to the notability. On the whole (unlike the Celts) they insisted on strict chastity among girls. Tacitus speaks with particular warmth of the inviolability of the matrimonial bond among the Germans. He gives adultery on the part of the woman as the sole reason of a divorce. But his report contains many gaps here, and furthermore, it too openly holds up the mirror of virtue to the dissipated Romans. So much is certain: if the Germans in their forests were such exceptional models of virtue, only a slight contact with the outer world was required to bring them down to the level of the other, average, Europeans. In the whirl of Roman life the last trace of strict morality disappeared even faster than the German language. It is enough to read Gregory of Tours. It goes without saying that refined voluptuousness could not exist in the primeval forests of Germany as it did in Rome, and so in this respect also the Germans were superior enough to the Roman world without ascribing to them a continence in carnal matters that has never prevailed among any people as a whole.

From the gentile system arose the obligation to inherit the feuds as well as the friendships of one's father and relatives; and also *wergild*, the fine paid in atonement for murder or injury, in place of blood revenge. A generation ago this *wergild* was regarded as a specifically German institution, but it has since been proved that hundreds of peoples practised this milder form of blood revenge which had its origin in the gentile system. Like the obligation of hospitality, it is found, for instance, among the American Indians. Tacitus' description of the manner in which hospitality was observed (*Germania*, c. 21) is almost identical, even in details, with Morgan's relating to his Indians.

The heated and ceaseless controversy as to whether or not the Germans in Tacitus' time had already finally divided up the cultivated land and how the pertinent passages should be interpreted is now a thing of the past. After it had been established that the cultivated land of nearly all peoples was tilled in common by the gens and later on by communistic family communities, a practice which Caesar still found among the Suevi; that later the land was allotted and periodically re-allotted to the individual families; and that this periodical re-allotment of the cultivated land has been preserved in parts of Germany down to this day, we need not waste any more breath on the subject. If the Germans in one hundred and fifty years passed from common cultivation, such as Caesar expressly attributes to the Suevi—they have no divided or private tillage whatsoever, he says—to individual cultivation with the annual redistribution of the land in Tacitus' time, it is surely progress enough; a transition from that stage to the complete private ownership of land in such a short period and without any outside intervention was an utter impossibility. Hence I can read in Tacitus only what he states in so many words: They change (or redivide) the cultivated land every year, and enough common land is left in the process. It is the stage of agriculture and appropriation of the soil which exactly tallies with the gentile constitution of the Germans of that time.

I leave the preceding paragraph unchanged, just as it stood in former editions. Meantime the question has assumed another aspect. Since Kovalevsky has demonstrated (see above, p. 44*) that the patriarchal household community was widespread, if not universal, as the connecting link between the mother-right communistic family and the modern isolated family, the question is no longer whether the land was common or private property, as was still discussed between Maurer and Waitz, but what *form* common property assumed. There is no doubt whatever that in Caesar's time the Suevi not only owned their land in common, but also tilled it in common for common account. The questions whether their economic unit was the gens or the household community or an intermediate communistic kinship group, or whether all three of these groups existed as a result of different local land conditions will remain subjects of controversy for a long time yet. Kovalevsky maintains that the conditions described by Tacitus were not based on the Mark or village community, but on the household community, which, much later, developed into the village community, owing to the growth of the population.

Hence, it is claimed, the German settlements on the territory they occupied in the time of the Romans, and on the territory they later took from the Romans, must have been not villages, but large family communities comprising several generations, which cultivated a correspondingly large tract of land and used the surrounding wild land as a common Mark with their neighbours. The passage in Tacitus concerning the changing of the cultivated land would

---

* See pp. 489-90 of this volume.—*Ed.*

then actually have an agronomic meaning, namely, that the community cultivated a different piece of land every year, and the land cultivated during the previous year was left fallow or entirely abandoned. The sparsity of the population would have left enough spare wild land to make all disputes about land unnecessary. Only after the lapse of centuries, when the members of the household had increased to such an extent that common cultivation became impossible under prevailing conditions of production, did the household communities allegedly dissolve. The former common fields and meadows were then divided in the well-known manner among the various individual households that had now formed, at first periodically, and later once for all, while forests, pastures and bodies of water remained common property.

As far as Russia is concerned, this process of development appears to have been fully proved historically. As for Germany, and secondarily, for other Germanic countries, it cannot be denied that in many respects, this view affords a better interpretation of the sources and an easier solution of difficulties than the former idea of tracing the village community down to the time of Tacitus. The oldest documents, for instance, the *Codex Laureshamensis*,[399] are on the whole more easily explained by the household community than by the village Mark community. On the other hand, it presents new difficulties and new problems that need solution. Here, only further investigation can decide. I cannot deny, however, that it is highly probable that the household community was also the intermediate stage in Germany, Scandinavia and England.

While in Caesar the Germans had partly just taken up settled abodes, and partly were still seeking such, they had been settled for a full century in Tacitus' time; the resulting progress in the production of means of subsistence is unmistakable. They lived in log houses; their clothing was still of the primitive forest type consisting of rough woollen cloaks and animal skins, and linen underclothing for the women and the notables. They lived on milk, meat, wild fruit and, as Pliny adds, oatmeal porridge (the Celtic national dish in Ireland and Scotland to this day). Their wealth consisted of cattle, of an inferior breed, however, the animals being small, uncouth and hornless; the horses were small ponies, not fast runners. Money, Roman coin only, was little and rarely used. They made no gold or silver ware, nor did they attach any value to these metals. Iron was scarce and, at least among the tribes on the Rhine and the Danube, was apparently almost wholly imported, not mined by themselves. The runic script (imitations of Greek and Latin letters) was only used as a secret code and exclusively for religious sorcery. Human sacrifices were still in vogue. In short, they were a people just emerged from the middle stage of barbarism into the upper stage. While, however, the tribes whose immediate contact with the Romans facilitated the import of Roman industrial products were thereby prevented from developing a metal and textile industry of their own, there is not the least doubt that the tribes of the North-East, on the Baltic, developed these industries. The pieces of armour found in the bogs of Schleswig—a long iron sword, a coat of mail, a silver helmet, etc., together with Roman coins from the close of the second century—and the German metal ware spread by the migration of peoples represent a peculiar type of fine workmanship, even such as were modelled after Roman originals. With the exception of England, emigration to the civilised Roman Empire everywhere put an end to this native industry. How uniformly this industry arose and developed is shown, for instance, by the bronze spangles. The specimens found in Burgundy, in Rumania and along the Azov Sea might have been produced in the very same workshop as the British and the Swedish, and are likewise of undoubtedly Germanic origin.

Their constitution was also in keeping with the upper stage of barbarism. According to Tacitus, there was commonly a council of chiefs (*principes*) which decided matters of minor importance and prepared important matters for the decision of the popular assembly. The latter, in the lower stage of barbarism, at least in places where we know it, among the Americans, was held only in the gens, not yet in the tribe or the confederacy of tribes. The council chiefs (*principes*) were still sharply distinguished from the war chiefs (*duces*), just as among the Iroquois. The former were already living, in part, on honorary gifts, such as cattle, grain, etc., from their fellow tribesmen. As in America they were generally elected from the same family. The transition to father right favoured, as in Greece and Rome, the gradual transformation of elective office into hereditary office, thus giving rise to a noble family in each gens. Most of this old, so-called tribal nobility disappeared during the migration of peoples, or shortly after. The military leaders were elected solely on their merits, irrespective of birth. They had little power and had to rely on force of example. As Tacitus explicitly states, actual disciplinary power in the army was held by the priests. The popular assembly was the real power. The king or tribal chief presided; the people decided: a murmur signified "no," acclamation and clanging of weapons meant "aye." The popular assembly was also the court of justice. Complaints were brought up here and decided; and death sentences were pronounced, the latter only in cases of cowardice, treason or unnatural vices. The gentes and other subdivisions also judged in a body, presided over by the chief, who, as in all original German courts, could be only director of the proceedings and questioner. Among the Germans, always and everywhere, sentence was pronounced by the entire community.

Confederacies of tribes came into existence from Caesar's time. Some of them already had kings. The supreme military commander began to aspire to despotic power, as among the Greeks and Romans, and sometimes succeeded in achieving it. These successful usurpers were by no means absolute rulers; nevertheless, they began to break the fetters of the gentile constitution. While freed slaves generally occupied an inferior position, because they could not be members of any gens, they often gained rank, wealth and honours as favourites of the new kings. The same occurred after the conquest of the Roman Empire in the case of the military leaders who had now become kings of large countries. Among the Franks, the king's slaves and freedmen played a great role first at court and then in the state; a large part of the new aristocracy was descended from them.

There was one institution that especially favoured the rise of royalty: the retinue. We have already seen how among the American Redskins private associations were formed alongside of the gens for the purpose of waging war on their own. Among the Germans, these private associations had developed into standing bodies. The military commander who had acquired fame gathered around his person a host of booty-loving young warriors pledged to loyalty to him personally, as he was to them. He fed them, gave them gifts and organised them on hierarchical principles: a bodyguard and a troop ready for immediate action in short expeditions, a trained corps of officers for larger campaigns. Weak as these retinues must have been, as indeed they proved to be later, for example, under Odoacer in Italy, they, nevertheless, served as the germ of decay of the old popular liberties, and proved to be such during and after the migration of peoples. Because, first, they created favourable soil for the rise of the royal power. Secondly, as Tacitus observed, they could be held together only by continuous warfare and plundering expeditions. Loot became the main object. If the chieftain found nothing to do in his neighbourhood, he marched his troops to other countries, where there was war and the prospect of booty. The German auxiliaries, who under the Roman standard even fought Germans in large numbers, partly consisted of such retinues. They were the first germs of the Landsknecht* system, the shame and curse of the Germans. After the conquest of the Roman Empire, these kings' retainers, together with the bonded and the Roman court attendants, formed the second main constituent part of the nobility of later days.

In general, then, the German tribes, combined into peoples, had the same constitution that had developed among the Greeks of the Heroic Age and among the Romans at the time of the so-called

---

* Mercenary soldiers.—*Ed.*

kings: popular assemblies, councils of gentile chiefs and military commanders who were already aspiring to real kingly power. It was the most highly-developed constitution the gentile order could produce; it was the model constitution of the higher stage of barbarism. As soon as society passed beyond the limits for which this constitution sufficed, the gentile order was finished. It burst asunder and the state took its place.

VIII

THE FORMATION OF THE STATE AMONG THE GERMANS

According to Tacitus the Germans were a very numerous people. An approximate idea of the strength of the different German peoples is given by Caesar; he puts the number of Usipetans and Tencterans, who appeared on the left bank of the Rhine, at 180,000, including women and children. Thus, about 100,000 to a single people,* considerably more than, say, the Iroquois numbered in their most flourishing period, when not quite 20,000 became the terror of the whole country, from the Great Lakes to the Ohio and Potomac. If we were to attempt to group on a map the individual peoples of the Rhine country, who are better known to us from reports, we would find that such a people would occupy on the average the area of a Prussian administrative district, about 10,000 square kilometres, or 182 geographical square miles. The *Germania Magna*** of the Romans, reaching to the Vistula, comprised, however, roundly 500,000 square kilometres. Counting an average of 100,000 for any single people, the total population of *Germania Magna* would have amounted to five million—a rather high figure for a barbarian group of peoples, although 10 inhabitants to the square kilometre, or 550 to the geographical square mile, is very little when compared with present conditions. But this does not include all the Germans then living. We know that German peoples of Gothic origin, Bastarnians, Peukinians and others, lived along the Carpathian Mountains all the way down to the mouth of the Danube. They were so numerous that Pliny designated them as the fifth main tribe of the Germans; in 180 B.C. they were already serving as mercenaries of the Macedonian King Perseus, and in the first years of the reign of Augustus they were still push-

---

* The number taken here is confirmed by a passage in Diodorus on the Celts of Gaul: "In Gaul live numerous peoples of unequal strength. The biggest of them numbers about 200,000, the smallest 50,000." (Diodorus Siculus; V, 25.) That gives an average of 125,000. The individual Gallic peoples, being more highly developed, must certainly have been more numerous than the German. [*Note by Engels.*]

** *Germania Magna*: Greater Germany.—*Ed.*

ing their way as far as the vicinity of Adrianople. If we assume
that they numbered only one million, then, at the beginning of the
Christian era, the Germans numbered probably not less than six
million.

After settling in Germany [*Germanien*], the population must have
grown with increasing rapidity. The industrial progress mentioned
above is sufficient to prove it. The objects found in the bogs of
Schleswig, to judge by the Roman coins found with them, date from
the third century. Hence at that time the metal and textile industry
was already well developed on the Baltic, a lively trade was carried on with the Roman Empire, and the wealthier class enjoyed
a certain luxury—all evidences of a greater density of population.
At this time, however, the Germans started their general assault
along the whole line of the Rhine, the Roman frontier rampart
and the Danube, a line stretching from the North Sea to the Black
Sea—direct proof of the ever-growing population striving outwards.
During the three centuries of struggle, the whole main body of the
Gothic peoples (with the exception of the Scandinavian Goths and
the Burgundians) moved towards the South-East and formed the
left wing of the long line of attack; the High Germans (Hermino-
nians) pushed forward in the centre of this line, on the Upper
Danube, and the Istaevonians, now called Franks, on the right wing,
along the Rhine. The conquest of Britain fell to the lot of the
Ingaevonians. At the end of the fifth century the Roman Empire,
exhausted, bloodless and helpless, lay open to the invading Germans.

In preceding chapters we stood at the cradle of ancient Greek
and Roman civilisation. Now we are standing at its grave. The
levelling plane of Roman world power had been passing for centuries over all the Mediterranean countries. Where the Greek language offered no resistance all national languages gave way to a
corrupt Latin. There were no longer any distinctions of nationality, no more Gauls, Iberians, Ligurians, Noricans[400]; all had become Romans. Roman administration and Roman law had everywhere dissolved the old bodies of *consanguinei* and thus crushed
the last remnants of local and national self-expression. The new-
fangled Romanism could not compensate for this loss; it did not
express any nationality, but only lack of nationality. The elements
for the formation of new nations existed everywhere. The Latin
dialects of the different provinces diverged more and more; the
natural boundaries that had once made Italy, Gaul, Spain, Africa
independent territories, still existed and still made themselves
felt. Yet nowhere was there a force capable of combining these
elements into new nations; nowhere was there the least trace of
any capacity for development or any power of resistance, much
less of creative power. The immense human mass of that enor-

mous territory was held together by one bond alone—the Roman state; and this, in time, had. become their worst enemy and oppressor. The provinces had ruined Rome; Rome itself had become a provincial town like all the others, privileged, but no longer ruling, no longer the centre of the world empire, no longer even the seat of the emperors and vice-emperors, who lived in Constantinople, Treves and Milan. The Roman state had become an immense complicated machine, designed exclusively for the exploitation of its subjects. Taxes, services for the state and levies of all kinds drove the mass of the people deeper and deeper into poverty. The extortionate practices of the procurators, tax collectors and soldiers caused the pressure to become intolerable. This is what the Roman state with its world domination had brought things to: it had based its right to existence on the preservation of order in the interior and protection against the barbarians outside. But its order was worse than the worst disorder, and the barbarians, against whom the state pretended to protect its citizens, were hailed by them as saviours.

Social conditions were no less desperate. During the last years of the republic, Roman rule was already based on the ruthless exploitation of the conquered provinces. The emperors had not abolished this exploitation; on the contrary, they had regularised it. The more the empire fell into decay, the higher rose the taxes and compulsory services, and the more shamelessly the officials robbed and blackmailed the people. Commerce and industry were never the business of the Romans who lorded it over entire peoples. Only in usury did they excel all others, before and after them. The commerce that existed and managed to maintain itself for a time was reduced to ruin by official extortion; what survived was carried on in the eastern, Grecian, part of the empire, but this is beyond the scope of our study. Universal impoverishment; decline of commerce, handicrafts, the arts, and of the population; decay of the towns; retrogression of agriculture to a lower stage—this was the final result of Roman world supremacy.

Agriculture, the decisive branch of production throughout antiquity, now became so more than ever. In Italy, the immense aggregations of estates (*latifundia*) which had covered nearly the whole territory since the end of the republic, had been utilised in two ways: either as pastures, on which the population had been replaced by sheep and oxen, the care of which required only a few slaves; or as country estates, on which large-scale horticulture had been carried on with masses of slaves, partly to serve the luxurious needs of the owners and partly for sale in the urban markets. The great pastures had been preserved and probably even enlarged. But the country estates and their horticulture fell into ruin owing to the impoverishment of their owners and the decay of the towns.

Latifundian economy based on slave labour was no longer profitable; but at that time it was the only possible form of large-scale agriculture. Small-scale farming again became the only profitable form. Estate after estate was parcelled out and leased in small lots to hereditary tenants, who paid a fixed sum, or to *partiarii*,* farm managers rather than tenants, who received one-sixth or even only one-ninth of the year's product for their work. Mainly, however, these small plots were distributed to *coloni*, who paid a fixed amount annually, were attached to the land and could be sold together with the plots. These were not slaves, but neither were they free; they could not marry free citizens, and intermarriage among themselves was not regarded as valid marriage, but as mere concubinage (*contubernium*), as in the case of the slaves. They were the forerunners of the medieval serfs.

The slavery of antiquity became obsolete. Neither in large-scale agriculture in the country, nor in the manufactories of the towns did it any longer bring in a return worth while—the market for its products had disappeared. Small-scale agriculture and small handicrafts, to which the gigantic production of the flourishing times of the empire was now reduced, had no room for numerous slaves. Society found room only for the domestic and luxury slaves of the rich. But moribund slavery was still sufficiently virile to make all productive work appear as slave labour, unworthy of the dignity of free Romans—and everybody was now a free Roman. On this account, on the one hand, there was an increase in the number of superfluous slaves who, having become a drag, were emancipated; on the other hand, there was an increase in the number of *coloni* and of beggared freemen (similar to the poor whites in the ex-slave states of America). Christianity is perfectly innocent of this gradual dying out of ancient slavery. It had partaken of the fruits of slavery in the Roman Empire for centuries, and later did nothing to prevent the slave trade of Christians, either of the Germans in the North, or of the Venetians on the Mediterranean, or the Negro slave trade of later years.** Slavery no longer paid, and so it died out; but dying slavery left behind its poisonous sting by branding as ignoble the productive work of the free. This was the blind alley in which the Roman world was caught: slavery was economically impossible, while the labour of the free was under a moral ban. The one could no longer, the other could not yet, be the basic form of social production. Only a complete revolution could be of help here.

---

* Sharecroppers.—*Ed.*

** According to Bishop Liutprand of Cremona, the principal industry of Verdun in the tenth century, that is, in the Holy German Empire,[181] was the manufacture of eunuchs, who were exported with great profit to Spain for the harems of the Moors. [*Note by Engels.*]

Things were no better in the provinces. Most of the reports we have concern Gaul. By the side of the *coloni*, free small peasants still existed there. In order to protect themselves against the brutal extortions of the officials, judges and usurers, they frequently placed themselves under the protection, the patronage, of men possessed of power; and they did this not only singly, but in whole communities, so much so that the emperors of the fourth century often issued decrees prohibiting this practice. How did this help those who sought this protection? The patron imposed the condition that they transfer the title of their lands to him, and in return he ensured them the usufruct of their land for life—a trick which the Holy Church remembered and freely imitated during the ninth and tenth centuries, for the greater glory of God and the enlargement of its own landed possessions. At that time, however, about the year 475, Bishop Salvianus of Marseilles still vehemently denounced such robbery and related that the oppression of the Roman officials and great landlords became so intolerable that many "Romans" fled to the districts already occupied by the barbarians, and the Roman citizens who had settled there feared nothing so much as falling under Roman rule again. That poor parents frequently sold their children into slavery in those days is proved by a law forbidding this practice.

In return for liberating the Romans from their own state, the German barbarians appropriated two-thirds of the entire land and divided it among themselves. The division was made in accordance with the gentile system; as the conquerors were relatively small in number, large tracts remained, undivided, partly in the possession of the whole people and partly in that of the tribes or gentes. In each gens fields and pastures were distributed among the individual households in equal shares by lot. We do not know whether repeated redivisions took place at that time; at all events, this practice was soon discarded in the Roman provinces, and the individual allotment became alienable private property, allodium. Forests and pastures remained undivided for common use; this use and the mode of cultivating the divided land were regulated by ancient custom and the will of the entire community. The longer the gens existed in its village, and the more Germans and Romans merged in the course of time, the more the consanguineous character of the ties retreated before territorial ties. The gens disappeared in the Mark community, in which, however, sufficient traces of the original kinship of the members were visible. Thus, the gentile constitution, at least in those countries where Mark communes were preserved—in the North of France, in England, Germany and Scandinavia—was imperceptibly transformed into a territorial constitution, and thus became capable of being fitted into the state. Nevertheless, it retained the natural democratic character which distinguishes the whole gentile order, and thus preserved a piece of the gentile constitution even in its degeneration, forced upon it in later times, thereby leaving a weapon in the hands of the oppressed, ready to be wielded even in modern times.

The rapid disappearance of the blood tie in the gens was due to the fact that its organs in the tribe and the whole people had also degenerated as a result of the conquest. We know that rule over subjugated people is incompatible with the gentile order. Here we see it on a large scale. The German peoples, masters of the Roman provinces, had to organise their conquest; but one could neither absorb the mass of the Romans into the gentile bodies nor rule them with the aid of the latter. A substitute for the Roman state had to be placed at the head of the Roman local administrative bodies, which at first largely continued to function, and this substitute could only be another state. Thus, the organs of the gentile constitution had to be transformed into organs of state, and owing to the pressure of circumstances, this had to be done very quickly. The first representative of the conquering people was, however, the military commander. The internal and external safety of the conquered territory demanded that his power be increased. The moment had arrived for transforming military leadership into kingship. This was done.

Let us take the kingdom of the Franks. Here, not only the wide dominions of the Roman state, but also all the very large tracts of land that had not been assigned to the large and small *gau* and Mark communities, especially all the large forests, fell into the hands of the victorious Salian people as their unrestricted possession. The first thing the king of the Franks, transformed from an ordinary military commander into a real monarch, did was to convert this property of the people into a royal estate, to steal it from the people and to donate or grant it in fief to his retainers. This retinue, originally composed of his personal military retainers and the rest of the subcommanders of the army, was soon augmented not only by Romans, that is, Romanised Gauls, who quickly became almost indispensable to him owing to their knowledge of writing, their education and familiarity with the Romance vernacular and literary Latin as well as with the laws of the land, but also by slaves, serfs and freedmen, who constituted his Court and from among whom he chose his favourites. All these were granted tracts of public land, first mostly as gifts and later in the form of benefices[401]—originally in most cases for the period of the life of the king—and so the basis was laid for a new nobility at the expense of the people.

But this was not all. The far-flung empire could not be governed by means of the old gentile constitution. The council of chiefs, even if it had not long become obsolete, could not have assembled and was soon replaced by the king's permanent retinue. The old popular assembly was still ostensibly preserved, but more and more as an assembly of the subcommanders of the army and the newly-rising notables. The free land-owning peasants, the mass of the Frankish people, were exhausted and reduced to penury by continuous civil war and wars of conquest, the latter particularly under Charlemagne, just as the Roman peasants had been during the last period of the republic. These peasants, who originally had formed the whole army, and after the conquest of the Frankish lands had been its core, were so impoverished at the beginning of the ninth century that scarcely one out of five could provide the accoutrements of war. The former army of free peasants, called up directly by the king, was replaced by an army composed of the servitors of the newly-arisen magnates. Among these servitors were also villeins, the descendants of the peasants who formerly had acknowledged no master but the king, and a little earlier had acknowledged no master at all, not even a king. Under Charlemagne's successors the ruin of the Frankish peasantry was completed by internal wars, the weakness of the royal power and corresponding usurpations of the magnates, whose ranks were augmented by the *gau* counts,[402] established by Charlemagne and eager to make their office hereditary, and finally by the incursions of the Normans.[362] Fifty years after the death of Charlemagne, the Frankish Empire lay as helpless at the feet of the Normans as four hundred years previously the Roman Empire had lain at the feet of the Franks.

Not only the external impotence, but the internal order, or rather disorder, of society, was almost the same. The free Frankish peasants found themselves in a position similar to that of their predecessors, the Roman *coloni*. Ruined by war and plunder, they had to seek the protection of the new magnates or the Church, for the royal power was too weak to protect them; they had to pay dear for this protection. Like the Gallic peasants before them, they had to transfer the property in their land to their patrons, and received it back from them as tenants in different and varying forms, but always on condition of performing services and paying dues. Once driven into this form of dependence, they gradually lost their personal freedom; after a few generations most of them became serfs. How rapidly the free peasants were degraded is shown by Irminon's land records of the Abbey Saint-Germain-des-Prés, then near, now in, Paris. Even during the life of Charlemagne, on the vast estates of this abbey, stretching into the surrounding country, there were 2,788 households, nearly all Franks with German names; 2,080 of them were *coloni*, 35 liti, 220 slaves and only 8 freeholders! The custom by which the patron had the land of the peasants transferred to himself, giving to them only the usufruct of it for life, the custom denounced as ungodly by Salvianus, was now universally practised by the Church in its dealings with the peasants. Feudal servitude, now coming more and more into vogue, was modelled as much on the lines of the Roman *angariae*, compulsory services for the state,[403] as on the services rendered by the members of the German Mark in bridge and road building and other work for common purposes. Thus, it looked as if, after four hundred years, the mass of the population had come back to the point it had started from.

This proved only two things, however: First, that the social stratification and the distribution of property in the declining Roman Empire corresponded entirely to the then prevailing stage of production in agriculture and industry, and hence was unavoidable; secondly, that this stage of production had not sunk or risen to any material extent in the course of the following four hundred years, and, therefore, had necessarily produced the same distribution of property and the same class division of population. During the last centuries of the Roman Empire, the town lost its supremacy over the country, and did not regain it during the first centuries of German rule. This presupposes a low stage of agriculture, and of industry as well. Such a general condition necessarily gives rise to big ruling landowners and dependent small peasants. How almost impossible it was to graft either· the Roman latifundian economy run with slave labour or the newer large-scale farming run with serf labour on to such a society, is proved by Charlemagne's very extensive experiments with his famous imperial estates, which passed away leaving hardly a trace. These· experiments were continued only by the monasteries and were fruitful only for them; but the monasteries were abnormal social bodies founded on celibacy. They could do the exceptional, and for that very reason had to remain exceptions.

Nevertheless, progress was made during these four hundred years. Even if in the end we find almost the same main classes as in the beginning, still, the people who constituted these classes had changed. The ancient slavery had disappeared; gone were also the beggared poor freemen, who had despised work as slavish. Between the Roman *colonus* and the new serf there had been the free Frankish peasant. The "useless reminiscences and vain strife" of doomed Romanism were dead and buried. The social classes of the ninth century had taken shape not in the bog of a declining civilisation, but in the travail of a new. The new race, masters as well as servants, was a race of men compared with its Roman predecessors. The relation of powerful landlords and serving peasants, which for the latter had been the hopeless form of the decline of the world of antiquity, was now for the former the starting-point of a new development. Moreover, unproductive as these four hundred years appear to have been, they, nevertheless, left *one* great product behind them: the modern nationalities, the reashioning and regrouping of West-European humanity for impending history. The Germans, in fact, had infused new life into Europe; and that is why the dissolution of the states in the German period ended, not in Norse-Saracen subjugation, but in the development from the royal benefices and patronage (commendation[404]) to feudalism, and in such a tremendous increase in the population that the drain of blood caused by the Crusades barely two centuries later could be borne without injury.

What was the mysterious charm with which the Germans infused new vitality into dying Europe? Was it the innate magic power of the German race, as our jingo historians would have it? By no means. Of course, the Germans were a highly gifted Aryan tribe, especially at that time, in full process of vigorous development. It was not their specific national qualities that rejuvenated Europe, however, but simply—their barbarism, their gentile constitution.

Their personal efficiency and bravery, their love of liberty, and their democratic instinct, which regarded all public affairs as its own affairs, in short, all those qualities which the Romans had lost and which were alone capable of forming new states and of raising new nationalities out of the muck of the Roman world—what were they but the characteristic features of barbarians in the upper stage, fruits of their gentile constitution?

If they transformed the ancient form of monogamy, moderated male rule in the family and gave a higher status to women than the classic world had ever known, what enabled them to do so if not their barbarism, their gentile customs, their still living heritage of the time of mother right?

If they were able in at least three of the most important countries —Germany, Northern France and England—to preserve and carry over to the feudal state a piece of the genuine constitution in the form of the Mark communities, and thus give to the oppressed class, the peasants, even under the hardest conditions of medieval serfdom, local cohesion and the means of resistance which neither the slaves of antiquity nor the modern proletarians found ready at hand—to what did they owe this if not to their barbarism, their exclusively barbarian mode of settling in gentes?

And lastly, if they were able to develop and universally introduce the milder form of servitude which they had been practising at home, and which more and more displaced slavery also in the Roman Empire—a form which, as Fourier first emphasised, gave to the oppressed the means of gradual emancipation *as a class* (*fournit aux cultivateurs des moyens d'affranchissement* collectif et progressif) and is therefore far superior to slavery, which permits only of the immediate manumission of the individual without any transitory stage (antiquity did not know any abolition of slavery by a victorious rebellion), whereas the serfs of the Middle Ages, step by step, achieved their emancipation as a class—to what was this due if not their barbarism, thanks to which they had not yet arrived at complete slavery, either in the form of the ancient labour slavery or in that of the Oriental domestic slavery?

All that was vital and life-bringing in what the Germans infused into the Roman world was barbarism. In fact, only barbarians are capable of rejuvenating a world labouring in the throes of a dying civilisation. And the highest stage of barbarism, to which and in which the Germans worked their way up previous to the migration of peoples, was precisely the most favourable one for this process. This explains everything.

IX

BARBARISM AND CIVILISATION

We have traced the dissolution of the gentile order in the three great separate examples: Greek, Roman, and German. We shall investigate, in conclusion, the general economic conditions that had already undermined the gentile organisation of society in the upper stage of barbarism and completely abolished it with the advent of civilisation. For this, Marx's *Capital* will be as necessary as Morgan's book.

Growing out of the middle stage and developing further in the upper stage of savagery, the gens reached its prime, as far as our sources enable us to judge, in the lower stage of barbarism. With this stage, then, we shall begin our investigation.

At this stage, for which the American Indians must serve as our example, we find the gentile system fully developed. A tribe was divided up into several, in most cases two, gentes; with the increase of the population, these original gentes again divided into several daughter gentes, in relation to which the mother gens appeared as the phratry; the tribe itself split up into several tribes, in each of which, in most cases, we again find the old gentes. In some cases, at least, a confederacy united the kindred tribes. This simple organisation was fully adequate for the social conditions from which it sprang. It was nothing more than a peculiar natural grouping capable of smoothing out all internal conflicts likely to arise in a society organised on these lines. In the realm of the external, conflicts were settled by war, which could end in the annihilation of a tribe, but never in its subjugation. The grandeur and at the same time the limitation of the gentile order was that it found no place for rulers and ruled. In the realm of the internal, there was as yet no distinction between rights and duties; the question of whether participation in public affairs, blood revenge or atonement for injuries was a right or a duty never confronted the Indian; it would have appeared as absurd to him as the question of whether eating, sleeping or hunting was a right or a duty. Nor could any tribe or gens split up into different classes. This leads us to the investigation of the economic basis of those conditions.

The population was very sparse. It was dense only in the habitat of the tribe, surrounded by its wide hunting grounds and beyond these the neutral protective forest which separated it from other tribes. Division of labour was a pure and simple outgrowth of nature; it existed only between the two sexes. The men went to war, hunted, fished, provided the raw material for food and the tools necessary for these pursuits. The women cared for the house, and prepared food and clothing; they cooked, weaved and sewed. Each was master in his or her own field of activity: the men in the forest, the women in the house. Each owned the tools he or she made and used: the men, the weapons and the hunting and fishing tackle, the women, the household goods and utensils. The household was communistic, comprising several, and often many, families.* Whatever was produced and used in common was common property: the house, the garden, the long boat. Here, and only here, then, do we find the "earned property" which jurists and economists have falsely attributed to civilised society—the last mendacious legal pretext on which modern capitalist property rests.

But man did not everywhere remain in this stage. In Asia he found animals that could be domesticated and propagated in captivity. The wild buffalo cow had to be hunted down; the domestic cow gave birth to a calf once a year, and also provided milk. A number of the most advanced tribes—Aryans, Semites, perhaps also the Turanians—made the domestication, and later the raising and tending of cattle, their principal occupation. Pastoral tribes separated themselves from the general mass of the barbarians: *first great social division of labour.* These pastoral tribes not only produced more articles of food, but also a greater variety than the rest of the barbarians. They not only had milk, milk products and meat in greater abundance than the others, but also skins, wool, goat's hair, and the spun and woven fabrics which the increasing quantities of the raw material brought into commoner use. This, for the first time, made regular exchange possible. At the preceding stages, exchange could only take place occasionally; exceptional ability in the making of weapons and

---

* Especially on the North-West coast of America; see Bancroft. Among the Haidas of the Queen Charlotte Islands some households gather as many as seven hundred members under one roof. Among the Nootkas, whole tribes lived under one roof. [*Note by Engels.*]

tools may have led to a transient division of labour. Thus, unquestionable remains of workshops for stone implements of the neolithic period have been found in many places. The artificers who developed their ability in those workshops most probably worked for the community, as the permanent handicraftsmen of the Indian gentile communities still do. At any rate, no other exchange than that within the tribe could arise in that stage, and even that was an exception. After the crystallisation of the pastoral tribes, however, we find here all the conditions favourable for exchange between members of different tribes, and for its further development and consolidation as a regular institution. Originally, tribe exchange with tribe through their respective gentile chiefs. When, however, the herds began to be converted into separate property, exchange between individuals predominated more and more, until eventually it became the sole form. The principal article which the pastoral tribes offered their neighbours for exchange was cattle; cattle became the commodity by which all other commodities were appraised, and was everywhere readily taken in exchange for other commodities—in short, cattle assumed the function of money and served as money already at this stage. Such was the necessity and rapidity with which the demand for a money commodity developed at the very beginning of commodity exchange.

Horticulture, probably unknown to the Asiatic barbarians of the lower stage, arose, among them, at the latest, at the middle stage, as the forerunner of field agriculture. The climate of the Turanian Highlands does not admit of a pastoral life without a supply of fodder for the long and severe winter. Hence, the cultivation of meadows and grain was here indispensable. The same is true of the steppes north of the Black Sea. Once grain was grown for cattle, it soon became human food. The cultivated land still remained tribal property and was assigned first to the gens, which, later, in its turn distributed it to the household communities for their use, and finally to individuals; these may have had certain rights of possession, but no more.

Of the industrial achievements of this stage two are particularly important. The first is the weaving loom, the second, the smelting of metal ore and the working up of metals. Copper, tin, and their alloy, bronze, were by far the most important; bronze furnished useful tools and weapons, but could not displace stone implements. Only iron could do that, but its production was as yet unknown. Gold and silver began to be used for ornament and decoration, and must already have been of far higher value than copper and bronze.

The increase of production in all branches—cattle breeding, agriculture, domestic handicrafts—enabled human labour power to produce more than was necessary for its maintenance. At the same time, it increased the amount of work that daily fell to the lot of every member of the gens or household community or single family. The addition of more labour power became desirable. This was furnished by war; captives were made slaves. Under the given general historical conditions, the first great social division of labour, by increasing the productivity of labour, that is, wealth, and enlarging the field of production, necessarily carried slavery in its wake. Out of the first great social division of labour arose the first great division of society, into two classes: masters and slaves, exploiters and exploited.

How and when the herds and flocks were converted from the common property of the tribe or gens into the property of the individual heads of families we do not know to this day; but it must have occurred, in the main, at this stage. The herds and the other new objects of wealth brought about a revolution in the family. Gaining a livelihood had always been the business of the man; he produced and owned the means therefore. The herds were the new means of gaining a livelihood, and their original domestication and subsequent tending was his work. Hence, he owned the cattle, and the commodities and slaves obtained in exchange for them. All the surplus now resulting from production fell to the man; the woman shared in consuming it, but she had no share in owning it. The "savage" warrior and hunter had been content to occupy second place in the house and give precedence to the woman. The "gentler" shepherd, presuming upon his wealth, pushed forward to first place and forced the woman into second place. And she could not complain. Division of labour in the family had regulated the distribution of property between man and wife. This division of labour remained unchanged, and yet it now put the former domestic relationship topsy-turvy simply because the division of labour outside the family had changed. The very cause that had formerly made the woman supreme in the house, namely, her being confined to domestic work, now assured supremacy in the house for the man: the woman's housework lost its significance compared with the man's work in obtaining a livelihood; the latter was everything, the former an insignificant contribution. Here we see already that the emancipation of women and their equality with men are impossible and must remain so as long as women are excluded from socially productive work and restricted to housework, which is private. The emancipation of women becomes possible only when women are enabled to take part in production on a large, social scale, and when domestic duties require their attention only to a minor degree. And this has become possible only as a result of modern large-scale industry, which not only permits of the participation of women in production in large numbers, but

actually calls for it and, moreover, strives to convert private
domestic work also into a public industry.

His achievement of actual supremacy in the house threw down the
last barrier to the man's autocracy. This autocracy was confirmed
and perpetuated by the overthrow of mother right, the introduction of father right and the gradual transition from the pairing
family to monogamy. This made a breach in the old gentile order:
the monogamian family became a power and rose threateningly
against the gens.

The next step brings us to the upper stage of barbarism, the
period in which all civilised peoples passed through their Heroic
Age: it is the period of the iron sword, but also of the iron plough-
share and axe. Iron became the servant of man, the last and most
important of all raw materials that played a revolutionary role in
history, the last—if we except the potato. Iron made possible field
agriculture on a larger scale and the clearing of extensive forest
tracts for cultivation; it gave the craftsman a tool of such hardness
and sharpness that no stone, no other known metal, could withstand it. All this came about gradually; the first iron produced
was often softer than bronze. Thus, stone weapons disappeared
but slowly; stone axes were still used in battle not only in the
Hildebrand Song, but also at the battle of Hastings, in 1066.[405] But
progress was now irresistible, less interrupted and more rapid. The
town, inclosing houses of stone or brick within its turreted and
crenellated stone walls, became the central seat of the tribe or confederacy of tribes. It marked rapid progress in the art of building;
but it was also a symptom of increased danger and need for protection. Wealth increased rapidly, but it was the wealth of single
individuals. Weaving, metalworking and the other crafts that were
becoming more and more specialised displayed increasing variety
and artistic finish in their products; agriculture now provided not
only cereals, leguminous plants and fruit, but also oil and wine,
the preparation of which had now been learned. Such diverse activities could no longer be conducted by any single individual; *the
second great division of labour* took place; handicrafts separated
from agriculture. The continued increase of production and with
it the increased productivity of labour enhanced the value of
human labour power. Slavery, which had been a nascent and sporadic factor in the preceding stage, now became an essential part
of the social system. The slaves ceased to be simply assistants, but
they were now driven in scores to work in the fields and workshops.
The division of production into two great branches, agriculture and
handicrafts, gave rise to production for exchange, the production
of commodities; and with it came trade, not only in the interior
and on the tribal boundaries, but also overseas. All this was still
very undeveloped; the precious metals gained preference as the

universal money commodity, but it was not yet minted and was exchanged merely by bare **weight.**

The distinction between rich and poor was added to that between freemen and slaves—with the new division of labour came a new division of society into classes. The differences in the wealth of the various heads of families caused the old communistic household communities to break up wherever they had still been preserved; and this put an end to the common cultivation of the soil for the account of the community. The cultivated land was assigned for use to the several families, first for a limited time and later in perpetuity; the transition to complete private ownership was accomplished gradually and simultaneously with the transition from the pairing family to monogamy. The individual family began to be the economic unit of society.

The increased density of the population necessitated closer union internally and externally. Everywhere the federation of kindred tribes became a necessity, and soon after, their amalgamation; and thence the amalgamation of the separate tribal territories into a single territory of the people. The military commander of the people—*rex, basileus, thiudans*—became an indispensable and permanent official. The popular assembly was instituted wherever it did not yet exist. The military commander, the council and the popular assembly formed the organs of the military democracy into which gentile society had developed. A military democracy—because war and organisation for war were now regular functions of the life of the people. The wealth of their neighbours excited the greed of the peoples who began to regard the acquisition of wealth as one of the main purposes in life. They were barbarians: plunder appeared to them easier and even more honourable than productive work. War, once waged simply to avenge aggression or as a means of enlarging territory that had become inadequate, was now waged for the sake of plunder alone, and became a regular profession. It was not for nothing that formidable walls were reared around the new fortified towns: their yawning moats were the graves of the gentile constitution, and their turrets already reached up into civilisation. Internal affairs underwent a similar change. The robber wars increased the power of the supreme military commander as well as of the subcommanders. The customary election of successors from one family, especially after the introduction of father right, was gradually transformed into hereditary succession, first tolerated, then claimed and finally usurped; the foundation of hereditary royalty and hereditary nobility was laid. In this manner the organs of the gentile constitution were gradually torn from their roots in the people, in gens, phratry and tribe, and the whole gentile order was transformed into its opposite: from an organisation of tribes for the free administration of their own affairs it

became an organisation for plundering and oppressing their neigh
bours; and correspondingly its organs were transformed from in
struments of the will of the people into independent organs fo
ruling and oppressing their own people. This could not have hap
pened had not the greed for wealth divided the members of th
gentes into rich and poor; had not "property differences in a gen
changed the community of interest into antagonism between mem
bers of a gens" (Marx)*; and had not the growth of slavery alread·
begun to brand working for a living as slavish and more ignomi
nious than engaging in plunder.

* * *

This brings us to the threshold of civilisation. This stage i
inaugurated by further progress in division of labour. In the low
est stage men produced only for their own direct needs; exchang·
was confined to sporadic cases when a surplus was accidentall·
obtained. In the middle stage of barbarism we find that the pas·
toral peoples had in their cattle a form of property which, with
sufficiently large herds and flocks, regularly provided a surplu·
over and above their needs; and we also find a division of labou·
between the pastoral peoples and backward tribes without herds·
so that there were two different stages of production side by side
which created the conditions for regular exchange. The upper stag·
of barbarism introduced a further division of labour, between agri·
culture and handicrafts, resulting in the production of a continually
increasing portion of commodities especially for exchange, so tha·
exchange between individual producers reached the point where i·
became a vital necessity for society. Civilisation strengthened and·
increased all the established divisions of labour, particularly by
intensifying the contrast between town and country (either the
town exercising economic supremacy over the country, as in antiq·
uity, or the country over the town, as in the Middle Ages) and
added a third division of labour, peculiar to itself and of decisive
importance: it created a class that took no part in production, but
engaged exclusively in exchanging products—the *merchants*. All
previous inchoative formations of classes were exclusively connected
with production; they divided those engaged in production into
managers and performers, or into producers on a large scale and
producers on a small scale. Here a class appears for the first time
which, without taking any part in production, captures the
management of production as a whole and economically subjugates
the producers to its rule; a class that makes itself the indispensable
intermediary between any two producers and exploits them

---

* See *Marx-Engels Archive*, Vol. IX, pp. 153-54.—*Ed.*

both. On the pretext of saving the producers the trouble and risk of exchange, of finding distant markets for their products, and of thus becoming the most useful class in society, a class of parasites arises, genuine social sycophants, who, as a reward for very insignificant real services, skim the cream off production at home and abroad, rapidly amass enormous wealth and corresponding social influence, and for this very reason are destined to reap ever new honours and gain increasing control over production during the period of civilisation, until they at last create a product of their own—periodic commercial crises.

At the stage of development we are discussing, the young merchant class had no inkling as yet of the big things that were in store for it. But it took shape and made itself indispensable, and that was sufficient. With it, however, *metal money*, minted coins, came into use, and with this a new means by which the non-producer could rule the producer and his products. The commodity of commodities, which conceals within itself all other commodities, was discovered; the charm that can transform itself at will into anything desirable and desired. Whoever possessed it ruled the world of production; and who had it above all others? The merchant. In his hands the cult of money was safe. He took care to make it plain that all commodities, and hence all commodity producers, must grovel in the dust before money. He proved in practice that all other forms of wealth were mere semblances compared with this incarnation of wealth as such. Never again has the power of money revealed itself with such primitive crudity and violence as it did in this period of its youth. After the sale of commodities for money came the lending of money, entailing interest and usury. And no legislation of any later period throws the debtor so pitilessly and helplessly at the feet of the usurious creditor as that of ancient Athens and Rome—both sets of law arose spontaneously, as common law, without other than economic compulsion.

Besides wealth in commodities and slaves, besides money wealth, wealth in the form of land came into being. The titles of individuals to parcels of land originally assigned to them by the gens or tribe were now so well established that these parcels became their hereditary property. The thing they had been striving for most just before that time was liberation from the claim of the gentile community to their parcels of land, a claim which had become a fetter for them. They were freed from this fetter—but soon after also from their new landed property. The full, free ownership of land implied not only possibility of unrestricted and uncurtailed possession, but also possibility of alienating it. As long as the land belonged to the gens there was no such possibility. But when the new landowner shook off the chains of the paramount title of the gens and tribe, he also tore the bond that had so long tied him

inseverably to tne soil. What that meant was made plain to him
by the money invented simultaneously with the advent of private
property in land. Land could now become a commodity which could
be sold and pledged. Hardly had the private ownership of land been
introduced when mortgage was discovered (see Athens). Just as
hetaerism and prostitution clung to the heels of monogamy, so
from now on mortgage clung to the ownership of land. You cla-
moured for free, full, alienable ownership of land. Well, here you
have it—*tu l'as voulu*,* Georges Dandin!

Commercial expansion, money, usury, landed property and mortgage were thus accompanied by the rapid concentration and centralisation of wealth in the hands of a small class, on the one hand,
and by the increasing impoverishment of the masses and a growing
mass of paupers, on the other. The new aristocracy of wealth, in
so far as it did not from the outset coincide with the old tribal nobility, forced the latter permanently into the background (in Athens,
in Rome, among the Germans). And this division of freemen into
classes according to their wealth was accompanied, especially in
Greece, by an enormous increase in the number of slaves,** whose
forced labour formed the basis on which the superstructure of all
society was reared.

Let us now see what became of the gentile constitution as a result
of this social revolution. It stood powerless in face of the new
elements that had grown up without its aid. It was dependent
on the condition that the members of a gens, or, say, of a tribe,
should live together in the same territory, be its sole inhabitants.
This had long ceased to be the case. Gentes and tribes were everywhere commingled; everywhere slaves, dependents and foreigners
lived among the citizens. The sedentary state, which had been
acquired only towards the end of the middle stage of barbarism,
was time and again interrupted by the mobility and changes of
abode upon which commerce, changes of occupation and the transfer of land were conditioned. The members of the gentile organisation could no longer meet for the purpose of attending to their
common affairs; only matters of minor importance, such as religious ceremonies, were still observed, indifferently. Beside the wants
and interests which the gentile organs were appointed and fitted to
take care of, new wants and interests had arisen from the revolution
in the conditions of earning one's living and the resulting change in

---

* You wanted it. This expression is taken from Molière's comedy *Georges
Dandin.—Ed.*
** For the number of slaves in Athens, see above, p. 126. In Corinth, at the
city's zenith, it was 460,000, and in Aegina 470,000; in both, ten times the number of free burghers. [*Note by Engels.*]
Engels gives the page of the fourth German edition. See p. 536 of this
volume.—*Ed.*

cial structure. These new wants and interests were not only alien
the old gentile order, but thwarted it in every way. The interests
f the groups of craftsmen created by division of labour, and the
pecial needs of the town as opposed to the country, required new
rgans; but each of these groups was composed of people from
ifferent gentes, phratries and tribes; they even included aliens.
lence, the new organs necessarily had to take form outside the gen-
le constitution, parallel with it, and that meant against it. And
gain, in every gentile organisation the conflict of interests made
:self felt and reached its apex by combining rich and poor, usurers
nd debtors, in the same gens and tribe. Then there was the mass
f new inhabitants, strangers to the gentile associations, which,
s in Rome, could become a power in the land, and was too
umerous to be gradually absorbed by the consanguine gentes
nd tribes. The gentile associations confronted these masses as
xclusive, privileged bodies; what had originally been a natu-
ally-grown democracy was transformed into a hateful aristocra-
y. Lastly, the gentile constitution had grown out of a society
hat knew no internal antagonisms, and was adapted only for
:uch a society. It had no coercive power except public opinion.
3ut now a society had come into being that by the force of all
ts economic conditions of existence had to split up into freemen
and slaves, into exploiting rich and exploited poor; a society
that was not only incapable of reconciling these antagonisms,
but had to drive them more and more to a head. Such a society
could only exist either in a state of continuous, open struggle of
these classes against one another or under the rule of a third
power which, while ostensibly standing above the classes struggling with each other, suppressed their open conflict and permitted
a class struggle at most in the economic field, in a so-called legal
form. The gentile constitution had outlived its usefulness. It was
burst asunder by the division of labour and by its result, the division
of society into classes. Its place was taken by the *state*.

* * *

Above we discussed separately each of the three main forms
in which the state was built up on the ruins of the gentile constitution. Athens represented the purest, most classical form.
Here the state sprang directly and mainly out of the class antagonisms that developed within gentile society. In Rome gentile
society became an exclusive aristocracy amidst a numerous plebs,
standing outside of it, having no rights but only duties. The victory of the plebs burst the old gentile constitution asunder and
erected on its ruins the state, in which both the gentile aristocracy and the plebs were soon wholly absorbed. Finally, among

the German vanquishers of the Roman Empire, the state sprang up as a direct result of the conquest of large foreign territories which the gentile constitution had no means of ruling. As this conquest did not necessitate either a serious struggle with the old population or a more advanced division of labour, and as conquered and conquerors were almost at the same stage of economic development and thus the economic basis of society remained the same as before, therefore, the gentile constitution could continue for many centuries in a changed, territorial form in the shape of a Mark constitution, and even rejuvenate itself for a time in enfeebled form in the noble and patrician families of later years, and even in peasant families, as in Dithmarschen.*

The state is, therefore, by no means a power forced on society from without; just as little is it "the reality of the ethical idea," "the image and reality of reason," as Hegel maintains.[407] Rather it is a product of society at a certain stage of development; it is the admission that this society has become entangled in an insoluble contradiction with itself, that it has split into irreconcilable antagonisms which it is powerless to dispel. But in order that these antagonisms and classes with conflicting economic interests might not consume themselves and society in fruitless struggle, it became necessary to have a power seemingly standing above society that would alleviate the conflict, and keep it within the bounds of "order"; and this power, arisen out of society but placing itself above it, and alienating itself more and more from it, is the state.

As distinct from the old gentile order, the state, first, divides its subjects *according to territory*. As we have seen, the old gentile associations, built upon and held together by ties of blood, became inadequate, largely because they presupposed that the members were bound to a given territory, a bond which had long ceased to exist. The territory remained, but the people had become mobile. Hence, division according to territory was taken as the point of departure, and citizens were allowed to exercise their public rights and duties wherever they settled, irrespective of gens and tribe. This organisation of citizens according to locality is a feature common to all states. That is why it seems natural to us; but we have seen what long and arduous struggles were needed before it could replace, in Athens and Rome, the old organisation according to gentes.

---

* The first historian who had at least an approximate idea of the nature of the gens was Niebuhr, thanks to his knowledge of the Dithmarschen families—to which, however, he also owes the errors he mechanically copied from there.[406] [*Note by Engels.*]

The second distinguishing feature is the establishment of a *public power* which no longer directly coincides with the population organising itself as an armed force. This special public power is necessary because a self-acting armed organisation of the population has become impossible since the split into classes. The slaves also belonged to the population; the 90,000 citizens of Athens formed only a privileged class as against the 365,000 slaves. The people's army of the Athenian democracy was an aristocratic public power against the slaves, whom it kept in check; however, a gendarmerie also became necessary to keep the citizens in check, as we related above. This public power exists in every state; it consists not merely of armed men but also of material adjuncts, prisons and institutions of coercion of all kinds, of which gentile [clan] society knew nothing. It may be very insignificant, almost infinitesimal, in societies where class antagonisms are still undeveloped and in out-of-the-way places as was the case at certain times and in certain regions in the United States of America. It [the public power] grows stronger, however, in proportion as class antagonisms within the state become more acute, and as adjacent states become larger and more populous. We have only to look at our present-day Europe, where class struggle and rivalry in conquest have tuned up the public power to such a pitch that it threatens to swallow the whole of society and even the state.

In order to maintain this public power, contributions from the citizens become necessary—*taxes*. These were absolutely unknown in gentile society; but we know enough about them today. As civilisation advances, these taxes become inadequate; the state makes drafts on the future, contracts loans, *public debts*. Old Europe can tell a tale about these, too.

Having public power and the right to levy taxes, the officials now stand, as organs of society, *above* society. The free, voluntary respect that was accorded to the organs of the gentile [clan] constitution does not satisfy them, even if they could gain it; being the vehicles of a power that is becoming alien to society, respect for them must be enforced by means of exceptional laws by virtue of which they enjoy special sanctity and inviolability. The shabbiest police servant in the civilised state has more "authority" than all the organs of gentile society put together; but the most powerful prince and the greatest statesman, or general, of civilisation may well envy the humblest gentile chief for the unstrained and undisputed respect that is paid to him. The one stands in the midst of society, the other is forced to attempt to represent something outside and above it.

Because the state arose from the need to hold class antagonisms in check, but because it arose, at the same time, in the midst of the conflict of these classes, it is, as a rule, the state of the most powerful, economically dominant class, which, through the medium of the state, becomes also the politically dominant class, and thus acquires new means of holding down and exploiting the oppressed class. Thus, the state of antiquity was above all the state of the slave owners for the purpose of holding down the slaves, as the feudal state was the organ of the nobility for holding down the peasant serfs and bondsmen, and the modern representative state is an instrument of exploitation of wage labour by capital. By way of exception, however, periods occur in which the warring classes balance each other so nearly that the state power, as ostensible mediator, acquires, for the moment, a certain degree of independence of both. Such was the àbsolute monarchy of the seventeenth and eighteenth centuries, which held the balance between the nobility and the class of burghers; such was the Bonapartism of the First, and still more of the Second French Empire, which played off the proletariat against the bourgeoisie and the bourgeoisie against the proletariat. The latest performance of this kind, in which ruler and ruled appear equally ridiculous, is the new German Empire of the Bismarck nation: here capitalists and workers are balanced against each other and equally cheated for the benefit of the impoverished Prussian cabbage junkers.

In most of the historical states, the rights of citizens are, besides, apportioned according to their wealth, thus directly expressing the fact that the state is an organisation of the possessing class for its protection against the non-possessing class. It was so already in the Athenian and Roman classification according to property. It was so in the medieval feudal state, in which the alignment of political power was in conformity with the amount of land owned. It is seen in the electoral qualifications of the modern representative states. Yet this political recognition of property distinctions is by no means essential. On the contrary, it marks a low stage of state development. The highest form of the state, the democratic republic, which under our modern conditions of society is more and more becoming an inevitable necessity, and is the form of state in which alone the last decisive struggle between proletariat and bourgeoisie can be fought out—the democratic republic officially knows nothing any more of property distinctions. In it wealth exercises its power indirectly, but all the more surely. On the one hand, in the form of the direct corruption of officials, of which America provides the classical example; on the other hand, in the form of an alliance between government and Stock Exchange, which become the easier to achieve the more the public debt increases and the more joint-stock companies concentrate in their hands not only transport but also production itself, using the Stock Exchange as their centre. The latest French republic as well as the United States is a striking example of this; and good old Switzerland has contributed its share in this field. But that a democratic republic is not essential for this fraternal alliance between government and Stock Exchange is proved by England and also by the new German Empire, where one cannot tell who was elevated more by universal suffrage, Bismarck or Bleichröder. And lastly, the possessing class rules directly through the medium of universal suffrage. As long as the oppressed class, in our case, therefore, the proletariat, is not yet ripe to emancipate itself, it will in its majority regard the existing order of society as the only one possible and, politically, will form the tail of the capitalist class, its extreme Left wing. To the extent, however, that this class matures for its self-emancipation, it constitutes itself as its own party and elects its own representatives, and not those of the capitalists. Thus, universal suffrage is the gauge of the maturity of the working class. It cannot and never will be anything more in the present-day state; but that is sufficient. On the day the thermometer of universal suffrage registers boiling point among the workers, both they and the capitalists will know what to do.

The state, then, has not existed from all eternity. There have been societies that did without it, that had no idea of the state and state power. At a certain stage of economic development, which was necessarily bound up with the split of society into classes, the state became a necessity owing to this split. We are now rapidly approaching a stage in the development of production at which the existence of these classes not only will have ceased to be a necessity, but will become a positive hindrance to production. They will fall as inevitably as they arose at an earlier stage. Along with them the state will inevitably fall. Society, which will reorganise production on the basis of a free and equal association of the producers, will put the whole machinery of state where it will then belong: into the museum of antiquities, by the side of the spinning-wheel and the bronze axe.

*   *   *

Thus, from the foregoing, civilisation is that stage of development of society at which division of labour, the resulting exchange between individuals, and commodity production, which combines the two, reach their complete unfoldment and revolutionise the whole hitherto existing society.

Production at all former stages of society was essentially collective and likewise consumption took place by the direct distribution of the products within larger or smaller communistic communities. This production in common was carried on within the narrowest limits, but concomitantly the producers were masters of their process of production and of their product. They knew what became of the product: they consumed it, it did not leave their hands; and as long as production was carried on on this basis, it could not grow beyond the control of the producers, and it could not raise any strange, phantom powers against them, as is the case regularly and inevitably under civilisation.

But, slowly, division of labour crept into this process of production. It undermined the collective nature of production and appropriation, it made appropriation by individuals the largely prevailing rule, and thus gave rise to exchange between individuals—how, we examined above. Gradually, the production of commodities became the dominant form.

With the production of commodities, production no longer for one's own consumption but for exchange, the products necessarily pass from hand to hand. The producer parts with his product in the course of exchange; he no longer knows what becomes of it. As soon as money, and with it the merchant, steps in as a middleman between the producers, the process of exchange becomes still more complicated, the ultimate fate of the product still more uncertain. The merchants are numerous and none of them knows what the other is doing. Commodities now pass not only from hand to hand, but also from market to market. The producers have lost control of the aggregate production of the conditions of their own life, and the merchants have not acquired it. Products and production become the playthings of chance.

But chance is only one pole of an interrelation, the other pole of which is called necessity. In nature, where chance also seems to reign, we have long ago demonstrated in each particular field the inherent necessity and regularity that asserts itself in this chance. What is true of nature holds good also for society. The more a social activity, a series of social processes, becomes too powerful for conscious human control, grows beyond human reach, the more it seems to have been left to pure chance, the more do its peculiar and innate laws assert themselves in this chance, as if by natural necessity. Such laws also control the fortuities of the production and exchange of commodities; these laws confront the individual producer and exchanger as strange and, in the beginning, even as unknown powers, the nature of which must first be laboriously investigated and ascertained. These economic laws of commodity production are modified at the different stages of development of this form of production; on the whole, however, the entire period of civilisation has been dominated by these laws. To this day, the product is master of the producer; to this day, the total production of society is regulated, not by a collectively thought-out plan, but by blind laws, which operate with elemental force, in the last resort in the storms of periodic commercial crises.

We saw above how human labour power became able, at a rather early stage of development of production, to produce considerably more than was needed for the producer's maintenance, and how this stage, in the main, coincided with that of the first appearance of the division of labour and of exchange between individuals. Now, it was not long before the great "truth" was discovered that man, too, may be a commodity; that human power may be exchanged and utilised by converting man into a slave. Men had barely started to engage in exchange when they themselves were exchanged. The active became a passive, whether man wanted it or not.

With slavery, which reached its fullest development in civilisation, came the first great cleavage of society into an exploiting and an exploited class. This cleavage has continued during the whole period of civilisation. Slavery was the first form of exploitation, peculiar to the world of antiquity; it was followed by serfdom in the Middle Ages, and by wage labour in modern times. These are the three great forms of servitude, characteristic of the three great epochs of civilisation; open, and, latterly, disguised slavery, are its steady companions.

The stage of commodity production, with which civilisation began, is marked economically by the introduction of 1) metal money and, thus, of money capital, interest and usury; 2) the merchants acting as middlemen between producers; 3) private ownership of land and mortgage; 4) slave labour as the prevailing form of production. The form of the family corresponding to civilisation and under it becoming the definitely prevailing form is monogamy, the supremacy of the man over the woman, and the individual family as the economic unit of society. The cohesive force of civilised society is the state, which in all typical periods is exclusively the state of the ruling class, and in all cases remains essentially a machine for keeping down the oppressed, exploited class. Other marks of civilisation are: on the one hand, fixation of the contrast between town and country as the basis of the entire division of social labour; on the other hand, the introduction of wills, by which the property holder is able to dispose of his property even after his death. This institution, which was a direct blow at the old gentile constitution, was unknown in Athens until the time of Solon; in Rome it was introduced very early, but we do not know when.* Among the Germans it was introduced by the priests in order that the good honest

---

* Lassalle's *Das System der erworbenen Rechte* (*System of Acquired Rights*) turns, in its second part, mainly on the proposition that the Roman testament is

German might without hindrance bequeath his property to the Church.

With this constitution as its foundation civilisation has accomplished things with which the old gentile society was totally unable to cope. But it accomplished them by playing on the most sordid instincts and passions of man, and by developing them at the expense of all his other faculties. Naked greed has been the moving spirit of civilisation from the first day of its existence to the present time; wealth, more wealth and wealth again; wealth, not of society, but of this shabby individual was its sole and determining aim. If, in the pursuit of this aim, the increasing development of science and repeated periods of the fullest blooming of art fell into its lap, it was only because without them the ample present-day achievements in the accumulation of wealth would have been impossible.

Since the exploitation of one class by another is the basis of civilisation, its whole development moves in a continuous contradiction. Every advance in production is at the same time a retrogression in the condition of the oppressed class, that is, of the great majority. What is a boon for the one is necessarily a bane for the other; each new emancipation of one class always means a new oppression of another class. The most striking proof of this is furnished by the introduction of machinery, the effects of which are well known today. And while among barbarians, as we have seen, hardly any distinction could be made between rights and duties, civilisation makes the difference and antithesis between these two plain even to the dullest mind by assigning to one class pretty nearly all the rights, and to the other class pretty nearly all the duties.

But this is not as it ought to be. What is good for the ruling class should be good for the whole of the society with which the ruling class identifies itself. Therefore, the more civilisation advances, the more it is compelled to cover the ills it necessarily creates with the cloak of love, to embellish them, or to deny their existence; in short, to introduce conventional hypocrisy—unknown both in previous forms of society and even in the earliest stages of civilisation—that culminates in the declaration:

---

as old as Rome itself, that in Roman history there was never "a time when testaments did not exist"; that the testament arose rather in pre-Roman times out of the cult of the dead. As a confirmed Hegelian of the old school, Lassalle derived the provisions of the Roman law not from the social conditions of the Romans, but from the "speculative conception" of the will, and thus arrived at this totally unhistoric assertion. This is not to be wondered at in a book that from the same speculative conception draws the conclusion that the transfer of property was purely a secondary matter in Roman inheritance. Lassalle not only believes in the illusions of Roman jurists, especially of the earlier period, but he even excels them. [*Note by Engels.*]

The exploiting class exploits the oppressed class solely and exclusively in the interest of the exploited class itself; and if the latter fails to appreciate this, and even becomes rebellious, it thereby shows the basest ingratitude to its benefactors, the exploiters.*

And now, in conclusion, Morgan's verdict on civilisation:

"Since the advent of civilisation, the outgrowth of property has been so immense, its forms so diversified, its uses so expanding and its management so intelligent in the interests of its owners that it *has become,* on the part of the people, *an unmanageable power. The human mind stands bewildered in the presence of its own creation.* The time will come, nevertheless, when human intelligence will rise to the mastery over property, and define the relations of the state to the property it protects, as well as the obligations and the limits of the rights of its owners. The interests of society are paramount to individual interests, and the two must be brought into just and harmonious relation. A mere property career is not the final destiny of mankind, if progress is to be the law of the future as it has been of the past. The time which has passed away since civilisation began is but a fragment of the past duration of man's existence; and but a fragment of the ages yet to come. The dissolution of society bids fair to become the termination of a career of which property is the end and aim, because such a career contains the elements of self-destruction. Democracy in government, brotherhood in society, equality in rights and privileges, and universal education, foreshadow the next higher plane of society to which experience, intelligence and knowledge are steadily tending. *It will be a revival, in a higher form, of the liberty, equality and fraternity of the ancient gentes.*" (Morgan, *Ancient Society,* p. 552.)**

Written at the end of
March-May 26, 1884

Published as a separate
publication in Zurich in 1884
Signed: *Friedrich Engels*

Printed according to the
text of the fourth German
edition, 1891

Translated from the
German

---

* I had intended at the outset to place the brilliant critique of civilisation, scattered through the works of Fourier, by the side of Morgan's and my own. Unfortunately, I cannot spare the time. I only wish to remark that Fourier already considered monogamy and property in land as the main characteristics of civilisation, and that he described it as a war of the rich against the poor. We also find already in his work the deep appreciation of the fact that in all imperfect societies, those torn by conflicting interests, the individual families (*les familles incohérentes*), are the economic units. [*Note by Engels.*]

** See also *Marx-Engels Archive,* Vol. IX, p. 56-57.—*Ed.*

Frederick Engels

LUDWIG FEUERBACH AND THE END OF CLASSICAL GERMAN PHILOSOPHY[408]

FOREWORD

In the preface to *A Contribution to the Critique of Political Economy*, published in Berlin, 1859, Karl Marx relates how the two of us in Brussels in the year 1845 set about "to work out in common the opposition of our view"—the materialist conception of history which was elaborated mainly by Marx—"to the ideological view of German philosophy, in fact, to settle accounts with our erstwhile philosophical conscience. The resolve was carried out in the form of a criticism of post-Hegelian philosophy. The manuscript, two large octavo volumes, had long reached its place of publication in Westphalia when we received the news that altered circumstances did not allow of its being printed. We abandoned the manuscript to the gnawing criticism of the mice all the more willingly as we had achieved our main purpose—self-clarification."*

Since then more than forty years have elapsed and Marx died without either of us having had an opportunity of returning to the subject. We have expressed ourselves in various places regarding our relation to Hegel, but nowhere in a comprehensive, connected account. To Feuerbach, who after all in many respects forms an intermediate link between Hegelian philosophy and our conception, we never returned.

In the meantime the Marxist world outlook has found representatives far beyond the boundaries of Germany and Europe and in all the literary languages of the world. On the other hand, classical German philosophy is experiencing a kind of rebirth abroad, especially in England and Scandinavia, and even in Germany itself people appear to be getting tired of the pauper's broth of eclecticism which is ladled out in the universities there under the name of philosophy.

In these circumstances a short, coherent account of our relation to the Hegelian philosophy, of how we proceeded, as well as of how we separated, from it, appeared to me to be re-

---

* See pp. 182-83 of this volume.—*Ed.*

quired more and more. Equally, a full acknowledgement of the influence which Feuerbach, more than any other post-Hegelian philosopher, had upon us during our period of storm and stress, appeared to me to be an undischarged debt of honour. I therefore willingly seized the opportunity when the editors of the *Neue Zeit*[409] asked me for a critical review of Starcke's book on Feuerbach. My contribution was published in that journal in the fourth and fifth numbers of 1886 and appears here in revised form as a separate publication.

Before sending these lines to press I have once again ferreted out and looked over the old manuscript of 1845-46.* The section dealing with Feuerbach is not completed. The finished portion consists of an exposition of the materialist conception of history which proves only how incomplete our knowledge of economic history still was at that time. It contains no criticism of Feuerbach's doctrine itself; for the present purpose, therefore, it was unusable. On the other hand, in an old notebook of Marx's I have found the eleven theses on Feuerbach** printed here as an appendix. These are notes hurriedly scribbled down for later elaboration, absolutely not intended for publication, but invaluable as the first document in which is deposited the brilliant germ of the new world outlook.

Frederick Engels

London, February 21, 1888

Published in the book:
F. Engels. *Ludwig Feuerbach und der Ausgang der klassischen deutschen Philosophie.*
Stuttgart, 1888

Printed according to the text of the book
Translated from the German

---

* The reference is to *The German Ideology.—Ed.*
** K. Marx, "Theses on Feuerbach" (see pp. 28-30 of this volume).—*Ed.*

LUDWIG FEUERBACH AND THE END
OF CLASSICAL GERMAN PHILOSOPHY[408]

I

The volume* before us carries us back to a period which, although in time no more than a generation behind us, has become as foreign to the present generation in Germany as if it were already a hundred years old. Yet it was the period of Germany's preparation for the Revolution of 1848; and all that has happened since then in our country has been merely a continuation of 1848, merely the execution of the last will and testament of the revolution.

Just as in France in the eighteenth century, so in Germany in the nineteenth, a philosophical revolution ushered in the political collapse. But how different the two looked! The French were in open combat against all official science, against the church and often also against the state; their writings were printed across the frontier, in Holland or England, while they themselves were often in jeopardy of imprisonment in the Bastille. On the other hand, the Germans were professors, state-appointed instructors of youth; their writings were recognised textbooks, and the terminating system of the whole development—the Hegelian system—was even raised, as it were, to the rank of a royal Prussian philosophy of state! Was it possible that a revolution could hide behind these professors, behind their obscure, pedantic phrases, their ponderous, wearisome sentences? Were not precisely those people who were then regarded as the representatives of the revolution, the liberals, the bitterest opponents of this brain-confusing philosophy? But what neither the government nor the liberals sav was seen at least by one man as early as 1833, and this man was indeed none other than Heinrich Heine.[410]

Let us take an example. No philosophical proposition has earned more gratitude from narrow-minded governments and wrath from equally narrow-minded liberals than Hegel's famous statement:

"All that is real is rational; and all that is rational is real."[411]

That was tangibly a sanctification of things that be, a philosophical benediction bestowed upon despotism, police government,

---

* *Ludwig Feuerbach*, by K. N. Starcke, Ph. D., Stuttgart, Ferd. Encke. 1885. [*Note by Engels.*]

Star Chamber proceedings and censorship. That is how Frederick William III and how his subjects understood it. But according to Hegel certainly not everything that exists is also real, without further qualification. For Hegel the attribute of reality belongs only to that which at the same time is necessary:

"In the course of its development reality proves to be necessity."

A particular governmental measure—Hegel himself cites the example of "a certain tax regulation"—is therefore for him by no means real without qualification. That which is necessary, however, proves itself in the last resort to be also rational; and, applied to the Prussian state of that time, the Hegelian proposition, therefore, merely means: this state is rational, corresponds to reason, in so far as it is necessary; and if it nevertheless appears to us to be evil, but still, in spite of its evil character, continues to exist, then the evil character of the government is justified and explained by the corresponding evil character of its subjects. The Prussians of that day had the government that they deserved.

Now, according to Hegel, reality is, however, in no way an attribute predicable of any given state of affairs, social or political, in all circumstances and at all times. On the contrary. The Roman Republic was real, but so was the Roman Empire, which superseded it. In 1789 the French monarchy had become so unreal, that is to say, so robbed of all necessity, so irrational, that it had to be destroyed by the Great Revolution, of which Hegel always speaks with the greatest enthusiasm. In this case, therefore, the monarchy was the unreal and the revolution the real. And so, in the course of development, all that was previously real becomes unreal, loses its necessity, its right of existence, its rationality. And in the place of moribund reality comes a new, viable reality—peacefully if the old has enough intelligence to go to its death without a struggle; forcibly if it resists this necessity. Thus the Hegelian proposition turns into its opposite through Hegelian dialectics itself: All that is real in the sphere of human history becomes irrational in the process of time, is therefore irrational by its very destination, is tainted beforehand with irrationality; and everything which is rational in the minds of men is destined to become real, however much it may contradict existing apparent reality. In accordance with all the rules of the Hegelian method of thought, the proposition of the rationality of everything which is real resolves itself into the other proposition: All that exists deserves to perish.*

But precisely therein lay the true significance and the revolutionary character of the Hegelian philosophy (to which, as the close

---

* A paraphrase of Mephistopheles' words from Goethe's *Faust*, Part I, Scene 3 (Faust's study).—*Ed.*

of the whole movement since Kant, we must here confine ourselves), that it once for all dealt the death blow to the finality of all products of human thought and action. Truth, the cognition of which is the business of philosophy, was in the hands of Hegel no longer an aggregate of finished dogmatic statements, which, once discovered, had merely to be learned by heart. Truth lay now in the process of cognition itself, in the long historical development of science, which mounts from lower to ever higher levels of knowledge without ever reaching, by discovering so-called absolute truth, a point at which it can proceed no further, where it would have nothing more to do than to fold its hands and gaze with wonder at the absolute truth to which it had attained. And what holds good for the realm of philosophical knowledge holds good also for that of every other kind of knowledge and also for practical action. Just as knowledge is unable to reach a complete conclusion in a perfect, ideal condition of humanity, so is history unable to do so; a perfect society, a perfect "state," are things which can only exist in imagination. On the contrary, all successive historical systems are only transitory stages in the endless course of development of human society from the lower to the higher. Each stage is necessary, and therefore justified for the time and conditions to which it owes its origin. But in the face of new, higher conditions which gradually develop in its own womb, it loses its validity and justification. It must give way to a higher stage which will also in its turn decay and perish. Just as the bourgeoisie by large-scale industry, competition and the world market dissolves in practice all stable time-honoured institutions, so this dialectical philosophy dissolves all conceptions of final, absolute truth and of absolute states of humanity corresponding to it. For it [dialectical philosophy] nothing is final, absolute, sacred. It reveals the transitory character of everything and in everything; nothing can endure before it except the uninterrupted process of becoming and of passing away, of endless ascendancy from the lower to the higher. And dialectical philosophy itself is nothing more than the mere reflection of this process in the thinking brain. It has, of course, also a conservative side: it recognises that definite stages of knowledge and society are justified for their time and circumstances; but only so far. The conservatism of this mode of outlook it relative; its revolutionary character is absolute—the only absolute dialectical philosophy admits.

It is not necessary, here, to go into the question of whether this mode of outlook is thoroughly in accord with the present state of natural science, which predicts a possible end even for the earth, and for its habitability a fairly certain one; which therefore recognises that for the history of mankind, too, there is not only an ascending but also a descending branch. At any rate we still find ourselves a considerable distance from the turning-point at which the historical course of society becomes one of descent, and we cannot expect Hegelian philosophy to be concerned with a subject which natural science, in its time, had not at all placed upon the agenda as yet.

But what must, in fact, be said here is this: that in Hegel the views developed above are not so sharply delineated. They are a necessary conclusion from his method, but one which he himself never drew with such explicitness. And this, indeed, for the simple reason that he was compelled to make a system and, in accordance with traditional requirements, a system of philosophy must conclude with some sort of absolute truth. Therefore, however much Hegel, especially in his *Logic*, emphasised that this eternal truth is nothing but the logical, or, the historical, process itself, he nevertheless finds himself compelled to supply this process with an end, just because he has to bring his system to a termination at some point or other. In his *Logic* he can make this end a beginning again, since here the point of conclusion, the absolute idea—which is only absolute in so far as he has absolutely nothing to say about it—"alienates," that is, transforms, itself into nature and comes to itself again later in the mind, that is, in thought and in history. But at the end of the whole philosophy a similar return to the beginning is possible only in one way. Namely, by conceiving of the end of history as follows: mankind arrives at the cognition of this selfsame absolute idea, and declares that this cognition of the absolute idea is reached in Hegelian philosophy. In this way, however, the whole dogmatic content of the Hegelian system is declared to be absolute truth, in contradiction to his dialectical method, which dissolves all dogmatism. Thus the revolutionary side is smothered beneath the overgrowth of the conservative side. And what applies to philosophical cognition applies also to historical practice. Mankind, which, in the person of Hegel, has reached the point of working out the absolute idea, must also in practice have gotten so far that it can carry out this absolute idea in reality. Hence the practical political demands of the absolute idea on contemporaries may not be stretched too far. And so we find at the conclusion of the *Philosophy of Right* that the absolute idea is to be realised in that monarchy based on social estates which Frederick William III so persistently but vainly promised to his subjects, that is, in a limited, moderate, indirect rule of the possessing classes suited to the petty-bourgeois German conditions of that time; and, moreover, the necessity of the nobility is demonstrated to us in a speculative fashion.

The inner necessities of the system are, therefore, of themselves sufficient to explain why a thoroughly revolutionary method of thinking produced an extremely tame political conclusion. As a matter of fact the specific form of this conclusion springs from this, that Hegel was a German, and like his contemporary Goethe had a bit of the Philistine's queue dangling behind. Each of them was an Olympian Zeus in his own sphere, yet neither of them ever quite freed himself from German Philistinism.

But all this did not prevent the Hegelian system from covering an incomparably greater domain than any earlier system, nor from developing in this domain a wealth of thought which is astounding even today. The phenomenology of mind (which one may call a parallel of the embryology and palaeontology of the mind, a development of individual consciousness through its different stages, set in the form of an abbreviated reproduction of the stages through which the consciousness of man has passed in the course of history), logic, natural philosophy, philosophy of mind, and the latter worked out in its separate, historical subdivisions: philosophy of history, of right, of religion, history of philosophy, aesthetics, etc.—in all these different historical fields Hegel laboured to discover and demonstrate the pervading thread of development. And as he was not only a creative genius but also a man of encyclopaedic erudition, he played an epoch-making role in every sphere. It is self-evident that owing to the needs of the "system" he very often had to resort to those forced constructions about which his pigmy opponents make such a terrible fuss even today. But these constructions are only the frame and scaffolding of his work. If one does not loiter here needlessly, but presses on farther into the immense building, one finds innumerable treasures which today still possess undiminished value. With all philosophers it is precisely the "system" which is perishable; and for the simple reason that it springs from an imperishable desire of the human mind—the desire to overcome all contradictions. But if all contradictions are once for all disposed of, we shall have arrived at so-called absolute truth—world history will be at an end. And yet it has to continue, although there is nothing left for it to do—hence, a new, insoluble contradiction. As soon as we have once realised—and in the long run no one has helped us to realise it more than Hegel himself—that the task of philosophy thus stated means nothing but the task that a single philosopher should accomplish that which can only be accomplished by the entire human race in its progressive development—as soon as we realise that, there is an end to all philosophy in the hitherto accepted sense of the word. One leaves alone "absolute truth," which is unattainable along this path or by any single individual; instead, one pursues attainable relative truths along the path of the positive sciences, and the summation of their results by means of dialectical thinking. At any rate, with Hegel philosophy comes to an end: on the one hand, because in his system he summed up its whole development in the most splendid fashion; and on the other hand, because, even though unconsciously, he showed us the way out of the labyrinth of systems to real positive knowledge of the world.

One can imagine what a tremendous effect this Hegelian system must have produced in the philosophy-tinged atmosphere of Germany. It was a triumphal procession which lasted for decades and which by no means came to a standstill on the death of Hegel. On the contrary, it was precisely from 1830 to 1840 that "Hegelianism" reigned most exclusively, and to a greater or lesser extent infected even its opponents. It was precisely in this period that Hegelian views, consciously or unconsciously, most extensively penetrated the most diversified sciences and leavened even popular literature and the daily press, from which the average "educated consciousness" derives its mental pabulum. But this victory along the whole front was only the prelude to an internal struggle.

As we have seen, the doctrine of Hegel, taken as a whole, left plenty of room for giving shelter to the most diverse practical party views. And in the theoretical Germany of that time, two things above all were practical: religion and politics. Whoever placed the chief emphasis on the Hegelian *system* could be fairly conservative in both spheres; whoever regarded the dialectical *method* as the main thing could belong to the most extreme opposition, both in politics and religion. Hegel himself, despite the fairly frequent outbursts of revolutionary wrath in his works, seemed on the whole to be more inclined to the conservative side. Indeed, his system had cost him much more "hard mental plugging" than his method. Towards the end of the thirties, the cleavage in the school became more and more apparent. The Left wing, the so-called Young Hegelians, in their fight with the pietist[412] orthodox and the feudal reactionaries, abandoned bit by bit that philosophical-genteel reserve in regard to the burning questions of the day which up to that time had secured state toleration and even protection for their teachings. And when, in 1840, orthodox pietism and absolutist feudal reaction ascended the throne with Frederick William IV, open partisanship became unavoidable. The fight was still carried on with philosophical weapons, but no longer for abstract philosophical aims. It turned directly on the destruction of traditional religion and of the existing state. And while in the *Deutsche Jahrbücher*[413] the practical ends were still predominantly put forward in philosophical disguise, in the *Rheinische Zeitung*[115] of 1842 the Young Hegelian school revealed itself directly as the philosophy of the aspiring radical bourgeoisie and used the meagre cloak of philosophy only to deceive the censorship.

At that time, however, politics was a very thorny field, and hence the main fight came to be directed against religion; this fight, particularly since 1840, was indirectly also political. Strauss' *Life of Jesus*, published in 1835, had provided the first impulse. The theory therein developed of the formation of the gospel myths was combated later by Bruno Bauer with proof that a whole series of

evangelic stories had been fabricated by the authors themselves. The
controversy between these two was carried out in the philosophical
disguise of a battle between "self-consciousness" and "substance."
The question whether the miracle stories of the gospels came into
being through unconscious-traditional myth-creation within the bosom
of the community or whether they were fabricated by the evangelists
themselves was magnified into the question whether, in world history,
"substance" or "self-consciousness" was the decisive operative force.
Finally came Stirner, the prophet of contemporary anarchism—
Bakunin has taken a great deal from him—and capped the sovereign
self-consciousness" by his sovereign "ego."[414]

We will not go further into this side of the decomposition process
of the Hegelian school. More important for us is the following: the
main body of the most determined Young Hegelians was, by the
practical necessities of its fight against positive religion, driven back
to Anglo-French materialism. This brought them into conflict with
their school system. While materialism conceives nature as the sole
reality, nature in the Hegelian system represents merely the "alienation" of the absolute idea, so to say, a degradation of the idea. At
all events, thinking and its thought-product, the idea, is here the
primary, nature the derivative, which only exists at all by the
condescension of the idea. And in this contradiction they floundered
as well or as ill as they could.

Then came Feuerbach's *Essence of Christianity*. With one blow it
pulverised the contradiction, in that without circumlocutions it
placed materialism on the throne again. Nature exists independently
of all philosophy. It is the foundation upon which we human beings,
ourselves products of nature, have grown up. Nothing exists outside
nature and man, and the higher beings our religious fantasies have
created are only the fantastic reflection of our own essence. The
spell was broken; the "system" was exploded and cast aside, and
the contradiction, shown to exist only in our imagination, was
dissolved. One must himself have experienced the liberating effect
of this book to get an idea of it. Enthusiasm was general; we all
became at once Feuerbachians. How enthusiastically Marx greeted
the new conception and how much—in spite of all critical reservations—he was influenced by it, one may read in *The Holy Family*.

Even the shortcomings of the book contributed to its immediate
effect. Its literary, sometimes even high-flown, style secured for it
a large public and was at any rate refreshing after long years of
abstract and abstruse Hegelianising. The same is true of its extravagant deification of love, which, coming after the now intolerable
sovereign rule of "pure reason," had its excuse, if not justification.
But what we must not forget is that it was precisely these two
weaknesses of Feuerbach that "true Socialism,"[109] which had been
spreading like a plague in "educated" Germany since 1844, took as

ts starting-point, putting literary phrases in the place of scientific knowledge, the liberation of mankind by means of "love" in place of the emancipation of the proletariat through the economic trans-formation of production—in short, losing itself in the nauseous fine writing and ecstasies of love typified by Herr Karl Grün.

Another thing we must not forget is this: the Hegelian school disintegrated, but Hegelian philosophy was not overcome through criticism; Strauss and Bauer each took one of its sides and set it polemically against the other. Feuerbach broke through the sys-tem and simply discarded it. But a philosophy is not disposed of by the mere assertion that it is false. And so powerful a work as Hegelian philosophy, which had exercised so enormous an influ-ence on the intellectual development of the nation, could not be disposed of by simply being ignored. It had to be "sublated" in its own sense, that is, in the sense that while its form had to be annihilated through criticism, the new content which had been won through it had to be saved. How this was brought about we shall see below.

But in the meantime the Revolution of 1848 thrust the whole of philosophy aside as unceremoniously as Feuerbach had thrust aside Hegel. And in the process Feuerbach himself was also pushed into the background.

II

The great basic question of all philosophy, especially of more recent philosophy, is that concerning the relation of thinking and being. From the very early times when men, still completely igno-rant of the structure of their own bodies, under the stimulus of dream apparitions* came to believe that their thinking and sensa-tion were not activities of their bodies, but of a distinct soul which inhabits the body and leaves it at death—from this time men have been driven to reflect about the relation between this soul and the outside world. If upon death it took leave of the body and lived on, there was no occasion to invent yet another distinct death for it. Thus arose the idea of its immortality, which at that stage of de-velopment appeared not at all as a consolation but as a fate against which it was no use fighting, and often enough, as among the Greeks, as a positive misfortune. Not religious desire for consola-tion, but the quandary arising from the common universal igno-rance of what to do with this soul, once its existence had been

---

* Among savages and lower barbarians the idea is still universal that the human forms which appear in dreams are souls which have temporarily left their bodies; the real man is, therefore, held responsible for acts committed by his dream apparition against the dreamer. Thus Im Thurn found this belief current, for example, among the Indians of Guiana in 1884. [*Note by Engels.*]

accepted, after the death of the body, led in a general way to the tedious notion of personal immortality. In an exactly similar manner the first gods arose through the personification of natural forces. And these gods in the further development of religions assumed more and more an extra-mundane form, until finally by a process of abstraction, I might almost say of distillation, occurring naturally in the course of man's intellectual development, out of the many more or less limited and mutually limiting gods there arose in the minds of men the idea of the one exclusive God of the monotheistic religions.

Thus the question of the relation of thinking to being, the relation of the spirit to nature—the paramount question of the whole of philosophy—has, no less than all religion, its roots in the narrow-minded and ignorant notions of savagery. But this question could for the first time be put forward in its whole acuteness, could achieve its full significance, only after humanity in Europe had awakened from the long hibernation of the Christian Middle Ages. The question of the position of thinking in relation to being, a question which, by the way, had played a great part also in the scholasticism of the Middle Ages, the question: which is primary, spirit or nature—that question, in relation to the church, was sharpened into this: Did God create the world or has the world been in existence eternally?

The answers which the philosophers gave to this question split them into two great camps. Those who asserted the primacy of spirit to nature and, therefore, in the last instance, assumed world creation in some form or other—and among the philosophers, Hegel, for example, this creation often becomes still more intricate and impossible than in Christianity—comprised the camp of idealism. The others, who regarded nature as primary, belong to the various schools of materialism.

These two expressions, idealism and materialism, originally signify nothing else but this; and here too they are not used in any other sense. What confusion arises when some other meaning is put into them will be seen below.

But the question of the relation of thinking and being has yet another side: in what relation do our thoughts about the world surrounding us stand to this world itself? Is our thinking capable of the cognition of the real world? Are we able in our ideas and notions of the real world to produce a correct reflection of reality? In philosophical language this question is called the question of the identity of thinking and being, and the overwhelming majority of philosophers give an affirmative answer to this question. With Hegel, for example, its affirmation is self-evident; for what we cognise in the real world is precisely its thought-content—that which makes the world a gradual realisation of the absolute idea, which absolute

dea has existed somewhere from eternity, independent of the world
and before the world. But it is manifest without further proof that
thought can know a content which is from the outset a thought-
content. It is equally manifest that what is to be proved here is already tacitly contained in the premises. But that in no way prevents
Hegel from drawing the further conclusion from his proof of the
identity of thinking and being that his philosophy, because it is correct for his thinking, is therefore the only correct one, and that the
identity of thinking and being must prove its validity by mankind
immediately translating his philosophy from theory into practice
and transforming the whole world according to Hegelian principles.
This is an illusion which he shares with well-nigh all philosophers.

In addition there is yet a set of different philosophers—those
who question the possibility of any cognition, or at least of an exhaustive cognition, of the world. To them, among the more modern
ones, belong Hume and Kant, and they have played a very important
role in philosophical development. What is decisive in the refutation of this view has already been said by Hegel, in so far as this
was possible from an idealist standpoint. The materialistic additions
made by Feuerbach are more ingenious than profound. The most
telling refutation of this as of all other philosophical crotchets is
practice, namely, experiment and industry. If we are able to prove
the correctness of our conception of a natural process by making it
ourselves, bringing it into being out of its conditions and making it
serve our own purposes into the bargain, then there is an end to
the Kantian ungraspable "thing-in-itself." The chemical substances
produced in the bodies of plants and animals remained just such
"things-in-themselves" until organic chemistry began to produce
them one after another, whereupon the "thing-in-itself" became a
thing for us, as, for instance, alizarin, the colouring matter of the
madder, which we no longer trouble to grow in the madder roots
in the field, but produce much more cheaply and simply from coal
tar. For three hundred years the Copernican solar system was a
hypothesis with a hundred, a thousand or ten thousand chances to
one in its favour, but still always a hypothesis. But when Leverrier,
by means of the data provided by this system, not only deduced the
necessity of the existence of an unknown planet, but also calculated
the position in the heavens which this planet must necessarily occupy, and when Galle really found this planet,[415] the Copernican
system was proved. If, nevertheless, the Neo-Kantians are attempting to resurrect the Kantian conception in Germany and the agnostics[416] that of Hume in England (where in fact it never became extinct), this is, in view of their theoretical and practical refutation
accomplished long ago, scientifically a regression and practically
merely a shamefaced way of surreptitiously accepting materialism,
while denying it before the world.

But during this long period from Descartes to Hegel and from Hobbes to Feuerbach, the philosophers were by no means impelled, as they thought they were, solely by the force of pure reason. On the contrary, what really pushed them forward most was the powerful and ever more rapidly onrushing progress of natural science and industry. Among the materialists this was plain on the surface, but the idealist systems also filled themselves more and more with a materialist content and attempted pantheistically to reconcile the antithesis between mind and matter. Thus, ultimately, the Hegelian system represents merely a materialism idealistically turned upside down in method and content.

It is, therefore, comprehensible that Starcke in his characterisation of Feuerbach first of all investigates the latter's position in regard to this fundamental question of the relation of thinking and being. After a short introduction, in which the views of the preceding philosophers, particularly since Kant, are described in unnecessarily ponderous philosophical language, and in which Hegel, by an all too formalistic adherence to certain passages of his works, gets far less than his due, there follows a detailed description of the course of development of Feuerbach's "metaphysics" itself, as this course was successively reflected in those writings of this philosopher which have a bearing here. This description is industriously and lucidly elaborated; only, like the whole book, it is loaded with a ballast of philosophical phraseology by no means everywhere unavoidable, which is the more disturbing in its effect the less the author keeps to the manner of expression of one and the same school, or even of Feuerbach himself, and the more he interjects expressions of very different tendencies, especially of the tendencies now rampant and calling themselves philosophical.

The course of evolution of Feuerbach is that of a Hegelian—a never quite orthodox Hegelian, it is true—into a materialist; an evolution which at a definite stage necessitates a complete rupture with the idealist system of his predecessor. With irresistible force Feuerbach is finally driven to the realisation that the Hegelian premundane existence of the "absolute idea," the "pre-existence of the logical categories" before the world existed, is nothing more than the fantastic survival of the belief in the existence of an extramundane creator; that the material, sensuously perceptible world to which we ourselves belong is the only reality; and that our consciousness and thinking, however suprasensuous they may seem, are the product of a material, bodily organ, the brain. Matter is not a product of mind, but mind itself is merely the highest product of matter. This is, of course, pure materialism. But, having got so far, Feuerbach stops short. He cannot overcome the customary philosophical prejudice, prejudice not against the thing but against the name materialism. He says:

"To me materialism is the foundation of the edifice of human essence and
knowledge; but to me it is not what it is to the physiologist, to the natural
scientist in the narrower sense, for example, to Moleschott, and necessarily is
from their standpoint and profession, namely, the edifice itself. Backwards I
fully agree with the materialists; but not forwards."

Here Feuerbach lumps together the materialism that is a general
world outlook resting upon a definite conception of the relation between matter and mind, and the special form in which this world
outlook was expressed at a definite historical stage, namely, in the
eighteenth century. More than that, he lumps it with the shallow,
vulgarised form in which the materialism of the eighteenth century
continues to exist today in the heads of naturalists and physicians,
the form which was preached on their tours in the fifties by Büchner, Vogt and Moleschott. But just as idealism underwent a series
of stages of development, so also did materialism. With each epoch-
making discovery even in the sphere of natural science it has to
change its form; and after history also was subjected to materialistic
treatment, a new avenue of development has opened here too.

The materialism of the last century was predominantly mechanical, because at that time, of all natural sciences, only mechanics,
and indeed only the mechanics of solid bodies—celestial and terrestrial—in short, the mechanics of gravity, had come to any definite
close. Chemistry at that time existed only in its infantile, phlogistic
form.[269] Biology still lay in swaddling clothes; vegetable and animal
organisms had been only roughly examined and were explained as
the result of purely mechanical cause. What the animal was to
Descartes, man was to the materialists of the eighteenth century—
a machine. This exclusive application of the standards of mechanics
to processes of a chemical and organic nature—in which processes
the laws of mechanics are, indeed, also valid, but are pushed into
the background by other, higher laws—constitutes the first specific
but at that time inevitable limitation of classical French materialism.

The second specific limitation of this materialism lay in its inability to comprehend the universe as a process, as matter undergoing uninterrupted historical development. This was in accordance
with the level of the natural science of that time, and with the
metaphysical, that is, anti-dialectical manner of philosophising connected with it. Nature, so much was known, was in eternal motion.
But according to the ideas of that time, this motion turned, also
eternally, in a circle and therefore never moved from the spot; it
produced the same results over and over again. This conception
was at that time inevitable. The Kantian theory of the origin of the
solar system had been put forward but recently and was still regarded merely as a curiosity. The history of the development of
the earth, geology, was still totally unknown, and the conception
that the animate natural beings of today are the result of a long

sequence of development from the simple to the complex could n
at that time scientifically be put forward at all. The unhistoric
view of nature was therefore inevitable. We have the less reas
to reproach the philosophers of the eighteenth century on this a
count since the same thing is found in Hegel. According to hi
nature, as a mere "alienation" of the idea, is incapable of develo
ment in time—capable only of extending its manifoldness in spac
so that it displays simultaneously and alongside of one another a
the stages of development comprised in it, and is condemned to a
eternal repetition of the same processes. This absurdity of a develo
ment in space, but outside of time—the fundamental condition
all development—Hegel imposes upon nature just at the very tin
when geology, embryology, the physiology of plants and animal
and organic chemistry were being built up, and when everywhe
on the basis of these new sciences brilliant foreshadowings of th
later theory of evolution were appearing (for instance, Goethe an
Lamarck). But the system demanded it; hence the method, for th
sake of the system, had to become untrue to itself.

This same unhistorical conception prevailed also in the domai
of history. Here the struggle against the remnants of the Middl
Ages blurred the view. The Middle Ages were regarded as a mer
interruption of history by a thousand years of universal barbarism
The great progress made in the Middle Ages—the extension of th
area of European culture, the viable great nations taking forn
there next to each other, and finally the enormous technical progres
of the fourteenth and fifteenth centuries—all this was not seen. Thu
a rational insight into the great historical interconnections was mad
impossible, and history served at best as a collection of example
and illustrations for the use of philosophers.

The vulgarising pedlars, who in Germany in the fifties dabble
in materialism, by no means overcame this limitation of thei
teachers. All the advances of natural science which had been mad
in the meantime served them only as new proofs against the existence of a creator of the world; and, indeed, they did not in th
least make it their business to develop the theory any further
Though idealism was at the end of its tether and was dealt a death-
blow by the Revolution of 1848, it had the satisfaction of seeing
that materialism had for the moment fallen lower still. Feuerbach
was unquestionably right when he refused to take responsibility for
this materialism; only he should not have confounded the doctrines
of these itinerant preachers with materialism in general.

Here, however, there are two things to be pointed out. First, even
during Feuerbach's lifetime, natural science was still in that process
of violent fermentation which only during the last fifteen years had
reached a clarifying, relative conclusion. New scientific data were
acquired to a hitherto unheard-of extent, but the establishing of

terrelations, and thereby the bringing of order into this chaos of scoveries following closely upon each other's heels, has only quite cently become possible. It is true that Feuerbach had lived to see l three of the decisive discoveries—that of the cell, the transfor-ation of energy and the theory of evolution named after Darwin. ut how could the lonely philosopher, living in rural solitude, be le sufficiently to follow scientific developments in order to appre-ate at their full value discoveries which natural scientists them-lves at that time either still contested or did not know how to make lequate use of? The blame for this falls solely upon the wretched nditions in Germany, in consequence of which cobweb-spinning lectic fleacrackers had taken possession of the chairs of philosophy, hile Feuerbach, who towered above them all, had to rusticate and row sour in a little village. It is therefore not Feuerbach's fault that e historical conception of nature, which had now become possible nd which removed all the one-sidedness of French materialism, emained inaccessible to him.

Secondly, Feuerbach is quite correct in asserting that exclusively atural-scientific materialism is indeed "the foundation of the edifice f human knowledge, but not the edifice itself." For we live not nly in nature but also in human society, and this also no less than ature has its history of development and its science. It was there-ore a question of bringing the science of society, that is, the sum otal of the so-called historical and philosophical sciences, into har-nony with the materialist foundation, and of reconstructing it there-pon. But it did not fall to Feuerbach's lot to do this. In spite of he "foundation," he remained here bound by the traditional idealist etters, a fact which he recognises in these words: "Backwards I gree with the materialists, but not forwards!" But it was Feuer-ach himself who did not go "forwards" here, in the social domain, who did not get beyond his standpoint of 1840 or 1844. And this was again chiefly due to this reclusion which compelled him, who, of all philosophers, was the most inclined to social intercourse, to produce thoughts out of his solitary head instead of in amicable and hostile encounters with other men of his calibre. Later we shall see in detail how much he remained an idealist in this sphere.

It need only be added here that Starcke looks for Feuerbach's idealism in the wrong place.

"Feuerbach is an idealist; he believes in the progress of mankind." (P. 19.) "The foundation, the substructure of the whole, remains nevertheless idealism. Realism for us is nothing more than a protection against aberrations, while we follow our ideal trends. Are not compassion, love and enthusiasm for truth and justice ideal forces?" (P. VIII.)

In the first place, idealism here means nothing but the pursuit of ideal aims. But these necessarily have to do at the most with Kantian idealism and its "categorical imperative"; however, Kant himself called his philosophy "transcendental idealism"; by ▪ means because he dealt therein also with ethical ideals, but for qui other reasons, as Starcke will remember. The superstition that ph losophical idealism is pivoted round a belief in ethical, that is, s cial, ideals, arose outside philosophy, among the German Philistine who learned by heart from Schiller's poems the few morsels of ph losophical culture they needed. No one has criticised more severe the impotent "categorical imperative" of Kant—impotent becau it demands the impossible, and therefore never attains to any reali ▪ —no one has more cruelly derided the Philistine sentimental e thusiasm for unrealisable ideals purveyed by Schiller than precise the complete idealist Hegel. (See, for example, his *Phenomenology*

In the second place, we simply cannot get away from the fa that everything that sets men acting must find its way throug their brains—even eating and drinking, which begins as a cons quence of the sensation of hunger or thirst transmitted through th brain, and ends as a result of the sensation of satisfaction likewis transmitted through the brain. The influences of the external worl upon man express themselves in his brain, are reflected therein ⅎ feelings, thoughts, impulses, volitions—in short, as "ideal tenden cies," and in this form become "ideal powers." If, then, a man ▪ to be deemed an idealist because he follows "ideal tendencies" an admits that "ideal powers" have an influence over him, then ever person who is at all normally developed is a born idealist and how in that case, can there still be any materialists?

In the third place, the conviction that humanity, at least at th present moment, moves on the whole in a progressive direction ha absolutely nothing to do with the antagonism between materialisn and idealism. The French materialists no less than the deists[30] Voltaire and Rousseau held this conviction to an almost fanatica degree, and often enough made the greatest personal sacrifices fo it. If ever anybody dedicated his whole life to the "enthusiasm fo truth and justice"—using this phrase in the good sense—it was Di derot, for instance. If, therefore, Starcke declares all this to be ideal ism, this merely proves that the word materialism, and the whole antagonism between the two trends, has lost all meaning for him here.

The fact is that Starcke, although perhaps unconsciously, in this makes an unpardonable concession to the traditional Philistine prejudice against the word materialism resulting from its long-continued defamation by the priests. By the word materialism the Philistine understands gluttony, drunkenness, lust of the eye, lust of the flesh, arrogance, cupidity, avarice, covetousness, profit-hunting and stock-exchange swindling—in short, all the filthy vices in which he himself indulges in private. By the word idealism he understands the belief in virtue, universal philanthropy and in a

neral way a "better world," of which he boasts before others but
which he himself at the utmost believes only so long as he is
ving the blues or is going through the bankruptcy consequent
on his customary "materialist" excesses. It is then that he sings
s favourite song, What is man?—Half beast, half angel.

For the rest, Starcke takes great pains to defend Feuerbach
ainst the attacks and doctrines of the vociferous assistant profes-
rs who today go by the name of philosophers in Germany. For
ople who are interested in this afterbirth of classical German phi-
sophy this is, of course, a matter of importance; for Starcke him-
lf it may have appeared necessary. We, however, will spare the
ader this.

III

The real idealism of Feuerbach becomes evident as soon as we
me to his philosophy of religion and ethics. He by no means
ishes to abolish religion; he wants to perfect it. Philosophy itself
ust be absorbed in religion.

"The periods of humanity are distinguished only by religious changes. A his-
rical movement is fundamental only when it is rooted in the hearts of men.
he heart is not a form of religion, so that the latter should exist *also* in the
art; the heart is the essence of religion." (Quoted by Starcke, p. 168.)

According to Feuerbach, religion is the relation between human
eings based on the affections, the relation based on the heart, which
lation until now has sought its truth in a fantastic mirror image
f reality—in the mediation of one or many gods, the fantastic mir-
or images of human qualities—but now finds it directly and with-
ut any mediation in the love between "I" and "Thou." Thus,
nally, with Feuerbach sex love becomes one of the highest forms,
f not the highest form, of the practice of his new religion.

Now relations between human beings, based on affection, and
specially between the two sexes, have existed as long as mankind
as. Sex love in particular has undergone a development and won
place during the last eight hundred years which has made it a
ompulsory pivotal point of all poetry during this period. The
xisting positive religions have limited themselves to the bestowal
f a higher consecration upon state-regulated sex love, that is, upon
he marriage laws, and they could all disappear tomorrow without
hanging in the slightest the practice of love and friendship. Thus
he Christian religion in France, as a matter of fact, so completely
isappeared in the years 1793-98 that even Napoleon could not
e-introduce it without opposition and difficulty; and this without
ny need for a substitute, in Feuerbach's sense, making itself felt
n the interval.

Feuerbach's idealism consists here in this: he does not simp
accept mutual relations based on reciprocal inclination betwee
human beings, such as sex love, friendship, compassion, self-sac
fice, etc., as what they are in themselves—without associating the
with any particular religion which to him, too, belongs to the pa:
but instead he asserts that they will attain their full value only wh
consecrated by the name of religion. The chief thing for him is n
that these purely human relations exist, but that they shall be co
ceived of as the new, true religion. They are to have full val
only after they have been marked with a religious stamp. Religi
is derived from *religare** and meant originally a bond. Therefor
every bond between two people is a religion. Such etymologic:
tricks are the last resort of idealist philosophy. Not what the wor
means according to the historical development of its actual use, be
what it ought to mean according to its derivation is what count
And so sex love and the intercourse between the sexes is apothec
sised to a *religion*, merely in order that the word religion, which
so dear to idealistic memories, may not disappear from the lar
guage. The Parisian reformers of the Louis Blanc trend used t
speak in precisely the same way in the forties. They likewise coul
conceive of a man without religion only as a monster, and used t
say to us: *"Donc, l'athéisme c'est votre religion!"*** If Feuerbac
wishes to establish a true religion upon the basis of an essentiall
materialist conception of nature, that is the same as regardin
modern chemistry as true alchemy. If religion can exist without it
god, alchemy can exist without its philosopher's stone. By the way
there exists a very close connection between alchemy and religion
The philosopher's stone has many godlike properties and the Egyp
tian-Greek alchemists of the first two centuries of our era had
hand in the development of Christian doctrines, as the data give
by Kopp and Berthelot have proved.

Feuerbach's assertion that "the periods of humanity are distin
guished only by religious changes" is decidedly false. Great histo
rical turning-points have been *accompanied* by religious change
only so far as the three world religions which have existed up to
the present—Buddhism, Christianity and Islam—are concerned
The old tribal and national religions, which arose spontaneously
did not proselytise and lost all their power of resistance as soon as
the independence of the tribe or people was lost. For the German
it was sufficient to have simple contact with the decaying Roman
world empire and with its newly adopted Christian world religion
which fitted its economic, political and ideological conditions. Only
with these world religions, arisen more or less artificially, partic-

---

* *Religare*: To bind.—*Ed.*
** "Well, then atheism is your religion!"—*Ed.*

arly Christianity and Islam, do we find that the more general
storical movements acquire a religious imprint. Even in regard
Christianity the religious stamp in revolutions of really universal
gnificance is restricted to the first stages of the bourgeoisie's strug-
e for emancipation—from the thirteenth to the seventeenth cen-
ry—and is to be accounted for, not as Feuerbach thinks by the
arts of men and their religious needs, but by the entire previous
story of the Middle Ages, which knew no other form of ideology
an precisely religion and theology. But when the bourgeoisie of
e eighteenth century was strengthened enough likewise to possess
a ideology of its own, suited to its own class standpoint, it made
great and conclusive revolution, the French, appealing exclusively
juristic and political ideas, and troubling itself with religion only
so far as it stood in its way. But it never occurred to it to put
new religion in place of the old. Everyone knows how Robespierre
iled in his attempt.*

The possibility of purely human sentiments in our intercourse
ith other human beings has nowadays been sufficiently curtailed
y the society in which we must live, which is based upon class
ntagonism and class rule. We have no reason to curtail it still
ore by exalting these sentiments to a religion. And similarly the
nderstanding of the great historical class struggles has already
een sufficiently obscured by current historiography, particularly
a Germany, so that there is also no need for us to make such an
nderstanding totally impossible by transforming the history of
nese struggles into a mere appendix of ecclesiastical history. Al-
eady here it becomes evident how far today we have moved beyond
euerbach. His "finest passages" in glorification of his new religion
f love are totally unreadable today.

The only religion which Feuerbach examines seriously is Chris-
anity, the world religion of the Occident, based upon monotheism.
Ie proves that the Christian god is only a fantastic reflection, a
nirror image, of man. Now, this god is, however, himself the
roduct of a tedious process of abstraction, the concentrated quint-
ssence of the numerous earlier tribal and national gods. And man,
vhose image this god is, is therefore also not a real man, but like-
vise the quintessence of the numerous real men, man in the abstract,
herefore himself again a mental image. Feuerbach, who on every
age preaches sensuousness, absorption in the concrete, in actuality,
ecomes thoroughly abstract as soon as he begins to talk of any other
han mere sex relations between human beings.

Of these relations only one aspect appears to him: morality. And
ere we are again struck by Feuerbach's astonishing poverty when

---

* The reference is to Robespierre's attempt to set up a religion of the "highest
eing."—Ed.

compared with Hegel. The latter's ethics, or doctrine of moral co
duct, is the philosophy of right and embraces: 1) abstract rig^r
2) morality; 3) social ethics [Sittlichkeit], under which again a
comprised: the family, civil society and the state. Here the conte
is as realistic as the form is idealistic. Besides morality the whc
sphere of law, economy, politics is here included. With Feuerba
it is just the reverse. In form he is realistic since he takes his sta
from man; but there is absolutely no mention of the world in whi
this man lives; hence, this man remains always the same abstra
man who occupied the field in the philosophy of religion. For tl
man is not born of woman; he issues, as from a chrysalis, from tl
god of the monotheistic religions. He therefore does not live in
real world historically come into being and historically determine
True, he has intercourse with other men; however, each one
them is just as much an abstraction as he himself. In his philosopl
of religion we still had men and women, but in his ethics even th
last distinction disappears. Feuerbach, to be sure, at long interva
makes such statements as:

> "Man thinks differently in a palace and in a hut." "If because of hunger,
> misery, you have no stuff in your body, you likewise have no stuff for morali
> in your head, in your mind or heart." "Politics must become our religion," et

But Feuerbach is absolutely incapable of achieving anything wit
these maxims. They remain mere phrases, and even Starcke has *
admit that for Feuerbach politics constituted an impassable frontie
and

> the "science of society, sociology, was *terra incognita* to him."

He appears just as shallow, in comparison with Hegel, in h
treatment of the antithesis of good and evil.

> "One believes one is saying something great," Hegel remarks, "if one say
> that 'man is naturally good.' But one forgets that one says something far great
> when one says 'man is naturally evil.' "

With Hegel evil is the form in which the motive force of historica
development presents itself. This contains the twofold meánin
that, on the one hand, each new advance necessarily appears as
sacrilege against things hallowed, as a rebellion against condition
though old and moribund, yet sanctified by custom; and that, o
the other hand, it is precisely the wicked passions of man—gree
and lust for power—which, since the emergence of class antagon
isms, serve as levers of historical development—a fact of which th
history of feudalism and of the bourgeoisie, for example, constitute
a single continual proof. But it does not occur to Feuerbach to in
vestigate the historical role of moral evil. To him history is al
together an uncanny domain in which he feels ill at ease. Even hi
dictum:

"Man as he sprang originally from nature was only a mere creature of nature, not a man. Man is a product of man, of culture, of history"—

with him even this dictum remains absolutely sterile.

What Feuerbach has to tell us about morals can, therefore, only be extremely meagre. The urge towards happiness is innate in man, and must therefore form the basis of all morality. But the urge towards happiness is subject to a double correction. First, by the natural consequences of our actions: after the debauch come the "blues," and habitual excess is followed by illness. Secondly, by their social consequences: if we do not respect the similar urge of other people towards happiness they will defend themselves, and so interfere with our own urge towards happiness. Consequently, in order to satisfy our urge, we must be in a position to appreciate rightly the results of our conduct and must likewise allow others an equal right to seek happiness. Rational self-restraint with regard to ourselves, and love—again and again love!—in our intercourse with others—these are the basic laws of Feuerbach's morality; from them all others are derived. And neither the most spirited utterances of Feuerbach nor the strongest eulogies of Starcke can hide the tenuity and banality of these few propositions.

Only very exceptionally, and by no means to his and other people's profit, can an individual satisfy his urge towards happiness by preoccupation with himself. Rather it requires preoccupation with the outside world, means to satisfy his needs, that is to say, food, an individual of the opposite sex, books, conversation, argument, activities, objects for use and working up. Feuerbach's morality either presupposes that these means and objects of satisfaction are given to every individual as a matter of course, or else it offers only inapplicable good advice and is, therefore, not worth a brass farthing to people who are without these means. And Feuerbach himself states this in plain terms:

"Man thinks differently in a palace and in a hut. If because of hunger, of misery, you have no stuff in your body, you likewise have no stuff for morality in your head, in your mind or heart."

Do matters fare any better in regard to the equal right of others to satisfy their urge towards happiness? Feuerbach posed this claim as absolute, as holding good for all times and circumstances. But since when has it been valid? Was there ever in antiquity between slaves and masters, or in the Middle Ages between serfs and barons, any talk about an equal right to the urge towards happiness? Was not the urge towards happiness of the oppressed class sacrificed ruthlessly and "by right of law" to that of the ruling class? Yes, that was indeed immoral; nowadays, however, equality of rights is recognised. Recognised in words ever since and inasmuch as the bourgeoisie, in its fight against feudalism and in the development

of capitalist production, was compelled to abolish all privileges o
estate, that is, personal privileges, and to introduce the equality o
all individuals before the law, first in the sphere of private law
then gradually also in the sphere of public law. But the urge to
wards happiness thrives only to a trivial extent on ideal rights. T
the greatest extent of all it thrives on material means; and capitalis
production takes care to ensure that the great majority of thos
with equal rights shall get only what is essential for bare existence
Capitalist production has, therefore, little more respect, if indeec
any more, for the equal right to the urge towards happiness of th
majority than had slavery or serfdom. And are we better of
in regard to the mental means of happiness, the educationa
means? Is not even "the schoolmaster of Sadowa"[417] a mythica
person?

More. According to Feuerbach's theory of morals the Stock Exchange is the highest temple of moral conduct, provided only tha
one always speculates right. If my urge towards happiness leads
me to the Stock Exchange, and if there I correctly gauge the consequences of my actions so that only agreeable results and no disadvantages ensue, that is, if I always win, then I am fulfilling Feuerbach's precept. Moreover, I do not thereby interfere with the equal
right of another person to pursue his happiness; for that other man
went to the Exchange just as voluntarily as I did and in concluding
the speculative transaction with me he has followed his urge towards happiness as I have followed mine. If he loses his money,
his action is *ipso facto* proved to have been unethical, because of
his bad reckoning, and since I have given him the punishment he
deserves, I can even slap my chest proudly, like a modern Rhada-
manthus. Love, too, rules on the Stock Exchange, in so far as it is
not simply a sentimental figure of speech, for each finds in others
the satisfaction of his own urge towards happiness, which is just
what love ought to achieve and how it acts in practice. And if I
gamble with correct prevision of the consequences of my operations, and therefore with success, I fulfil all the strictest injunctions
of Feuerbachian morality—and become a rich man into the bargain. In other words, Feuerbach's morality is cut exactly to the
pattern of modern capitalist society, little as Feuerbach himself
might desire or imagine it.

But love!—yes, with Feuerbach love is everywhere and at all
times the wonder-working god who should help to surmount all
difficulties of practical life—and at that in a society which is split
into classes with diametrically opposite interests. At this point the
last relic of its revolutionary character disappears from his philosophy, leaving only the old cant: Love one another—fall into each
other's arms regardless of distinctions of sex or estate—a universal
orgy of reconciliation!

In short, the Feuerbachian theory of morals fares like all its predecessors. It is designed to suit all periods, all peoples and all conditions, and precisely for that reason it is never and nowhere applicable. It remains, as regards the real world, as powerless as Kant's categorical imperative. In reality every class, even every profession, has its own morality, and even this it violates whenever it can do so with impunity. And love, which is to unite all, manifests itself in wars, altercations, lawsuits, domestic broils, divorces and every possible exploitation of one by another.

Now how was it possible that the powerful impetus given by Feuerbach turned out to be so unfruitful for himself? For the simple reason that Feuerbach himself never contrives to escape from the realm of abstraction—for which he has a deadly hatred —into that of living reality. He clings fiercely to nature and man; but nature and man remain mere words with him. He is incapable of telling us anything definite either about real nature or real men. But from the abstract man of Feuerbach one arrives at real living men only when one considers them as participants in history. And that is what Feuerbach resisted, and therefore the year 1848,[20] which he did not understand, meant to him merely the final break with the real world, retirement into solitude. The blame for this again falls chiefly on the conditions then obtaining in Germany, which condemned him to rot away miserably.

But the step which Feuerbach did not take had nevertheless to be taken. The cult of abstract man, which formed the kernel of Feuerbach's new religion, had to be replaced by the science of real men and of their historical development. This further development of Feuerbach's standpoint beyond Feuerbach was inaugurated by Marx in 1845 in *The Holy Family*.

IV

Strauss, Bauer, Stirner, Feuerbach—these were the offshoots of Hegelian philosophy, in so far as they did not abandon the field of philosophy. Strauss, after his *Life of Jesus* and *Dogmatics*, produced only literary studies in philosophy and ecclesiastical history after the fashion of Renan. Bauer only achieved something in the field of the history of the origin of Christianity, though what he did here was important. Stirner remained a curiosity, even after Bakunin blended him with Proudhon and labelled the blend "anarchism." Feuerbach alone was of significance as a philosopher. But not only did philosophy—claimed to soar above all special sciences and to be the science of sciences connecting them—remain to him an impassable barrier, and inviolable holy thing, but as a philosopher, too, he stopped halfway, was a materialist below and an idealist above. He was incapable of disposing of Hegel through criticism;

he simply threw him aside as useless, while he himself, compare
with the encyclopaedic wealth of the Hegelian system, achieve
nothing positive beyond a turgid religion of love and a meagre
impotent morality.

Out of the dissolution of the Hegelian school, however, there de
veloped still another tendency, the only one which has borne rea
fruit. And this tendency is essentially connected with the name o
Marx.*

The separation from Hegelian philosophy was here also the resul
of a return to the materialist standpoint. That means it was resolve
to comprehend the real world—nature and history—just as i
presents itself to everyone who approaches it free from preconceive
idealist crotchets. It was decided mercilessly to sacrifice ever
idealist crotchet which could not be brought into harmony with th
facts conceived in their own and not in a fantastic interconnection
And materialism means nothing more than this. But here the ma
terialistic world outlook was taken really seriously for the first tim
and was carried through consistently—at least in its basic feature
—in all domains of knowledge concerned.

Hegel was not simply put aside. On the contrary, one started
out from his revolutionary side, described above, from the dialectical method. But in its Hegelian form this method was unusable.
According to Hegel, dialectics is the self-development of the concept. The absolute concept does not only exist—unknown where—
from eternity, it is also the actual living soul of the whole existing
world. It develops into itself through all the preliminary stages
which are treated at length in the *Logic* and which are all included
in it. Then it "alienates" itself by changing into nature, where,
without consciousness of itself, disguised as the necessity of nature,
it goes through a new development and finally comes again to self-
consciousness in man. This self-consciousness then elaborates itself
again in history from the crude form until finally the absolute concept again comes to itself completely in the Hegelian philosophy.
According to Hegel, therefore, the dialectical development apparent

---

* Here I may be permitted to make a personal explanation. Lately repeated reference has been made to my share in this theory, and so I can hardly avoid saying
a few words here to settle this point. I cannot deny that both before and during my
forty years' collaboration with Marx I had a certain independent share in laying the
foundations of the theory, and more particularly in its elaboration. But the greater
part of its leading basic principles, especially in the realm of economics and history, and, above all, their final trenchant formulation, belong to Marx. What I contributed—at any rate with the exception of my work in a few special fields—Marx
could very well have done without me. What Marx accomplished I would not have
achieved. Marx stood higher, saw further, and took a wider and quicker view than
all the rest of us. Marx was a genius; we others were at best talented. Without him
the theory would not be by far what it is today. It therefore rightly bears his name.
[*Note by Engels.*]

in nature and history, that is, the causal interconnection of the progressive movement from the lower to the higher, which asserts itself through all zigzag movements and temporary retrogressions, is only a copy [*Abklatsch*] of the self-movement of the concept going on from eternity, no one knows where, but at all events independently of any thinking human brain. This ideological perversion had to be done away with. We comprehended the concepts in our heads once more materialistically—as images [*Abbilder*] of real things instead of regarding the real things as images of this or that stage of the absolute concept. Thus dialectics reduced itself to the science of the general laws of motion, both of the external world and of human thought—two sets of laws which are identical in substance, but differ in their expression in so far as the human mind can apply them consciously, while in nature and also up to now for the most part in human history, these laws assert themselves unconsciously, in the form of external necessity, in the midst of an endless series of seeming accidents. Thereby the dialectic of concepts itself became merely the conscious reflex of the dialectical motion of the real world and thus the dialectic of Hegel was placed upon its head; or rather, turned off its head, on which it was standing, and placed upon its feet. And this materialist dialectic, which for years has been our best working tool and our sharpest weapon, was, remarkably enough, discovered not only by us but also, independently of us and even of Hegel, by a German worker, Joseph Dietzgen.*

In this way, however, the revolutionary side of Hegelian philosophy was again taken up and at the same time freed from the idealist trimmings which with Hegel had prevented its consistent execution. The great basic thought that the world is not to be comprehended as a complex of ready-made *things*, but as a complex of *processes*, in which the things apparently stable no less than their mind images in our heads, the concepts, go through an uninterrupted change of coming into being and passing away, in which, in spite of all seeming accidentality and of all temporary retrogression, a progressive development asserts itself in the end—this great fundamental thought has, especially since the time of Hegel, so thoroughly permeated ordinary consciousness that in this generality it is now scarcely ever contradicted. But to acknowledge this fundamental thought in words and to apply it in reality in detail to each domain of investigation are two different things. If, however, investigation always proceeds from this standpoint, the demand for final solutions and eternal truths ceases once for all; one is always conscious of the necessary limitation of all acquired knowledge, of the fact that

---

* See *Das Wesen der menschlichen Kopfarbeit, dargestellt von einem Handarbeiter* [*The Nature of Human Brainwork, Described by a Manual Worker*]. Hamburg, Meissner. [*Note by Engels*.]

it is conditioned by the circumstances in which it was acquired
On the other hand, one no longer permits oneself to be imposed
upon by the antitheses, insuperable for the still common old metaphysics, between true and false, good and bad, identical and different, necessary and accidental. One knows that these antitheses
have only a relative validity; that that which is recognised now as
true has also its latent false side which will later manifest itself,
just as that which is now regarded as false has also its true side by
virtue of which it could previously be regarded as true. One knows
that what is maintained to be necessary is composed of sheer accidents and that the so-called accidental is the form behind which
necessity hides itself—and so on.

The old method of investigation and thought which Hegel calls
"metaphysical," which preferred to investigate *things* as given, as
fixed and stable, a method the relics of which still strongly haunt
people's minds, had a great deal of historical justification in its
day. It was necessary first to examine things before it was possible
to examine processes. One had first to know what a particular
thing was before one could observe the changes it was undergoing.
And such was the case with natural science. The old metaphysics,
which accepted things as finished objects, arose from a natural
science which investigated dead and living things as finished objects.
But when this investigation had progressed so far that it became
possible to take the decisive step forward, that is, to pass on to the
systematic investigation of the changes which these things undergo
in nature itself, then the last hour of the old metaphysics struck
in the realm of philosophy also. And in fact, while natural science
up to the end of the last century was predominantly a *collecting*
science, a science of finished things, in our century it is essentially
a *systematising* science, a science of the processes, of the origin and
development of these things and of the interconnection which binds
all these natural processes into one great whole. Physiology, which
investigates the processes occurring in plant and animal organisms;
embryology, which deals with the development of individual organisms from germ to maturity; geology, which investigates the
gradual formation of the earth's surface—all these are the offspring
of our century.

But, above all, there are three great discoveries which have
enabled our knowledge of the interconnection of natural processes
to advance by leaps and bounds: first, the discovery of the cell as
the unit from whose multiplication and differentiation the whole
plant and animal body develops, so that not only is the development
and growth of all higher organisms recognised to proceed according
to a single general law, but also, in the capacity of the cell to change,
the way is pointed out by which organisms can change their species
and thus go through a more than individual development. Second,

the transformation of energy, which has demonstrated to us that all the so-called forces operative in the first instance in inorganic nature—mechanical force and its complement, so-called potential energy, heat, radiation (light, or radiant heat), electricity, magnetism and chemical energy—are different forms of manifestation of universal motion, which pass into one another in definite proportions so that in place of a certain quantity of the one which disappears, a certain quantity of another makes its appearance and thus the whole motion of nature is reduced to this incessant process of transformation from one form into another. Finally, the proof which Darwin first developed in connected form that the stock of organic products of nature environing us today, including man, is the result of a long process of evolution from a few originally unicellular germs, and that these again have arisen from protoplasm or albumen, which came into existence by chemical means.

Thanks to these three great discoveries and the other immense advances in natural science, we have now arrived at the point where we can demonstrate the interconnection between the processes in nature not only in particular spheres but also the interconnection of these particular spheres on the whole, and so can present in an approximately systematic form a comprehensive view of the interconnection in nature by means of the facts provided by empirical natural science itself. To furnish this comprehensive view was formerly the task of so-called natural philosophy. It could do this only by putting in place of the real but as yet unknown interconnections ideal, fancied ones, filling in the missing facts by figments of the mind and bridging the actual gaps merely in imagination. In the course of this procedure it conceived many brilliant ideas and foreshadowed many later discoveries, but it also produced a considerable amount of nonsense, which indeed could not have been otherwise. Today, when one needs to comprehend the results of natural scientific investigation only dialectically, that is, in the sense of their own interconnection, in order to arrive at a "system of nature" sufficient for our time; when the dialectical character of this interconnection is forcing itself against their will even into the metaphysically-trained minds of the natural scientists, today natural philosophy is finally disposed of. Every attempt at resurrecting it would be not only superfluous but a *step backwards*.

But what is true of nature, which is hereby recognised also as a historical process of development, is likewise true of the history of society in all its branches and of the totality of all sciences which occupy themselves with things human (and divine). Here, too, the philosophy of history, of right, of religion, etc., has consisted in the substitution of an interconnection fabricated in the mind of the philosopher for the real interconnection to be demonstrated in the events; has consisted in the comprehension of history as a whole as well as in its separate parts, as the gradual realisation of ideas—and naturally always only the pet ideas of the philosopher himself. According to this, history worked unconsciously but of necessity towards a certain ideal goal set in advance—as, for example, in Hegel, towards the realisation of his absolute idea—and the unalterable trend towards this absolute idea formed the inner interconnection in the events of history. A new mysterious providence—unconscious of gradually coming into consciousness—was thus put in the place of the real, still unknown interconnection. Here, therefore, just as in the realm of nature, it was necessary to do away with these fabricated, artificial interconnections by the discovery of the real ones—a task which ultimately amounts to the discovery of the general laws of motion which assert themselves as the ruling ones in the history of human society.

In one point, however, the history of the development of society proves to be essentially different from that of nature. In nature—in so far as we ignore man's reaction upon nature—there are only blind, unconscious agencies acting upon one another, out of whose interplay the general law comes into operation. Nothing of all that happens—whether in the innumerable apparent accidents observable upon the surface, or in the ultimate results which confirm the regularity inherent in these accidents—happens as a consciously desired aim. In the history of society, on the contrary, the actors are all endowed with consciousness, are men acting with deliberation or passion, working towards definite goals; nothing happens without a conscious purpose, without an intended aim. But this distinction, important as it is for historical investigation, particularly of single epochs and events, cannot alter the fact that the course of history is governed by inner general laws. For here, also, on the whole, in spite of the consciously desired aims of all individuals, accident apparently reigns on the surface. That which is willed happens but rarely; in the majority of instances the numerous desired ends cross and conflict with one another, or these ends themselves are from the outset incapable of realisation or the means of attaining them are insufficient. Thus the conflicts of innumerable individual wills and individual actions in the domain of history produce a state of affairs entirely analogous to that prevailing in the realm of unconscious nature. The ends of the actions are intended, but the results which actually follow from these actions are not intended; or when they do seem to correspond to the end intended, they ultimately have consequences quite other than those intended. Historical events thus appear on the whole to be likewise governed by chance. But where on the surface accident holds sway, there actually it is always governed by inner, hidden laws and it is only a matter of discovering these laws.

Men make their own history, whatever its outcome may be, in

that each person follows his own consciously desired end, and it is precisely the resultant of these many wills operating in different directions and of their manifold effects upon the outer world that constitutes history. Thus it is also a question of what the many individuals desire. The will is determined by passion or deliberation. But the levers which immediately determine passion or deliberation are of very different kinds. Partly they may be external objects, partly ideal motives, ambition, "enthusiasm for truth and justice," personal hatred or even purely individual whims of all kinds. But, on the one hand, we have seen that the many individual wills active in history for the most part produce results quite other than those intended—often quite the opposite; that their motives, therefore, in relation to the total result are likewise of only secondary importance. On the other hand, the further question arises: What driving forces in turn stand behind these motives? What are the historical causes which transform themselves into these motives in the brains of the actors?

The old materialism never put this question to itself. Its conception of history, in so far as it has one at all, is therefore essentially pragmatic; it judges everything according to the motives of the action; it divides men who act in history into noble and ignoble and then finds that as a rule the noble are defrauded and the ignoble are victorious. Hence, it follows for the old materialism that nothing very edifying is to be got from the study of history, and for us that in the realm of history the old materialism becomes untrue to itself because it takes the ideal driving forces which operate there as ultimate causes, instead of investigating what is behind them, what are the driving forces of these driving forces. The inconsistency does not lie in the fact that *ideal* driving forces are recognised, but in the investigation not being carried further back behind these into their motive causes. On the other hand, the philosophy of history, particularly as represented by Hegel, recognises that the ostensible and also the really operating motives of men who act in history are by no means the ultimate causes of historical events; that behind these motives are other motive powers, which have to be discovered. But it does not seek these in history itself, it imports them rather from outside, from philosophical ideology, into history. Hegel, for example, instead of explaining the history of ancient Greece out of its own inner interconnections, simply maintains that it is nothing more than the working out of "forms of beautiful individuality," the realisation of a "work of art" as such. He says much in this connection about the old Greeks that is fine and profound, but that does not prevent us today from refusing to be put off with such an explanation, which is a mere manner of speech.

When, therefore, it is a question of investigating the driving powers which—consciously or unconsciously, and indeed very often unconsciously—lie behind the motives of men who act in history and which constitute the real ultimate driving forces of history, then it is not a question so much of the motives of single individuals, however eminent, as of those motives which set in motion great masses, whole peoples, and again whole classes of the people in each people; and this, too, not momentarily, for the transient flaring up of a straw-fire which quickly dies down, but for a lasting action resulting in a great historical transformation. To ascertain the driving causes which here in the minds of acting masses and their leaders—the so-called great men—are reflected as conscious motives, clearly or unclearly, directly or in ideological, even glorified, form—that is the only path which can put us on the track of the laws holding sway both in history as a whole, and at particular periods and in particular lands. Everything which sets men in motion must go through their minds; but what form it will take in the mind will depend very much upon the circumstances. The workers have by no means become reconciled to capitalist machine industry, even though they no longer simply break the machines to pieces as they still did in 1848 on the Rhine.

But while in all earlier periods the investigation of these driving causes of history was almost impossible—on account of the complicated and concealed interconnections between them and their effects—our present period has so far simplified these interconnections that the riddle could be solved. Since the establishment of large-scale industry, that is, at least since the European peace of 1815, it has been no longer a secret to any man in England that the whole political struggle there turned on the claims to supremacy of two classes: the landed aristocracy and the bourgeoisie (middle class). In France, with the return of the Bourbons, the same fact was perceived, the historians of the Restoration period,[418] from Thierry to Guizot, Mignet and Thiers, speak of it everywhere as the key to the understanding of all French history since the Middle Ages. And since 1830 the working class, the proletariat, has been recognised in both countries as a third competitor for power. Conditions had become so simplified that one would have had to close one's eyes deliberately not to see in the fight of these three great classes and in the conflict of their interests the driving force of modern history—at least in the two most advanced countries.

But how did these classes come into existence? If it was possible at first glance still to ascribe the origin of the great, formerly feudal landed property—at least in the first instance—to political causes, to taking possession by force, this could not be done in regard to the bourgeoisie and the proletariat. Here the origin and development of two great classes was seen to lie clearly and palpably in purely economic causes. And it was just as clear that in the struggle between landed property and the bourgeoisie, no less than in the struggle between the bourgeoisie and the proletariat, it was a question, first and foremost, of economic interests, to the further-ance of which political power was intended to serve merely as a means. Bourgeoisie and proletariat both arose in consequence of a transformation of the economic conditions, more precisely, of the mode of production. The transition, first from guild handicrafts to manufacture, and then from manufacture to large-scale industry, with steam and mechanical power, had caused the development of these two classes. At a certain stage the new productive forces set in motion by the bourgeoisie—in the first place the division of labour and the combination of many detail labourers [*Teilarbeiter*] in one general manufactory—and the conditions and requirements of exchange, developed through these productive forces, became in-compatible with the existing order of production handed down by history and sanctified by law, that is to say, incompatible with the privileges of the guild and the numerous other personal and local privileges (which were only so many fetters to the unprivileged estates) of the feudal order of society. The productive forces repre-sented by the bourgeoisie rebelled against the order of production represented by the feudal landlords and the guildmasters. The result is known: the feudal fetters were smashed, gradually in England, at one blow in France. In Germany the process is not yet finished. But just as, at a definite stage of its development, manufacture came into conflict with the feudal order of production, so now large-scale industry has already come into conflict with the bourgeois order of production established in its place. Tied down by this order, by the narrow limits of the capitalist mode of production, this industry produces, on the one hand, an ever-increasing proletarianisation of the great mass of the people, and on the other hand, an ever greater mass of unsaleable products. Overproduction and mass misery, each the cause of the other—that is the absurd contradiction which is its outcome, and which of necessity calls for the liberation of the productive forces by means of a change in the mode of produc-tion.

In modern history at least it is, therefore, proved that all political struggles are class struggles, and all class struggles for emancipa-tion, despite their necessarily political form—for every class strug-gle is a political struggle—turn ultimately on the question of *eco-nomic* emancipation. Therefore, here at least, the state—the political order—is the subordinate, and civil society—the realm of economic relations—the decisive element. The traditional conception, to which Hegel, too, pays homage, saw in the state the determining element, and in civil society the element determined by it. Appearances cor-respond to this. As all the driving forces of the actions of any indi-vidual person must pass through his brain, and transform themselves into motives of his will in order to set him into action, so also all the needs of civil society—no matter which class happens to be the ruling one—must pass through the will of the state in order to secure general validity in the form of laws. That is the formal aspect of the matter—the one which is self-evident. The question arises, however, what is the content of this merely formal will—of the individual as well as of the state—and whence is this content derived? Why is just this willed and not something else? If we enquire into this we discover that in modern history the will of the state is, on the whole, determined by the changing needs of civil society, by the supremacy of this or that class, in the last resort, by the development of the productive forces and relations of exchange.

But if even in our modern era, with its gigantic means of production and communication, the state is not an independent domain with an independent development, but one whose existence as well as development is to be explained in the last resort by the economic conditions of life of society, then this must be still more true of all earlier times when the production of the material life of man was not yet carried on with these abundant auxiliary means, and when, therefore, the necessity of such production must have exercised a still greater mastery over men. If the state even today, in the era of big industry and of railways, is on the whole only a reflection, in concentrated form, of the economic needs of the class controlling production, then this must have been much more so in an epoch when each generation of men was forced to spend a far greater part of its aggregate lifetime in satisfying material needs, and was therefore much more dependent on them than we are today. An examination of the history of earlier periods, as soon as it is seriously undertaken from this angle, most abundantly confirms this. But, of course, this cannot be gone into here.

If the state and public law are determined by economic relations, so, too, of course is private law, which indeed in essence only sanctions the existing economic relations between individuals which are normal in the given circumstances. The form in which this happens can, however, vary considerably. It is possible, as happened in England, in harmony with the whole national development, to retain in the main the forms of the old feudal laws while giving them a bourgeois content; in fact, directly reading a bourgeois meaning into the feudal name. But, also, as happened in western continental Europe, Roman Law, the first world law of a commodity-producing society, with its unsurpassably fine elaboration of all the essential legal relations of simple commodity owners (of buyers and sellers, debtors and creditors, contracts, obligations, etc.), can be taken as the foundation. In which case, for the benefit of a still petty-bourgeois and semi-feudal society, it can either be reduced to the level of such a society simply through judicial practice (common law) or, with the help of allegedly enlightened, moralising jurists, it can be worked into a special code of law to correspond with such social level—a code which in these circumstances will be a bad one also from the legal standpoint (for instance, Prussian *Landrecht*). In which case, however, after a great bourgeois revolution, it is also possible for such a classic law code of bourgeois society as the French *Code Civil*[312] to be worked out upon the basis of this same Roman Law. If, therefore, bourgeois legal rules merely express the economic life conditions of society in legal form, then they can do so well or ill according to circumstances.

The state presents itself to us as the first ideological power over man. Society creates for itself an organ for the safeguarding of its common interests against internal and external attacks. This organ is the state power. Hardly come into being, this organ makes itself independent *vis-à-vis* society; and, indeed, the more so, the more it becomes the organ of a particular class, the more it directly enforces the supremacy of that class. The fight of the oppressed class against the ruling class becomes necessarily a political fight, a fight first of all against the political dominance of this class. The consciousness of the interconnection between this political struggle and its economic basis becomes dulled and can be lost altogether. While this is not wholly the case with the participants, it almost always happens with the historians. Of the ancient sources on the struggles within the Roman Republic only Appian tells us clearly and distinctly what was at issue in the last resort—namely, landed property.

But once the state has become an independent power *vis-à-vis* society, it produces forthwith a further ideology. It is indeed among professional politicians, theorists of public law and jurists of private law that the connection with economic facts gets lost for fair. Since in each particular case the economic facts must assume the form of juristic motives in order to receive legal sanction; and since, in so doing, consideration of course has to be given to the whole legal system already in operation, the juristic form is, in consequence, made everything and the economic content nothing. Public law and private law are treated as independent spheres, each having its own independent historical development, each being capable of and needing a systematic presentation by the consistent elimination of all inner contradictions.

Still higher ideologies, that is, such as are still further removed from the material, economic basis, take the form of philosophy and religion. Here the interconnection between conceptions and their material conditions of existence becomes more and more complicated, more and more obscured by intermediate links. But the interconnection exists. Just as the whole Renaissance period,[41] from the middle of the fifteenth century, was an essential product of the towns and, therefore, of the burghers, so also was the subsequently newly-awakened philosophy. Its content was in essence only the philosophical expression of the thoughts corresponding to the development of the small and middle burghers into a big bourgeoisie. Among last century's Englishmen and Frenchmen who in many cases were just as much political economists as philosophers, this is clearly evident; and we have proved it above in regard to the Hegelian school.

We will now in addition deal only briefly with religion, since the latter stands furthest away from material life and seems to be most alien to it. Religion arose in very primitive times from erroneous, primitive conceptions of men about their own nature and external nature surrounding them. Every ideology, however, once it has arisen, develops in connection with the given concept-material, and develops this material further; otherwise it would not be an ideology, that is, occupation with thoughts as with independent entities, developing independently and subject only to their own laws. That the material life conditions of the persons inside whose heads this thought process goes on in the last resort determine the course of this process remains of necessity unknown to these persons, for otherwise there would be an end to all ideology. These original religious notions, therefore, which in the main are common to each group of kindred peoples, develop, after the group separates, in a manner peculiar to each people, according to the conditions of life falling to their lot. For a number of groups of peoples, and particularly for the Aryans (so-called Indo-Europeans), this process has been shown in detail by comparative mythology. The gods thus fashioned within each people were national gods, whose domain extended no farther than the national territory which they were to protect; on the other side of its boundaries other gods held undisputed sway. They could continue to exist, in imagination, only as long as the nation existed; they fell with its fall. The Roman world empire, the economic conditions of whose origin we do not need to examine here, brought about this downfall of the old nationalities. The old national gods decayed, even those of the Romans, which also were patterned to suit only the narrow confines of the city of Rome. The need to complement the world empire by means of a world religion was clearly revealed in the attempts made to provide in Rome recognition and altars for all the foreign gods to the slightest degree respectable alongside of the indigenous ones. But a new world religion is not to be made in this fashion, by imperial decree. The new world religion, Christianity, had already quietly come into being, out of a mixture of generalised Oriental, particularly Jewish, theology, and vulgarised Greek, particularly Stoic, philosophy. What it originally looked like has to be first laboriously discovered, since its official form, as it has been handed down to us, is merely that in which it became the state religion to which purpose it was adapted by the Council of Nicaea.[419] The fact that already after 250 years it became the state religion suffices to show that it was the religion in correspondence with the conditions of the time. In the Middle Ages, in the same measure as feudalism developed, Christianity grew into the religious counterpart to it, with a corresponding feudal hierarchy. And when the burghers began to thrive, there developed, in opposition to feudal Catholicism, the Protestant heresy, which first appeared in Southern France, among the Albigenses,[420] at the time the cities there reached the highest point of their florescence. The Middle Ages had attached to theology all the other forms of ideology—philosophy, politics, jurisprudence—and made them subdivisions of theology. It thereby constrained every social and political movement to take on a theological form. The sentiments of the masses were fed with religion to the exclusion of all else; it was therefore necessary to put forward their own interests in a religious guise in order to produce an impetuous movement. And just as the burghers from the beginning brought into being an appendage of propertyless urban plebeians, day labourers and servants of all kinds, belonging to no recognised social estate, precursors of the later proletariat, so likewise heresy soon became divided into a burgher-moderate heresy and a plebeian-revolutionary one, the latter an abomination to the burgher heretics themselves.

The ineradicability of the Protestant heresy corresponded to the invincibility of the rising burghers. When these burghers had become sufficiently strengthened, their struggle against the feudal nobility, which till then had been predominantly local, began to assume national dimensions. The first great action occurred in Germany—the so-called Reformation. The burghers were neither powerful enough nor sufficiently developed to be able to unite under their banner the remaining rebellious estates—the plebeians of the towns, the lower nobility and the peasants on the land. At first the nobles were defeated; the peasants rose in a revolt which formed the peak of the whole revolutionary struggle; the cities left them in the lurch, and thus the revolution succumbed to the armies of the secular princes who reaped the whole profit. Thenceforward Germany disappears for three centuries from the ranks of countries playing an independent active part in history. But beside the German Luther appeared the Frenchman Calvin. With true French acuity he put the bourgeois character of the Reformation in the forefront, republicanised and democratised the Church. While the Lutheran Reformation in Germany degenerated and reduced the country to rack and ruin, the Calvinist Reformation served as a banner for the republicans in Geneva, in Holland and in Scotland, freed Holland from Spain and from the German Empire[421] and provided the ideological costume for the second act of the bourgeois revolution, which was taking place in England. Here Calvinism justified itself as the true religious disguise of the interests of the bourgeoisie of that time, and on this account did not attain full recognition when the revolution ended in 1689 in a compromise between one part of the nobility and the bourgeoisie.[308] The English state Church was re-established; but not in its earlier form of a Catholicism which had the king for its pope, being, instead, strongly Calvinised. The old state Church had celebrated the merry Catholic Sunday and had fought against the dull Calvinist one. The new, bourgeoisified Church introduced the latter, which adorns England to this day.

In France, the Calvinist minority was suppressed in 1685 and either Catholicised or driven out of the country.[422] But what was the good? Already at that time the freethinker Pierre Bayle was at the height of his activity, and in 1694 Voltaire was born. The forcible measures of Louis XIV only made it easier for the French bourgeoisie to carry through its revolution in the irreligious, exclusively political form which alone was suited to a developed bourgeoisie. Instead of Protestants, freethinkers took their seats in the national assemblies. Thereby Christianity entered into its final stage. It had become incapable for the future of serving any progressive class as the ideological garb of its aspirations. It became more and more the exclusive possession of the ruling classes and these apply it as a mere means of government, to keep the lower classes within bounds. Moreover, each of the different classes uses its own appropriate religion: the landed nobility—Catholic Jesuitism or Protestant orthodoxy; the liberal and radical bourgeoisie—rationalism; and it makes little difference whether these gentlemen themselves believe in their respective religions or not.

We see, therefore: religion, once formed, always contains traditional material, just as in all ideological domains tradition forms a great conservative force. But the transformations which this material undergoes spring from class relations, that is to say, out of the economic relations of the people who execute these transformations. And here that is sufficient.

In the above it could only be a question of giving a general sketch of the Marxist conception of history, at most with a few illustrations, as well. The proof must be derived from history itself; and in this regard I may be permitted to say that it has been sufficiently furnished in other writings. This conception, however, puts an end to philosophy in the realm of history, just as the dialectical conception of nature makes all natural philosophy both unnecessary and impossible. It is no longer a question anywhere of inventing interconnections from out of our brains, but of discovering them in the facts. For philosophy, which has been expelled from nature and history, there remains only the realm of pure thought, so far as it is left: the theory of the laws of the thought process itself, logic and dialectics.

* * *

With the Revolution of 1848, "educated" Germany said farewell to theory and went over to the field of practice. Small production and manufacture, based upon manual labour, were superseded by real large-scale industry. Germany again appeared on the world market. The new little German Empire[423] abolished at least the most crying of the abuses with which this development had been obstructed by the system of petty states, the relics of feudalism, and bureaucratic management. But to the same degree that speculation abandoned the philosopher's study in order to set up its temple in the Stock Exchange, educated Germany lost the great aptitude for theory which had been the glory of Germany in the days of its deepest political humiliation—the aptitude for purely scientific investigation, irrespective of whether the result obtained was practically applicable or not, whether likely to offend the police authorities or not. Official German natural science, it is true, maintained its position in the front rank, particularly in the field of specialised research. But even the American journal *Science* rightly remarks that the decisive advances in the sphere of the comprehensive correlation of particular facts and their generalisation into laws are now being made much more in England, instead of, as formerly, in Germany. And in the sphere of the historical sciences, philosophy included, the old fearless zeal for theory has now disappeared completely, along with classical philosophy. Inane eclecticism and an anxious concern for career and income, descending to the most vulgar job-hunting, occupy its place. The official representatives of these sciences have become the undisguised ideologists of the bourgeoisie and the existing state—but at a time when both stand in open antagonism to the working class.

Only among the working class does the German aptitude for theory remain unimpaired. Here it cannot be exterminated. Here there is no concern for careers, for profit-making, or for gracious patronage from above. On the contrary, the more ruthlessly and disinterestedly science proceeds the more it finds itself in harmony with the interests and aspirations of the workers. The new tendency, which recognised that the key to the understanding of the whole history of society lies in the history of the development of labour, from the outset addressed itself by preference to the working class and here found the response which it neither sought nor expected from officially recognised science. The German working-class movement is the inheritor of German classical philosophy.

Written early in 1886

Published in the journal
Die Neue Zeit Nos. 4 and 5,
1886, and as a separate
publication in Stuttgart
in 1888

Printed according to the text
of the 1888 edition
Translated from the German

Frederick Engels

THE PEASANT QUESTION
IN FRANCE AND GERMANY[424]

The bourgeois and reactionary parties greatly wonder why everywhere among Socialists the peasant question has now suddenly been placed upon the order of the day. What they should be wondering at, by rights, is that this has not been done long ago. From Ireland to Sicily, from Andalusia to Russia and Bulgaria, the peasant is a very essential factor of the population, production and political power. Only two regions of Western Europe form an exception. In Great Britain proper big landed estates and large-scale agriculture have totally displaced the self-supporting peasant; in Prussia east of the Elbe the same process has been going on for centuries; here too the peasant is being increasingly "turned out"* or at least economically and politically forced into the background.

The peasant has so far largely manifested himself as a factor of political power only by his apathy, which has its roots in the isolation of rustic life. This apathy on the part of the great mass of the population is the strongest pillar not only of the parliamentary corruption in Paris and Rome but also of Russian despotism. Yet it is by no means insuperable. Since the rise of the working-class movement in Western Europe, particularly in those parts where small peasant holdings predominate, it has not been particularly difficult for the bourgeoisie to render the socialist workers suspicious and odious in the minds of the peasants as *partageux*, as people who want to "divide up," as lazy greedy city dwellers who have an eye on the property of the peasants. The hazy socialistic aspirations of the Revolution of February 1848 were rapidly disposed of by the reactionary ballots of the French peasantry; the peasant, who wanted peace of mind, dug up from his treasured memories the legend of Napoleon, the emperor of the peasants, and created the Second Empire. We all know what this one feat of the peasants cost the people of France; it is still suffering from its aftermath.

But much has changed since then. The development of the capitalist form of production has cut the life-strings of small produc-

---

* *Wird "gelegt". Bauernlegen*—a technical term from German history meaning eviction, expropriation of peasants. [*Lenin's note to his translation of the beginning of Engels's work.*]

tion in agriculture; small production is irretrievably going to rack and ruin. Competitors in North and South America and in India, too, have swamped the European market with their cheap grain, so cheap that no domestic producer can compete with it. The big landowners and small peasants alike see ruin staring them in the face. And since they are both owners of land and country folk, the big landowners assume the role of champions of the interests of the small peasants, and the small peasants by and large accept them as such.

Meanwhile a powerful socialist workers' party has sprung up and developed in the West. The obscure presentiments and feelings dating back to the February Revolution have become clarified and acquired the broader and deeper scope of a programme that meets all scientific requirements and contains definite tangible demands; and a steadily growing number of Socialist deputies fight for these demands in the German, French and Belgian parliaments. The conquest of political power by the Socialist Party has become a matter of the not too distant future. But in order to conquer political power this party must first go from the towns to the country, must become a power in the countryside. This party, which has an advantage over all others in that it possesses a clear insight into the interconnections between economic causes and political effects and long ago descried the wolf in the sheep's clothing of the big landowner, that importunate friend of the peasant—may this party calmly leave the doomed peasant in the hands of his false protectors until he has been transformed from a passive into an active opponent of the industrial workers? This brings us right into the thick of the peasant question.

I

The rural population to which we can address ourselves consists of quite different parts, which vary greatly with the various regions.

In the West of Germany, as in France and Belgium, there prevails the small-scale cultivation of small-holding peasants, the majority of whom own and the minority of whom rent their parcels of land.

In the Northwest—in Lower Saxony and Schleswig-Holstein—we have a preponderance of big and middle peasants who cannot do without male and female farm servants and even day labourers. The same is true of part of Bavaria.

In Prussia east of the Elbe and in Mecklenburg we have the region of big landed estates and large-scale cultivation with hinds, cotters and day labourers, and in between small and middle peasants in relatively unimportant and steadily decreasing proportion.

In central Germany all these forms of production and ownership
are found mixed in various proportions, depending upon the local-
y, without the decided prevalence of any particular form over a
arge area.

Besides there are localities varying in extent where the arable
and owned or rented is insufficient to provide for the subsistence
f the family, but can serve only as the basis for operating a do-
aestic industry and enabling the latter to pay the otherwise incom-
rehensibly low wages that ensure the steady sale of its products
lespite all foreign competition.

Which of these subdivisions of the rural population can be won
ver by the Social-Democratic Party? We, of course, investigate this
question only in broad outline; we single out only clearcut forms.
We lack space to give consideration to intermediate stages and
aixed rural populations.

Let us begin with the small peasant. Not only is he, of all peasants,
he most important for Western Europe in general, but he is also
he critical case that decides the entire question. Once we have
clarified in our minds our attitude to the small peasant we have
all the data needed to determine our stand relative to the other
constituent parts of the rural population.

By small peasant we mean here the owner or tenant—particularly
the former—of a patch of land no bigger, as a rule, than he and
his family can till, and no smaller than can sustain the family. This
small peasant, just like the small handicraftsman, is therefore a
toiler who differs from the modern proletarian in that he still possesses his instruments of labour; hence a survival of a past mode of
production. There is a threefold difference between him and his
ancestor, the serf, bondman or, quite exceptionally, the free peasant
liable to rent and feudal services. First, in that the French Revolution freed him from the feudal services and dues that he owed to
the landlord and in the majority of cases, at least on the left bank
of the Rhine, assigned his peasant farm to him as his own free
property. Secondly, in that he lost the protection of and the right
to participate in the self-administering Mark community, and hence
his share in the emoluments of the former common Mark. The common Mark was whisked away partly by the erstwhile feudal lord
and partly by enlightened bureaucratic legislation patterned after
Roman law. This deprives the small peasant of modern times of the
possibility of feeding his draft animals without buying fodder.
Economically, however, the loss of the emoluments derived from
the Mark by far outweighs the benefits accruing from the abolition
of feudal services. The number of peasants unable to keep draft
animals of their own is steadily increasing. Thirdly, the peasant
of today has lost half of his former productive activity. Formerly
he and his family produced, from raw material he had made himself,

the greater part of the industrial products that he needed; the re:
of what he required was supplied by village neighbours who plie
a trade in addition to farming and were paid mostly in articles o
exchange or in reciprocal services. The family, and still more th
village, was self-sufficient, produced almost everything it neede
It was natural economy almost unalloyed; almost no money wa
necessary. Capitalist production put an end to this by its mone
economy and large-scale industry. But if the Mark emolument
represented one of the basic conditions of his existence, his industri
side line was another. And thus the peasant sinks ever lower. Taxe:
crop failures, divisions of inheritance and litigations drive on
peasant after another into the arms of the usurer; the indebtednes
becomes more and more general and steadily increases in amoun
in each case—in brief, our small peasant, like every other surviva
of a past mode of production, is hopelessly doomed. He is a futur
proletarian.

As such he ought to lend a ready ear to socialist propaganda
But he is prevented from doing so for the time being by his deep
rooted sense of property. The more difficult it is for him to defen
his endangered patch of land the more desperately he clings to i
the more he regards the Social-Democrats, who speak of transferrin;
landed property to the whole of society, as just as dangerous a fo
as the usurer and lawyer. How is the Social-Democracy to over
come this prejudice? What can it offer to the doomed small peasan
without becoming untrue to itself?

Here we find a practical point of support in the agrarian pro
gramme of the French Socialists of the Marxian trend, a programm
which is the more noteworthy as it comes from the classical land o:
small peasant economy.

The Marseilles Congress of 1892[425] adopted the first agrarian pro
gramme of the Party. It demands for propertyless rural *worker*.
(that is to say, day labourers and hinds): minimum wages fixed by
trade unions and community councils; rural trade courts consisting
half of workers; prohibition of the sale of common land; and the
leasing of public domain land to communities which are to rent al
this land, whether owned by them or rented, to associations of pro
pertyless families of farm labourers for common cultivation, on
condition that the employment of wage-workers be prohibited and
that the communities exercise control; old-age and invalid pensions,
to be defrayed by means of a special tax on big landed estates.

On behalf of the *small peasants*, with special consideration for
tenant farmers and share croppers (*métayers*), acquisition of
machinery by the community to be leased at cost price to the peasants; the formation of peasant co-operatives for the purchase of
manure, drain-pipes, seed, etc., and for the sale of the produce;
abolition of the real estate transfer tax if the value involved does

ot exceed 5,000 francs; arbitration commissions on the Irish pattern
» reduce exorbitant rentals and compensate quitting tenant farmers
nd share croppers (*métayers*) for appreciation of the land due to
1em; repeal of Article 2,102 of the Civil Code[312] which allows a
1ndlord to distrain on the crop, and the abolition of the right of
reditors to levy on growing crops; exemption from levy and
istraint of a definite amount of farm implements and of the crop,
eed, manure, draft animals, in short, whatever is indispensable to
1e peasant for carrying on his business; revision of the general
adastre, which has long been out of date, and until such time a
ocal revision in each community; lastly, free instruction in farming,
nd agricultural experimental stations.

As we see, the demands made in the interests of the peasants—
hose made in the interests of the workers do not concern us here
or the time being—are not very far-reaching. Part of them has
lready been realised elsewhere. The tenants' arbitration courts
ollow the Irish prototype by express mention. Peasant co-operatives
lready exist in the Rhine provinces. The revision of the cadastre has
een a constant pious wish of all liberals and even bureaucrats
hroughout Western Europe. The other points, too, could be carried
nto effect without any substantial impairment of the existing
apitalist order. So much simply in characterisation of the pro-
;ramme. No reproach is intended; quite the contrary.

The Party did such a good business with this programme among
he peasants in the most diverse parts of France that—since appetite
omes with eating—one felt constrained to suit it still more to their
aste. It was felt, however, that this would be treading on dangerous
;round. How was the peasant to be helped, not the peasant as a
uture proletarian but as a present propertied peasant, without
iolating the basic principles of the general socialist programme?
In order to meet this objection the new practical proposals were
orefaced by a theoretical preamble, which seeks to prove that it is
n keeping with the principles of socialism to protect small-peasant
oroperty from destruction by the capitalist mode of production
although one is perfectly aware that this destruction is inevitable.
Let us now examine more closely this preamble as well as the
demands themselves, which were adopted by the Nantes Congress
in September of this year.

The preamble begins as follows:

"Whereas according to the terms of the general programme of the Party
producers can be free only in so far as they are in possession of the means of
production;

"Whereas in the sphere of industry these means of production have already
reached such a degree of capitalist centralisation that they can be restored to the
producers only in collective or social form, but in the sphere of agriculture—at
least in present-day France—this is by no means the case, the means of produc-

tion, namely, the land, being in very many localities still in the hands of th
individual producers themselves as their individual possession;

"Whereas even if this state of affairs characterised by small-holding owne
ship is irretrievably doomed (*est fatalement appelé à disparaître*), still it is ne
for socialism to hasten this doom, as its task does not consist in separating pre
perty from labour but, on the contrary, in uniting both of these factors of a
production by placing them in the same hands, factors the separation of whic
entails the servitude and poverty of the workers reduced to proletarians;

"Whereas, on the one hand, it is the duty of socialism to put the agricultur:
proletarians again in possession—collective or social in form—of the great d
mains after expropriating their present idle owners, it is, on the other hand, n
less its imperative duty to maintain the peasants themselves tilling their patche
of land in possession of the same as against the fisk, the usurer and the encroach
ments of the newly-arisen big landowners;

"Whereas it is expedient to extend this protection also to the producers wh
as tenants or share croppers (*métayers*) cultivate the land owned by others an
who, if they exploit day labourers, are to a certain extent compelled to do s
because of the exploitation to which they themselves are subjected—

"Therefore the Workers' Party—which unlike the anarchists does not cou
on an increase and spread of poverty for the transformation of the social orde
but expects labour and society in general to be emancipated only by the organi
sation and concerted efforts of the workers of both country and town, by thei
taking possession of the government and legislation—has adopted the followin
agrarian programme in order thereby to bring together all the elements of rura
production, all occupations which by virtue of various rights and titles utilise th
national soil, to wage an identical struggle against the common foe: the feudalit
of landownership."

Now for a closer examination of these "whereases."

To begin with, the statement in the French programme tha
freedom of the producers presupposes the possession of the mean
of production must be supplemented by those immediately follow
ing: that the possession of the means of production is possible only
in two forms: either as individual possession, which form never an
nowhere existed for the producers in general, and is daily being
made more impossible by industrial progress; or as common posses
sion, a form the material and intellectual preconditions of whicl
have been established by the development of capitalist society itself
that therefore taking *collective* possession of the means of produc
tion must be fought for by all means at the disposal of the pro
letariat.

The common possession of the means of production is thus se
forth here as the sole principal goal to be striven for. Not only in
industry, where the ground has already been prepared, but in
general, hence also in agriculture. According to the programme
individual possession never and nowhere obtained generally for all
producers; for that very reason and because industrial progress
removes it anyhow, socialism is not interested in maintaining but
rather in removing it; because where it exists and in so far as it
exists it makes common possession impossible. Once we cite the
programme in support of our contention we must cite the entire
programme, which considerably modifies the proposition quoted in

Nantes; for it makes the general historical truth expressed in it dependent upon the conditions under which alone it can remain a truth today in Western Europe and North America.

Possession of the means of production by the individual producers nowadays no longer grants these producers real freedom. Handicraft has already been ruined in the cities; in metropolises like London it has already disappeared entirely, having been superseded by large-scale industry, the sweatshop system and miserable bunglers who thrive on bankruptcy. The self-supporting small peasant is neither in the safe possession of his tiny patch of land nor is he free. He as well as his house, his farmstead and his few fields belong to the usurer; his livelihood is more uncertain than that of the proletarian, who at least does have tranquil days now and then, which is never the case with the eternally tortured debt slave. Strike out Article 2,102 of the Civil Code, provide by law that a definite amount of a peasant's farm implements, cattle, etc., shall be exempt from levy and distraint; yet you cannot ensure him against an emergency in which he is compelled to sell his cattle "voluntarily," in which he must sign himself away body and soul to the usurer and be glad to get a reprieve. Your attempt to protect the small peasant in his property does not protect his liberty but only the particular form of his servitude; it prolongs a situation in which he can neither live nor die. It is, therefore, entirely out of place here to cite the first paragraph of your programme as authority for your contention.

The preamble states that in present-day France the means of production, that is, the land, is in very many localities still in the hands of individual producers as their individual possession; that, however, it is not the task of socialism to separate property from labour, but, on the contrary, to unite these two factors of all production by placing them in the same hands. As has already been pointed out, the latter in this general form is by no means the task of socialism. The latter's task is rather only to transfer the means of production to the producers as their *common possession*. As soon as we lose sight of this the above statement becomes directly misleading in that it implies that it is the mission of socialism to convert the present sham property of the small peasant in his fields into real property, that is to say, to convert the small tenant into an owner and the indebted owner into a debtless owner. Undoubtedly socialism is interested to see that the false semblance of peasant property should disappear, but not in this manner.

At any rate we have now got so far that the preamble can straightforwardly declare it to be the duty of socialism, indeed, its imperative duty,

"to maintain the peasants living by their own labour in possession of the same as against the fisk, the usurer and the encroachments of the newly-arisen big landowners."

The preamble thus imposes upon socialism the imperative duty to carry out something which it had declared to be impossible in the preceding paragraph. It charges it to "maintain" the small-holding ownership of the peasants although it itself states that this form of ownership is "irretrievably doomed." What are the fisk, the usurer and the newly-arisen big landowners if not the instruments by means of which capitalist production brings about this inevitable doom? What means "socialism" is to employ to protect the peasant against this trinity we shall see below.

But not only the small peasant is to be protected in his property. It is likewise

"expedient to extend this protection also to the producers who as tenants or share croppers (*métayers*) cultivate land owned by others and who, if they exploit day labourers, are to a certain extent compelled to do so because of the exploitation to which they themselves are subjected."

Here we are entering upon ground that is passing strange. Socialism is particularly opposed to the exploitation of wage labour. And here it is declared to be the imperative duty of socialism to protect the French tenants when they "*exploit* day labourers," as the text literally states! And that because they are compelled to do so to a certain extent "by the exploitation to which they themselves are subjected"!

How easy and pleasant it is to keep on coasting once you are on the toboggan slide! When now the big and middle peasants of Germany come to ask the French Socialists to intercede with the German Party Executive to get the German Social-Democratic Party to protect them in the exploitation of their male and female farm servants, citing in support of their contention the "exploitation to which they themselves are subjected" by usurers, tax collectors, grain speculators and cattle dealers, what will they answer? What guarantee have they that our agrarian big landlords will not send them Count Kanitz (as he also submitted a proposal like theirs providing for a state monopoly of grain importation) and likewise ask for socialist protection of their exploitation of the rural workers, citing in support "the exploitation to which they themselves are subjected" by stock-jobbers, money lenders and grain speculators?

Let us say here at the outset that the intentions of our French friends are not as bad as one would suppose. The above sentence, we are told, is intended to cover only a quite special case, namely the following: In Northern France, just as in our sugar-beet districts, land is leased to the peasants subject to the obligation to cultivate beets, on conditions which are extremely onerous. They must deliver the beets to a stated factory at a price fixed by it, must buy definite seed, use a fixed quantity of prescribed fertiliser and on delivery are badly cheated into the bargain. We know all about this in

Germany, as well. But if this sort of peasant is to be taken under one's wing this must be said openly and expressly. As the sentence reads now, in its unlimited general form, it is a direct violation not only of the French programme but also of the fundamental principle of socialism in general, and its authors will have no cause for complaint if this careless piece of editing is used against them in various quarters contrary to their intention.

Also capable of such misconstruction are the concluding words of the preamble according to which it is the task of the Socialist Workers' Party

"to bring together all the elements of rural production, all occupations which by virtue of various rights and titles utilise the national soil, to wage an identical struggle against the common foe: the feudality of landownership."

I flatly deny that the socialist workers' party of any country is charged with the task of taking into its fold, in addition to the rural proletarians and the small peasants, also the middle and big peasants and perhaps even the tenants of big estates, the capitalist cattle breeders and the other capitalist exploiters of the national soil. To all of them the feudality of landownership may appear to be a common foe. On certain questions we may make common cause with them and be able to fight side by side with them for definite aims. We can use in our Party individuals from every class of society, but have no use whatever for any groups representing capitalist, middle-bourgeois or middle-peasant interests. Here too what they mean is not as bad as it looks. The authors evidently never even gave all this a thought. But unfortunately they allowed themselves to be carried away by their zeal for generalisation and they must not be surprised if they are taken at their word.

After the preamble come the newly-adopted addenda to the programme itself. They betray the same cursory editing as the preamble.

The article providing that the communities must procure farming machinery and lease it at cost to the peasants is modified so as to provide that the communities are, in the first place, to receive state subsidies for this purpose and, secondly, that the machinery is to be placed at the disposal of the small peasants gratis. This further concession will not be of much avail to the small peasants, whose fields and mode of production permit of but little use of machinery.

Furthermore,

substitution of a single progressive tax on all incomes upward of 3,000 francs for all existing direct and indirect taxes.

A similar demand has been included for many years in almost every Social-Democratic programme. But that this demand is raised in the special interests of the small peasants is something new and shows only how little its real scope has been calculated. Take Great

Britain. There the state budget amounts to 90 million pounds sterling, of which $13^{1}/_{2}$ to 14 million are accounted for by the income tax. The smaller part of the remaining 76 million is contributed by taxing business (post and telegraph charges, stamp tax), but by far the greater part of it by imposts on articles of mass consumption, by the constantly repeated clipping of small, imperceptible amounts totalling many millions from the incomes of all members of the population, but particularly of its poorer sections. In present-day society it is scarcely possible to defray state expenditures in any other way. Suppose the whole 90 million are saddled in Great Britain on the incomes of 120 pounds sterling=3,000 francs and in excess thereof by the imposition of a progressive direct tax. The average annual accumulation, the annual increase of the aggregate national wealth, amounted in 1865 to 1875, according to Giffen, to 240 million pounds sterling. Let us assume it now equals 300 million annually; a tax burden of 90 million would consume almost one-third of the aggregate accumulation. In other words, no government except a Socialist one can undertake any such thing. When the Socialists are at the helm there will be things for them to carry into execution alongside of which that tax reform will figure as a mere, and quite insignificant, settlement for the moment while altogether different prospects open up before the small peasants.

One seems to realise that the peasants will have to wait rather long for this tax reform so that "in the meantime" (*en attendant*) the following prospect is held out to them:

"abolition of taxes on land for all peasants living by their own labour, and reduction of these taxes on all mortgaged plots."

The latter half of this demand can refer only to peasant farms *too big* to be operated by the family itself; hence it is again a provision in favour of peasants who "exploit day labourers."
Again:

"hunting and fishing rights without restrictions other than such as may be necessary for the conservation of game and fish and the protection of growing crops."

This sounds very popular but the concluding part of the sentence wipes out the introductory part. How many rabbits, partridges, pikes and carps are there even today per peasant family in all the rural localities? Would you say more than would warrant giving each peasant just *one* day a year for free hunting and fishing?

"Lowering of the legal and conventional rate of interest"—

hence renewed usury laws, a renewed attempt to introduce a police measure that has always failed everywhere for the last two thousand years. If a small peasant finds himself in a position where recourse to a usurer is the lesser evil to him, the usurer will always find ways and means of sucking him dry without falling foul of the usury laws. This measure could serve at most to soothe the small peasant but he will derive no advantage from it; on the contrary, it makes it more difficult for him to obtain credit precisely when he needs it most.

"Medical service free of charge and medicines at cost price"—

This at any rate is not a measure for the special protection of the peasants. The German programme goes further and demands that medicine too should be free of charge.

"Compensation for families of reservists called up for military duty for the duration of their service"—

This already exists, though most inadequately, in Germany and Austria and is likewise no special peasant demand.

"Lowering of the transport charges for fertiliser and farm machinery and products"—

is on the whole in effect in Germany, and mainly in the interests— of the big landowners.

"Immediate preparatory work for the elaboration of a plan of public works for the amelioration of the soil and the development of agricultural production"—

leaves everything in the realm of uncertitude and beautiful promises and is also above all in the interest of the big landed estates.

In brief, after the tremendous theoretical effort exhibited in the preamble the practical proposals of the new agrarian programme are even more unrevealing as to the way in which the French Workers' Party expects to be able to maintain the small peasants in possession of their small holdings, which, on its own testimony, are irretrievably doomed.

II

In one point our French comrades are absolutely right: No lasting revolutionary transformation is possible in France *against* the will of the small peasant. Only it seems to me they have not got the right leverage if they mean to bring the peasant under their influence.

They are bent, it seems, to win over the small peasant forthwith, possibly even for the next general elections. This they can hope to achieve only by making very risky general assurances in defence of which they are compelled to set forth even much more risky theoretical considerations. Then, upon closer examination, it appears that the general assurances are self-contradictory (promise to maintain a state of affairs which, as one declares oneself, is irretrievably doomed) and that the various measures are either wholly without effect (usury-laws), or are general workers' demands or demands which also benefit the big landowners or finally are such as are of no great importance by any means in promoting the interests of the small peasants. In consequence, the directly practical part of the programme of itself corrects the erroneous initial part and reduces the apparently formidable grandiloquence of the preamble to actually innocent proportions.

Let us say it outright: in view of the prejudices arising out of their entire economic position, their upbringing and their isolated mode of life, prejudices nurtured by the bourgeois press and the big landowners, we can win the mass of the small peasants forthwith only if we make them a promise which we ourselves know we shall not be able to keep. That is, we must promise them not only to protect their property in any event against all economic forces sweeping upon them but also to relieve them of the burdens which already now oppress them: to transform the tenant into a free owner and to pay the debts of the owner succumbing to the weight of his mortgage.[155] If we could do this we should again arrive at the point from which the present situation would necessarily develop anew. We shall not have emancipated the peasant but only given him a reprieve.

But it is not in our interests to win the peasant overnight only to lose him again on the morrow if we cannot keep our promise. We have no more use for the peasant as a Party member if he expects us to perpetuate his property in his small holding than for the small handicraftsman who would fain be perpetuated as a master. These people belong to the anti-Semites. Let them go to them and let them promise to salvage their small enterprises. Once they learn there what these glittering phrases really amount to and what melodies are fiddled down from the anti-Semitic heavens they will realise in ever-increasing measure that we who promise less and look for salvation in entirely different quarters are after all more reliable people. If the French had the strident anti-Semitic demagogy we have they would hardly have committed the Nantes mistake.

What, then, is our attitude towards the small peasantry? How shall we have to deal with it on the day of our accession to power?

To begin with, the French programme is absolutely correct in stating: that we foresee the inevitable doom of the small peasant but that it is not our mission to hasten it by any interference on our part.

Secondly, it is just as evident that when we are in possession of state power we shall not even think of forcibly expropriating the small peasants (regardless of whether with or without compensation), as we shall have to do in the case of the big landowners. Our task relative to the small peasant consists, in the first place, in

:ffecting a transition of his private enterprise and private possession
o co-operative ones, not forcibly but by dint of example and the
)roffer of social assistance for this purpose. And then of course we
hall have ample means of showing to the small peasant prospective
idvantages that must be obvious to him even today.

Almost twenty years ago the Danish Socialists, who have only
)ne real city in their country—Copenhagen—and therefore have to
ely almost exclusively on peasant propaganda outside of it, were
ilready drawing up such plans. The peasants of a village or parish
—there are many big individual homesteads in Denmark—were
,o pool their land to form a single big farm in order to cultivate it
or common account and distribute the yield in proportion to the
and, money and labour contributed. In Denmark small landed
)roperty plays only a secondary role. But if we apply this idea to
i region of small holdings we shall find that if these are pooled
ind the aggregate area cultivated on a large scale, part of the la-
)our power employed hitherto is rendered superfluous. It is pre-
:isely this saving of labour that represents one of the main ad-
/antages of large-scale farming. Employment can be found for this
abour power in two ways. Either additional land taken from big
estates in the neighbourhood is placed at the disposal of the peasant
:o-operative or the peasants in question are provided with the
means and the opportunity of engaging in industry as an accessory
:alling, primarily and as far as possible for their own use. In either
:ase their economic position is improved and simultaneously the
general social directing agency is assured the necessary influence
:o transform the peasant co-operative to a higher form, and to
equalise the rights and duties of the co-operative as a whole as
well as of its individual members with those of the other departments of the entire community. How this is to be carried out in
practice in each particular case will depend upon the circumstances
of the case and the conditions under which we take possession of
political power. We may thus possibly be in a position to offer these
co-operatives yet further advantages: assumption of their entire
mortgage indebtedness by the national bank with a simultaneous
sharp reduction of the interest rate; advances from public funds
for the establishment of large-scale production (to be made not
necessarily or primarily in money but in the form of required products: machinery, artificial fertiliser, etc.), and other advantages.

The main point is and will be to make the peasants understand
that we can save, preserve their houses and fields for them only by
transforming them into co-operative property operated co-operative-
ly. It is precisely the individual farming conditioned by individual
ownership that drives the peasants to their doom. If they insist on
individual operation they will inevitably be driven from house and
home and their antiquated mode of production superseded by

capitalist large-scale production. That is how the matter stands. Now
we come along and offer the peasants the opportunity of introducing
large-scale production themselves, not for account of the capitalist
but for their own, common account. Should it really be impossible
to make the peasants understand that this is in their own interest
that it is the sole means of their salvation?

Neither now nor at any time in the future can we promise the
small-holding peasants to preserve their individual property and in
dividual enterprise against the overwhelming power of capitalist
production. We can only promise them that we shall not interfere
in their property relations by force, against their will. Moreover, we
can advocate that the struggle of the capitalists and big landlord
against the small peasants should be waged from now on with a
minimum of unfair means and that direct robbery and cheating
which are practised only too often, be as far as possible prevented
In this we shall succeed only in exceptional cases. Under the
developed capitalist mode of production nobody can tell where
honesty ends and cheating begins. But always it will make a considerable difference whether public authority is on the side of the cheater
or the cheated. We of course are decidedly on the side of the small
peasant; we shall do everything at all permissible to make his lot
more bearable, to facilitate his transition to the co-operative should
he decide to do so, and even to make it possible for him to remain
on his small holding for a protracted length of time to think the
matter over, should he still be unable to bring himself to this decision. We do this not only because we consider the small peasant
living by his own labour as virtually belonging to us, but also in
the direct interest of the Party. The greater the number of peasants
whom we can save from being actually hurled down into the proletariat, whom we can win to our side while they are still peasants,
the more quickly and easily the social transformation will be accomplished. It will serve us nought to wait with this transformation
until capitalist production has developed everywhere to its utmost
consequences, until the last small handicraftsman and the last small
peasant have fallen victim to capitalist large-scale production. The
material sacrifice to be made for this purpose in the interest of
the peasants and to be defrayed out of public funds can, from the
point of view of capitalist economy, be viewed only as money
thrown away, but it is nevertheless an excellent investment because
it will effect a perhaps tenfold saving in the cost of the social reorganisation in general. In this sense we can, therefore, afford to
deal very liberally with the peasants. This is not the place to go
into details, to make concrete proposals to that end; here we can
deal only with general principles.

Accordingly we can do no greater disservice to the Party as well
as to the small peasants than to make promises that even only

eate the impression that we intend to preserve the small holdings
ermanently. It would mean directly to block the way of the
easants to their emancipation and to degrade the Party to the
vel of rowdy anti-Semitism. On the contrary, it is the duty of our
arty to make clear to the peasants again and again that their posi-
on is absolutely hopeless as long as capitalism holds sway, that
is absolutely impossible to preserve their small holdings for them
such, that capitalist large-scale production is absolutely sure
run over their impotent antiquated system of small production
s a train runs over a pushcart. If we do this we shall act in con-
ormity with the inevitable trend of economic development, and this
evelopment will not fail to bring our words home to the small
easants.

Incidentally, I cannot leave this subject without expressing my
onviction that the authors of the Nantes programme are also es-
entially of my opinion. Their insight is much too great for them
ot to know that areas now divided into small holdings are also
ound to become common property. They themselves admit that
mall-holding ownership is destined to disappear. The report of
he National Council drawn up by Lafargue and delivered at the
Congress of Nantes likewise fully corroborates this view. It has
een published in German in the Berlin *Sozialdemokrat* of October
8 of this year.[426] The contradictory nature of the expressions used
n the Nantes programme itself betrays the fact that what the
uthors actually say is not what they want to say. If they are not
nderstood and their statements misused, as actually has already
appened, that is of course their own fault. At any rate, they will
ave to elucidate their programme and the next French congress
evise it thoroughly.

We now come to the bigger peasants. Here as a result of the
divisions of inheritance as well as of indebtedness and forced sales
of land we find a variegated pattern of intermediate stages, from
mall-holding peasant to big peasant proprietor, who has retained
is old patrimony intact or even added to it. Where the middle
peasant lives among small-holding peasants his interests and views
will not differ greatly from theirs; he knows from his own experience how many of his kind have already sunk to the level of
mall peasants. But where middle and big peasants predominate
and the operation of the farms requires, generally, the help of male
and female servants it is quite a different matter. Of course a
workers' party has to fight, in the first place, on behalf of the wage-
workers, that is, for the male and female servantry and the day
labourers. It is unquestionably forbidden to make any promises to
the peasants which include the continuance of the wage slavery of
the workers. But as long as the big and middle peasants continue to
exist as such they cannot manage without wage-workers. If it

would, therefore, be downright folly on our part to hold out pr
spects to the small-holding peasants of continuing permanently
be such, it would border on treason were we to promise the san
to the big and middle peasants.

We have here again the parallel case of the handicraftsmen
the cities. True, they are more ruined than the peasants but the:
still are some who employ journeymen in addition to apprentic
or for whom apprentices do the work of journeymen. Let those
these master craftsmen who want to perpetuate their existence
such cast in their lot with the anti-Semites until they have co
vinced themselves that they get no help in that quarter either. T
rest, who have realised that their mode of production is inevitab
doomed, are coming over to us and, moreover, are ready in futu
to share the lot that is in store for all other workers. The sam
applies to the big and middle peasants. It goes without saying th:
we are more interested in their male and female servants and da
labourers than in them themselves. If these peasants want to k
guaranteed the continued existence of their enterprises we are i
no position whatever to assure them of that. They must then tak
their place among the anti-Semites, peasant leaguers and simila
parties who derive pleasure from promising everything and keepin
nothing. We are economically certain that the big and midd
peasant must likewise inevitably succumb to the competition o
capitalist production and the cheap overseas corn, as is proved b
the growing indebtedness and the everywhere evident decay of thes
peasants as well. We can do nothing against this decay except ,re
commend here too the pooling of farms to form co-operative enter
prises, in which the exploitation of wage labour will be eliminate
more and more, and their gradual transformation into branches o
the great national producers' co-operative with each branch enjoy
ing equal rights and duties can be instituted. If these peasant
realise the inevitability of the doom of their present mode of pro
duction and draw the necessary conclusions they will come to u
and it will be incumbent upon us to facilitate to the best of ou
ability also their transition to the changed mode of production
Otherwise we shall have to abandon them to their fate and addres:
ourselves to their wage-workers, among whom we shall not fail tc
find sympathy. Most likely we shall be able to abstain here as wel
from resorting to forcible expropriation, and as for the rest to coun
on future economic developments making also these harder pates
amenable to reason.

Only the big landed estates present a perfectly simple case. Here
we are dealing with undisguised capitalist production and nc
scruples of any sort need restrain us. Here we are confronted by
rural proletarians in masses and our task is clear. As soon as our
Party is in possession of political power it has simply to expropriate

he big landed proprietors just like the manufacturers in industry. Whether this expropriation is to be compensated for or not will to great extent depend not upon us but the circumstances under which we obtain power, and particularly upon the attitude adopted by these gentry, the big landowners, themselves. We by no means consider compensation as impermissible in any event; Marx told me and how many times!) that in his opinion we would get off cheapest if we could buy out the whole lot of them. But this does not concern us here. The big estates thus restored to the community are to be turned over by us to the rural workers who are already cultivating them and are to be organised into co-operatives. They are to be assigned to them for their use and benefit under the control of the community. Nothing can as yet be stated as to the terms of their tenure. At any rate the transformation of the capitalist enterprise into a social enterprise is here fully prepared for and can be carried into execution overnight, precisely as in Mr. Krupp's or Mr. von Stumm's factory. And the example of these agricultural co-operatives would convince also the last of the still resistant small-holding peasants, and surely also many big peasants, of the advantages of co-operative, large-scale production.

Thus we can open up prospects here before the rural proletarians as splendid as those facing the industrial workers, and it can be only a question of time, and of only a very short time, before we win over to our side the rural workers of Prussia east of the Elbe. But once we have the East-Elbe rural workers a different wind will blow at once all over Germany. The actual semi-servitude of the East-Elbe rural workers is the main basis of the domination of Prussian Junkerdom[19] and thus of Prussia's specific overlordship in Germany. It is the Junkers east of the Elbe who have created and preserved the specifically Prussian character of the bureaucracy as well as of the body of army officers—the Junkers, who are being reduced more and more to ruin by their indebtedness, impoverishment and parasitism at state and private cost and for that very reason cling the more desperately to the dominion which they exercise; the Junkers, whose haughtiness, bigotry and arrogance have brought the German Reich of the Prussian nation[158] within the country into such hatred—even when every allowance is made for the fact that at present this Reich is inevitable as the sole form in which national unity can now be attained—and abroad so little respect despite its brilliant victories. The power of these Junkers is grounded on the fact that within the compact territory of the seven old Prussian provinces—that is, approximately one-third of the entire territory of the Reich—they have at their disposal the landed property, which here brings with it both social and political power. And not only the landed property but, through their beet-sugar refineries and liquor distilleries, also the most important in-

dustries of this area. Neither the big landowners of the rest
Germany nor the big industrialists are in a similarly favourab
position. Neither of them have a compact kingdom at their disposa
Both are scattered over a wide stretch of territory and compe
among themselves and with other social elements surrounding the
for economic and political predominance. But the economic founda
tion of this domination of the Prussian Junkers is steadily dete
riorating. Here too indebtedness and impoverishment are spreadin
irresistibly despite all state assistance (and since Frederick II th
item is included in every regular Junker budget). Only the actua
semi-serfdom sanctioned by law and custom, and the resulting po
sibility of the unlimited exploitation of the rural workers, sti
barely keeps the drowning Junkers above water. Sow the seed
Social-Democracy among these workers, give them the courage an
cohesion to insist upon their rights, and the glory of the Junke
will be at an end. The great reactionary power, which to German
represents the same barbarous, predatory element as Russian tsar
dom does to the whole of Europe, will collapse like a pricked bubble
The "picked regiments" of the Prussian army will become Socia
Democratic, which will result in a shift in power that is pregnan
with an entire upheaval. But for this reason it is of vastly greate
importance to win the rural proletariat east of the Elbe than th
small peasants of Western Germany or yet the middle peasants o
Southern Germany. It is here, in East-Elbe Prussia, that the de
cisive battle of our cause will have to be fought and for this ver
reason both government and Junkerdom will do their utmost t
prevent our gaining access here. And should, as we are threatened
new violent measures be resorted to to impede the spread of ou
Party, their primary purpose will be to protect the East-Elbe rura
proletariat from our propaganda. It's all the same to us. We sha
win it nevertheless.

Written between November 15
and 22, 1894

Published in the journal
Die Neue Zeit, Bd. 1, No. 10,
1894-95
Signed: *Friedrich Engels*

Printed according to the tex
of the journal
Translated from the Germa

FREDERICK ENGELS

INTRODUCTION TO KARL MARX'S WORK
THE CLASS STRUGGLES IN FRANCE,
1848 TO 1850[427]

The work here republished was Marx's first attempt to explain a section of contemporary history by means of his materialist conception, on the basis of the given economic situation. In the *Communist Manifesto*, the theory was applied in broad outline to the whole of modern history; in the articles by Marx and myself in the *Neue Rheinische Zeitung*,[27] it was constantly used to interpret political events of the day. Here, on the other hand, the question was to demonstrate the inner causal connection in the course of a development which extended over some years, a development as critical, for the whole of Europe, as it was typical; hence, in accordance with the conception of the author, to trace political events back to effects of what were, in the final analysis, economic causes.

If events and series of events are judged by current history, it will never be possible to go back to the *ultimate* economic causes. Even today, when the specialised press concerned provides such rich material, it still remains impossible even in England to follow day by day the movement of industry and trade in the world market and the changes which take place in the methods of production in such a way as to be able to draw a general conclusion, for any point of time, from these manifold, complicated and ever-changing factors, the most important of which, into the bargain, generally operate a long time in secret before they suddenly make themselves violently felt on the surface. A clear survey of the economic history of a given period can never be obtained contemporaneously, but only subsequently, after a collecting and sifting of the material has taken place. Statistics are a necessary auxiliary means here, and they always lag behind. For this reason, it is only too often necessary, in current history, to treat this, the most decisive, factor as constant, and the economic situation existing at the beginning of the period concerned as given and unalterable for the whole period, or else to take notice of only such changes in this situation as arise out of the patently manifest events themselves, and are, therefore, likewise patently manifest. Hence, the materialist method has here quite often to limit itself to tracing political conflicts back to the struggles between the interests of the existing social classes and fractions of classes created by the economic development, and to prove the particular political parties to be the more or less adequate political expression of these same classes and fractions of classes.

It is self-evident that this unavoidable neglect of contemporaneous changes in the economic situation, the very basis of all the processes to be examined, must be a source of error. But all the conditions of a comprehensive presentation of current history unavoidably include sources of error—which, however, keeps nobody from writing current history.

When Marx undertook this work, the source of error mentioned was even more unavoidable. It was simply impossible during the period of the Revolution of 1848-49 to follow up the economic transformations taking place at the same time or even to keep them in view. It was the same during the first months of exile in London, in the autumn and winter of 1849-50. But that was just the time when Marx began this work. And in spite of these unfavourable circumstances, his exact knowledge both of the economic situation in France before, and of the political history of that country after the February Revolution made it possible for him to give a picture of events which laid bare their inner connections in a way never attained ever since, and which later brilliantly stood the double test applied by Marx himself.

The first test resulted from the fact that after the spring of 1850 Marx once again found leisure for economic studies, and first of all took up the economic history of the last ten years. Thereby what he had hitherto deduced, half *a priori*, from gappy material, became absolutely clear to him from the facts themselves, namely, that the world trade crisis of 1847 had been the true mother of the February and March Revolutions, and that the industrial prosperity, which had been returning gradually since the middle of 1848 and attained full bloom in 1849 and 1850, was the revitalising force of the newly strengthened European reaction. That was decisive. Whereas in the first three articles* (which appeared in the January, February and March issues of the *Neue Rheinische Zeitung. Politisch-ökonomische Revue*,[146] Hamburg, 1850) there was still the expectation of an early new upsurge of revolutionary energy, the historical review written by Marx and myself for the last issue, a double issue (May to October), which was published in the autumn of 1850, breaks once and for all with these illusions: "A new revolution is possible only in the wake of a new crisis. It is, however, just as certain as this crisis."** But that was the only es-

---

* K. Marx, *The Class Struggles in France, 1848 to 1850* (see Marx and Engels, *Selected Works*, Vol. I, Moscow, 1962, pp. 139-227).—*Ed.*
** Ibid., p. 231.—*Ed.*

sential change which had to be made. There was absolutely nothing to alter in the interpretation of events given in the earlier chapters, or in the causal connections established therein, as the continuation of the narrative from March 10 up to the autumn of 1850 in the review in question proves. I have, therefore, included this continuation as the fourth article in the present new edition.

The second test was even more severe. Immediately after Louis Bonaparte's *coup d'état* of December 2, 1851,[40] Marx worked out anew the history of France from February 1848 up to this event, which concluded the revolutionary period for the time being. (*The Eighteenth Brumaire of Louis Bonaparte.* Third edition, Hamburg, Meissner, 1885.*) In this pamphlet the period depicted in our present publication is again dealt with, although more briefly. Compare this second presentation, written in the light of the decisive event which happened over a year later, with ours and it will be found that the author had very little to change.

What, besides, gives our work quite special significance is the circumstance that it was the first to express the formula in which, by common agreement, the workers' parties of all countries in the world briefly summarise their demand for economic transformation: the appropriation of the means of production by society. In the second chapter, in connection with the "right to work," which is characterised as "the first clumsy formula wherein the revolutionary demands of the proletariat are summarised," it is said: "But behind the right to work stands the power over capital; behind the power over capital, the *appropriation of the means of production*, their subjection to the associated working class and, therefore, the abolition of wage labour as well as of capital and of their mutual relations."** Thus, here, for the first time, the proposition is formulated by which modern workers' socialism is equally sharply differentiated both from all the different shades of feudal, bourgeois, petty-bourgeois, etc., socialism and also from the confused community of goods of utopian and of spontaneous workers' communism. If, later, Marx extended the formula to include appropriation of the means of exchange, this extension, which in any case was self-evident after the *Communist Manifesto*, only expressed a corollary to the main proposition. A few wiseacres in England have of late added that the "means of distribution" should also be handed over to society. It would be difficult for these gentlemen to say what these economic means of distribution are, as distinct from the means of production and exchange; unless *political* means of distribution are meant, taxes, poor relief, including the *Sachsenwald*[428] and other

---

* See pp. 96-179 of this volume.—*Ed.*
** K. Marx, *The Class Struggles in France, 1848 to 1850* (see Marx and Engels, *Selected Works*, Vol. I, Moscow, 1962, p. 171).—*Ed.*

endowments. But, first, these are already now means of distribution in possession of society in the aggregate, either of the state or of the community, and secondly, it is precisely the abolition of these that we desire.

* * *

When the February Revolution broke out, all of us, as far as our conceptions of the conditions and the course of revolutionary movements were concerned, were under the spell of previous historical experience, particularly that of France. It was, indeed, the latter which had dominated the whole of European history since 1789, and from which now once again the signal had gone forth for general revolutionary change. It was, therefore, natural and unavoidable that our conceptions of the nature and the course of the "social" revolution proclaimed in Paris in February 1848, of the revolution of the proletariat, should be strongly coloured by memories of the prototypes of 1789 and 1830. Moreover, when the Paris uprising found its echo in the victorious insurrections in Vienna, Milan and Berlin; when the whole of Europe right up to the Russian frontier was swept into the movement; when thereupon in Paris, in June, the first great battle for power between the proletariat and the bourgeoisie was fought; when the very victory of its class so shook the bourgeoisie of all countries that it fled back into the arms of the monarchist-feudal reaction which had just been overthrown—there could be no doubt for us, under the circumstances then obtaining, that the great decisive combat had commenced, that it would have to be fought out in a single, long and vicissitudinous period of revolution, but that it could only end in the final victory of the proletariat.

After the defeats of 1849 we in no way shared the illusions of the vulgar democracy grouped around the future provisional governments *in partibus*.[53] This vulgar democracy reckoned on a speedy and finally decisive victory of the "people" over the "tyrants"; we looked to a long struggle, after the removal of the "tyrants," among the antagonistic elements concealed within this "people" itself. Vulgar democracy expected a renewed outbreak any day; we declared as early as autumn 1850 that at least the *first* chapter of the revolutionary period was closed and that nothing was to be expected until the outbreak of a new world economic crisis. For which reason we were excommunicated, as traitors to the revolution, by the very people who later, almost without exception, made their peace with Bismarck—so far as Bismarck found them worth the trouble.

But history has shown us too to have been wrong, has revealed our point of view of that time to have been an illusion. It has done even more: it has not merely dispelled the erroneous notions

ve then held; it has also completely transformed the conditions
under which the proletariat has to fight. The mode of struggle of
1848 is today obsolete in every respect, and this is a point which
deserves closer examination on the present occasion.

All revolutions up to the present day have resulted in the displacement of one definite class rule by another; but all ruling classes
up to now have been only small minorities in relation to the
ruled mass of the people. One ruling minority was thus overthrown;
another minority seized the helm of state in its stead and re-
fashioned the state institutions to suit its own interests. This was
on every occasion the minority group qualified and called to rule
by the given degree of economic development; and just for that
reason, and only for that reason, it happened that the ruled majority
either participated in the revolution for the benefit of the former
or else calmly acquiesced in it. But if we disregard the concrete
content in each case, the common form of all these revolutions was
that they were minority revolutions. Even when the majority took
part, it did so—whether wittingly or not—only in the service of a
minority; but because of this, or even simply because of the passive,
unresisting attitude of the majority, this minority acquired the appearance of being the representative of the whole people.

As a rule, after the first great success, the victorious minority
divided; one half was satisfied with what had been gained, the other
wanted to go still further, and put forward new demands, which,
partly at least, were also in the real or apparent interest of the great
mass of the people. In individual cases these more radical demands
were actually forced through, but often only for the moment; the
more moderate party would regain the upper hand, and what had
last been won would wholly or partly be lost again; the vanquished
would then shriek of treachery or ascribe their defeat to accident.
In reality, however, the truth of the matter was largely this: the
achievements of the first victory were only safeguarded by the
second victory of the more radical party; this having been attained, and, with it, what was necessary for the moment, the radicals
and their achievements vanished once more from the stage.

All revolutions of modern times, beginning with the great English
Revolution of the seventeenth century, showed these features,
which appeared inseparable from every revolutionary struggle.
They appeared applicable, also, to the struggle of the proletariat for
its emancipation; all the more applicable, since precisely in 1848
there were but a very few people who had any idea at all of the
direction in which this emancipation was to be sought. The proletarian masses themselves, even in Paris, after the victory, were
still absolutely in the dark as to the path to be taken. And yet the
movement was there, instinctive, spontaneous, irrepressible. Was
not this just the situation in which a revolution had to succeed, led,

true, by a minority, but this time not in the interest of the minority
but in the veriest interest of the majority? If, in all the longer revolutionary periods, it was so easy to win the great masses of the
people by the merely plausible false representations of the forward-
thrusting minorities, why should they be less susceptible to ideas
which were the truest reflection of their economic condition, which
were nothing but the clear, rational expression of their needs, of
needs not yet understood but merely vaguely felt by them? To be
sure, this revolutionary mood of the masses had almost always, and
usually very speedily, given way to lassitude or even to a revulsion
of feeling as soon as illusion evaporated and disappointment set in.
But here it was not a question of false representations, but of giving
effect to the highest special interests of the great majority itself,
interests which, true, were at that time by no means clear to this
great majority, but which soon enough had to become clear to it
in the course of giving practical effect to them, by their convincing
obviousness. And when, as Marx showed in his third article, in the
spring of 1850, the development of the bourgeois republic that arose
out of the "social" Revolution of 1848 had even concentrated real
power in the hands of the big bourgeoisie—monarchistically inclined
as it was into the bargain—and, on the other hand, had grouped
all the other social classes, peasantry as well as petty bourgeoisie,
round the proletariat, so that, during and after the common victory,
not they but the proletariat grown wise by experience had to become the decisive factor—was there not every prospect then of
turning the revolution of the minority into a revolution of the
majority?

History has proved us, and all who thought like us, wrong. It
has made it clear that the state of economic development on the
Continent at that time was not, by a long way, ripe for the elimination of capitalist production; it has proved this by the economic revolution which, since 1848, has seized the whole of the Continent,
and has caused big industry to take real root in France, Austria,
Hungary, Poland and, recently, in Russia, while it has made
Germany positively an industrial country of the first rank—all on
a capitalist basis, which in the year 1848, therefore, still had great
capacity for expansion. But it is just this industrial revolution which
has everywhere produced clarity in class relations, has removed a
number of intermediate forms handed down from the period of
manufacture and in Eastern Europe even from guild handicraft,
has created a genuine bourgeoisie and a genuine large-scale industrial proletariat and has pushed them into the foreground of social
development. However, owing to this, the struggle between these
two great classes, a struggle which, apart from England, existed
in 1848 only in Paris and, at the most, in a few big industrial
centres, has spread over the whole of Europe and reached an in-

ensity still inconceivable in 1848. At that time the many obscure evangels of the sects, with their panaceas; today the *one* generally recognised, crystal-clear theory of Marx, sharply formulating the ultimate aims of the struggle. At that time the masses, sundered and differing according to locality and nationality, linked only by the feeling of common suffering, undeveloped, helplessly tossed to and fro from enthusiasm to despair; today the *one* great international army of Socialists, marching irresistibly on and growing daily in number, organisation, discipline, insight and certainty of victory. If even this mighty army of the proletariat has still not reached its goal, if, far from winning victory by one mighty stroke, it has slowly to press forward from position to position in a hard, tenacious struggle, this only proves, once and for all, how impossible it was in 1848 to win social transformation by a simple surprise attack.

A bourgeoisie split into two dynastic-monarchist sections,[429] a bourgeoisie, however, which demanded, above all, peace and security for its financial operations, faced by a proletariat vanquished, indeed, but still always a menace, a proletariat round which petty bourgeois and peasants grouped themselves more and more—the continual threat of a violent outbreak, which, nevertheless, offered absolutely no prospect of a final solution—such was the situation, as if specially created for the *coup d'état* of the third, the pseudo-democratic pretender, Louis Bonaparte. On December 2, 1851, by means of the army, he put an end to the tense situation and secured Europe domestic tranquillity in order to confer upon it the blessing of a new era of wars.[430] The period of revolutions from below was concluded for the time being; there followed a period of revolutions from above.

The reversion to the empire in 1851 gave new proof of the unripeness of the proletarian aspirations of that time. But it was itself to create the conditions under which they were bound to ripen. Internal tranquillity ensured the full development of the new industrial boom; the necessity of keeping the army occupied and of diverting the revolutionary currents outwards produced the wars in which Bonaparte, under the pretext of asserting "the principle of nationality,"[431] sought to hook annexations for France. His imitator, Bismarck, adopted the same policy for Prussia; he made his *coup d'état*, his revolution from above, in 1866, against the German Confederation[149] and Austria, and no less against the Prussian *Konfliktskammer*.* But Europe was too small for two Bonapartes and the irony of history so willed it that Bismarck overthrew Bonaparte, and King William of Prussia not only established the little German empire,[423] but also the French republic. The general result,

* *Konfliktskammer*, that is, the Prussian Chamber then in conflict with the government.—*Ed.*

however, was that in Europe the independence and internal unity
of the great nations, with the exception of Poland, had become a
fact. Within relatively modest limits, it is true, but, for all that
on a scale large enough to allow the development of the working
class to proceed without finding national complications any longer
a serious obstacle. The grave-diggers of the Revolution of 1848 had
become the executors of its will. And alongside of them already rose
threateningly the heir of 1848, the proletariat, in the shape of the
International.

After the war of 1870-71, Bonaparte vanishes from the stage and
Bismarck's mission is fulfilled, so that he can now sink back again
into the ordinary *Junker*. The period, however, is brought to a close
by the Paris Commune.[8] An underhand attempt by Thiers to steal
the cannon of the Paris National Guard called forth a victorious
rising.[432] It was shown once more that in Paris none but a proletarian revolution is any longer possible. After the victory power
fell, quite of itself and quite undisputed, into the hands of the
working class. And once again it was proved how impossible even
then, twenty years after the time described in our work, this rule
of the working class still was. On the one hand, France left Paris
in the lurch, looked on while it bled profusely from the bullets of
MacMahon; on the other hand, the Commune was consumed in unfruitful strife between the two parties which split it, the Blanquists
(the majority) and the Proudhonists (the minority), neither of
which knew what was to be done. The victory which came as a gift
in 1871 remained just as unfruitful as the surprise attack of 1848.

It was believed that the militant proletariat had been finally buried
with the Paris Commune. But, completely to the contrary, it dates
its most powerful resurgence from the Commune and the Franco-
Prussian War. The recruitment of the whole of the population able
to bear arms into armies that henceforth could be counted only in
millions, and the introduction of fire-arms, projectiles and explosives
of hitherto undreamt-of efficacy, created a complete revolution in
all warfare. This revolution, on the one hand, put a sudden end to
the Bonapartist war period and ensured peaceful industrial development by making any war other than a world war of unheard-of
cruelty and absolutely incalculable outcome an impossibility. On the
other hand, it caused military expenditure to rise in geometrical
progression and thereby forced up taxes to exorbitant levels and so
drove the poorer classes of people into the arms of socialism. The
annexation of Alsace-Lorraine, the immediate cause of the mad competition in armaments, was able to set the French and German
bourgeoisie chauvinistically at each other's throats; for the workers
of the two countries it became a new bond of unity. And the anniversary of the Paris Commune became the first universal day of
celebration of the whole proletariat.

The war of 1870-71 and the defeat of the Commune transferred
the centre of gravity of the European workers' movement for the
time being from France to Germany, as Marx had foretold. In
France it naturally took years to recover from the blood-letting of
May 1871. In Germany, on the other hand, where industry—
fostered, in addition, in positively hothouse fashion by the blessing
of the French milliards[170]—developed more and more rapidly, Social-Democracy experienced a still more rapid and enduring growth.
Thanks to the intelligent use which the German workers made of
the universal suffrage introduced in 1866, the astonishing growth
of the party is made plain to all the world by incontestable figures:
1871, 102,000; 1874, 352,000; 1877, 493,000 Social-Democratic votes.
Then came recognition of this advance by high authority in the
shape of the Anti-Socialist Law[167]; the party was temporarily broken
up, the number of votes dropped to 312,000 in 1881. But that was
quickly overcome, and then, under the pressure of the Exceptional
Law, without a press, without a legal organisation and without the
right of combination and assembly, rapid expansion really began:
1884, 550,000; 1887, 763,000; 1890, 1,427,000 votes. Thereupon the
hand of the state was paralysed. The Anti-Socialist Law disappeared; socialist votes rose to 1,787,000, over a quarter of all the
votes cast. The government and the ruling classes had exhausted all
their expedients—uselessly, purposelessly, unsuccessfully. The tangible proofs of their impotence, which the authorities, from night
watchman to the imperial chancellor, had had to accept—and that
from the despised workers!—these proofs were counted in millions.
The state was at the end of its tether, the workers only at the beginning of theirs.

But, besides, the German workers rendered a second great service
to their cause in addition to the first, a service performed by their
mere existence as the strongest, best disciplined and most rapidly
growing Socialist Party. They supplied their comrades in all countries with a new weapon, and one of the sharpest, when they showed
them how to make use of universal suffrage.

There had long been universal suffrage in France, but it had
fallen into disrepute through the misuse to which the Bonapartist
government had put it. After the Commune there was no workers'
party to make use of it. It also existed in Spain since the republic,
but in Spain boycott of elections was ever the rule of all serious
opposition parties. The experience of the Swiss with universal suffrage was also anything but encouraging for a workers' party. The
revolutionary workers of the Latin countries had been wont to
regard the suffrage as a snare, as an instrument of government
trickery. It was otherwise in Germany. The *Communist Manifesto*
had already proclaimed the winning of universal suffrage, of democracy, as one of the first and most important tasks of the militant

proletariat, and Lassalle had again taken up this point.[1] Now, whe:
Bismarck found himself compelled to introduce this franchise[433] a
the only means of interesting the mass of the people in his plan:
our workers immediately took it in earnest and sent August Bebe
to the first, constituent Reichstag. And from that day on, they hav
used the franchise in a way which has paid thém a thousandfol
and has served as a model to the workers of all countries. Th
franchise has been, in the words of the French Marxist programm∈
*transformé, de moyen de duperie qu'il a été jusqu'ici, en instrumer.
d'émancipation*—tranformed by them from a means of deceptior
which it was before, into an instrument of emancipation.[434] And i
universal suffrage had offered no other advantage than that :
allowed us to count our numbers every three years; that by th
regularly established, unexpectedly rapid rise in the number o
our votes it increased in equal measure the workers' certainty o
victory and the dismay of their opponents, and so became our be:
means of propaganda; that it accurately informed us concerning ou
own strength and that of all hostile parties, and thereby provide
us with a measure of proportion for our actions second to non∈
safeguarding us from untimely timidity as much as from untimel
foolhardiness—if this had been the only advantage we gained fror
the suffrage, it would still have been much more than enough. Bu
it did more than this by far. In election agitation it provided us wit
a means, second to none, of getting in touch with the mass of th
people where they still stand aloof from us; of forcing all parti∈
to defend their views and actions against our attacks before all th
people; and, further, it provided our representatives in the Reich
stag with a platform from which they could speak to their opponen:
in parliament, and to the masses without, with quite other authorit
and freedom than in the press or at meetings. Of what avail wa
their Anti-Socialist Law to the government and the bourgeois
when election campaigning and socialist speeches in the Reichsta
continually broke through it?

With this successful utilisation of universal suffrage, howeve
an entirely new method of proletarian struggle came into operatior
and this method quickly developed further. It was found that th
state institutions, in which the rule of the bourgeoisie is organise
offer the working class still further opportunities to fight these ver
state institutions. The workers took part in elections to particul:
Diets, to municipal councils and to trades courts; they conteste
with the bourgeoisie every post in the occupation of which a su
ficient part of the proletariat had a say. And so it happened th:
the bourgeoisie and the government came to be much more afrai
of the legal than of the illegal action of the workers' party, of th
results of elections than of those of rebellion.

For here, too, the conditions of the struggle had essentiall changed. Rebellion in the old style, street fighting with barricades, which decided the issue everywhere up to 1848, was to a considerable extent obsolete.

Let us have no illusions about it: a real victory of an insurrection over the military in street fighting, a victory as between two armies, is one of the rarest exceptions. And the insurgents counted on it just as rarely. For them it was solely a question of making the troops yield to moral influences which, in a fight between the armies of two warring countries, do not come into play at all or do so to a much smaller extent. If they succeed in this, the troops fail to respond, or the commanding officers lose their heads, and the insurrection wins. If they do not succeed in this, then, even where the military are in the minority, the superiority of better equipment and training, of single leadership, of the planned employment of the military forces and of discipline makes itself felt. The most that an insurrection can achieve in the way of actual tactical operations is the proper construction and defence of a single barricade. Mutual support, the disposition and employment of reserves—in short, concerted and co-ordinated action of the individual detachments, indispensable even for the defence of one section of a town, not to speak of the whole of a large town, will be attainable only to a very limited extent, and most of the time not at all. Concentration of the military forces at a decisive point is, of course, out of question here. Hence passive defence is the prevailing form of fighting; the attack will rise here and there, but only by way of exception, to occasional thrusts and flank assaults; as a rule, however, it will be limited to occupation of positions abandoned by retreating troops. In addition, the military have at their disposal artillery and fully equipped corps of trained engineers, resources of war which, in nearly every case, the insurgents entirely lack. No wonder, then, that even the barricade fighting conducted with the greatest heroism—Paris, June 1848[6]; Vienna, October 1848[36]; Dresden, May 1849[30]—ended in the defeat of the insurrection as soon as the leaders of the attack, unhampered by political considerations, acted from the purely military standpoint, and their soldiers remained reliable.

The numerous successes of the insurgents up to 1848 were due to a great variety of causes. In Paris, in July 1830 and February 1848, as in most of the Spanish street fighting, a citizens' guard stood between the insurgents and the military. This guard either sided directly with the insurrection, or else by its lukewarm, indecisive attitude caused the troops likewise to vacillate, and supplied the insurrection with arms into the bargain. Where this citizens' guard opposed the insurrection from the outset, as in June 1848 in Paris, the insurrection was vanquished. In Berlin in 1848, the people were victorious partly through a considerable accession of new fighting forces during the night and the morning of [March] the 19th, partly as a result of the exhaustion and bad victualling of the troops, and, finally, partly as a result of the paralysis that was seizing the command. But in all cases the fight was won because the troops failed to respond, because the commanding officers lost the faculty to decide or because their hands were tied.

Even in the classic time of street fighting, therefore, the barricade produced more of a moral than a material effect. It was a means of shaking the steadfastness of the military. If it held out until this was attained, victory was won; if not, there was defeat. This is the main point, which must be kept in view, likewise, when the chances of possible future street fighting are examined.*

Already in 1849, these chances were pretty poor. Everywhere the bourgeoisie had thrown in its lot with the governments, "culture and property" had hailed and feasted the military moving against insurrection. The spell of the barricade was broken; the soldier no longer saw behind it "the people," but rebels, agitators, plunderers, levellers, the scum of society; the officer had in the course of time become versed in the tactical forms of street fighting, he no longer marched straight ahead and without cover against the improvised breastwork, but went round it through gardens, yards and houses. And this was now successful, with a little skill, in nine cases out of ten.

But since then there have been very many more changes, and all in favour of the military. If the big towns have become considerably bigger, the armies have become bigger still. Paris and Berlin have, since 1848, grown less than fourfold, but their garrisons have grown more than that. By means of the railways, these garrisons can, in twenty-four hours, be more than doubled, and in forty-eight hours they can be increased to huge armies. The arming of this enormously increased number of troops has become incomparably more effective. In 1848 the smooth-bore, muzzle-loading percussion gun, today the small-calibre, breech-loading magazine rifle, which shoots four times as far, ten times as accurately and ten times as fast as the former. At that time the relatively ineffective round shot and grape-shot of the artillery; today the percussion shells, of which one is sufficient to demolish the best barricade. At that time the pick-axe of the sapper for breaking through firewalls; today the dynamite cartridge.

On the other hand, all the conditions of the insurgents' side have grown worse. An insurrection with which all sections of the people sympathise will hardly recur; in the class struggle all the middle strata will probably never group themselves round the proletariat

---

* In *Die Neue Zeit* and in the 1895 edition of *The Class Struggles in France*, this sentence is omitted.—*Ed.*

so exclusively that in comparison the party of reaction gathered round the bourgeoisie will well-nigh disappear. The "people," therefore, will always appear divided, and thus a most powerful lever, so extraordinarily effective in 1848, is gone. If more soldiers who have seen service came over to the insurrectionists, the arming of them would become so much the more difficult. The hunting and fancy guns of the munitions shops—even if not previously made unusable by removal of part of the lock by order of the police— are far from being a match for the magazine rifle of the soldier, even in close fighting. Up to 1848 it was possible to make the necessary ammunition oneself out of powder and lead; today the cartridges differ for each gun, and are everywhere alike only in one point, namely, that they are a complicated product of big industry, and therefore not to be manufactured *ex tempore*, with the result that most guns are useless as long as one does not possess the ammunition specially suited to them. And, finally, since 1848 the newly built quarters of the big cities have been laid out in long, straight, broad streets, as though made to give full effect to the new cannon and rifles. The revolutionist would have to be mad who himself chose the new working-class districts in the North or East of Berlin for a barricade fight.

Does that mean that in the future street fighing will no longer play any role? Certainly not. It only means that the conditions since 1848 have become far more unfavourable for civilian fighters and far more favourable for the military. In future, street fighting can, therefore, be victorious only if this disadvantageous situation is compensated by other factors. Accordingly, it will occur more seldom in the beginning of a great revolution than in its further progress, and will have to be undertaken with greater forces. These, however, may then well prefer, as in the whole great French Revolution or on September 4[291] and October 31, 1870, in Paris,[209] the open attack to the passive barricade tactics.*

Does the reader now understand why the powers that be positively want to get us to go where the guns shoot and the sabres slash? Why they accuse us today of cowardice, because we do not betake ourselves without more ado into the street, where we are certain of defeat in advance? Why they so earnestly implore us to play for once the part of cannon fodder?

The gentlemen pour out their prayers and their challenges for nothing, for absolutely nothing. We are not so stupid. They might just as well demand from their enemy in the next war that he should accept battle in the line formation of old Fritz,** or in the

---

* In *Die Neue Zeit* and in the 1895 edition of *The Class Struggles in France*, this paragraph is omitted.—*Ed.*
** Frederick II, King of Prussia (1740-86).—*Ed.*

columns of whole divisions *à la* Wagram[435] and Waterloo,[333] and with the flint-lock in his hands at that. If conditions have changed in the case of war between nations, this is no less true in the case of the class struggle. The time of surprise attacks, of revolutions carried through by small conscious minorities at the head of unconscious masses, is past. Where it is a question of a complete transformation of the social organisation, the masses themselves must also be in it, must themselves already have grasped what is at stake, what they are going in for, body and soul.* The history of the last fifty years has taught us that. But in order that the masses may understand what is to be done, long, persistent work is required, and it is just this work that we are now pursuing, and with a success which drives the enemy to despair.

In the Latin countries, also, it is being realised more and more that the old tactics must be revised. Everywhere the German example of utilising the suffrage, of winning all posts accessible to us, has been imitated; everywhere the unprepared launching of an attack has been relegated to the background.** In France, where for more than a hundred years the ground has been undermined by revolution after revolution, where there is not a single party which has not done its share in conspiracies, insurrections and all other revolutionary actions; in France, where, as a result, the government is by no means sure of the army and where, in general, the conditions for an insurrectionary *coup de main* are far more favourable than in Germany—even in France the Socialists are realising more and more that no lasting victory is possible for them, unless they first win the great mass of the people, that is, in this case, the peasants. Slow propaganda work and parliamentary activity are recognised here, too, as the immediate tasks of the party. Successes were not lacking. Not only have a whole series of municipal councils been won; fifty Socialists have seats in the Chambers, and they have already overthrown three ministries and a president of the republic. In Belgium last year the workers forced the adoption of the franchise, and have been victorious in a quarter of the constituencies. In Switzerland, in Italy, in Denmark, yes, even in Bulgaria and Rumania the Socialists are represented in the parliaments. In Austria all parties agree that our admission to the *Reichsrat* can no longer be withheld. We will get in, that is certain; the only question still in dispute is: by which door? And even in

---

* In *Die Neue Zeit* and in the 1895 edition of *The Class Struggles in France*, the words "what they should fight for" are given instead of "what they are going in for, body and soul".—*Ed.*

** In *Die Neue Zeit* and the 1895 edition of *The Class Struggles in France*, the words "everywhere the unprepared launching of an attack has been relegated to the background" are omitted.—*Ed.*

Russia, when the famous *Zemsky Sobor* meets—that National Assembly to which young Nicholas offers such vain resistance—even there we can reckon with certainty on being represented in it.

Of course, our foreign comrades do not thereby in the least renounce their right to revolution. The right to revolution is, after all, the only *really* "historical right," the only right on which all modern states without exception rest, Mecklenburg included, whose aristocratic revolution was ended in 1755 by the "hereditary settlement" ["Erbvergleich"], the glorious charter of feudalism still valid today.[436] The right to revolution is so incontestably recognised in the general consciousness that even General von Boguslawski derives the right to a *coup d'état*, which he vindicates for his Kaiser, solely from this popular right.

But whatever may happen in other countries, the German Social-Democracy occupies a special position and therewith, at least in the immediate future, has a special task. The two million voters whom it sends to the ballot box, together with the young men and women who stand behind them as non-voters, form the most numerous, most compact mass, the decisive "shock force" of the international proletarian army. This mass already supplies over a fourth of the votes cast; and as the by-elections to the *Reichstag*, the Diet elections in individual states, the municipal council and trades court elections demonstrate, it increases incessantly. Its growth proceeds as spontaneously, as steadily, as irresistibly, and at the same time as tranquilly as a natural process. All government intervention has proved powerless against it. We can count even today on two and a quarter million voters. If it continues in this fashion, by the end of the century we shall conquer the greater part of the middle strata of society, petty bourgeois and small peasants, and grow into the decisive power in the land, before which all other powers will have to bow, whether they like it or not. To keep this growth going without interruption until it of itself gets beyond the control of the prevailing governmental system, not to fritter away this daily increasing shock force in vanguard skirmishes, but to keep it intact until the decisive day,* that is our main task. And there is only one means by which the steady rise of the socialist fighting forces in Germany could be temporarily halted, and even thrown back for some time: a clash on a big scale with the military, a blood-letting like that of 1871 in Paris. In the long run that would also be overcome. To shoot a party which numbers millions out of existence is too much even for all the magazine rifles of Europe and America. But the normal development

---

* In *Die Neue Zeit* and the 1895 edition of *The Class Struggles in France*, the words "not to fritter away this daily increasing shock force in vanguard skirmishes, but to keep it intact until the decisive day" are omitted.—*Ed.*

would be impeded, the shock force would, perhaps, not be available at the critical moment, the decisive combat* would be delayed, protracted and attended by heavier sacrifices.

The irony of world history turns everything upside down. We, the "revolutionists," the "overthrowers"—we are thriving far better on legal methods than on illegal methods and overthrow. The parties of Order, as they call themselves, are perishing under the legal conditions created by themselves. They cry despairingly with Odilon Barrot: *la légalité nous tue,* legality is the death of us; whereas we, under this legality, get firm muscles and rosy cheeks and look like life eternal. And if *we* are not so crazy as to let ourselves be driven to street fighting in order to please them, then in the end there is nothing left for them to do but themselves break through this fatal legality.

Meanwhile they make new laws against overthrows. Again everything is turned upside down. These anti-overthrow fanatics of today, are they not themselves the overthrowers of yesterday? Have *we* perchance evoked the civil war of 1866? Have *we* driven the King of Hanover, the Elector of Hesse, and the Duke of Nassau from their hereditary lawful domains and annexed these hereditary domains? And these overthrowers of the German Confederation and three crowns by the grace of God complain of overthrow! *Quis tulerit Gracchos de seditione querentes?*** Who could allow the Bismarck worshippers to rail at overthrow?

Let them, nevertheless, put through their anti-overthrow bills, make them still worse, transform the whole penal law into indiarubber, they will gain nothing but new proof of their impotence. If they want to deal Social-Democracy a serious blow they will have to resort to quite other measures, in addition. They can cope with the Social-Democratic overthrow, which just now is doing so well by keeping the law, only by an overthrow on the part of the parties of Order, an overthrow which cannot live without breaking the law. Herr Rössler, the Prussian bureaucrat, and Herr von Boguslawski, the Prussian general, have shown them the only way perhaps still possible of getting at the workers, who simply refuse to let themselves be lured into street fighting. Breach of the constitution, dictatorship, return to absolutism, *regis voluntas suprema lex!**** Therefore, take courage, gentlemen; here half measures will not do; here you must go the whole hog!

---

* In *Die Neue Zeit* and the 1895 edition of *The Class Struggles in France,* the words "the shock force would, perhaps, not be available at the critical moment" are omitted, and the word "decision" is given instead of "the decisive combat".—*Ed.*

** Who would suffer the Gracchi to complain of sedition? (Juvenal, Satire II).—*Ed.*

*** The King's will is the supreme law!—*Ed.*

But do not forget that the German empire, like all small states and generally all modern states, is a *product of contract*; of the contract, first, of the princes with one another and, second, of the princes with the people. If one side breaks the contract, the whole contract falls to the ground; the other side is then also no longer bound, as Bismarck demonstrated to us so beautifully in 1866. If, therefore, you break the constitution of the Reich, the Social-Democracy is free, and can do as it pleases with regard to you. But it will hardly blurt out to you today what it is going to do then.*

It is now, almost to the year, sixteen centuries since a dangerous party of overthrow was likewise active in the Roman empire. It undermined religion and all the foundations of the state; it flatly denied that Caesar's will was the supreme law; it was without a fatherland, was international; it spread over all countries of the empire, from Gaul to Asia, and beyond the frontiers of the empire. It had long carried on seditious activities in secret, underground; for a considerable time, however, it had felt itself strong enough to come out into the open. This party of overthrow, which was known by the name of Christians, was also strongly represented in the army; whole legions were Christian. When they were ordered to attend the sacrificial ceremonies of the pagan established church, in order to do the honours there, the subversive soldiers had the audacity to stick peculiar emblems—crosses—on their helmets in protest. Even the wonted barrack bullying of their superior officers was fruitless. The Emperor Diocletian could no longer quietly look on while order, obedience and discipline in his army were being undermined. He interfered energetically, while there was still time. He promulgated an anti-Socialist—beg pardon, I meant to say anti-Christian—law. The meetings of the overthrowers were forbidden, their meeting halls were closed or even pulled down, the Christian emblems, crosses, etc., were, like the red handkerchiefs in Saxony, prohibited. Christians were declared incapable of holding public office; they were not to be allowed to become even corporals. Since there were not available at that time judges so well trained in "respect of persons" as Herr von Köller's anti-overthrow bill[437] assumes, Christians were forbidden out of hand to seek justice before a court. This exceptional law was also without effect. The Christians tore it down from the walls with scorn; they are even supposed to have burnt the Emperor's palace in Nicomedia over his head. Then the latter revenged himself by the great persecution of Christians in the year 303 of our era. It was the last of its kind. And

---

* In *Die Neue Zeit* and the 1895 edition of *The Class Struggles in France*, the words beginning with "as Bismarck demonstrated" and to the end of the paragraph are omitted.—*Ed.*

it was so effective that seventeen years later the army consisted overwhelmingly of Christians, and the succeeding autocrat of the whole Roman empire, Constantine, called the Great by the priests, proclaimed Christianity the state religion.

F. Engel

London, March 6, 1895

Published in abridged form in the journal *Die Neue Zeit*, Bd. 2, Nos. 27 and 28, 1894-95, and in the book: Karl Marx. *Die Klassenkämpfe in Frankreich 1848 bis 1850.* Berlin, 1895

Printed according to the galleys of the book checked with the manuscript

Translated from the German

Karl Marx and Frederick Engels

LETTERS

MARX TO P. V. ANNENKOV IN PARIS

Brussels, December 28[1846]

My Dear Monsieur Annenkov,
You would long ago have received my answer to your letter of November 1 but for the fact that my bookseller only sent me Monsieur Proudhon's book, *The Philosophy of Poverty*, last week. I have gone through it in two days in order to be able to give you my opinion about it at once. As I have read the book very hurriedly, I cannot go into details but can only tell you the general impression it has made on me. If you wish I could go into details in a second letter.

I must frankly confess that I find the book on the whole bad, and very bad. You yourself laugh in your letter at the "patch of German philosophy" which M. Proudhon parades in this formless and pretentious work, but you suppose that the economic argument has not been infected by the philosophic poison. I too am very far from imputing the faults in the economic argument to M. Proudhon's philosophy. M. Proudhon does not give us a false criticism of political economy because he is the possessor of an absurd philosophic theory, but he gives us an absurd philosophic theory because he fails to understand the social system of today in its *engrènement*, to use a word which, like much else, M. Proudhon has borrowed from Fourier.

Why does M. Proudhon talk about God, about universal reason, about the impersonal reason of humanity which never errs, which has always been equal to itself throughout all the ages and of which one need only have the right consciousness in order to know the truth? Why does he resort to feeble Hegelianism to give himself the appearance of a bold thinker?

He himself provides you with the clue to this enigma. M. Proudhon sees in history a series of social developments; he finds progress realised in history; finally he finds that men, as individuals, did not know what they were doing and were mistaken about their own movement, that is to say, their social development seems at the first glance to be distinct, separate and independent of their individual development. He cannot explain these facts, and so the hypothes of universal reason manifesting itself comes in very handy. Nothing is easier than to invent mystical causes, that is to say, phrases which lack common sense.

But when M. Proudhon admits that he understands nothing about the historical development of humanity—he admits this by using such high-sounding words as: Universal Reason, God, etc.— is he not implicitly and necessarily admitting that he is incapable of understanding *economic development*?

What is society, whatever its form may be? The product of men's reciprocal action. Are men free to choose this or that form of society? By no means. Assume a particular state of development in the productive faculties of man and you will get a particular form of commerce and consumption. Assume particular stages of development in production, commerce and consumption and you will have a corresponding social constitution, a corresponding organisation of the family, of orders or of classes, in a word, a corresponding civil society. Assume a particular civil society and you will get particular political conditions which are only the official expression of civil society. M. Proudhon will never understand this because he thinks he is doing something great by appealing from the state to civil society—that is to say, from the official résumé of society to official society.

It is superfluous to add that men are not free to choose *their productive forces*—which are the basis of all their history—for every productive force is an acquired force, the product of former activity. The productive forces are therefore the result of practical human energy; but this energy is itself conditioned by the circumstances in which men find themselves, by the productive forces already acquired, by the social form which exists before they do, which they do not create, which is the product of the preceding generation. Because of this simple fact that every succeeding generation finds itself in possession of the productive forces acquired by the previous generation, which serve it as the raw material for new production, a coherence arises in human history, a history of humanity takes shape which is all the more a history of humanity as the productive forces of man and therefore his social relations have been more developed. Hence it necessarily follows that the social history of men is never anything but the history of their individual development, whether they are conscious of it or not. Their material relations are the basis of all their relations. These material relations are only the necessary forms in which their material and individual activity is realised.

M. Proudhon mixes up ideas and things. Men never relinquish what they have won, but this does not mean that they never relinquish the social form in which they have acquired certain productive forces. On the contrary, in order that they may not be deprived of the result attained and forfeit the fruits of civilisation,

MARX TO P. V. ANNENKOV, DECEMBER 28, 1846

they are obliged, from the moment when their mode of carrying on commerce no longer corresponds to the productive forces acquired, to change all their traditional social forms. I am using the word "commerce" here in its widest sense, as we use *Verkehr* in German. For example: the privileges, the institution of guilds and corporations, the regulatory regime of the Middle Ages, were social relations that alone corresponded to the acquired productive forces and to the social condition which had previously existed and from which these institutions had arisen. Under the protection of the regime of corporations and regulations, capital was accumulated, overseas trade was developed, colonies were founded. But the fruits of this men would have forfeited if they had tried to retain the forms under whose shelter these fruits had ripened. Hence burst two thunderclaps—the Revolutions of 1640 and 1688. All the old economic forms, the social relations corresponding to them, the political conditions which were the official expression of the old civil society, were destroyed in England. Thus the economic forms in which men produce, consume, and exchange, are *transitory and historical*. With the acquisition of new productive faculties, men change their mode of production and with the mode of production all the economic relations which are merely the necessary relations of this particular mode of production.

This is what M. Proudhon has not understood and still less demonstrated. M. Proudhon, incapable of following the real movement of history, produces a phantasmagoria which presumptuously claims to be dialectical. He does not feel it necessary to speak of the seventeenth, the eighteenth or the nineteenth century, for his history proceeds in the misty realm of imagination and rises far above space and time. In short, it is not history but old Hegelian junk, it is not profane history—a history of man—but sacred history—a history of ideas. From his point of view man is only the instrument of which the idea or the eternal reason makes use in order to unfold itself. The *evolutions* of which M. Proudhon speaks are understood to be evolutions such as are accomplished within the mystic womb of the absolute idea. If you tear the veil from this mystical language, what it comes to is that M. Proudhon is offering you the order in which economic categories arrange themselves inside his own mind. It will not require great exertion on my part to prove to you that it is the order of a very disorderly mind.

M. Proudhon begins his book with a dissertation on *value*, which is his pet subject. I will not enter on an examination of this dissertation today.

The series of economic evolutions of the eternal reason begins with *division of labour*. To M. Proudhon division of labour is a perfectly simple thing. But was not the caste regime also a particular division of labour? Was not the regime of the corporations another division of labour? And is not the division of labour under the system of manufacture, which in England begins in the middle of the seventeenth century and comes to an end in the last part of the eighteenth, also totally different from the division of labour in large-scale, modern industry?

M. Proudhon is so far from the truth that he neglects what even the profane economists attend to. When he talks about division of labour he does not feel it necessary to mention the world *market*. Good. Yet must not the division of labour in the fourteenth and fifteenth centuries, when there were still no colonies, when America did not as yet exist for Europe, and Eastern Asia only existed for her through the medium of Constantinople, have been fundamentally different from what it was in the seventeenth century when colonies were already developed?

And that is not all. Is the whole inner organisation of nations, are all their international relations anything else than the expression of a particular division of labour? And must not these change when the division of labour changes?

M. Proudhon has so little understood the problem of the division of labour that he never even mentions the separation of town and country, which took place in Germany, for instance, from the ninth to the twelfth century. Thus, to M. Proudhon, this separation is an eternal law since he knows neither its origin nor its development. All through his book he speaks as if this creation of a particular mode of production would endure until the end of time. All that M. Proudhon says about the division of labour is only a summary, and moreover a very superficial and incomplete summary, of what Adam Smith and a thousand others have said before him.

The second evolution is *machinery*. The connection between the division of labour and machinery is entirely mystical to M. Proudhon. Each kind of division of labour had its specific instruments of production. Between the middle of the seventeenth and the middle of the eighteenth century, for instance, people did not make everything by hand. They had instruments, and very complicated ones at that, such as looms, ships, levers, etc.

Thus there is nothing more absurd than to derive machinery from division of labour in general.

I may also remark, by the way, that M. Proudhon has understood very little the historical origin of machinery, but has still less understood its development. One can say that up to the year 1825—the period of the first general crisis—the demands of consumption in general increased more rapidly than production, and the development of machinery was a necessary consequence of the needs of the market. Since 1825, the invention and application of machinery has been simply the result of the war between workers and employers. But this is only true of England. As for the European nations, they were driven to adopt machinery owing to English competition both in their home markets and on the world market. Finally, in North America the introduction of machinery was due both to competition with other countries and to lack of hands, that is, to the disproportion between the population of North America and its industrial needs. From these facts you can see what sagacity Monsieur Proudhon develops when he conjures up the spectre of competition as the third evolution, the antithesis to machinery!

Lastly and in general, it is altogether absurd to make *machinery* an economic category alongside with division of labour, competition, credit, etc.

Machinery is no more an economic category than the ox which draws the plough. The *application* of machinery in the present day is one of the relations of our present economic system, but the way in which machinery is utilised is totally distinct from the machinery itself. Powder is powder whether used to wound a man or to dress his wounds.

M. Proudhon surpasses himself when he allows competition, monopoly, taxes or police, balance of trade, credit and property to develop inside his head in the order in which I have mentioned them. Nearly all credit institutions had been developed in England by the beginning of the eighteenth century, before the invention of machinery. Public credit was only a fresh method of increasing taxation and satisfying the new demands created by the rise of the bourgeoisie to power.

Finally, the last category in M. Proudhon's system is constituted by *property*. In the real world, on the other hand, the division of labour and all M. Proudhon's other categories are social relations forming in their entirety what is today known as *property*; outside these relations bourgeois property is nothing but a metaphysical or juristic illusion. The property of a different epoch, feudal property, develops in a series of entirely different social relations. M. Proudhon, by establishing property as an independent relation, commits more than a mistake in method: he clearly shows that he has not grasped the bond which holds together all forms of *bourgeois* production, that he has not understood the *historical* and *transitory* character of the forms of production in a particular epoch. M. Proudhon, who does not regard our social institutions as historical products, who can understand neither their origin nor their development, can only produce dogmatic criticism of them.

M. Proudhon is therefore obliged to take refuge in a *fiction* in order to explain development. He imagines that division of labour, credit, machinery, etc., were all invented to serve his fixed idea, the idea of equality. His explanation is sublimely naïve. These things were invented in the interests of equality but unfortunately they turned against equality. This constitutes his whole argument. In other words, he makes a gratuitous assumption and then, as the actual development contradicts his fiction at every step, he concludes that there is a contradiction. He conceals from you the fact that the contradiction exists solely between his fixed ideas and the real movement.

Thus, M. Proudhon, mainly because he lacks the historical knowledge, has not perceived that as men develop their productive faculties, that is, as they live, they develop certain relations with one another and that the nature of these relations must necessarily change with the change and growth of the productive faculties. He has not perceived that *economic categories* are only *abstract expressions* of these actual relations and only remain true while these relations exist. He therefore falls into the error of the bourgeois economists, who regard these economic categories as eternal and not as historical laws which are only laws for a particular historical development, for a definite development of the productive forces. Instead, therefore, of regarding the political-economic categories as abstract expressions of the real, transitory, historic social relations, Monsieur Proudhon, thanks to a mystic inversion, sees in the real relations only embodiments of these abstractions. These abstractions themselves are formulas which have been slumbering in the heart of God the Father since the beginning of the world.

But here our good M. Proudhon falls into severe intellectual convulsions. If all these economic categories are emanations from the heart of God, are the hidden and eternal life of man, how does it come about, first, that there is such a thing as development, and secondly, that M. Proudhon is not a conservative? He explains these evident contradictions by a whole system of antagonisms.

To throw light on this system of antagonisms let us take an example.

Monopoly is a good thing, because it is an economic category and therefore an emanation of God. Competition is a good thing because it is also an economic category. But what is not good is the reality of monopoly and the reality of competition. What is still worse is the fact that competition and monopoly devour each other. What is to be done? As these two eternal ideas of God contradict each other, it seems obvious to him that there is also within the bosom of God a synthesis of them both, in which the evils of monopoly are balanced by competition and *vice versa*. As a result of the struggle between the two ideas only their good side will come into view. One must snatch this secret idea from God and then apply it and everything will be for the best; the synthetic formula which lies hidden in the darkness of the impersonal reason of man must be revealed. M. Proudhon does not hesitate for a moment to come forward as the revealer.

But look for a moment at real life. In the economic life of the present time you find not only competition and monopoly but also their synthesis, which is not a *formula* but a *movement*. Monopoly produces competition, competition produces monopoly. But this equation, far from removing the difficulties of the present situation, as the bourgeois economists imagine it does, results in a situation still more difficult and confused. If therefore you alter the basis on which present-day economic relations rest, if you destroy the present *mode* of production, then you will not only destroy competition, monopoly and their antagonism, but also their unity, their synthesis, the movement which is the real equilibrium of competition and monopoly.

Now I will give you an example of Monsieur Proudhon's dialectics.

Freedom and *slavery* constitute an antagonism. I need not speak of the good and bad sides of freedom nor, speaking of slavery, need I dwell on its bad sides. The only thing that has to be explained is its good side. We are not dealing with indirect slavery, the slavery of the proletariat, but with direct slavery, the slavery of the black races in Surinam, in Brazil, in the Southern States of North America.

Direct slavery is as much the pivot of our industrialism today as machinery, credit, etc. Without slavery no cotton; without cotton no modern industry. Slavery has given value to the colonies; the colonies have created world trade; world trade is the necessary condition of large-scale machine industry. Thus, before the traffic in Negroes began, the colonies supplied the Old World with only very few products and made no visible change in the face of the earth. Slavery is therefore an economic category of the highest importance. Without slavery North America, the most progressive country, would be transformed into a patriarchal land. You have only to wipe North America of the map of the nations and you get anarchy, the total decay of trade and of modern civilisation. But to let slavery disappear is to wipe North America off the map of the nations. And therefore, because it is an economic category, we find slavery in every nation since the world began. Modern nations have merely known how to disguise slavery of their own countries while they openly imported it into the New World. After these observations on slavery, how will our worthy M. Proudhon proceed? He will look for the synthesis between freedom and slavery, the golden mean or equilibrium between slavery and freedom.

Monsieur Proudhon has very well grasped the fact that men produce cloth, linen, silks, and it is a great merit on his part to have grasped this small amount! What he has not grasped is that these men, according to their abilities, also produce the *social relations* amid which they prepare cloth and linen. Still less has he understood that men, who produce their social relations in accordance with their material productivity, also produce *ideas, categories,* that is to say, the abstract, ideal expressions of these same social relations. Thus the categories are no more eternal than the relations they express. They are historical and transitory products. To M. Proudhon, on the contrary, abstractions, categories are the primordial cause. According to him they, and not men, make history. The *abstraction,* the *category taken as such,* i.e., apart from men and their material activities, is of course immortal, unchangeable, unmoved; it is only one form of the being of pure reason; which is only another way of saying that the abstraction as such is abstract. An admirable *tautology*!

Thus, regarded as categories, economic relations for M. Proudhon are eternal formulas without origin or progress.

Let us put it in another way: M. Proudhon does not directly state that *bourgeois life* is for him an *eternal verity*; he states it indirectly by deifying the categories which express bourgeois relations in the form of thought. He takes the products of bourgeois society for spontaneously arisen eternal beings, endowed with lives of their own, as soon as they present themselves to his mind in the form of categories, in the form of thought. So he does not rise above the bourgeois horizon. As he is operating with bourgeois ideas, the eternal truth of which he presupposes, he seeks a synthesis, an equilibrium of these ideas, and does not see that the present method by which they reach equilibrium is the only possible one.

Indeed he does what all good bourgeois do. They all tell you that in principle, that is, considered as abstract ideas, competition, monopoly, etc., are the only basis of life, but that in practice they leave much to be desired. They all want competition without the lethal effects of competition. They all want the impossible, namely, the conditions of bourgeois existence without the necessary consequences of those conditions. None of them understands that the bourgeois form of production is historical and transitory, just as the feudal form was. This mistake arises from the fact that the bourgeois man is to them the only possible basis of every society; they cannot imagine a society in which men have ceased to be bourgeois.

M. Proudhon is therefore necessarily *doctrinaire*. To him the historical movement, which is turning the present-day world upside down, reduces itself to the problem of discovering the correct equilibrium, the synthesis, of two bourgeois thoughts. And so the clever fellow by virtue of his subtlety discovers the hidden thought of God, the unity of two isolated thoughts—which are only isolated because M. Proudhon has isolated them from practical life, from present-day production, which is the combination of the realities which they express. In place of the great historical movement arising from the conflict between the productive forces already acquired by men and their social relations, which no longer correspond to these productive forces; in place of the terrible wars which are being prepared between the different classes within each nation and between different nations; in place of the practical and violent action of the masses by which alone these conflicts can be resolved—in place of this vast, prolonged and complicated movement, Monsieur Proudhon supplies the whimsical motion of his own head. So it is the men of learning that make history, the men who know how to purloin God's secret thoughts. The common people have only to apply their revelations.

You will now understand why M. Proudhon is the declared enemy of every political movement. The solution of present problems does not lie for him in public action but in the dialectical rotations of his own head. Since to him the categories are the motive force, it is not necessary to change practical life in order to change the categories. Quite the contrary. One must change the categories and the consequence will be a change in the existing society.

In his desire to reconcile the contradictions Monsieur Proudhon does not even ask if the very basis of those contradictions must not be overthrown. He is exactly like the political doctrinaire who wants to have the king and the chamber of deputies and the chamber of peers as integral parts of social life, as eternal categories. All he is looking for is a new formula by which to establish an equilibrium between these powers whose equilibrium consists precisely in the actual movement in which one power is now the conqueror and now the slave of the other. Thus in the eighteenth century a number of mediocre minds were busy finding the true formula which would bring the social estates, nobility, king, parliament, etc., into equilibrium, and they woke up one morning to find that there was in fact no longer any king, parliament or nobility. The true equilibrium in this antagonism was the overthrow of all the social relations which served as a basis for these feudal existences and for the antagonisms of these feudal existences.

Because M. Proudhon places eternal ideas, the categories of pure reason, on the one side and human beings and their practical life, which, according to him, is the application of these categories, on the other, one finds with him from the beginning a *dualism* between life and ideas, between soul and body, a dualism which recurs in many forms. You can see now that this antagonism is nothing but the incapacity of M. Proudhon to understand the profane origin and the profane history of the categories which he deifies.

My letter is already too long for me to speak of the absurd case which M. Proudhon puts up against communism. For the moment you will grant me that a man who has not understood the present state of society may be expected to understand still less the movement which is tending to overthrow it, and the literary expressions of this revolutionary movement.

The *sole point* on which I am in complete agreement with Monsieur Proudhon is in his dislike for sentimental socialistic daydreams. I had already, before him, drawn much enmity upon myself by ridiculing this sentimental, utopian, mutton-headed socialism. But is not M. Proudhon strangely deluding himself when he sets up his petty-bourgeois sentimentality—I am referring to his declamations about home, conjugal love and all such banalities—in opposition to socialist sentimentality, which in Fourier, for example, goes much deeper than the pretentious platitudes of our worthy Proudhon? He himself is so thoroughly conscious of the emptiness of his arguments, of his utter incapacity to speak about these things, that he bursts into violent explosions of rage, vociferation and righteous wrath, foams at the mouth, curses, denounces, cries shame and murder, beats his breast and boasts before God and man that he is not defiled by the socialist infamies! He does not seriously criticise socialist sentimentalities, or what he regards as such. Like a holy man, a pope, he excommunicates poor sinners and sings the glories of the petty bourgeoisie and of the miserable patriarchal and amorous illusions of the domestic hearth. And this is no accident. From head to foot M. Proudhon is the philosopher and economist of the petty bourgeoisie. In an advanced society the *petty bourgeois* necessarily becomes from his very position a Socialist on the one side and an economist on the other; that is to say, he is dazed by the magnificence of the big bourgeoisie and has sympathy for the sufferings of the people. He is at once both bourgeois and man of the people. Deep down in his heart he flatters himself that he is impartial and has found the right equilibrium, which claims to be something different from the golden mean. A petty bourgeois of this type glorifies *contradiction* because contradiction is the basis of his existence. He is himself nothing but social contradiction in action. He must justify in theory what he is in practice, and M. Proudhon has the merit of being the scientific interpreter of the French petty bourgeoisie—a genuine merit, because the petty bourgeoisie will form an integral part of all the impending social revolutions.

I wish I could send you my book on political economy[438] with this letter, but it has so far been impossible for me to get this

vork, and the criticism of the German philosophers and Socialists* of which I spoke to you in Brussels, printed. You would never
believe the difficulties which a publication of this kind comes up
against in Germany, from the police on the one hand and from
the booksellers, who are themselves the interested representatives
of all tendencies I am attacking, on the other. And as for our own
Party, it is not merely that it is poor, but a large section of the
German Communist Party is also angry with me for opposing
their utopias and declamations. . . .

First published in the original   Printed according to the book
French in the book: Translated from the French
*M. M. Stasyulevich and
His Contemporaries in
Their Correspondence*, Vol. III,
St. Petersburg, 1912

MARX TO J. WEYDEMEYER IN NEW YORK

London, March 5, 1852

. . .And now as to myself, no credit is due to me for discovering
the existence of classes in modern society or the struggle between
them. Long before me bourgeois historians had described the
historical development of this class struggle and bourgeois economists the economic anatomy of the classes. What I did that was
new was to prove: 1) that the *existence of classes* is only bound
up with *particular historical phases in the development of production*, 2) that the class struggle necessarily leads to *the dictatorship of the proletariat*, 3) that this dictatorship itself only con-
situtes the transition to the *abolition of all classes* and to a
classless society. . . .

First published in full
in the journal   Printed according to the
Jungsozialistische   manuscript
Blätter, 1930   Translated from the German

MARX TO L. KUGELMANN IN HANOVER

London, April 12, 1871

. . .Yesterday we received the by no means tranquillising news
that Lafargue (not Laura) was at present in Paris.
If you look at the last chapter of my *Eighteenth Brumaire*,** you

---

* Marx is referring to *Die deutsche Ideologie* (see Marx and Engels, *The
German Ideology*, Moscow, 1964).—*Ed.*
** See pp. 166-79 of this volume.—*Ed.*

will find that I declare that the next attempt of the French Revolution will be no longer, as before, to transfer the bureaucratic
military machine from one hand to another, but *to smash* it, an
this is the preliminary condition for every real people's revolutio
on the Continent. And this is what our heroic Party comrades i
Paris are attempting. What elasticity, what historical initiative
what a capacity for sacrifice in these Parisians! After six month
of hunger and ruin, caused by internal treachery more even than
by the external enemy, they rise, beneath Prussian bayonets, as
if there had never been a war between France and Germany and
the enemy were not still at the gates of Paris! History has no like
example of like greatness! If they are defeated only their "good
nature" will be to blame. They should have marched at once on
Versailles after first Vinoy and then the reactionary section of the
Paris National Guard had themselves retreated. They missed their
opportunity because of conscientious scruples. They did not want
to start a civil war, as if that mischievous abortion Thiers had not
already started the civil war with his attempt to disarm Paris!
Second mistake: The Central Committee[439] surrendered its power
too soon, to make way for the Commune. Again from a too "honourable" scrupulosity! However that may be, the present rising in
Paris—even if it be crushed by the wolves, swine, and vile curs
of the old society—is the most glorious deed of our Party since the
June insurrection in Paris.[6] Compare these Parisians, storming
heaven, with the slaves to heaven of the German-Prussian Holy
Roman Empire, with its posthumous masquerades reeking of the
barracks, the Church, cabbage-Junkerdom[19] and, above all, of the
philistine.

A propos. In the *official publication* of the list of those receiving
direct subsidies from L. Bonaparte's treasury there is a note that
Vogt received 40,000 francs in August 1859! I have informed
Liebknecht of this fact for further use.

You can send me the Haxthausen[440] as *lately* I have been receiving undamaged various pamphlets, etc., not only ˙from Germany
but even from Petersburg.

Thanks for the various newspapers you sent me. (Please let me
have more of them, for I want to write something about Germany,
the Reichstag, etc.)

First published in abridged
form in the journal
Die Neue Zeit, Bd. 1,
No. 23, Stuttgart, 1901-02,
and in full in Russian
in the book: *Marx's
Letters to Kugelmann*, 1928

Printed according to the
manuscript
Translated from the German

MARX TO L. KUGELMANN IN HANOVER

[London], April 17, 1871

Your letter duly received. Just at present I have my hands full. Hence only a few words. How you can compare pretty bourgeois demonstrations à la June 13, 1849,[288] etc., with the present struggle in Paris is quite incomprehensible to me.

World history would indeed be very easy to make if the struggle were taken up only on condition of infallibly favourable chances. It would on the other hand be of a very mystical nature, if "accidents" played no part. These accidents naturally form part of the general course of development and are compensated by other accidents. But acceleration and delay are very much dependent upon such "accidents," including the "accident" of the character of the people who first head the movement.

The decisively unfavourable "accident" this time is by no means to be sought in the general conditions of French society, but in the presence of the Prussians in France and their position right before Paris. Of this the Parisians were well aware. But of this, the bourgeois *canaille* of Versailles were also well aware. Precisely for that reason they presented the Parisians with the alternative of either taking up the fight or succumbing without a struggle. The demoralisation of the working class in the latter case would have been a far greater misfortune than the succumbing of any number of "leaders." With the struggle in Paris the struggle of the working class against the capitalist class and its state has entered upon a new phase. Whatever the immediate outcome may be, a new point of departure of world-wide importance has been gained.

First published in abridged
form in the journal
Die Neue Zeit, Bd. 1,
No. 23, Stuttgart, 1901-02,
and in full in Russian
in the book: *Marx's
Letters to Kugelmann*, 1928

Printed according to the
manuscript
Translated from the German

MARX TO F. BOLTE IN NEW YORK

[London], November 23, 1871

...The *International* was founded in order to replace the socialist or semi-socialist sects by a real organisation of the working class for struggle. The original Rules* and the Inaugural Address** show this at a glance. On the other hand the International could not have maintained itself if the course of history had not already smashed sectarianism. The development of socialist sectarianism and that of the real working-class movement always stand in inverse ratio to each other. Sects are justified (historically) so long as the working class is not yet ripe for an independent historical movement. As soon as it has attained this maturity all sects are essentially reactionary. Nevertheless, what history exhibits everywhere was repeated in the history of the International. What is antiquated tries to re-establish itself and maintain its position within the newly acquired form.

And the history of the International was a *continual struggle* *of the General Council* against the sects and amateur experiments which sought to assert themselves within the International against the real movement of the working class. This struggle was conducted at the *congresses*, but far more in the private negotiations between the General Council and the individual sections.

In Paris, as the Proudhonists (Mutualists[441]) were co-founders of the Association, they naturally held the reins there for the first few years. Later, of course, collectivist, positivist, etc., groups were formed there in opposition to them.

In Germany—the Lassalle clique. I myself corresponded with the notorious Schweitzer for two years and proved to him irrefutably that Lassalle's organisation was a mere sectarian organisation and, as such, hostile to the organisation of the *real* workers' movement striven for by the International. He had his "reasons" for not understanding.

At the end of 1868 the Russian Bakunin joined the *International* with the aim of forming inside it *a second International* under the name of *"Alliance de la Démocratie Socialiste"*[243] *and with himself as leader.* He—a man devoid of all theoretical knowledge—laid claim to representing in that separate body the *scientific* propaganda of the International, and wanted to make such propaganda the special function of that second *International within the International.*

His programme was a hash superficially scraped together from the Right and from the Left—*equality of classes* (!), *abolition of the right of inheritance* as the *starting point* of the social movement (St. Simonist nonsense), *atheism* as a *dogma* dictated to the

---

* Provisional Rules of the International Working Men's Association drawn up by Marx.—*Ed.*
** The Inaugural Address of the International Working Men's Association drawn up by Marx.—*Ed.*

members, etc., and as the main dogma (*Proudhonist*): *abstention from the political movement.*

This children's primer found favour (and still has a certain hold) in Italy and Spain, where the real conditions for the workers' movement are as yet little developed, and among a few vain, ambitious, and empty doctrinaires in Latin Switzerland and in Belgium.

To Mr. Bakunin doctrine (the mess he has brewed from bits of Proudhon, St. Simon, and others) was and is a secondary matter —merely a means to his personal self-assertion. Though a nonentity as a theoretician he is in his element as an intriguer.

For years the General Council had to fight against this conspiracy (supported up to a certain point by the French Proudhonists, especially in the *South of France*). At last, by means of Conference Resolutions 1, 2, and 3, IX, XVI, and XVII, it delivered its long-prepared blow.[442]

It goes without saying that the General Council does not support in America what it combats in Europe. Resolutions 1, 2, 3 and IX now give the New York Committee the legal weapons with which to put an end to all sectarianism and amateur groups, and, if necessary, to expel them.

...The political movement of the working class has as its ultimate object, of course, the conquest of political power for this class, and this naturally requires a previous organisation of the working class developed up to a certain point and arising precisely from its economic struggles.

On the other hand, however, every movement in which the working class comes out as a *class* against the ruling classes and tries to coerce them by pressure from without is a political movement. For instance, the attempt in a particular factory or even in a particular trade to force a shorter working day out of individual capitalists by strikes, etc., is a purely economic movement. On the other hand the movement to force through an eight-hour, etc., *law*, is a *political* movement. And in this way, out of the separate economic movements of the workers there grows up everywhere a *political* movement, that is to say, a movement of the *class*, with the object of enforcing its interests in a general form, in a form possessing general, socially coercive force. While these movements presuppose a certain degree of previous organisation, they are in turn equally a means of developing this organisation.

Where the working class is not yet far enough advanced in its organisation to undertake a decisive campaign against the collective power, i.e., the political power of the ruling classes, it must at any rate be trained for this by continual agitation against this power and by a hostile attitude toward the policies of the

ruling classes. Otherwise it remains a plaything in their hands
as the September revolution in France[291] showed, and as is also
proved to a certain extent by the game that Messrs. Gladstone &
Co. have been successfully engaged in in England up to the
present time.

First published in abridged form
in the book: *Briefe und Auszüge aus
Briefen von Joh. Phil. Becker, Jos.
Dietzgen, Friedrich Engels, Karl
Marx u. A. an F. A. Sorge und
Andere*. Stuttgart, 1906, and in
full in Russian in the *Works* of
K. Marx and F. Engels, First
edition, Vol. XXVI, 1935

Printed according
to the manuscript and
the text of the book
Translated from the German

ENGELS TO A. BEBEL IN HUBERTUSBURG

London, June 20, 1873

I am answering your letter first because Liebknecht's is still with
Marx, who cannot locate it just now.

It was not Hepner but York's letter to him, signed by the Committee, which caused us here to be afraid that your imprisonment
would be used by the Party authorities, which unfortunately are
entirely Lassallean, to transform the *Volksstaat*[162] into an "honest"
Neuer Social-Demokrat.[443] York plainly confessed to such an intention, and as the Committee claimed to have the right to appoint and remove the editors the danger was surely big enough.
Hepner's impending deportation further strengthened these plans.
Under these circumstances it was absolutely necessary for us to
know what the situation was; hence this correspondence....

With regard to the attitude of the Party towards Lassalleanism, you of course can judge better than we what tactics should
be adopted, especially in particular cases. But there is also this
to be considered. When, as in your case, one is to a certain extent
in the position of a competitor to the General Association of
German Workers,[444] one is easily too considerate of one's rival
and gets into the habit of always thinking of him first. But both
the General Association of German Workers and the Social-Democratic Workers' Party together still form only a very small minority of the German working class. Our view, which we have found
confirmed by long practice, is that the correct tactics in propaganda are not to entice away a few individuals and memberships
here and there from one's opponent, but to work on the great
mass, which is not yet taking part in the movement. The raw force
of a single individual whom one has oneself reared from the raw

s worth more than ten Lassallean turncoats, who always bring
he germs of their false tendencies into the Party with them. And
f one could only get the masses without their *local leaders* it
would still be all right. But one always has to take along a whole
crowd of these leaders into the bargain, who are bound by their
previous public utterances, if not by their previous views, and
now must   prove above all things that they have not deserted their
principles but that on the contrary the Social-Democratic Workers' Party preaches *true* Lassalleanism. This was the unfortunate
thing at Eisenach,[251] which could not be avoided at that   time,
perhaps, but there is no doubt at all that these elements have done
harm to the Party and I am not sure that the Party would not
have been at least as strong today without that accession. In any
case, however, I should regard it as a misfortune if these elements
were to receive reinforcements.

One must not allow oneself to be misled by the cry for "unity."
Those who have this word most often on their lips are the ones
who sow the most dissension, just as at present the Jura Bakuninists
in Switzerland, who have provoked all the splits, clamour for
nothing so much as for unity. These unity fanatics are either
people of limited intelligence who want to stir everything into one
nondescript brew, which, the moment it is left to settle, throws
up the differences again but in much sharper   contrast because
they will then be all in one pot (in Germany you have a fine example of this in the people who preach reconciliation of the workers
and the petty bourgeoisie)—or else they are people who unconsciously (like Mühlberger, for instance) or consciously want to
adulterate the movement. For this reason the biggest sectarians
and the biggest brawlers and rogues at   times shout loudest for
unity. Nobody in our lifetime has given us more trouble and been
more treacherous than the shouters for unity.

Naturally every party leadership wants to see successes, and
this is quite a good thing. But there are circumstances in which
one must have the courage to sacrifice *momentary* success for
more important things. Especially for a party like ours, whose
ultimate success is so absolutely certain, and which has developed
so enormously in our own lifetime and before our own eyes,
momentary success is by no means always and absolutely necessary. Take the International,[120] for instance. After the Commune[8]
it had a colossal success. The bourgeois, struck all of a heap,
ascribed omnipotence to it. The great mass of the membership
believed things would stay like that for all eternity. We knew very
well that the bubble *must* burst. All the riff-raff attached themselves to it. The sectarians within it became arrogant and misused
the International in the hope that the meanest and most stupid
actions would be permitted them. We did not allow that. Know-

ing well that the bubble must burst some time our concern was
not to delay the catastrophe but to take care that the International emerged from it pure and unadulterated. The bubble burst at
the Hague[250] and you know that the majority of the Congress
members went home sick with disappointment. And yet nearly all
these disappointed people, who imagined they would find the ideal
of universal brotherhood and reconciliation in the International,
had far more bitter quarrels at home than those which broke out
at the Hague. Now the sectarian quarrel-mongers are preaching
reconciliation and decrying us as being cantankerous and dicta-
tors. And if we had come out in a conciliatory way at the Hague,
if we had hushed up the breaking out of the split—what would
have been the result? The sectarians, especially the Bakuninists,
would have got another year in which to perpetrate, in the name
of the International, even much greater stupidities and infamies;
the workers of the most developed countries would have turned
away in disgust; the bubble would not have burst but, pierced by
pinpricks, would have slowly collapsed, and the next Congress
which would have been bound to bring the crisis anyhow, would
have turned into the lowest kind of personal row, because *principles* would already have been sacrificed at the Hague. Then the
International would indeed have gone to pieces—gone to pieces
through "unity"! Instead of this we have now got rid of the rotten elements with honour to ourselves—the members of the Commune who were present at the last and decisive session say that
no session of the Commune left such a terrible impression upon
them as this session of the tribunal which passed judgement on
the traitors to the European proletariat. For ten months we let
them expend all their energies on lies, slander and intrigue—and
where are they? They, the alleged representatives of the great
majority of the International, now themselves announce that they
do not dare to come to the next Congress. (More details in an
article which is being sent off to the *Volksstaat** with this letter.)
And if we had to do it again we should not, taking it all together,
act any differently—tactical mistakes are always made, of course.

In any case, I think the efficient elements among the Lassalleans will fall to you of themselves in the course of time and it
would, therefore, be unwise to break off the fruit before it is ripe,
as the unity crowd wants to.

Moreover, old man Hegel said long ago: A party proves itself
victorious by *splitting* and being able to stand the split.[445] The
movement of the proletariat necessarily passes through different
stages of development; at every stage part of the people get stuck

* F. Engels, "*Aus der Internationalen*" (see Marx/Engels, *Werke*, Bd. 18, Dietz
Verlag, Berlin, 1962, S. 472-75).—*Ed.*

and do not join in the further advance; and this alone explains why it is that actually the "solidarity of the proletariat" is everywhere being realised in different party groupings, which carry on life-and-death feuds with one another, as the Christian sects in the Roman Empire did amidst the worst persecutions.

You must also not forget that if the *Neuer Social-Demokrat* for example has more subscribers than the *Volksstaat*, this is due to the fact that each *sect* is necessarily fanatic and through this fanaticism obtains, particularly in regions where it is new (as for instance the General Association of German Workers in Schleswig-Holstein), much greater momentary successes than the Party, which simply represents the real movement, without any sectarian vagaries. On the other hand, fanaticism does not last long.

I have to close my letter as the mail is about to close. Let me only add hurriedly: Marx cannot tackle Lassalle[446] until the French translation* is finished (approx. end of July), after which he will absolutely need a rest as he has greatly overworked himself....

First published in abridged
form in the book: F. Engels.
Politisches Vermächtnis.
Aus unveröffentlichten Briefen.
Berlin, 1920, and in full in
Russian in the journal
Bolshevik No. 10, 1932.

Printed according to the
manuscript
Translated from the
German

MARX TO W. BLOS IN HAMBURG

London, November 10, 1877

...I am "not angry" (as Heine puts it) and neither is Engels.[447] Neither of us cares a straw for popularity. A proof of this is, for example, that, because of aversion to any personality cult, I have never permitted the numerous expressions of appreciation from various countries, with which I was pestered during the existence of the International,[120] to reach the realm of publicity, and have never answered them, except occasionally by a rebuke. When Engels and I first joined the secret Communist Society** we made it a condition that everything tending to encourage superstitious belief in authority was to be removed from the statutes.[448] (Later on Lassalle exerted his influence in the opposite direction.)

First published in
the journal *Der wahre
Jacob* No. 565 (6), March 17,
1908

Printed according to the manuscript
Translated from the German

---

* Of Vol. I of *Capital.—Ed.*
** The Communist League.—*Ed.*

ENGELS TO K. KAUTSKY IN VIENNA

London, September 12, 1882

... You ask me what the English workers think about colonial policy. Well, exactly the same as they think about politics in general: the same as the bourgeois think. There is no workers' party here, you see, there are only Conservatives and Liberal-Radicals, and the workers gaily share the feast of England's monopoly of the world market and the colonies. In my opinion the colonies proper, i.e., the countries occupied by a European population— Canada, the Cape, Australia—will all become independent; on the other hand, the countries inhabited by a native population, which are simply subjugated—India, Algeria, the Dutch, Portuguese and Spanish possessions—must be taken over for the time being by the proletariat and led as rapidly as possible towards independence. How this process will develop is difficult to say. India will perhaps, indeed very probably, make a revolution, and as a proletariat in process of self-emancipation cannot conduct any colonial wars, it would have to be allowed to run its course; it would not pass off without all sorts of destruction, of course, but that sort of thing is inseparable from all revolutions. The same might also take place elsewhere, e.g., in Algeria and Egypt, and would certainly be the best thing *for us*. We shall have enough to do at home. Once Europe is reorganised, and North America, that will furnish such colossal power and such an example that the semi-civilised countries will of themselves follow in their wake; economic needs, if anything, will see to that. But as to what social and political phases these countries will then have to pass through before they likewise arrive at socialist organisation, I think we today can advance only rather idle hypotheses. One thing alone is certain: the victorious proletariat can force no blessings of any kind upon any foreign nation without undermining its own victory by so doing. Which of course by no means excludes defensive wars of various kinds. ...

First published in full   Printed according to the
in Russian in *Marx-Engels*   manuscript
Archive, Vol. I (VI), 1932   Translated from the German

ENGELS TO C. SCHMIDT IN BERLIN

London, August 5, 1890

... I saw a review of Paul Barth's book[449] by that bird of ill omen, Moritz Wirth, in the Vienna *Deutsche Worte*,[450] and *this* criticism left on my mind an unfavourable impression of the book itself, as well. I will have a look at it, but I must say that if "little Moritz" is right when he quotes Barth as stating that the sole example of the dependence of philosophy, etc., on the material conditions of existence which he can find in all Marx's works is that Descartes declares animals to be machines, then I am sorry for the man who can write such a thing. And if this man has not yet discovered that while the material mode of existence is the *primum agens** this does not preclude the ideological spheres from reacting upon it in their turn, though with a secondary effect, he cannot possibly have understood the subject he is writing about. However, as I have said, all this is second-hand and little Moritz is a dangerous friend. The materialist conception of history has a lot of them nowadays, to whom it serves as an excuse for *not* studying history. Just as Marx used to say, commenting on the French "Marxists" of the late seventies: "All I know is that I am not a Marxist."

There has also been a discussion in the *Volkstribüne*[451] about the distribution of products in future society, whether this will take place according to the amount of work done or otherwise. The question has been approached very "materialistically" in opposition to certain idealistic phraseology about justice. But strangely enough it has not struck anyone that, after all, the method of distribution essentially depends on *how much* there is to distribute, and that this must surely change with the progress of production and social organisation, so that the method of distribution may also change. But to everyone who took part in the discussion, "socialist society" appeared not as something undergoing continuous change and progress but as a stable affair fixed once for all, which must, therefore, have a method of distribution fixed once for all. All one can reasonably do, however, is 1) to try and discover the method of distribution to be used *at the beginning,* and 2) to try and find the *general tendency* of the further development. But about this I do not find a single word in the whole debate.

In general, the word "materialistic" serves many of the younger writers in Germany as a mere phrase with which anything and everything is labelled without further study, that is, they stick on this label and then consider the question disposed of. But our conception of history is above all a guide to study, not a lever for construction after the manner of the Hegelian. All history must be studied afresh, the conditions of existence of the different formations of society must be examined individually before the attempt is made to deduce from them the political, civil-law, aesthetic, philosophic, religious, etc., views corresponding to them. Up to now but little has been done here because only a few people have got down to it seriously. In this field we can utilise heaps of help, it is im-

---

* Primary agent, prime cause.—*Ed.*

mensely big, and anyone who will work seriously can achieve much and distinguish himself. But instead of this too many of the younger Germans simply make use of the phrase historical materialism (and *everything* can be turned into a phrase) only in order to get their own relatively scanty historical knowledge—for economic history is still in its swaddling clothes!—constructed into a neat system as quickly as possible, and they then deem themselves something very tremendous. And after that a Barth can come along and attack the thing itself, which in his circle has indeed been degraded to a mere phrase.

However, all this will right itself. We are strong enough in Germany now to stand a lot. One of the greatest services which the Anti-Socialist Law[167] did us was to free us from the obtrusiveness of the German intellectual who had got tinged with socialism. We are now strong enough to digest the German intellectual too, who is giving himself great airs again. You, who have really done something, must have noticed yourself how few of the young literary men who fasten themselves on to the Party give themselves the trouble to study economics, the history of economics, the history of trade, of industry, of agriculture, of the formations of society. How many know anything of Maurer except his name! The self-sufficiency of the journalist must serve for everything here and the result looks like it. It often seems as if these gentlemen think anything is good enough for the workers. If these gentlemen only knew that Marx thought his best things were still not good enough for the workers, how he regarded it as a crime to offer the workers anything but the very best! ...

First published in full
in the journal
Sozialistische Monatshefte
Nos. 18-19, 1920

Printed according to the
manuscript
Translated from the German

ENGELS TO OTTO VON BOENIGK IN BRESLAU

Folkestone, near Dover
August 21, 1890

... I can reply only briefly and in general terms to your enquiries, for as concerns the first question I should otherwise have to write a treatise.

Ad.I. To my mind, the so-called "socialist society" is not anything immutable. Like all other social formations, it should be conceived in a state of constant flux and change. Its crucial difference from the present order consists naturally in production organised on the basis of common ownership by the nation of all means of production. To begin this reorganisation tomorrow, but performing it gradually, seems to me quite feasible. That our workers are capable of it is borne out by their many producer and consumer co-operatives which, whenever they are not deliberately ruined by the police, are equally well and far more honestly run than the bourgeois stock companies. I cannot see how you can speak of the ignorance of the masses in Germany after the brilliant evidence of political maturity shown by the workers in their victorious struggle against the Anti-Socialist Law.[167] The patronising and errant lecturing of our so-called intellectuals seems to me a far greater impediment. We are still in need of technicians, agronomists, engineers, chemists, architects, etc., it is true, but if the worst comes to the worst we can always buy them just as well as the capitalists buy them, and if a severe example is made of a few of the traitors among them—for traitors there are sure to be—they will find it to their own advantage to deal fairly with us. But apart from these specialists, among whom I also include schoolteachers, we can get along perfectly well without the other "intellectuals". The present influx of literati and students into the party, for example, may be quite damaging if these gentlemen are not properly kept in check.

The Junker latifundia east of the Elbe could be easily leased under the due technical management to the present day-labourers and the other retinue, who would work the estates jointly. If any disturbances occur, the Junkers, who have brutalised people by flouting all the existing school legislation, will alone be to blame.

The biggest obstacle are the small peasants and the importunate super-clever intellectuals who always think they know everything so much the better, the less they understand it.

Once we have a sufficient number of followers among the masses, the big industries and the large-scale latifundia farming can be quickly socialised, provided we hold the political power. The rest will follow shortly, sooner or later. And we shall have it all our own way in large-scale production.

You speak of an absence of uniform insight. This exists—but on the part of the intellectuals who stem from the aristocracy and the bourgeoisie and who do not suspect how much they still have to learn from the workers.

First published in full
in Russian in the journal
Voprosy istorii KPSS (The
Problems of the C.P.S.U.
History) No. 2, 1964, and in
German in the journal *Beiträge
zur Geschichte der deutschen
Arbeiterbewegung* No. 2, 1964

Printed according to the
manuscript
Translated from the German

ENGELS TO J. BLOCH IN KÖNIGSBERG

London, September 21 [-22], 1890

... According to the materialist conception of history, the *ultimately* determining element in history is the production and reproduction of real life. More than this neither Marx nor I have ever asserted. Hence if somebody twists this into saying that the economic element is the *only* determining one, he transforms that proposition into a meaningless, abstract, senseless phrase. The economic situation is the basis, but the various elements of the superstructure—political forms of the class struggle and its results, to wit: constitutions established by the victorious class after a successful battle, etc., juridical forms, and even the reflexes of all these actual struggles in the brains of the participants, political, juristic, philosophical theories, religious views and their further development into systems of dogmas—also exercise their influence upon the course of the historical struggles and in many cases preponderate in determining their *form*. There is an interaction of all these elements in which, amid all the endless host of accidents (that is, of things and events whose inner interconnection is so remote or so impossible of proof that we can regard it as nonexistent, as negligible), the economic movement finally asserts itself as necessary. Otherwise the application of the theory to any period of history would be easier than the solution of a simple equation of the first degree.

We make our history ourselves, but, in the first place, under very definite assumptions and conditions. Among these the economic ones are ultimately decisive. But the political ones, etc., and indeed even the traditions which haunt human minds also play a part, although not the decisive one. The Prussian state also arose and developed from historical, ultimately economic, causes. But it could scarcely be maintained without pedantry that among the many small states of North Germany, Brandenburg was specifically determined by economic necessity to become the great power embodying the economic, linguistic and, after the Reformation, also the religious difference between North and South, and not by other elements as well (above all by its entanglement with Poland, owing to the possession of Prussia, and hence with international political relations—which were indeed also decisive in the formation of the Austrian dynastic power). Without making oneself ridiculous it would be a difficult thing to explain in terms of economics the existence of every small state in Germany, past and present, or the origin of the High German consonant permutations, which widened the geographic partition wall formed by the mountains from the Sudetic range to the Taunus to form a regular fissure across all Germany.

In the second place, however, history is made in such a way that the final result always arises from conflicts between many individual wills, of which each in turn has been made what it is by a host of particular conditions of life. Thus there are innumerable intersecting forces, an infinite series of parallelograms of forces which give rise to one resultant—the historical event. This may again itself be viewed as the product of a power which works as a whole *unconsciously* and without volition. For what each individual wills is obstructed by everyone else, and what emerges is something that no one willed. Thus history has proceeded hitherto in the manner of a natural process and is essentially subject to the same laws of motion. But from the fact that the wills of individuals —each of whom desires what he is impelled to by his physical constitution and external, in the last resort economic, circumstances (either his own personal circumstances or those of society in general)—do not attain what they want, but are merged into an aggregate mean, a common resultant, it must not be concluded that they are equal to zero. On the contrary, each contributes to the resultant and is to this extent included in it.

I would furthermore ask you to study this theory from its original sources and not at second-hand; it is really much easier. Marx hardly wrote anything in which it did not play a part. But especially *The Eighteenth Brumaire of Louis Bonaparte* is a most excellent example of its application. There are also many allusions to it in *Capital.* Then may I also direct you to my writings: *Herr Eugen Dühring's Revolution in Science* and *Ludwig Feuerbach and the End of Classical German Philosophy,* in which I have given the most detailed account of historical materialism which, as far as I know, exists.

Marx and I are ourselves partly to blame for the fact that the younger people sometimes lay more stress on the economic side than is due to it. We had to emphasise the main principle *vis-à-vis* our adversaries, who denied it, and we had not always the time, the place or the opportunity to give their due to the other elements involved in the interaction. But when it came to presenting a section of history, that is, to making a practical application, it was a different matter and there no error was permissible. Unfortunately, however, it happens only too often that people think they have fully understood a new theory and can apply it without more ado from the moment they have assimilated its main principles, and even those not always correctly. And I cannot exempt many of the more recent "Marxists" from this reproach, for the most amazing rubbish has been produced in this quarter, too. . . .

First published in
the journal *Der sozialistische*
Akademiker No. 19, 1895

Printed according to the
text of the journal
Translated from the German

ENGELS TO C. SCHMIDT IN BERLIN

London, October 27, 1890

Dear Schmidt,

I am taking advantage of the first free moments to reply to you. I think you would do very well to accept the offer of the *Züricher Post*.[452] You could always learn a good deal about economics there, especially if you bear in mind that Zurich is after all only a third-rate money and speculation market, so that the impressions which make themselves felt there are weakened by two-fold or three-fold reflection or are deliberately distorted. But you will get a practical knowledge of the mechanism and be obliged to follow the stock exchange reports from London, New York, Paris, Berlin and Vienna at first-hand, and thus the world market, in its reflex as money and stock market, will reveal itself to you. Economic, political and other reflections are just like those in the human eye: they pass through a condensing lens and therefore appear upside down, standing on their heads. Only the nervous apparatus which would put them on their feet again for presentation to us is lacking. The money market man sees the movement of industry and of the world market only in the inverted reflection of the money and stock market and so effect becomes cause to him. I noticed that already in the forties in Manchester: the London stock exchange reports were utterly useless for understanding the course of industry and its periodical maxima and minima because these gentry tried to explain everything by crises on the money market, which of course were themselves generally only symptoms. At that time the point was to disprove temporary over-production as the origin of industrial crises, so that the thing had in addition its tendentious side, provocative of distortion. This point now ceases to exist—for us, at any rate, for good and all—besides which it is indeed a fact that the money market can also have its own crises, in which direct disturbances of industry play only a subordinate part or no part at all. Here there is still much to be established and examined, especially in the history of the last twenty years.

Where there is division of labour on a social scale there the separate labour processes become independent of each other. In the last instance production is the decisive factor. But as soon as trade in products becomes independent of production proper, it follows a movement of its own, which, while governed as a whole by that of production, still in particulars and within this general dependence again follows laws of its own inherent in the nature of this new factor; this movement has phases of its own and in its turn reacts on the movement of production. The discovery of America was due to the thirst for gold which had previously driven the Portuguese to Africa (cf. Soetbeer's *Production of Precious*

Metals), because the enormously extended European industry of the fourteenth and fifteenth centuries and the trade corresponding to it demanded more means of exchange than Germany, the great silver country ˙from 1450 to 1550, could provide. The conquest of India by the Portuguese, Dutch and English between 1500 and 1800 had *imports from* India as its object—nobody dreamt of exporting anything there. And yet what a colossal reaction these discoveries and conquests, brought about solely by trade interests, had upon industry: it was only the need for *exports to* these countries that created and developed modern large-scale industry.

So it is, too, with the money market. As soon as trade in money becomes separate from trade in commodities it has—under certain conditions imposed by production and commodity trade and within these limits—a development of its own, special laws determined by its own nature and separate phases. If to this is added that money trade, developing further, comes to include trade in securities and that these securities are not only government papers but also industrial and transport stocks, so that money trade gains direct control over a portion of the production by which, taken as a whole, it is itself controlled, then the reaction of money trading on production becomes still stronger and more complicated. The traders in money are the owners of railways, mines, iron works, etc. These means of production take on a double aspect: their operation has to be directed sometimes in the interests of direct production but sometimes also according to the requirements of the shareholders, so far as they are money traders. The most striking example of this is furnished by the North American railways, whose operation is entirely dependent on the daily stock exchange operations of a Jay Gould or a Vanderbilt, etc., which have nothing whatever to do with the particular railway and its interests as a means of communication. And even here in England we have seen contests lasting decades between different railway companies over the boundaries of their respective territories—contests on which an enormous amount of money was thrown away, not in the interests of production and communication but simply because of a rivalry whose sole object usually was to facilitate the stock exchange transactions of the share-holding money traders.

With these few indications of my conception of the relation of production to commodity trade and of both to money trade, I have answered, in essence, your questions about "historical materialism" generally. The thing is easiest to grasp from the point of view of the division of labour. Society gives rise to certain common functions which it cannot dispense with. The persons appointed for this purpose form a new branch of the division of labour *within society*. This gives them particular interests, distinct, too, from the interests of those who empowered them; they make themselves in-

dependent of the latter and—the state is in being. And now things
proceed in a way similar to that in commodity trade and later in
money trade: the new independent power, while having in the main
to follow the movement of production, reacts in its turn, by virtue
of its inherent relative independence—that is, the relative independence once transferred to it and gradually further developed—upon
the conditions and course of production. It is the interaction of two
unequal forces: on the one hand, the economic movement, on the
other, the new political power, which strives for as much independence as possible, and which, having once been established, is endowed with a movement of its own. On the whole, the economic
movement gets its way, but it has also to suffer reactions from the
political movement which it itself established and endowed with
relative independence, from the movement of the state power, on
the one hand, and of the opposition simultaneously engendered, on
the other. Just as the movement of the industrial market is, in the
main and with the reservations already indicated, reflected in the
money market and, of course, in *inverted* form, so the struggle between the classes already existing and fighting with one another is
reflected in the struggle between government and opposition, but
likewise in inverted form, no longer directly but indirectly, not as
a class struggle but as a fight for political principles, and so distorted
that it has taken us thousands of years to get behind it.

The reaction of the state power upon economic development can
be of three kinds: it can run in the same direction, and then development is more rapid; it can oppose the line of development,
in which case nowadays it will go to pieces in the long run in
every great people; or it can prevent the economic development
from proceeding along certain lines, and prescribe other lines.
This case ultimately reduces itself to one of the two previous ones.
But it is obvious that in cases two and three the political power
can do great damage to the economic development and cause a great
squandering of energy and material.

Then there is also the case of the conquest and brutal destruction of economic resources, by which, in certain circumstances, a
whole local or national economic development could formerly be
ruined. Nowadays such a case usually has the opposite effect, at
least with great peoples: in the long run the vanquished often gains
more economically, politically and morally than the victor.

Similarly with law. As soon as the new division of labour which
creates professional lawyers becomes necessary, another new and
independent sphere is opened up which, for all its general dependence on production and trade, has also a special capacity for
reacting upon these spheres. In a modern state, law must not only
correspond to the general economic condition and be its expression,
but must also be an *internally coherent* expression which does not,

owing to inner contradictions, reduce itself to nought. And in order to achieve this, the faithful reflection of economic conditions suffers increasingly. All the more so the more rarely it happens that a code of law is the blunt, unmitigated, unadulterated expression of the domination of a class—this in itself would offend the "conception of right." Even in the *Code Napoléon*[312] the pure, consistent conception of right held by the revolutionary bourgeoisie of 1792-96 is already adulterated in many ways, and, in so far as it is embodied there, has daily to undergo all sorts of attenuations owing to the rising power of the proletariat. This does not prevent the *Code Napoléon* from being the statute book which serves as the basis of every new code of law in every part of the world. Thus to a great extent the course of the "development of right" consists only, first, in the attempt to do away with the contradictions arising from the direct translation of economic relations into legal principles, and to establish a harmonious system of law, and then in the repeated breaches made in this system by the influence and compulsion of further economic development, which involves it in further contradictions. (I am speaking here for the moment only of civil law.)

The reflection of economic relations as legal principles is necessarily also a topsy-turvy one: it goes on without the person who is acting being conscious of it; the jurist imagines he is operating with *a priori* propositions, whereas they are really only economic reflexes; so everything is upside down. And it seems to me obvious that this inversion, which, so long as it remains unrecognised, forms what we call *ideological outlook*, reacts in its turn upon the economic basis and may, within certain limits, modify it. The basis of the right of inheritance—assuming that the stages reached in the development of the family are the same—is an economic one. Nevertheless, it would be difficult to prove, for instance, that the absolute liberty of the testator in England and the severe restrictions in every detail imposed upon him in France are due to economic causes alone. Both react back, however, on the economic sphere to a very considerable extent, because they influence the distribution of property.

As to the realms of ideology which soar still higher in the air—religion, philosophy, etc.—these have a prehistoric stock, found already in existence by and taken over in the historical period, of what we should today call bunk. These various false conceptions of nature, of man's own being, of spirits, magic forces, etc., have for the most part only a negative economic element as their basis; the low economic development of the prehistoric period is supplemented and also partially conditioned and even caused by the false conceptions of nature. And even though economic necessity was the main driving force of the progressive knowledge of nature and has become ever more so, it would surely be pedantic to try and find economic causes for all this primitive nonsense. The history of science is the history of the gradual clearing away of this nonsense or rather of its replacement by fresh but always less absurd nonsense. The people who attend to this belong in their turn to special spheres in the division of labour and appear to themselves to be working in an independent field. And to the extent that they form an independent group within the social division of labour, their productions, including their errors, react upon the whole development of society, even on its economic development. But all the same they themselves are in turn under the dominating influence of economic development. In philosophy, for instance, this can be most readily proved true for the bourgeois period. Hobbes was the first modern materialist (in the eighteenth century sense) but he was an absolutist in a period when absolute monarchy was at its height throughout Europe and in England entered the lists against the people. Locke, both in religion and politics, was the child of the class compromise of 1688.[308] The English deists[304] and their more consistent continuators, the French materialists, were the true philosophers of the bourgeoisie, the French even of the bourgeois revolution. The German philistine runs through German philosophy from Kant to Hegel, sometimes positively and sometimes negatively. But as a definite sphere in the division of labour, the philosophy of every epoch presupposes certain definite thought material handed down to it by its predecessors, from which it takes its start. And that is why economically backward countries can still play first fiddle in philosophy: France in the eighteenth century as compared with England, on whose philosophy the French based themselves, and later Germany as compared with both. But in France as well as Germany philosophy and the general blossoming of literature at that time were the result of a rising economic development. I consider the ultimate supremacy of economic development established in these spheres too, but it comes to pass within the limitations imposed by the particular sphere itself: in philosophy, for instance, by the operation of economic influences (which again generally act only under political, etc., disguises) upon the existing philosophic material handed down by predecessors. Here economy creates nothing anew, but it determines the way in which the thought material found in existence is altered and further developed, and that too for the most part indirectly, for it is the political, legal and moral reflexes which exert the greatest direct influence on philosophy.

About religion I have said what was most necessary in the last section on Feuerbach.*

If therefore Barth supposes that we deny any and every reaction of the political, etc., reflexes of the economic movement upon

---

* See pp. 618-21 of this volume.—*Ed.*

the movement itself, he is simply tilting at windmills. He has only got to look at Marx's *Eighteenth Brumaire*,* which deals almost exclusively with the *particular* part played by political struggles and events, of course within their *general* dependence upon economic conditions. Or *Capital*, the section on the working day,** for instance, where legislation, which is surely a political act, has such a trenchant effect. Or the section on the history of the bourgeoisie. (Chapter XXIV***) Or why do we fight for the political dictatorship of the proletariat if political power is economically impotent? Force (that is, state power) is also an economic power!

But I have no time to criticise the book[449] now. I must first get Volume III*) out and besides I think that Bernstein, for instance, could deal with it quite effectively.

What these gentlemen all lack is dialectics. They always see only here cause, there effect. That this is a hollow abstraction, that such metaphysical polar opposites exist in the real world only during crises, while the whole vast process goes on in the form of interaction—though of very unequal forces, the economic movement being by far the strongest, most primordial, most decisive—that here everything is relative and nothing absolute—this they never begin to see. As far as they are concerned Hegel never existed. . . .

First published in full in
the journal *Sozialistische
Monatshefte* Nos. 20-21,
1920

Printed according to the
manuscript
Translated from the German

ENGELS TO F. MEHRING IN BERLIN

London, July 14, 1893

Dear Herr Mehring,

Today is my first opportunity to thank you for the *Lessing Legend* you were kind enough to send me. I did not want to reply with a bare formal acknowledgement of receipt of the book but intended at the same time to tell you something about it, about its contents. Hence the delay.

I shall begin at the end—the appendix on historical materialism,[453] in which you have lined up the main things excellently and for any unprejudiced person convincingly. If I find anything to object to it is that you give me more credit than I deserve, even if I

* See pp. 96-179 of this volume.—*Ed.*
** See Marx/Engels, *Werke*, Bd. 23, Dietz Verlag, Berlin, 1962, S. 245-320.—*Ed.*
*** Ibid., S. 741-91—*Ed.*
*) Of *Capital*.—*Ed.*

count in everything which I might possibly have found out for
myself—in time—but which Marx with his more rapid *coup d'œil*
and wider vision discovered much more quickly. When one had the
good fortune to work for forty years with a man like Marx, one
usually does not during his lifetime get the recognition one thinks one
deserves. Then, when the greater man dies, the lesser easily gets
overrated and this seems to me to be just my case at present; history will set all this right in the end and by that time one will have
quietly turned up one's toes and not know anything any more about
anything.

Otherwise only one more point is lacking, which, however, Marx
and I always failed to stress enough in our writings and in regard
to which we are all equally guilty. That is to say, we all laid, and
were bound to lay, the main emphasis, in the first place, on the *derivation* of political, juridical and other ideological notions, and of
actions arising through the medium of these notions, from basic
economic facts. But in so doing we neglected the formal side—the
ways and means by which these notions, etc., come about—for the
sake of the content. This has given our adversaries a welcome opportunity for misunderstandings and distortions, of which Paul
Barth[449] is a striking example.

Ideology is a process accomplished by the so-called thinker consciously, it is true, but with a false consciousness. The real motive
forces impelling him remain unknown to him; otherwise it simply
would not be an ideological process. Hence he imagines false or
seeming motive forces. Because it is a process of thought he derives its form as well as its content from pure thought, either his
own or that of his predecessors. He works with mere thought material, which he accepts without examination as the product of thought,
and does not investigate further for a more remote source independent of thought; indeed this is a matter of course to him, because,
as all action is *mediated* by thought, it appears to him to be ultimately based upon thought.

The historical ideologist (historical is here simply meant to comprise the political, juridical, philosophical, theological—in short,
all the spheres belonging to *society* and not only to nature) thus possesses in every sphere of science material which has formed itself
independently out of the thought of previous generations and has
gone through its own independent course of development in the
brains of these successive generations. True, external facts belonging
to one or another sphere may have exercised a codetermining influence on this development, but the tacit presupposition is that these
facts themselves are also only the fruits of a process of thought, and
so we still remain within that realm of mere thought, which apparently has successfully digested even the hardest facts.

It is above all this semblance of an independent history of state constitutions, of systems of law, of ideological conceptions in every separate domain that dazzles most people. If Luther and Calvin "overcome" the official Catholic religion or Hegel "overcomes" Fichte and Kant or Rousseau with his republican *Contrat social*[324] indirectly "overcomes" the constitutional Montesquieu, this is a process which remains within theology, philosophy or political science, represents a stage in the history of these particular spheres of thought and never passes beyond the sphere of thought. And since the bourgeois illusion of the eternity and finality of capitalist production has been added as well, even the overcoming of the mercantilists[454] by the physiocrats[130] and Adam Smith is accounted as a sheer victory of thought; not as the reflection in thought of changed economic facts but as the finally achieved correct understanding of actual conditions subsisting always and everywhere—in fact, if Richard Cœur-de-Lion and Philip Augustus had introduced free trade instead of getting mixed up in the crusades[12] we should have been spared five hundred years of misery and stupidity.

This aspect of the matter, which I can only indicate here, we have all, I think, neglected more than it deserves. It is the old story: form is always neglected at first for content. As I say, I have done that too and the mistake has always struck me only later. So I am not only far from reproaching you with this in any way—as the older of the guilty parties I certainly have no right to do so; on the contrary. But I would like all the same to draw your attention to this point for the future.

Hanging together with this is the fatuous notion of the ideologists that because we deny an independent historical development to the various ideological spheres which play a part in history we also deny them any *effect upon history*. The basis of this is the common undialectical conception of cause and effect as rigidly opposite poles, the total disregarding of interaction. These gentlemen often almost deliberately forget that once an historic element has been brought into the world by other, ultimately economic causes, it reacts, can react on its environment and even on the causes that have given rise to it. For instance, Barth on the priesthood and religion, your page 475. I was very glad to see how you settled this fellow, whose banality exceeds all expectations; and him they make professor of history in Leipzig! I must say that old man Wachsmuth—also rather a bonehead but greatly appreciative of facts—was quite a different chap.

- As for the rest, I can only repeat about the book what I repeatedly said about the articles when they appeared in the *Neue Zeit*[409]: it is by far the best presentation in existence of the genesis of the Prussian state. Indeed, I may well say that it is the only good presentation, correctly developing in most matters their interconnections down to the veriest details. One regrets only that you were unable to include the entire further development down to Bismarck and one hopes involuntarily that you will do this another time and present a complete coherent picture, from the Elector Frederick William down to old William.* You have already made your preliminary investigations and, in the main at least, they are as good as finished. The thing has to be done sometime anyhow before the shaky old shanty comes tumbling down. The dissipation of the monarchical-patriotic legends, while not directly a necessary preliminary for the abolition of the monarchy which screens class domination (inasmuch as a *pure*, bourgeois republic in Germany was outstripped by events before it came into existence), will nevertheless be one of the most effective levers for that purpose.

Then you will have more space and opportunity to depict the local history of Prussia as part of the general misery that Germany has gone through. This is the point where I occasionally depart some-what from your view, especially in the conception of the preliminary conditions for the dismemberment of Germany and of the failure of the bourgeois revolution in Germany during the sixteenth century. When I get down to reworking the historical introduction to my *Peasant War,*** which I hope will be next winter, I shall be able to develop there the points in question. Not that I consider those you indicated incorrect, but I put others alongside them and group them somewhat differently.

In studying German history—the story of a continuous state of wretchedness—I have always found that only a comparison with the corresponding French periods produces a correct idea of propor-tions, because what happens there is the direct opposite of what hap-pens in our country. There, the establishment of a national state from the scattered parts of the feudal state precisely at the time we pass through the period of our greatest decline. There, a rare objective logic during the whole course of the process; with us, more and more dismal dislocation. There, during the Middle Ages, foreign interven-tion is represented by the English conqueror who intervenes in favour of the Provençal nationality against the Northern French nationa-lity. The wars with England represent, in a way, the Thirty Years' War,[455] which, however, ends in the ejection of the foreign invaders and the subjugation of the South by the North. Then comes the strug-gle between the central power and vassal Burgundy, supported by its foreign possessions, which plays the part of Brandenburg-Prussia, a struggle which ends, however, in the victory of the central power and conclusively establishes the national state. And precisely at that moment the national state completely collapses in our country (in

---

* Wilhelm I.—*Ed.*
** See Friedrich Engels, "Der deutsche Bauernkrieg" (Marx/Engels, *Werke*, Bd. 7, Dietz Verlag, Berlin, 1960, S. 327-413).—*Ed.*

far as the "German kingdom" within the Holy Roman Empire[181] can be called a national state) and the plundering of German territory on a large scale sets in. This comparison is most humiliating for Germans but for that very reason the more instructive; and since our workers have put Germany back again in the forefront of the historical movement it has become somewhat easier for us to swallow the ignominy of the past.

Another especially significant feature of the development of Germany is the fact that neither of the partial states which in the end partitioned Germany between them was purely German—both were colonies on conquered Slav territory: Austria a Bavarian and Brandenburg a Saxon colony—and that they acquired power *within* Germany only by relying upon the support of foreign, non-German possessions: Austria upon that of Hungary (not to mention Bohemia) and Brandenburg that of Prussia. On the Western border, the one in greatest jeopardy, nothing of the kind took place; on the Northern border it was left to the Danes to protect Germany against the Danes; and in the South there was so little to protect that the frontier guard, the Swiss, even succeeded in tearing themselves loose from Germany!

But I have allowed myself to drift into all kinds of extraneous matter. Let this palaver at least serve you as proof of how stimulating an effect your work has upon me.

Once more cordial thanks and greetings from

Yours,

F. Engels

First published in abridged
form in the book: F. Mehring.
*Geschichte der Deutschen
Sozialdemokratie*, Bd. III,
Th. II, Stuttgart, 1898, and
in full in Russian in the *Works*
of K. Marx and F. Engels, first
edition. Vol. XXIX, 1946

Printed according to the
manuscript
Translated from the German

ENGELS TO W. BORGIUS[456] IN BRESLAU

London, January 25, 1894

Dear Sir,

Here is the answer to your questions:

1. What we understand by the economic relations, which we regard as the determining basis of the history of society, is the manner and method by which men in a given society produce their means of subsistence and exchange the products among themselves (in so far as division of labour exists). Thus the *entire technique* of production

and transport is here included. According to our conception this tec**nique also determines the manner and method of exchange and, fu**ther, of the distribution of products and with it, after the dissolutio**of gentile society, also the division into classes, and hence the rel**tions of lordship and servitude and with them the state, politics, la**etc. Further included in economic relations are the *geographical bas*on which they operate and those remnants of earlier stages of ec**nomic development which have actually been transmitted and hav**survived—often only through tradition or by force of inertia; also **course the external environment which surrounds this form of societ**

If, as you say, technique largely depends on the state of scienc**science depends far more still on the *state* and the *requirements* **technique. If society has a technical need, that helps science fo**ward more than ten universities. The whole of hydrostatics (Torr**celli, etc.) was called forth by the necessity for regulating the moun**tain streams of Italy in the sixteenth and seventeenth centuries. **have known anything reasonable about electricity only since its tech**nical applicability was discovered. But unfortunately it has becom**the custom in Germany to write the history of the sciences as if the**had fallen from the skies.

2. We regard economic conditions as that which ultimately con**ditions historical development. But race is itself an economic factor Here, however, two points must not be overlooked:

a) Political, juridical, philosophical, religious, literary, artistic etc., development is based on economic development. But all these react upon one another and also upon the economic basis. It is no**that the economic situation is *cause, solely active*, while everything else is only passive effect. There is, rather, interaction on the basis of economic necessity, which *ultimately* always asserts itself. The state, for instance, exercises an influence by protective tariffs, free trade, good or bad fiscal system; and even the deadly inanition and impotence of the German philistine, arising from the miserable economic condition of Germany from 1648 to 1830 and expressing themselves at first in pietism, then in sentimentality and cringing servility to princes and nobles, were not without economic effect. That was one of the greatest hindrances to recovery and was not shaken until the revolutionary and Napoleonic wars made the chronic misery an acute one. So it is not, as people try here and there conveniently to imagine, that the economic situation produces an automatic effect. No. Men make their history themselves, only they do so in a given environment, which conditions it, and on the basis of actual relations already existing, among which the economic relations, however much they may be influenced by the other—the political and ideological relations, are still ultimately the decisive ones, forming the keynote which runs through them and alone leads to understanding.

b) Men make their history themselves, but not as yet with a col-
-ctive will according to a collective plan or even in a definite, delim-
-ed given society. Their aspirations clash, and for that very reason
-ll such societies are governed by *necessity*, the complement and
-orm of appearance of which is *accident*. The necessity which here
-sserts itself athwart all accident is again ultimately economic neces-
-ity. This is where the so-called great men come in for treatment.
-hat such and such a man and precisely that man arises at a partic-
-lar time in a particular country is, of course, pure chance. But cut
-im out and there will be a demand for a substitute, and this substi-
-ute will be found, good or bad, but in the long run he will be found.
-hat Napoleon, just that particular Corsican, should have been the
-ilitary dictator whom the French Republic, exhausted by its own
-varfare, had rendered necessary, was chance; but that, if a Napoleon
-ad been lacking, another would have filled the place, is proved by
-he fact that the man was always found as soon as he became neces-
-ary: Caesar, Augustus, Cromwell, etc. While Marx discovered the
-materialist conception of history, Thierry, Mignet, Guizot and all the
-English historians up to 1850 are evidence that it was being striven
-or, and the discovery of the same conception by Morgan proves that
-he time was ripe for it and that it simply *had* to be discovered.

So with all the other accidents, and apparent accidents, of history.
The further the particular sphere which we are investigating is
removed from the economic sphere and approaches that of pure
abstract ideology, the more shall we find it exhibiting accidents in
its development, the more will its curve run zigzag. But if you plot
the average axis of the curve, you will find that this axis will run
more and more nearly parallel to the axis of economic development
the longer the period considered and the wider the field dealt
with.

In Germany the greatest hindrance to correct understanding is
the irresponsible neglect by literature of economic history. It is so
hard not only to disaccustom oneself to the ideas of history drilled
into one at school but still more to take up the necessary material for
doing so. Who, for instance, has read at least old G. von Gülich,
whose dry collection of material[457] nevertheless contains so much
stuff for the clarification of innumerable political facts!

For the rest, the fine example which Marx has given in *The Eighteenth Brumaire** should, I think, provide you fairly well with information on your questions, just because it is a practical example. I
have also, I believe, already touched on most of the points in *Anti-
Dühring*, I, chs. 9-11, and II, 2-4, as well as in III, 1, or Introduction,
and also in the last section of *Feuerbach*.**

---

* See pp. 96-179 of this volume.—*Ed.*
** See pp. 586-622 of this volume.—*Ed.*

Please do not weigh each word in the above too scrupulously, but keep the general connection in mind; I regret that I have not the time to word what I am writing to you as exactly as I should be obliged to do for publication....

First published in
the journal *Der
sozialistische
Akademiker* No. 20, 1895

Printed according to the
text of the journal
Translated from the German

NOTES
INDEXES

NOTES

¹ *Theses on Feuerbach* were written by Karl Marx in Brussels in the spring of 1845 when he had elaborated the main outlines of his materialist theory of history and application of materialism in order to analyse human society. Engels described it "as the first document in which is deposited the brilliant germ of the new world outlook" (see p. 585 of this volume).

In this work Marx points out the principal drawback of Feuerbach's materialism and of earlier materialism, namely, their contemplative character and failure to understand that man's activity is revolutionary and "practically critical". Marx emphasises the decisive role of revolutionary practice in acquiring knowledge of the world and changing it.—28

² *Manifesto of the Communist Party*—the first policy document of scientific communism which provides an integral and well-composed exposition of the fundamental principles of the great teachings of Marx and Engels. "With the clarity and brilliance of genius, this work outlines a new world conception, consistent materialism, which also embraces the realm of social life; dialectics, as the most comprehensive and profound doctrine of development; the theory of the class struggle and of the world-historic revolutionary role of the proletariat—the creator of a new, communist society" (V. I. Lenin, *Collected Works*, Vol. 21, Moscow, 1964, p. 48).

The *Manifesto of the Communist Party* armed the proletariat with scientific proofs of the inevitability of the collapse of capitalism and the triumph of the proletarian revolution and defined the tasks and aims of the revolutionary working-class movement.—31, 35

³ *The Communist League*—the first international communist organisation of the proletariat founded by Marx and Engels; it existed from 1847 till 1852. See F. Engels's article "On the History of the Communist League" (pp. 431-48 of this volume).—31

⁴ This refers to the February revolution of 1848 in France.—31, 71, 105, 183, 281, 437

⁵ *The Red Republican*—a Chartist weekly published in London by George Julian Harney from June to November 1850. It carried an abridged version of the *Manifesto* in Nos. 21-24, November 1850.—31

⁶ The reference is to the heroic uprising of the Paris workers of June 23-26, 1848, which was suppressed by the French bourgeoisie with extreme brutality. This insurrection was the first great civil war between the proletariat and the bourgeoisie.—31, 71, 102, 239, 250, 269, 275, 281, 367, 389, 651, 670

⁷ *Le Socialiste*—a weekly newspaper published in New York from October 1871 till May 1873 in French. It was an organ of the French sections of the North-American Federation of the International (see Note 120); after the Hague Congress (see Note 250) it broke away from the International.

The French translation of the *Manifesto of the Communist Party* referre to in the text was published in *Le Socialiste* between January and Mar 1872.—31

8 *The Paris Commune of 1871*—the revolutionary government of the workir class, which was in power from March 28 till May 28, 1871 and provide the first historical experience of the dictatorship of the proletariat. Loosel this term is applied to the actual proletarian revolution of March 18, 187 and also to the period of proletarian dictatorship that followed. *The Civ War in France* treats the history of the Paris Commune and analyses its es sential features in great detail (see pp. 248-309 of this volume).—31, 246, 31 323, 370, 648, 675

9 *The Cologne Communist trial* (October 4-November 12, 1852)—a frame-u trial of 11 members of the Communist League, staged by the Prussian Govern ment. Charged with high treason on the basis of faked documents and fals evidence, seven of the accused were sentenced to terms of imprisonment in fortress varying from three to six years. The vile provocations of the Prussia police state against the international working-class movement were expose by Marx and Engels (see Engels, "Der Kommunisten-Prozess zu Köln", an also Marx's pamphlet *Revelations about the Cologne Communist Trial*).—32 368, 431

10 This refers to the June insurrection in Paris in 1848 (see Note 6).—34

11 This preface was written by Engels on May 1, 1890, the day when, in ac cordance with the decision of the Paris Congress of the Second International (July 1889), mass demonstrations, strikes and meetings were held in a number of countries of Europe and America. The workers put forward the demand for the 8-hour working day and other demands set forth by the Congress. From that time onwards the First of May began to be celebrated annually by the workers of all countries as the day of international solidarity of the proleta- riat.—34

12 This refers to military colonialist expeditions to the East by the West- European big feudal lords, knights and Italian merchants in the eleventh- thirteenth centuries with the religious goal of recovering shrines in Jerusa- lem and other "holy places" from the Mohammedans. The crusades were inspired and justified by the Catholic Church and papacy which were striving for world domination, while the knights made up their main fighting force. Peasants who sought liberation from the feudal yoke also took part in the crusades. The crusaders resorted to plunder and violence against both the Moslem and Christian population of the countries through which they marched. The objects of their predatory aspirations were not only the Moslem states in Syria, Palestine, Egypt and Tunisia, but the orthodox Byzantine Empire. Their conquests in the Eastern Mediterranean area were, however, not lasting and soon they were recovered by the Moslems.—38, 691

13 In their later works Marx and Engels used the more exact terms "the value of labour power" and "the price of labour power" introduced by Marx instead of "the value of labour" and "the price of labour" (see in this connection Engels's introduction to Marx's *Wage Labour and Capital*, pp. 64-70 of this volume).—41

14 This refers to the French bourgeois revolution at the end of the eighteenth century.—47

15 This refers to the movement for a reform of the electoral law which, under pressure from the people, was passed by the House of Commons in 1831 and was finally endorsed by the House of Lords in June 1832. This reform was directed against the monopoly rule of the landed and financial aristocracy and

opened the way to Parliament for the representatives of the industrial bourgeoisie. The proletariat and the petty bourgeoisie who were the main force in the struggle for the reform were deceived by the liberal bourgeoisie and were not granted electoral rights.—*53, 388, 390*

16 *The Restoration of 1660-89*—the period of the second rule in England of the Stuart dynasty, which was overthrown by the English bourgeois revolution of the seventeenth century (see Note 104).

The Restoration of 1814-30—a period of the second reign in France of the Bourbon dynasty. The reactionary regime of the Bourbons which supported the interests of the nobles and the clericals was overthrown by the July revolution of 1830.—*54, 110*

17 *The Legitimists*—the adherents of the "legitimate" Bourbon dynasty overthrown in 1830, which represented the interests of the big landed nobility. In their struggle against the reigning Orleans dynasty (1830-48), which relied on the financial aristocracy and big bourgeoisie, a section of the Legitimists resorted to social demagogy and projected themselves as defenders of the working people against the exploitation by the bourgeoisie.—*54, 110, 277, 300*

18 *"Young England"*—a group of British Conservatives—men of politics and literature—formed in the early 1840s (see Note 81). While expressing the dissatisfaction of the landed aristocracy with the growing economic and political might of the bourgeoisie, the "Young England" leaders resorted to demagogic ruses in order to subjugate the working class to their influence and to turn it into a tool in their struggle against the bourgeoisie.—*54*

19 *Squirearchy* or *Junkerdom*—in the narrow sense, landed nobility in East Prussia; in the broad sense this means a class of German landowners.—*54, 239, 639, 670*

20 This refers to the bourgeois-democratic revolution of 1848-49 in Germany.—*58, 607*

21 *Jerusalem*—famous city and religious centre in Palestine, a Christian and Judaean holy place.

New Jerusalem is a synonym of Paradise according to the Christian tradition.—*59*

22 *Chartism*—a political movement of the British workers in the period from the thirties to the middle fifties of the nineteenth century which arose as a result of the hard economic conditions of the workers and their lack of political rights. The watchword of the movement was the struggle for the implementation of the People's Charter (see Note 315), which included the demand for universal suffrage and a number of provisions guaranteeing this right for the workers. Lenin said that Chartism was "the first broad, truly mass and politically organised proletarian revolutionary movement" (V. I. Lenin, *Collected Works*, Vol. 29, Moscow, 1965, p. 309).—*62, 389, 435*

23 This refers to petty-bourgeois republican democrats and petty-bourgeois socialists who were adherents of the French newspaper *La Réforme*. They came out for a republic and democratic and social reforms.—*62, 437*

24 *La Réforme*—French daily newspaper published in Paris from 1843 to 1850.—*62*

25 In February 1846 preparations were made for an insurrection throughout the Polish territories with the aim of achieving national liberation. Polish revolutionary democrats (Dembowski and others) were the main inspirers of the insurrection. However, as a result of the betrayal by a section of the Polish gentry and the arrest of the leaders of the insurrection by the Prussian police, only isolated risings broke out. Only in Cracow, which from 1815

onwards was jointly controlled by Austria, Russia and Prussia, did the in-surgents gain a victory on February 22 and establish a national government, which issued a manifesto repealing obligatory services to the feudal lords. The Cracow uprising was crushed early in March 1846. In November 1846 Austria, Prussia and Russia signed a treaty according to which Cracow was annexed to the Austrian Empire.—62

26 In preparing this work for the press, Marx set himself the task of provid-ing a popular outline of the economic relations forming the material basis for the class struggle in capitalist society. His purpose was to arm the pro-letariat with a theoretical weapon—a profound understanding of the fact that the class rule of the bourgeoisie in capitalist society rests on the wage slavery of the workers. In elaborating the postulates of his theory of surplus value, Marx formulated a general thesis on the relative and absolute impoverishment of the working class under capitalism.

The present edition of this pamphlet is printed according to the text of the 1891 edition, edited by Engels.—64, 71

27 *Neue Rheinische Zeitung. Organ der Demokratie*—daily newspaper published in Cologne from June 1, 1848 to May 19, 1849; its editor-in-chief was Marx, and Engels was a member of the editorial board.—64, 183, 367, 430, 443, 641

28 *The German Workers' Society* in Brussels was founded by Marx and Engels at the end of August 1847 to further the political enlightenment of German workers residing in Belgium and the dissemination of the ideas of scientific communism among them. The Society guided by Marx and Engels and their associates became the legal rallying centre for the German revolutionary work-ers in Belgium. The outstanding members of the Society were also members of the Brussels branch of the Communist League. The activities of the German Workers' Society in Brussels ceased soon after the February bourgeois revolu-tion of 1848 in France because of the arrests and deportation of its members by the Belgian police.—64, 183, 366, 437

29 This refers to the intervention of the tsarist troops in Hungary in 1849 for the purpose of suppressing the Hungarian bourgeois revolution and restoring the Austrian Hapsburg dynasty.—64

30 This refers to the people's uprisings in Germany in May-July 1849 in sup-port of the imperial Constitution (adopted by the Frankfurt parliament on March 28, 1849, but rejected by a number of German states). These uprisings were spontaneous and disunited, and were therefore crushed in mid-July 1849.—64, 368, 443, 651

31 Later among Marx's papers was found the manuscript of a rough outline of the conclusion to a series of lectures on the subject of wage labour and capi-tal bearing the heading "Wages" and a note on the cover "Brussels, December 1847". As regards its contents, the manuscript represents, in some respects, a continuation of the unfinished work *Wage Labour and Capital*. But the final chapters of this work ready for the press were never found among Marx's manuscripts.—64

32 Marx wrote in *Capital*: "...by classical Political Economy, I understand that economy which, since the time of W. Petty, has investigated the real relations of production in bourgeois society...." (Karl Marx, *Capital*, Vol. I, Moscow, 1965, p. 81.) The most prominent representatives of classical political economy in Britain were Adam Smith and David Ricardo.—65

33 Engels wrote in *Anti-Dühring*: "Although it first took shape in the minds of a few men of genius towards the end of the seventeenth century, political economy in the narrow sense, in its positive formulation by the physiocrats

and Adam Smith, is nevertheless essentially a child of the eighteenth century. . . ." (F. Engels, *Anti-Dühring*, Moscow, 1962, p. 209.)—65

34 Engels is referring to the celebration of May Day in 1891. In some countries (Britain and Germany) May Day was celebrated on the first Sunday after May 1, which in 1891 fell on May 3.—70

35 This refers to the March revolution of 1848 in Prussia.—71

36 On November 1, 1848, after a week of fierce fighting the Austrian Emperor's troops crushed the people's insurrection in Vienna and seized the city.

In November and December 1848 a reactionary coup d'état took place in Prussia; on November 1, an openly counter-revolutionary government came to power. On November 9, the sessions of the Prussian National Assembly were transferred from Berlin to the town of Brandenburg; the majority of the National Assembly who continued to hold their sittings in Berlin were dispersed by troops on November 15. The coup d'état ended with the dissolution of the National Assembly on December 5, and the proclamation of a reactionary constitution.—71, 367, 651

37 Marx is referring to the national liberation uprisings in 1848 and 1849 in Hungary, Italy and Poland.—71

38 This is an allusion to the legend about a very intricate knot by which Gordius, King of Phrygia, attached a yoke to a chariot pole; according to the oracle he who untied the knot would become the Ruler of Asia; Alexander the Great cut the knot with his sword instead of untying it.—76

39 This work, written on the basis of a concrete analysis of the revolutionary events in France from 1848 to 1851, is one of the most important Marxist writings. In it Marx gives a further elaboration of all the basic tenets of historical materialism—the theory of the class struggle and proletarian revolution, the state and the dictatorship of the proletariat. Of extremely great importance is the conclusion which Marx arrived at on the question of the attitude of the proletariat to the bourgeois state. He says, "All revolutions perfected this machine instead of smashing it" (see p. 169 of this volume). Lenin described it as one of the most important propositions in the Marxist teaching on the state.

In *The Eighteenth Brumaire of Louis Bonaparte* Marx continued his analysis of the question of the peasantry as a potential ally of the working class in the imminent revolution, outlined the role of the political parties in the life of society and exposed for what they were the essential features of Bonapartism.—94, 96

40 On December 2, 1851 a counter-revolutionary coup d'état in France was carried out by Louis Bonaparte and his adherents.—94, 98, 119, 250, 261, 284, 389, 643

41 *Renaissance*—a period in the cultural and ideological development of a number of countries in Western and Central Europe called forth by the emergence of capitalist relations, which covers the second half of the fifteenth and the sixteenth century. This period is usually associated with a rapid development in the arts and sciences and the revival of interest in the culture of classical Greece and Rome (hence the name of the period). For Engels's description of the Renaissance see his "Introduction to *Dialectics of Nature*" (pp. 338-40 of this volume).—94, 617

42 The Second Republic existed in France from 1848 to 1852. For Marx's description of this period see *The Class Struggles in France, 1848 to 1850* and *The Eighteenth Brumaire of Louis Bonaparte*.—95·

[43] *The Montagne* (1793-95)—a revolutionary-democratic group in the National Convention during the French bourgeois revolution of the late 18th century (see also Notes 76 and 106).—96

[44] *Brumaire*—a month in the French republican calendar.
The Eighteenth Brumaire (November 9, 1799)—the coup d'état which took place on this day and resulted in the establishment of Napoleon Bonaparte's military dictatorship. By "the second edition of the eighteenth Brumaire" Marx means the coup d'état of December 2, 1851.—96

[45] *The Old Testament*—a greater portion of the Bible comprising the Books of the Law and the Prophets.—97

[46] This refers to the English bourgeois revolution of the seventeenth century (see also Note 104).—97

[47] *Bedlam*—a lunatic asylum in London.—98

[48] On December 10, 1848, Louis Bonaparte was elected President of the French Republic by plebiscite.—98

[49] The expression "to long for the fleshpots of Egypt" comes from the biblical legend according to which during the exodus of the Israelites from Egypt the faint-hearted among them were driven by the hardships of the journey and hunger to long for the days of captivity when at least they had enough to eat.—98

[50] *Hic Rhodus, hic salta!* (Here is Rhodes, leap here!)—the words are taken from a fable by Aesop about a swaggerer who claimed to be able to produce witnesses to prove that he had once made a remarkable leap in Rhodes, to which he received the reply: "Why cite witnesses if it is true? Here is Rhodes, leap here!" In other words, "Show us right here what you can do!"
Here is the rose, dance here!— this paraphrase of the preceding quotation (in Greek Rhodes, the name of the island, also means "rose") is used by Hegel in the preface to his work *Grundlinien der Philosophie des Rechts* (Principles of the Philosophy of Right).—99

[51] According to the French Constitution of 1848 presidential elections were to take place every four years on the second Sunday in May. In May 1852 Louis Bonaparte's term as president expired.—99, 161

[52] *Chiliasts* (from the Greek word *chilias*, a thousand)—preachers of a mystical religious doctrine concerning the second coming of Christ and the establishment of the millennium, when justice, universal equality and prosperity will be triumphant.—99

[53] *In ,partibus infidelium* (literally in the country of the infidels)—an addition to the title of Catholic bishops appointed to a purely nominal diocese in non-Christian countries. This expression is frequently used in Marx's and Engels's writings to describe émigré governments formed abroad without taking into consideration the real situation in a country.—99, 123, 161, 644

[54] *The Capitol*—a temple of Jupiter on a hill in Rome, which was a citadel. According to legend, in 390 B.C., during the Gallic invasion, Rome was saved only thanks to the cackle of geese from the temple of Juno which awoke the sleeping guards of the Capitol.—100

[55] This refers to the so-called "Africans" or "Algerians", French generals and officers, who won military fame during colonial wars against the Algerian tribes fighting for their liberation. In the Legislative Assembly African generals Cavaignac, Lamoricière and Bedeau headed the Republicans.—100, 116

[56] *Dynastic opposition*—a group, led by Odilon Barrot, in the French Chamber of Deputies during the July monarchy. Its representatives voiced the senti-

ments of the liberal industrial and commercial bourgeoisie and advocated moderate electoral reform as a means of averting the revolution and preserving the Orleans dynasty.—100, 111

57 *July monarchy*—a period of the reign of Louis Philippe (1830-48), which derived its name from the July revolution.—101, 115

58 On May 15, 1848, during a popular demonstration Paris workers and artisans forced their way into the hall where the Constituent Assembly was in session, proclaimed it dissolved and formed a revolutionary government. The demonstrators, however, were soon dispersed by the National Guard and troops which came to the rescue. The leaders of the workers (Blanqui, Barbès, Albert, Raspail and others) were arrested.—101, 111

59 According to the Roman historian Eusebius, Emperor Constantine I in 312, on the eve of a victory over his rival Maxentius, saw in the sky the sign of the Cross with the words on it: "By this sign thou shalt conquer!"—103

60 Pythia, a Greek oracle and priestess in the temple of Apollo at Delphi who is said to have proclaimed her prophecies from a special tripod.—103

61 *Le National*—a French daily published in Paris from 1830 to 1851, the organ of moderate bourgeois republicans. Their main representatives in the provisional government were Marrast, Bestide and Garnier Pagès.—104, 134, 281, 308

62 *Journal des Débats politiques et littéraires*—a French bourgeois daily newspaper founded in Paris in 1789. At the time of the July monarchy—a government paper, the organ of the pro-Orleans bourgeoisie. During the 1848 revolution the newspaper expressed the views of the counter-revolutionary bourgeoisie, the so-called Party of Order.—104, 164

63 This refers to treaties signed in Vienna in May and June 1815 by the countries who took part in the Napoleonic wars. In conclusion the Vienna Congress of 1814-15 restored France within the boundaries of 1792 and placed it under strict control by other states. France was also barred from making any territorial annexations in Europe.—104

64 *The Constitutional Charter*, adopted after the bourgeois revolution of 1830 in France, was the basic law of the July monarchy. Nominally the Charter proclaimed the sovereign rights of the nation and made some restrictions on the king's power.—105

65 *The Elysian Fields (Champs Élysées)*—the main street in Paris where the Elysée Palace is situated, which, in accordance with the 1848 Constitution, was the official residence of the President of the Republic. In this instance Marx makes an ironic allusion to the resemblance between the names of the street and the paradise of classical mythology.—107

66 *Clichy*—from 1826 to 1867 a debtors' prison in Paris.—107, 141

67 Immediately after the establishment of the French Republic the question of choosing the national standard arose. The revolutionary workers of Paris demanded that the red flag hoisted by the workers of the suburbs of Paris during the June insurrection of 1832 be made the national standard. The representatives of the bourgeoisie insisted on the tricolor (blue, white and red) flag, which had been the national standard of France during the bourgeois revolution of the late 18th century and at the time of Napoleon I. The tricolor had been the banner of bourgeois republicans who supported *Le National* even prior to the 1848 revolution. The workers' representatives had to agree to making the tricolor the national standard of the Republic of France but they attached a red rosette to the flagstaff.—109

[68] *Praetorians*—in ancient Rome the life-guards of the general or emperor, maintained by him and enjoying various privileges. They constantly took part in internal disturbances and not infrequently enthroned their henchmen. The allusion here is to the Society of December 10 (for this see pp. 136-38 of this volume).—109, 305

[69] From May to July 1849 the Kingdom of Naples together with Austria participated in the intervention against the Republic of Rome.—110

[70] Marx is referring to the following events in Louis Bonaparte's life: in 1832 Louis Bonaparte became a Swiss citizen in the canton Thurgau; in 1848 during his stay in Britain he voluntarily joined the special constabulary (in Britain a police reserve comprised of civilians).—110

[71] *Orleanists*—supporters of the House of Orleans, a cadet branch of the Bourbon dynasty that came to power during the July revolution of 1830 and was overthrown by the revolution of 1848. They defended the interests of the finance aristocracy and the big bourgeoisie.—110, 269, 277, 300

[72] *The Party of Order*—a party of the conservative big bourgeoisie founded in 1848. It was a coalition of the two French monarchist factions—the Legitimists and Orleanists (see Notes 17 and 71); from 1849 till the coup d'état of December 2, 1851, it held the leading position in the Legislative Assembly of the Second Republic.—110, 275, 293, 305

[73] Caligula, a Roman emperor (A.D. 37-41) who was enthroned by the Praetorian Guard.—112

[74] *Le Moniteur universel*—French daily newspaper, official government organ published in Paris from 1789 to 1901. It printed all government acts, parliamentary proceedings and other official documents.—113, 145

[75] *Questor* of the Legislative Assembly is the name given to every deputy charged by the Assembly with handling economic and financial matters and safeguarding its security (by analogy with Roman questors). The reference is to the bill granting the president of the National Assembly the right to direct requisition of troops which was tabled on November 6, 1851 by the royalist questors Le Flô, Baze and Panat, and rejected after a heated debate on November 17.—113

[76] *Constitutionalists*—adherents of constitutional monarchy, representatives of the big bourgeoisie closely connected with the king, and of liberal nobility.
    Girondins—a bourgeois political group at the time of the French bourgeois revolution at the end of the 18th century. The Girondins expressed the interests of the moderate bourgeoisie, wavered between the revolutionary and counter-revolutionary forces and compromised with the royalists. The name is derived from the Department of Gironde because its representatives in the Legislative Assembly and the National Convention were leaders of this group.
    Jacobins—Left-wing bourgeois political group during the French bourgeois revolution at the end of the 18th century; they resolutely and consistently advocated the necessity of the abolition of feudalism and absolutism.—114, 289

[77] On April 16, 1848 a peaceful demonstration of Paris workers arranged in order to hand in a petition to the provisional government on the "organisation of labour" and the "abolition of exploitation of man by man" was dispersed by the bourgeois National Guard specially mobilised for this purpose.—114

[78] *The Fronde*—a movement against absolutism among the French nobility and bourgeoisie which was active between 1648 and 1653. Its leaders from among the aristocracy relied on the support of their vassals and foreign troops and

utilised peasant revolts and the democratic movement in the cities to further their own objectives.—115

79 *The Phrygian cap*—a headdress worn by the ancient Phrygians which was red in colour; subsequently it was taken as a model for the Jacobin hat (see Note 76) during the French bourgeois revolution at the end of the 18th century; from then on it became the symbol of freedom.—115

80 *Lily*—a heraldic emblem of the Bourbon dynasty.—117

81 *The Tories*—a political party in England which was founded at the end of the 17th century; it defended the interests of the landed aristocracy and the upper Church hierarchy, upheld the old feudal traditions and fought against liberal and progressive demands. In the mid-19th century the Conservative Party evolved from it.—118, 391

82 *Ems*—a town in West Germany, one of the permanent residences of the Count of Chambord, the pretender to the French throne (who called himself Henry V) and a descendant of a branch of the Bourbon dynasty.
Claremont—a castle near London Louis Philippe's residence after his escape from France after the February revolution of 1848.—118

83 *Jericho*—according to biblical tradition, the first town to be occupied by the Israelites when they came to Palestine. Its walls collapsed at the trumpet-blasts of the besiegers.—121

84 An allusion to the plans of Louis Bonaparte, who expected that Pope Pius IX would crown him King of France. According to biblical tradition David, the king of Israel, was anointed king by the prophet Samuel.—124

85 The battle of Austerlitz (in Moravia) on December 2, 1805, ended in a victory for Napoleon I over the Russo-Austrian troops.—124

86 This refers to the July revolution of 1830.—125, 250

87 An allusion to Louis Bonaparte's book *Des idées napoléoniennes*, published in Paris in 1839.—129

88 *Burgraves* was the name given to the 17 leading Orleanists and Legitimists (see Notes 17 and 71), who were members of the Legislative Assembly's committee for drafting a new electoral law, for their unwarranted claim to power and their reactionary aspirations. The name was taken from the title of Victor Hugo's historical drama. Its action is set in medieval Germany where Burg-Graf was the title of the ruler of a "burg" (fortified town or castle), who was appointed by the emperor.—132

89 The press law passed by the Legislative Assembly in July 1850 considerably increased the deposits which newspaper publishers had to pay, and introduced a stamp duty applicable to pamphlets as well.—134

90 *La Presse*—a daily newspaper published in Paris from 1836 onwards; during the July monarchy it belonged to the opposition; in 1848 and 1849 it was the organ of the bourgeois republicans and afterwards a Bonapartist paper.—134

91 *Lazzaroni*—a nickname of the declassed lumpenproletariat in Italy who were repeatedly drawn by the reactionary monarchist circles into the struggle against liberal and democratic movements.—137

92 This refers to the following two incidents in the life of Louis Bonaparte: on October 30, 1836, he attempted to stir up a revolt in Strasbourg with the help of two artillery regiments, but the insurgents were disarmed and Louis Bonaparte was arrested and deported to America. On August 6, 1840, he again attempted to instigate a rebellion among the troops of the local garri-

son in Boulogne. This attempt also proved a failure. He was sentenced to life imprisonment, but escaped to England in 1846.—137

93 *Elysée newspapers*—newspapers of a Bonapartist trend; the name is taken from the Elysée Palace, the residence of Louis Bonaparte while president.—139

94 For his play on words Marx cites here a line from Schiller's *Lied an die Freude* (Ode to Joy), in which the poet sings of joy as the "daughter of Elysium". In classical mythology Elysium or the Elysian fields is equivalent to paradise. Champs Elysées (Elysian Fields), the name of the Paris avenue, where Louis Bonaparte s residence stood.—143

95 Parliaments were the supreme judicial bodies in France before the bourgeois revolution of 1789. They registered the royal decrees and possessed the so-called right of remonstrance, i.e., the right to protest against decrees which infringed the customs and legislation of the country.—146

96 *Belle Isle*—an island in the Bay of Biscay; a place of detention for political prisoners.—149

97 Here Marx is paraphrasing a story which the Greek writer Athenaeus (2nd and 3rd centuries A.D.) recounts in his book *Deipnosophistae* (Dinner-Table Philosophers). The Egyptian Pharaoh Tachos, alluding to the small stature of the Spartan King Agesilaus who had come with his troops to Pharaoh's assistance, said: "The mountain was in labour. Zeus was scared. But the mountain has brought forth a mouse." Agesilaus replied: "I seem to thee now but a mouse, but the time will come when I will appear to thee as a lion."—150

98 *L'Assemblée nationale*—a daily French newspaper of a monarchist Legitimist trend; it appeared in Paris from 1848 to 1857. Between 1848 and 1851 it supported the fusion of the two dynastic parties—the Legitimists and the Orleanists (see Notes 17 and 71).—153

99 In the 1850s the Count of Chambord, the Legitimist pretender to the French throne, lived in Venice.—153

100 This is a reference to the tactical disagreements in the camp of the Legitimists during the Restoration period from 1814 to 1830 (see Note 16). Villèle (supporter of Louis XVIII) favoured a more cautious introduction of reactionary measures, while Polignac (adherent of the Comte d'Artois—King Charles X from 1824) advocated the unqualified restoration of the pre-revolutionary regime.

The *Palace of the Tuileries* in Paris was Louis XVIII's residence; during the Restoration the Comte d'Artois lived in the *Pavillon Marsan*, one of the wings of the palace.—154

101 *The Economist*—an English economic and political weekly journal, organ of the big industrial bourgeoisie; it has been published in London ever since 1843.—156

102 The first international trade and industrial exhibition was held in London from May to October 1851.—160, 380

103 *Le Messager de l'Assemblée*—French anti-Bonapartist daily published in Paris from February 16 to December 2, 1851.—162

104 *The Long Parliament* (1640-53)—English parliament convened by King Charles I at the outbreak of the bourgeois revolution; it became its constituent body. In 1649 the parliament passed a death sentence on Charles I and proclaimed a republic. The parliament was dissolved by Cromwell in 1653.—165

105 *Cévennes*—a mountainous region of the Languedoc province in France where an uprising of peasants took place from 1702 to 1705. The revolt, which began as a protest against the persecution of Protestants, assumed an openly anti-feudal character.

An allusion to a counter-revolutionary revolt in Vendée (a Western province of France), which was instigated in 1793 by the French royalists who used the backward peasants as a tool in the struggle against the French revolution.—171

106 *National Convention*—supreme representative body in France during the bourgeois revolution at the end of the 18th century, which existed from September 1792 to October 1795. When the revolution was asserting itself, the Convention was progressive in its policy, expressed the interests of the French bourgeoisie which strove to consolidate the gains of the revolution and to abolish the feudal social structure.—172

107 *Mount Sinai*—a mountain range on the Sinai Peninsula in Arabia. According to biblical tradition prophet Moses received the tablets on which were written the ten Commandments from God on Mount Sinai.—176

108 *The Council of Constance* (1414-18) was convened in order to strengthen the weakened position of the Catholic Church during the rise of the Reformation movement. The Council condemned the doctrines of John Wycliffe and Jan Hus, leaders of the Reformation, and put an end to the schism in the Catholic Church by electing a new head of the Church in place of the three popes then contending for power.—176

109 A reference to German, or "True", Socialism—a reactionary trend which became widespread mainly among petty-bourgeois intellectuals in Germany in the 1840s. Marx and Engels gave a description of this trend in the *Manifesto of the Communist Party* (see pp. 56-58 of this volume).—176, 592

110 This refers to the regency of Philippe d'Orleans in France from 1715 to 1723 during the infancy of Louis XV.—178

111 *The Holy Tunic of Treves*—one of the "sacred" relics (alleged to be a garment of Christ, doffed at the time of the crucifixion) exhibited in the Catholic Cathedral at Trier (an old town in West Germany sometimes called Treves in English). Whole generations of pilgrims came to pay homage to it.—179

112 *The Vendôme Column* was erected between 1806 and 1810 in Paris in honour of the victories of Napoleon and was made out of the bronze from captured enemy guns and crowned by a statue of Napoleon. On May 16, 1871, by order of the Paris Commune, the Vendôme Column was destroyed, but in 1875 it was restored by the reactionaries.—179, 294

113 Marx's book *A Contribution to the Critique of Political Economy* represents an important stage in the creation of Marxist political economy. Before setting out to write this book Marx carried out fifteen years of research work in the course of which he studied a vast amount of literature and worked out the basis of his economic doctrine. Marx planned to set forth the results of his investigation in a major work devoted to economics. In August and September 1857 he started to systematise his material and make the first rough draft of his work. During the ensuing months Marx made a detailed plan and decided to publish his future work in parts, in separate issues. Having concluded a preliminary contract with F. Duncker, a Berlin publisher, he began to work on the first article which was printed in June 1859.

Soon after the first article Marx planned to publish a second, which was to deal with the problems of capital. His subsequent studies, however, prompted

Marx to change his original plan. Instead of the planned articles he wrote *Capital* in which he included, in a revised form, the main ideas of his book *A Contribution to the Critique of Political Economy.*—180

[114] This is a reference to the unfinished introduction which Marx had planned to write for his major work on economics.—180

[115] *Rheinische Zeitung für Politik, Handel und Gewerbe* (Rhenish Gazette on Questions of Politics, Trade and Industry)—daily newspaper published in Cologne from January 1, 1842 to March 31, 1843. From April 1842 onwards Marx contributed to the newspaper and in October of the same year he became one of its editors.—180, 365, 430, 591

[116] *Allgemeine Zeitung* (General Journal)—German reactionary daily newspaper; it started publication in 1798. From 1810 to 1882 it was published in Augsburg. In 1842 it carried an article distorting the ideas of utopian communism and socialism which was exposed by Marx in his article, "Der Kommunismus und die *Augsburger Allgemeine Zeitung*" (Communism and the *Augsburg General Journal*).—181

[117] *Deutsch-Französische Jahrbücher* (German-French Yearbooks) was published in German in Paris; its editors were Karl Marx and Arnold Ruge. Only one, double issue appeared in February 1844. It carried writings by Marx and Engels which marked Marx's and Engels's final transition to the standpoint of materialism and communism. The publication of the journal ceased mainly as a result of differences of opinion between Marx and the bourgeois radical Ruge.—181, 366, 436

[118] *The New York Daily Tribune*—progressive bourgeois newspaper published from 1841 to 1924. Marx and Engels contributed to it from August 1851 to March 1862.—183, 368, 430

[119] This work is the report delivered by Marx at the meetings of the General Council of the First International in June 1865. In this report Marx set forth for the first time in public the basis of his theory of surplus value. Though the address was directed against the mistaken views of a member of the International, John Weston, who maintained that higher wages cannot improve the condition of the workers and that the trade unions' activity must be considered detrimental to their interests, it at the same time dealt a blow at the Proudhonists, and also at the Lassalleans, who had a negative attitude towards the economic struggle of the workers and the trade unions. Marx resolutely opposed the preaching of passivity and submissiveness of the proletarians in face of the capitalist exploiters; he provided a theoretical substantiation of the role and significance of the workers' economic struggle and stressed the necessity of its subordination to the ultimate aim of the proletariat—abolition of wage slavery. The manuscript of the paper has been preserved. The paper was first published in London in 1898 by Marx's daughter Eleanor under the title *Value, Price and Profit* with a preface by her husband Eduard Aveling, English socialist. The introduction and first six chapters had no headings in the manuscript, for which Aveling provided the titles. In the present edition all these headings except the main one have been retained.—185

[120] *The International Working Men's Association* (The First International)—the first international organisation of the proletariat, which was guided by Marx and Engels (1864-76). It disseminated among the advanced workers of the major capitalist countries the ideas of scientific socialism and "laid the foundation of an international organisation of the workers for the preparation of their revolutionary attack on capital" (V. I. Lenin, *Collected Works*, Vol. 29, Moscow, p. 306). For a description of the International see Engels's Preface to the German edition of the *Manifesto of the Communist Party* of 1890 and Marx's letter to F. Bolte of November 23, 1871 (see pp. 32-34 and 671-74 of this volume).—185, 255, 430, 431, 675, 677

121 The struggle of the working class for the official restriction of the working day to ten hours began in England at the end of the 18th century, and from the 1830s onwards it involved broad masses of the proletariat.

The Ten Hours' Bill for youths and women was passed by the Parliament on June 8, 1847. Many factory-owners, however, did not apply it in practice.—191

122 At the time of the French bourgeois revolution in 1793 and 1794 the Jacobin Convention (see Notes 76 and 106) introduced fixed price limits on some commodities and fixed maximum wages.—191

123 The English Society for the Advancement of Science was founded in 1831 and exists to this day. Marx refers here to a speech delivered by W. Newmarch (whose name is misspelt by Marx) at a meeting of the economic section of the Society in September 1861.—191

124 See Robert Owen, *Observations on the Effect of the Manufacturing System,* London, 1817, p. 76.—192

125 This refers to the Crimean War of 1853-56.—193

126 In the middle of the last century the extensive demolition of dwelling houses in rural localities can to some extent be explained by the fact that the amount of the taxes paid by the landowners for the benefit of the poor largely depended on the number of poor people residing on their land. The landowners demolished on purpose those houses they had no need of but which could still be used as a shelter by the "surplus" agricultural population.—193

127 *Society of Arts*—a bourgeois educationalist and philanthropic society founded in London in 1754. The paper referred to was read by John Chalmers Morton, son of John Morton.—193

128 *The Corn Laws,* aimed at restricting or prohibiting the importing of grain from abroad, were introduced in England to safeguard the interests of the big landlords. In 1838 Manchester factory-owners Cobden and Bright founded the Anti-Corn Law League which put forward the demand for unrestricted Free Trade. The League fought for the abolition of the Corn Laws for the purpose of reducing workers' wages and weakening the economic and political positions of the landed aristocracy. As a result of this struggle the Corn Laws were abolished in 1846, which signified the victory of the industrial bourgeoisie over the landed aristocracy.—193, 218

129 *The Civil War in the United States* (1861-65) was waged between the industrial States of the North and the insurgent slaveowners' States of the South. The working class of England came out against the policy of its bourgeoisie which supported the slaveowners, and prevented England's interference in the Civil War.—193, 229, 270, 368, 446

130 *Physiocrats*—a trend in bourgeois classical political economy (see Note 32), which arose in France in the 1850s. Physiocrats were staunch advocates of large-scale capitalist agriculture, abolition of class privileges and protectionism. They realised the need for abolishing the feudal system but wanted to bring it about through peaceful reforms without detriment to the ruling classes and absolutism. The physiocrats' philosophic views were close to those of the 18th-century French bourgeois Enlighteners. A number of economic reforms proposed by the physiocrats were put into effect during the French bourgeois revolution.—205, 691

131 Adam Smith, *An Inquiry into the Nature and Causes of the Wealth of Nations,* Vol. I, Edinburgh, 1814, p. 93.—206

[132] This refers to the wars which England waged against France during the French bourgeois revolution at the end of the 18th century. At the time there was a reign of terror in England introduced by the government to suppress the people, for example, a number of revolts were crushed and laws prohibiting workers' unions were promulgated.—219

[133] Karl Marx refers here to a pamphlet by Malthus, *An Inquiry into the Nature and Progress of Rent, and the Principles by Which It Is Regulated*, London, 1815.—219

[134] Workhouses were established in England in the 17th century. After the introduction of the Poor Laws in 1834 the workhouses became the only form of aid to the poor; they were notorious for their rigid prison-like discipline and were called "bastilles for the poor" by the people.—219

[135] *Juggernaut*—one of the personifications of the Indian god Vishnu. The cult of Juggernaut was distinguished by magnificent ritual, and also extreme religious fanaticism which manifested itself in self-tortures and suicides of the believers. At major festivals some of them would throw themselves under the wheels of the chariot carrying the image of Vishnu-Juggernaut.—220

[136] In accordance with the poor laws that had existed in England since the 16th century each parish had to pay a special tax for the benefit of the poor. Those parishioners who were unable to support themselves received grants through the societies of aid to the poor.—223

[137] David Ricardo, *On the Principles of Political Economy, and Taxation*, London, 1821, p. 479—224

[138] *Capital*—the outstanding Marxist classic. It was the work of Marx's lifetime; he started work on it early in the forties which lasted for forty years, right up till the end of his life.

Marx began his systematic study of political economy at the end of 1843 in Paris. The fruits of his first research into this field are to be found in such works as *Economic and Philosophic Manuscripts of 1844, The German Ideology, The Poverty of Philosophy, Wage Labour and Capital, Manifesto of the Communist Party*, and others. It was in these early works that Marx first revealed the foundations of capitalist exploitation, the irreconcilable contradictions between the interests of the capitalists and those of the wage workers, the antagonistic and transient nature of all capitalist economic relations.

After an interval due to the revolution of 1848-49 Marx was next able to resume his economic studies in London where he had to emigrate to in August 1849.

In 1857 and 1858 Marx wrote a manuscript of over 50 signatures, which was a rough draft of his future *Capital*. It was first published between 1939 and 1941 in German by the Institute of Marxism-Leninism of the Central Committee of the C.P.S.U. under the title *Grundrisse der Kritik der politischen Oekonomie* (Principal Features of Criticism of Political Economy). At the same time he made the first outline of the entire work, which he elaborated in detail in the following months. In April 1858 he made up his mind to write this book in six volumes. Soon, however, Marx decided to issue his work in parts, in separate volumes.

In 1858 he began to write his first book which he entitled *A Contribution to the Critique of Political Economy* (see Note 113). The book was published in 1859. Between 1861 and 1863, while working on the following sections, he wrote a large book of about 200 signatures, in 23 notebooks. It had the same title as the book of 1859 and the majority of it (notebooks VI-XV and XVIII) deals with the history of economic theories. It was prepared for the press and printed in Russian by the Institute of Marxism-Leninism under the title *Theories of Surplus Value* (Volume IV of *Capital*). Other notebooks deal to some degree or other with the topics elaborated in the three volumes of *Capital.*

In the course of his further work Marx changed the original composition of the work so as to cover four books instead of six as originally planned. Between 1863 and 1865 he wrote a new comprehensive manuscript which was the first detailed version of the three theoretical volumes of *Capital.* Only after the whole work had been written (January 1866) did Marx begin the final editing. Moreover, on Engels's advice, he decided to prepare for the press not the whole work at once but to concentrate on the first volume. The final editing was carried out by Marx so thoroughly that the result was a new version of the first volume of *Capital.*

After the first volume had come out (in September 1867), Marx continued to work on it while preparing new editions in German and editing its translations into other languages. He introduced many changes into the second (1872) edition and gave detailed directions for the Russian edition which was published in St. Petersburg in 1872 and was the first translation of *Capital* into a foreign language. He made important revisions when editing the French translation which was printed in separate issues from 1872 to 1875.

At the same time Marx continued to work on the remaining volumes with the aim of completing the entire work in a short time. However he did not manage to achieve this because much of his time was taken up by his diverse activities in the Genneal Council of the First International. Moreover, he had to interrupt his work more and more frequently because of ill health. The following two volumes were prepared for the press and published by Engels after Karl Marx's death, the second volume in 1885 and the third in 1894. In carrying out this work Engels made an invaluable contribution to the treasure-store of scientific communism.

In the present edition of an extract from Volume I of *Capital*, the footnotes given by Marx have been retained.—227, 232

[139] Marx refers here to the first chapter ("Commodities and Money") in the first German edition of *Capital*, Volume I. In the second and the following German editions of this volume Part I corresponds to this chapter.—227

[140] The reference is to Chapter 3 of Ferdinand Lassalle's work, *Herr Bastiat-Schulze von Delitzsch, der ökonomische Julian, oder: Kapital und Arbeit,* Berlin, 1864.—227

[141] *The American War of Independence* (1775-83) against British rule was caused by the struggle of the emergent American bourgeois nation to win independence and to abolish barriers to the development of capitalism. The victory of the North Americans resulted in the birth of an independent bourgeois state—the United States of America.—229

[142] *The Established Church*—a state church.—230

[143] *Blue Books*—a general title for printed matter of the English Parliament and of the Foreign Office which derived its name from the blue covers. Their publication began in England in the 17th century. They are the principal official source of information on the country's economy and foreign policy. The Blue Book referred to came out in London in 1867.—230

[144] C. Pecqueur, *Théorie nouvelle d'économie sociale et politiques, ou Études sur l'organisation des sociétés,* Paris, 1842, p. 435.—232

[145] In the preface which he wrote in February 1870 to the second edition of *The Peasant War in Germany* dealing with the anti-feudal revolt of the German peasants in the 16th century, Engels analysed the changes that had taken place in the economic and political life of the country since 1848 and the role of the different classes and parties during this period of German

history. A most important theoretical and political conclusion on the necessity of the alliance of the proletariat and the peasantry which Marx and Engels formulated in a number of their works on the basis of the experience of the revolutions of 1848-49 is here further elaborated and set forth in great detail. Engels demonstrates the need for a discriminating approach to the peasantry and analyses which strata of the peasantry may become the proletariat's allies in the revolutionary struggle and for what reasons. While preparing the third edition of *The Peasant War in Germany* for the press in 1874, Engels supplemented the 1870 preface with important notes on the significance of theory in the socialist and workers' movement, emphasised the importance of the education of the masses in the spirit of proletarian internationalism and outlined valuable theoretical directions on the character, tasks and forms of the struggle of the working class and its party.—235, 242

146 *Neue Rheinische Zeitung. Politisch-ökonomische Revue* (New Rhenish Gazette. Politico-Economic Review)—journal, theoretical organ of the Communist League (see Note 3), founded by Marx and Engels. It was published from December 1849 to November 1850; altogether six issues appeared.—235, 367, 445, 642

147 The book referred to is W. Zimmermann's *Allgemeine Geschichte des grossen Bauernkrieges* (General History of the Great Peasant War), in three volumes, which was published in Stuttgart in 1841-43.—235

148 This refers to the extreme Left wing in the all-German National Assembly which held its sessions in Frankfurt am Main during the revolution of 1848-49. It represented mainly the interests of the petty bourgeoisie but also had the support of a section of the German workers. The chief task of the National Assembly was to put an end to the political disunity of Germany and to work out a general Constitution. Because of the cowardice and vacillation of its liberal majority, however, the National Assembly failed to take power in its hands and was unable to take a resolute stand on the principal questions of the German revolution. On May 30, 1849, the National Assembly had to move to Stuttgart. On June 18, 1849, it was dispersed by troops.—235, 443

149 The war of 1866 between Austria and Prussia ended in the victory of Prussia and put an end to the rivalry of long standing between these countries, thus paving the way for the unification of Germany under the hegemony of Prussia. A number of German states took part in the war on the side of Austria, while Prussia had Italy as its ally. In accordance with the Prague peace treaty, Austria ceded to Prussia its rights in Schleswig and Holstein, paid it moderate indemnities and ceded Venice to the Kingdom of Italy; the German Union set up as far back as 1815 by the Vienna Congress (see Note 63) and uniting over 30 German states was annulled and instead the North-German Confederation was established (see Note 159) headed by Prussia; Austria stayed out of the Confederation. As a result of the war Prussia also annexed the Kingdom of Hanover, the electorate of Hesse-Cassel, the grand duchy of Nassau and the free town of Frankfurt am Main.

In conditions of the political crisis aggravated by Austria's rout in the war and of the growing national liberation movement the country's reactionary circles had to come to terms with Hungary and form a joint monarchy—Austria-Hungary, on the one hand, and on the other, they had to make a number of political concessions to the bourgeoisie. The new constitution of 1867 extended the rights of the Reichsrat, defined the duties of ministers, and introduced universal military conscription and central government. The government formed on the basis of this constitution included both representatives of the aristocracy and the liberal bourgeoisie.—236, 242, 251, 647

150 *National-Liberals*—the party of the German bourgeoisie formed in the autumn of 1866. The National-Liberals put forward as their main goal the unification

of Germany under Prussia's hegemony. Their policy reflected the German liberal bourgeoisie's capitulation to Bismarck.—237

151 *The People's Party* (*Volkspartei*), founded in 1865, consisted of the democratic elements from among the petty bourgeoisie and, partly, of the bourgeoisie, chiefly from the South-German states. The *Volkspartei* opposed Prussian hegemony in Germany and advocated a "Greater Germany" that would include Prussia and Austria. By advocating a federative German state, it actually . opposed the unification of Germany as an integral centralised democratic republic.—237, 313, 327, 333

152 In the mid-sixties of the 19th century a system of special licenses (concessions) was introduced in a number of industries in Prussia without which it was forbidden to engage in industry. This semi-feudal law restricted the development of capitalism.—238

153 This refers to the parliamentary reform of 1831 (see Note 15).—238

154 *The battle of Sadowa* (known also as the battle of Königgrätz, now Hradec Králové) took place on July 3, 1866. It was a turning-point in the Austro-Prussian War of 1866 (see Note 149).—239, 242, 262

155 *Mortgage*—conveyance of property, chiefly land or houses, by the debtor to the creditor as security for debt.—240, 530, 634

156 This refers to the *Basle Congress* of the International (see Note 120) which was held from September 6 to 11, 1869. On September 10, the Basle Congress adopted the following resolution on landed property, which was submitted by Marx's adherents:

"1) The society has the right to abolish private property on land and to transform it into common, national property;

"2) It is necessary to abolish private property on land and to transform it into common, national property."

The Congress also adopted decisions on the unification of trade unions on a national and international scale, and a number of decisions on organisational measures aimed at strengthening the International and extending the rights of the General Council.—241

157 During the Franco-Prussian War of 1870-71, at the battle of Sedan, the French army led by Napoleon III was defeated by the German troops and surrendered on September 2, 1870. The Emperor and the commanding staff were kept prisoner in Wilhelmshöhe (near Cassel), in a castle of the Prussian kings, from September 5, 1870 to March 19, 1871. The defeat at Sedan accelerated the downfall of the Second Empire and led to the proclamation of the republic in France on September 4, 1870. A new government, called the Government of National Defence, was set up.—242, 251, 254, 264, 272

158 Engels here paraphrases the name of the medieval Holy Roman Empire of the German nation (see Note 181) and emphasises that the unification of Germany, i.e., the formation of the German Empire in 1871 as a result of the victory over France, took place under Prussia's hegemony and was accompanied by the Prussianisation of all German states.—242, 639

159 *The North-German Union* or *Confederation* with Prussia at its head comprised 19 states and three free towns of North and Central Germany and was formed in 1867 on Bismarck's recommendation. Its formation represented a most decisive stage in the reunification of Germany under Prussia's hegemony. In January 1871 the Confederation ceased to exist as a result of the formation of the German Empire.—242, 267

160 This refers to the annexation of Bavaria, Baden, Württemberg and Hessen-Darmstadt by the North-German Confederation in 1870.—242

[161] In the battle at *Spichern* (Lorraine) on August 6, 1870 the Prussian troops inflicted a defeat on the French. It has also gone down in history as the battle at Forbach.

At *Mars-la-Tour* (also known as the battle of Vionville) on August 16, 1870 the German troops succeeded in checking the retreat of the French Rhine army from Metz and, subsequently, in cutting it off.—245

[162] *Der Volksstaat* (People's State)—central organ of the German Social-Democratic Workers' Party (Eisenachers), which was published in Leipzig from October 2, 1869 to September 29, 1876. Wilhelm Liebknecht carried out the general direction of the newspaper, and August Bebel was its manager. Marx and Engels contributed to the newspaper and assisted in its editing. Until 1869 the newspaper appeared under the title *Demokratisches Wochenblatt* (see Note 264).—245, 314, 333, 674

[163] On January 10, 1874, during the Reichstag elections, nine Social-Democrats were elected, among them Bebel and Liebknecht, who were serving their prison terms at the time.—245

[164] *The Civil War in France*—a most important work of scientific communism, in which the main Marxist tenets in relation to the class struggle, the state, revolution and dictatorship of the proletariat were further elaborated on the basis of the experience of the Paris Commune. It was written as an address of the General Council to all the Association members in Europe and the United States with the purpose of arming the workers of all countries with a clear understanding of the character and world-wide significance of the heroic struggle of the Communards and spreading their historic experience to the entire proletariat.

In this work Marx corroborated and further developed his idea on the necessity for the proletariat to break up the bourgeois state machine, set forth in *The Eighteenth Brumaire of Louis Bonaparte* (see pp. 96-179 of this volume). Marx drew the conclusion that "the working class cannot simply lay hold of the ready-made state machinery, and wield it for its own purposes" (see p. 285 of this volume). The proletariat should break it up and supersede it by a state of the Paris Commune type. Marx's conclusion on a new, Paris Commune type of state as the state form of the dictatorship of the proletariat constitutes the essence of his new contribution to revolutionary theory.

Marx's *The Civil War in France* was very widely circulated. In 1871 and 1872 it was translated into a number of languages and published in various countries of Europe and in the U.S.A. In 1905 its Russian translation, edited by Lenin, was put out in Odessa.—248, 271

[165] This introduction was written by Engels for the third German edition of Marx's *The Civil War in France*, published in 1891 to mark the twentieth anniversary of the Paris Commune. Having emphasised the historical significance of the experience of the Paris Commune and Marx's theoretical analysis of it in *The Civil War in France*, Engels added a number of supplementary comments on the history of the Paris Commune, on the activity of the Blanquists and Proudhonists. In this edition Engels included the first and second addresses of the General Council of the International Working Men's Association on the Franco-Prussian War written by Marx which were also included in the later editions of this work in different languages when published in pamphlet form.—248

[166] This refers to the national liberation war of the German people against Napoleon's occupation in 1813-14.—248, 263

[167] *The Exceptional Law* (or *the Anti-Socialist Law*) was introduced in Germany on October 21, 1878. According to this law all organisations of the Social-Democratic Party, mass workers' organisations and workers press were

prohibited, socialist publications were made subject to confiscation and Social-Democrats were persecuted. Under pressure from the mass labour movement the law was repealed on October 1, 1890.—248, 394, 447, 649, 680, 681

168 In the 1820s in Germany this term was applied to the participants in the Opposition movement among the German intelligentsia, who came out against the reactionary political system in the German states and advocated the unification of Germany. "Demagogues" were ruthlessly persecuted by the authorities.—248, 432

169 The reference is to the Legitimists, Orleanists (see Notes 17 and 71) and Bonapartists—supporters of the Bonaparte dynasty.—250

170 This refers to the preliminary peace treaty between France and Germany signed at Versailles on February 26, 1871 by Thiers and Jules Favre, on the one hand, and Bismarck, on the other. According to the terms of this treaty France ceded Alsace and East Lorraine to Germany and paid it indemnities to the sum of 5,000,000,000 francs. The final peace treaty was signed in Frankfurt am Main on May 10, 1871.—252, 278, 649

171 In October 1870 the French army under the command of Marshal Bazaine surrendered Metz to the besieging German troops.—254

172 This refers to Proudhon's book *Idée générale de la Révolution au XIX siècle,* Paris, 1851. For the criticism of Proudhon's views set forth in this book, see Marx's letter to Engels of August 8, 1851 and Engels's "Critical Remarks on Proudhon's *General Conception of the 19th-Century Revolution*" (*Marx-Engels Archive,* Vol. X, pp. 13-17).—256

173 *Possibilism*—an opportunist trend in the French socialist movement led by Bruce, Malon and others who brought about a split in the French Workers' Party in 1882. Its leaders proclaimed a reformist principle—to achieve only that which is "possible", hence the name.—256

174 When publishing Engels's Introduction in *Die Neue Zeit* (Bd. 2, issue No. 28, 1890-91) the editorial board of the journal changed the original text, substituting the words "German philistine" for the expression "the Social-Democratic philistine" used in the manuscript. As can be seen from Fischer's letter to Engels of March 17, 1891, Engels disapproved of this arbitrary change but apparently to avoid different readings of the one-time publications of this work he retained a changed version in a pamphlet-form edition. In the present volume the original wording has been restored.—258

175 The *First Address* on the International's attitude towards the Franco-Prussian war, written by Marx on the instructions of the General Council immediately after the outbreak of the war, as well as the *Second Address* written by him in September 1870 reflected the attitude of the working class towards militarism and war and the struggle which Marx and Engels were waging against wars of aggression and for the implementation of the principles of proletarian internationalism. Marx provided convincing proof to substantiate the most important propositions of his teaching on the social causes of predatory wars waged by the exploiting classes for mercenary ends and pointed out that these wars also pursued the aim of suppressing the revolutionary workers' movement. He stressed, in particular, the unity of the interests of the German and the French workers and called for their joint struggle against the aggressive policy of the ruling classes of both countries.

With exceptional foresight Marx drew in the First Address the conclusion that the establishment of workers' rule would put an end to all wars and that peace among nations would be a great internationalist principle of the future communist society.—260, 264

[176] The plebiscite was conducted by Napoleon III in May 1870 for the alleged purpose of ascertaining the attitude of the popular masses to the empire. The questions were so worded that it was impossible to express disapproval of the policy of the Second Empire without at the same time declaring opposition to all democratic reforms. The sections of the First International in France exposed the demagogic manoeuvre and instructed its members to abstain from voting. On the eve of the plebiscite the Paris Section members were arrested on a charge of conspiring against Napoleon III; this pretext was used by the government to launch a campaign of persecution and baiting of the members of the International in various towns of France. At the trial of the Paris Section members which took place from June 22 to July 5, 1870, the frame-up of the charge of conspiracy was fully exposed; nevertheless a number of the International's members were sentenced to imprisonment merely for being members of the International Working Men's Association. The working class of France responded with mass protests to these persecutions.—260

[177] On July 19, 1870 the Franco-Prussian War broke out.—261

[178] *Le Réveil*—Left republican newspaper founded by Louis Charles Delescluze. It was published in Paris from July 1868 to January 1871. It carried the documents of the International and other material on the workers' movement.—261

[179] *La Marseillaise*—Left republican daily newspaper published in Paris from December 1869 to September 1870. It carried reports on the activities of the International and on the working-class movement.—261

[180] This refers to the *Society of December 10*—a secret Bonapartist society organised mainly from among declassed elements, political gamblers, representatives of the military, etc.; its members assisted Louis Bonaparte's election as President of the Republic of France on December 10, 1848 (hence the name of the society). For a detailed description of this society see Karl Marx, *The Eighteenth Brumaire of Louis Bonaparte* (pp. 136-38 of this volume).—261

[181] This refers to the *Holy Roman Empire of the German nation*—a medieval empire formed in 962, comprising the territory of Germany and part of Italy. Subsequently, the Empire included also some French territories, Bohemia, Austria, the Netherlands, Switzerland and other countries. The Empire was not a centralised state. It was a loose union of feudal principalities and free towns which recognised the supreme authority of the Emperor. It fell apart in 1806 when the Hapsburgs had to renounce the title of Emperor of the Holy Roman Empire after the defeat in the war against France.—265, 560, 693

[182] In 1618 the Electorate of Brandenburg united with the Prussian duchy (East Prussia), which had been formed early in the 16th century out of the Teutonic Order possessions and which was still a feudal vassal of the Kingdom of Poland. The Elector of Brandenburg, a Prussian duke at the same time, remained a Polish vassal until 1657 when, taking advantage of Poland's difficulties in the war against Sweden, he secured sovereign rights to Prussian possessions.—265

[183] This refers to the separate *Basle Peace Treaty* concluded by Prussia, a member of the first anti-French coalition of the European states, with the French Republic on April 5, 1795.—266

[184] *The Treaty of Tilsit* was concluded between July 7 and 9, 1807 between Napoleonic France and Russia and Prussia, participants of the fourth anti-French coalition, who sustained a defeat in the war. The peace terms were very onerous for Prussia who lost a considerable part of her territory. Russia suffered no territorial losses but had to recognise the consolidation of France's position in Europe and to take part in the blockade of England (the so-

called continental blockade). The predatory peace treaty of Tilsit imposed by Napoleon I aroused bitter indignation among the population of Germany and sowed the seeds of the national liberation movement against the rule of Napoleon, which started in 1813.—266

185 *Teutons*—ancient tribes of German origin; in the widest sense it is applied to all Germanic peoples. Marx here makes an ironic allusion to the use of this word by the German nationalists.—267

186 Marx refers here to the triumph of feudal reaction in Germany after the downfall of Napoleon. Feudal disunity of Germany was restored, feudal monarchies were established in the German states, which retained all the privileges of the nobility and intensified the semi-feudal exploitation of the peasantry.—268

187 The reference is to the Tuileries Palace in Paris, a residence of Napoleon III at the time of the Second Empire.—268, 369

188 Marx is referring to a campaign of the English workers for securing recognition of the French Republic proclaimed on September 4, 1870. On September 5 a series of meetings and demonstrations began in London and other big cities, the demonstrators adopting resolutions and petitions demanding that the British Government immediately recognise the French Republic. The General Council of the First International took a direct part in the organisation of this movement.—269

189 Marx is alluding to England's active part in forming a coalition of feudal monarchies which started a war against revolutionary France in 1792, and also to the fact that the English oligarchy was the first in Europe to recognise the Bonapartist regime in France, established as a result of the coup d'état of Louis Bonaparte on December 2, 1851.—269

190 *Journal Officiel de la République Française*—official organ of the Paris Commune, which was published from March 20 to May 24, 1871; the newspaper retained the name of the official organ of the government of the French Republic which had appeared in Paris from September 5, 1870 onwards (at the time of the Paris Commune the Thiers government at Versailles put out a newspaper under the same title). The issue of March 30 came out under the title *Journal Officiel de la Commune de Paris*. Simon's letter was published in the newspaper on April 25, 1871.—272

191 On January 28, 1871 Favre, on behalf of the Government of National Defence, and Bismarck signed a Convention on the Armistice and the Capitulation of Paris—this ignominious act amounted to the betrayal of the national interests of France. Under this Convention Favre agreed to humiliating terms demanded by the Prussians, i.e., to pay a 200 million francs indemnity within a fortnight, to surrender a greater part of the Paris forts and to hand over the field artillery and munitions of the Paris Army to the Prussians.—272

192 *Capitulards*—a contemptuous nickname of the advocates of the capitulation of Paris during the siege of 1870-71. Subsequently, it came to denote in French anyone who favoured surrender in general.—272

193 *L'Étendard*—French newspaper of Bonapartist leanings; it was published in Paris from 1866 to 1868. Its publication was discontinued after the discovery of fraud to acquire more funds.—273

194 *Société Générale du Crédit Mobilier*—a large French joint-stock bank founded in 1852. Its main source of income was speculation in securities. The bank was closely linked with the government circles of the Second Empire. In 1867 it went bankrupt and was liquidated in 1871.—273

195 *L'Électeur libre*—Right republican organ published in Paris from 1868 to 1871. During 1870 and 1871 it was linked up with the Ministry of Finance of the Government of National Defence.—273

196 On February 14 and 15, 1831, the Paris mob plundered the church of Saint Germain l'Auxerrois and the Archbishop's palace in protest against the Legitimist demonstration during the requiem mass for the Duke de Berry. Thiers who was present when the rioting crowd was committing excesses in the church and the Archbishop's palace persuaded the National Guards not to interfere.

In 1832, by the order of Thiers, the then Minister of the Interior, the Duchess de Berry, mother of the Comte de Chambord, the Legitimist pretender to the French throne, was arrested and subjected to a humiliating medical examination aimed at giving publicity to her secret marriage and in this way ruining her political career.—274

197 An allusion to the ignominious role of Thiers, the then Minister of the Interior, in suppressing the people's insurrection in Paris against the July monarchy on April 13-14, 1834. The insurrection was put down with savage brutality by the military, for example, the inhabitants of one of the houses on Rue Transnonain were massacred.

September Laws—reactionary laws against the press introduced by the French Government in September 1835. They provided for imprisonment and large fines for publications criticising the existing social and political system. —274

198 In January 1841 Thiers submitted to the Chamber of Deputies a plan for building a ring of military fortifications around Paris. Revolutionary-democratic sections saw this move as a preparatory step for the crushing of popular demonstrations. The plan provided for the building of particularly strong fortifications in the vicinity of the workers' districts.—274

199 In January 1848 the Neapolitan troops of Ferdinand II, subsequently nicknamed King Bomba for his bombardment of the town of Messina in the autumn of the same year, bombarded Palermo in an attempt to suppress the people's revolt, which served to spark off the bourgeois revolution in the various Italian states in 1848 and 1849.—274

200 In April 1849 France in conjunction with Austria and Naples organised an intervention campaign against the Republic of Rome in order to crush it and restore the Pope's temporal power. French troops severely bombarded Rome. Despite heroic resistance, the Republic was crushed and Rome occupied by French troops. For Marx's description of this, see *The Eighteenth Brumaire of Louis Bonaparte* (pp. 113, 124 and 126 of this volume).—275, 283

201 On July 15, 1840, England, Russia, Prussia, Austria and Turkey signed the London convention, without the participation of France, on rendering aid to the Turkish Sultan against the Egyptian Ruler Mohammed Ali, who enjoyed the support of France. As a result, a threat of war between France and the coalition of European powers arose, but King Louis Philippe did not dare begin hostilities and abandoned his support of Mohammed Ali.—276

202 In order to suppress the Paris Commune Thiers appealed to Bismarck for permission to supplement the Versailles army with French prisoners of war most of whom had been serving in the armies that surrendered at Sedan and Metz (see Notes 157 and 171).—276

203 *Chambre introuvable*—Chamber of Deputies in France in 1815 and 1816 (during the first years of the Restoration—see Note 16), which consisted of extreme reactionaries.—277, 295

204 *Landlord Chamber*, the *Assembly of "Rurals"*—nickname of the National Assembly of 1871, which met in Bordeaux and was largely made up of reac-

tionary monarchists: provincial landlords, officials, rentiers and merchants elected in rural districts. There were about 430 monarchists among the 630 deputies of the Assembly.—277

205 On March 10, 1871, the National Assembly passed a law on the deferred payment of overdue bills; under this law the payments of debts on obligations concluded between August 13 and November 12, 1870 could be deferred; as for payments on obligations concluded after November 12, no deferment was granted. Thus, the law of March 10 dealt a heavy blow at the workers and poorer sections of the population and led to the bankruptcy of many minor industrialists and merchants.—278

206 Décembriseur—participant in the Bonapartist coup d'état of December 2, 1851 and supporter of acts in the spirit of this coup.—278

207 According to the newspapers, the internal loan, which the Thiers government wanted to float, gave Thiers and members of his government over 300 million francs "commission". On June 20, 1871, after the suppression of the Paris Commune, the law on the loan was passed.—278

208 Cayenne—town in French Guiana (South America), penal settlement and place of exile.—280

209 On October 31, 1870, upon the receipt of the news that the Government of National Defence had decided to start negotiations with the Prussians, the Paris workers and the revolutionary sections of the National Guard rose up in revolt. They seized the Town Hall and set up their revolutionary government—the Committee of Public Safety, headed by Blanqui. Under pressure from the workers the Government of National Defence had to promise to resign and schedule elections to the Commune for November 1. The Paris revolutionary forces, however, were not sufficiently well organised and there were disagreements among the leaders of the uprising—the followers of Blanqui and the petty-bourgeois Jacobin democrats. The government took advantage of the situation and, with the aid of some loyal battalions of the National Guard, seized the Town Hall and re-established its power.—281, 653

210 Bretons—Breton Mobile Guard (one of the types of military formations in France at the time of the Franco-Prussian War of 1870-71) which Trochu used as gendarmes to put down the revolutionary movement in Paris.
    Corsicans—during the Second Empire, they constituted a considerable part of the gendarme corps.—281

211 On January 22, 1871, the Paris proletariat and the National Guards held a revolutionary demonstration initiated by the Blanquists. They demanded the overthrow of the government and the establishment of a Commune. By order of the Government of National Defence, the Breton Mobile Guard, which was defending the Town Hall, opened fire on the demonstrators. After suppressing the revolutionary movement by means of terror, the government began preparations to surrender Paris.—282

212 Sommations (a preliminary demand to disperse)—under the laws of a number of bourgeois states the demand was repeated three times, following which the authorities were entitled to resort to force.
    The Riot Act was introduced in England in 1715. It prohibited "rebel gatherings" of more than 12 people, giving the authorities the right to use force if the crowd did not disperse within an hour after the reading out of a special warning three times.—282

213 On October 31 (see Note 209), Flourens prevented the members of the Government of National Defence from being shot, as had been demanded by one of the insurrectionists.—284

214 The reference is to the decree on hostages adopted by the Commune on April 5, 1871. (Marx gives the date of its publication in the English press.) Under this decree, all persons charged with keeping in contact with Versailles, if found guilty, were declared hostages. By this decree the Commune sought to prevent Communards from being shot by the Versaillists.—284

215 *The Times*—English conservative daily published in London ever since 1785.—284

216 *Investiture*—a system of appointing officials, under which persons in the lower rungs of the hierarchy were fully dependent on higher officials.—289

217 *Kladderadatsch*—illustrated satirical weekly first published in Berlin in 1848. *Punch, or the London Charivari*—English bourgeois-liberal humorous weekly published in London since 1841.—290

218 The reference is to the Paris Commune's decree of April 16, 1871, providing for payment of all debts in instalments for three years and abolishing payment of interest on them.—292

219 On August 22, 1848, the Constituent Assembly rejected the bill on "amiable agreements" ("*concordats à l'amiable*") aimed to introduce the deferred payment of debts. As a result of this measure, a considerable section of the petty bourgeoisie were utterly ruined and found themselves completely dependent on the creditors from among the big bourgeoisie.—292

220 *Frères Ignorantins* (ignorant brothers)—nickname of a religious order, founded in Rheims in 1680, whose members pledged themselves to educate the children of the poor. The pupils received a predominantly religious education and very scanty knowledge in other fields. In this context, this expression alludes to the low level and clerical character of primary education in bourgeois France.—292

221 This refers to the *Alliance républicaine des Départements*—a political association of petty-bourgeois representatives from the various departments of France, who lived in Paris; it called on the people to fight against the Versailles government and the monarchist National Assembly and to support the Commune throughout the country.—292

222 This refers to the law of April 27, 1825 on the payment of compensation to the former émigrés for the landed estates confiscated from them during the French bourgeois revolution. — 292

223 In the Picpus nunnery cases of nuns incarcerated in cells for many years were exposed and instruments of torture were found; in the Church of Saint Laurent there was found a secret cemetery attesting to the murders that had been committed there. These facts were made public in the Commune's newspaper *Mot d'Ordre* on May 5, 1871, and also in the pamphlet *Les Crimes des congrégations religieuses*.—295

224 *Absentees*—big landowners who hardly ever visited their estates which were managed by land agents or leased to middlemen who, in their turn, subleased them to subtenants at high rents.—296

225 On June 20, 1789, when the government of Louis XVI made an attempt to interrupt the session of the *States Géneral*, which had proclaimed themselves to be the National Assembly, the representatives of the third estate (the bourgeoisie) gathered in Versailles in the hall for ball games and swore to stay there until a constitution had been drafted. This was one of the events that led up to the French bourgeois revolution at the end of the 18th century.—296

226 *Francs-fileurs* (literally: "free absconders")—nickname given to the Paris bourgeois who fled from the city during the siege. The name sounded all the

more ironical as a result of its resemblance to the word *"francs-tireurs"* ("free sharpshooters")—French guerrillas who actively fought against the Prussians. —297

227 *Coblenz*—a city in Germany; during the French bourgeois revolution at the end of the 18th century it was the centre where the landlord-monarchist émigrés made preparations for intervention against revolutionary France. Coblenz was the seat of the émigré government headed by the rabid reactionary de Calonne, a former minister of Louis XVI.—297

228 This name was given to the Versailles soldiers of royalist sympathies recruited in Brittany, by analogy with those who took part in the counter-revolutionary royalist insurrection in North-Western France during the French bourgeois revolution at the end of the 18th century.—297

229 The reference is to the regiment of the papal guard, recruited from the sons of the French gentry. It was organised and trained on the pattern of the French light infantry (Zouaves). In September 1870, following the abolition of the Pope's temporal power, the papal Zouaves were brought to France where they took part in the Franco-Prussian War. After the war the regiment was used for suppressing the Paris Commune.—297

230 Under the impact of the proletarian revolution in Paris which led to the establishment of the Commune, revolutionary mass actions of a similar nature took place in Lyons and Marseilles. However, mass revolutionary demonstrations were brutally crushed by government troops.—298

231 Under the law concerning the procedure of military courts, submitted by Dufaure to the National Assembly, it was ruled that cases were to be investigated and sentences carried out within 48 hours.—299

232 This trade treaty between England and France was concluded on January 23, 1860. Under this treaty France was to abandon her prohibitive customs policy and replace it by introducing new import duties. As a result of the influx of English goods to France, competition in the home market sharply increased, causing much dissatisfaction among French manufacturers.—300

233 *Insurgent*—participant in an armed uprising against the government.—301

234 This refers to the reign of terror and bloody repressions in Ancient Rome at the various stages of the crisis of the slaveowning Roman Republic in the first century B.C. *Sulla's dictatorship* (82-79 B.C.). *The First and second triumvirates* (60-53 and 43-36 B.C.)—periods of dictatorship by the Roman generals: Pompey, Caesar and Crassus—the first triumvirate; Octavianus, Antonius and Lepidus—the second triumvirate.—302

235 *Journal de Paris*—weekly newspaper of a monarchist-Orleanist orientation; its publication started in Paris in 1867.—302

236 In August 1814, during the war between Britain and the United States, British troops seized Washington and burnt the Capitol, the White House and other public buildings.
   In October 1860 during the war waged by Britain and France against China, British and French troops pillaged and then burnt down the summer palace of the Chinese Emperors, a treasure-house of Chinese art and architecture.—303

237 In the autumn of 1812, the people of Moscow burnt down a considerable portion of the city occupied by Napoleon's army so as to deprive the enemy troops of warm quarters and food supplies.—304

238 This is what Marx called the Prussian Assembly by analogy with the French *Chambre introuvable* (see Note 203). The Assembly elected in January and

February 1849 consisted of two chambers: the first was a privileged aristocratic "chamber of the gentry"; the composition of the second was determined by two-stage elections in which only the so-called "independent" Prussians took part. Elected to the second chamber, Bismarck became one of the
leaders of the extremely reactionary Junker group.—305

239 *The Daily News*—English liberal newspaper, organ of the industrial bourgeoisie, published in London from 1846 to 1930.—307

240 *Le Temps*—French conservative daily, organ of the big bourgeoisie; it was
published in Paris from 1861 to 1943.—308

241 *The Evening Standard*—the evening edition of the *Standard*, an English
conservative newspaper; it was published in London from 1857 to 1905.—308

242 The authors of this letter were Karl Marx and Frederick Engels.—308

243 *The Alliance of Socialist Democracy*—an organisation founded by Bakunin
in 1868 in Geneva. In their programme the members of the Alliance declared
that they were in favour of the equality of classes and of abolishing the state;
they rejected the necessity for the working class to wage a political struggle.
The petty-bourgeois anarchist programme of the Alliance found support in
areas with a low level of industrial development in Italy, Switzerland, Spain
and other countries. In 1869 the Alliance approached the General Council with
a request to be admitted to the International. The General Council agreed to
admit individual sections of the Alliance provided the latter dissolved as an
independent organisation. However, on entering the International, the members of the Alliance preserved their secret organisation within the International Working Men's Association and with Bakunin as their leader launched
a campaign against the General Council. This campaign intensified still more
after the defeat of the Paris Commune when Bakunin and his followers
denounced the idea of the dictatorship of the proletariat and the consolidation
of the independent political party of the working class, a party founded on
the principles of democratic centralism. The Hague Congress of the First International which took place in September 1872 expelled the Alliance's leaders,
Bakunin and Guillaume, by an overwhelming majority.—309, 672

244 *The Spectator*—English liberal weekly; it has been published in London ever
since 1828.—309

245 *The London Conference* of the First International met between September 17
and 23, 1871. Since the Conference convened at a time of harsh repressions
against the members of the International, which set in after the defeat of the
Paris Commune, its attendance numbers were rather depleted: it was attended
by 22 delegates with the right to vote and 10 delegates with voice but no vote.
Countries that could not send their delegates were represented by corresponding
secretaries of the General Council. Marx represented Germany, Engels—Italy.
    The London Conference marked an important stage in the struggle which
Marx and Engels waged for the foundation of a proletarian party. The Conference adopted a resolution on the "Political Action of the Working Class",
the main part of which, on the decision of the Hague Congress of the International (see Note 250), was incorporated in the General Rules of the International Working Men's Association. Many important tactical and organisational principles of the proletarian party were formulated in the Conference decisions, which dealt a heavy blow at sectarianism and reformism. The London
Conference played a major role in upholding the principles of proletarian commitment over anarchism and opportunism.—310

246 *Critique of the Gotha Programme*, written by Marx in 1875, contains critical
remarks in relation to the draft programme of a united workers' party of
Germany. This draft suffered from serious mistakes and concessions of principle to Lassalleanism. Marx and Engels approved the idea of founding a

united socialist party of Germany but denounced the ideological compromise
with Lassalleans and subjected it to withering criticism. In this work Marx
formulated many ideas on the major issues of scientific communism, such
as the socialist revolution, the dictatorship of the proletariat, a period of
transition from capitalism to communism, the two phases of communist society, the production and distribution of the social product under socialism
and the principal features of communism, proletarian internationalism and
the party of the working class.

Marx also further elaborates his theory of the state and the dictatorship
of the proletariat. He puts forward an important proposition about the historical inevitability of a special stage of transition from capitalism to communism with the corresponding form of state which he calls the "revolutionary dictatorship of the proletariat" (see p. 327 of this volume). "The great
significance of Marx's explanations is," Lenin wrote with regard to Critique
of the Gotha Programme, "that here, too, he consistently applies materialist
dialectics, the theory of development, and regards communism as something
which develops out of capitalism. Instead of scholastically invented, 'concocted'
definitions and fruitless disputes over words (What is socialism? What is communism?), Marx gives an analysis of what might be called the stages of the
economic maturity of communism" (V. I. Lenin, Collected Works, Vol. 25,
p. 471).—311, 315

247 This foreword was written by Engels in connection with the publication of
Marx's Critique of the Gotha Programme in 1891. Engels undertook the publication of this major policy document in order to deal a blow at the opportunist elements which became active in the German Social-Democratic Party. At
that time such a move was particularly important because the party was about
to discuss and adopt at the Erfurt Congress a new programme which was to
replace the Gotha Programme. When preparing Critique of the Gotha Programme for the press Engels met with opposition on the part of German
Social-Democratic leaders, Dietz, the publisher of Die Neue Zeit, and the editor
K. Kautsky, who insisted on certain changes and omissions, to which he had
to agree. The rank-and-file members of the German Social-Democratic Party
and the socialists from other countries met Marx's Critique of the Gotha Programme with approval and regarded it as a worthy policy document for the
international socialist movement. Together with Critique of the Gotha Programme Engels published Marx's letter to Bracke of May 5, 1875, which was
directly bound up with the work.

In Engels's lifetime there existed only one edition of Critique of the Gotha
Programme and his foreword to it. The complete text of Critique of the Gotha
Programme was first published in 1932 in the Soviet Union.—311

248 At the Gotha Congress which met between May 22 and 27, 1875, the two
trends in the German working-class movement—the Social-Democratic Workers' Party (Eisenachers) led by August Bebel and Wilhelm Liebknecht (see
Note 251) and the Lassallean General German Workers' Union—united to
form the Socialist Workers' Party of Germany. This put an end to the split
in the German working class. The draft programme of the united party, which
Marx and Engels subjected to withering criticism, was adopted by the Congress with only insignificant corrections.—311, 375

249 The German Social-Democratic Congress in Halle met between October 12
and 18, 1890. It adopted a decision to draft a new programme and publish
it three months before the next Party Congress in Erfurt so as to discuss it first
in local party organisations and in the press.—311

250 The Hague Congress of the International Working Men's Association (see
Note 120) took place between September 2 and 7, 1872. It was attended by
65 delegates from 15 national organisations, including Marx and Engels who

directed the entire work of the Congress. The Congress witnessed the cul
mination of the struggle which Marx, Engels and their followers waged fc
many years against all kinds of petty-bourgeois sectarianism in the working
class movement. The sectarian activities of the anarchists were denounced an
their leaders expelled from the International. The decisions of the Hague Con
gress paved the way for the foundation of independent political parties of th
working class in various countries.—311, 369, 676

251 The German Social-Democratic Workers' Party, which was formed at a Con
gress of Social-Democrats from Germany, Austria and Switzerland, held i
Eisenach between August 7 and 9, 1869, became known as the Eisenachers
The programme adopted at the Congress corresponded in the main to the prin
ciples advanced by the First International.—313, 332, 675

252 The reference is to Bakunin's book *Statehood and Anarchy*, published ir
Switzerland in 1873.—313

253 After the holiday, that is, with some delay. The Gotha Unity Congress
took place between May 22 and 27, 1875, the Congress of the Lassalleans—
earlier in May, and the Congress of the Eisenachers in Hamburg on June 8.—
314

254 *The League of Peace and Freedom*—a bourgeois pacifist organisation founded
by petty-bourgeois republicans and liberals in Switzerland in 1867. By asserting that it was possible to prevent wars by creating "the United States
of Europe" the League of Peace and Freedom spread false illusions among
the masses and diverted the proletariat from the class struggle.—323, 333

255 *Norddeutsche Allgemeine Zeitung*—daily reactionary newspaper published in
Berlin from 1861 to 1918. Between the 1860s and 1880s it was the official
organ of Bismarck's government. Marx is referring to an article in its issue
of March 20, 1875.—323

256 Malthus maintained in his work, *An Essay on the Principle of Population*,
that the population has a tendency to grow in geometrical progression whereas
the production of consumer goods can grow at most in arithmetical progression.—324

257 *L'Atelier*—monthly magazine published in Paris from 1840 to 1850. It was
the organ of artisans and workers of Christian socialist sympathies.—326

258 *Kulturkampf*—the name given by bourgeois liberals to a system of reforms
implemented in the seventies of the last century by Bismarck's government
under the banner of a campaign for secular culture. In the eighties, however,
in order to consolidate reactionary forces, Bismarck repealed the greater part
of these reforms.—330

259 Engels's letter to Bebel written between March 18 and 28, 1875, which is
closely connected with Marx's work, *Critique of the Gotha Programme* (see
Notes 246 and 247), expressed the common opinion of Marx and Engels concerning the draft programme of the future united Social-Democratic Workers'
Party of Germany. Engels sharply criticised the compromise draft programme
—the entire system of its Lassallean dogmas, its opportunist postulates on
the state and its rejection of the principles of proletarian internationalism.—332

260 *Frankfurter Zeitung und Handelsblatt* (Frankfurt Gazette and Commercial
Sheet)—daily petty-bourgeois democratic newspaper published from 1856
(under this name from 1866) to 1943.—333

261 Engels is here referring to the following articles of the draft Gotha Programme:
"The German Workers' Party demands as the free basis of the state:
"1. Universal, equal and direct suffrage by secret ballot for all males who

have reached the age of twenty-one, for all elections, national and local. 2. Direct legislation by the people including the right to initiate and to reject bills. 3. Universal military training. The standing army to be replaced by a people's militia. Decisions regarding war and peace are to be taken by a representative assembly of the people. 4. Abolition of all exceptional laws, in particular the laws on the press, association and assembly. 5. Jurisdiction by the people. Administration of justice without fees.

"The German Workers' Party demands as the intellectual and moral basis of the state:

"1. Universal and equal public education to be provided by the state. Compulsory education. Free instruction. 2. Freedom of scientific thought. Freedom of conscience."—333

262 The reference is to the Franco-Prussian War of 1870-71.—333

263 Cf. W. Bracke, *Der Lassall'sche Vorschlag* (Lassalle's Proposal), Braunschweig, 1873.—334

264 *Demokratisches Wochenblatt* (Democratic Weekly)—German workers' newspaper published in Leipzig from January 1868 to September 1869; it was edited by Wilhelm Liebknecht. The paper played an important part in creating the German Social-Democratic Workers' Party. In 1869, at the Eisenach Congress, it was made the central organ of the party and became known as *Volksstaat* (see Note 162). Marx and Engels were among its contributors.—336

265 *Dialectics of Nature*, one of the main works of Frederick Engels, contains a dialectical-materialist analysis of the most important discoveries in natural science in the mid-19th century; it elaborates materialist dialectics and offers critical analysis of metaphysical and idealist conceptions in natural science.

The materials used for *Dialectics of Nature* were not published in Engels's lifetime. The complete edition of the book was put out for the first time in the U.S.S.R. in 1925 in German with a parallel Russian translation.—338

266 According to a Greek myth the large stables of King Augeas of Elis which had been in a state of filth for many years were cleaned out by Hercules in one day. The expression Augean stables is a synonym of any heap of refuse and filth or extreme neglect and disorder.—339

267 Engels is referring to Luther's choral, *Ein feste Burg ist unser Gott*. Heinrich Heine called this song "the *Marseillaise* of the Reformation" in his work *Zur Geschichte der Religion und Philosophie in Deutschland* (On the History of Religion and Philosophy in Germany), Book II.—339

268 Copernicus received a copy of his book *De revolutionibus orbium coelestium* (On the Rotation of Celestial Bodies), in which he set forth his heliocentric system of the Universe, on the day of his death—May 24, 1543.—340

269 According to the views current in chemistry in the 18th century phlogiston was considered to be the principle of inflammability supposed to exist in combustible bodies and released during combustion. The untenability of this theory was demonstrated by Lavoisier, outstanding French chemist, who supplied a correct explanation of the process of combustion as a chemical combination of combustible substances with oxygen.—341, 597

270 *Theology*—a teaching of religion attempting to arrange in a system and "scientifically" substantiate religious morals, dogmas and cults.—342, 378

271 Pseudo-scientific idealist doctrine which maintains that every development is predetermined in advance; it provided and still provides theoretical justification for the religious world outlook.—342

272 The reference is to Kant's *Allgemeine Naturgeschichte und Theorie des Himmels* (General Natural History and the Theory of the Heaven), published

anonymously in 1755. In it Kant set forth his cosmogonic hypothesis, according to which the solar system originated from primal nebular matter. Laplace first expounded his hypothesis on the formation of the solar system in the last chapter of his work, *Exposition du système du monde* (Exposition of th[e] Universe), Vol. I-II, Paris, 1796.—342

273 *Encyclopaedists* or *Enlighteners* were ideologists of the French bourgeoisie on the eve of the bourgeois revolution of the 18th century who joined force[s] to publish the *Encyclopaedia of Arts and Crafts.* The editor-in-chief of th[e] publication was Diderot, a materialist philosopher. Despite certain difference[s] in political and philosophical views, the contributors were united in thei[r] negative attitude towards feudalism, in their advocacy of the rights of th[e] third estate (see Note 331) headed by the bourgeoisie and their hatred o[f] medieval scholasticism and the Catholic Church. For Engels's description of their activity see *Socialism: Utopian and Scientific* (pp. 394-97 of this volume).—342

274 An allusion to the idea expounded by Isaac Newton in his *Mathematical Principles of Natural Science*, Book III, General Theory. When quoting this idea of Newton's in his *Encyclopaedia of Philosophic Science*, § 98, Addendum I, Hegel wrote: "Newton ... directly warned physics not to slip into metaphysics...."—343

275 *Amphioxus* (the lancelet)—a small fish-like animal. It is an intermediary form between the invertebrates and the vertebrates; it breeds in seas and oceans.

Lepidosiren belongs to the subclass of the lung fishes or Dipnoi, having both lungs and gills. It is found in South America.—345

276 *Ceratodus* (barramunda)—a dipnoan, breeding in Australia.

Archaeopteryx—a fossil vertebrate, the oldest representative of the bird class which at the same time possessed features of the reptiles.—345

277 This refers to C. F. Wolff's thesis "Theoria generationis" (Theory of Origin), published in 1759.—346

278 Charles Darwin's *Origin of Species* came out in 1859.—346

279 *Protista*, according to Haeckel's classification, is a large group of protozoa (unicellular and cellularless) forming a third kingdom of organic nature alongside the two other kingdoms (of multi-cellular organisms—animals and plants).—346

280 *Eozoon canadense*—fossil remains supposedly of extremely primitive organisms found in Canada. In 1878 German zoologist K. Möbius refuted the hypothesis with regard to their organic origin.—348

281 Originally this article was planned as an introduction to a more extensive work under the title of *Three Main Forms of Enslavement*. The project, however, was not carried out, and Engels, in the end, supplied his introductory section with a heading, "The Part Played by Labour in the Transition from Ape to Man". Engels analyses the vital role of labour and the production of tools in forming the human physical type and in creating human society; he shows how, as a result of a long historical process, the ape was transformed into a qualitatively new being—man.—354

282 See Charles Darwin, *The Descent of Man and Selection in Relation to Sex*, published in London, 1871.—354

283 This is a reference to the world economic crisis of 1873. In Germany it began with an "immense crash" in May 1873 which was a prelude to a protracted crisis which lasted till the end of the seventies.—364, 372

³⁴ *Kölnische Zeitung* (Cologne Newspaper)—German daily newspaper the publication of which began in Cologne in 1802; during the 1848-49 revolution and the period of reaction that followed it, the newspaper reflected the cowardly and treacherous policy of the Prussian liberal bourgeoisie; in the late 19th century it was associated with the National-Liberal Party.—365

³⁵ The order to deport Marx from France was issued by the French Government on January 16, 1845 under pressure from the Prussian Government.—366

³⁶ *Deutsche Brüsseler Zeitung* (German Brussels Newspaper) was founded by German political émigrés in Brussels and published from January 1847 to February 1848. From September 1847 onwards Marx and Engels were regular contributors to the paper and exerted a strong influence on its editorial policy. Under their guidance it became the organ of the Communist League.— 367, 430, 437

³⁷ *Kreuzzeitung* (Cross Newspaper)—a name given to the German daily, *Neue Preussische Zeitung* (New Prussian Newspaper), because the sign of the cross, the emblem of Landwehr, was used in its heading. The paper, which appeared in Berlin from June 1848 to 1939, was the organ of the counter-revolutionary court clique and the Prussian Junkers.—367

³⁸ *On June 13, 1849,* the petty-bourgeois party of the Mountain organised in Paris a peaceful demonstration of protest against the despatch of French troops to Italy to suppress the revolution. The demonstration was dispersed by the troops. Many leaders of the Mountain were arrested and deported or were forced to emigrate from France.—368, 443, 671

³⁹ *The Italian War*—a war between France and Piedmont against Austria in 1859. It was unleashed by Napoleon III allegedly to further the liberation of Italy, but in fact he was aspiring after territorial conquests and the consolidation of the Bonapartist regime in France, Napoleon III, however, was frightened by the mounting tide of the national liberation movement in Italy and concluded a separate peace treaty with Austria to preserve Italy's dismemberment. In accordance with this treaty France annexed Savoy and Nice, Lombardy was transferred to Sardinia, and Venice was left under Austrian rule.—368

⁹⁰ *Das Volk*—weekly newspaper published in German in London between May 7 and August 20, 1859, with Marx's direct participation. Marx in fact became its editor in early July.—368

⁹¹ The mass revolutionary insurrection of September 4, 1870 brought about the downfall of the Second Empire: the republic was proclaimed and a provisional government, the so-called Government of National Defence, was formed, which included both moderate Republicans and monarchists. This government headed by Trochu, Governor-General of Paris, and actually inspired by Thiers was set on betraying national interests and concluding treacherous agreements with the enemy.—369, 653, 674

⁹² Engels's *Socialism: Utopian and Scientific* consists of three chapters from *Anti-Dühring*, which were rewritten by Engels for the express purpose of providing the workers with a popular exposition of the Marxist teaching as an integral world outlook. In it Engels describes the three component parts of Marxism. He shows what led up to the appearance of dialectical and historical materialism and demonstrates that it was solely thanks to Marx's two great discoveries—his elaboration of the materialist conception of history and the creation of the theory of surplus-value—that socialism was given a scientific basis.

After pointing out the fundamental difference between scientific socialism and utopian socialism and remarking on the latter's role in history and its shortcomings, Engels goes on to reveal the sources of scientific socialism.

In the last chapter Engels proves that the main contradiction of capitalis
—the contradiction between the social character of production and the priva
character of appropriation—can be done away with only through a proletaria
revolution.—*375, 394*

293 *Bimetallism*—a system in which two metals, gold and silver, are simu
taneously used to fulfil the function of money.—*376*

294 *Vorwärts*—the central organ of the Socialist Workers' Party of German
published in Leipzig from October 1, 1876 to October 27, 1878. Engels
Anti-Dühring was printed in it between January 3, 1877 and July 7, 1878.—*37*

295 *The Mark* was an ancient German village community. Under this title Enge
published his brief outline of the history of German peasantry from ancier
times as an Appendix to the first German edition of *Socialism: Utopian an
Scientific*.—*376*

296 Engels makes a reference here to M. M. Kovalevsky's works *Tableau des or
gines et de l'évolution de la famille et de la propriété*, published in Stockhol
in 1890, and *Primitive Law, Book I, The Gens*, published in Moscow in 1886.-
376

297 *Agnosticism* (from Gr. *a*—not, and *gnóstikos*—good at knowing)—an ideali
doctrine according to which the world is unknowable, and man's reason r
stricted and unable to know anything beyond human sensations. Some ag
nostics recognise the objective existence of the material world but deny th
possibility of getting to know it, while others deny the existence of the ma
terial world for the simple reason that man cannot know whether anythin
exists beyond his sensations.—*377*

298 *Schoolman*—a proponent of scholasticism, medieval religious philosophy whic
was notable for its extreme abstractness, complete divorcement from livin
reality, and which sought to justify the dogmas of the Christian Church b
means of diverse logical subterfuges.—*377*

299 *Nominalists* represented a trend in medieval philosophy, according to whic
general concepts are merely the names of individual things. Unlike medieva
realists, they held that general concepts do not exist independently and ar
only names, words or abstractions. This means they recognised that object
were primary and concepts secondary. In this sense, nominalism was th
first expression of materialism in the Middle Ages.—*378*

300 *Homoiomeriae* (Homoeomeries)—the minutest, qualitatively definite materia
particles subject to endless division. According to Anaxagoras, homoeomerie
were the primary basis of all that exists and their combinations gave rise t
a multiplicity of things.—*378*

301 John Locke's book *An Essay concerning Human Understanding* was firs
published in London in 1690.—*379*

302 Inherent in theism, a religious dogma recognising the existence of a persona
God, the creator of the universe.—*379*

303 *Sensationalism* (from Lat. *sensus*—to feel), a trend in philosophy, according
to which sensibility (sensations, perceptions, desires, etc.) is held to be th
unique basis and source of all knowledge and of all man's psychical faculties
—*379*

304 *Deism*—a religious philosophical doctrine which recognises God to be an
impersonal but reasonable prime cause of the universe and denies his intervention in nature and human life.—*379, 600, 688*

305 *Baptists*—one of the most widespread Christian sects. Baptists approve of
baptising only for adults who consciously profess their faith in Christ. They

reject most sacraments and rituals of the Christian Church and champion
the community members' right to interpret the holy writings. The first baptist
communities were founded in England and the English colonies in America
in the 17th century.

Salvation Army—a reactionary religious and philanthropic organisation
founded in England in 1865 and reorganised on a military model in 1880 (hence
its name). Relying on widespread support from the bourgeoisie, this organisation set up a network of charitable institutions in many countries for the
purpose of diverting the working people from the struggle against the exploiters.—380

⁵ *Spiritualism* (from Lat. *spiritus*—a breath)—an idealistic teaching concerning
the spiritual primary basis of the world. Adherents of spiritualism hold that
the soul exists independently of the body.—382

⁷ This means dissident; it is derived from the Greek word *schisma* (to split),
which was adopted in Christian and historical literature to designate division
in the Christian Church in the Middle Ages.—383

⁸ The English Revolution of 1688 is referred to in British bourgeois historiography as the Glorious Revolution. The 1688 coup d'état resulted in the expulsion of James II, the deposition of the Stuart House and the establishment
of a constitutional monarchy (in 1689) with William of Orange at its head.
This monarchy represented a compromise between the landed aristocracy and
the big bourgeoisie.—385, 620, 688

⁹ *Wars of the Roses*—a dynastic struggle in England (1455-85) between the
feudal Houses of Lancaster and York, the name being derived from their
emblems, the red and the white rose. The Yorks were supported by big
feudal landowners from the southern, more economically developed part of
the country and also by the knighthood and the townspeople, while the Lan-
casters were backed by the feudal aristocracy from the northern counties.
The wars culminated in an almost complete wiping out of the ancient feudal
families and in the rise to power of a new dynasty, that of the Tudors, who
set up an absolute monarchy in the country.—385

¹⁰ *Cartesianism*—a doctrine propounded by the followers of the French 17th-
century philosopher René Descartes (in Lat. *Cartesius*), who drew materialist
conclusions from his philosophical system.—386

¹¹ *Declaration of the Rights of Man* was adopted by the French Constituent Assembly in 1789. It expounded the political principles of a new bourgeois
system and was incorporated in the French Constitution of 1791. The Jacobins
used this Constitution as a model when formulating their own version of
the Declaration of the Rights of Man in 1793. The National Convention included this Declaration as an introduction to the republican Constitution of
1793.—387

¹² Here and in subsequent references by the *Code Civil* (*Code Napoléon*) Engels
implies the entire system of bourgeois law as represented by five codes (civil,
civil procedure, commercial, criminal and criminal procedure) promulgated
in the period 1804-10 under Napoleon Bonaparte. These codes were introduced
in the western and south-western parts of Germany seized by Napoleonic
France and continued to operate in the Rhine Province even after it was
ceded to Prussia in 1815.—387, 492, 617, 627, 687

¹³ *Reign of terror*—a period of the revolutionary-democratic dictatorship wielded
by the Jacobins (see Note 76) from June 1793 to July 1794.—388, 396

¹⁴ In 1824, under mass pressure the English Parliament adopted an act repealing the ban on the trade unions.—389

[315] *The People's Charter*, which contained the demands of the Chartists (s
Note 22), was published on May 8, 1838 in the form of a bill to be submitt
to Parliament. It consisted of six clauses, namely, universal suffrage (f
men over 21), annual elections to Parliament, secret ballot, equal constitue
cies, abolition of property qualifications for candidates for Parliament, ar
salaries for M.P.s. The Chartists presented three petitions to Parliament
this effect, but they were rejected in 1839, 1842 and 1849.
The Anti-Corn Law League—see Note 128.—389

[316] The mass demonstration in London, which the Chartists (see Note 22) stag
on April 10, 1848 in order to hand in a petition to Parliament requesting t
adoption of a People's Charter, ended in fiasco due to the indecision ar
wavering of its organisers. The failure of the demonstration was exploite
by the reactionaries to make an assault on the workers and to apply r
pressions against the Chartists.—389

[317] *Brother Jonathan* (humorous)—a collective nickname given by the Englis
to the North Americans during the war waged by the English colonies i
America for independence (1775-83).
Revivalism—a movement in Protestantism which made its appearance i
the first half of the 18th century in England and later spread to Nor
America. Its adherents sought to strengthen and widen the influence c
Christianity by delivering religious sermons and organising new communiti
of believers. Moody and Sankey, two American preachers, were organise
of this movement.—389

[318] *The Second Parliamentary Reform*—a campaign for this was carried on i
England until it was introduced in 1867 under mass pressure of the labou
movement. An active part in this movement for the reform was played b
the General Council of the First International. The reform more than double
the number of electors and granted franchise to a section of skilled workers.-
391

[319] *Whigs*—a name applied to members of one of the great English political par
ties founded in the early 1680s. The Whig Party expressed the interests o
the bourgeois aristocracy and the big commercial and financial bourgeoisi
who sought to restrict royal authority. It ceased to exist as such in the 1850s
when the Whigs joined together with other political groupings of the bour
geoisie to form a new party, the Liberal Party.—391

[320] *Katheder-Socialism* (socialism of the chair)—a trend in bourgeois ideolog
between the 1870s and 1890s. Its representatives, primarily professors of Ger
man universities, preached bourgeois reformism under the guise of socialisn
from the university chairs (this trend was ironically called "Kathedersozialis
mus"). They (A. Wagner, G. Schmoller, L. Brentano, W. Sombart and others
claimed that the state was a supra-class institution, which was able to re
concile the hostile classes and gradually introduce socialism without infring
ing on the interests of the capitalists. Their aim was to better the condition
of the workers by organising insurance against sickness and accident an
by adopting factory acts. They insisted that well-organised trade unions mak
political struggle and a working-class party superfluous. This trend was on
of the ideological forerunners of revisionism.—391

[321] *Ritualism*—a trend in the Church of England which first appeared in the
1830s. Its adherents campaigned for the restoration of Catholic rituals and
certain Catholic dogmas in the Anglican Church (hence its name).—392

[322] The reference is to the eastern part of London inhabited by the proletaria
and the poor.—393

[323] This conclusion concerning the possibility of the concurrent victory of proletarian revolutions in the advanced capitalist countries and hence the impossibility of the victory of a proletarian revolution in one country alone was formulated by Engels in 1847 in his work *Principles of Communism.* It was valid for the period of pre-monopoly capitalism. Under new historical conditions of the period of monopoly capitalism, Lenin, drawing on the law he already formulated to the effect that in the era of imperialism the economic and political development of capitalism was uneven, came to a new conclusion, namely, that a socialist revolution could quite well triumph either in several countries at one and the same time or even in a single country, and that a simultaneous victory of socialist revolutions in all countries or in the majority of them was impossible. This conclusion was first formulated by Lenin in his article "On the Slogan for a United States of Europe" (1915).—393

[324] According to Rousseau's theory enunciated in his famous work *Du contrat social*, in primitive society people lived in natural conditions under which all men were equal. The appearance of private property and the development of material inequality were responsible for the people's transition from the natural to the civil condition and also for the establishment of the state based as it was on a social contract. Subsequently, however, the evolution of political inequality led to the break-down of the social contract and the emergence of a new underprivileged class. This phenomenon could be done away with, Rousseau argued, by a reasonable state based on a new social contract.— 395, 691

[325] *Anabaptists*—members of a sect which held that baptism should be for adults only and, therefore, that those baptised in infancy must be baptised again.—395

[326] Engels makes a reference here to the *True Levellers,* or *Diggers,* who represented the ultra-Left forces in the period of the English revolution of the 17th century and voiced the interests of the poor sections of the people in town and country. They demanded abolition of private landownership, propagated the ideas of primitive, levelling communism and attempted to implement them in practice through the collective ploughing of common lands.—395

[327] Engels refers here to the works by the outstanding representatives of utopian communism—*Utopia* by Thomas More and *City of the Sun* by Tomaso Campanella.—395

[328] *Directoire*—the French Directorate of 1795-99. This leading executive body consisted of 5 Directors, one of whom was re-elected every year. This institution opposed the democratic movement, supported the regime of terror employed against it and upheld the interests of the big bourgeoisie.—397

[329] Reference is made to the famous slogan of the French Revolution: *"Liberté, Egalité, Fraternité."*—397

[330] *New Lanark*—a cotton-spinning factory near the Scottish town of Lanark; it was built in 1784 together with a small township.—397

[331] *Third estate*—the underprivileged taxable class in feudal France (peasants, merchants, artisans and later bourgeoisie). This concept was to acquire particular significance on the eve of the French Revolution, when the bourgeoisie needed mass support and rallied the people around it to form a single "third estate", opposed to the privileged estates, those of the nobility and clergy.—398

[332] *Hundred days*—a period which saw the temporary restoration of Napoleon's Empire, lasting from his return from exile (on the island of Elba) to Paris on March 20, 1815 to his second abdication on June 22 of that year.—400

[333] *Waterloo*—a place near Brussels where Napoleon was finally defeated on

June 18, 1815 by the Anglo-Dutch armies led by Wellington and the Prussiar army led by Blücher.—400, 654

334 *The Grand National Consolidated Trades Union of Great Britain and Ireland* was formally set up at a congress of co-operative societies and trade unions which was held in October 1833 in London with Robert Owen in the chair. After meeting with strong opposition from the bourgeois state and society, the Union was dissolved in August 1834.—404

335 Engels refers here to the so-called markets for the fair exchange of labour products which were founded by pro-Owen co-operative societies of workers in various cities of England. The products of labour were exchanged there through the medium of labour-notes, whose unit was measured in terms of an hour of working time. These markets, however, soon went bankrupt.—404

336 An attempt to found a special bank to carry out the exchange of goods between petty producers without using money and to grant free credit to workers was made by Proudhon during the revolution of 1848-49. His *Banque du Peuple,* founded on January 31, 1849, existed for about two months, and was doomed to failure before it started to operate. The bank was closed at the beginning of April.—404

337 The reference is to the period extending from the third century B.C. to the seventh century A.D., which came to be known in history as the Alexandrian era (after the Egyptian city of Alexandria, a major centre of international trade of that time). This era saw the swift progress of a number of sciences, including mathematics, mechanics, geography, astronomy, anatomy and physiology.—406

338 The reference is to the great discoveries made by European merchants and seafarers in the period ranging from the latter half of the 15th century to the first half of the 17th century, the most important of which were the discovery of America, Australia, of a sea route to India round Africa, etc. The great geographical discoveries contributed to the collapse of feudalism and accelerated the emergence of capitalist relations in Western Europe.—417

339 The reference is to the wars waged in the latter half of the 17th century and the beginning of the 18th century. These were pursued by the coalitions of European powers led by France, on the one hand, and by Holland and, later, England, on the other. The underlying causes were the striving of the bourgeoisie and nobility, chiefly of France, to achieve territorial expansion and secure political and economic hegemony in Europe. These wars and the War of the Spanish Succession (1701-14) which France lost and which was the last in this series of "commercial wars" heavily undermined her economic and military positions and deprived her of vast colonial possessions.—417

340 *The Royal Maritime Company (Seehandlung)*—a commercial and credit society founded in Prussia in 1772. It enjoyed important government privileges and granted large loans to the Prussian Government.—422

341 *Vorwärts*—German radical newspaper which was issued in Paris twice a week from January to December 1844. Among its contributors were Marx and Engels.—430, 435

342 Engels wrote "On the History of the Communist League" as an introduction to the German edition (1885) of Marx's pamphlet *Revelations about the Co-*

logne Communist Trial. In the period of the operation of the Exceptional Law (see Note 167) it was essential for the working class of Germany to learn of the revolutionary experience gleaned during the onslaught of reaction in 1849-52. For this reason Engels deemed it necessary to reprint Marx's pamphlet.

In his work Engels highlights the historic role and place of the first international working-class organisation in the international labour movement, which proclaimed for the first time in history scientific communism to be its ideological weapon. Basing himself on the example of the Communist League which signified an important stage in the struggle for the creation of a proletarian party, Engels shows that the triumph of Marxism over various sectarian trends was due to its ability to reflect, right from its inception, all the needs of the revolutionary struggle of the proletariat, and to the fact that this theory was an inseparable part of the revolutionary struggle.—431

343 *Babouvism*—the theory of utopian, egalitarian communism, propounded by the 18th-century French revolutionary Gracchus Babeuf and his followers.—432

344 *Société des saisons* (Society of the Seasons)—a republican, socialist conspiratorial organisation acting in Paris from 1837 to 1839 under the leadership of Auguste Blanqui and Armand Barbès.

The Paris uprising of May 12, 1839, in which revolutionary workers played a major role, was prepared by this society. This uprising was not supported by the masses and was defeated by government troops and the National Guard.—432

345 The reference is to an episode in the struggle of German democrats on the home front against reaction. On April 3, 1833 a group of radicals demonstrated against the Federal Assembly in Frankfurt am Main in an attempt to stage a coup d'état and proclaim a German Republic. This poorly organised coup was suppressed by German troops.—432

346 In February 1834, the Italian bourgeois democrat Giuseppe Mazzini organised a march from Switzerland to Savoy, drawing on the support of the "Young Italy" society, which he founded in 1831, and also a group of revolutionary émigrés. Their aim was to start a popular uprising in the name of Italian unity and to proclaim an independent bourgeois republic. On entering Savoy the detachment was smashed by Piedmontese troops.—432

347 The reference is to the *London Educational Society of German Workers.* It was founded in February 1840 by Karl Schapper, Joseph Moll and other leaders of the League of the Just. In 1849 and 1850, Marx and Engels played an active part in its activities. On September 17, 1850, Marx, Engels and their adherents left the society, for a large section of its members took the side of the sectarian and adventurist group of Willich-Schapper (see Note 355). With the foundation of the International in 1864, this society became the German section of the International Working Men's Association in London. The London Educational Society existed till 1918, when it was closed down by the British Government.—433

348 *The Northern Star*—English weekly, the central organ of the Chartists, founded in 1837. Till November 1844 it appeared in Leeds and from November 1844 to 1852 in London. Feargus O'Connor was its founder and editor. George Harney was also on the staff of the paper. It printed articles by Engels between 1843 and 1850.—437

349 *Democratic Society*—founded in Brussels in the autumn of 1847. Its membership was made up of proletarian revolutionaries, primarily from among the German revolutionary émigrés, and progressive sections of the bour-

geois and petty-bourgeois democrats. Marx and Engels played an active role in its foundation. On November 15, 1847, Marx was elected its Vice-President the President being the Belgian democrat L. Jotran. As a result of Marx's work the Brussels Democratic Society became an important centre of international democratic movement. After Marx was deported from Brussels early in March 1848 and the Belgian authorities suppressed the most revolutionary elements of the society, its activities acquired a more restricted, purely local character and in 1849 it ceased to exist.—437

350 *Der Volks-Tribun*—New York weekly founded by German "true socialists"; it appeared between January 5 and December 31, 1846.—438

351 "Demands of the Communist Party in Germany"—a leaflet written by Marx and Engels in Paris between March 21 and 29, 1848. It was a political platform of the Communist League in the German revolution. This policy document was distributed among the members of the League who were to leave for their native country. In the course of the revolution Marx and Engels and their supporters propagated this document among the people.—441

352 The reference is to the German Workers' Club opened in Paris on March 8-9, 1848 on the initiative of the Communist League. The leading role in this club was played by Marx. The purpose of the club was to consolidate the ranks of the German workers who had emigrated to Paris and to explain to them the tactics of the proletariat in the impending bourgeois-democratic revolution.—442

353 The 1885 edition of Marx's *Revelations about the Cologne Communist Trial,* which carries the present article, written by Engels as an introduction, was supplemented by him with some documents, including the Addresses of the Central Committee to the Communist League dated March and June 1850.—444

354 *Progressives*—representatives of the Prussian bourgeois Progressive Party that was set up in June 1861. This party demanded that Germany be united under the hegemony of Prussia, that an all-German Parliament be convened, and that a strong liberal ministry responsible to the Chamber of Deputies be set up. In 1866, the Right wing of the party capitulated before Bismarck and split away to form the National-Liberal Party. Unlike the National-Liberals the Progressives continued to play the part of an opposition party even after Germany was unified in 1871, but their role was limited to the sphere of oratory. Out of fear of the working class and hostility to the socialist movement the Progressive Party reconciled itself to the rule of the Prussian Junkers in the conditions of semi-absolutist Germany. The indecisive behaviour of the party leadership reflected the instability of the commercial bourgeoisie, small industrialists and handicraftsmen on whom it relied for support. In 1844, the Progressives joined the Left wing of the National-Liberals to form the German Freethinking Party.—446

355 An ironical name given by Marx and Engels to the sectarian and adventurist group under Willich-Schapper by way of analogy with the separate union of the reactionary Catholic cantons in Switzerland in the 1840s. This group, that seceded from the Communist League after the split on September 15, 1850, formed an independent organisation with its own Central Committee. By its activities it helped the Prussian police to disclose the illegal communities of the Communist League in Germany and gave it a pretext for framing evidence in a trial against the prominent leaders of the Communist League in Cologne in 1852 (see Note 9).—447

356 *The Origin of the Family, Private Property and the State*—a fundamental work of Marxism. It provides a scientific analysis of the history of mankind

in the early stages of its development, reveals the process of the disintegration of the primitive-communal system and the formation of a class society based on private property, outlines the general features of this society, explains the peculiarities of the family relations in different socio-economic formations, discloses the origin and essence of the state and demonstrates the historical inevitability of its withering away with the final victory of a classless communist society.

This book was written by Engels in the space of two months, between the end of March and the end of May, 1884. While sorting out Marx's manuscripts Engels found a detailed synopsis of Lewis Morgan's book, *Ancient Society*, made by Marx in 1880-81. It contained many of his critical notes and his own points of analysis and also additions taken from other sources. After acquainting himself with this synopsis of the book by the progressive American scholar and realising that Morgan's book confirmed his and Marx's materialist understanding of history and their analysis of primitive society, Engels deemed it necessary to write a special book. He made a wide use of Marx's notes and also his propositions and the factual material derived from Morgan's book. Engels regarded this work as a partial fulfilling of Marx's last will and testament. When he worked on his book, Engels used much additional material taken from his study of the history of Greece and Rome, ancient Ireland, the ancient Germans, etc. (see Engels's works *The Mark, On the History of the Ancient Germans* and *The Franconian Period).*

In 1890, after compiling a vast amount of material on primitive society, Engels proceeded to prepare a new, fourth edition of his book. In the course of his preliminary research he studied all the latest literature, in particular the works of the Russian scientist M. M. Kovalevsky, and introduced many changes in his original text, and also considerable addenda, particularly to the chapter on the family.

The fourth, revised edition of Engels's book appeared in Stuttgart towards the end of 1891 and was not subjected to any further changes.—449, 461

357 *Contemporanul*—Rumanian journal of a socialist trend, which appeared in the town of Jassy in 1881-90.—451

358 *Magars*—a tribe in the 19th century, now a nationality populating the western part of Nepal.—455

359 Engels made a trip to the United States and Canada in August and September 1888.—459

360 *Pueblo*—a group of Indian tribes of North America which resided on the territory of New Mexico (at present the south-western part of the U.S. and Northern Mexico) and which shared a common history and culture. Their name is derived from the Spanish word *pueblo* (a people, community, village), which Spanish colonisers applied to these Indians and their villages. They lived in large communal fortified houses of 5 or 6 storeys, each inhabited by some thousand people.—463

361 This is a reference to the ancient names of the Central Asian rivers: the Amu Darya and the Syr Darya.—464

362 *Normans*—Scandinavian tribes which settled in Northern Europe. In the early Middle Ages this name was commonly used for the predecessors of the present-day Norwegians, Swedes and Danes.

Vikings—Scandinavian pirates and seafarers who made plundering raids on the shores of European countries and sailed via the Northern Atlantic as far as America in the period extending from the late 8th to the mid-11th century.—465, 551, 563

363 *Dravidians*—a group of Indian peoples who settled in Southern India. In ancient times they comprised the bulk of the population of the Indian subcontinent.
Gaura (or *Gauda*)—Indian tribes in West Bengal.—466

364 *Caribbeans*—a group of Indian tribes inhabiting areas in the northern part of South America: Brazil and the adjacent areas of Venezuela, Guiana and Colombia.—471

365 This letter of Marx's has not been preserved. Engels mentioned it in his letter of April 11, 1884, addressed to Kautsky.—472

366 The reference is to the text of the operatic tetralogy *Ring of the Nibelung* written by Richard Wagner, the subject of which was taken from the Scandinavian epic *Edda* and the German epic *Nibelungenlied*.—472

367 *Edda* and *Ögisdrecka*—a collection of ancient mythological stories and heroic songs of the Scandinavian peoples.—473

368 *Aesir* and *Vanir*—two groups of gods in Scandinavian mythology. The Ynglinga saga is the first saga in the book written by Snorri Sturluson, a medieval Icelandic poet and chronicler, about Norwegian kings from ancient times to the 12th century.—473

369 The reference is to special groups among most of the Australian aboriginal tribes. Men of each group could marry women belonging to a definite group. Each tribe had 4 to 8 such groups.—476

370 *Saturnalia*—the festival of Saturn in mid-December in ancient Rome, when the harvest was celebrated. During this festival people enjoyed the freedom of sexual intercourse. The word is now used to imply an orgy, a frantic unrestrained celebration.—483

371 See L. H. Morgan, *Ancient Society*, London, 1877, pp. 465-66.—488

372 Ibid., p. 470.—489

373 The reference is to M. M. Kovalevsky's work *Primitive Law, Book I, Gens*, Moscow, 1886. The author cites the data on the family community in Russia collected by Orshansky in 1875 and Yefimenko in 1878.—490

374 *Pravda of Yaroslav* is the first part of the old version of *Russian Pravda*, the code of laws of ancient Rus which appeared in the 11th and 12th centuries on the basis of traditional laws which reflected the socio-economic relations of that society.
Dalmatian Laws were in force in the 15th-17th centuries in Politz (part of Dalmatia). They were known as the Politz Statute.—490

375 *Calpulli*—the family community of Mexican Indians at the time of the Spanish conquest of Mexico. Every family community, whose members had common ancestors, owned a common plot of land which was not subject to alienation or division among heirs.—490

376 *Das Ausland* (Foreign Lands)—German journal concerned with geography, ethnography and natural science, published in 1828-93. Since 1873 it was issued in Stuttgart.—490

377 The reference is to Article 230 of the Civil Code (see Note 312).—492

378 *Spartiates*—a class of citizens of ancient Sparta enjoying full civil rights.
Helots—a class of underprivileged inhabitants of ancient Sparta attached to land and obliged to pay duties to Spartan landholders.—493

³⁷⁹ Aristophanes, *Thesmophoria zuasae.*—493

³⁸⁰ *Hierodules*—temple slaves of both sexes in ancient Greece and the Greek colonies. In many places, including Asia Minor and Corinth, the female slaves were engaged in prostitution.—495

³⁸¹ *Taifali*—a Germanic tribe, kindred to the Goths. By the 3rd century it had settled on the Northern shores of the Black Sea and was later, in the latter half of the 4th century, ejected by the Huns.

Heruli—a Germanic tribe which before the new era settled on the Scandinavian Peninsula. In the 3rd century, part of them moved to the Northern shores of the Black Sea from where they were driven out by the Huns.—498

³⁸² *Gudrun*—a German epic poem of the 13th century.—504

³⁸³ The reference is to the conquest of Mexico by Spanish colonisers in 1519-21.—514

³⁸⁴ L. H. Morgan, *Ancient Society*, London, 1877, p. 115.—515

³⁸⁵ *Neutral Nations*—a military alliance formed in the 17th century by the Indian tribes which were akin to Iroquois and lived on the Northern shore of Lake Erie. The French colonists applied this name to them because this alliance remained neutral in the wars between the Iroquois proper and the Hurons.—519

³⁸⁶ The reference is to the national liberation struggle waged by the Zulus against the British colonialists in 1879-87.

The Nubians, Arabs and other nationalities of the Sudan participated in the national liberation struggle lasting from 1881 to 1884. Under the leadership of the Muslim preacher Mohammed Ahmed their uprising culminated in the establishment of an independent centralised state. The Sudan was conquered by the British only in 1899.—520

³⁸⁷ The reference is to the so-called *metoikos*, or aliens who settled permanently in Attica. They were not slaves but they did not enjoy full rights of the Athenian citizens. They engaged chiefly in handicrafts and trade and had to pay a special tax and have "patrons" from among privileged citizens, through whom they could apply to the administration.—534

³⁸⁸ *Twelve Tables*—the code of Roman Law formulated in the mid-5th century B.C. as a result of the struggle waged by the plebs against the patricians. This code reflected the stratification of Roman society according to property, the evolution of slavery and the formation of a slaveowning state. The code of laws was inscribed on twelve tables, hence the name.—537

³⁸⁹ *Punic Wars*—the wars between the largest slaveowning states—Rome and Carthage—for domination in the Western Mediterranean and for the seizure of new territories and slaves. The Second Punic War (218-201 B.C.) ended in the rout of Carthage.—538

³⁹⁰ Wales was finally conquered by the English in 1283 but it still retained its autonomy at that time. It was ceded to England in the mid-16th century.—546

³⁹¹ In 1869-70 Engels was writing a work devoted to the history of Ireland but failed to complete it. While engaged in the study of Celtic history Engels analysed the old Welsh laws.—546

³⁹² Engels quotes here from the book *Ancient Laws and Institutes of Wales*, Vol. I, 1841, p. 93.—546

³⁹³ In September 1891 Engels toured Scotland and Ireland.—548

[394] In 1745-46 Scotland was the scene of an uprising of the mountainous clans against the oppression and dispossession of land practised by the English and Scottish landed aristocracy and bourgeoisie. The mountaineers upheld the traditional social structure based on the clans. After the uprising was suppressed the clan system in the highlands of Scotland was smashed and the survivals of clan landownership eliminated. More and more Scottish peasants were driven away from their land; the clan courts of law were abolished and certain clan customs forbidden.—548

[395] L. H. Morgan, *Ancient Society*, London, 1877, pp. 357-58.—548

[396] *Alamannian Law*—a code of common laws of the Germanic tribal alliance of the Alamanni who settled on the territory of contemporary Alsace, Eastern Switzerland and the South-Western part of Germany in the 5th century. They date back to the period between the end of the 6th and the 8th century. Here Engels refers to Law LXXXI (LXXXIV) of the Alamannian Law.—549

[397] *Song of Hildebrand*—a heroic poem, a specimen of ancient Germanic epic poetry of the 8th century. Only fragments of it have been preserved to the present day.—549

[398] The rebellion of the Germanic and Gallic tribes against Roman domination took place in A.D. 69-70 (according to some sources, in 69-71). Led by Civilis, it extended to a large part of Gaul and the Germanic areas under Roman rule, thus threatening to deprive Rome of these territories. The rebels were defeated and forced to come to terms with Rome.—552

[399] *Codex Laureshamensis*—a collection of the copies of letters patent and privileges belonging to the Lorch Monastery. It was compiled in the 12th century and is an important historical document with regard to the system of peasant and feudal landownership of the 8th-9th centuries.—554

[400] *Iberians*—a group of tribes, which in ancient times populated part of the Iberian Peninsula, the adjacent islands in the Mediterranean and the South-East of contemporary France.

Ligurians—a group of tribes that resided in the greater part of the Italian Peninsula in ancient times. In the 6th century B.C. they were driven away by Italic tribes to the North-Western section of the peninsula and to the coastal South-Eastern part of Gaul.

Noricans—a group of Illyrian and Celtic tribes which settled on the territory of the ancient Roman province of Noricum (now part of Styria and part of Carinthia).—558

[401] *Benefices*—grants of land bestowed as rewards. This form of remuneration was a common practice in the Franconian state in the first half of the 8th century. Plots of land with peasants attached to them were transferred in the form of benefices to the beneficiaries for life, in return for service, usually of the military variety. The system of benefices contributed to the formation of a feudal class, consisting in the main of small and middle nobility, to the transformation of peasants into serfs and to the development of vassal relations and the feudal hierarchy. Later, the benefices were made into fiefs, or hereditary estates.—562

[402] *Gau counts (Gaugrafen)*—royal officers appointed to administer counties in the Franconian state. They were invested with judicial power, collected taxes and led the troops during military campaigns. For their service they received one-third of the royal income collected in a given country and were rewarded with landed estates. In particular after 877, after the official decision to transfer the office by right of succession, the counts were gradually turning into powerful hereditary landowners.—563

[403] *Angariae*—compulsory services performed by residents of the Roman Empire, who were obliged to supply carriers and horses for state undertakings. In due course these services were used on a larger scale and were a heavy burden on the people.—564

[404] *Commendation*—an act by which a peasant or a small landowner commended himself to the protection of a powerful landowner in accordance with established practice (military service, transfer of a plot of land in return for a conventional holding). For peasants who were often compelled to do this by force this meant the loss of personal freedom and for small landowners, becoming vassals of the powerful feudal lords. This practice, widespread in Europe from the 8th and 9th centuries onwards, helped to consolidate feudal relations.—565

[405] *Hastings*—the place where Duke William of Normandy defeated Harold, the Anglo-Saxon king, on October 14, 1066. The Anglo-Saxon military organisation retained the survivals of gentile system and was armed primitively. William became King of England and came to be known as William the Conqueror.—570

[406] *Dithmarschen*—an area in the South-West of present-day Schleswig-Holstein. In ancient times it was populated by Saxons; in the 8th century it was seized by Charlemagne and subsequently belonged to various church dignitaries and secular lords. In the mid-12th century, the people of Dithmarschen, the majority of whom were free peasants, began to gain their independence. Between the 13th and the mid-16th century they enjoyed virtual independence. In that period Dithmarschen was a conglomeration of self-governing peasant communities based on the old peasant clans. Until the 14th century supreme power was exercised by an assembly of all free landholders and later it passed to the three elected collegiums. In 1559, the troops of the Danish King Frederick II and the Holstein Dukes Johann and Adolf broke down the resistance of the people of Dithmarschen and the area was divided between the conquerors. However, the communal administration and partial self-government continued to exist up to the second half of the 19th century.—576

[407] See Hegel's *Grundlinien der Philosophie des Rechts* (Principles of the Philosophy of Right), §§ 257 and 360.—576

[408] Engels's book *Ludwig Feuerbach and the End of Classical German Philosophy* shows how the Marxist world outlook evolved and what were its essential features. It expounds systematically the fundamentals of dialectical and historical materialism and reveals the relationship between Marxism and its philosophical predecessors as represented by Hegel and Feuerbach, the prominent representatives of German classical philosophy.

Engels demonstrates the most essential feature of philosophy throughout its history—the struggle between the two camps: materialism and idealism. For the first time Engels gives here a classical definition of the fundamental issue of philosophy, that of the relation of thinking and being, of spirit and nature.

The way a philosopher approaches the fundamental issue of philosophy determines his allegiance to one or the other philosophical camp.

While emphasising the fact that attempts to reconcile materialism and idealism and thereby to create an intermediate philosophy (dualism or agnosticism) are futile, Engels refutes agnosticism in all its manifestations and points out that "the most telling refutation of this as of all other philosophical crotchets is practice, namely, experiment and industry" (see p. 595 of this volume).

Engels reveals the essence of the revolution wrought by Marx in philosophy by his formulation of dialectical materialism. He thoroughly scrutinises the gist of historical materialism, which contributed to the definition of the general laws of development which operate in human society. While noting the fact that economic relations determine the historical process and the nature of a political system and all forms and types of social consciousness, including religion and philosophy, Engels at the same time emphasises the active role played by the ideological superstructures, their ability to develop independently and exert a reciprocal influence on the economic basis.

Much credit is due to Engels for his substantiation of the partisan principle of philosophy against a background of the struggle waged between philosophical trends throughout the history of class societies and reflecting the struggle of classes and parties. This work of Engels is a model of proletarian commitment and principled philosophical thinking.—584, 586

409 *Die Neue Zeit*—theoretical journal of German Social-Democracy; it appeared in Stuttgart from 1883 to 1923. Between 1885 and 1894 Engels published a series of his articles in this journal.—585, 691

410 In 1833-34, Heinrich Heine published his works *Die romantische Schule* (Romantic School) and *Zur Geschichte der Religion und Philosophie in Deutschland* (On the History of Religion and Philosophy in Germany), in which he put forward the idea that the German philosophical revolution, the culminating stage of which was Hegel's philosophy, was a prelude to the impending democratic revolution in Germany.—586

411 See Hegel's *Philosophy of Right, Preface.*—586

412 *Pietism* (from Lat. *pietas*—pity)—a name applied to a movement of religious and mystic reformers among the West-European Protestants in the late 17th and the first half of the 18th centuries, which was initiated in the Netherlands and Germany. Pietism was not a sect but a reactionary movement directed against rationalism and the philosophy of the Enlightenment.—591

413 *Deutsche Jahrbücher für Wissenschaft und Kunst* (German Annuals of Science and Art)—literary and philosophical journal of the Young Hegelians published in Leipzig from July 1841 to January 1843.—591

414 This reference is to Max Stirner's *Der Einzige und sein Eigenthum* (The Unique and His Property) which appeared in Leipzig in 1845.—592

415 The planet referred to is Neptune, discovered in 1846 by the German astronomer Johann Galle.—595

416 *Agnostics, adherents of agnosticism* (see Note 297).—595

417 *The schoolmaster of Sadowa*—an expression currently used by German bourgeois publicists after the victory of the Prussians at Sadowa (see Note 154), the implication being that the Prussian victory was to be attributed to the superiority of the Prussian system of public education.—606

418 The reference is to the epoch of the Restoration (1814-30). See Note 16.—614

419 *The Council of Nicaea*—the first ecumenical council of the Christian Bishops of the Roman Empire, convened by Emperor Constantine I in the town of Nicaea (Asia Minor) in 325. The Council adopted the so-called Nicene Creed, the acceptance of which was obligatory for all Christians.—619

420 *Albigenses* (the name is derived from the town of Albi)—a religious sect which was active in the towns of Southern France and Northern Italy in the 12th and 13th centuries. It directed a movement against the rich Catholic rituals and the Church hierarchy and gave a religious form to the protest of

urban merchants and handicraftsmen against the feudal system of land-ownership.—619

421 Between 1477 and 1555, Holland was part of the Holy Roman Empire (see Note 181). After the Empire broke up the country was annexed to Spain. Towards the end of the 16th-century bourgeois revolution Holland freed herself from Spanish rule and became an independent bourgeois republic.—620

422 In 1685, in the midst of the political and religious persecution of the Calvinists (Huguenots), which mounted in the 1620s, Louis XIV repealed the Nantes Edict promulgated in 1598. The Edict ensured the Huguenots freedom of belief and religious practice. After its repeal several hundred thousand Huguenots left France.—620

423 This term is applied to the German Empire (without Austria) that arose as a result of the victory of Prussia over France during the Franco-Prussian War of 1870-71. (For the little German Empire see Note 158).—621, 647

424 Engels's *The Peasant Question in France and Germany* is a major Marxist work on the agrarian question. The immediate cause for writing this work was the attempt by Vollmar and other opportunists to make use of the discussion of the draft agrarian programme at the Frankfurt Congress of German Social-Democrats in 1894 in order to smuggle in an anti-Marxist theory on the socialist transformation of rich peasants. Engels was also prompted to write this work by his striving to correct the mistakes committed by the French socialists, who deviated from Marxism and made concessions to opportunism in their agrarian programme adopted in Marseilles in 1892 and supplemented in Nantes in 1894.

Alongside this Engels elucidates the revolutionary principles of the proletarian policy vis-à-vis the various groups of peasants and elaborates the idea of the alliance between the working class and the working peasantry.—623

425 The 10th Congress of the French Workers' Party was held in Marseilles from September 24 to 28, 1892. It reviewed the situation in the Party, the celebration of May Day, participation in the International Socialist Workers' Congress in Zurich (1893), participation in the forthcoming parliamentary elections and other questions.

A major point on the Congress agenda was party work in the countryside, which was dictated by the rapid growth of the peasant movement throughout the country and the desire of the party to secure the support of the peasants in the parliamentary elections. The Congress adopted the agrarian programme, in which it put forward a number of concrete demands to suit the interests of the rural workers and small peasants. However, this programme deviated in some respects from the principles of socialism and made certain concessions to the wealthier sections of the rural population in the spirit of petty-bourgeois utopianism. These mistakes, which reflected opportunist influences, came still more to the fore in the programme and the supplements to it that were adopted at the Congress of Nantes.—626

426 *Sozialdemokrat*—weekly of the Social-Democratic Party of Germany, which appeared in Berlin in 1894-95.

Paul Lafargue's report "Peasant Property and Economic Progress", which Engels mentions, was published in the supplement to the newspaper on October 18, 1894.—637

427 Engels's introduction to *The Class Struggles in France, 1848 to 1850* by Marx was written for a separate publication of the booklet in Berlin in 1895.

By demonstrating the vast importance of the analysis of the revolution of 1848-49 and of its lessons provided for in Marx's work Engels devotes a great part of his introduction to the synthesis of the experience gleaned in the class struggle of the proletariat, chiefly in Germany. Engels underlines the necessity of utilising all the legal means for the sake of preparing the proletariat for a socialist revolution, of skilfully combining the struggle for democracy with the struggle for socialist revolution and of subordinating the first task to the second. In his introduction Engels once again demonstrates the fundamental Marxist principles of using tactical methods and forms of struggle appropriate to concrete historical conditions and of replacing the peaceful forms of revolutionary struggle, which the proletariat prefers, by coercive forms in cases when the ruling reactionary classes resort to violence.

Before the introduction was published, the Board of the German Social-Democratic Party insistently urged Engels to tone down the "over-revolutionary" spirit of the work and make it more prudent. Engels subjected the indecisive position of the party's leadership and its efforts to "act exclusively within the framework of legality" to scathing criticism. However, under pressure from the Board Engels was compelled to delete some passages in the proofs and change some formulations (these changes and deletions are provided in footnotes. The proofs that have been handed down to us and reference to the actual manuscript make it possible to restore the original text).

At the same time, relying on this abridged introduction, some leaders of Social-Democracy made an attempt to present Engels as a defender of a peaceful seizure of power by the working class at all costs, as a worshipper of "legality *quand même*" (at any price). Filled with indignation, Engels then insisted on the publication of this introduction in the *Neue Zeit* in full. Nevertheless, it was published in that journal with the same cuts which the author had been compelled to make for the separate edition mentioned above. However, even the abridged introduction retained its revolutionary character.

The unabridged text of Engels's introduction was published for the first time in the Soviet Union in the 1930 edition of *The Class Struggles in France, 1848 to 1850.*—641

428 The reference is to government subsidies which Engels ironically names after the estate in Sachsenwald near Hamburg, granted to Bismarck by Emperor Wilhelm I.—643

429 The reference is to the Legitimists and the Orleanists (see Notes 17 and 71).—647

430 During the reign of Napoleon III, France took part in the Crimean Campaign (1854-55), waged war with Austria on account of Italy (1859), participated together with Britain in the wars against China (1856-58 and 1860), began the conquest of Indo-China (1860-61), organised an expedition to Syria (1860-61) and Mexico (1862-67), and finally, in 1870-71, fought against Prussia.—647

431 The term applied by Engels expressed one of the principles of the foreign policy conducted by the ruling circles of Louis Napoleon's Second Empire (1852-70). This so-called principle of nationality was widely used by the ruling classes of big powers as an ideological mask for their plans of conquest and adventures abroad. It had nothing in common with the recognition of the right to national self-determination and was used to stir up national hatred and transform the national movements, especially of minor peoples, into the instrument of counter-revolutionary policies pursued by the vying powers.—647

432 For this episode, which started the insurrection of March 18, 1871, see *The Civil War in France*, included in the present volume (p. 280).—648

433 Universal suffrage was introduced by Bismarck in 1866, when elections to

the North-German Reichstag were held, and again in 1871, when elections to the Reichstag of the united German Empire were held.—650

434 This phrase was taken by Engels from Marx's introduction to the programme of the French Workers' Party. The programme was adopted at the Havre Congress of the party in 1880.—650

435 *The battle of Wagram* took place on July 5-6, 1809, during the Austro-French War of 1809. The French troops led by Napoleon Bonaparte defeated the Austrian army of Archduke Charles.—654

436 Engels refers here to the long struggle that was waged between the Dukes and nobility in Mecklenburg-Schwerin and Mecklenburg-Strelitz and which culminated in the signing of a Constitutional Treaty in Rostock in 1755. The Treaty confirmed the nobility's freedoms, hereditary rights and privileges and secured their leading role in the Landtags, which were organised on the social estate principle. It also exempted half of their land from taxes, fixed taxes on trade and handicrafts, and determined their contribution to state expenditure. —655

437 A new Anti-Socialist Bill, introduced in the German Reichstag on December 5, 1894, was rejected by the legislature on May 11, 1895.—657

438 Reference to *Critique of Politics and Economics*, a work which Marx planned to write.—668

439 *The Central Committee of the Paris National Guard* was formed in February 1871. During the siege of Paris in the Franco-Prussian War of 1870-71 the National Guard was joined by a large mass of democratically-minded people. Its Committee headed the insurrection of March 18, 1871 and exercised the functions of the history's first proletarian government till the establishment of the Paris Commune (see Note 8) on March 28.—670

440 Reference is to A. Haxthausen's book *Ueber den Ursprung und die Grundlagen der Verfassung in den ehemals slavischen Ländern Deutschlands im allgemeinen und des Herzogthums Pomern im besondern* (On the Origin and the Basis of Communal System in the Former Slav Lands of Germany in General and the Duchy of Pomerania in Particular), published in Berlin in 1842.—670

441 *Mutualists*—the Proudhonists referred to themselves as such in the 1860s, because they put forward a petty-bourgeois reformist plan of liberating the working people by organising mutual aid (co-operatives, mutual-aid societies, etc.).—672

442 The reference is to the resolutions passed by the London Conference of the First International held on September 17-23, 1871 (see Note 245): "Designations of National Councils, etc." (Resolution II, §§ 1, 2, 3), "Political Action of the Working Class" (Resolution IX), "The Alliance of Socialist Democracy" (Resolution XVI), and "Split in the French-Speaking Part of Switzerland" (Resolution XVII).—673

443 *Neuer Social-Demokrat*—German newspaper, which appeared in Berlin between 1871 and 1876. It was the organ of the General Association of German Workers led by Lassalle, which opposed the Marxist leadership of the First International and the German Social-Democratic Workers' Party and supported the Bakuninists and representatives of other anti-proletarian currents in the labour movement.—674

444 *The General Association of German Workers*—a political organisation set up in 1863 with the active participation of Lassalle. It functioned till 1875

when at the Gotha Congress the Lassalleans and Eisenachers (the party headed by Liebknecht and Bebel) united to form the Socialist Workers' Party of Germany.—674

445 See Hegel's *Phenomenology of Mind*, section "The Truth of Education".—676

446 On several occasions in 1872 and 1873, Liebknecht and Hepner addressed Marx with a request to write a pamphlet or an article for *Volksstaat* (see Note 162) and criticise Lassalle's views in it.—677

447 Referring to the outburst by Dühring's supporters at the Gotha Congress in 1877, Blos asked Marx in his letter dated October 30-November 6, 1877, whether Marx and Engels were angry with party members in Germany. Noting the fact that German workers were paying greater attention to articles by Marx and Engels than ever before, Blos wrote that thanks to the agitation carried on by Social-Democrats Marx and Engels had become more popular than they themselves could possibly imagine.—677

448 The reference is to the Statutes of the League of the Just. Marx and Engels took an active part in formulating the League Statutes in June 1847 at its first Congress. After it had been discussed by the League communities, it was scrutinised at the second Congress and finally approved on December 8, 1847.—677

449 The book referred to is *Die Geschichtsphilosophie Hegels und der Hegelianer bis auf Marx und Hartmann* (The Philosophy of History of Hegel and the Hegelians up to Marx and Hartmann), published in Leipzig in 1890.—678, 689, 690

450 *Deutsche Worte* (German Word)—Austrian economic and socio-political journal, which appeared in Vienna between 1881 and 1904.
   M. Wirth's article "Outrages in Respect of Hegel and Persecution of Him in Contemporary Germany" was published in the journal's issue No. 5 for 1890.—678

451 *Berliner Volkstribüne* (Berlin Popular Tribune)—weekly of Social-Democrats, which gravitated towards the semi-anarchist group of the "Young"; it appeared between 1887 and 1892.
   The discussion material for the subject "Full Product of Labour to Everybody" was published in the newspaper between June 14 and July 12, 1890—679

452 *Züricher Post*—Swiss daily of democratic leanings, which appeared between 1879 and 1936.—684

453 Franz Mehring's article *Über den historischen Materialismus* (On Historical Materialism) was printed in 1893 as an appendix to his book *Lessing Legende* (The Lessing Legend).—689

454 The reference is to the adherents of mercantilism, a system of economic views current in the epoch of primitive accumulation. The theoreticians of mercantilism, who represented commercial capital, identified the national wealth with accumulation of money and saw foreign trade as its sole source. In the 17th and 18th centuries mercantilism exerted a great influence on the economic policies of the absolutist states.—691

455 *Thirty Years' War* (1618-48)—a general European war, caused by the feud between Protestants and Catholics. Germany was the chief scene of the

fighting and was made the object of much military plunder and the expansionist ambitions of foreign powers. The war ended in 1648 when the Westphalian Peace Treaty, which sealed the political fragmentation of Germany, was signed.—692

456 This letter was first published without any mention of the addressee in the journal *Der sozialistische Akademiker* No. 20, 1895, by its contributor H. Starkenburg. As a result Starkenburg was wrongly identified as the addressee in all previous editions.—693

457 Engels has in mind the following work by G. Gülich, consisting of many volumes: *Geschichtliche Darstellung des Handels, der Gewerbe und des Ackerbaus der bedeutendsten handeltreibenden Staaten unserer Zeit* (Historical Description of Trade, Industry and Agriculture of the Most Important Commercial States of Our Time), published in Jena between 1830 and 1845.—695

NAME INDEX

A

Adler, Victor (1852-1918)—one of the organisers and leaders of the Austrian Social-Democratic Party—20

Aeschylus (525-456 B.C.)—outstanding playwright of ancient Greece, author of classic tragedies—453, 492, 525

Affre, Denis Auguste (1793-1848)— French clergyman, Archbishop of Paris (1840-48), was shot by order of the revolutionary government during the June 1848 uprising—305

Agassiz, Jean Louis Rodolphe (1807-1873)—Swiss geologist and zoologist; propagated the idealist doctrine of cataclysms and the idea of divine creation of the world—483

Agesilaus (c. 442-c. 358 B.C.)—King of Sparta (c. 399-c. 358 B.C.)—150

Agis I (died c. 399 B.C.)—King of Sparta (c. 426-c. 399 B.C.)—150

Ailly, Pierre d' (1350-1420 or 1425)— French cardinal, played an important role at the Constance Council—176

Alais, Louis Pierre Constant (born c. 1821)—French police agent—138, 141

Albrecht, Karl (1788-1844)—German merchant: was sentenced to six years' imprisonment for his participation in the opposition movement of "demagogues". From 1841 he lived in Switzerland, preached ideas which were close to the utopian communism of Weitling, but vested them in religious-mystical attire—438

Alexander of Macedon (356-323 B.C.)— great soldier and statesman—76, 138, 406, 490

Alexander II (1818-1881)—Russian Emperor (1855-81)—267

Alexandra (1844-1925)—daughter of Christian IX, King of Denmark; in 1863 she married Edward, Prince of Wales, who in 1901 became King Edward VII of Great Britain—282

Ammianus Marcellinus (c. 332-c. 400)— Roman historian—498, 516

Anacreon (second half of the 6th cent. B.C.)—ancient Greek poet—503

Anaxagoras of Clazomenae (c. 500-428 B.C.)—Greek materialist philosopher —378, 394

Anaxandridas (6th cent. B.C.)—King of Sparta (since 560 B.C.); ruled together with Ariston—493

Anglès, François Ernest (1807-1861)— French landowner, deputy of the Legislative Assembly (1850-51), member of the Party of Order—157

Annenkov, Pavel Vasilyevich (1812-1887)—Russian liberal landowner and man of letters—659-69

Appian (end of 1st cent.-the 170s)— ancient Roman historian—617

Appius Claudius (died c. 448 B.C.)— Roman statesman, one of the Committee of Decemvirs (451, 450), which promulgated the laws of the Twelve Tables—538

Aristides (c. 540-467 B.C.)—ancient Greek statesman and soldier—534, 545

Ariston (6th cent. B.C.)—King of Sparta (574-520 B.C.), ruled together with Anaxandridas—493

Aristophanes (c. 446-c. 385 B.C.)— ancient Greek playwright, author of political comedies—493

Aristotle (384-322 B.C.)—great thinker of ancient times, ideologist of the class of slave-holders; vacillated between materialism and idealism—405, 527

Arkwright, Richard (1732-1792)— English industrialist, plagiarised a number of inventions in Britain—388

Artaxerxes—name of three Persian kings of the Achaemenian dynasty—543

Auer, Ignaz (1846-1907)—one of the leaders of the German Social-Democratic Party, was several times elected to the Reichstag; subsequently adhered to reformism—311, 313

Augustus (63 B.C.-A.D. 14)—Roman Emperor (27 B.C.-A.D. 14)—538, 539, 557, 695

Aurelle de Paladines, Louis Jean Baptiste d' (1804-1877)—French general, Clerical, Commander-in-Chief of the Paris National Guard (March 1871), deputy of the National Assembly of 1871—278-80

Aveling, Eleanor (1855-1898)—prominent figure in the British and international working-class movement; Marx's youngest daughter, wife of the British Socialist Edward Aveling—14

B

Babeuf, François Noël (Gracchus) (1760-1797)—French revolutionary, utopian communist, organiser of "Conspiracy of Equals"—59, 395

Bachofen, Johann Jacob (1815-1887)—prominent Swiss historian and lawyer, author of Mother Right—451-55, 457, 459, 468, 475-76, 482, 483, 484, 487, 507

Bacon, Francis, de Verulam (1561-1626)—great English philosopher, founder of English materialism—378-79, 406

Baer, Karl Ernst (Karl Maximovich) (1792-1876)—outstanding Russian naturalist, founder of scientific embryology; worked in Germany and Russia—346

Bailly, Jean Sylvain (1736-1793)—prominent figure in the French bourgeois revolution at the end of the 18th century and a leader of the liberal constitutional bourgeoisie—97

Bakunin, Mikhail Alexandrovich (1814-1876)—Russian democrat and publicist, one of the ideologists of anarchism; took part in the 1848-49 revolution in Germany; being member of the First International revealed himself as a sworn enemy of Marxism and was expelled from the International for his schismatic activities by the Hague Congress in 1872—14, 33, 246, 311, 313, 336, 592, 607, 672-73

Balzac, Honoré de (1799-1850)—great French realist writer—179

Bancroft, Hubert Howe (1832-1918)—American bourgeois historian, author

of works on history and ethnography —471, 482, 484, 567

Bang, Anton Christian (1840-1913)—Norwegian theologian, author of works on Scandinavian, mythology, and history of Christianity in Norway—551

Baraguay d'Hilliers, Achille (1795-1878)—French Bonapartist general; during the Second Republic was deputy of the Constituent and the Legislative Assembly; in 1851, Commander-in-Chief of the Paris Garrison—145-46, 155

Barbès, Armand (1809-1870)—French petty-bourgeois revolutionary democrat; took an active part in the 1848 revolution; was sentenced to life imprisonment for his participation in the events of May 15, 1848 and pardoned in 1854—432

Baroche, Pierre Jules (1802-1870)—French politician and statesman, member of the Party of Order, subsequently Bonapartist; in 1849 was appointed Attorney General of Court of Appeal—132, 142, 146, 150

Barrot, Odilon (1791-1873)—French bourgeois politician, leader of liberal monarchist opposition until February 1848; from December 1848 to October 1849 headed the ministry supported by the Party of Order—111-13, 115, 126-28, 135, 147, 149, 154, 162, 656

Barth, Paul (1858-1922)—German bourgeois philosopher and sociologist, professor of Leipzig University—678-80, 688, 690, 691

Barton, John (end of the 18th-beginning of the 19th cent.)—English economist, theoretician of classical bourgeois political economy—225

Bauer, Bruno (1809-1882)—German idealist philosopher, prominent Young Hegelian, bourgeois radical; after 1866, National-Liberal—11, 19, 366, 591, 593, 607

Bauer, Edgar (1820-1886)—German publicist, Young Hegelian, brother of Bruno Bauer—18, 19

Bauer, Heinrich—prominent figure in the German working-class movement, a leader of the League of the Just, member of the Central Committee of the Communist League—432, 441, 444, 446

Bayle, Pierre (1647-1706)—French sceptical philosopher—620

Blanc, Louis (1811-1882)—French petty-bourgeois Socialist, historian; in 1848 —member of the Provisional Government and Chairman of the Luxemburg Commission; since August 1848, one of the leaders of petty-bourgeois émigrés in London—62, 96, 443, 445, 602

Blanchet, Stanislas (real name *Pourille*) (b. 1833)—French monk, police agent provocateur; he made his way into the Paris Commune, but was exposed and arrested—295

Blanqui, Louis Auguste (1805-1881)— French revolutionary, utopian communist: during the 1848 revolution adhered to the extreme Left of the democratic and proletarian movement in France; was several times sentenced to imprisonment—101, 254, 278, 281, 305, 432

Bleichröder, Gerson (1822-1893)— German financier, Bismarck's personal banker, his unofficial adviser in financial matters and negotiator in various machinations—579

Bloch, Joseph—editor of the magazine *Sozialistische Monatshefte*—682-83

Blos, Wilhelm (1849-1927)—German Social-Democrat, journalist and historian; in 1872-74, an editor of *Volksstaat*; member of the Reichstag; during the First World War adopted a social-chauvinist stand—677

Boenigk, Otto von—German public figure, read lectures on socialism at Breslau University—680-81

Boguslawski, Albert (1834-1905)—German general and writer on war—655-56

Böhme, Jacob (1575-1624)—German handicraftsman; mystical philosopher —378

Bolingbroke, Henry (1678-1751)— English deist philosopher and politician, a leader of the Tories—386

Bolte, Friedrich—prominent figure of the American labour movement, German-born; in 1872 Secretary of the Federal Council of North-American sections of the International; member of the General Council (1872-74); in 1874 expelled from the General Council—671-74

Bonaparte, See *Napoleon III*.

Bonaparte, Napoleon Joseph Charles Paul (1822-1891)—son of Jérôme Bonaparte and cousin of Louis Bonaparte; Deputy of the Constituent and the Legislative Assembly during the Second Republic—369

Bonapartes—dynasty of emperors in France (1804-14, 1815, 1852-70)—98, 170-73

Bonnier, Charles (b. 1863)—French Socialist, journalist—473

Borgius, W.—693-96

Born, Stephan (real name *Buttermilch*) (1824-1898)—German worker, member of the Communist League, during the 1848-49 revolution in Germany was one of the first representatives of reformism in the German working-class movement—443

Bornsted, Adalbert (1808-1851)—German petty-bourgeois democrat, founded and edited the *Deutsche Brüsseler Zeitung* in 1847-48; member of the Communist League until March 1848, when he was expelled; one of the organisers of the volunteer legion of German émigrés in Paris, which participated in the Baden uprising in April 1848—442

Börnstein, Arnold Bernhard Karl (1808-1849)—German petty-bourgeois democrat, a leader of the volunteer legion of German émigrés in Paris, which took part in the Baden uprising in April 1848—442

Bourbons—French royal dynasty (1589-1792, 1814-15 and 1815-30)—110, 117, 151, 152-53, 170, 614

Bracke, Wilhelm (1842-1880)—German Social-Democrat, one of the founders (1869) and leaders of the Social-Democratic Workers' Party (Eisenachers); was close to Marx and Engels, waged struggle against the Lassalleans—311, 313-14, 334, 337

Brentano, Lujo (1844-1931)—German vulgar bourgeois economist, one of the chief representatives of Katheder-socialism—393

Bright, John (1811-1889)—English industrialist, advocate of Free Trade, one of the founders of the Anti-Corn Law League; since the end of the 60s a leader of the liberal Party, Minister in several Liberal governments—238, 391

Broglie, Achille Charles (1785-1870)— French statesman, Prime Minister (1835-36), deputy of the Legislative Assembly (1849-51), Orleanist—132, 154

June 1848, commander of the garrison and the National Guard of Paris; took part in dispersing a demonstration in Paris on June 13, 1849—112-13, 115, 121, 124-25, 138-39, 141, 142, 144-48, 150, 155, 157, 162, 163, 165, 283

Charles I (1600-1649)—King of England (1625-49); was executed during the 17th-century bourgeois revolution in England—385

Charles the Great (Charlemagne) (c. 742-814)—King of the Franks (768-800) and Empemr (800-814)—563-64

Charras, Jean Baptiste Adolphe (1810-1865)—French colonel and politician, moderate bourgeois republican; took part in suppressing the June uprising of Paris workers in 1848; opposed Louis Bonaparte; expelled from France—165

Cherbuliez, Antoine Elisée (1797-1869) —Swiss economist, follower of Sismondi—225

Civilis, Julius (1st cent. A.D.)—leader of the German tribe of Batavians, headed the revolt of German and Gallic tribes against Roman rule (69-70 or 69-71)—552

Claudian gens—Roman patricians—538

Cleisthenes—Athenian politician, in 510-507 B.C. carried out reforms aimed at abolishing the remnants of the clan system and establishing democracy based on slaveholding—535

Cobden, Richard (1804-1865)—English bourgeois politician and industrialist, a leader of Free Traders and founder of the Anti-Corn Law League, M.P. —391

Coëtlogon, Louis Charles Emmanuel, Count (1814-1886)—French official, Bonapartist, one of the organisers of the counter-revolutionary action against Paris on March 22, 1871—282

Collins, Anthony (1676-1729)—English materialist philosopher—379

Columbus, Christopher (1451-1506)—great seafarer, discovered America—363

Constant, Benjamin (1767-1830)—French writer and liberal politician—97

Constantine I (c. 274-337)—Roman Emperor (306-337)—658

Copernicus, Nicholaus (1473-1543)—great Polish astronomer, founder of

the theory of heliocentric system of the world—340, 342, 595

Corbon, Claude Anthime (1808-1891)—French politician, republican, member of the Constituent Assembly (1848-49); subsequently mayor of one of the Paris districts, and member of the National Assembly of 1871—272

Coulanges, de. See *Fustel de Coulanges.*

Cousin, Victor (1792-1867)—French idealist, eclectic philosopher—97

Cousin-Montauban, Charles Guillaume Marie-Appolinaire-Antoine, comte de Palikao (1796-1878)—French general, Bonapartist; in 1860 commanded Anglo-French expeditionary forces in China; War Minister and head of the government (August-September 1870) —278

Coward, William (c. 1656-1725)—English physician, materialist philosopher—379

Creton, Nicolas Joseph (1798-1864)—French lawyer; during the Second Republic member of the Constituent and the Legislative Assembly, Orleanist—152,

Cromwell, Oliver (1599-1658)— leader of the bourgeoisie and the nobility that joined the ranks of the bourgeoisie in the English bourgeois revolution of the 17th century; from 1653, Lord Protector of the Commonwealth —97, 165, 385, 695

Cunow, Heinrich Wilhelm Karl (1862-1936)—German Social-Democrat, historian, sociologist and ethnographer; in the 80s and 90s adhered to Marxism, later revisionist—490

Cuvier, Georges (1769-1832)—French naturalist, author of unscientific idealist theory of cataclysms—344, 467

D

Dąbrowski, Yaroslaw (1836-1871)—Polish revolutionary democrat, participant in the national liberation movement in Poland in the 1860s; general of the Paris Commune; from the beginning of May 1871 Commander-in-Chief of all its armed forces; was killed on the barricades—294

Dalton, John (1766-1844)—English chemist and physicist, developed atomic ideas in chemistry—345

Daniels, Roland (1819-1855)—German physician, member of the Communist

League, was prosecuted at the Cologne Communist trial (1852); was among the first who tried to apply dialectical materialism in natural science; friend of Marx and Engels—446

Dante, Alighieri (1265-1321)—great Italian poet—184, 231, 365

Danton, Georges Jacques (1759-1794)—prominent figure in the French bourgeois revolution at the end of the 18th century; leader of the Right wing of Jacobins—96

Darboy, Georges (1813-1871)—French theologian, Archbishop of Paris since 1863; in May 1871 shot by the Commune as a hostage—254, 274, 304-05

Darwin, Charles Robert (1809-1882)—great English naturalist, founder of scientific evolutionary biology—346, 348, 354-55, 376, 407, 417, 429, 458, 599, 611

Deflotte, Paul (1817-1860)—French naval officer, Blanquist, participant in the events of May 15 and the insurrection of June 1848 in Paris, deputy of the Legislative Assembly (1850-51)—132

Democritus (c. 460-c. 370 B.C.)—ancient Greek materialist philosopher, one of the founders of the atomic theory—378

Demosthenes (384-322 B.C.)—famous ancient Greek orator and politician—521

Deprez, Marcel (1843-1918)—French physicist, electrical engineer, worked on the problem of transmission of electric power over long distances—430

Descartes, René (1596-1650)—outstanding French dualist philosopher, mathematician and naturalist—340, 345, 405, 596, 597, 679

Desmarêt—French officer of gendarmes, killed Gustave Flourens—283

Desmoulins, Camille (1760-1794)—French publicist, prominent figure in the French bourgeois revolution at the end of the 18th century, belonged to the Right wing of Jacobins—96

Dicaearchus (4th cent. B.C.)—Greek scholar, Aristotle's disciple, author of a number of works on history, politics, philosophy, geography, etc.—522

Diderot, Denis (1713-1784)—great French atheist philosopher, mechanical materialist, one of the ideologists of the French revolutionary bourgeois,

head of the Encyclopaedists—405, 600

Dietz, Johann Heinrich Wilhelm (1843-1922)—German Social-Democrat, founder of a Social-Democratic publishing house, deputy of the Reichstag since 1881—451

Dietzgen, Joseph (1828-1888)—German Social-Democrat, philosopher, who, without any previous schooling, arrived at the fundamental principles of dialectical materialism; leather worker by trade—609

Diocletian (c. 245-313)—Roman Emperor (284-305)—657

Diodorus of Sicily (c. 80-29 B.C.)—ancient Greek historian, author of works on world history, Historical Library—550, 557

Dionysius of Halicarnassus (1st cent. B.C.-1st cent. A.D.)—ancient Greek historian and rhetorician, author of Roman Ancient History—525

Disraeli, Benjamin, Lord Beaconsfield (1804-1881)—English statesman and writer, Tory, leader of the Conservative Party, Prime Minister (1868-70 and 1874-80)—391

Dodwell, Henry (d. 1784)—English materialist philosopher—379

Dolleschall, Laurenz (b. 1790)—police official in Cologne (1819-47); censor of the Rheinische Zeitung—365

Douay, Félix (1816-1879)—French general, taken prisoner at Sedan, one of the commanders of the Versailles troops, a hangman of the Paris Commune—301

Duchâtel, Charles (1803-1867)—French statesman, Orleanist, Minister of the Interior (1839-40, 1840-February 1848)—153

Dufaure, Jules Armand Stanislas (1798-1881)—French lawyer and statesman, Orleanist, Minister of the Interior (1848 and 1849), Minister of Justice (1871-73, 1875-76 and 1877-79), hangman of the Paris Commune, Chairman of the Council of Ministers (1876, 1877-79)—278, 283, 298, 299

Dühring, Eugen (1833-1921)—German eclectic philosopher and vulgar economist, representative of reactionary petty-bourgeois socialism; metaphysician; in his philosophy combined idealism, vulgar materialism and positivism; privatdocent at Berlin University, 1863-77—20, 24, 375-76

Duncker, Franz (1822-1888)—German

bourgeois politician and publisher—368

Duns, Scotus Johannus (c. 1265-1308)—English scholastic philosopher, representative of nominalism, which was the earliest form of materialism in the Middle Ages; author of *Oxford Opus* —377

Dupin, André Marie (1783-1865)—French jurist and politician,Orleanist, Chairman of the Legislative Assembly (1849-51), subsequently Bonapartist—138, 141, 142

Duprat, Pascal (1815-1885)—French journalist, bourgeois Republican, deputy of the Constituent and the Legislative Assembly under the Second Republic, was against Louis Bonaparte—143, 144

Dureau de la Malle, Adolphe (1777-1857)—French poet and historian—544

Dürer, Albrecht (1471-1528)—German painter of the Renaissance—339

Duval, Émile Victor (1841-1871)—prominent figure in the French working-class movement, founder by trade; member of the International, member of the Central Committee of the National Guard and Paris Commune, general of the National Guard; on April 4, 1871 was taken prisoner and shot by Versailles troops—283

E

Eccarius, Johann Georg (1818-1889)—German tailor, prominent figure in the international working-class movement, member of the League of the Just and, later, of the Communist League; member of the General Council of the First International; subsequently participant in the British trade union movement—439

Ehrhard, Johann Ludwig Albert (born c. 1820)—German commercial clerk, member of the Communist League, involved in the Cologne Communist trial (1852)—446

Engels, Friedrich (1820-1895)—11, 13, 15-22, 24, 32, 34, 64, 65, 182-83, 235, 247, 310-13, 332-37, 366, 376, 378, 393, 430, 431, 441-50, 460, 495, 498, 527, 546, 548, 582-85, 608, 622, 630, 636, 640, 642, 658, 674-85, 689, 693, 696

Epicurus (c. 341-c. 270 B.C.)—outstanding materialist philosopher of Ancient Greece, atheist—11

Eschenbach. See *Wolfram von Eschenbach.*

Espartero, Baldomero (1793-1879)—Spanish general and statesman, Regent of Spain (1841-43) and Premier (1854-56), leader of the Progressist Party—275

Espinas, Alfred Victor (1844-1922)—French bourgeois philosopher and sociologist, advocate of the theory of evolution—469-70

Euclid (end of the 4th-beginning of the 3rd cent. B.C.)—outstanding ancient Greek mathematician—340

Eudes, Émile Desirée François (1843-1888)—French revolutionary, Blanquist, general of the National Guard and member of the Paris Commune; after the suppression of the Commune emigrated to Switzerland and then to England; upon his return to France (under the amnesty of 1880) became an organiser of the Central Revolutionary Committee of the Blanquists —254

Euripides (c. 480-c. 406 B.C.)—ancient Greek playwright, author of classical tragedies—494

Everbeck, August Hermann (1816-1860)—German physician and man of letters, leader of the Paris communities of the League of the Just; later on, member of the Communist League from which he withdrew in 1850—437, 446

F

Fabian gens—Roman patricians—542

Falloux, Alfred (1811-1886)—French politician, Legitimist and clerical; initiated the dissolution of National *ateliers* in 1848 and inspired the suppression of the June uprising in Paris; Minister of Education (1848-49) —115, 126, 127, 154, 156

Faucher, Léon (1803-1854)—French bourgeois politician, Orleanist, economist (follower of Malthus), Minister of the Interior (December 1848-May 1849, 1851); later on Bonapartist—133, 150, 154

Favre, Jules (1809-1880)—French lawyer and politician, one of the leaders of moderate bourgeois republicans; as Foreign Minister (1870-71) he conducted negotiations on the capitulation of Paris and peace with Germany; hangman of the Paris Commune and instigator of the struggle against the International—261, 271-73, 276, 278, 281, 295, 300, 308-10

Ferdinand II (1810-1859)—King of Naples (1830-59), nicknamed "King Bomba" for bombarding Messina in 1848—274-75

Ferdinand V (the Catholic) (1452-1516) —King (1474-1504) and Governor (1507-16) of Castile, King of Aragon under the name of Ferdinand II (1479-1516)—484

Ferry, Jules François Camille (1832-1893)—French lawyer, publicist and politician, one of the leaders of moderate bourgeois republicans; member of the Government of National Defence, Mayor of Paris (1870-71), took an active part in the struggle against the revolutionary movement; Chairman of the Council of Ministers (1880-81 and 1883-85), pursued colonial policy—273

Feuerbach, Ludwig (1804-1872)—great German materialist philosopher of the pre-Marxian period—11, 20, 24, 28-30, 584-85, 586-607, 688

Fichte, Johann Gottlieb (1762-1814)—representative of classical German philosophy, subjective idealist—691

Fison, Lorimer (1832-1907)—British ethnographer, expert on Australia, missionary; author of several works on Australian and Fijian tribes—477-78

Flocon, Ferdinand (1800-1866)—French politician and publicist, petty-bourgeois democrat, an editor of *Réforme*, member of the Provisional Government (1848)—367, 442

Flourens, Gustave (1838-1871)—French revolutionary and naturalist, Blanquist, leader of the Paris uprising on October 31, 1870 and January 22, 1871; member of the Paris Commune; was killed by the Versaillists in April 1871—278, 281, 283

Forster, William Edward (1818-1886)—British manufacturer and politician, Liberal M.P.; as Secretary of State for Ireland (1880-82) he pursued a policy of severe suppression of the national liberation struggle—390-91

Fould, Achille (1800-1867)—French banker, Orleanist, later Bonapartist;

in 1849-67 repeatedly held the post of Finance Minister—128, 146, 150, 156

Fourier, Charles (1772-1837)—great French utopian socialist—60, 61, 246, 396-97, 400, 401, 417, 420, 460, 499, 565, 583, 659, 668

Frankel, Leo (1844-1896)—prominent figure in the Hungarian and international working-class movement, member of the Paris Commune where he headed the Labour and Exchange Commission, member of the General Council of the First International (1871-72); one of the founders of the General Workers' Party of Hungary, comrade-in-arms of Marx and Engels —294

Franklin, Benjamin (1706-1790)—outstanding American politician, scientist and diplomat, bourgeois democrat, participant in the American War of Independence—202

Frederick II (the Great) (1712-1786)—King of Prussia (1740-86)—309, 640, 653

Frederick William (1620-1688)—Kurfürst von Brandenburg (1640-88)—692

Frederick William III (1770-1840)—King of Prussia (1797-1840)—365, 422, 587, 589

Frederick William IV (1795-1861)—King of Prussia (1840-61)—591

Freeman, Edward Augustus (1823-1892) —English bourgeois historian, Liberal, professor at Oxford University—450

Freiligrath, Ferdinand (1810-1876)—German poet, first romanticist and then revolutionary poet; in 1848-49 was an editor of *Neue Rheinische Zeitung*, member of the Communist League; in the 1850s, left the revolutionary struggle—446

Fustel de Coulanges, Numa-Denis (1830-1889)—French bourgeois historian, author of the book *La Cité antique*—524

G

Gaius (2nd cent. A.D.)—Roman jurist, compiler of a book on Roman law—488

Galle, Johann Gottfried (1812-1910)—German astronomer, in 1846 discovered Neptune on the basis of Leverrier's calculations—595

ian and statesman, actually directed French home and foreign policy from 1840 to 1848—35, 97, 107, 153, 154, 168, 178, 181, 275, 366, 614, 695

Gülich, Gustav (1791-1847)—German bourgeois economist and historian, author of works on the history of national economy—695

H

Hales, John (b. 1839)—British trade union leader, member of the General Council of the International (1866-72) and its Secretary; member of the Reform League and 'of the Land and Labour League; in early 1872 began to head the reformist wing of the British Federal Council, waged a struggle against Marx and his followers with a view to taking over the leadership of the International's organisations in England—309

Hansemann, David (1790-1864)—big German capitalist, one of the leaders of the Rhenish liberal bourgeoisie; in March-September 1848, Prussian Minister of Finance—365

Harney, George Julian (1817-1897)—leader of the Left wing of the Chartist movement, edited a number of Chartist periodicals, was connected with Marx and Engels—437

Harring, Harro (1798-1870)—German writer, petty-bourgeois radical; from 1828 (with intervals) lived as an emigrant in various countries—438

Hartley, David (1705-1757)—English physician and materialist philosopher—379

Hasenclever, Wilhelm (1837-1889)—German Social-Democrat, Lassallean, President of the General German Workers' Union (1871-75)—332, 337

Hasselmann, Wilhelm (b. 1844)—one of the leaders of the Lassallean General German Workers' Union; editor of the Neuer Social-Demokrat (1871-75), member of the German Social-Democratic Party from 1875 to 1880 when he was expelled as an anarchist—322, 332, 337

Haupt, Herman Wilhelm (born c. 1831)—German trading official, member of the Communist League; involved in the Cologne Communist trial, he gave treacherous evidence; released until the trial, he fled to Brazil—446

Haussmann, Eugène Georges (1809-1891)—French politician, Bonapartist, prefect of the Seine Department (1853-70); directed work on the reconstruction of Paris—294, 304

Hautpoul, Alphonse Henri d' (1789-1865)—French general, Legitimist, and later—Bonapartist; War Minister (1849-50)—128, 132, 139-40

Haxthausen, August (1792-1866)—Prussian official and writer, author of a book describing vestiges of communal system in Russian land relations—36, 670

Heckeren (d'Anthès) Georges Charles (1812-1895)—French politician, murderer of Alexander Pushkin; Bonapartist since 1848; one of the organisers of the counter-revolutionary action in Paris on March 22, 1871—282

Hegel, Georg Wilhelm Friedrich (1770-1831)—great classical German philosopher, objective idealist—11, 16, 17, 24, 96, 181, 246, 342, 381, 394, 401, 405, 408, 409, 410, 576, 584, 586, 587, 588-91, 593, 594-96, 597, 600, 604, 607, 609, 612, 613, 615, 661, 676, 688-89, 691

Heine, Heinrich (1797-1856)—great German revolutionary poet—586, 677

Henry II of Lorraine, Duke Guise (1614-1664)—one of the leaders of Fronde—177

Henry V. See Chambord.

Henry VI (1421-1471)—King of England (1422-61)—152

Henry VII (1457-1509)—King of England (1485-1509)—385

Henry VIII (1491-1547)—King of England (1509-47)—385

Hepner, Adolf (1846-1923)—German Social-Democrat, editor of the Volksstaat, delegate to the Hague Congress of the International (1872); subsequently a social-chauvinist—674

Heraclitus (c. 540-c. 480 B. C.)—ancient Greek philosopher, one of the founders of dialectics, spontaneous materialist—405

Herod (73-4 B.C.)—King of Judaea (40-4 B.C.)—543

Herodotus (c. 484-c. 425 B.C.)—ancient Greek historian—475, 493

Herschel, William (1738-1822)—English astronomer—343

Hervé, Edouard (1835-1899)—French publicist, one of the founders and

Kautsky, Karl (1854-1938)—German Social-Democrat, publicist, editor of *Die Neue Zeit* (1883-1917); in the 80s adhered to Marxism but subsequently went over to the camp of opportunists and became ideologist of Centrism in the German Social-Democratic Party and the Second International—678

Kaye, John William (1814-1876)—English colonial official, author of a number of works on the history and ethnography of India, and on the history of British colonial wars in Afghanistan and India—475

Kepler, Johannes (1571-1630)—great German astronomer, discovered laws of planetary movement—340

Kinkel, Gottfried (1815-1882)—German poet and publicist, petty-bourgeois democrat, participated in the Baden-Pfalz uprising in 1849; later, was a leader of petty-bourgeois émigrés in London; fought against Marx and Engels—445

Klein, Johann Jacob (born c. 1818)——physician in Cologne, member of the Communist League, was prosecuted at the Cologne Communist trial—446

Köller, Ernst Matthias (1841-1928)—German reactionary statesman, member of the Reichstag (1881-88) and Prussian Minister of the Interior (1894-95); persecuted the Social-Democratic Party—657

Kopp, Hermann Franz Moritz (1817-1892)—German chemist—602

Kossuth, Lajos (Ludwig) (1802-1894)—leader of Hungarian national liberation movement, in the 1848-49 revolution took leadership of bourgeois-democratic forces, headed the Hungarian revolutionary government; after the defeat of the revolution emigrated abroad—445

Kovalevsky, Maxim Maximovich (1851-1916)—Russian sociologist, historian and politician, bourgeois liberal, author of works on history of the primitive communal system—376, 377, 488, 489, 490-91, 545, 549, 553

Kriege, Hermann (1820-1850)—German journalist, representative of "True Socialism", in the late 40s headed a group of German "True Socialists" in New York—438

Krupp, Friedrich Alfred (1854-1902)—magnate in German steel and armament industry—639

Kugelmann, Ludwig (1830-1902)—German physician, participant in the 1848-49 revolution, member of the International, attended several congresses of the International; friend of Marx's family—669-71

Kuhlmann, Georg—agent provocateur in the service of the Austrian Government; passed himself off as a "prophet"; in the 40s, preached "True Socialism" among German artisans—supporters of Weitling—in Switzerland in the guise of religious phraseology—438

L

Lafargue, Laura (1845-1911)—prominent figure in the French working-class movement, wife of Paul Lafargue, Marx's daughter—14, 669

Lafargue, Paul (1842-1911)—prominent figure in the international working-class movement and propagator of Marxism; member of the General Council of the International, Corresponding Secretary for Spain (1866-69); took part in organising the International's sections in France (1869-70), Spain and Portugal (1871-72); delegate to the Hague Congress (1872); one of the founders of the Workers' Party in France; disciple and associate of Marx and Engels—376, 637, 669

Laffitte, Jacques (1767-1844)—big French banker and politician, Orleanist—274

La Hitte, Jean Ernest (1789-1878)—French general, Bonapartist, member of the Legislative Assembly (1850-51), Minister of Foreign Affairs (1849-51)—132

Lamarck, Jean Baptiste Pierre Antoine (1744-1829)—great French naturalist, founder of the first doctrine of evolution in biology, forerunner of Darwin—346, 598

Lamartine, Alphonse (1790-1869)—French poet, historian and politician; in 1848, Minister of Foreign Affairs and virtually head of provisional government—149, 367, 442

Lamoricière, Christophe Louis Léon (1806-1865)—French general, moderate bourgeois republican; in 1848

Roman historian, author of *History of Rome from Its Foundation*—540, 541

Lochner, Georg (born c. 1824)—prominent figure in the German and international working-class movement; turner by trade; member of the Communist League and of the General Council of the First International; friend and associate of Marx and Engels—439

Locke, John (1632-1704)—great English dualist philosopher, sensualist—97, 379, 406, 688

Longus (end of the 2nd-beginning of the 3rd cent.)—ancient Greek writer—503

Longuet, Jean (1876-1938)—grandson of Marx, son of Jenny Marx, one of the reformist leaders of the French Socialist Party and the Second International—14

Longuet, Jenny (1844-1883)—Marx's eldest daughter, wife of Charles Longuet (French Socialist)—14

Louis XIV (1638-1715)—King of France (1643-1715)—171, 620

Louis XV (1710-1774)—King of France (1715-74)—178

Louis XVI (1754-1793)—King of France (1774-92), executed during the French bourgeois revolution at the end of the 18th century—253

Louis XVIII (1755-1824)—King of France (1814-15 and 1815-24)—97

Louis Bonaparte. See *Napoleon III.*

Louis Napoleon. See *Napoleon III.*

Louis Philippe (1773-1850)—Duke of Orleans, King of France (1830-48)—100, 102, 104, 105, 110, 111, 115, 125, 126, 136, 153, 154, 155, 156, 169, 250, 274, 275, 276, 281, 289, 299, 326, 328, 385, 389, 432

Louis Philippe Albert of Orleans, Count of Paris (1838-1894)—grandson of Louis Philippe, pretender to the French throne—152

Lubbock, John (1834-1913)—British biologist, follower of Darwin, ethnographer and archeologist, wrote several works on primitive society—455-56, 458

Lucian (c. 120-c. 180)—ancient Greek writer, atheist—473

Luther, Martin (1483-1546)—prominent figure in the Reformation period, founder of Protestantism (Lutheranism) in Germany, ideologist of German burghers—96, 339, 340, 384, 619, 691

Lyell, Charles (1797-1875)—outstanding English geologist—344

M

Mably, Gabriel (1709-1785)—outstanding French sociologist, representative of utopian equalitarian communism—395

Macfarlane, Helen—active correspondent of Chartist newspapers in 1849-50, translated the *Manifesto of the Communist Party* into English—31

Machiavelli, Niccolò (1469-1527)—Italian politician, historian and author—339

McLennan, John Ferguson (1827-1881)—Scottish bourgeois lawyer and historian; wrote several works on the history of marriage and the family—454-60, 467, 481, 491, 511, 545

MacMahon, Marie Edme Patrice Maurice (1808-1893)—French reactionary militarist and politician, Bonapartist; one of the hangmen of the Paris Commune; President of the Third Republic (1873-79)—301, 304, 305, 648

Mädler, Johann Heinrich (1794-1874)—German astronomer—343, 347, 351

Magnan, Bernard Pierre (1791-1865)—French marshal, Bonapartist, one of the organisers of the coup d'état on December 2, 1851—155, 163, 165

Maine, Henry James Sumner (1822-1888)—English lawyer, writer—505

Maleville, Léon (1803-1879)—French politician, Orleanist, deputy of the Constituent and the Legislative Assembly during the Second Republic, Home Minister (late December 1848)—149

Malthus, Thomas Robert (1766-1834)—English clergyman and economist; advocate of the misanthropic theory of population—219, 324, 334

Manners, John James Robert (1818-1906)—British politician, Tory; Conservative M.P., repeatedly held ministerial posts in the Conservative governments—391

Mantell, Gideon Algernon (1790-1852)—English geologist and paleontologist; in his works he sought to recon-

Pic, Jules—French journalist, Bonapartist, responsible publisher of the newspaper *L'Étendard*—273

Picard, Ernest (1821-1877)—French lawyer and politician, moderate bourgeois republican Finance Minister in the Government of National Defence (1870-71), Minister of Internal Affairs in the Thiers government (1871), one of the hangmen of the Paris Commune—273, 278, 283, 306

Picard, Eugène Arthur (b. 1825)—French politician and stock-broker, moderate bourgeois republican, brother of Ernest Picard—273

Pietri, Joseph Marie (1820-1902)—French politician, Bonapartist, Prefect of the Paris police (1866-70)—261, 297

Pisistratus (c. 600-527 B.C.)—King of Athens (560-527 B.C., with intervals)—537

Pius IX (1792-1878)—Pope of Rome (1846-78)—127

Plekhanov, Georgi Valentinovich (1856-1918)—prominent figure in the Russian and international socialist movement, outstanding propagandist of Marxism; in 1883, founded abroad the first Russian Marxist organisation—the Emancipation of Labour group; afterwards he became a Menshevik—20

Pliny (Gaius Plinius Secundus) (23-79)—Roman scientist, author of 37-volume *Natural History*—554, 557

Plutarch (c. 46-c. 125)—ancient Greek writer and idealist philosopher—493

Polignac, Auguste Jules Armand Marie, Prince (1780-1847)—French statesman, Legitimist and Clerical, Foreign Minister and Prime Minister (1829-30)—154

Pouyer-Quertier, Auguste-Thomas (1820-1891)—big French manufacturer and politician, Finance Minister (1871-72)—278, 300

Priestley, Joseph (1733-1804)—famous English chemist, materialist philosopher and progressive public figure—379

Procopius of Caesarea (end of the 5th cent.-c. 562)—Byzantine historian, author of the *History of the Wars of Justinian with Persians, Vandals and Goths*—498

Proudhon, Pierre-Joseph (1809-1865)—French publicist, economist and sociologist, ideologist of the petty bourgeoisie and one of the founders of anarchism—12, 14, 58, 123, 183, 255-56, 335, 366, 404, 443, 607, 659-68, 673

Ptolemy, Claudius (2nd cent.)—ancient Greek mathematician, astronomer and geographer, founder of the heliocentric theory—340

Publicola (Publius Valeri Publicola) (d. 503 B.C.)—semi-legendary statesman of the Roman Republic—97

Pyat, Félix (1810-1889)—French publicist and petty-bourgeois democrat, participant in the revolution of 1848, émigré (from 1849); for a number of years, carried on a slander campaign against Marx and the International using for this end the French section in London; member of the Paris Commune—310

Q

Quintilian gens—Roman patricians—588

R

Rafael, Santi (1483-1520)—great Italian painter of the Renaissance—355

Ramm, Hermann—German Social-Democrat, member of the *Volksstaat* editorial board (1875)—337

Ramsey, George (1800-1871)—English economist, one of the last representatives of classical bourgeois political economy—225

Rateau, Jean Pierre (1800-1887)—French lawyer, deputy of the Constituent and the Legislative Assembly during the Second Republic, Bonapartist—112

Ravé, Henri—French journalist, translator of Engels's works into French—451

Regnaud de Saint-Jean d'Angély, Auguste-Michel-Étienne, Count (1794-1870)—French general, Bonapartist, War Minister (January 1851)—145, 146

Reiff, Wilhelm Joseph (b. 1824)—member of the Cologne Workers' Union and of the Communist League from which he was expelled in 1850; was involved in the Cologne Communist trial (1852)—446

Rémusat, Charles François Maria, Count (1797-1875)—French statesman and writer. Orleanist, Minister of the

Say, Jean Baptiste (1767-1832)—French bourgeois economist, representative of vulgar political economy—97

Schaper, von—representative of the Prussian reactionary bureaucracy, Lord Lieutenant of the Rhine Province (1842-45)—180

Schapper, Karl (1812-1870)—prominent figure in the German and international working-class movement, one of the leaders of the League of the Just, member of the Central Committee of the Communist League, participant in the 1848-49 revolution in Germany; in 1850 was among the leaders of the sectarian-adventurist group during the split in the Communist League; in 1856 again joined Marx; member of the General Council of the First International—432-33, 437, 441, 444, 446-47

Schiller, Friedrich (1759-1805)—great German writer—600

Schmidt, Konrad (1863-1932)—German economist and philosopher, author of works which served as a source of revisionism—678-80, 684-89

Schömann, Georg Friedrich (1793-1879) —German philologist and historian, author of several works on the history of ancient Greece—493, 525

Schramm, Jean Paul Adam (1789-1884) —French general and politician, Bonapartist, War Minister (1850-51)—140

Schulze-Delitzsch, Franz Hermann (1808-1883)—German politician and vulgar bourgeois economist; deputy of the Prussian National Assembly (1848); a leader of the bourgeois Progressist Party in the 1860s; sought to divert the workers from the revolutionary struggle by organising co-operative societies—227

Schurz, Karl (1829-1906)—German petty-bourgeois democrat, participant in the Baden uprising of 1849; emigrant in Switzerland; later, U.S. statesman—445

Schweitzer, Johann Baptist (1833-1875) —one of the prominent exponents of Lassalleanism in Germany, President of the General German Workers' Union (1867-71), hindered the affiliation of German workers to the First International, waged a struggle against the Social-Democratic Workers' Party; in 1872 was expelled from the Union for his ties with the Prussian authorities—672

Scott, Walter (1771-1832)—famous British novelist—548

Secchi, Angelo (1818-1878)—Italian astronomer, known for his research on the sun and stars; Jesuit—347, 350-51

Servetus, Miguel (1511-1553)—outstanding Spanish scientist of the Renaissance; physician who made important discoveries in the research of blood circulation—340

Servius Tullius (578-534 B.C.)—semilegendary King of ancient Rome—544

Shaftesbury, Anthony, Count (1671-1713)—English philosopher, moralist, prominent exponent of deism; politician, Whig—386

Shakespeare, William (1564-1616)—great English writer—169, 223, 337

Sickingen, Franz von (1481-1523)—German knight who joined the ranks of the Reformation; led the knights' uprising in 1522-23—384

Simon, Jules (1814-1896)—French statesman, moderate bourgeois republican, Minister of Public Education (1870-73), an instigator of the struggle against the Commune; Chairman of the Council of Ministers (1876-77)—278

Sismondi, Jean Charles Simonde de (1773-1842)—Swiss economist, petty-bourgeois critic of capitalism—55, 225, 233

Smith, Adam (1723-1790)—English economist, one of the great representatives of classical bourgeois political economy—25, 200, 205, 224, 662, 691

Soetbeer, Georg Adolf (1814-1892)—German bourgeois economist and statistician—684

Solon (c. 638-c. 558 B.C.)—famous Athenian legislator; under pressure from the popular masses carried out a number of reforms directed against the aristocracy—523, 532, 533-34, 544, 581

Soulouque, Faustin (c. 1782-1867)—President of the Negro Republic of Haiti; in 1849, proclaimed himself Emperor, assuming the name of Faustin I—178

Spinoza, Baruch (Benedictus) (1632-1677)—outstanding Dutch materialist philosopher, atheist—342, 405

Thorwaldsen, Bertel (1768-1844)—famous Danish sculptor—355

Thucydides (c. 460-c. 395 B.C.)——famous ancient Greek historian, author of *The History of the Peloponnesian War*—527

Tiberius (42 B.C.-A.D. 37)—Roman Emperor (14-37)—543, 554

Timur (*Tamerlane*) (1336-1405)—Central Asian general and conqueror, founder of a large state in the East—284

Tocqueville, Alexis (1805-1859)—French bourgeois historian and politician, Legitimist, deputy of the Constituent and the Legislative Assembly during the Second Republic, Foreign Minister (June-October 1849)—154

Tolain, Henri Louis (1828-1897)—French engraver, Right-wing Proudhonist, one of the leaders of the Paris section of the International, delegate at the London Conference (1865) and several congresses of the International; deputy of the National Assembly of 1871; during the Paris Commune went over to the side of Versailles and was expelled from the International—289

Tölcke, Karl Wilhelm (1817-1893)—German Social-Democrat, one of the leaders of the Lassallean General German Workers' Union—332, 337

Tooke, Thomas (1774-1858)—English bourgeois economist, belonging to the classical school; critic of Ricardo's theory of money—191, 206

Torricelli, Evangelista (1608-1647)—outstanding Italian physicist and mathematician—340, 694

Trier, Gerson (b. 1851)—Danish Social-Democrat, one of the leaders of the revolutionary minority of the Social-Democratic Party; waged a struggle against the party's opportunist wing; translator of Engels's works into Danish—451

Trochu, Louis Jules (1815-1896)—French general and politician, Orleanist; head of the Government of National Defence, Commander-in-Chief of the Paris armed forces (September 1870-January 1871), sabotaged the defence of Paris; deputy of the National Assembly of 1871—271-72, 277, 280-81, 304

U

Ulfila (or *Wulfila*) (c. 311-383)—West-Gothic church leader, conducted Christianisation of the Goths, creator of the Gothic alphabet, translator of the Scriptures into Gothic—543

Ure, Andrew (1778-1857)—British chemist, vulgar economist—191, 194

Urquhart, David (1805-1877)—British diplomat, reactionary publicist and politician, Turkophile; M.P. (1847-52)—193

V

Vaïsse, Claude Marius (1799-1864)—French statesman, Bonapartist; Minister of the Interior (January-April 1851)—149

Valentin, Louis Ernest—French Bonapartist general, Prefect of the Paris police on the eve of the uprising of March 18, 1871—278-79, 297

Vanderbilts—dynasty of American financial and industrial magnates—685

Varus, Publius Quintilius (c. 53 B.C.-A.D. 9)—Roman political figure and soldier, governor in Germany (A.D. 7-9); was killed in the battle with the rebellious German tribes in the Teutoburger Wald—538

Vatimesnil, Antoine (1789-1860)—French political figure, Legitimist, deputy of the Legislative Assembly (1849-51)—149

Veleda—priestess and prophetess from the German tribe of Bructers; actively participated in the uprising against Roman rule—551

Veneday, Jacob (1805-1871)—German radical publicist; in 1848-49, deputy of the Frankfort National Assembly, adhered to the Left wing; subsequently a liberal—432

Véron, Louis Désiré (1798-1867)—French journalist and politician, Bonapartist; owner of the newspaper *Constitutionnel*—178, 179

Victoria (1819-1901)—Queen of Great Britain (1837-1901)—403

Vidal, François (1814-1872)—French economist, petty-bourgeois socialist; in 1848, Secretary of the Luxembourg Commission, deputy of the Legislative Assembly (1850-51)—133

INDEX OF LITERARY AND MYTHOLOGICAL NAMES

land, fiancé and then husband of Gudrun—504

Hettel—hero of the ancient German national epic and of the 13th-century German poem *Gudrun*, king of the Hegelingen—504

Hilde—heroine of the ancient German national epic and of the 13th-century German poem *Gudrun*, daughter of the Irish King, wife of Hettel, King of the Hegelingen—504

Hildebrand—hero of the ancient German heroic epic *Hildebrandslied* (Song of Hildebrand)—549, 570

Job (Bible)—image of a long-suffering poor man whom God rewarded for his patience and meekness—276

Joshua (*Yehoshua ben Nun*) (Bible)—hero who ruined the walls of Jericho by the sounds of sacred trumpets and cries of his warriors—282

Juggernaut (*Jagannath*) (Indian myth.)—a form of Vishnu—220

Kriemhild—heroine of the ancient German national epic and of the medieval German poem *Nibelungenlied*, sister of Gunther, the Burgundian King; bride and later wife of Siegfried; after the latter's death, wife of Etzel, King of the Huns—504

Loki (Scandinavian myth.)—evil demon and god of fire, hero of the ancient Scandinavian epic *Elder Edda*—473

Medusa (Greek myth.)—monster which had the power of changing its onlooker to stone—229

Megaera—one of the three goddesses of vengeance, embodiment of wrath and envy; used figuratively—a malicious shrew—303

Meleager (Greek myth.)—son of Oeneus, legendary king of Calydon, and of Althaea who killed her mother's brothers—550

Mephistopheles—character from Goethe's tragedy *Faust*—100, 350, 411, 473, 587

Moses (Bible)—prophet and law-giver who freed the Jews from Egyptian captivity and gave them laws—157, 451, 486

Mulios—personage from Homer's poem *Odyssey*—527

Mylitta—Greek name of *Ishtar*, goddess of love and fertility in Babylonian mythology—483

Nestor (Greek myth.)—eldest and wisest of Greek heroes who took part in the Trojan war—524

Nick Bottom—personage from Shakespeare's comedy *A Midsummer Night's Dream*—137

Njord (Scandinavian myth.)—god of fertility, hero from the ancient Scandinavian national epic *Elder Edda*—473

Odysseus—hero from Homer's epics *Iliad* and *Odyssey*, mythical King of Ithaka, one of the leaders of the Greek troops in the Trojan war, was known for his bravery, cunning and oratory—526-27

Orestes (Greek myth.)—son of Agamemnon and Clytemnestra who revenged himself on his mother and Aegisthus for the murder of his father; hero of Aeschylus's tragedies *Choephoroe* and *Eumenides* (second and third parts of the trilogy *Oresteia*)—453

Paul (Bible)—one of Christian apostles—96

Perseus (Greek myth.)—son of Zeus and Danae; performed many deeds, cut off Medusa's head—229

Phineus (Greek myth.)—blind prophet; instigated by his second wife he tortured his children born by his first wife, Cleopatra (daughter of Boreas), for which he was punished by gods—550

Pistol—character from Shakespeare's *Henry IV*, *Henry V* and *Merry Wives of Windsor*; cheat, coward and braggard—307

Polyneices (Greek myth.)—one of the sons of Oedipus (King of Thebes); fighting for power he killed his brother Eteocles and himself perished in the fight; the myth served as a basis for Aeschylus's tragedy *Seven Against Thebes*—525

Pourceaugnac—chief character from Molière's comedy *Monsieur de Pourceaugnac*, image of a dull and ignorant provincial noble—277

Prometheus (Greek myth.)—one of the titans; he stole fire from the gods and gave it to people, for which he was punished by being chained to a rock where every day an eagle ate his liver—418

SUBJECT INDEX

A

Abstraction—29, 180, 228, 357, 594, 603, 607, 664, 666, 689
Accident (chance)—65, 645, 671
Accident (chance) and necessity—580, 609, 612, 682, 695
Accumulation of capital—45, 87, 90, 224, 374
—its historical tendency—232-34
Agnosticism—377, 380-83, 595
Agrarian question—240-41, 623-24, 629-31, 633-40
Agriculture—172, 570
Albumen—348, 382
—as a bearer of life—348, 361, 382
Alchemy—340-41, 602
Algebra—340
Algeria—678
Alliance of Socialist Democracy (L'Alliance de la Démocratie Socialiste)—308-09, 672
Alsace and Lorraine—248, 265, 266, 268, 648
America
—discovery of—36-37, 84, 384, 684-85
—United States of America—34, 44, 61, 62, 103, 190, 193, 224, 230, 257, 328, 390, 446, 517, 560, 577, 579, 663, 665, 673, 678
—War of Independence—229
—Civil War—193, 229, 368, 446
—South America—390, 665
Amortisation of means of production—78, 204
Anarchists—33, 168, 311, 335, 424
Anarchy of capitalist production—55-56, 78, 290, 394, 413, 416-19, 424, 581, 685, 695
Anatomy—341, 345, 383
Ancient society—80, 182, 465, 488, 497, 521-46, 550-53, 557-61, 563, 565, 574-77, 581

Annexation—249, 648
Antagonism—45, 47, 51, 60, 120, 130, 152, 182, 228, 371, 415, 536, 665, 667
Anti-Jacobin War—219, 223, 269
Anti-Socialist (Exceptional) Law—248, 447, 649-50, 657, 680-81
Antithesis—407, 689
—between industrial and agricultural labour—53
Arabs—338-40, 363, 406
Aristocracy—43, 53-55, 385, 388
Arming of the proletariat—441, 652-53
Army—80, 175, 647, 648, 651-52
Art—38, 339, 355, 360, 694
Asiatic mode of production—182
Astronomy—346-48, 351-52, 383
—its history—340-43, 345-47, 380, 383
Australia—183, 446, 678
Austria—236-37, 644, 646, 651, 654, 682, 693
Austro-Prussian War (1866)—236-37, 239, 251, 267
Average rate of profit—189, 223

B

Bakuninists, Bakuninism—311, 370, 672-73, 675-76
Banks, bank capital—155-57, 194-95, 685
Barbarism—39, 40, 401, 449, 462-66, 474, 476, 479, 481-82, 484, 486, 491, 495, 501-02, 515, 529, 531, 555-57, 565-73, 574
Barricade fight—651-53
Basic question of philosophy—592-96
Basis and superstructure—38, 40, 49, 50-51, 71-72, 95, 117, 181-82, 228, 285, 371-72, 392-93, 400, 409, 429, 436, 574, 616, 641, 646, 661, 666, 668, 682-83, 685-89, 690-91, 693-95
See also: State, Art, Morality, Law (Right), Religion, Philosophy, Economics and politics